Black Greek-Letter Organizations
in the Twenty-first Century

Black Greek-Letter Organizations in the Twenty-first Century

Our Fight Has Just Begun

Edited by
Gregory S. Parks

UNIVERSITY PRESS OF KENTUCKY

Copyright © 2008 by The University Press of Kentucky
Paperback edition 2017

Scholarly publisher for the Commonwealth,
serving Bellarmine University, Berea College, Centre College of Kentucky,
Eastern Kentucky University, The Filson Historical Society, Georgetown
College, Kentucky Historical Society, Kentucky State University, Morehead
State University, Murray State University, Northern Kentucky University,
Transylvania University, University of Kentucky, University of Louisville,
and Western Kentucky University.
All rights reserved.

Editorial and Sales Offices: The University Press of Kentucky
663 South Limestone Street, Lexington, Kentucky 40508-4008
www.kentuckypress.com

The Library of Congress has cataloged the hardcover edition as follows:

Black Greek-letter organizations in the twenty-first century : our fight has
just begun / edited by Gregory S. Parks.
       p. cm.
  Includes bibliographical references and index.
  ISBN 978-0-8131-2491-9 (hardcover : alk. paper)
  1. Greek letter societies—United States. 2. African American college
students—Societies, etc. I. Parks, Gregory, 1974-
LJ34.B58 2008
378.1'98508996073—dc22   2007052578
  ISBN 978-0-8131-6975-0 (pbk. : alk. paper)

This book is printed on acid-free paper meeting the requirements of the American
National Standard for Permanence in Paper for Printed Library Materials.
∞

Manufactured in the United States of America.

Member of the Association of
American University Presses

To the Extension and affiliated brothers and chapters

CONTENTS

FOREWORD
Julianne Malveaux

If you were to call the roll of prominent African American people, the prevalence of sorority or fraternity affiliations would underscore the importance of black Greek-letter organizations (BGLOs) in African American life. The father of African American intellectuals, W. E. B. DuBois, was a member of Alpha Phi Alpha Fraternity, as was Dr. Martin Luther King Jr. The first African American woman to earn a PhD in economics was also the first national president of Delta Sigma Theta Sorority Inc. Delta's political footprint is well documented, what with the civil rights work of its tenth president, Dorothy Irene Height; the pioneering legal work of fourteenth president and attorney Frankie Muse Freeman; the phenomenal and historic leadership of Texas congresswoman Barbara Jordan; the educational leadership of its seventeenth president, Mona Humphries Bailey; and the social action and civic participation of twenty-first president Marcia Fudge.

My obvious pride at the accomplishments of my sisters in the nation's largest African American sorority may be obvious, but no Greek-letter organization is missing from this honor roll of African American notables. Novelist Toni Morrison and tennis pioneer Zina Garrison are members of Alpha Kappa Alpha Sorority. Novelist Zora Neal Hurston was a member of Zeta Phi Beta. Omega Psi Phi Fraternity can claim Dr. William H. ("Bill") Cosby, the Reverend Jesse Jackson, and the extraordinary poet Langston Hughes. Wall Street pioneer and billionaire Reginald F. Lewis was a member of Kappa Alpha Psi Fraternity, and labor activist A. Philip Randolph was a member of Phi Beta Sigma Fraternity. Whether the sector is academia, arts, culture, journalism, science, or sports, there are African Americans of achievement who have belonged to Greek-letter organizations.

Why, then, has there been so little scholarship about these organizations? Do college rituals, often shrouded in secrecy and controversy (e.g., branding, hazing), make such organizations more likely targets of ridicule than scholarship? Do the loyalties that some scholars have to their organizations dampen intellectual curiosity about them? Do national organizations seek and encourage scholarship, or do they avoid and discourage it, based on their own lack of knowledge about the outcomes that unbiased studies might provide? Certainly, there is significant conjecture about the role of sororities and fraternities in undergraduate life at both historically black colleges and universities and predominantly white institutions. There is also debate about whether these organizations have a unifying or a divisive influence among African American people. Although the data do not establish what percentage of the African American leadership, broadly construed, are members of Greek-letter organizations, casual empiricism suggests that a significant number of African American leaders and activists have some background in BGLOs. But can research establish that members of BGLOs are more activist, more public-service oriented, or more philanthropic than other African Americans? Are they more or less likely to finish their undergraduate studies? To earn graduate and professional degrees? Are they more or less likely to contribute to African American organizations? To make an impact in our community? Is the BGLO experience instrumental in, or incidental to, the development of African American leadership? These are questions that could be answered with the development of scholarship around BGLOs. This is a scholarship that Gregory S. Parks has begun and that emerges in this edited volume, *Black Greek-Letter Organizations in the Twenty-first Century*.

This is an important time to undertake this work. As the social and economic organization of both the United States and the developing world undergoes change due to global and technological pressures, the status of African American people is also evolving. In the United States, African Americans are no longer the largest or the most favored minority group, yet issues of social and economic justice—holdover issues from the nineteenth and twentieth centuries—are unresolved and, in many cases, ignored. Thus, two years after New Orleans drowned from the broken levees that followed Hurricane Katrina, the city's population, which was once mostly black, had not been restored, and the federal government had all but abandoned relief efforts. Our nation's failure to "fix" New Orleans echoed its failure, in the global arena, to resolve the fiasco created by the invasion of Iraq in 2002. "No Child Left Behind" legislation has, in fact, left thousands of inner-city schools behind, and gaps in the educational achievements of African American students and others remain wide. Indeed, an array of disparities—in income, education, health status, employment, wealth, political participation, and other areas—remains, despite the efforts of many African American organizations to effect change. There was a time when sorority and fraternity programs were at least partially focused on closing these gaps, but in the twenty-first century, it is appropriate to assess whether sororities and fraternities are really improving the quality of life not only for their own members but also for African American people across the board. Indeed, with a series of impending crises shaping the status of the African American community, one might argue that this is a community that can ill afford to expend resources on outdated and ineffective organizations. Any inquiry that challenges BGLOs to embrace their highest and best manifestations may have positive and productive benefits for the community at large.

Parks has assembled an impressive group of scholars to focus on some of these issues, and they tackle vital topics in their essays. Parks explores an important set of parameters in his introduction, noting how important "critical BGLO scholarship" may be for the African American community, and he explains the methodology and resources that lie at the foundation of this work. This compendium includes histories of the BGLOs, as well as incisive explorations of different aspects of BGLO life. Authors discuss feminism, homophobia, eating disorders, academic advising, and philanthropy, among other topics, and they often raise as many questions as they answer about BGLOs. Most important, they establish BGLOs as an area of scholarship and inquiry. Further research in these areas may well reveal critical information about the manner and method of African American social organization in the twenty-first century. It may determine that these organizations have an impact on the lives of a cross section of African American children and families. Or research may show that class biases in the African American community are so entrenched that these organizations, perceived as elitist, have only a limited impact on the quality of life of African Americans.

It has been exciting to review this work and consider its broader implications. I look forward to the next steps in this interesting, important, and heretofore limited exploration of black Greek-letter organizations.

PREFACE

The task of researching and writing about black Greek-letter organizations (BGLOs) is a difficult one that is as much political as it is scholarly. BGLO leaders at every level, as well as rank-and-file members, have a vested interest in making sure that their organizations are represented in the best light possible. What amounts to good scholarship in this area may result in a very candid but not entirely flattering depiction of BGLOs in general or one BGLO in particular. Conversely, what amounts to good storytelling about BGLOs may border on mere advertising for the organizations and ultimately poor scholarship. As a member of a BGLO—Alpha Phi Alpha Fraternity—and coeditor of a previously published book on BGLOs, I am well aware of the challenges involved in a scholarly inquiry into these organizations. Two key questions that must be addressed at the outset are likely to be posed by BGLO members who read this book: Why are the nine National Pan-Hellenic Council (NPHC) organizations not equally represented among the contributing authors? Why do some organizations seem to get more coverage than others? To answer these questions, let me shed some light on my methodological approach as the editor of this book and allay any concerns about my bias for or against any BGLO.

My first step was to identify either pressing or interesting BGLO topics that could be addressed in a book. I then set out to locate individuals who were already conducting such research. Employing various university library search engines, I identified individuals who had written scholarly journal articles, scholarly books or book chapters, dissertations, and, in some instances, theses on BGLOs or relevant topics. I then contacted these individuals and invited them to contribute to the book, regardless of whether they were BGLO members. For some topics, this methodological approach was fruitless, and I failed to find appropriate authors. In that case, I identified either academicians or practitioners who, in my opinion, could write well and adequately address a particular topic. My hope was to have at least one contributing author from each NPHC organization, but quite honestly, the vast majority of research being conducted on BGLOs has been carried out by members of Alpha Phi Alpha, Alpha Kappa Alpha, and Delta Sigma Theta. I reached out to each NPHC organization that lacked sufficient contributor representation on this project, contacting national headquarters as well as regional, provincial, district, and state officers to help identify academicians within their respective organizations who might be willing and able to contribute to this book. Not all organizations responded with the same level of enthusiasm, but for those that provided the names of potential contributors, I contacted each individual and requested a copy of his or her curriculum vitae. If their scholarship looked sound, I invited them to contribute to the project. Some accepted; others did not.

Many of the original contributors produced their chapters and met the submission deadline, but some failed to do so. In the latter case, in an attempt to save such chapters, I had to begin the selection process anew. Again, I had to draw from a pool of potential contributors in which certain NPHC organizations were better represented than others. Given the time constraints, I ultimately had to select authors who were fairly easy to locate.

In addition to selecting the contributors, I was very hands-on when it came to content. In several instances, I provided the authors with outlines for their chapters, as well as a list of resources I expected them to consult. Ultimately, however, contributors were free to determine the course of their own chapters. Given the nature of some BGLO topics, certain groups warranted more coverage than others. This is a hard truth. For instance, a chapter on womanist identity and BGLOs must necessarily focus on sororities to the exclusion of fraternities. There is also an accessibility issue. Some NPHC organizations have far more publicly accessible information than others. I personally contacted the national offices of several NPHC organizations to request certain documents and information to assist the contributing authors with their research. Again, some organizations were more forthcoming than others. Thus, those BGLOs that provided greater access to information or were more willing to share information receive broader coverage in this book. For the same reason, certain chapters, particularly those providing biographies of NPHC organizations' founders, are not equally substantive.

As a final note, it is important to clarify that this project was not commissioned by any organization—NPHC or otherwise. The goal of this book is not to paint a positive picture but to paint an accurate one. Although many of the contributors are BGLO members, I believe that they approached the writing of their chapters as scholars. Their thoughts, their research, and their writing are their own. None of them are representing their respective BGLOs in an official capacity, and I do not believe that any of them sought permission from their respective national organizations to contribute to this book. As such, this book is not the official position of any NPHC group or of the NPHC itself.

ACKNOWLEDGMENTS

First and foremost, all praises are due to the Creator. Thank you to my parents, sisters, and other relatives who provided tremendous support throughout this project. Thanks to Jen for consistently being there with support, encouragement, and advice.

My Alpha brothers have also been a huge support and impetus for this project: my dean, assistant dean of pledges, dean of hell, spesh, and every Extension line have been the epitome of brotherhood. Also, thanks to my big brother, the Reverend Barry Hargrove. Because of you, I know what true brotherhood is. Thanks to brother Rashid Darden for his insight and guidance, especially with regard to the chapter on homosexuality in black fraternities. Thank you to brothers Robert Harris and Zollie Stevenson for your advice in the latter stages of the project. Thanks to the various Alpha Phi Alpha Fraternity Inc. chapters that inspired this work: Omicron Omicron (University of the District of Columbia), Nu Beta (George Washington, Georgetown, and American universities), Eta Zeta (Bowie State University), Iota Zeta (University of Maryland–College Park), Nu Kappa (University of Maryland–Baltimore County), Rho Rho (SUNY Stony Brook), Epsilon Chi (University of Kentucky), and Beta (Howard University). Thank you to Dr. Walter Kimbrough for his suggestions about the direction this book should take. And to Sonya, thanks for all the support and for listening to me talk endlessly about this book.

This book would have been impossible to bring into fruition if it were not for the efforts of the contributing authors. Edited books are not easy to pull off, and as an editor, I can be a bit demanding. Thanks to all the authors who took my feedback into consideration, wrote and rewrote, and ultimately stuck with me on this project. I believe that we have a great book here and the beginning of something even greater.

The leadership and national staff from a number of National Pan-Hellenic Council organizations aided me in finding potential contributors, providing research materials, and identifying funding sources for this project. Thank you to Alpha Phi Alpha's Darryl Matthews (general president), Dr. Robert Harris (national historian), Willard Hall (executive director), William Lyle (communications director), Darryl Peal (Midwestern Region vice president), Michael Blake (chair, College Brothers' Affairs), and Horace Dawson (chair, World Policy

Council); Kappa Alpha Psi's Richard Snow (executive director) and Andre Early (director of undergraduate affairs); Alpha Kappa Alpha's Dr. Betty James (executive director); Zeta Phi Beta's Lois Sylver (executive director); and Sigma Gamma Rho's Dr. Mynora Bryant (international Grand Basileus) and Jennifer Jones (executive director).

Also, I am grateful to the Association of Fraternity Advisors Foundation for its generous gift, which allowed this work to be completed.

Last but not least, I owe a huge debt of gratitude to the University Press of Kentucky staff: Steven Wrinn, Melinda Wirkus, Hap Houlihan, Mack McCormick, Allison Webster, Wyn Morris, Leila Salisbury, and Anne Watkins. You captured the essence of this project and ran with it. I appreciate all the support, hard work, and friendship.

Introduction
Toward a Critical Scholarship
Gregory S. Parks

Here we are, approximately 100 years from the time black Greek-letter organizations (BGLOs) began. During much of the twentieth century, these groups loomed large and cast a long shadow across the American landscape. They brought together a cadre of men and women dedicated to uplifting blacks and provided them a space to pool their individual efforts, resources, and ideals. Their work in the last century (and continuing in this one) comprised various philanthropic, civic, and community service activities. Moreover, BGLOs taught college-educated black men and women how to commit themselves to personal excellence and achievement as well as to one another. Despite their tremendous efforts, at the twilight of the last century, there was a growing commentary that questioned the relevance of these groups. Today, some contend that BGLOs' golden age has long passed. It is true that the level of interest in these groups has waned in recent decades, but does this mean that BGLOs are no longer relevant?

We now live in an era in which the BGLO presence is evident in popular culture. Music videos such as Jay-Z's *99 Problems*; hip-hop albums such as Kanye West's *High School Dropout* and *Late Registration*; the movies *School Daze, Drumline,* and *Stomp the Yard*; and step shows from coast to coast have introduced tens if not hundreds of thousands of people to BGLO culture. However, and quite regrettably, BGLOs have been reduced to two elements among the general public: stepping and hazing. Collectively, BGLOs have not done a very good job of staving off such a reductionist image, despite their various uplift activities. What may be most troubling is not the general public's lack of knowledge about BGLOs but that these organizations' members do not have a particularly nuanced, broad, or deep understanding of their own groups. To some, such a statement amounts to heresy, because most BGLO members consider themselves to be gurus on their respective organizations. But even if this is true, BGLO members rarely have a robust understanding of the history and culture of their organizations and the broader issues they face. This paucity of understanding may have implications for how members function within these groups and how they perpetuate them.

There are challenges on the horizon for black Americans, and it will take an organized body of men and women to meet those challenges. The future calls to these groups. Despite this call, I do not naively assume that every organization in the National Pan-Hellenic Council (NPHC) will reach its centennial celebration. However, BGLOs can remain viable and relevant through a collaborative effort among BGLOs' hip-hop generation, those that came before, and those that will follow. Our fight has just begun. Both internally and externally, BGLOs must craft an identity that is relevant in the new millennium. Internally, these groups must wrestle with hazing, homophobia, petty intergroup competition, the divide between college and alumni members, and the like. Externally, BG-LOs must rededicate themselves to their communities and lead an aggressive and unwavering campaign against modern forms of racism, sexism, and other types of xenophobia. Knowledge is power, and I hope that this critical, scholarly look at BGLOs empowers them and aids them in their quest for viability, longevity, and relevance.

Toward this end, I propose that a critical study of BGLOs is not only warranted but also necessary. Despite their 100-year existence, little substantive research has been conducted on BGLOs, and even less has been published. This is surprising, given that these organizations' rolls serve as a veritable who's who of black achievers in almost every field of endeavor. Moreover, during the twentieth century, these organizations played a prominent role in various racial uplift activities in the United States and, in some cases, abroad. What is more surprising, though, is that although BGLO members are well educated and hold a respectable portion of faculty positions in American universities, few have considered their own organizations as an area of scholarship. Here, I recommend some parameters for this line of study, suggest mechanisms for its actualization, and highlight pitfalls that might hinder its development.

Form, Function, and Content

Broadly, there are three approaches that make up critical BGLO scholarship. First, a formal approach supposes that there are defining features that set the parameters and constitute the outer limits of this scholarship. Second, a functional approach supposes that there are certain underlying goals. Third, a content approach supposes that there are certain BGLO-related topics that are worth exploring. The integration of these three approaches leads to a holistic and scholarly analysis of BGLOs.

FORM: THE PARAMETERS OF SCHOLARSHIP

There are three features that should define the outer contours of critical BGLO scholarship: critical analysis, peer review, and citation. Critical analysis does not mean that works must deal harshly with BGLOs; however, they must provide a substantive and probing analysis of topics related, directly and indirectly, to BGLOs. Serious questions about these groups must be asked, and serious answers must be sought.

Second, scholars must submit their work for peer review and critique.[1] Peer review makes professional honesty more likely and instills humility in authors, as they are forced to acknowledge the gaps in their knowledge.[2] Additionally, before any scholarship is published, it should be revised based on the reviewers' comments, which are designed to ensure the academic integrity of the work. Works subjected to greater academic scrutiny should be accorded more weight. In this hierarchy, works from most weighty to least weighty are as follows: peer-reviewed journal articles, scholarly books, academic conference presentations, doctoral dissertations, master's theses.

Third, critical BGLO scholarship must cite sources, such that the reader can verify assertions and conclusions made within the body of the work. These core parameters rule out works of fiction and journalism; in addition, the fact that a work is nonfiction does not mean that it rises to the level of scholarship. To the degree that it does not conform to the three principles cited, it is merely a book about BGLOs and not critical scholarship on these groups.

In addition to these core principles, other attributes can lend nuance to critical scholarship. Research on BGLOs has traditionally been the province of people in the fields of higher education administration, history, psychology, and sociology; however, other disciplines may provide insight into BGLO culture, history, or the issues they face. As such, critical scholarship on BGLOs should take a multidisciplinary and interdisciplinary analytic approach. It should embrace the work and methodological approaches of all academic disciplines, because different approaches may yield different answers to the same question. Furthermore, certain disciplines and methodologies may be better adapted than others to answer certain questions. In addition, collaborative efforts by scholars in different fields may bear considerable fruit. For example, a sociology professor and an organizational behavior professor might provide an empirical analysis of the societal (external) factors and organizational (internal) factors that cause BGLO members to become inactive. Alternatively, professors in law, higher education administration, political science, and social psychology might quantitatively discern what type of membership intake process would be most acceptable to BGLO members, universities, and state legislatures enacting hazing laws.

Critical BGLO scholarship can also be defined by the type of individuals engaged in developing and perpetuating it. Academicians who are BGLO members may have a certain degree of understanding that nonmembers do not. Conversely, non-BGLO members may possess a greater degree of objectivity than members do. Hence, both members and nonmembers (including nonblacks) can provide useful insights and perspectives.[3] Moreover, as in many areas of scholarship, more seasoned academicians tend to dominate the field. However, critical BGLO scholarship may call for the expertise of younger scholars as well. The most pressing issue facing BGLOs is hazing, and younger scholars who are also BGLO members have an intimate knowledge of that issue. Therefore, younger scholars' research might be better focused on the root of the problem than that of scholars who are further removed from the realities of undergraduate BGLO life. Other current issues are related to the growth of the hip-hop generation within BGLO ranks, making members of that generation best suited to conduct research on those topics. Others may also have unique and valuable perspectives. For instance, BGLO national office staff, officers, and even university staff and administrators may not be familiar with research methodology or may not understand the rigors of academic writing and publishing, but if they partner with academicians as part of a research team, their insights may prove invaluable, guiding research in new directions.

It is important to make a distinction between experts and scholars. Whereas scholars conform to the above-mentioned principles, BGLO experts do not necessarily do so. The term *expert* merely denotes someone who is knowledgeable, and such a title may be bestowed for a variety of reasons: holding a national office in a BGLO or the NPHC, lecturing widely on BGLOs, or simply being acknowledged by the media as someone who gives interviews on the topic. However, an expert has not necessarily engaged in any original research. An expert is not necessarily a scholar, but a scholar is necessarily an expert. Scholars come in two varieties—generalists and specialists. Those who focus on one BGLO topic—hazing, stepping, civic action, feminism—are specialists. Those who broadly study various aspects of BGLO life are generalists.

FUNCTION: THE GOALS AND AIMS OF SCHOLARSHIP

Like any other scholarly enterprise, critical BGLO scholarship is a means by which university professors can fulfill one of their scholarly obligations: publishing. James Axtell notes twenty-five reasons why academicians must publish.[4] Among them is the notion that original scholarly work is the best indication of intellectual distinction and the best predictor that scholarship will not cease upon the granting of tenure or full professorship. Academic meritocracy is premised on the notion that peer-reviewed scholarship is the only reliable way to evaluate scholars' activities. Scholars are expected to advance knowledge, and scholarship serves to unite scholars across disparate disciplines. Also, scholarship can be more objectively evaluated than teaching. Because scholars are often nationally or internationally known, they tend to have a higher status than mere teaching professors. Scholarship is the defining feature of academic achievement. In addition, publications command higher salaries, speaking engagements, and wider audiences for one's ideas.

Certainly, professional writers are also compelled to write. However, the standards for evaluating scholarly writing and lay writing are quite different. In academic publishing, an author's work is largely evaluated on how well it will contribute to scholarship in a given area. In trade publishing, an author's work is largely evaluated on how well it will sell.[5] A critic of such a scholarly approach to understanding BGLOs once commented that such researchers are mere "ivory-tower thinkers engaged in intellectual masturbation."[6] However, scholars in this area should be committed to more than just advancing their march toward tenure or full professorship. They should also be interested in two other potential aspects of their research: providing the public (nonacademics) with substantive information about BGLOs, and influencing policies that relate to BGLOs.

Generally, there is a paucity of research on BGLOs. There may be a handful of dissertations, theses, and peer-reviewed journal articles on these groups. However, these works are largely inaccessible to the general public, including BGLO members. The most accessible scholarship on BGLOs consists of books published by academic presses, but there are few of these books.

In addition to informing people about BGLOs, scholarship should aim to influence policies affecting these organizations and how they function.[7] These policies may be developed externally by state legislatures or universities, or they may be developed within BGLOs themselves. With regard to internal policies and functioning, research may point the way toward more effective functioning. How can BGLOs retain a higher percentage of active, dues-paying members among those they initiate? How can they reclaim inactive members? How can they best inculcate organizational values in new initiates? How can organizational headquarters better serve members' needs and meet their expectations?

With regard to external polices, at the highest level, critical scholarship may effect laws affecting BGLOs—in particular, state hazing laws. On a smaller scale, scholarship may help universities to better engage and interact with their black Greek communities.

CONTENT: THE SUBSTANCE OF SCHOLARSHIP

Researchers have been studying predominantly white Greek-letter organizations for decades. Scholars have turned their attention to BGLOs only in the past decade or so, and this research has been limited. Aside from unpublished dissertations and theses, a paltry number of peer-reviewed journal articles have been published, along with only five scholarly books: Elizabeth Fine and Ricky Jones specifically addressed the topics of stepping and hazing, respectively; Felix Armfield authored a biography of Alpha Phi Alpha founder Eugene Kinckle Jones; Walter Kimbrough wrote a book broadly addressing the history and culture of BGLOs; and Tamara Brown, Clarenda Phillips, and I edited a broad text on the history, culture, and contemporary issues facing BGLOs.[8] There are many more topics and issues that should be explored. Here, I provide some examples of those areas that need coverage.

First and foremost, little is known about the men and women who founded these organizations. Charles Harris Wesley, noted historian and former general president and national historian of Alpha Phi Alpha, authored a book on Alpha founder Henry Arthur Callis, and Herman "Skip" Mason, Alpha's national archivist, wrote a book on the lives of Alpha's founders and general presidents.[9] However, the only academic book written on any of these groups' founders is the aforementioned work by Armfield. A review of each organization's archives and interviews with the founders' family members and former national leaders would unearth much information. Considerable research needs to be conducted on the men and women who propelled these organizations through history, with a special focus on national leaders and prominent members. Dissertations have been written on two prominent members of Alpha Phi Alpha—Raymond Pace Alexander and Kelly Miller—but they have yet to be published.[10] These works would be invaluable in understanding not only BGLOs but also black history in general. In addition, new research on these men and women needs to be conducted, especially when there are repositories of knowledge and archived papers available. For instance, the papers of Sadie Tanner Mosell Alexander (first national president of Delta Sigma Theta) are at the University of Pennsylvania.[11] It is surprising that no one has explored the life of this trailblazer.

Second, given the degree of interest in BGLOs by aspiring members, a substantive public history is needed. By this, I do not mean a condensation of the histories of each group into one book. Moreover, merely extracting information from organizational Web sites is not sufficient, because it is difficult to determine the accuracy of such information. What is needed is a well-researched book that draws on the histories of the groups, past issues of their national journals, archival information, and interviews with past leaders. Such a project should also place these groups in their proper historical context—situating them within the history of black Americans more broadly. Such a book would go a long way toward educating nonmembers about BGLOs and providing a cohesive history of the BGLO movement rather than nine distinct organizations. In addition, each NPHC organization would be well advised to have its own public history—broad, substantive, and scholarly, but accessible to nonmembers.[12] Regional, provincial, district, area, and chapter histories may also warrant attention.

Third, many topics that were explored in the earlier volume I coedited, as well as this one, deserve much more coverage. For instance, the origins of BGLOs—particularly their African and European roots—need further exploration. Literary societies played a prominent role in the development of fraternities and sororities (particularly Alpha Phi Alpha), warranting a historical assessment of these groups and their impact on Greek life. More work needs to be done on black college life during the early twentieth century to understand the milieu in which BGLOs developed and flourished. The parallels between black secret societies and BGLOs, and the former's impact on the development of the latter, require analysis.

Scholars at Cornell have conducted some great research on BGLO civic action, but this topic merits its own book. More work on BGLO public rituals is needed, especially with regard to hand signs. Some research has been conducted on little sister organizations, but not much is known about male auxiliary groups. These groups provide an important support network for members, and their role in local, state, and national politics needs to be explored. Clothing, artistic expression, and poetry are other potential avenues of research. For example, an oft-quoted poem among BGLOs is Rudyard Kipling's "If—." Kipling was a Freemason, and it is contended that Masonic doctrine often found its way into his writing, including "If—."[13] Did BGLO founders or members, some of whom were Masons, select this poem because of its Masonic imagery?

Empirical research is needed on topics such as BGLOs and womanist identity, racial identity, eating disorders, substance abuse, and date rape. In addition, is there any truth to the stereotypes associated with BGLOs? And if so, what does that ultimately mean? Work on BGLOs and diversity is required—specifically, non-Christian, nonblack, and nonheterosexual members. Whether there is any truth to the assertion that BGLOs practiced colorism deserves some treatment. Additionally, work needs to be done on the distinctions between BGLO chapters on white versus historically black campuses and on the gap between college and alumni members.

Developing a Critical BGLO Scholarship

A number of elements must be in place to create a sustainable critical BGLO scholarship; however, none is as important as accessibility to readers. Given that the vast majority of them are likely to be BGLO members and not academicians, the information has to be accessible to the general public, which is best accomplished by scholarly books.

MATERIALS: ACCESSING THE DATA

Many scholars turn to the typical data sources—books and journal articles. However, other data sources may yield more substantive answers to scholars' theories and hypotheses. Depending on the methodological approach, different data must be employed. Social scientists, for instance, will likely focus on members and chapters or perhaps broader units such as provinces or regions. As such, these scholars may work with student affairs personnel in contacting collegiate members or chapters, but they should not ignore alumni chapters. Certainly, at the macrolevel (and maybe even at the microlevel), support from a BGLO's national headquarters makes access to subjects more likely and more robust. Scholars in the humanities should look to collegiate yearbooks and newspapers, especially those at historically black colleges and universities. The text of these publications often casts a historical lens on these groups, and the photographs add to the richness of the historical analysis. The national journals of each NPHC group can serve as a valuable source of information about how they developed over time, their major programs and projects, and the issues that were most pressing at various points in history. They can be found in various university libraries throughout the country.[14] In addition, it is likely that each BGLO has its own archival materials preserved at its headquarters or with its national archivist. Whether they will make these documents accessible is another issue. Last, researchers should mine unpublished master's theses and doctoral dissertations for information; some of them are quite good, and most may be useful.

FACILITATORS: MAKING IT HAPPEN

Broadly, there are several entities that could stimulate a serious study of BGLOs. On college campuses, the Greek affairs office and various academic departments could play a significant role. Greek affairs is the repository for a great deal of information about the functioning of college chapters and is the best means of gaining access to students. Greek affairs offices may not be centers of scholarly research, but they should consider being more proactive, reaching out to faculty and sharing their data. Moreover, Greek affairs offices should encourage the academic departments on their respective campuses to establish courses on BGLOs. History, sociology, African American studies, and higher education administration programs could offer courses on BGLOs from different perspectives. Given the popularity of the topic generally, such classes would likely be popular. In addition to creating a body of potential fraternity and sorority members who are better versed on BGLOs, such classes might inspire undergraduates to go on to study these groups.

Nationally, BGLOs themselves as well as groups such as the Association of Fraternity Advisors (AFA), the National Association of Student Personnel Administrators (NASPA), and the Center for the Study of the College Fraternity (CSCF) could play a role in developing a critical BGLO scholarship. The NPHC and each constituent organization are likely the best facilitators, given their control over or access to archival information about the history and functioning of their organizations. They also have the ability to marshal members who are academicians to conduct research. Many of the most talented black professors in this nation are BGLO members, so it would not be difficult to pull together teams of researchers to write on any number of topics relevant to BGLOs. Additionally, AFA, NASPA, and CSCF could take a proactive role in identifying researchers and then encouraging and supporting their efforts to study BGLOs. These groups might also collaborate with one or more BGLO or the NPHC itself in pushing for substantive research on BGLOs.

OBSTACLES: OVERCOMING CHALLENGES

There is already an intellectual market for critical BGLO scholarship, so developing this line of scholarship seems promising. However, there are several factors that might militate against any substantive study of BGLOs. First is the attitude that a finite group of scholars should be the only ones engaged in this type of research. This may be particularly problematic when the people who determine this group are not academics but BGLO leaders or members or student affairs practitioners. The consequence is that if certain individuals are not deemed to be the *right* scholars, their scholarship may be undermined and hindered. An analogous obstacle is the belief by laypersons that anyone who lectures or claims to be an expert on BGLOs is necessarily a scholar. As noted earlier, certain formal characteristics identify scholars, and those who fail to possess them cannot be critical BGLO scholars. Placing nonscholars in the position of determining what is and is not scholarship may devalue the budding field and lower scholarly standards.

Second, BGLO members and leaders have a vested interest in ensuring that their organizations are well represented and well depicted in any book on BGLOs. Not surprisingly, they may be inclined to have unrealistic expectations from said publications. For example, they may want editorial control—demanding equal representation among organizations, the ability to review and sign off on the project before publication, and the right to alter the content, such as adding or deleting chapters. When authors or editors do not comply, organizations or members may attempt to regulate the project through formal and informal means. They may publicly—at least among their membership—boycott the project. They may deny researchers access to their membership. They may offer grants for research but make that funding conditional on altering the research project in some way that conforms to the organization's expectations. Any of these factors would undermine the scholarly integrity of a research project.

Third, there are several potential sources of funding for scholarship on BGLOs, but each has drawbacks. Institutional (university) sources may question the value of BGLOs as a research topic and thus be hesitant to fund research in that area. NASPA funds research on college student culture.[15] However, if the funds are used for any project garnering royalties, NASPA treats the grant as a loan, and the recipient must repay the money. This may exhaust royalties in some cases and thus be an untenable proposition for authors. The North American Inter-Fraternity Foundation (NIF) also provides grant funding, but only for projects that are "national" in scope.[16] The foundation's funding guidelines are unclear—for example, what is meant by "national"?—and it is unknown whether the NIF has supported any works on BGLOs. The CSCF provides grants for research, but its funding seems to be primarily for thesis and dissertation reaseach.[17] The AFA provides grants, and this may be the best alternative for critical BGLO scholars.[18]

The national bodies of NPHC organizations may be another source of funding. For instance, Alpha Kappa Alpha Sorority[19] and Delta Sigma Theta[20] both have national foundations that support research. Alpha Kappa Alpha's foundation functions at the regional level as well. However, such organizations tend to use their money for various philanthropic, community service, and civic activities, and any research they fund may need to be narrowly tailored. In fact, an organization may reject a proposal outright if the project is deemed too critical of BGLOs. Or funding may be refused if the organization providing the grant is not featured prominently in the project. Another pitfall is that a national organization may try to control the concept of a project or dictate what conclusions it draws.[21] BGLO chapters may be a source of funding for research that is local in nature, but the same concerns raised about the national bodies apply to chapters as well. In addition, chapters may be more inclined to see their funding of a project as a business investment, with an expectation of sharing in the profits.[22] This is not feasible with a scholarly book.

Fourth, it may be a challenge to find a publisher. Many publishers have no idea how substantial the potential market is for BGLO-related books. To date, the only academic presses to publish in this area are the University Press of Kentucky (two books), University of Illinois Press (two books), Fairleigh Dickinson University Press (one book), and the State University of New York Press (one book). Other practical concerns are royalty and advance rates, the quality of book preparation, and marketing of the book.[23] Academic presses often have limited budgets for marketing. The truth is that these presses commonly sell only a limited number of copies (200 to 700) of any book they publish, and more advertising usually does not significantly increase sales. Purchasing advertising space is often a fruitless endeavor, and direct mail is subject to increasing postage costs. Therefore, the responsibility for promoting, marketing, and selling the book is overwhelmingly the author's. BGLO scholars must provide potential publishers with a clear marketing strategy in their prospectus—delineating the market and the most strategic approaches to reaching it.

Despite the fact that books in this area must be scholarly, the reality of the market is that nonacademics are the main audience; this should influence how the author writes the book,[24] as well as how he or she pitches it to academic publishers. University press acquisition editors may be particularly concerned with whether a book on BGLOs is likely to be adopted for courses. Research suggests that university presses make the most revenue from sales to libraries or other institutions, related to college course adoptions, to general retailers, for export, direct to consumers, and to schools.[25] At this point, there are few if any courses on BGLOs; however, the majority of readers of books on BGLOs are BGLO members or aspiring members—a market that is quite robust. Another consideration is that academic presses necessarily price their books high, given that they typically sell a limited number of copies.[26] However, BGLO scholars should make the case for pricing their books more reasonably. The best rationale is that doing so will widen the market, allowing the press to sell enough copies at the lower price to still make a profit.

Conclusion

Critical BGLO scholarship is a viable area of research. Certain parameters, goals, and content define its features and move it beyond the realm of mere writing about BGLOs. Such research may provide individuals—members and nonmembers alike—with a better understanding of these groups and help these organizations capitalize on their strengths while minimizing their weaknesses. But if this line of research is to develop and flourish, interested parties must play an active role.

Notes

1. Such an approach is usually not feasible in legal academia, given that law-review submissions are reviewed by students. Scholarship must be submitted to the appropriate type of review in the particular discipline, and that review must meet the discipline's standard for ensuring that research is sound.

2. James Axtell, "Twenty-five Reasons to Publish," *Journal of Scholarly Publishing* (October 1997): 3–20.

3. Marybeth Gasman and Lucretia Payton-Stewart, "Twice Removed: A White Scholar Studies the History of Black Sororities and a Black Scholar Responds," *International Journal of Research and Method in Education* (October 2006): 129–49.

4. Axtell, "Twenty-five Reasons," 3–20.

5. Marcel Danesi, "From the (Ivory) Tower to the (Cold) Shower: A Tongue-in-Cheek Comparison of Academic versus Commercial and Trade Publishing," *Journal of Scholarly Publishing* (January 1999): 76.

6. Anonymous critic, e-mail to author, summer of 2005.

7. During the early twentieth century, a new area of jurisprudence, legal philoso-

phy, was developed that contravened the dominant notions of law at the time. This new model was called legal realism. Among their many arguments, the realists contended that law was insufficient in and of itself to answer legal questions; law must draw from other disciplines to effectively answer legal questions. The realists' focus was on social science. However, the progeny of legal realism, the law and society movement, broadened this scope to include other disciplines, such as the humanities. Realists were concerned with law in action—how the law impacts people in reality, not simply in theory. Also, realists believed that law should be employed to make public policy arguments. Though he may not have considered himself a realist, Charles Hamilton Houston was trained by the forerunner of legal realism—Harvard Law School's Roscoe Pound. Houston went on to become an exemplar of realist thinking and activity, serving as dean of Howard Law School while simultaneously practicing law—joining the academic and the practical. Also, in his battle to end school segregation, Houston employed both traditional legal tactics and social science. In a similar vein, critical BGLO scholarship should be both academic and practical; it should employ multiple research methodologies. See Roger A. Fairfax Jr., "Wielding the Double-edged Sword: Charles Hamilton Houston and Judicial Activism in the Age of Legal Realism," *Harvard Black Letter Law Journal* 14 (1998): 17–44; William W. Fisher III, Morton J. Horowitz, and Thomas A. Reed, eds., *American Legal Realism* (New York: Oxford University Press, 1993); Morton J. Horowitz, *The Transformation of American Law, 1870–1960* (New York: Oxford University Press, 1993); Lara Kalman, *Legal Realism at Yale, 1920–1960* (Chapel Hill: University of North Carolina Press, 1986); William E. Nelson, "*Brown v. Board of Education* and the Jurisprudence of Legal Realism," *St. Louis University Law Journal* 48 (2004): 795–838; John Henry Schlegel, *American Legal Realism and Empirical Social Science* (Chapel Hill: University of North Carolina Press, 1995); J. Clay Smith Jr. and E. Desmond Hogan, "Remembered Hero, Forgotten Contribution: Charles Hamilton Houston, Legal Realism, and Labor Law," *Harvard Black Letter Law Journal* 14 (1998): 1–16.

8. Elizabeth C. Fine, *Soulstepping: African American Step Shows* (Champaign: University of Illinois Press, 2003); Ricky Jones, *Black Haze: Violence and Manhood in Black Greek-Letter Fraternities* (Albany: State University of New York Press, 2004); Felix L. Armfield, *Eugene Kinckle Jones and the Rise of Professional Black Social Workers, 1910–1940* (Champaign: University of Illinois Press, 2007); Walter M. Kimbrough, *Black Greek 101: The Culture, Customs, and Challenges of Black Fraternities and Sororities* (Madison, N.J.: Fairleigh Dickinson University Press, 2003); Tamara L. Brown, Gregory S. Parks, and Clarenda M. Phillips, eds., *African American Fraternities and Sororities: The Legacy and the Vision* (Lexington: University Press of Kentucky, 2005).

9. Charles Harris Wesley, *Henry Arthur Callis: Life and Legacy* (Chicago: Foundation Publishers, 1977); Herman Mason Jr., *The Talented Tenth: The Founders and Presidents of Alpha*, 2d ed. (Winter Park, Fla.: Four-G Publishers, 1999).

10. David A. Canton, "The Struggle for Status and Justice: The Life of Judge Raymond Pace Alexander" (PhD diss., Temple University, 2001); Larry McGruder, "Kelly

Miller: The Life and Thoughts of a Black Intellectual, 1863–1939" (PhD diss., Miami University, 1984).

11. http://www.archives.upenn.edu/faids/upt/upt50/alexanderall.html (accessed July 4, 2006).

12. Although it does not conform to all the parameters of critical scholarship, for an example of a sound public history, see Paula Giddings, *In Search of Sisterhood: Delta Sigma Theta and the Challenge of the Black Sorority Movement* (New York: William Morrow, 1988).

13. Thomas Leroy Wendelmoot, "Masonic Allusions and Themes in the Works of Rudyard Kipling" (PhD diss., University of South Florida, 1980).

14. Among the fraternities' publications are Sigma Pi Phi's *Boule Journal* (Fisk University, Howard University); Alpha Phi Alpha's *Sphinx* (Howard University, Northern Illinois University, Ohio Historical Society, Ohio State University, Prairie View A&M University, Schomberg Library, University of Illinois, University of Michigan, West Virginia State College, Wisconsin Historical Society, Yale); the *Kappa Alpha Psi Journal* (California University of Pennsylvania, Cameron University, Central State University, Clarke Historical Library, Denver Public Library, Delaware State University, Dillard University, East Stroudsburg University, Florida A&M University, Grambling State University, Howard University, Kentucky State University, Lincoln University [Pa.], Lincoln University [Mo.], Lock Haven University of Pennsylvania, New York Institute of Technology–Central Islip, North Carolina A&T University, North Carolina Central University, Northeastern State University, Ohio State University, Old Dominion University, Prairie View A&M University, Southern Methodist University, SUNY Brockport, SUNY Old Westbury, Tennessee Tech University, Texas A&M University–Kingsville, Texas Southern University, University of Dayton, University of the District of Columbia, University of Illinois, University of Michigan, University of Southern Mississippi, University of South Florida, University of the Virgin Islands, Virginia Union University, West Virginia State College, Wilberforce University, Winston-Salem State University, Wisconsin Historical Society, Xavier University [La.]); Omega Psi Phi's *Oracle* (California State University–Sacramento, Central State University, Elizabeth City State University, Emory University, Fayetteville State University, Florida State University, Grambling State University, Howard University, Johnson C. Smith University, Kent State University, Lincoln University [Mo.], Morehead State University, Ohio State University, Ohio University, Norfolk State University, Schomberg Library, Southern University, SUNY Westbury, Texas Southern University, Tulane University, University of California–Santa Barbara, University of Illinois, Wilberforce University, Xavier University [La.]); and Phi Beta Sigma's *Crescent* (Central State University, Johnson C. Smith University, Lincoln University, Northwestern University, Schomberg Library, Wisconsin Historical Society, University of Michigan, University of Southern Mississippi, Winston Salem State University, Xavier University [La.]).

The sororities' publications are Alpha Kappa Alpha's *Ivy Leaf* (Baylor University,

Boston Public Library, Central State University, Chicago Public Library, College of New Jersey, Duke University, Emory University, Harvard University, Indiana University, Historical Society of West Pennsylvania, Illinois State University, Library of Congress, Michigan State University, North Carolina State University, Northern Illinois University, Ohio State University, Prairie View A&M University, Portland State University, Schomberg Library, Smith College, Southern University, SUNY Buffalo, Tulane University, University of Delaware, University of Illinois, University of Kentucky, University of Missouri–Kansas City, University of Oklahoma, University of Oregon, University of Pennsylvania, University of Pittsburgh, University of Tennessee, Virginia State University, Western Reserve Historical Society, Wisconsin Historical Society); Delta Sigma Theta's *Delta* (Angelo State University, Harvard University, Howard University, Northwestern University, Schomberg Library, Texas Southern University, University of Illinois, University of Virginia, Wisconsin University); Zeta Phi Beta's *Archon* (Central State University, Delaware State University, Harvard University, Schomberg Library, Southern University, University of the Virgin Islands, Wisconsin Historical Society, Xavier University [La.]); and Sigma Gamma Rho's *Aurora* (Balch Institute for Ethnic Studies, Central State University, Delaware State University, Florida State University, Historical Society of Pennsylvania, Indiana Historical Society, Johnson C. Smith University, Kent State University, Lincoln University [Mo.], Norfolk State University, Savannah State University, Southern University, Texas Southern University, University of Illinois, University of Memphis, Wilberforce University, Wisconsin Historical Society, Xavier University [La.]).

15. http://www.naspa.org/foundation/index.cfm (accessed July 4, 2006).

16. http://www.nif-inc.net/ (accessed July 4, 2006).

17. http://www.indiana.edu/~sao/cscfsite/ (accessed July 4, 2006).

18. http://www.fraternityadvisors.org/Foundation.aspx (accessed July 4, 2006).

19. http://www.akaeaf.org (accessed July 4, 2006).

20. http://www.deltafoundation.net (accessed July 4, 2006).

21. While I was preparing this book, an executive officer from one NPHC organization strongly encouraged me to remove certain chapters. The individual indicated that if I did not, the organization would informally boycott the book.

22. When I was soliciting grant funding for my earlier coedited work, *African American Fraternities and Sororities*, a BGLO alumni chapter considered providing such funds, but only if there were profit sharing involved, apparently assuming that academic publishing was as profitable as trade publishing.

23. Allan H. Pasco, "Basic Advice for Novice Authors," *Journal of Scholarly Publishing* (January 2002): 75–89; Albert N. Greco, Walter F. O'Connor, Sharon P. Smith, and Robert M. Wharton, "The Price of University Press Books, 1989–2000," *Journal of Scholarly Publishing* (October 2003): 4–39; Carolyn Wood, "The Marketing that Authors Really Want," *Journal of Scholarly Publishing* (April 2005): 133–38; James M. Lang, "Adventures in Trade Publishing," *Journal of Scholarly Publishing* (April 2005): 139–44.

24. Audrey Thompson, "How Scholarly Writing Makes Readers Work," *Journal of Scholarly Publishing* (January 1998): 88–100. This can be done by writing in a more reader-friendly tone or by placing the notes in the back of the book, as opposed to at the end of chapters.

25. Albert N. Greco, "The General Reader Market for University Press Books in the United States, 1990–1999, with Projections for years 2000 through 2004," *Journal of Scholarly Publishing* (January 2001): 61–86.

26. Pasco, "Basic Advice," 75–89.

Part I

The Founders

1

The First and Finest
The Founders of Alpha Phi Alpha Fraternity

Stefan Bradley

In creating a fraternity at a starkly white Ivy League university (Cornell), Alpha Phi Alpha's founders (affectionately known as the Jewels) were part of a black intelligentsia that created opportunities for black people in the United States. Established in 1906 as the first incorporated collegiate fraternity created explicitly for African Americans, Alpha was the offspring of two important historical movements that contested Jim Crow in America: the Niagara movement and the "uplift" movement.

The Niagara movement was led by some of black America's brightest minds. Men such as W. E. B. DuBois used their intellect to fight Jim Crow in all its ugly forms. In this way, the black intelligentsia was in the vanguard of the fight for total freedom. At the same time, black America's middle and elite classes took steps to help downtrodden black people in what was known as the uplift movement. This was an extension of the "self-help" program that leaders such as Booker T. Washington had propagated. To advance the uplift movement, class- and race-aware black activists formed various service societies and social clubs in their campaign against racism.

In the wake of the uplift and Niagara movements, the Jewels created a fraternal bond among black men that has endured for more than 100 years. The seven Jewels of the fraternity were Henry Arthur Callis, Charles Henry Chapman, Eugene Kinckle Jones, George Biddle Kelley, Nathaniel Allison Murray, Robert Harold Ogle, and Vertner Woodson Tandy.

A Lineage of Uplift

"First of all; servants of all; we shall transcend all." That is the motto of Alpha Phi Alpha Fraternity Inc. As the first official fraternity for African American college men, Alpha focused on service to the community and displayed many of the qualities of black America's elite class in the early twentieth century. Whether the Jewels realized it or not, Alpha, by way of its founding and programs, transcended much of black and white America at the time. As such, early Alpha represented the uplift movement by way of the founders' economic standing and social status and their politically charged push for racial equality—a lofty ideal at the time.

At a time when most black Americans (and much of America in general) concentrated on tilling, planting, cultivating, and harvesting, some Americans looked beyond the fields to make a life for themselves. For those who could afford it, there was the possibility of higher education. This was a relatively new option for African Americans, as many institutions for the education of black people had been established shortly after the Civil War.

By the beginning of the twentieth century, though, a majority of black people still lived in the South and worked at jobs associated with agriculture. Some owned the land on which they worked, but many others sharecropped or tenant-farmed the land they cultivated. Sharecropping and tenant farming, by most modern accounts, were glorified versions of slavery for many black people.[1] Because their agreements often consisted of written contracts, white owners frequently cheated black sharecroppers. This was possible, in part, because so many African American laborers were unable to read.[2] In addition, there was little recourse for those black sharecroppers who caught landowners cheating on their contracts. Indeed, Jim Crow justice prevailed throughout the court system and in much of the rest of the nation.

By the twentieth century, black leaders attempted to assist the race in different ways. Booker T. Washington tried to improve the lot of black farmers by offering agricultural, mechanical, and industrial training at institutions such as Tuskegee. He advocated a plan that socially accommodated racism but encouraged black people to help themselves by becoming indispensable to southern economic progress in agriculture and the service industry. To many African Americans, a liberal arts education at a university seemed unattainable. With that in mind, Washington pushed a platform of economic self-help for blacks through thrift and ownership.[3]

W. E. B. DuBois sought to provide different opportunities for African Americans. As a northerner born after slavery ended, DuBois had a different outlook from that of Washington. The first black person to earn a doctorate from the prestigious Harvard University, DuBois urged the best and brightest African American minds to pursue professional careers as doctors, lawyers, teachers, and the like.[4] He and Washington clashed in their approaches to social and political freedom, but they agreed that, to advance, black people must uplift themselves.

The idea of racial uplift took on different meanings in the early twentieth century. As historian Kevin Gaines explains in his work *Uplifting the Race,* to former slaves, uplift meant "transcendence of worldly oppression and misery." The founders of Alpha Phi Alpha also saw transcendence as a crucial step for fraternity members. Gaines notes that, in search of this uplift, "African Americans have, with almost religious fervor, regarded education as the key to liberation." Likewise, the education and advancement of black men was the basis for the initial interaction among the fraternity's founders. Finally, Gaines's analysis reveals an aspect of Alpha that has been underemphasized in the past. He suggests that "many black elites sought status, moral authority, and recognition of their humanity by distinguishing themselves, as bourgeois agents of civilization, from the presumably undeveloped black majority."[5] The founders of the fraternity attempted to prove that African Americans had a culturally relevant past and that they, as students at an elite university, represented the best of that legacy.

Welcome to Ithaca

The Jewels of Alpha created the fraternity in the shadows of these movements. In 1905, while most black people headed to the fields, several black men attended one of the nation's most esteemed institutions of higher education, Cornell University. Situated on a hill in Ithaca, New York, Cornell was one of several Ivy League universities that admitted African Americans at the time. Although it admitted black students, Cornell was, like the winters in Ithaca, cold for nonwhite learners. As a member of the Ivy League, Cornell's curriculum was broad and featured rigorous courses of study in many areas, and the school administered entrance examinations for incoming students. The opportunity to matriculate at such an institution was rare for many Americans but even more so for African Americans.

The initial intention of the Jewels was not to create a fraternity at Cornell but rather to fight the isolation of the black students. The university had graduated its first African Americans some sixteen years prior to the Jewels' arrival on campus in 1905.[6] The Jewels were part of a small minority population on campus—they were seven of eleven African Americans who arrived that year.[7] In all, there were sixteen black males at the universtiy.[8] At least six African Americans from the previous year's class had not returned. Indeed, the statistics were bleak. The rigors of the academic programs, racial isolation, and finances were all threats to the survival of African American students at Cornell.

Scholastic Socialization

To confront these threats, several black students formed a social/study group for the sake of networking. An older student, C. C. Poindexter, helped facilitate the social mixers that the founders attended. Jewel Murray remembered the mixers fondly and explained that the meetings "provided . . . wholesome recreation and amusement."[9]

At the time, black students did not live on campus, so they took up residence with the black citizens of Ithaca. It was in the homes of residents such as Edward Newton that the social/study group held its events. Although the black students may have been isolated on campus, they enjoyed the support of the larger African American community in town. According to Jewel Kelley, this was a blessing: "The social life among our group was carried on in the many comfortable homes of the Negroes [in Ithaca]. Nearly every Friday night, we were welcomed at the home of Mr. and Mrs. Wm. Cannon where we could meet their charming daughter and the other young women of the community. We were allowed to dance and good eats were always served us."[10] For college students, that was a blessing indeed.

In addition to socializing, the early group members worked to improve their academic opportunities by studying together. The students borrowed one study technique from the members of white fraternities on campus. They banked the tests they took so that black students who took the courses in the future would know how and what to study.[11]

Soon afterward, some leading members of this social/study group suggested that it become a literary society. The idea of a literary society was radical, in the sense that so many Americans were either illiterate or had little or no time for leisure reading. That these African American college men enjoyed such a luxury was telling. Although all the members of the group were amenable to adding literary discourse to their meetings, they could not agree on what to name the society. Some members, such as Jewels Callis and Jones, wanted to use Greek letters, like the white fraternities did. Poindexter, however, demurred, claiming that there were no Greek signifiers that could be used for African Americans. After some debate and research, the leading members of the society came up with the name Alpha Phi Alpha.[12]

To support themselves financially, some of the Jewels worked in white fraternity houses, so they were familiar with the idea of a fraternity. Callis and Kelley were employed as waiters at two different fraternity houses, and they made extra money by tutoring some of the fraternity men.[13] At the turn of the century, attending a college or a university was a feat that some black students had managed to accomplish, but creating a fraternity that paralleled white organizations would have been truly remarkable.

According to Murray, while the group was still meeting as a literary society, he and Jewel Ogle "thought that we (the members of the literary society) ought to try and band ourselves into a fraternal organization the same as the white boys on the hill."[14] Not surprisingly, some members considered the suggestion of a fraternity fantastic; they did not believe that Africans had enough history on which to base a fraternity. Because of institutional and cultural racial bias, many Americans believed that black people lacked the cultural background and sophistication necessary to create organizations that mirrored the best of white society. In spite of the uncertainty of a few, the idea of a fraternity became a goal for the majority of black men in the literary society.

Leading the early charge for a fraternity were all seven Jewels and society members James H. Morton and Morgan T. Phillips.[15] Those men participated in an initiation ceremony for the society that had been devised by several Jewels (with the help of white fraternity members at whose houses they worked), and the ritual took place at a local Masonic hall in Ithaca. The members of the society had the support of various white fraternities, professors, and black community members who offered moral and financial encouragement. Unfortunately, they did not enjoy the backing of society president Poindexter, but his discouragement actually fueled their desire to push forward with the idea of a fraternal brotherhood. In the weeks leading up to the official decision to become a fraternity, the society members debated vigorously whether to move ahead with the idea.[16]

"Our Dear Fraternal Bond"

On Tuesday, December 4, 1906, Poindexter submitted his resignation from the literary society, as did another member. With the main opposition removed, seven members of the literary society voted to create Alpha Phi Alpha Fraternity at Cornell University.[17] Although black physicians in Philadelphia had created a fraternity in 1904, and college fraternities had existed in the United States for more than 130 years, no previous fraternity had fashioned itself specifically for the fellowship of black college men. In 1905, Ogle had researched the potential existence of a fraternity at Ohio State University but found no evidence to prove as much. In *Black Greek 101*, author Walter Kimbrough mentions a fraternity that had a short life in another northern school, but neither it nor any other college organization got beyond the initial stages. In this singular act, Alpha distinguished itself. This black college fraternity quickly initiated its first members and set about the business of refining the experiment. Incidentally, the fraternity treated those first initiates to such fineries as demitasse, ladyfingers, and lamb chops—not a typical meal for the majority of Americans.[18]

Believing that other black college men needed the fellowship that the fraternity had to offer, Alpha sought to expand. Although not outright exclusionary, the fraternity was selective about opening its doors to members from other universities. Renowned historian and past general president of the fraternity Charles H. Wesley noted, "It was only natural that the thought of the master builders of this early period should be turned toward other colleges and universities of first rank."[19] The original members of the fraternity debated just how open Alpha should be to expansion. Kelley and Tandy believed it was their duty to guard the fraternity from members who would harm its ideals. Kelley wrote that Tandy "was anxious that we retain our custom of selecting members in our Chapters so that the organizations would not become packed with undesirables."[20] The founders eventually agreed that the fraternity should allow "the granting of charters to bodies that meet with their distinct approval."[21]

Toward that end, in 1907, Alpha expanded to Howard University. Established in 1867, Howard was described as an "institution of the 'higher grade for training colored preachers and teachers to help uplift some of the four million recently emancipated slaves and a quarter million Negroes who had been born free.'"[22] Considered in many circles to be the most elite of black colleges, Howard became the first of the historically black colleges and universities to recognize a Greek-letter fraternity. Thus, Alpha Phi Alpha was the first fraternity for black college men to be established at a historically black and a predominantly white university.

Alpha's expansion during its first twenty years of existence also indicated its desire to reach universities of "Grade A" recognition. As Alpha's official history explained, some of the new chapters to which the fraternity granted charters were "located at some of the best universities in the country."[23] By 1926, Alpha had formed chapters at six of the eight Ivy League universities—Cornell, Columbia, Yale, Pennsylvania, Brown, and Harvard. In the two decades after its founding, Alpha chartered forty-one chapters in twenty-four different states; eleven resided at historically black colleges and universities. In 1912, Alpha established a chapter at the very first historically black university, Lincoln University in Pennsylvania.

The fraternity established another first in 1908 when Alpha became the first international fraternity for black college men when it chartered a chapter at the University of Toronto.[24] Also in that year, the fraternity incorporated in the state of New York, and in 1912, it incorporated in the United States of America.

Early in its history, Alpha set about uplifting the race by establishing its first national program: "Go to High School; Go to College." As previously indicated, the members of the uplift movement placed immense value on education and service to the race. In creating such a program, Alpha sought to uplift the race through its youth. Although the education of black youth ranked high on the Alpha's agenda, the fraternity did not overlook the need for African Americans' participation in politics. Just as members of the Niagara movement attempted to do, Alpha Phi Alpha attempted to register black American voters with its campaign "A Voteless People Is a Hopeless People." That program illustrated Alpha's ability to look outside itself for answers to societal problems. The fact that a college fraternity, which is essentially an organization for social interaction, would take service to its racial community so seriously reflected Alpha's commitment to using social and economic status to improve the race.

The Crowned Jewels of Cornell

The fact that the Jewels could afford to attend Cornell spoke to their intellectual ability and class status in black America. To be sure, the Jewels were the sons of relatively established families. Various members of their families had served in the Civil War, attended college, taught at the college level, were ministers, owned businesses, and more.

HENRY ARTHUR CALLIS

Henry Arthur Callis's father attended Hampton Institute, took several courses at Cornell, and eventually became a prominent African Methodist Episcopal pastor. Jewel Callis (1887–1974) was also related to abolitionist Frederick Douglass. He remembered living in a former "station" of the Underground Railroad and discussing it with Douglass and Harriet Tubman.[25] Growing up in Binghamton, New York, Callis was a high school standout who won a state scholarship to attend Cornell. He claimed to have decided to attend Cornell when he was six years old.[26]

Although he was prominent among the founders, Callis preferred not to be addressed as a "Jewel," as he found the title somewhat pretentious. He was secretary of the social/study group, and with the help of professors on campus and Jewel Jones, he came up with the name Alpha Phi Alpha. Callis and Jones also created Alpha's ritual. Callis led the movement to incorporate the fraternity in 1908, served as the third president of Alpha's chapter on the Cornell campus, and assisted in organizing a chapter at the University of Michigan and in Chicago.[27] Incidentally, he was the only Jewel to ever hold the title of general president of the fraternity.

At one point, Callis had to leave Cornell due to his inability to pay tuition. As Roscoe C. Giles, one of the first initiates of the fraternity, remembered, "by his indefatigable determination," Callis "returned to secure his degree, setting an example for the faint hearted."[28] Indeed, Callis conquered one of the many threats that faced black students at Cornell.

After attaining his degree at Cornell, Callis attended the University of Chicago and in 1922 received a degree from Rush Medical College in Chicago.[29] He achieved national acclaim as a medical doctor and ardently advocated the training of African American physicians. In one article he explained that "the Negro physician is in a special class and bears a peculiar burden in this country only because of his racial identity."[30] He argued that the ratio of black doctors to black patients was too low and that colleges, particularly black colleges, should do more to train students in the sciences to prepare them for medical school. He did his best to solve that problem by taking a post as an associate professor at the Howard University Medical School. Throughout his career, Callis worked at the U.S. Veterans Hospital in Tuskegee, Alabama, and maintained a private practice in Chicago.

Callis was a member of the National Medical Association (NMA), which had been created in 1895 by seven black doctors because the American Medical Association (AMA) refused to accept black physicians.[31] When the AMA also refused to recognize the research of black doctors in its medical journal, the NMA created its own journal, and Callis was published frequently in the *Journal of the National Medical Association*. Thus, Callis was part of two pioneering black organizations at the turn of the century.

Callis had a very full life. On January 9, 1909, he eloped with Alice Dunbar, the former wife of Paul Lawrence Dunbar and a political activist in her own right.[32] The relationship did not last. Eventually, Callis married Myrna Colson, an educator, social worker, and member of Alpha Kappa Alpha Sorority.[33] Both Callis and his wife were life members of the Association for the Study of Negro Life and History (ASNLH). In fact, Mrs. Callis conducted a study on black employment in Washington, D.C., with famed historian Lorenzo Greene, and they presented their findings at an ASNLH conference. Another prominent historian (and Alpha member), Rayford Logan, used Callis's words as the title for a chapter in his seminal work, *Betrayal of the Negro*.[34] Callis had assessed the progress of race relations at the beginning of the twentieth century as stagnated on a "low, rugged plateau," and Logan used Callis's assessment to frame his explanation of the racism faced by African Americans.

Not surprisingly, Callis nurtured relationships with other black leaders who had a hand in advancing the status of the race. He corresponded with Alpha men such as scholar W. E. B. DuBois and activist and performer Paul Robeson. He also stayed in contact with community leaders and scholars such as Mary Church Terrell and Alain Locke.[35] Callis's communications with such influential people provided testimony to his role in shaping twentieth-century black America.

CHARLES HENRY CHAPMAN

With great sentimentality, Charles Henry Chapman (1877–1934)[36] observed, "There never was a more beautiful episode in my life than the small part I played in the organization of this fraternity in 1906."[37] Hailing from Cayuga County, New York, Chapman attended high school at Old Howard University Academy. He was older than many of the other Jewels, having enrolled at Cornell in 1900–1901, left school, and then reenrolled in 1902.[38] According to Callis, Chapman was "the proprietor of a small brickyard (and) of a private dining room for students."[39] His experience as either the manager or owner of Spencer Brickyard in Spencer, New York,[40] may have fueled his desire to move forward with the fraternity idea. While other members of the society (such as Poindexter and George Thompkins) "could accept inter-collegiate association, but not fraternity . . . the faith of Chapman had been increased by his own success in business."[41] Chapman helped oversee the first initiation ceremony for the society and spoke at the first initiation ceremony of the fraternity.

Chapman had a varied educational career. Before attending and graduating from Cornell, he spent some time at Hampton College and, at one point, took courses from Ohio State University. In school, he made his highest marks in agriculture, farm management, and soil mapping, so it was a logical step for him to become an educator along those lines.[42] He taught agriculture for a short while at Alabama Agricultural and Mechanical College and Jackson State College and joined the faculty at Florida Agricultural and Mechanical College in 1924.[43] Incidentally, Chapman won prizes for his dairy herds.

Chapman was an inspiration to many. In fact, his fraternity brothers claimed that, in 1932, they organized a chapter of Alpha at Florida A&M with his encouragement. Two years later, Chapman died. The *Baltimore Afro-American* reported that his "Wife Hurried from Cleveland to His Bedside."[44]

EUGENE KINCKLE JONES

Eugene Kinckle Jones's father attended what is now Colgate University; his mother graduated from Howard University and taught at Hartshorn Memorial College.[45] Jewel Jones (1885–1954) attended Wayland Academy in Virginia and later earned a bachelor's degree from Virginia Union. His first year at Cornell, he took up civil engineering to prove to university officials that he was capable of performing at the high level required to enter Cornell's graduate school.

Jones was a unique Jewel for several reasons. First, he had already received his bachelor's degree when he came to Cornell in the fall of 1906 to pursue a master's degree. Second, he was actually one of the first initiates in the literary society. Third, and most importantly for Alpha, Jones was not designated a Jewel until 1952.

According to Thomas Pawley III, longtime fraternity member and scholar, although fraternity members unofficially addressed the founders as "Jewels" before 1929, it was not until that year that the term became an official designation. From that time through the middle of the century, another brother, James H. Morton, held the esteemed title and was considered the seventh Jewel. Then, at the 1952 national convention in Ohio, Jewels Callis, Kelley, and Murray and fraternity historian Wesley decided that Jones deserved to take Morton's place as a Jewel.[46] Years later, Callis wrote a letter to Wesley justifying his position on the matter of designating Jones a Jewel. He explained, "E. K. Jones ranks as a founder because he with Vertner Tandy set up the three other chapters which, under our N.Y. incorporation, required the *first* general convention."[47]

Indeed, Jones did a great deal for the fraternity. He was on the committee to draft a constitution and to re-create the ritual of Alpha, and he acted as the second president of the original chapter. As indicated in Callis's letter, Jones and Tandy established the second chapter of Alpha at Howard University in 1907.

Shortly afterward, Jones set up a chapter at his alma mater, Virginia Union. During his winter travels, he chartered another chapter at the University of Toronto, making him responsible for internationalizing Alpha. In 1911, he chartered the first official alumni chapter in Louisville, Kentucky, where he taught at Louisville High School for a short time.[48]

After Cornell, Jones became a leader in the movement to improve life for African Americans. In 1916, he took a post as executive secretary of the National Urban League (NUL), an organization that sought to assist southern black migrants adjust to the industrial North through training and education.[49] In that capacity, he lobbied the U.S. secretary of labor to appoint an African American to the post of director of Negro economics.[50] During the Great Depression, Jones served on President Franklin Delano Roosevelt's "black cabinet," which advised the administration on matters of race.[51] Like several of the other founders, Jones was in contact with the shapers of black America. In fact, scholar (and Alpha member) E. Franklin Frazier worked under Jones's tutelage at the NUL, and Jones corresponded with opera singer Marian Anderson.[52]

Jones married Blanche Ruby Watson in 1909, and the couple had two children.[53] For the rest of his life, he took care of his family and other black families. Further, in his capacity as an NUL executive, National Conference of Social Work member, and member of Alpha, Jones did his best to help African Americans take care of themselves. He died two years after receiving the title of Jewel.

GEORGE BIDDLE KELLEY

George Biddle Kelley (1884–1962) was the son of a skilled craftsman who had been a fugitive slave and Union soldier during the Civil War.[54] He was the grandson of one of the most famous African Methodist Episcopal ministers of the nineteenth century. Kelley's uncle was a graduate of Harvard and had served during the Civil War with Company A of the esteemed Fifty-fourth Regiment of Massachusetts Volunteers, a unit consisting mostly of literate, free black men. Kelley graduated from the Troy Military Academy and took courses at Rensselaer Polytechnic Institute before enrolling at Cornell to study civil engineering.[55]

The first president of the original Alpha chapter, Kelley made the motion to approve the name Alpha Phi Alpha for the literary society. He worked at the Theta Beta Pi fraternity house, so the idea of a fraternity was at the forefront of his mind.[56] He also participated heavily in advancing the discussion of literature and was acting chair when the founders made the decision to become a fraternity.

Upon graduation from Cornell, Kelley gained employment with the New York State Engineering Department and worked on the Barge Canal. He later spent thirty-two years working for the State Department of Taxation and Finance and assisted with personal tax preparation.[57] He retired in 1952.

Kelley was rare among the founders, in that he frequently attended national conventions and participated in fraternity operations after he left Cornell. Kelley captured the spirit of Alpha with a story he liked to tell, and fraternity historian Skip Mason has done well to document it. As the story went, Kelley had set up a date in Utica, New York, but discovered that his paycheck would be delayed, leaving him unable to pay for the evening out. A desperate Kelley contacted the founding brothers who still attended Cornell and, within a day, he had enough money for his date.[58] The generosity of the other Jewels represented the meaning of fraternity for him. (By the way, Kelley never indicated how well the date went.)

Kelley maintained a busy life outside of Alpha. He was a thirty-third-degree Mason, a member of the Liberty Presbyterian Church, and a board member of his local YMCA. Carrying on the fight for the race, Kelley was the vice chairman of the Troy Council against Discrimination.[59] Finally, he maintained a loving marriage with Harriet Brooks Grossman, whom he wed in 1934. When Kelley died, his widow received telegrams from Governor Nelson Rockefeller, Attorney General Louis Lefkowits, and State Commissioner for Human Rights J. Edward Conway, testifying to Kelley's service to New York State.[60]

NATHANIEL ALLISON MURRAY

In many ways, Nathaniel Allison Murray (1884–1959) was born into black high society. Murray's family lived a relatively privileged life in Washington, D.C. At one time, Murray's father was one of the richest African Americans in Washington. His grandfather was a free black man and an abolitionist, and one of that grandfather's grandparents was Scottish royalty.[61] Murray also had an uncle who died during John Brown's raid on Harpers Ferry. His mother graduated from Oberlin College and taught at Howard; she was involved with the National League of Colored Women and the Colored Women's Club. Murray's siblings also attended college at Harvard, Cornell, and Oberlin. Like at least one other Jewel, Murray graduated from M Street High School in Washington D.C.[62]

Murray was important to Alpha in many different ways. Aside from founding the fraternity, his remembrances and recollections provided a good deal of the material that constitutes Alpha's written history. More than any other founder, Murray noted the events of the early years of the fraternity in his speeches, articles, and addresses. He, like Kelley, attended national conventions and continued to offer his opinions on the direction of the brotherhood.

As Murray reflected: "In the fall of 1905, your humble servant matriculated into Cornell University, Ithaca, New York, as a student in the College of Agriculture."[63] From the first meetings of the social/study group in his room, Murray was part of the contingent that wanted to create a fraternity. In fact, he seconded the first motion to move in that direction. At the first initiation of the literary society, he played the organ to set the mood. Murray even suggested a $1 initiation fee and seconded the motion that monthly dues be set at 50 cents. Murray never held a position in the national fraternity, but he made all elected positions possible with his work on the original constitution committee.[64]

After college, Murray, like Chapman, began a career as an educator. He returned to Washington, D.C., to teach botany at Dunbar High School and later Armstrong Technical High School, where he stayed until the 1940s. Murray also helped charter an alumni chapter in Washington. By the end of his career, he owned several homes from which he rented rooms. Upon retirement, he moved to Los Angeles, where he mentored young Alpha brothers and became involved with the local alumni chapter.[65]

Murray valued both family and fraternity. He stayed faithfully married to his wife, Mary, until his death; she died in 1974. The couple had two daughters. Coming from a proud and established family, it was fitting that Murray establish a brotherhood that endured for longer than a century, and several of his cousins and nephews were members. For Murray, the fraternity was his crowning achievement.

ROBERT HAROLD OGLE

Robert Harold Ogle (1886–1936) attended M Street High School, from which many students went on to higher education.[66] Upon his arrival in Ithaca, Ogle stayed in the home where Alpha as a fraternity was born: 411 East State Street. It was the residence of Archie and Annie Singleton, and they allowed the founders to meet there. The idea of a fraternity took hold of Ogle in 1905, when he saw an article in the *Chicago Defender* (one of the most widely read black periodicals in the early twentieth century) describing Pi Gamma Omicron, an alleged fraternity at Ohio State University. Although the registrar of the university informed him that no black fraternity existed there, Ogle and the other Jewels were intrigued.

As the social/study group transitioned into a literary society, Ogle acted as the organization's secretary. He made the initial motion to organize into a fraternity.[67] Soon after the fraternity came to life, he suggested that a chapter be raised at Howard University in his hometown of Washington, D.C. Brothers of Alpha will always remember Ogle, because he proposed that black and old gold be the official colors of the fraternity.[68] More than that, he chaired the fraternity's historical commission that oversaw the publication of Alpha's official history in 1929.[69]

By the time Alpha Phi Alpha became a fraternity, Ogle had already married Helen Moore, the daughter of one of the Ithaca families that welcomed the black students of Cornell into their homes. The couple had two daughters while Ogle continued his studies. Sorrowfully, Ogle's wife died in 1908. In spite of his deep grief, he dutifully finished his degree, leaving his daughters in the care of his mother-in-law. He and his daughters later moved back to Washington, D.C.[70]

There, in the nation's capital, Ogle established himself. He chartered an alumni chapter of Alpha and entered the field of politics. Under the chairmanship of Senator Francis E. Warren of Wyoming, Ogle held the position of secretary of the Senate Appropriations Committee. Later, he clerked for two municipal court judges, one of whom was a member of Alpha. His service undoubtedly fostered his uncanny knowledge of parliamentary procedure, and the brothers of his alumni chapter marveled at his ability to keep meetings running efficiently.[71]

In addition to his reputation as an excellent parliamentarian, according to Ogle's daughter, the fraternity founder had an even bigger reputation for being one of Washington's most eligible bachelors. In an interview with author Skip Mason, she explained that her father was extremely handsome and very well dressed, and he eventually remarried. Like Callis, he married an Alpha Kappa Alpha, Marea Scott.[72] The couple fit in well with black Washington high society and lived happily together.[73]

Unfortunately, Ogle passed away in 1936, becoming the first of the founders to die. He left behind his wife, who never remarried; his daughters (one of whom became an Alpha Kappa Alpha); and thousands of brothers. Ogle's attention to detail and his desire for a better life led to the creation of a lasting brotherhood.

VERTNER WOODSON TANDY

Vertner Woodson Tandy (1885–1949) was born in Lexington, Kentucky. His father owned a construction company and was a prominent member of

Lexington's black society. Tandy studied at Tuskegee under Booker T. Washington for a short time. Like Kelley and Jones, Tandy had attended another institution of higher learning before entering Cornell.[74]

Tandy had several characteristics that distinguished him from the other founders. First, he was born and reared in Lexington, which was the southernmost birth city and state of all the Jewels. Second, to many members of Alpha, Tandy seemed larger than life—literally. He stood taller than six feet and weighed some 230 pounds. His size, though, was apparently offset by his charming nature. Callis remembered the Kentucky native showing up at campus wearing his ROTC cadet uniform, complete with tightly fitting pants, and a saxophone tucked under his arm. From the beginning, Callis found Tandy to be a "jovial good natured, lovable fellow with a keen sense of humor."[75]

According to Giles, Tandy, "in his college days . . . was mischievous and full of tricks and fun." He recalled that roommates Tandy and Jones pulled a prank on their landlady, who was in the habit of bursting into their room unannounced, as if she expected to catch them doing something immoral. This aggravated the two Jewels, and they plotted to put an end to her interruptions. Knowing that the landlady was a devout Christian who abhorred gambling and games, the Jewels hatched a scheme and enlisted the help of several freshmen, who were instructed to enter the room and take off their clothes. Understandably hesitant, the freshmen were convinced to comply, "under the duress of some threatening gestures of . . . Tandy." The Jewels then pretended to be in the midst of a very loud and boisterous card game and waited for the landlady to come break it up. When she entered the room without knocking, she was treated to the sight of several naked freshmen.[76]

Giles relayed another story about the fun-loving Jewel, who was "not . . . a paragon of virtue" and was, on occasion, "a devotee to the Shrine of Becchus [sic] and Aphrodite." This time, Tandy went missing for a week and would not explain his whereabouts when he returned. Although the brothers were worried, they did not query him further. Soon afterward, though, a preacher from out of town came to Giles's room, inquiring about a "Reverend Vertner Tandy." When Giles and his roommates explained that no minister lived at their residence, the preacher insisted that Reverend Tandy did live there and then went on to describe him. Giles later conceded that "the F.B.I. could not have given a better description of the distinguished Jewel." As it turned out, during Tandy's weeklong absence, he had gone out of town and run out of traveling money. To make his fare back, he had preached a sermon at the minister's church, where the congregation took up a collection for him. Apparently thinking that he would never see the man again, Tandy had told the preacher to contact him if he were ever in Ithaca.[77]

Though not a minister, Tandy had the spirit of Alpha in his heart. Some brothers might remember Tandy's mischievous antics, but all members of Alpha remember his contribution to the fraternity. For instance, Tandy, a student of architecture, designed the fraternity pin that all Alphas wear. Tandy also acted as the first treasurer of the fraternity, and he, along with Jones, helped charter the second chapter of the fraternity at Howard University and the fourth chapter at the University of Toronto.

Tandy's determination to make life better for black people did not end when he graduated. When the dean of women at Sage College (an affiliate of Cornell) refused to admit black women to the college, Tandy and others led a movement to allow black women to enroll.[78] Their efforts were successful, and Sage reluctantly admitted black female students. Tandy was a Mason and an Elk, and in 1917, he became the first African American to be commissioned as an officer in the New York National Guard. He quickly moved up the ranks to captain and then major and eventually commanded a segregated unit of the Fifteenth Infantry.[79]

Aside from being an officer, a member of several fraternal orders, and an activist, Tandy was one of the first black architects registered in the state of New York. In that role, he became a prominent figure in the upper echelons of black society. He designed several buildings in New York City, including St. Phillip's Protestant Episcopal Church.[80] He gained membership in the National Negro Business League (NNBL), another organization that sought the progress of black people through work. The NNBL was the brainchild of men such as Booker T. Washington, who desired to uplift the race through business ownership.

Men were not the only ones who took Washington's and the NNBL's goals to heart. Madam C. J. Walker became a multimillionaire by patenting her hair care products and inventions. Based in New York City, she employed hundreds of black people, one of whom was Tandy. Biographer Tananarive Due notes that Walker "built her house with money she'd made from Negroes, and many of those Negroes earned their living from other Negroes." Her opulence, as it turns out, benefited the rest of New York City's black community. She hired Tandy to design her home, according to Due, to make the point that black people could advance if they united their efforts.[81]

Working with Walker certainly benefited Tandy, who expressed as much at a meeting of the NNBL. He stated, "I want to say to you (Walker), through your unselfish loyalty to your race and through your achievements and successes that a Negro has been successful and has achieved success in architecture."[82] Walker spared no expense on her home, and this worked well for Tandy. Another biographer of Walker maintained that "Tandy, it must be said, had profited handsomely from the arrangement, building commission fees into nearly every transaction, from the purchase of the organ to the acquisition of the roof tiles." In the end, the design was a marvel—"a stately building with a bowed red-brick-and-limestone Georgian façade."[83] Tandy maintained a relationship with Walker even after he completed the construction of her home. In 1919, both Tandy and Jones attended Walker's funeral.

Tandy shared his life's achievements with his wife, Sadie Dorsette, whom he married on June 3, 1912. The two had a son together. He spoke numerous times at national conventions of the fraternity and was affiliated with an alumni chapter. Tandy embodied all the potential of Alpha Phi Alpha.

"Onward and Upward toward the Light"

At the turn of the twentieth century, for seven young black men at Cornell University to believe that they could create an institution that was the equal of any white institution was certainly audacious in the eyes of many onlookers—both black and white. By establishing Alpha Phi Alpha and eventually incorporating the fraternity, the Jewels sparked a youth movement that led to the establishment of eight other fraternities and sororities. Moreover, the founders of Alpha cemented a precedent of service and excellence that has remained strong for more than a century. The positive acts of those seven Jewels are manifested in the 300 chapters and more than 150,000 fraternity members that exist today.

In the early 1900s, Alpha faced problems such as isolation, racism, and skepticism. In the early 2000s, the issues have changed somewhat, and Alpha now faces internal problems such as brutality, individualism, and apathy among its members. Time will tell how the fraternity addresses those issues. Externally, Alpha is leading the push to recognize one of its own, Martin Luther King Jr., with a monument in the nation's capital. In other arenas, chapters of Alpha are battling health issues, such as HIV and premature birth, that are crippling the black community. These local chapters are offering scholarships to low-income students and fostering the leaders of tomorrow with their leadership institutes. Indeed, the issues that Alpha faces in the future will be the same issues that affect the black community as a whole. Come what may, Alpha Phi Alpha Fraternity Inc. will continue to achieve its aims of "manly deeds, scholarship, and love for all mankind."

Notes

1. For excellent discussions of sharecropping and similar practices, see Peter Daniel, *The Shadow of Slavery: Peonage in the South, 1901–1969* (Urbana: University of Illinois Press, 1990), and David Oshinsky, *Worse than Slavery: Parchman Farm and the Ordeal of Jim Crow Justice* (New York: Free Press, 1996), 114–22.

2. During the 1940s, illiteracy rates exceeded 25 percent. Bill Jersey and Richard Wormser, *The Rise and Fall of Jim Crow*, Program Four: Terror and Triumph, 1940–1954, Quest and Video Line Productions, 2002.

3. Booker T. Washington, ed., *Tuskegee and Its People: Their Ideals and Achievements* (New York: Negro Universities Press, 1905), 1–15.

4. David Levering Lewis, *WEB Du Bois: Biography of a Race* (New York: Henry Holt, 1994), 79–116.

5. Kevin Gaines, *Uplifting the Race: Black Leadership, Politics, and Culture in the Twentieth Century* (Chapel Hill: University of North Carolina Press, 1996), 1, 2.

6. http://rmc.library.cornell.edu/alpha/sevenjewels/index.html.

7. Charles H. Wesley, *The History of Alpha Phi Alpha: A Development in College Life* (Washington, D.C.: Foundation Publishers, 1929), 18.

8. Herman "Skip" Mason, *The Talented Tenth: The Founders and Presidents of Alpha* (Winter Park, Fla.: Four-G Publishers, 1999), 104.

9. N. A. Murray, "The Early History and Ideals of the Founders," *Sphinx* 60, no. 2 (May–June 1974): 13.

10. George Biddle Kelley, "Reminisces of a Founder," *Sphinx* (November–December 1939), in John H. Johnson III, ed., *Centennial Book of Essays and Letters: Excerpts from the Brotherhood of Alpha Phi Alpha Fraternity, Inc.* (Baltimore: Foundation Publishers, 2006), 20.

11. Ibid.

12. Charles H. Wesley, *Henry Arthur Callis: Life and Legacy* (Baltimore: Foundation Publishers, 1977), 26.

13. Wesley, *History of Alpha Phi Alpha*, 25; Roscoe C. Giles, "Jewel Henry Arthur Callis ... A Drop-out with Indefatigable Determination Returned to Cornell University," *Sphinx* 60, no. 2 (May–June 1974): 11.

14. Murray, "Early History and Ideals of the Founders," 13.

15. Wesley, *History of Alpha Phi Alpha*, 14–16.

16. Ibid., 23.

17. "Minutes of the Alpha Phi Alpha Society," December 4, 1906, in Wesley, *History of Alpha Phi Alpha*, 508.

18. Ibid., 33; Walter Kimbrough, *Black Greek 101: The Culture, Customs, and Challenges of Black Fraternities and Sororities* (Madison, N.J.: Fairleigh Dickinson University Press, 2003), 29.

19. Wesley, *History of Alpha Phi Alpha*, 40–41.

20. George Biddle Kelley, "Jewel Kelley's Testimonial on Vertner W. Tandy," *Sphinx* 36, no. 1 (February 1950): 2.

21. Wesley, *History of Alpha Phi Alpha*, 41.

22. Rayford Logan, *Howard University: The First Hundred Years, 1867–1967* (New York: New York University Press, 1969); http://www.howard.edu/longwalk/!longwa11.htm.

23. Wesley, *History of Alpha Phi Alpha*, 89.

24. Ibid., 494–95.

25. Henry Arthur Callis, "Founder's Address," given at the Fiftieth Anniversary General Convention of Alpha Phi Alpha Fraternity Inc., Buffalo, N.Y., 1956, in Johnson, *Centennial Book of Essays and Letters*, 47.

26. Wesley, *Henry Arthur Callis*, 272, 276; Mason, *Talented Tenth*, 3–4.

27. "The Last Jewel Enters the Eternal Diadem: Brother Henry Arthur Callis, M.D.," *Sphinx* 60, no. 4 (December 1974): 19.

28. Giles, "Jewel Henry Arthur Callis," 11.

29. *Who's Who in Colored America*, 1927 ed., s.v. "Henry Arthur Callis."

30. Henry Arthur Callis, M.D., "The Need and Training of Negro Physicians," *Journal of Negro Education* 4 (1935): 32–41, in Wesley, *Henry Arthur Callis*, 227.

31. Vernon H. Ross, M.D., "History of the National Medical Association," *Journal of the American Society of Anesthesiology* 70, no. 3 (March 2006): 1.

32. Eleanor Alexander, *Lyrics of Sunshine and Shadow: The Courtship of Paul Lawrence Dunbar and Alice Ruth Moore* (New York: Plume, 2004), 174.

33. *Who's Who in Colored America*, 1927 ed., s.v. "Myrna Colson Callis"; *Negro Yearbook*, 1937–1938 ed., s.v. "Lorenzo J. Greene and Myrna Colson Callis."

34. Rayford Logan, *Betrayal of the Negro: From Rutherford B. Hayes to Woodrow Wilson* (New York: Collier Books, 1965), 341.

35. Henry Arthur Callis Papers, Moorland-Springarn Research Center, Howard University, Washington, D.C.

36. Chapman's Cornell University transcript indicates that he was born in 1877 rather than 1876, which is the conventionally accepted date of his birth. Johnson, *Centennial Book of Essays and Letters*, 51.

37. Charles H. Chapman, "A Founder Looks Back," *Sphinx* 18, no. 1 (February 1932): 7.

38. http://rmc.library.cornell.edu/alpha/sevenjewels/sevenjewels_2.html.

39. Henry A. Callis, "Founders' Address," Alpha Phi Alpha General Convention, 1950, in Johnson, *Centennial Book of Essays and Letters*, 47.

40. Wesley, *History of Alpha Phi Alpha*, 536.

41. Callis, "Founders' Address."

42. Cornell University transcript of Charles H. Chapman, in Johnson, *Centennial Book of Essays and Letters*, 51.

43. "Chapman, Alpha Founder Dies at 68," *Baltimore Afro-American*, November 24, 1934, 22.

44. Ibid.

45. Mason, *Talented Tenth*, 51–52.

46. Thomas D. Pawley III, "The Selection of the Seventh Jewel," *Sphinx* (spring 1994): 13.

47. Henry Arthur Callis to Charles Henry Wesley, May 23, 1965, in Wesley, *Henry Arthur Callis*, 26.

48. Wesley, *History of Alpha Phi Alpha*, 41–45, 71.

49. Felix L. Armfield, "Jewel Eugene Kinckle Jones & the Development of Early African-American Social Work," *Sphinx* 84, no. 1 (spring 1999): 23.

50. *Who's Who in Colored America*, 1927 ed., s.v. "Eugene Kinckle Jones."

51. Felix L. Armfield, "Eugene Kinckle Jones and the Rise of Professional Black Social Workers, 1910–1940" (PhD diss., Michigan State University, 1998), 22.

52. rmc.library.cornell.edu/alpha/sevenjewels/sevenjewels_3.html.

53. Armfield, "Jones and the Rise of Professional Black Social Workers," 22.

54. "Death Claims the Body of Brother Jewel George Biddle Kelley . . . But His Spirit Marches On," *Sphinx* (October 1962): 2, in Johnson, *Centennial Book of Essays and Letters,* 54.

55. Emilio Louis, *A Brave Black Regiment: Massachusetts Volunteer Infantry, 1863–1865*, 3d ed. (Salem, Mass.: Ayer Company Publishers, 1990), 339.

56. Wesley, *Henry Arthur Callis*, 24.

57. "Death Claims the Body of Brother Kelley," 2.

58. Mason, *The Talented Tenth*, 82–84.

59. "Death Claims the Body of Brother Kelley," 2.

60. "Death Claims the Body of Brother Kelley," in Johnson, *Centennial Book of Essays and Letters*, 53.

61. Mason, *Talented Tenth*, 95–99.

62. Leroy Graham, *Baltimore: The Nineteenth Century Black Capital* (Lanham, Md.: University Press of America, 1982), 269–72.

63. Murray, "Early History and Ideals of the Founders," 13.

64. "Minutes of the Social Study Club," "Minutes of Alpha Phi Alpha Society," and "Minutes of Alpha Phi Alpha," June 2, 1906, through April 3, 1912, in Wesley, *History of Alpha Phi Alpha*, 505–39.

65. Mason, *Talented Tenth*, 102–3, 119–23.

66. Callis, "Founders' Address," 47; Wesley, *Henry Arthur Callis*, 276.

67. Nathaniel A. Murray, "The Aims of Our Dear Fraternity . . .," *Sphinx* 45, no. 1 (February 1960): 28, 33.

68. "Minutes of the Social Study Club," October 23, 1906, in Wesley, *History of Alpha Phi Alpha*, 506.

69. Wesley, *History of Alpha Phi Alpha,* 169; Mason, *Talented Tenth*, 134.

70. Mason, *Talented Tenth*, 131.

71. Emory Smith, "Alpha Phi Alpha His First Love," *Sphinx* 23, no. 3 (February 1937): 3.

72. Ibid.

73. Mason, *Talented Tenth*, 133.

74. Wesley, *Henry Arthur Callis*, 20; Mason, *Talented Tenth*, 134.

75. Henry Arthur Callis, "Jewel Callis' Testimonial to Vertner W. Tandy, Founder," *Sphinx* 36, no. 1 (February 1950): 2.

76. Giles, "Jewel Henry Arthur Callis," 15.

77. Ibid, 11.

78. Ibid.

79. *Who's Who in Colored America*, 1927 ed., s.v. "Vertner W. Tandy."

80. Callis, "Callis' Testimonial to Tandy," 2.

81. Tananarive Due, *The Black Rose: The Dramatic Story of Madam C. J. Walker, America's First Black Female Millionaire* (New York: Ballantine Books, 2001), 345.

82. A'Lelia Perry Bundles, *On Her Own Ground: The Life and Times of Madame C. J. Walker* (New York: Scribner Books, 2002), 236–37.

83. Ibid., 171.

2

The Vision of Virtuous Women
The Twenty Pearls of Alpha Kappa Alpha Sorority

Stephanie Y. Evans

This chapter traces the lives of the founders, original members, and incorporators of the Alpha Kappa Alpha Sorority: the twenty "Pearls." The sorority brought together like-minded women from disparate paths to celebrate scholarship and provide dedicated "service to all mankind." On January 15, 1908, nine women, led by Ethel Hedgeman Lyle and advised by Ethel Esther Maria Tremain Robinson and Elizabeth Appo Cook at Howard University, brought forth an organization dedicated in sisterhood to live and work "by culture and by merit." The motto, translated into Greek, became *Askosis Kai Axiosis,* and the letters AKA, the ivy leaf, and pink for femininity and green for everlasting life became the signs of the first black women's collegiate sisterhood.[1]

The Alpha chapter expanded by inviting seven sophomore honor students to join the organization in late February 1908. The first initiation of new members took place in February 1909, and on January 29, 1913, six members banded together to incorporate and expand Alpha Kappa Alpha Sorority, making it the first national, incorporated Greek-letter organization for black college women.[2]

The First Nine

ETHEL OCTAVIA HEDGEMAN LYLE

Ethel Octavia Hedgeman (1887–1950) was born in St. Louis and graduated from Sumner High School there; she received that school's first scholarship to attend Howard University. Although Hedgeman made history as a founder of the first black sorority, she also had a clear sense of history from her distinguished family heritage. Her paternal grandfather, born in 1824, was an African Methodist Episcopal minister who helped establish churches from St. Paul, Minnesota, to

Denver, Colorado. Her maternal grandfather escaped enslavement to participate as a Union solider in the Civil War and became one of the founding members of Lincoln University in Missouri. Her mother, Maria Hubbard Hedgeman, was a certified teacher, but she stayed home to raise Ethel and her two sisters, Iota and Thelma. Ethel's father, Albert Hedgeman, born in 1858, was a respected community builder who worked for the YMCA.[3]

Ethel entered Howard in 1904 but had to withdraw after the first year due to illness. At Howard, she was active in the university choir, Christian Endeavor, drama productions, and the YWCA.[4] She was described as "a lively, charming, bubbling young woman, full of life and laughter, although somewhat delicate in health."[5]

Ethel's close friend George Lyle was a member of Alpha Phi Alpha Fraternity, and she was encouraged to develop a sorority by Ethel Robinson, a native of Providence, Rhode Island, who had graduated from Brown University and participated in sorority activities there. With an innovative spirit, Ethel convened eight Howard coeds and established the first sorority for African American women. In addition to being the originator, she worked with Margaret Flagg and Lavinia Norman to finalize the organization's constitution, which had been drafted by Lucy Diggs Slowe, and she designed the ivy leaf inscribed with "AKA" as their symbol. Lucy Slowe (the only senior in the new organization) became the first president; Hedgeman was elected president in the fall of 1908 and was succeeded by Lavinia Norman.[6]

After graduating in 1909 with a bachelor's degree in English and liberal arts, Hedgeman moved to Enfala, Oklahoma, where she taught music and English and stayed until 1910. She is recognized as the first college-trained black woman to teach in a normal school in Oklahoma and the first to receive a Life Teacher's Certificate from the Department of Education there. For the 1910–1911 school year, she taught at a public school in Centralia, Illinois.[7]

On celebrating the twentieth anniversary of the sorority's formation, Margaret Flagg Holmes recalled Hedgeman's personality, saying that Ethel "was a jolly, fun-loving loveable girl, whose outstanding charm was her gurgling, bubbling laughter. School work (for she was a brilliant student) and George Lyle vied with each other for Ethel's affections." Hedgeman's commitment to scholarship and community service continued to flourish, as did her love for Lyle. On June 21, 1911, Ethel Hedgeman married George Lyle in New York City. They moved immediately to Philadelphia, where George became a high school principal. They had one son, George Lyle Jr., who eventually married and had two children. When her daughter-in-law passed away, Ethel ensured that her two granddaughters, Murieal Jean and Andrea Joan, were dearly cared for. In addition to supporting her family, she enjoyed reading, working crossword puzzles, and playing bridge.[8]

While taking good care of family matters, Mrs. Lyle was also engaged in community affairs in Philadelphia. She founded the Mother's Club of the City, was a charter member of the West Philadelphia League of Women Voters, and was a member of the Republican Women's Committee of Ward 40. In 1937, she was appointed chairperson of the Mayor's Committee of One Hundred Women and charged with planning the sesquicentennial of the adoption of the Constitution. While her civic and social activities are widely known, it is lesser known that Ethel Hedgeman Lyle also attended graduate school at both the University of Pennsylvania and Temple University.[9]

Like most women who attended college in the early twentieth century, Lyle was a dedicated teacher. She taught English in the public schools of Philadelphia from 1921 to 1948, when she retired. With all her family and community responsibilities, she remained ever faithful to her sorority and supported many chapters, in addition to its growth on a national level. She was a charter member of the Mu Chapter (established in 1922 in Philadelphia); in 1923, she was elected Supreme Tamiouchos (national treasurer), a position she held until 1946. She also was a founder and Basileus of the Omega Omega Graduate Chapter (established in 1926 in Philadelphia).[10]

Ethel Hedgeman Lyle was honored many times through the years. She was named Honorary Supreme Basileus (national president) by Alpha Kappa Alpha in 1926 and held that title until her passing on November 28, 1950. No other member has been awarded this honor. Her funeral was held at Mount Pasgah African Methodist Episcopal Church on December 2, and she was buried in the city of Philadelphia. The Ethel Hedgeman Lyle Endowment Fund was named in her honor, and at the 1958 Golden Anniversary Boulé (the national convention) in Washington, D.C., her granddaughters were awarded a $1,000 scholarship to attend college and follow in their grandmother's footsteps.[11]

BEULAH ELIZABETH BURKE

Beulah Burke (1885–1975) was born in Hertford, North Carolina. She and her sister Lillie attended preparatory school in North Carolina, and Beulah entered Howard University at age fifteen in 1900. She graduated with a bachelor's degree in Latin in 1908. She also studied Greek, German, English, political science, chemistry, and physics. She taught for one year in Georgia and then in Kansas City, Kansas. She earned a master's degree in home economics from Columbia University and did further graduate study at the University of Chicago.[12]

Beulah was a vital force in the incorporation process and an advocate for the development of Alpha Kappa Alpha as a national organization. She used her proficiency in Greek to propose the name Alpha Kappa Alpha, which means "by merit and by culture." She also suggested that the sorority's colors be apple green and salmon pink. After incorporation, she chartered the first chapters at the University of Chicago (Beta Chapter, 1913), University of Illinois (Gamma Chapter, 1913), and University of Kansas (1914) and established graduate chapters in both Kansas City, Missouri (Beta Omega, 1920), and Kansas City, Kansas (Mu Omega, 1922). She was Basileus of both graduate chapters. She was involved as hostess Basileus at the 1922 Kansas City Boulé and was the Second Supreme Anti-Basileus during 1923. She served as midwestern regional director in 1925 and participated in many other local and national activities.[13]

Beulah taught at Delaware State College in Dover and then in Atlantic City, New Jersey, before returning to Washington, D.C., and joining the Xi Omega Chapter. In 1968, she attended the Sixtieth Founders' Day Celebration, where she, Norma Boyd, and Lavinia Norman were honored guests. In Washington, Burke was a member of the NAACP, YWCA, National Education Association, and Worker's Organization, which advocated for black women's employment opportunities. She was known for her sewing and tailoring and held a position at Howard University. Beulah passed away, after a long illness, on April 28, 1975, in Washington, and she rests eternal in Lincoln Cemetery. She was eighty-nine years old and a member of Alpha Kappa Alpha for sixty-seven years.[14]

LILLIE BURKE

Like her sister Beulah, Lillie Burke (?–1949) was born and raised in Hertford, North Carolina. Lillie entered the preparatory department of Howard University in 1900 and earned a bachelor's degree in English in 1908. Margaret Flagg Holmes described both sisters as "tall, fair, and good looking," with Lillie being "oh so serious" and, like her sister, proficient in Greek. Lillie attended the University of Pennsylvania for graduate study. She then began her teaching career in Downington, Pennsylvania, where she headed the Academic Department of the Downing Institute. In 1911, she returned to North Carolina and taught

English at the State Normal School in Fayetteville, but stayed for only one year. Lillie moved back to Washington, D.C., in 1912; Beulah would join her there in the 1940s. Lillie retired from teaching at the Garnet Patterson Junior High School and was very active in her church.[15]

Lillie Burke was one of the organizers of the Xi Omega Chapter in 1923, where she remained involved and dedicated until her death on December 16, 1949. She had difficulties with her eyesight in later years but was regarded as a valuable participant in chapter activities and was noted for contributing elaborate homegrown floral arrangements to brighten up events.[16]

ANNA EASTER BROWN

Anna Easter Brown (1879–1957) was born on Easter Sunday in New Jersey. She graduated with honors from West Orange High School in Orange, New Jersey, and began studying at Howard University's Teachers College Department. As one of the founding members of Alpha Kappa Alpha, she was elected its first treasurer and wrote the sorority song. While at Howard, she was known as being "solid, reliable, gentle, and sweet." She also worked as the head night librarian, which took up most of her spare time. She, along with Lavinia Norman and Ethel Hedgeman, graduated from Howard in 1909.[17]

Brown moved to North Carolina, where she taught for almost fifty years. First she taught at a private school in Bricks, North Carolina, where she also served as house mother and adviser to the YWCA. In 1926, she moved to the Booker T. Washington High School in Rocky Mount, North Carolina, where she taught in the Social Studies Department for thirty-one years. She worked closely with the YWCA and the American Teachers Association and was a charter member of the Chi Omega Graduate Chapter (established in 1925) in Rocky Mount.[18]

In addition to her teaching and community building, Brown was highly regarded for her research in African American history. She taught her students black history, even though the conservative curriculum and school officials prohibited it. Outside of school, she traveled widely to conduct research and wrote an article published in the National Urban League's *Opportunity* magazine. Her annual Negro History Exhibit always received wide acclaim, especially the 1951 exhibit, which marked her twenty-fifth anniversary in Rocky Mount; that year's exhibit received national attention and established her reputation as a rigorous scholar of the African American experience. Brown died in March 1957 and was buried in Rocky Mount, North Carolina.[19]

MARJORIE HILL

The surviving records of Marjorie Hill's life are sparse and meager. Marjorie Hill (?–1909) began at Howard in 1904 and graduated from the School of Arts and Sciences with a bachelor's degree in pedagogy and political science in 1908. In a reminiscence of the founders as she knew them, Margaret Flagg Holmes described Hill as a "very small, quaint, and sweet-voiced girl." She was remembered as quiet, unassuming, and always willing to help when a job had to be done. Holmes also recalled that when faced with any significant matter, Hill would simply respond, "my mother says . . . ," and that would be her basis for decision making.[20]

In October, after graduation, she left Washington, D.C., to teach at Morgan College in Lynchburg, Virginia. Marjorie died in the summer of 1909, becoming the first "Ivy beyond the Wall."[21]

MARGARET FLAGG HOLMES

Margaret Flagg Holmes (1886–1976) was born and raised in Greensboro, North Carolina, the daughter of the Reverend Lewis and Callie McAdoo Flagg. Although she attended elementary school in Greensboro, she went to high school in Washington, D.C. From 1904 to 1908, Margaret attended Howard on scholarship and concentrated on Latin, English, and history. She assisted Lucy Slowe in writing Alpha Kappa Alpha's original constitution. She described herself during the founding of the organization as "tall, thin, self-conscious, interested mainly in books, but with usually a beau in the offing." In a 1927–1928 edition of *Ivy Leaf*, she recorded her impressions of her fellow founders and provided an invaluable look into the personal side of the public figures who established and incorporated Alpha Kappa Alpha Sorority.[22]

After graduation, Margaret moved to Baltimore, where her parents were living. She began working as a substitute teacher and then taught at Baltimore High School for nine years, where Lucy Slowe was also on the faculty. She proved to be a stellar teacher: the North Central Association judged her the best Latin teacher in Baltimore. In 1917, she earned a master's degree in philosophy from Columbia University.[23]

Margaret Flagg married John Clay Holmes on August 1, 1917, and they moved to Chicago, where they were both engaged in community and activist affairs. Between 1921 and 1952, Margaret taught at Wendell Phillips High School and also at DuSable High School as head of the History Department, where she remained until she retired in 1953.

Margaret Holmes worked closely with the YWCA and the NAACP. She associated with high-ranking NAACP leaders and scholar-activists such as W. E. B. DuBois and Joel Spingarn and suffragist Mary White Ovington. Holmes traveled nationally and internationally, and in 1931, she and her husband toured Europe for six months, where she met Pope Pius XI in Rome and entertainer Josephine Baker in Paris.[24]

Margaret Flagg Holmes was a member of Theta Omega Chapter in Chicago from 1922 to 1953 and served as Anti-Basileus, Grammateus, and chapter delegate to two boulés. After retiring—right before the 1954 *Brown v. Board of Education* decision—she moved to New York City to live with her sister. Her husband had died in 1946, but she remained active and continued to contribute to the sorority by joining the Tau Omega Chapter in New York. In 1968, she was the guest of honor at a joint Founders' Day celebration in New York, where Atlantic regional director Thelma Derlack Boozer celebrated her legacy. Holmes responded, "Life is for the living, to love, to share and give one's self."[25]

After being of "service to all mankind" for more than sixty years, Margaret Flagg Holmes passed away on January 29, 1976, in New York.[26]

LAVINIA NORMAN

Lavania Norman (1882–1983) was born in Montgomery, West Virginia, the eighth of sixteen children.[27] She entered Howard's preparatory department in 1901. Because few women were admitted at the time, she recalled that during her junior year, she and Ethel Hedgeman were the only girls in her classes. Lavinia was central to the establishment of the sorority and worked with Margaret Flagg and Hedgeman to develop the constitution drafted by Lucy Diggs Slowe. After Hedgeman's graduation, Norman became president of the sorority and presided over the second Ivy Day exercises. In 1909, she graduated cum laude from Howard with a bachelor's degree in English and French and read the class history at the graduation ceremony.[28]

Although she was recognized as an outstanding teacher and had offers to teach in numerous locations, Norman remained at Douglass High School in Huntington, West Virginia, from 1909 until her retirement in 1950. She instructed junior and senior high school students in Latin, French, English, and dramatics, as well as supervising the students' drama productions and the Douglass High School newspaper. Norman earned an additional bachelor's degree in 1934 from West Virginia State College.[29]

Norman served the Beta Tau Omega Chapter in Huntington as secretary, speaker for Founders' Day activities, member of the Entertainment Committee, and director of chapter plays. After retiring in 1950, she returned to Washington, D.C., and joined the Xi Omega Chapter. She suffered a slight stroke in 1978 and did not venture out in public much after that, but she celebrated her 100th birthday on December 14, 1982, with a lavish affair. She passed away one month later on January 22, 1983. Her memorial service, held in the Andrew Rankin Chapel at Howard University, was attended by Alpha Kappa Alpha women from thirty-six states, who were in Washington to participate in the sorority's Diamond Jubilee celebration.[30]

LUCY DIGGS SLOWE

Lucy Diggs Slowe (1885–1937) was born in Berryville, Virginia, the daughter of Henry Slowe, a hotel owner, and Fannie Porter Slowe. Her father died when she was only nine months old; after her mother's death, six-year-old Lucy went to live with her aunt, Martha Slowe Price, in Lexington, Virginia. In 1904, she was the first female graduate of the Baltimore Colored High School to enroll in Howard University. She was recognized for being a gifted scholar, an outstanding singer, and a competitive tennis player, winning seventeen tennis cups.[31]

As one of the original group of sorority founders, she drafted the first constitution. The final document stipulated that the president have senior standing, and accordingly, Slowe was elected the first president of Alpha Kappa Alpha Sorority. Slowe graduated in 1908 and returned to Baltimore to teach English at Douglass High School for seven years. She earned a master's degree from Columbia University in 1915. She then taught at Armstrong High School in Washington, D.C., until 1919, when the board of education requested that she head Shaw Junior High School, the first junior high school for African Americans in Washington. The school's creed included a commitment to "the development of the highest ideals of character, wisdom, and worth . . . trustworthiness, dependability, regard for one's word, deference to elders, consideration of one's comrades, respect for oneself . . . and truth." She headed Shaw until 1922, when she became the first dean of women at Howard University. However, she continued to support Shaw for almost two decades after its founding.[32]

According to the Howard *Record*, Slowe was "the answer to a spiritual need in the life of the women of the university." As the number of women on campus grew, the dean of women's position was created to handle social issues, assist with campus policy, and provide academic guidance. Lucy Slowe held the position until her death in 1937. In an effort to improve women's education, she also worked to develop the National Association of Women Deans, Administrators, and Counselors, and she detailed many cocurricular opportunities that Howard students should have access to.[33]

In 1923, Slowe gave a talk at the Conference of College Women held at the Phillis Wheatley YWCA in Washington, D.C. In the speech, titled "The Training of College Women," she argued that members of organizations such as the College Alumnae Club, Association of Advisors to Women in Colored Schools, and National Federation of College Women were "charged with the responsibility of laying the foundation [and] have endeavored to lay it solidly, [so] that the superstructure—Service to humanity—may rise with confidence on a never-weakening base. Let us face the future boldly."[34]

As Slowe stated in her 1933 article "Higher Education of the Negro Woman," the industrial revolution, international connectedness, and women's suffrage altered what it meant to be an educated black woman. She argued that women's political independence garnered by suffrage in 1920 warranted an increased focus on political and economic studies. She lamented the fact that, because of lingering stereotypes, college women were limited to courses of study that prepared them for teaching or nursing; there were few opportunities for black women to gain leadership experience. Slowe's complaint was echoed widely by black women who wrote memoirs of their college experiences.[35]

Lucy Slowe worked with Mary McLeod Bethune to establish the National Council of Negro Women, an umbrella organization for black women's clubs, and served as its first executive secretary. In addition to being an effective organizer, Slowe was a prolific writer. The January 1939 edition of the *Journal of the College Alumnae Club of Washington D.C.* included speeches she had delivered in Washington, D.C., New York, South Carolina, Georgia, and Ohio; her administrative treatises; and a 1937 national radio address challenging racial segregation in the nation's capital.[36]

Margaret Flagg Holmes remembered Lucy Slowe as "serious, hard working, conscientious, and efficient in all that she did." Slowe died on October 21, 1937. One month before her passing, an article she wrote titled "The Colored Girl Enters College—What Shall She Expect?" was published in *Opportunity: Journal of Negro Life*. Slowe mused that although the college experience would be a struggle for black women, they should face the task with determination and maturity, because "students grow into well-rounded women through doing things that challenge their whole being." Slowe embodied the type of woman she dared other students to become. Lucy Diggs Slowe Hall at Howard University and Lucy Diggs Slowe Elementary School in Washington, D.C., were named in her honor.[37]

MARIE WOOLFOLK TAYLOR

Marie Woolfolk Taylor (1893–1960) was born in Atlanta, Georgia. She attended Stoors School and was enrolled for one year at Atlanta University before entering the preparatory department of Howard University in 1904. Marie was a lyric soprano in the Howard University chorus and performed in the drama club. She was also known as a southern belle with an extensive wardrobe. She was involved in the development of the sorority from the first planning meeting and joined Ethel Hedgeman in petitioning university officials to establish the organization; she was elected its first secretary. Later, Marie was chosen to approach the seven members of the sophomore class and encourage their membership. Margaret Flagg Holmes claimed, "On special occasions, when we felt that we needed some one to uphold the dignity of the group, we selected either Lucy [Slowe] or Marie Woolfolk. Marie was the member of the chapter whose name was synonymous with clothes and such goodlooking ones. . . . The combined wardrobe of the rest of us wouldn't equal Marie's at any time. And clever! She had the happy faculty of getting whatever she wanted." In 1908, Marie graduated magna cum laude in English, with honors in Latin and history. She then moved to Cleveland, Ohio, and integrated the Schauffler Training School for Social Service, where she majored in religion. She returned to Atlanta to work with Dr. Henry Procter as the community assistant to the pastor of the First Congregational Church.[38]

For four years she headed the inspection department of the Standard Life Insurance Company, and in 1917, she was one of two African Americans who partnered with the Red Cross after the Atlanta fire. In 1919, she married Dr. Alfred G. Taylor of Atlanta, and they had one daughter. She remained an active member in the First Congregational Church.[39]

Taylor assisted in the development of the Kappa Omega Chapter in 1923 and was the first chapter Basileus. She was very involved in Atlanta life; she served on the board of directors for the Carrie Steele Pitts foster home, worked on the Community Planning Council, chaired the Finance Committee of the YWCA, and was active in the Atlanta NAACP. She also worked with the Community Chest (which later became the United Way) and participated in an antituberculosis drive. She died on October 21, 1937, and her final resting place is in

Atlanta. She was survived by her daughter, Alfred Marie Taylor Anderson, also a member of Alpha Kappa Alpha Sorority.[40]

The Sophomores of 1908

NORMA ELIZABETH BOYD

Norma Boyd (1888–1985) was born in Washington, D.C., and attended school there. She entered Howard University in 1906 and graduated with a bachelor's degree in mathematics in 1910. She was elected president of the Alpha Chapter in 1910 and was the first to serve two terms as chapter president. In 1913, she worked with Nellie Quander and Minnie Smith on the incorporation committee for the organization. According to Margaret Flagg Holmes, she was someone who could be trusted with all the "hard jobs," because "Norma didn't mind work in the least, so long as she could express her opinions beforehand, and she always had decided opinions, usually practical ones."[41]

As recorded in the 1921 inaugural edition of the *Alpha Kappa Alpha Ivy Leaf*, Norma Boyd served as the first Supreme Epistoleus on the first directorate and joined Nellie Quander as one of the speakers at the Third Annual Boulé held in Cleveland, Ohio, in 1920. Boyd served as Basileus of the Alpha Chapter (twice), Basileus of the Xi Omega Graduate Chapter, and North Atlantic and East Central regional director; she also chaired the first committee to raise funds for the Mississippi Health Project. Her dedication to the sorority over the years was phenomenal, and her peers lauded her as being someone for whom "no task has been too difficult, no sacrifice too big" for the work of the organization. "Miss Boyd does not know the words failure and defeat."[42]

Norma Boyd was regarded as an organizational genius. She chaired the first fund-raising committee for the Mississippi Health Project, which, through the dedication of Alpha Kappa Alpha members Dr. Ida Jackson and Dr. Dorothy Ferebee, made a great social impact between 1934 and 1942. Boyd also led the Xi Omega Chapter in founding and directing the National Non-Partisan Council of Public Affairs lobbying group in 1938, with a paltry budget of $135; by 1948, the civil rights organization had grown into an influential African American body with an annual budget of $25,000. Similarly, she grew an international program founded in 1945 into a significant organization that was recognized by the United Nations. For her tireless national and international activism, Boyd was honored at the 1948 inaugural awards dinner of the American Council on Human Rights in Washington, D.C.; she was honored the same year by the National Council of Negro Women as "Woman of the Year in the Field of Legislation" for her political advocacy work. She organized the Women's International Religious Fellowship in 1959 and, during her career, traveled in the United States, Canada, Mexico, South America, and the West Indies, working with the United Nations, nongovernmental organizations, and local human rights initiatives.[43]

Like many of her peers, Boyd pursued higher education, taking graduate courses in education and public relations at Columbia, New York University, Berkeley, Middlebury Language School in Vermont, American University, and George Washington University. She also completed course work at the University of Mexico. Boyd taught mathematics in the Washington public schools until her retirement from Banneker Junior High School in 1948. She died in Washington on January 4, 1985—the last of the twenty Pearls to become an "Ivy beyond the Wall." Her travels, life, and work are recorded in her autobiography, *A Love That Equals My Labors: The Life Story of Norma E. Boyd*, published in 1980 by Alpha Kappa Alpha Sorority.[44]

ETHEL JONES MOWBRAY

Ethel Jones (?–1948) was born and educated in Baltimore, Maryland. After graduating from high school with honors, she enrolled in Howard University's College of Arts and Sciences in 1906. She was one of the seven sophomore honor students added to the sorority and, in the first semester of 1909, was elected vice president of Alpha Kappa Alpha. On May 25, 1909, she was one of those present at the first Ivy Day celebration, during which the participants planted ivy at the south end of Miner Hall. In March 1910, during the last semester of her senior year, she became president of the sorority. Ethel graduated from Howard with a major in mathematics and a minor in education. She then returned to Baltimore to teach math in the public school system, where she stayed for two years. Her sorority sister Holmes wrote, "Ethel's round face, rosy cheeks, and wonderful hair are the things I remember best about her, if I except her interest in Mowbray for she was wild about him."[45]

In 1913, Ethel Jones married George Mowbray and moved to Chicago. After spending the summer in Chicago, the Mowbrays moved to Kansas, where George was a teacher and Ethel was a caterer. They had two daughters. Ethel was involved during the incorporation process of the sorority and was active in expanding the program. It is recorded that she "resumed" her activity in 1924 with the establishment of the Mu Omega Chapter in Kansas City, insinuating that there was a lapse in her activity while she pursued her culinary business. However, she continued the spirit of the sorority's work by joining the local PTA, serving as a room mother at her daughters' school, and supporting her husband's career in education. Mowbray died on November 25, 1948, in Kansas City, where she was buried.[46]

ALICE PORTER MURRAY

There is little information available on Alice Murray's life. Even in Holmes's 1928 *Ivy Leaf* article, where she lovingly records the attributes of her founding sorors, Alice Murray is omitted. What is known is that she was born in Washington, D.C., and became a member of Alpha Kappa Alpha with the group of sophomores admitted in the spring of 1908; she was an "active participant in the early days."[47]

Her father was P. A. Murray, and her family lived on U Street in Washington, D.C. She entered Teachers College at Howard University in 1906 and graduated with a bachelor's degree in liberal arts and pedagogy in 1910, along the way taking classes in kindergarten teaching methods. She wrote articles on music and glee club performances that were published in the *Howard University Journal*. She also published short stories that, according to historian Marjorie Parker, reveal Murray as a "sensitive, cultivated person." The date and place of Murray's death are unconfirmed.[48]

SARAH MERRIWEATHER NUTTER

Sarah Merriweather (?–1950) was born in Washington, D.C., and attended public school there, graduating from the prestigious M Street High School in 1906. She graduated from Howard in 1910 with a major in English and history and earned a normal school degree in 1912. According to Holmes, Sarah was "brisk, always in more or less of a hurry, with her beautiful hair worn in a tight little knot at the back of her head [and she] could be depended upon always to see that things were right, just as they should be." Although she gave the impression of being conservative and something of an "old maid," Sarah was considered pleasant. In 1914, she represented Howard University at the World Student Federation Convention in Princeton, New Jersey.[49]

Sarah taught English at Dunbar High School and then mathematics at Howard University. She married attorney T. Gillis Nutter in 1920, and they moved to Charleston, West Virginia. She was the keynote speaker at the Eighteenth

Annual Boulé (1935) in Richmond, Virginia, and was active with three chapters of Alpha Kappa Alpha in Charleston. She helped establish the Nu Chapter at West Virginia State College (1922) and Beta Beta Omega (1934), which she worked with for twenty-seven years.[50]

Nutter organized the College Alumnae Club of Kanawha County and the Book Lover's Club and served both through their twenty-fifth anniversaries. She also worked for the NAACP and was chairman of its Educational Committee. Like many of her cohorts, she was an avid collector of poetry, an advocate of cultural appreciation, and an activist for African American rights.[51]

The Merriweather family was both benefactor and beneficiary of the Alpha Kappa Alpha legacy. Sarah's father, James Merriweather, was a graduate and trustee of Howard University, and he donated the table on which the charter creating the Xi Omega Chapter was signed in the 1920s; in 1941, the cherrywood table was placed in the Founders' Library. Sarah's mother, Mary, eventually became a member of Alpha Kappa Alpha Sorority's Xi Omega Chapter, signifying the family's integral and multigenerational ties to both Howard University and Alpha Kappa Alpha Sorority. It seems fitting, then, that after Sarah Merriweather Nutter died at her home in Charleston on May 10, 1950, her body was returned to Washington, D.C., for burial.[52]

JOANNA MARY BERRY SHIELDS

Joanna Mary Berry (1884–1965) was born in Catherpin, Virginia, to Charles and Carrie Lucas Berry. She was the oldest of eleven children and attended private school in Prince William County. She was related to Lavinia Norman. Joanna scored 98 out of 100 on her Howard entrance examination and entered the preparatory department in 1901.[53]

Joanna Berry graduated cum laude from Howard University in 1910 and then taught social science for two years at Winston-Salem State Teachers College in North Carolina. She met Samuel J. Shields of Darlington, South Carolina, while visiting New York City, and they married in 1913; they had six children. After her marriage, she changed careers and became the personal secretary to Assemblyman E. A. Johnson. She resumed teaching in 1920 and held positions in South Carolina, Virginia, North Carolina, and then New York City, where she taught remedial English at Christopher Columbus High School in the Bronx from 1937 to 1943.[54]

Shields was active in three sorority chapters: Alpha in Washington, D.C. (1909–1910), Phi Omega in North Carolina (1924–1937), and Tau Omega in

New York (1937–1958), but she served as consultant to chapters nationwide. In 1935, she attended the Eighteenth Annual Boulé in Richmond, Virginia, as a delegate of Phi Omega Chapter; there, she was honored as a founder with a diamond pin. She was also involved in the Howard University Alumni Club of New York, Upper Manhattan YWCA, NAACP, National Council of Negro Women, American Women's Volunteer Service, Negro History Club, and Consumers Protective Committee.[55]

Shields died on February 2, 1965, in New York City, where all her children lived. She was survived by her six children—Vivian Ida Shields, Samuel J. Shields Jr., Thomas Shields, Landrum Shields, Hanna Morgan, and Claristine Martha Brisbane—and nine grandchildren. Joanna's daughter Claristine was a highly respected member of the Tau Omega Chapter of Alpha Kappa Alpha. Members from seven metropolitan area chapters participated in a memorial ceremony for Shields on February 4, 1965, at Williams Memorial Chapel. She was buried at the Frederick Douglass Memorial Cemetery in Staten Island.[56]

CARRIE E. SNOWDEN

Carrie Snowden (?–1948) entered the School of Arts and Sciences at Howard University in 1906. Snowden, who was remembered by Margaret Flagg Holmes as "small, slim, and gracious," was close friends with Harriet Terry and expressed great interest in joining the sorority. Snowden was elected Epistoleus (corresponding secretary) and served beginning in the fall of 1909.[57]

Snowden studied English, French, German, history, geography, and science; she graduated from Howard University with a bachelor's degree in May 1910. She was a charter member of the Xi Omega Chapter, where she served on the membership and amenities committees and was remembered by those who knew her as "shy and retiring." Snowden embraced the concept of lifelong learning and enrolled in classes at Howard for three decades after her graduation. In addition to taking classes in commerce, economics, social work, and mathematics, she enrolled in a typing course in 1943 and worked at Howard as a switchboard operator, demonstrating students' commitment to the institution at all levels. She died in 1948 and was buried in Washington, D.C.[58]

HARRIETT JOSEPHINE TERRY

Harriet Terry (1885–1967) was born in Cornwall-on-Hudson, New York. After graduation from Cornwall-on-Hudson High School, she enrolled at Howard University in 1906. She was recommended as one of the seven sophomore sorority members because of her "quiet charm and ever-present smile." On October 30, 1908, she was elected treasurer, and she wrote the initiation hymn "Hail Alpha Kappa Alpha Dear," which was sung at the first official initiation ceremony in Miner Hall on February 11, 1909. She was widely recognized for her many talents and was elected secretary of Howard's class of 1910. She earned her bachelor's degree in liberal arts, specializing in English, but also excelled at Latin, French, German, political science, pedagogy, history, and chemistry.[59]

After leaving Howard, Terry moved to Virginia, where he headed the English and history departments at Gloucester High School in Capahoasic. She then taught English at the Alabama Agricultural and Mechanical College in Normal for thirty-seven years, before retiring in 1959. She also taught extension courses for teachers in Athens and Limestone counties and, during World War I, made and inspected money at the Bureau of Engraving in the Government Printing Office in Washington, D.C. Like other sorority women, she was involved in many organizational networks, including the National Federated Women's Club.[60]

She was a charter member and served as Basileus of Epsilon Gamma Omega, founded in 1949 in Normal. After her retirement, Terry moved back to Washington, where she was active in Xi Omega. She passed away there on August 15, 1967. Terry Hall at Alabama A&M University was named in her honor.[61]

The Incorporators

During the 1934 Founders' Day celebration, Ethel Hedgeman Lyle honored Nellie Quander for upholding the Alpha Kappa Alpha pledge and for guarding against "treachery and faithlessness" of those who attempted to change the organization in 1912. Two of the sophomores, Norma Boyd and Ethel Mowbray (see above), joined four other members to incorporate the organization to ensure perpetuity. Though she took pride in the fact that no harsh words were exchanged during the meeting that precipitated the split by the emerging Delta Sigma Theta sorority, Quander nonetheless found it imperative to take steps toward incorporation and expansion of the original ideals, principles, and culture of Alpha Kappa Alpha Sorority. The organization was incorporated on January 29, 1913.[62]

JULIA EVANGELINE BROOKS

Margaret Holmes wrote of Julia Brooks (?–1948): She was "charming in sport-clothes long before sport clothes became the rage. How we envied Julia because she had a job and a salary. She was a public school teacher. Then, again, Julia had an 'air' and she was popular with the men folk, another reason for envy on our part." Julia Brooks was born in New Orleans, Louisiana, and attended Miner Normal School to train as a teacher. After teaching elementary school, she enrolled in Howard University and graduated in 1908. Brooks was listed on the incorporation documents as the first Tamiouchus (treasurer) and served until turning the position over to Ethel Hedgeman Lyle in 1923; Lyle held the position for the next twenty years. After assisting in the incorporation, Julia Brooks remained very active in Alpha Kappa Alpha: she was a founding member of the Xi Omega Chapter in 1923 and the Anti-Basileus of the Epsilon Omega Chapter of Baltimore, Maryland. Also in 1923, she wrote "The History of Alpha Kappa Alpha Sorority," which she presented at the boulé, the first meeting to be held in Baltimore.[63]

From 1916 to 1922, Brooks taught English and Spanish at Dunbar High School (formerly M Street High School), in Washington, D.C. She earned a master's degree from Columbia University in 1928. Brooks also served as assistant principal at Dunbar High School until 1948 and was eventually appointed dean of girls. On November 24, 1948, Brooks passed away unexpectedly. In addition to her civic and social contributions, she was still very active in Xi Omega at the time.[64]

NELLIE M. QUANDER

Nellie Quander (1880–1961) was born in Washington, D.C. She could trace her family roots to the Quander (Guan-do) family, which in 1984 documented 300 years of residence in Maryland and Virginia—recognized as the longest recorded African American lineage in America. Nellie's parents were John Pierson Quander and Hanna Bruce Ford Quander. These Quanders were related to Nancy Quander, the slave that former president George Washington freed in his will. Nellie was also the granddaughter of Daniel and Hanna Bruce, prominent free blacks, and the grandniece of Blanche K. Bruce, a Mississippi senator during the Reconstruction era.[65]

Nellie Quander attended public school in Washington, graduated with honors from Minor Normal School, and then taught at Garrison Elementary School while attending Howard University. She joined Alpha Kappa Alpha in 1911 and graduated from Howard in June 1912, majoring in history, economics, and political science. Upon receiving notice of intended changes to the organization in October 1912, she spearheaded the incorporation process that was finalized in January 1913. After incorporation, Quander was Basileus of the first directorate. She served as national Basileus between 1913 and 1919 and remained dedicated to Alpha Kappa Alpha, setting up chapters in Illinois, Ohio, and Kansas.[66]

In 1916, Quander was commissioned by the Children's Bureau (then under the Department of Labor) in Delaware to study economic and social conditions affecting the developmentally disabled in that state. In 1918, the Women's War Work Council asked her to survey industrial conditions of women in Detroit.[67]

Quander completed work for a master's degree from Columbia University and also earned a certificate from the New York School of Social Work. She studied economics for ten summers at the University of Washington in Seattle and in 1936 was awarded a diploma from Uppsala University in Sweden. Quander taught the social sciences at Shaw Junior High School (headed by Lucy Slowe) for more than thirty years and retired in 1950. She initiated the first School Safety Patrol Unit in Washington, D.C., and remained involved in the program for twenty-five years. Quander also had a full civic life: she was on the board of directors for the Phyllis Wheatley YWCA, chairperson of the Young Women's Department for twelve years, and YWCA special field secretary for the national office. She was active in the teachers' union and was asked to be a representative to the Women's Trade Union League.[68]

In 1958, commemorating the fiftieth anniversary of Alpha Kappa Alpha, she recalled that she saw "the conspicuous achievements, emphasized both in words and personal conduct of the Alpha Kappa Alpha women . . . moral and spiritual values, peace and friendship, scholastic attainment, courage and fortitude in remaining faithful to Alpha Kappa Alpha's high original principles."[69]

When Nellie Quander passed away unexpectedly at her home on October 23, 1961, more than 100 sorority members attended the memorial and funeral services, including founders Beulah Burke and Lavinia Norman. Supreme Basileus Marjorie Parker read a resolution of sorrow on behalf of the 40,000 members of Alpha Kappa Alpha for the woman who had dedicated herself to the endurance of the sorority.[70]

NELLIE PRATT RUSSELL

Nellie Pratt (1890–1979) was born in Macon, Georgia. She entered Howard University's College of Arts and Sciences in 1907 and became an initiate in her second year. She was the only incorporator in the February 1909 class. Nellie graduated with a bachelor's degree in English in 1911.[71]

She contributed much to the Episcopal Church Women in Virginia and was described as possessing "qualities of humanness, friendliness, and the capacity to organize and get things done." She had "a keen sense of humor, rare brand of intelligence, and an appreciation for things aesthetic," in addition to being a voracious reader. Her favorite authors were William Shakespeare, Rudyard Kipling, Samuel Taylor Coleridge, Omar Khayyam, Langston Hughes, and James Weldon Johnson, among others. Holmes recalled that "Nellie Pratt Russell never knew what boredom was." In addition to reading, she kept herself busy with sewing, gardening, working crossword puzzles, and socializing, despite her arthritis. Nellie Pratt married James Alvin Russell, and they had five children who lovingly nicknamed her "Command Central" for her ability to organize, delegate, and strengthen them with a sense of purpose.[72] Nellie Pratt Russell crossed over on December 13, 1979, in Lawrenceville, Virginia.

MINNIE BEATRICE SMITH

Minnie Smith (?–1919) was a native of Washington, D.C., and graduated from Howard in 1912. In addition to being one of the incorporators, she became the first Supreme Grammateus. She was on the committee, with Norma Boyd and Nellie Quander, to pursue legal incorporation. Minnie Smith assisted in the effort toward program sustainability by writing letters to graduate members, informing them of the proposed changes to the organization and soliciting their support to maintain the origins of Alpha Kappa Alpha. Smith was present at the January 29, 1913, meeting to sign the articles of incorporation for the first national sorority of black women. Smith was close to Quander, and when Quander took a leave of absence from teaching in 1916 to pursue research in Delaware, Smith served as acting Basileus in her place. Minnie Smith died in Washington during the influenza epidemic of 1919.[73]

Portrait of the Twenty Pearls

Historian Marjorie Parker observed that most of the founders, sophomores, and incorporators were born in North Carolina, Washington, D.C., and Virginia, with some hailing from New York, New Jersey, Georgia, Missouri, and West Virginia. Twelve of the twenty Pearls never married. Twelve were teachers, and others were employed in schools, churches, or social work, in addition to their homemaking and child-care responsibilities. Significantly, the twenty Pearls remained dedicated to the growth and expansion of Alpha Kappa Alpha Sorority. Parker noted that "founders were charter members of at least twelve different chapters, and four served as the first Basileus."

The first sororities built on the history of networking and community building established early in antebellum black communities. Accordingly, many organizations built on the solid network of sororities founded mainly at historically black colleges and universities. Lucy Slowe's 1922 copy of the *Howard University Student Manual* reveals that all Howard students were expected to perform, academically and personally, in a manner that displayed "all that is best and noblest in all the outreachings of humanity." The larger environment in which the women of Alpha Kappa Alpha developed was one of high expectation, challenge, and excellence. For the fiftieth anniversary celebration, the theme of "Pride in the Past, Gratitude for the Present, Faith in the Future—Forward to a New Era of Service" reflected the organization's dedication to both tradition and innovation.[74]

Although factions formed in the sorority movement, black women effectively organized and coalesced for community empowerment, but they also pushed for individual achievement. All four of the first African American women to earn PhDs were in sororities: two in Alpha Kappa Alpha (Georgiana Simpson and Anna Julia Cooper), and two in Delta Sigma Theta (Sadie T. M. Alexander and Eva Dykes). The twenty Pearls of Alpha Kappa Alpha began an organization that subsequently counted many well-known women among its members, including educators such as Charlotte Hawkins Brown; scholars such as Maya Angelou, Toni Morrison, and Mae Jamison; and entertainers Ella Fitzgerald and Alicia Keys.[75]

On the eve of its 100th anniversary, Alpha Kappa Alpha Sorority boasts more than 170,000 members in 930 chapters. Much work "in service to all mankind" has been done in the memory of the original founders; much work remains to be done. By gaining a clearer picture of the founders' lives, members can reflect on current practices to ensure that they are in line with original goals. But these stories are valuable for scholarly research as well. Interest in research on black Greek-letter organizations is essential to a better understanding of organizational, African American, and educational history. These women's personal histories illuminate the gendered, social, cultural, economic, and political dimensions of the United States during a crucial point in the development of the Jim Crow and civil rights eras. By closely investigating founders' lives, we may increase historical understanding beyond organizations and construct useful portraits of African Americans in history that honor the complexity of their lives, community service, cultural mores, and social justice movements. Contemporary visions of merit, culture, and service will be clearer when focused on these virtuous women.

Notes

The author would like to thank the excellent staff at the Moorland-Spingarn Research Center (especially Jo Ellen Bashir) for access to its collections and for assistance with archival research. I also thank Soror Yvonne Rawls of the Mu Upsilon Omega Chapter of Alpha Kappa Alpha (Gainesville, Florida) for sharing rare primary resources from her personal collection and Soror Gloria Dickinson in New Jersey for her invaluable research.

1. André McKenzie, "In the Beginning: The Early History of the Divine Nine," in *African American Fraternities and Sororities: The Legacy and the Vision*, ed. Tamara L. Brown, Gregory S. Parks, and Clarenda M. Phillips (Lexington: University Press of Kentucky, 2005), 184–86; Marjorie H. Parker, *Past Is Prologue: The History of Alpha Kappa Alpha, 1908–1999* (Washington, D.C.: Alpha Kappa Alpha Sorority, 1999), 3–4, 21. Note that Lawrence C. Ross, in *The Divine Nine* (New York: Kensington Publishing, 2000), mistakenly lists Hedgeman's adviser's name as Ethel Aremain Robinson.

2. McKenzie, "In the Beginning," 184–86; Parker, *Past Is Prologue*, 3–4, 21.

3. *Ivy Leaf* (December 1948): 33; *Ivy Leaf* (1958): 5; Marjorie H. Parker, *Alpha Kappa Alpha: Sixty Years of Service* (Washington, D.C.: Alpha Kappa Alpha Sorority, 1966), 7; Marjorie H. Parker, *Alpha Kappa Alpha through the Years, 1908–1988* (Chicago: Mobium Press, 1990), 15; Parker, *Past Is Prologue*, 7–8; Paula Giddings, *In Search of Sisterhood: Delta Sigma Theta and the Challenge of the Black Sorority Movement* (New York: William Morrow, 1988), 44; Ross, *The Divine Nine*, 179–80; Ernestine Green McNealey, "Lyle," in *Black Women in America: Historical Encyclopedia*, ed. Darlene Clark Hine, Elsa Barkley Brown, and Rosalyn Terbourg-Penn (Bloomington: Indiana University Press, 1994), 737. Ernestine Green McNealey, *Pearls of Service: The Legacy of America's First Black Sorority, Alpha Kappa Alpha* (Chicago: Alpha Kappa Alpha Sorority, 2006), and *Black Women in America* list Lyle's birth year as 1887, but the *Ivy Leaf* sources cite 1885 as the correct date.

4. Ross, *The Divine Nine*, 180.

5. Parker, *Through the Years*, 15; Ross, *The Divine Nine*, 180.

6. *Ivy Leaf* (June 1958): 9; *Ivy Leaf* (spring 1980): 7; McKenzie, "In the Beginning," 184; Giddings, *In Search of Sisterhood*, 44.

7. Parker, *Through the Years*, 15; Ross, *The Divine Nine*, 180.

8. *Ivy Leaf* (March 1951): 5; *Ivy Leaf* (summer 1976): 4; Parker, *Through the Years*,

15; McKenzie, "In the Beginning," 184. Margaret Flagg Holmes accounts for many of the original members of Alpha Kappa Alpha in *Ivy Leaf* 6, no. 4 (November 1928): 37–38, reprinted as "Our Founders in Retrospect—by One of Them," *Ivy Leaf* 52, no. 2 (summer 1976): 4.

    9. *Ivy Leaf* (March 1951): 5; Parker, *Through the Years*, 15; Ross, *The Divine Nine*, 180.

    10. *Ivy Leaf* (1927): 1; *Ivy Leaf* (March 1951): 5; Parker, *Through the Years*, 15; Ross, *The Divine Nine*, 180.

    11. *Ivy Leaf* (May 1928): 49; Parker, *Through the Years*, 15; Ross, *The Divine Nine*, 181.

    12. Although some sources cite 1883 as her birth date, the 1880 census confirms the date as 1885. *Ivy Leaf* (June 1958): 6; *Ivy Leaf* (summer 1975): 40; *Ivy Leaf* (fall 1975): 36; Parker, *Sixty Years of Service*, 8; Parker, *Through the Years*, 17; Ross, *The Divine Nine*, 181. In Margaret Holmes's 1920s reflection on the founders, she lists Beulah's last name as Gowens. *Ivy Leaf* (summer 1976): 4.

    13. *Ivy Leaf* (June 1958): 9; *Ivy Leaf* (summer 1975): 40; *Ivy Leaf* (fall 1975): 36; Parker, *Through the Years*, 17; Ross, *The Divine Nine*, 181. The 1958 *Ivy Leaf* incorrectly lists the Gamma founding date as 1914; the correct date is given in *Through the Years*, 295.

    14. *Ivy Leaf* (fall 1975): 36; Parker, *Past Is Prologue*, 182; Parker, *Through the Years*, 17–18; Ross, *The Divine Nine*, 181. The sources disagree on the actual date of her passing: Parker and Ross both cite April 8, but the fall 1975 *Ivy Leaf* lists April 28, 1975. I cite April 28 because the 1975 primary source gives much more detail and is probably more accurate. It is possible, however, that the 28 is a typographical error.

    15. Parker, *Past Is Prologue*, 7; Parker, *Sixty Years of Service*, 8; Parker, *Through the Years*, 18–19; Ross, *The Divine Nine*, 186–87.

    16. Parker, *Through the Years*, 18–19; Ross, *The Divine Nine*, 187.

    17. Parker, *Through the Years*, 15; Ross, *The Divine Nine*, 184.

    18. Parker, *Through the Years*, 15; Ross, *The Divine Nine*, 185.

    19. Ibid.; McNealey, *Pearls of Service*, 30–31.

    20. *Ivy Leaf* (summer 1976): 4; Parker, *Sixty Years of Service*, 7; Parker, *Through the Years*, 13; Ross, *The Divine Nine*, 179.

    21. Parker, *Through the Years*, 13; Ross, *The Divine Nine*, 179.

    22. *Ivy Leaf* (June 1958): 6; *Ivy Leaf* (spring 1976): 36; *Ivy Leaf* (summer 1976): 4; Parker, *Sixty Years of Service*, 8; Parker, *Through the Years*, 18; Ross, *The Divine Nine*, 185. Here again, the sources disagree on the details. The 1958 *Ivy Leaf* and Ross both list her majors as Latin, English, and history; Parker lists English and Latin; and the 1976 *Ivy Leaf* claims that she majored in Spanish and Latin.

    23. *Ivy Leaf* (June 1958): 6; *Ivy Leaf* (spring 1976): 36; Parker, *Through the Years*, 18; Ross, *The Divine Nine*, 185. Parker and Ross say that her degree was in philosophy, but the *Ivy Leaf* says social science.

    24. Parker, *Through the Years*, 18; Ross, *The Divine Nine*, 186.

    25. Parker, *Through the Years*, 18; *Ivy Leaf* (June 1958): 6; Ross, *The Divine Nine*, 186.

26. Parker, *Through the Years*, 18; Ross, *The Divine Nine*, 186.

27. Parker, *Through the Years*, 18; Ross, *The Divine Nine*, 189.

28. *Ivy Leaf* (June 1958): 6; Parker, *Through the Years*, 18; Ross, *The Divine Nine*, 189.

29. Parker, *Through the Years*, 19; Ross, *The Divine Nine*, 189.

30. *Ivy Leaf* (spring 1980): 7; Parker, *Through the Years*, 19; Ross, *The Divine Nine*, 189–90.

31. *Ivy Leaf* (summer 1976): 4; Parker, *Through the Years*, 13; Ross, *The Divine Nine*, 182; Linda Perkins, "Slowe, Lucy Diggs," *American National Biography Online*, http://www.anb.org (accessed November 16, 2007); Kathleen Thompson, "Slowe, Lucy" in *Black Women in America*, 1071–72.

32. *Ivy Leaf* (June 1958): 9; Parker, *Through the Years*, 13; Ross, *The Divine Nine*, 183; Lucy Slowe, "My Creed for Life," *Journal of the College Alumnae Club of Washington D.C.*, memorial edition (January 1939): 34–35, Lucy Slowe Papers, Moorland-Spingarn Research Center.

33. Elizabeth Ihle, *Black Women in Higher Education: An Anthology of Essays, Studies, and Documents* (New York: Garland, 1992), xxviii; Lucy Slowe, "Higher Education of the Negro Woman," *Journal of Negro Education* (July 1933): 352–58; Lucy Slowe, "Colored Girl Enters College—What Shall She Expect?" *Opportunity: Journal of Negro Life* (September 1937): 276–79; Slowe, "My Creed for Life," 34–35; Parker, *Through the Years*, 13; Ross, *The Divine Nine*, 183.

34. Association of College Women, *Proceedings of the Conference of College Women, April 6 and 7, 1923*, 28, Lucy Diggs Slowe Collection, Moorland-Spingarn Research Center.

35. Deborah Gray White, *Too Heavy a Load: Black Women in Defense of Themselves, 1894–1994* (New York: W. W. Norton, 1999), 40–41; Ihle, *Black Women in Higher Education*, 189–90; Slowe, "Higher Education of the Negro Woman," 354, 356; Mary Church Terrell, *A Colored Woman in a White World* (1940; reprint, New York: Arno Press, 1980), 52–53. For examples of memoirs, see "Reminiscences of School Life: Six College Memoirs," in Stephanie Y. Evans, *Black Women in the Ivory Tower, 1850–1954: An Intellectual History* (Gainesville: University Press of Florida, 2007).

36. College Alumnae Club, *Journal of the College Alumnae Club of Washington D.C.* (January 1939); Ihle, *Black Women in Higher Education*, 185; Anna Julia Cooper, "Higher Education of Women," in *The Voice of Anna Julia Cooper: Including A Voice from the South and Other Important Essays, Papers, and Letters* (Lanham, Md.: Rowman and Littlefield, 1998), 84; Linda Perkins, "Education," in *Black Women in America*, 386–87.

37. Slowe, "Colored Girl Enters College," 279; *Ivy Leaf* (summer 1976): 4; Thompson, "Slowe," in *Black Women in America*, 1071–72. In her encyclopedia entry, Thompson incorrectly lists Slowe's date of death as 1936.

38. *Ivy Leaf* (summer 1976): 4; Parker, *Through the Years*, 16; Ross, *The Divine Nine*, 187–88. In the *Ivy Leaf*, Holmes refers to Marie Woolfolk's last name as "Young"; there

is no evidence of her marrying a Young, so the name could be an error on Holmes's part.

39. Parker, *Through the Years*, 16; Ross, *The Divine Nine*, 188.

40. *Ivy Leaf* (June 1958): 6; Parker, *Through the Years*, 16.

41. *Ivy Leaf* (June 1958): 6; *Ivy Leaf* (summer 1976): 4; *Ivy Leaf* (spring 1980): 5; Parker, *Past Is Prologue*, 15–16; Parker, *Through the Years*, 18, 25; Ross, *The Divine Nine*, 190.

42. *Ivy Leaf* (1921): 6–7, 13; *Ivy Leaf* (1927): 1; *Ivy Leaf* (June 1958): 6–7; *Ivy Leaf* (spring 1980): 5; Ross, *The Divine Nine*, 190.

43. *Ivy Leaf* (March 1940): 9; *Ivy Leaf* (December 1948): 37; *Ivy Leaf* (spring 1980): 5; *Ivy Leaf* (summer 1976): 16–17; Parker, *Through the Years*, 25–26; Ross, *The Divine Nine*, 191; Robert L. Harris Jr., "Lobbying Congress for Civil Rights: The American Council on Human Rights, 1948–1963," in *African American Fraternities and Sororities*, 214.

44. *Ivy Leaf* (June 1958): 6; *Ivy Leaf* (spring 1980): 5; Parker, *Through the Years*, 25; Parker, *Past Is Prologue*, 16; Ross, *The Divine Nine*, 190–91. *Pearls of Service* (49) states that Boyd passed away in New York City.

45. *Ivy Leaf* (summer 1976): 4; Parker, *Through the Years*, 22; Parker, *Past Is Prologue*, 12–13; Ross, *The Divine Nine*, 191.

46. Parker, *Through the Years*, 22; Parker, *Past Is Prologue*, 12–13; Ross, *The Divine Nine*, 191.

47. Parker, *Through the Years*, 21; Parker, *Past Is Prologue*, 12; Ross, *The Divine Nine*, 194.

48. Ibid.

49. *Ivy Leaf* (December 1935): 5; *Ivy Leaf* (December 1950): 55–56; *Ivy Leaf* (June 1958): 9; *Ivy Leaf* (summer 1976): 4; Parker, *Past Is Prologue*, 13. Holmes spelled her sorority sister's name "Sara Merriwether." While at the Princeton conference, Merriweather sent Nellie Quander a piece of ivy from former president Grover Cleveland's grave site; the leaf was planted near the Manual Arts Building at Howard University.

50. *Ivy Leaf* (December 1935): 5; *Ivy Leaf* (December 1950): 55–56; *Ivy Leaf* (June 1958): 9; *Ivy Leaf* (summer 1976): 4; McNealey, *Pearls of Service*, 53.

51. *Ivy Leaf* (September–December 1950): 55; *Ivy Leaf* (June 1958): 9; Parker, *Past Is Prologue*, 13–14; Ross, *The Divine Nine*, 195–96.

52. *Ivy Leaf* (June 1950): 46; *Ivy Leaf* (September–December 1950): 55; *Ivy Leaf* (June 1958): 9; Parker, *Through the Years*, 22–23; Parker, *Past Is Prologue*, 13–14; Ross, *The Divine Nine*, 195–96. The June *Ivy Leaf* lists her date of death as May 8; the date given in the September–December 1950 issue is probably more accurate because it provides explicit details of her life.

53. *Ivy Leaf* (February–March 1965): 40; *Ivy Leaf* (spring 1980): 7; Ross, *The Divine Nine*, 192.

54. *Ivy Leaf* (February–March 1965): 40.

55. *Ivy Leaf* (June 1958): 6; *Ivy Leaf* (February–March 1965): 40.

56. *Ivy Leaf* (February–March 1965): 40; *Ivy Leaf* (spring 1980): 7; Parker, *Past Is Prologue*, 15; Ross, *The Divine Nine*, 193. Claristine attended Winston-Salem State Teachers College, earned a bachelor's degree from Columbia University, and worked as a librarian and public servant in New York until her death in 1977.

57. *Ivy Leaf* (summer 1976): 4; *Ivy Leaf* (June 1958): 9; Parker, *Through the Years*, 21–22; Parker, *Past Is Prologue*, 12–13; Ross, *The Divine Nine*, 197.

58. *Ivy Leaf* (June 1958): 9; Parker, *Past Is Prologue*, 12–13; Ross, *The Divine Nine*, 197.

59. *Ivy Leaf* (June 1958): 6; *Ivy Leaf* (summer 1976): 4; Parker, *Past Is Prologue*, 15; Ross, *The Divine Nine*, 196. The 1958 *Ivy Leaf* incorrectly lists her graduation date as 1914.

60. *Ivy Leaf* (June 1958): 6; *Ivy Leaf* (September 1967): 46; Ross, *The Divine Nine*, 196.

61. Ibid.

62. *Ivy Leaf* (December 1948): 32; Parker, *Through the Years*, 254; McKenzie, "In the Beginning," 185–86.

63. *Ivy Leaf* (summer 1976): 4; Parker, *Past Is Prologue*, 18, 24, 67; Ross, *The Divine Nine*, 198–99.

64. Ibid.

65. Parker, *Through the Years*, 41–43; Parker, *Past Is Prologue*, 72–73.

66. *Ivy Leaf* (June 1958): 7; *Ivy Leaf* (December 1961): 2; Ross, *The Divine Nine*, 197.

67. *Ivy Leaf* (1921): 12.

68. Ibid.; *Ivy Leaf* (June 1958): 7; *Ivy Leaf* (December 1961): 2; Ross, *The Divine Nine*, 197–98.

69. *Ivy Leaf* (June 1958): 7, 24.

70. *Ivy Leaf* (December 1961): 32; Ross, *The Divine Nine*, 197; Giddings, *In Search of Sisterhood*, 50.

71. *Ivy Leaf* (spring 1980): 6.

72. Ibid.

73. *Ivy Leaf* (June 1958): 9.

74. *Howard University Student Manual*, July 1922, 3, Lucy Diggs Slowe Collection, Moorland-Spingarn Research Center; Parker, *Sixty Years of Service*, vii.

75. Linda Perkins, "Black Feminism and 'Race Uplift,' 1890–1900" (Radcliffe Institute working paper, Mary Ingraham Bunting Institute, Cambridge, Mass., 1981); Linda Perkins, "Black Women and the Philosophy of 'Racial Uplift' prior to Emancipation" (Radcliffe Institute working paper, Mary Ingraham Bunting Institute, Cambridge, Mass., 1980); Francille Wilson, "'All of the Glory . . . Faded . . . Quickly': Sadie T. M. Alexander and Black Professional Women, 1920–50," in *Sister Circle: Black Women and Work,* ed. Sharon Harley (New Brunswick, N.J.: Rutgers University Press, 2002), 164–83; Catherine Johnson, "Georgiana Simpson," in *Black Women in America*, 1038–39.

3

The Last Shall Be First
The Founders of Omega Psi Phi Fraternity
Judson L. Jeffries

Omega Psi Phi Fraternity Inc. has the distinction of being the first black fraternity founded at a historically black college. Within its ranks are some of the most highly regarded men in the fields of education, science, medicine, music, architecture, and civil rights. The men of Omega include Clifford Alexander, the first black secretary of the army; L. Douglas Wilder, the first black governor elected in U.S. history; Dr. Daniel Hale Williams, the first black to successfully perform open-heart surgery; Dr. Robert Lawrence, the first black astronaut; Dr. Carter G. Woodson, founder of the Association for the Study of Negro Life and History and the *Journal of Negro History;* and Dr. Ernest Everett Just, considered by many to be one of the most important scientists of the twentieth century.

Founded in the nation's capital in 1911 on the campus of America's most prestigious black college, Omega Psi Phi Fraternity Inc. grew from a regional fraternity to an international one within a relatively short period. Whereas other fraternities and sororities boast of their huge membership, the men of Omega have always taken pride in the fact that earning membership in their organization is an extremely daunting undertaking. Indeed, Omega Psi Phi does not seek men; rather, quality men seek it. Few aspirants have demonstrated the level of manhood, scholarship, perseverance, and uplift necessary to merit consideration by those who wear the royal purple and old gold.

The story of Omega began on a brisk fall afternoon in November 1911. On that day, Edgar A. Love, Oscar J. Cooper, and Frank Coleman, all of whom were juniors, met in the office of Dr. Ernest E. Just (located in Science Hall; now known as Thirkield Hall) to hammer out an idea that the three students had been knocking around for the past several months—the creation of a black fraternity. Although Howard University was already home to the first black sorority, the idea of a black fraternity initially found no support when Love, Cooper, and Coleman approached the school's administration. Unable to bore through the mountainous pile of red tape required to establish a new organization, and unable to secure the backing of key school officials, the three men solicited the assistance of the highly respected and accomplished Professor Just. Despite resistance from school administrators, Love, Cooper, Coleman, and Just persevered, and out of the meeting held on November 17 in Dr. Just's office, Omega Psi Phi Fraternity Inc. was born. Given the bond among the three students—especially Cooper and Coleman, who had attended the same high school—"friendship is essential to the soul" was chosen as the group's motto, hence the name Omega Psi Phi. Manhood, scholarship, perseverance, and uplift were adopted as the fraternity's cardinal principles.

What follows are the personal histories of four men who set the standard against which all other Omega men are measured.

Frank Coleman

A native of the District of Columbia, Frank Coleman (1890–1967) was an inquisitive child. Seldom did young Frank waste an opportunity to inquire about the world and its confines, which led to a love of science. Coleman attended the famous M Street High School (now Dunbar High School), considered the nation's best high school for blacks during the first half of the twentieth century. M Street graduates include such luminaries as William Hastie, the first black nominated to the Third Circuit Court of Appeals; Dr. Charles Drew; Robert Weaver; and Sterling Brown, all of whom would eventually join the ranks of Omega men. In high school, Coleman became keenly interested in physics and "conducted many an experiment to discover some new secret of nature."[1] He looked at every day as an opportunity to discover something new. After graduating from high school, Coleman attended Howard University, where he earned a bachelor's degree in physics in 1913. Officials at Howard were so impressed with Coleman that they wasted no time in offering him a position as an instructor of physics. Though flattered by the offer, Coleman believed that additional training was imperative for any self-respecting professor, and he left to pursue a graduate degree at the University of Chicago. Coleman missed his hometown of Washington, D.C., but he basked in the wonders of Chicago. Upon completing his master's degree, Coleman set out to continue his studies at the University of Pennsylvania. However, Coleman never finished his dissertation because his work was interrupted by World War I and his enlistment in the army. Commissioned as a first lieutenant at Fort Des Moines, Iowa, Coleman was one of only a handful of black officers in the U.S. Army at the time. Most notably, Coleman served with the American Expeditionary Forces in France and carried out his responsibilities with honor and valor. He served as an exemplary role model for black enlisted men.

Coleman led a life characterized by a strong sense of community. He was a member of the Boys' Committee of the YMCA and a Mason. However, Coleman is perhaps best known for his role in launching the illustrious Omega Psi Phi Fraternity. Said Coleman: "I with Oscar Cooper and Edgar Love envisioned a land down in the valley that was purple and gold. The light we saw shined from beyond time itself. We took our light to Dr. Ernest Everett Just who assisted us in giving our foster mother life. The four of us combined gave all our love, peace and happiness to Omega."[2] Coleman's commitment to Omega was steadfast at the outset and unwavering throughout his life. He served as the fraternity's first Grand Keeper of Seal (national treasurer). His loyalty to and love for the Omega Psi Phi were matched by few who have worn the royal purple and old gold. Coleman died in February 1967.

Oscar J. Cooper

Like Coleman, Oscar J. Cooper (1888–1972) was a native of Washington, D.C., and attended M Street High School. Cooper was quiet and studious—a lover of books and a voracious reader. Raised to be humble, reserved, and meticulous in appearance, he was also a gentleman.[3] The summer after graduating from high school, Cooper left home to find work to help pay for his college tuition. In 1909, after amassing a decent sum of money, Cooper enrolled at Howard University, where he would remain until 1917, when he earned a doctor of medicine degree. Cooper knew early on that he wanted to be a doctor, and his love of science led him to excel in biology. In Dr. Ernest Everett Just, Cooper found a mentor and wasted no time in impressing his professor. Before long, Just made Cooper his laboratory assistant. Just recognized in Cooper a trait that he wished all his students possessed—a willingness to work hard. Cooper not only worked hard but also enjoyed doing so. He liked the feeling that came from a job well done.

Clearly, Cooper's upbringing and his tutelage under Just formed the foundation for his relentless pursuit of scientific inquiry. Likewise, his colleagues were not surprised when Cooper worked just as diligently to bring Omega Psi Phi into being. For his efforts, he was made the fraternity's first Grand Keeper of Records (national secretary). In the fraternity's second year, Cooper served as its Grand Basileus.

Cooper's penchant for hard work would also pay dividends when he entered medical school at Howard. The fact that he was able to achieve such a lofty goal at a time when blacks were discouraged and at times prevented from pursuing occupations traditionally held by whites is a testament to his will and character. Upon earning his MD, Cooper moved to Philadelphia, where he practiced medicine for half a century. Fraternity brothers who visited Cooper over the years marveled at his extensive library and were impressed by his reputation as an outstanding physician not only in Philadelphia but in the state of Pennsylvania as well. Herman Dreer submits that Cooper's practice "exhibited the democratic spirit and the love of the humanitarian."[4] He is said to have had one of the most successful medical practices in the City of Brotherly Love. Cooper died in 1972.

Ernest Everett Just

A zoologist, biologist, and research scientist in the field of physical chemistry, Ernest Everett Just (1883–1941) was born in the old seaport town of Charleston, South Carolina. Raised in a Christian household with love and support, Just was urged to "reach for the stars." His parents were industrious but far from prosperous. His mother, Mary Matthews, was a schoolteacher, and his father, Charles Frazier, worked on the docks, a highly sought-after job. Unfortunately, Charles Frazier died when Ernest was only four years old, forcing the young Just to help compensate for the family's lost income at an early age. Just began working in the fields every day after school. In many places in the South, black schools did not go past the eighth grade. Desperate to see her son further his education, Mary Matthews scraped together enough money to send young Just to Kimball Union Academy, an elite boarding school in Meriden, New Hampshire. Fortunately for Just, his mother was an educator, which afforded him opportunities that were not available to many other young blacks. In 1896 at the age of thirteen he enrolled in the Industrial School of the State College of Orangeburg (now South Carolina State University), graduating in three years. Determined to prove his mettle and make his mark at Kimball, Just graduated in only three years, earning degrees in both biology and history. While there, he worked on the school's newspaper and was captain of the debate team. As class valedictorian, Just was poised to attend a prestigious college, matriculating at nearby Dartmouth College in Hanover in 1903. It was at Dartmouth that he decided to become a research biologist specializing in cytology, the study of cells. Confident that he could perform on a par with his white counterparts, and not one to rest on his laurels, Just was elected to Phi Beta Kappa and graduated magna cum laude in 1907—the only one in his class to earn such an honor.

Just encountered the same difficulties that plagued all black college graduates of his era: regardless of how bright they were or how high their grades were, it was nearly impossible for blacks to get teaching posts at predominantly white colleges or universities. In 1909, Dr. Frank R. Lille, head of the Biology Department at the University of Chicago and chief of the Marine Biological Laboratory at Woods Hole, Massachusetts, invited Just to spend the summer at Woods Hole as his research assistant. One year later, officials at both Howard University and Morehouse College recognized Just's brilliance, and both schools set their sights on him. Howard won, offering Just a position in its newly formed Biology Department. By 1910, he was in charge of that department, and in 1912, Just was chosen to head the Department of Zoology, a position he held until his death. That same year, Just's personal life was significantly enhanced when he married Ethel Highwarden, who taught German at Howard University.

At Howard, Just developed a reputation as a tough but fair-minded instructor. This reputation proved to be both a blessing and a curse. The more his reputation grew, the more was asked of him. Among those who made additional demands on Just's time were Edgar Love, Frank Coleman, and Oscar Cooper, when they approached Just with the idea of creating a black Greek-letter fraternity on campus. Within a short time, Omega Psi Phi Fraternity Inc. was born, with Professor Just serving as its faculty adviser.

Just wore several other hats at Howard; he chaired the physiology and zoology departments and served on the faculty of the medical school. Always seeking to better himself, Just took a short sabbatical to pursue doctoral studies at the University of Chicago, completing his PhD in experimental psychology in 1916.

Just made numerous contributions to the world of science. For approximately twenty years, he studied and conducted experiments on the reproductive cells of marine life at the Marine Biological Laboratory in Massachusetts. Just believed that if scientists understood the functions of normal as well as abnormal cells, it would lead to the ability to treat many human ills, such as cancer, leukemia, and sickle cell anemia. In his book *The Biology of Cell Surface*, Just argues that the cell membrane is as important to the life of a cell as its nucleus. Just received many honors for his accomplishments. He was a fellow of the American Association for the Advancement of Science and a member of the American Society of Naturalists, the Washington Academy of Sciences, and La Societe des Sciences Naturelles et Mathematiques of France. In 1915, he was awarded the Spingarn Medal, the highest honor given by the NAACP to individuals of notable achievement.[5]

Despite his genius, Just was never invited to conduct research at any notable U.S. laboratories or esteemed American universities. Convinced that racial discrimination would forever restrict him, Just set out for Europe in 1929 and conducted experiments at the Zoological Station in Naples, Italy. Then, in 1930, he became the first American—black or white—to be invited to serve as a scholar in residence at the Kaiser Wilhelm Institute in Germany, the most highly regarded academy of physics, chemistry, and biology in the world. Just also received a similar invitation from the Sorbonne in Paris.

Although Just remained employed by Howard University, he spent the bulk of his time in Germany. Just ceased his work there in 1933, when the Nazis took over Germany. In 1934, he conducted most of his research in Italy and at the Sorbonne. In 1938, Just moved to France, where he began to experience poor health. After Germany invaded France in 1940, Just was briefly held in a prisoner of war camp. The State Department negotiated his release, and he returned home in September 1940. However, Just had fallen gravely ill while imprisoned, and his condition worsened back in the States. Just died of cancer on October 27, 1941, at the young age of fifty-eight. That same year, the Schomberg Collection of Black History selected Just for its Honor Roll of the twelve most outstanding African Americans, citing him as "the best investigator in the field of biology that the Negro people have produced in America." Fifty-five years later, in 1996, Just was immortalized with a commemorative U.S. postage stamp, making him the only founder of a black fraternity or sorority who can lay claim to that honor.

Edgar A. Love

Edgar A. Love (1891–1974) was the first Grand Basileus of Omega Psi Phi Fraternity Inc. He was elected Grand Basileus again in 1913 at the Washington, D.C., conclave and served in that capacity for two years. In the words of Herman Dreer, "it was Rev. Edgar Love in the germ, the stripling in his teens, the youth of promise and vision who helped organize the Omega Psi Phi Fraternity and start it on its pioneering way."[6]

Born in Richmond, Virginia, the capital of the Confederacy, Love was raised in the small town of Harrisburg, Virginia. The son of a Methodist minister, Love was educated in the public schools of Maryland and Virginia. Upon graduating from high school, he entered the college that most East Coast blacks clamored to attend—Howard University. In 1913, Love graduated from Howard with honors (cum laude), and in 1916, he received a second undergraduate degree in divinity. He followed that up with a third degree—a bachelor of sacred theology from Boston University. Equipped with an insatiable thirst for knowledge, Love entered graduate school at the University of Chicago. However, his studies were cut short by World War I. When the call was issued for youth to serve in France, Love entered the Officers' Training School in Des Moines, Iowa. After receiving his commission, Love was put in charge of 3,000 men. Love's most important responsibility came when he was assigned as chaplain to the 368th Infantry, which saw action in the Vosges Mountains and the Argonne Forest. Lieutenant Love displayed tremendous courage under fire, especially during what has become known as the "great offensive," which lasted eight days and during which Love and his men were gassed.

Aside from tending to the spiritual needs of the soldiers, Love helped organize a school for soldiers who were considered functional illiterates in the 809th Pioneer Infantry. The school's curriculum included subjects ranging from reading and writing to philosophy to automotive repair.

Love was discharged from the army in 1919, at which time he was hired by Morgan State College in Baltimore as professor of Bible and history. In addition to his full-time teaching duties, he served as the school's athletic director.

While in Baltimore, Love pastored at several churches: for one year in Fairmount, Maryland; for four years in Washington, D.C.; for three years in Annapolis, Maryland; and for three years in the blue-collar town of Wheeling, West Virginia. However, he would earn wide recognition as director of the famous John Wesley M. C. Church in Baltimore. Love's work in disadvantaged communities in Maryland, Washington, and West Virginia impacted the lives of hundreds, perhaps thousands, of indigent blacks. It was because of his dedication to humankind, and his prowess as an instructor of religion, that Morgan State College bestowed on Love an honorary doctorate of divinity in 1935.

Many others acknowledged Love as a giant among social engineers. At a time when racial problems were on the rise, Maryland governor Albert C. Ritchie appointed him to the Maryland Interracial Commission. Love also participated in many other important community-oriented endeavors, such as serving as president of the Interdenominational Ministers Alliance of Washington and as district superintendent of the Washington District for the Methodist Episcopal Church. Later in his life, Love joined the Masons, where he rose to the rank of thirty-second degree.

When Love died in 1974, the ecumenical world suffered a great loss. As a civic and religious leader, Love "made the church, wherever he was, function as a community center for the people of the neighborhood, as well as a temple of worship for the Most High God."[7]

Conclusion

Just, Love, Cooper, and Coleman exhibited extraordinary perseverance, keen intellect, and an unwavering commitment to service, and they attracted men of similar ilk. With the founding of Omega Psi Phi Fraternity Inc., Just, Love, Cooper, and Coleman set in motion a chain of events that would impact nearly every aspect of American life. Indeed, since World War I, no major movement in which blacks have figured prominently has not been influenced by the men of Omega. In fact, there are likely few Americans whose lives have not been touched by the men of Omega in some way.

Notes

1. Herman Dreer, *The History of Omega Psi Phi Fraternity* (Washington, D.C.: Omega Psi Phi Fraternity, 1940), 7.
2. http://www.vsu.edu/students/organization/omega/_private/coleman.htm.
3. Dreer, *History of Omega Psi Phi,* 4.
4. Ibid., 5.
5. Robert C. Hayden, *A Salute to Black Scientists and Inventors* (Chicago: Empak Enterprises, 1985), 13.
6. Dreer, *History of Omega Psi Phi,* 3.
7. Ibid.

4

Women of Vision, Catalysts for Change
The Founders of Delta Sigma Theta Sorority

Jessica Harris

Lifting as they climb, onward and upward they go struggling and striving and hoping that the buds and blossoms of their desires may burst into glorious fruition ere long.

—Mary Church Terrell

This chapter traces the lives of the twenty-two founders of Delta Sigma Theta Sorority Inc. In 1913, these twenty-two Howard University students embarked on a journey that forever changed the trajectory of the black sorority movement. Together, they formed an organization dedicated to service and committed to the bonds of sisterhood and the achievement of academic excellence. Taking a stand at a time and in an era marred by legalized racial and gender inequality, the visionary twenty-two set forth to challenge and upset the white patriarchal order of their day. Memorialized most pointedly through their participation in the March 1913 demonstration for women's suffrage in Washington, D.C., the conviction, courage, and tenacity of the founders were put on display, and the impetus of Delta Sigma Theta Sorority as a national organization and movement was congealed.

Because the present and future goals of Delta Sigma Theta Sorority are so closely tied to the pioneering efforts of the organization's twenty-two founders, it is only fitting to examine their trailblazing lives. Unfortunately, there are few readily available sources on which to base extensive biographical sketches of the founders. As such, the scholarly inquiry of Paula Giddings provides much of the context for the ensuing account. In spite of these constraints, I hope to show the contribution of these dynamic women to the expansion of the black sorority movement and pay tribute to their persistent pursuit of racial justice and gender equality.

Osceola Macarthy Adams

"There were, of course, many differences of opinion and conflicting notions as to how things should be done; but regarding matters of principle and ideal, there was a rare degree of unanimity."[1] These words by founder Osceola Macarthy Adams (1890–1983) reveal much about the founders of Delta Sigma Theta. Individually, the young women spanned a wide range of academic disciplines, life experiences, and backgrounds. Collectively, however, they were resolved to see the founding and expansion of Delta Sigma Theta Sorority become a reality.

Osceola Macarthy (Adams) was a senior majoring in dramatics at the time of Delta's founding. Born in Albany, Georgia, she came to Howard with aspirations of becoming a star of the theater. At a time when African Americans were just beginning to showcase their talents on Broadway and other major stages, Adams spent a wealth of time and energy preparing to take her place amid the challenging yet invigorating world of American theater. As a leader of the Howard College Dramatic Club and through her roles in plays such as *For One Night Only*, she was poised for a successful career.[2]

After graduating from Howard, Adams, a highly qualified and skilled actress, was denied admittance to her preferred drama school. She recalled, "I wanted to go to the American Academy of Dramatic Arts, but was refused because of my race. Finally I was accepted by the American Repertory Theater."[3] As a student with the Repertory Theater, Adams was finally able to live out her dream of being a working actress. During the Depression, she made her Broadway debut and soon ventured into the role of director—directing plays for a number of theaters, among them the American Negro Theater. As a director and teacher at the American Negro Theater, Adams witnessed the acting debuts of two world-renowned artists of the stage and screen: Sidney Poitier and Harry Belafonte. Additionally, she served as director of the Harlem School of the Arts and taught drama courses at Bennett College in Greensboro, North Carolina. Throughout her life, she remained dedicated to the theater, continuing to perform when opportunities availed themselves and assisting others in their pursuit of acting. Moreover, abiding in her commitment to public service and social activism, in 1921, Adams, fellow founder Marguerite Young Alexander, and five other members of the sorority chartered the Lambda Chapter of Delta Sigma Theta in Chicago, Illinois. Adams served as the first president of the Lambda Chapter and subsequently as Delta's national treasurer.[4]

Although committed to life as an artist and a public servant, Osceola Macarthy Adams was also a devoted wife and mother. In 1915, she married Numa P. G.

Adams, himself a Howard University alumnus and member of Alpha Phi Alpha Fraternity. After graduating from the University of Chicago's School of Medicine, Dr. Adams returned to Howard as a professor and served as the first black dean of the university's medical school.[5] Together they parented one child.

Described by her fellow Delta founders as "the most dramatic and elegant among them in manner, speech, and dress," consummate artist Osceola Macarthy Adams died in 1983.[6]

Marguerite Young Alexander

Unfortunately, not much is known about the life of Marguerite Young (Alexander). However, what can be deduced from her involvement in the founding of Delta Sigma Theta Sorority is that she was a woman of foresight, purpose, and deed. Coming to Howard University from Chicago, Illinois, Alexander established herself as a true renaissance woman on campus. Aside from her active membership in myriad campus organizations, Alexander was a student of romance and classical languages. Putting her training to use after graduating in 1913, she launched a career as a French and Spanish correspondence secretary for a prestigious Chicago business firm.[7] Apart from her career, marriage, and motherhood, Alexander held fast to her commitment to seeing Delta thrive and expand into a sustainable national organization. In addition to being a supporter of Alpha Chapter's projects and programs, she was a charter member of the sorority's Lambda Chapter in her hometown of Chicago.

Winona Cargile Alexander

Winona Cargile (1893–1984) was born in Columbus, Georgia, on June 21, 1893. The daughter and niece of Howard University alumni, she graduated high school as class salutatorian and then made the trip north to attend Howard, just as her father and uncle before her.[8]

During her four years at Howard, Alexander made a name for herself, becoming active as a student leader and garnering popularity. She was a member and at one point secretary of the Social Science Club, a member of the College Classical Club, class vice president, and the first custodian of the Alpha Chapter of Delta Sigma Theta Sorority.[9]

After graduating from Howard in 1913, she taught for a couple of years before entering New York University's School of Social Work. A pioneer in the field, she was the first black social worker with the New York City and New York County Charities. Alexander moved to Florida after completing her course work and became a social worker with the Duval County Welfare Board. After the death of her husband, Florida attorney Edward Alexander, in 1943, Winona Cargile Alexander made her home in Jacksonville, Florida, until her death in 1984.[10]

Ethel Cuff Black

Ethel Cuff (Black) was born in Wilmington, Delaware, in 1890. Her grandparents were second-generation free blacks and landowners, and her father was an entrepreneur in the banking and retail industries. Ethel was thus among the upper echelon of the black community. While at Howard, she was a member of Howard University's choir, chairperson of the YWCA's collegiate committee, and the first vice president of Alpha Chapter.[11]

After graduating from Howard in 1915, Black taught social studies in the public schools in Sedalia, Missouri, and Oklahoma City; she also taught courses at Delaware State College in Dover.[12] She spent much of her career in the New York City school system and was the first black teacher in Richmond County, New York. In 1939, while teaching at P.S. 108 in Queens, she married New York City real estate agent David Horton Black. Very active in community affairs, particularly programs oriented toward youth, Black helped charter the Queens Alumnae Chapter of Delta Sigma Theta Sorority in June 1951.[13]

Bertha Pitts Campbell

Bertha Pitts (1889–1990) was born in Winfield, Kansas. Soon after her birth, she and her family moved westward, finally settling in Montrose, Colorado.[14] Highly intelligent and an incessant studier, by the time she enrolled in Montrose High School in 1903—the only black student in her class—she had mastered three foreign languages and could translate them fluently. In high school, Campbell maintained top grades in all her subjects and graduated as valedictorian of her class. She was awarded a four-year scholarship to attend Colorado College in Colorado Springs. However, with the financial support of the Montrose Congregational Church and a little persuading by a church trustee, in the fall of

1909, she instead boarded a train headed for Washington, D.C., and Howard University.[15]

At Howard, Campbell developed the racial and gender consciousness that inspired much of her later activism. Participating in what was known as Howard Night, she and her fellow classmates engaged issues plaguing African Americans in Washington and across the nation. Among the main topics of discourse was the subject of racism. According to Giddings: "For the young Bertha Pitts Campbell, who was spared the cruder aspects of discrimination in Montrose, the experience of not being able to eat in the city's 'White' restaurants, or try on a dress before buying it, was a new one."[16] Moreover, Campbell and other Howard students were exposed to the workings of the women's suffrage movement. Campbell's growing awareness, coupled with the influence of human rights advocate Mary Church Terrell, led her and the other founders of Delta Sigma Theta to participate in a women's suffrage march in 1913. Campbell commented, "If they [white women] get the vote, we will too, someday."[17]

In the spring of 1913, Campbell graduated with honors from the Teachers College, earning a bachelor's degree in education. At the urging of the university's placement office, Campbell accepted a teaching position at the Topeka Industrial Educational Institute in Kansas. After one year there, Campbell returned to Washington, D.C., and Howard University, securing a job with the Teachers College; soon after, she was appointed assistant dean of women in Minor Hall. Just as Campbell was becoming reacquainted with Howard, she received word that her sister Minnie had died. Campbell traveled to her sister's home in Dillon, Montana, gathered her nieces and nephew, and journeyed with them to Grand Junction, Colorado, where they would be residing with their father's family.[18]

While in Grand Junction, Bertha met Earl Allen Campbell, and the two married in 1917. While her husband was off at work, Campbell kept busy fulfilling her role as wife and mother to their son, Earl Jr. In 1923, the Campbell family moved to Seattle, where Campbell was an active member of the First African Methodist Episcopal Church and heavily involved in community affairs.[19]

"An act of discrimination against one black is discrimination against us all."[20] These words spoken by Campbell just months shy of her ninety-second birthday speak volumes about her undying faithfulness to the struggle for racial equality. With a strong interest in race relations, Campbell was an active member of the Ladies' Auxiliary of the Seattle Urban League. After that group dissolved, Campbell became a member of the parent organization, the National Urban League, and remained so until her death. In addition, Campbell was a member of the YWCA and in 1936 became the first African American at the Seattle branch to become a voting member of its board of directors. With Delta ever present in her heart and in the forefront of her mind, Campbell helped create the Alpha Omicron Chapter (now the Seattle Alumnae Chapter), chartered on April 17, 1933.[21]

Continuing her work in the realm of race relations, Campbell was a charter member of the Christian Friends for Racial Equality, an interracial group devoted to encouraging understanding among racial groups.[22] Moreover, the group examined cases of racial discrimination in public spaces and demanded a response from local and state officials. Through the tireless efforts of its members, the organization gained much success.

The 1950s brought tragedy to Campbell. Earl Jr. was killed in 1951 by an accidental explosion while serving in the military. Three years later, Earl Sr. died of a heart attack. Though mourning the loss of her only child and husband, Campbell pressed forward and continued to serve the community as she had her entire life.[23]

In 1980, Campbell rallied in support of the equal rights amendment, and a year later, she led a delegation of 10,000 Deltas down Pennsylvania Avenue in Washington to commemorate the founders' participation in the march for women's suffrage back in 1913.[24]

Bertha Pitts Campbell departed this life in 1990 at the age of 101. When reflecting on her age, she made the following remarks: "I never thought I'd live to get this old. I've outlived all of my relatives except my one niece, Vessie Branson of Los Angeles, California. I'm grateful to God to be alive and of sound mind and good health. I don't know how long I'll live; no one knows. I remember the quip that says, 'The success to living to become one hundred is to get to ninety-nine and then being very careful.'" Referred to by many as the most viable Delta, "too young to be old," Bertha Pitts Campbell was "a remarkable, spirited, and giving legend."[25]

Zephyr Chisom Carter

Zephyr Chisom (1891–1976) was born in El Paso, Texas. A member of Howard's class of 1913, Carter developed a close relationship with Bertha Pitts Campbell and Naomi Sewell Richardson. Like her good friend Campbell, Carter was also a lover of the arts and a member of the Howard College Dramatics Club. As an actress, she was best known for her role as Mistress Quickly in Shakespeare's

The Merry Wives of Windsor. Carter was also involved with the Literary and Social Club on campus, serving as the group's critic.[26]

As was the case with a number of Howard University students, issues of race were the catalyst for their activism. Carter joined fellow Delta founders Vashti Turley Murphy, Winona Cargile Alexander, and Madree Penn White as members of the Howard branch of the National Association for the Advancement of Colored People (NAACP). Because of her charisma and drive, an issue of *Crisis Magazine* described Carter as the "leading spirit in the organization."[27] These qualities extended to Carter's involvement with Delta, as she served as Alpha Chapter's reporter.

After graduation, Carter moved back to Texas and taught briefly in San Antonio before relocating to California. According to Giddings, while in California, she "worked as a security officer for the state's Department of Employment—perhaps to help support her love for singing chorus background music for films and television shows."[28]

Remembered by her fellow founders and sorors for her good nature, Zephyr Chisom Carter died in 1976.

Edna Brown Coleman

Howard University was not new territory for Delta founder Edna Brown Coleman, a native of Washington, D.C. Her father, Sterling Nelson Brown, had been a professor of religion at Howard for thirty-one years. Coleman was Howard Academy valedictorian in 1909—a graduating class that included fellow Delta founders Ethel Cuff Black and Jimmie Bugg Middleton.[29]

During Coleman's tenure at Howard University, she was active in a number of campus organizations and held a number of leadership positions, among them, class president. Described by many as brilliant, Coleman was, once again, valedictorian of the class of 1913. After leaving Howard, she attended graduate school at Oberlin College and married Omega Psi Phi founder and future Howard physics professor Frank Coleman.[30]

Jessie McGuire Dent

Hailing from Galveston, Texas, Jessie McGuire (Dent) graduated from East District High School, one of the first black high schools in the state of Texas.

Although quite active while at Howard, Dent's most important contributions took place in her hometown of Galveston. During the 1940s, a time when African American teachers throughout the South were lobbying for better pay, Dent successfully sued the Galveston Independent School District and won equal pay for black teachers in the city.[31]

Although Dent married and gave birth to a son, he passed away at a very young age. With no heir, Dent and longtime friend and sorority sister Frederica Chase Dodd created a "survivor's will," stating that the surviving sister would inherit the other's estate. Sadly, Dent died in 1948, and Dodd outlived her by twenty-four years.[32]

Frederica Chase Dodd

Frederica Chase (1892–1972), educator, social worker, and activist, was born in Dallas, Texas. Bertha Pitts Campbell described Dodd as "very aristocratic in her speech and carriage, and soft-spoken in manner." Dodd's father was a successful Texas attorney and her mother, a well-known teacher. After graduating from the Dallas Colored School Number 2 in 1910, she arrived at Howard that fall. There she quickly befriended Naomi Sewell Richardson, Myra Davis Hemmings, and Jessie McGuire Dent, with whom she would remain the closest.[33]

After graduating from Howard in 1914, Dodd returned to her hometown and worked as an English instructor at Dallas High School. She married Dallas physician and Howard University Medical School graduate Dr. John Horace Dodd in 1920, after which she stopped teaching and became very active in civic and service organizations.[34] Dodd was influential in helping to establish a YWCA branch for black women in Dallas. Through the efforts of Dodd and others, that organization, initially an after-school group for girls, would become the Maria Morgan branch of the YWCA. Moreover, owing to her diligence, the Eta Beta Chapter (now the Dallas Alumnae Chapter) of Delta Sigma Theta was chartered. With the formation of the graduate chapter, Delta Sigma Theta became the first Greek-letter organization in Dallas.[35]

Dodd went on to attend Atlanta University (now Clark Atlanta University) for graduate school. In the 1930s, she began a career as a social worker and, like Winona Cargile Alexander in New York, Dodd became one of her state's first black social workers. Dodd began her career with the Texas Relief Commission, becoming director of the Emergency Relief Station for African Americans; she later worked for United Charities.[36]

A devoted friend and dedicated activist, Frederica Chase Dodd died in January 1972 at age eighty.

Myra Davis Hemmings

Myra Lillian Davis (1895–1968) was born in Gonzales, Texas. She grew up in San Antonio and in 1909 graduated from the city's Riverside High School. While a student at Howard, Hemmings was a member of the Alpha Phi Literary Society and worked very closely with Howard's instructor of music, Lulu Vere Childers.[37] Although quite an active coed on campus, Hemmings is best remembered for her leadership and guidance with regard to the founding of Delta Sigma Theta Sorority Inc.

In 1912, when the idea for the new sorority was conceived, Hemmings and some of the other twenty-two founders were members of Alpha Kappa Alpha Sorority (AKA). Hemmings, AKA president at the time, supported the idea proposed by Madree Penn (White) and others to reorganize and revamp the structure of the sorority: "The younger members of Alpha Kappa Alpha decided that their affiliation should be devoted to larger matters than those with which they previously had been concerned. It was felt that the times demanded of women everywhere evidence of their emancipated thinking and acting."[38] Inspired by the call to respond to the issues and concerns facing African Americans and women, the twenty-two moved to form what would become Delta Sigma Theta Sorority Inc. Simultaneously, graduate members of Alpha Kappa Alpha, under the leadership of Nellie Quander (former president of the sorority), moved to preserve AKA and its original mission.

The twenty-two former AKA members held an official meeting to reorganize themselves in 1913. The date of that meeting, January 13, serves as the founding date and the dawn of Delta Sigma Theta. Elections were held, and because of her leadership ability and adeptness, Hemmings was elected first president of the Alpha Chapter, a position she held until May 1913, when she graduated from Howard University.

Over the course of her life, Hemmings earned a master's degree in speech and dramatic arts from Northwestern University and taught school in her hometown of San Antonio. Her teaching career spanned fifty-one years, during which time she received many accolades for her oratorical gifts and for her stage productions of works ranging from Shakespeare to modern writers. She married John "Pop" Hemmings, a former Broadway actor, in 1922.[39] Together, they organized dramatic guilds and produced a number of plays, enhancing the cultural lives of black San Antonians.[40] Moreover, in 1944 Hemmings coproduced, codirected, and starred in *Go Down Death*, now a black film classic.[41] Aside from her life as an educator and actress, Hemmings also made vital contributions to the civic vitality of the city. She was an active member of the NAACP and the National Council of Negro Women and a charter member of the San Antonio Alumnae Chapter of Delta Sigma Theta Sorority. Hemmings also served as the sorority's grand vice president during the tenure of sixth national president Jeannette Triplett Jones.[42]

When the sorority's nineteenth convention was held in San Antonio in 1947, Hemmings was the cochair. And on the occasion of the sorority's golden anniversary in 1963, Hemmings, a consummate leader, once again served as cochair of the convention. Myra Davis Hemmings passed away in December 1968 in San Antonio. Though a "blustery one," according to fellow founder Bertha Pitts Campbell, Hemmings proved to be a perpetual leader in Delta and in her community.

Olive C. Jones

Like fellow founder Edna Brown Coleman, Olive C. Jones was a native of Washington, D.C. A member of Howard's class of 1913 and an accomplished pianist, she went on to teach music in the D.C. public school system.[43] Although she held no position on the executive board of Alpha Chapter and spent only three months on campus after the sorority's founding, Jones continued her support of the chapter. Unfortunately, she lost touch with the sorority, and little is known about her life after Howard. Nonetheless, Jones stands among the circle of twenty-two founders of a dynamic institution.

Jimmie Bugg Middleton

A native of Lynchburg, Virginia, Jimmie Bugg (Middleton) arrived on Howard's campus in 1909. Middleton, like all of Delta's founders, was a very active member of the Howard community. She notes: "as positions in campus life opened to women, Delta girls were always in the vanguard of those seeking to fill them; in fact no aspect of Howard University's campus life open to women was unattended by the presence of some soror." The efforts of the founders were not confined to campus leadership, but "Delta women of the period declared that they studied night and day to maintain superiority in numbers on the university's honor roll." And in true Delta form, in 1913, Middleton graduated from Howard's Teachers College with honors.[44] She returned to Howard during the 1930s to acquire a master's degree.

After receiving her bachelor's degree, Jimmie married Dr. Charles Clayton Middleton.[45] Their first daughter, Catherine Brown Middleton, born in January 1916, had the distinction of being the first child born to a founder. Her second daughter, Amanda Belle, was born in 1917.[46]

Middleton enjoyed an extensive career as an educator; first as a teacher, then as a librarian, and finally as dean of girls at a high school in Raleigh, North Carolina. Steadfast in her loyalty to Delta, Middleton helped establish the Alpha Zeta Sigma Chapter (now the Raleigh Alumnae Chapter) of the sorority on May 7, 1938.[47]

Active in myriad civic and educational endeavors, Middleton served as president and national treasurer of the National Association of College Women, a cadre of college-educated, professional African American women committed to training others like them for leadership. Because of her trailblazing efforts in the realm of education, Middleton was appointed to the Scholarship Board of New York State's Twenty-second Congressional District in 1944, during the first term of Congressman Adam Clayton Powell Jr.[48]

Pauline Oberdorfer Minor

The first treasurer of Alpha Chapter, Pauline Oberdorfer Minor (?–1963) was born in Charlottesville, Virginia. According to Giddings, "by her own submitted biography to the sorority, [she] did not know who her parents were or the exact date of her birth . . . [and] was reared by an aunt and uncle in Philadelphia." She graduated from the Philadelphia High School for Girls in 1910 and, with financial assistance from her church, enrolled in the Teachers College at Howard University that fall. Besides her teaching career, which took her to Alabama, South Carolina, and Pennsylvania, Minor was also a gifted musician. After graduating as valedictorian of the class of 1914, she embarked on a career as a mezzo-soprano recitalist and published hymn writer. Among her publications was a book entitled *Soul Echoes* that featured forty of her own compositions, including "My Lord Is a Refuge" and "Get Off the Judgment Seat."[49] Minor passed away in 1963.

Vashti Turley Murphy

Lula Vashti Turley (1884–1960) was born in the nation's capital, graduated from Dunbar High School, and went on to teach elementary school.[50] When Howard opened its doors to Washington schoolteachers, Murphy became a member of the class of 1914. During her four years in college, Murphy not only kept teaching but also was an active member of the student branch of the NAACP and, at one time, her class vice president.[51] After graduation, she married Carl Murphy, alumnus of Howard and Harvard; professor and chair of the German Department at Howard; and editor and publisher of the *Baltimore Afro-American,* the paper his father founded in 1892.[52] Carl Murphy was a member of Alpha Phi Alpha Fraternity and at one time served as editor of the fraternity's national organ, the *Sphinx*. Together, Carl and Vashti Murphy were the parents of five daughters, four of whom became Deltas. Their granddaughter, the Reverend Vashti Murphy McKenzie, is the current national chaplain of Delta Sigma Theta, as well as the first female bishop of the African Methodist Episcopal Church.

Vashti Turley Murphy was at the core of an enduring legacy extending to her daughters and grandchildren, but her service and contributions to the sorority stretch far beyond the familial sphere. Murphy was an active member of the Baltimore Alumnae Chapter and is fondly remembered by its members. Delta's ninth national president, Mae Wright Peck, herself a member of the Baltimore Alumnae Chapter, said the following about "Miss Vash": "Sorors who have grown to maturity in the city where a founder of Delta Sigma Theta has resided are most fortunate. They have been able to capture the enthusiasm for our sisterhood from one who was there at Howard University in 1913 and who caught the glorious vision that became Delta Sigma Theta. I was one who was privileged to sit at the font. 'Miss Vash,' as Founder Vashti Turley Murphy was affectionately known to the sorors who lived in Baltimore, taught us by example what it meant to be a good, loyal stalwart Delta." In addition to her service to Delta, Murphy was a member of the Baltimore branch of the National Association of College Women and a member of the NAACP. With an interest in the plight of delinquent girls, Murphy was involved with the Maryland School for Girls and a staunch supporter of the YWCA.[53]

Vashti Turley Murphy passed away in 1960. Remembered by those who knew and loved her as the epitome of grace, dignity, and fortitude, Murphy's life, works, and deeds exemplified the words of her favorite hymn:

Be strong! We are not here to play, to dream, to drift;
We have hard work to do and loads to lift;
Shun not the struggle; face it, 'tis God's gift.
Be strong, be strong, be strong! Be Strong!

Say not the days are evil, who's to blame?
And fold the hands and acquiesce, O shame!
Stand up, speak out, and bravely in God's Name.
Be strong, be strong, be strong!

Be strong! It matters not how deep intrenched the wrong.
How hard the battle goes, the day, how long;
Faint not, fight on! Tomorrow comes the song.
Be strong, be strong, be strong! Amen.[54]

Naomi Sewell Richardson

Naomi Sewell (1892–1993), Delta's longest surviving founder, was born in Washingtonville, New York. The first African American graduate of the Washingtonville High School, Richardson entered Howard as a student in its Teachers College.[55] After graduation, she was appointed to teach elementary-aged students in the segregated public school system of East St. Louis, Missouri. Later in her career, she taught in Princeton, New Jersey, and New York City. While in New Jersey, she became friends with noted actor, singer, activist, and, at the time, Rutgers University student Paul Robeson; there, she met and married Clarence Richardson, one of Robeson's fraternity brothers in Alpha Phi Alpha.[56] The Richardsons lived in New York City for more than twenty years and were very active in the community. After a life of service, Richardson died in 1993 in her hometown of Washingtonville.

Mamie Reddy Rose

During the train ride from Gonzales, Texas, Myra Davis Hemmings met her future sorority sister Mamie Reddy (?–1919), a native of Beta, South Carolina, and a resident of Mount Vernon, Illinois. As a student at Howard, Mamie was very active and served as president of the literary and social club.[57] She graduated from Howard in 1913 and soon after married the Reverend James E. Rose and became a homemaker. After four years of marriage, Mamie Reddy Rose became very ill and was the first of Delta's founders to depart this earthly life. She died on February 17, 1919.[58]

Eliza Pearl Shippen

Eliza Pearl Shippen (1888–1981) was born in Washington, D.C., where her family was well known. Her father was an alumnus of Howard University. Shippen was educated at the Minor Normal School and graduated first in her senior class.[59] At Howard, she was a member of the Teacher's Club and graduated from the Howard College of Arts and Sciences, magna cum laude, in 1912. Although Delta Sigma Theta was not formally chartered until 1913, after she graduated, Shippen was among the circle of twenty-two women who gathered in 1912 with the hope of reorganizing AKA. She went on to earn a master's degree from the Teachers College at Columbia University in 1928 and a PhD in English language and literature from the University of Pennsylvania in 1944.[60] After devoting much of her life to education and service to youth, Shippen died in 1981.

Florence Letcher Toms

Another native of Washington, D.C., Florence Letcher (?–1972) graduated from the Armstrong Manual Training High School. According to Giddings, the graduation ceremony was particularly memorable because Toms was awarded a diploma and scholarship by President William Howard Taft.[61] Toms was active in a number of student organizations on campus, in addition to her role in the founding of Delta Sigma Theta Sorority Inc.

After graduating from Howard, Florence married attorney Charles H. Toms and began a successful career in education, including the position of assistant principal at Garnet-Patterson Junior High School in Washington, D.C. Toms also attained a master's degree from New York University.[62] Throughout her life, she was active in a plethora of civic groups and organizations oriented toward education. She was a member of the board of directors of the Family Welfare Association and a member of the Federation of Parent-Teacher Associations and the Intercultural Vocation School. Toms, a lifelong educator and public servant, died in 1972.

Ethel Carr Watson

Ethel Carr grew up in Parkersburg, West Virginia. She graduated from the Sumner School and, at the urging of her principal, entered Howard University as a freshman. At Howard, Watson was a member of the College Classical Club and treasurer of the literary and social club, an organization to which other Delta founders belonged as well.[63] After graduating from Howard, she entered the teaching profession and remained in that field until May 1948, at which time she became a dramatic performer.[64] One of her most well-known dramatic performances was the presentation of *She Stoops to Conquer* at the Smoot Theater in her hometown of Parkersburg. In recalling her performance, Watson remarked, "I have been the only colored who has ever given a performance at Smoot Theater for Warner Brothers in Parkersburg, West Virgina."[65] Although the date of Watson's death is uncertain, it is known that by the time of the sorority's golden anniversary in 1963, she had passed away.

Wertie Blackwell Weaver

Wertie Blackwell was born in Kansas City, Missouri. After graduating from Howard, she returned to her home state and, along with cofounder Naomi Sewell Richardson, taught elementary school in East St. Louis, Missouri. After marrying Dr. Darrington Weaver, the two made their home in Los Angeles, California, and were the parents of three sons. While in Los Angeles, she was an active member of the Nu Sigma Chapter of Delta. Weaver was the author of a novel entitled *The Valley of the Poor,* which shed light on issues of racism and class in the South. Shortly before her death, Weaver said of Delta, "You will never know just how happy and proud, I, as one of the founders of Delta, feel watching the remarkable progress you and other sorors have made, thus making Deltas stand out as one of the greatest beacon lights of the many fraternal organizations."[66]

Madree Penn White

According to Delta historian Mary Vroman, "Madree Penn (White) was a young woman endowed with some noteworthy characteristics, who was no doubt as important an influence on the campus as she was in the sorority."[67] When Madree Penn (?-1967) arrived at Howard University after graduating with honors from Omaha, Nebraska's Central High School, she never would have guessed that she would be the catalyst behind the formation of what would one day become the largest African American women's organization. Moreover, she would not have prophesied that her mark on Howard's campus would be so indelible and enduring.

White had turned down scholarships to the University of Iowa and the University of Nebraska so that she could attend Howard, a university that had produced a plethora of premier African American scholars, leaders, and activists.[68] As a student at Howard, White began the process of placing herself among these well-known and notable men and women, as she became an effective leader and student advocate. White has the distinction of being the first woman to hold office in a student organization, becoming the first female editor of the campus newspaper, the *Howard University Journal*.[69] Her name and face were known throughout the campus, owing to her participation and leadership in so many activities; she was a member of the College Classical Club, president of the campus chapter of the YWCA, vice president of the student branch of the NAACP, vice president of the Social Science Club, and, during her four years at Howard, class journalist, vice president, and treasurer. Therefore, it comes as no surprise that White was named "Most Popular" of her graduating class and came in third for "Who Has Done the Most for Howard."[70]

Characterized by fellow founder Bertha Pitts Campbell as the "inspiration to the whole Delta movement," it would be Madree Penn (White) who first conceived the idea of founding what became Delta Sigma Theta. In the fall of 1912, White went to chapter president Myra Davis (Hemmings) with her grand idea. Consequently, Hemmings named White as chair of the committee to draft the new sorority's constitution and bylaws and formulate the new sorority's initiation ritual; because she was an accomplished linguist, White was also put in charge of selecting the Greek-letter symbols of the new sorority.[71]

When Hemmings graduated from Howard in 1913, White was named her successor as president of Alpha Chapter, and she quickly set the wheels in motion for the creation of other chapters of Delta. During her presidency, on February 5, 1914, the sorority's second chapter, Beta Chapter, was established at Wilberforce University.[72] White's service to the sorority continued long after her days at Howard. During the tenure of Delta's third national president, Ethel LaMay Calimese, White served as the sorority's journalist. She also had a hand in founding a chapter of the sorority in St. Louis and, after moving to Cleveland in 1955, became an active member of the Omega Chapter there (now the Greater Cleveland Alumnae Chapter).[73]

After Howard, White was executive secretary of the YWCA in Charlotte, North Carolina, before launching a career in journalism. She was associate editor and business manager of the *Omaha Monitor* and later formed her own company—the Triangle Press Company—a publishing and printing firm in St. Louis.[74]

Madree Penn married Dr. James E. White and they had two children, James E. White and Grace White Ware (also a Delta). Madree Penn White, an exemplary architect of change, died in 1967.

Edith Motte Young

Native North Carolinian Edith Motte Young was an accomplished pianist. She graduated from Howard University's Teachers College a year earlier than antici-pated and began working at Claflin University in Orangeburg, South Carolina. Shortly thereafter, she married and made her home in Youngstown, Ohio. She and her husband had four children, two girls and two boys. After detecting the musical talent of her two daughters, Young and her family moved to Oberlin, Ohio, where the girls were enrolled in the Oberlin Conservatory of Music.[75] While in Oberlin, Young worked on her master's degree in biblical literature.

Conclusion: Forward through the Ages

Delta founder Bertha Pitts Campbell said of Delta in 1950, "It is a source of great satisfaction and pride to me to see that Delta has grown and prospered through the years, so that now it stands as a beacon, to light the way for good living. May Delta Sigma Theta continue its good work for the benefit of all people."[76] Since those remarks more than half a century ago, Delta Sigma Theta's membership has grown to more than 200,000 predominantly African American, college-educated women. Through Delta chapters all over the world, the vision of the twenty-two founders lives on, as Delta sisters continue to show their commitment to social change. With a lineage and a heritage encompassing such exemplars of leadership and service as Sadie T. M. Alexander, Mary McLeod Bethune, and Dorothy I. Height, the future of the sorority promises to be one of continued assessment, progress, and change. Mirroring the words of the hymn "Forward through the Ages"—"Not alone we conquer—not alone we fall. In each loss or triumph, lose or triumph all. Bound by God's far purpose, in one living whole, move we on together, to the shining goal"— the women of Delta Sigma Theta move onward and upward, adhering to and inspired by their ancestors' directive to stand as catalysts for change.[77]

Notes

Epigraph from Mary Church Terrell, "The Progress of Colored Women (an address delivered before the National American Women's Suffrage Association at the Columbia Theater, Washington, D.C., February 18, 1898, on the occasion of its fiftieth anniversary)" (Washington, D.C.: Smith Brothers Printers, 1898), 15.

1. Mary Elizabeth Vroman, *Shaped to Its Purpose: Delta Sigma Theta: The First Fifty Years* (New York: Random House, 1965), 15.
2. Paula Giddings, *In Search of Sisterhood: Delta Sigma Theta and the Challenge of the Black Sorority Movement* (New York: William Morrow, 1988), 36–37.
3. Ibid., 67.
4. Ibid., 67, 90.
5. Ibid., 66–67.
6. Ibid., 36.
7. Ibid., 65.
8. Ibid., 32.
9. Ibid., 39, 41, 47–48.
10. *Delta,* January–February 1979, 4.
11. Giddings, *In Search of Sisterhood,* 34, 36, 39, 48.
12. *Delta,* January–February 1979, 4.
13. Giddings, *In Search of Sisterhood,* 189, 259.
14. Ibid., 28.
15. Pauline Anderson Simmons Hill and Sherrilyn Johnson Jordan, *Too Young to Be Old: The Story of Bertha Pitts Campbell, a Founder of Delta Sigma Theta Sorority, Inc.* (Seattle: Peanut Butter Publishing, 1981), 8–12.
16. Giddings, *In Search of Sisterhood,* 42.
17. Ibid., 57.
18. Hill and Jordan, *Too Young to Be Old,* 23, 24–26, 27.
19. Ibid., 29, 33.
20. Ibid., 58.
21. Ibid., 33–35.
22. *Delta,* January–February 1979, 4.
23. Hill and Jordan, *Too Young to Be Old,* 57.
24. Ibid.
25. Ibid., 52.

26. Giddings, *In Search of Sisterhood,* 33, 37, 39.

27. Ibid., 41.

28. Ibid., 69.

29. Ibid., 34.

30. Ibid., 66.

31. Ibid., 35, 208.

32. Ibid., 261.

33. Ibid., 35.

34. Ibid., 94.

35. *Delta,* January–February 1979, 4.

36. Ibid.

37. Giddings, *In Search of Sisterhood,* 35, 39.

38. Vroman, *Shaped to Its Purpose,* 12.

39. Handbook of Texas Online, http://www.tsha.utexas.edu/handbook/online/articles/HH/fhe64.html (accessed September 24, 2006).

40. Giddings, *In Search of Sisterhood,* 68.

41. Handbook of Texas Online, http://www.tsha.utexas.edu/handbook/online/articles/HH/fhe64.html (accessed September 24, 2006).

42. Giddings, *In Search of Sisterhood,* 259, 154.

43. Ibid., 36.

44. Ibid., 38, 54, 48.

45. *Delta,* January–February 1979, 5.

46. Giddings, *In Search of Sisterhood,* 67.

47. Ibid., 189.

48. Ibid., 191.

49. Ibid., 36, 69.

50. Elizabeth Murphy Moss, *Be Strong! The Life of Vashti Turley Murphy* (Baltimore: Wells Printers, 1980), 4–5.

51. Giddings, *In Search of Sisterhood,* 41.

52. Kwame Anthony Appiah and Henry Louis Gates, *The Encyclopedia of the African and African American Experience* (New York: Perseus Books Group, 1999), 1359.

53. Moss, *Be Strong,* 36.

54. Ibid., 80.

55. *Delta,* January–February 1979, 5.

56. Giddings, *In Search of Sisterhood,* 65, 66.

57. Ibid., 35, 39.

58. *Delta,* January–February 1979, 5.

59. Giddings, *In Search of Sisterhood,* 38.

60. *Delta,* January–February 1979, 5.

61. Giddings, *In Search of Sisterhood,* 38.

62. Ibid., 189.

63. Ibid., 34, 39.

64. *Delta,* January–February 1979, 5.

65. Giddings, *In Search of Sisterhood,* 68.

66. *Delta,* January–February 1979, 5.

67. Vroman, *Shaped to Its Purpose,* 19.

68. Giddings, *In Search of Sisterhood,* 42.

69. Vroman, *Shaped to Its Purpose,* 19.

70. Giddings, *In Search of Sisterhood,* 65.

71. Ibid., 50.

72. Vroman, *Shaped to Its Purpose,* 20.

73. Giddings, *In Search of Sisterhood,* 260.

74. *Delta,* January–February 1979, 5.

75. Giddings, *In Search of Sisterhood,* 36.

76. Ibid., 4.

77. Frederick Lucian Hosmer, "Forward through the Ages."

5

Constitutionally Bound
The Founders of Phi Beta Sigma Fraternity and Zeta Phi Beta Sorority

Matthew W. Hughey

> The world of humanity has two wings—one is women and the other men. Not until both wings are equally developed can the bird fly. Should one wing remain weak, flight is impossible. Not until the world of women becomes equal to the world of men in the acquisition of virtues and perfections, can success and prosperity be attained as they ought to be.
>
> —Abdu'l-Bahá, *Bahá'í World Faith*

Of all the National Pan-Hellenic Council (NPHC) organizations,[1] only two can claim an authentic brother-sister association: Phi Beta Sigma Fraternity Inc. and Zeta Phi Beta Sorority Inc. Seven years after the founding of Phi Beta Sigma, its sister sorority was organized and set into motion. Almost a century later, with Sigma now boasting more than 125,000 members in 650 chapters all over the United States, Switzerland, and Africa, and Zeta boasting more than 125,000 members in 800 chapters in the United States, Africa, Europe, Asia, and the Caribbean, they work closely together as they attempt to materialize what their founders envisioned: a deep and abiding dedication to enhancing and promoting systematic fellowship, African American self-determination, justice, equal rights, and service to all humankind. Such a relationship endures, in part, because they are the only two constitutionally bound black Greek-letter organizations (BGLOs).[2]

Phi Beta Sigma Fraternity Inc.

On Saturday, October 18, 1913, Howard University student A. L. Taylor approached L. F. Morse, his former roommate, with the idea of forming a new fraternity.[3] After careful discussion, they jointly chose one of their mutual friends, C. I. Brown, to be the third founder. Taylor recorded for posterity the events that led to the fraternity's formation: "The first meeting of the organizing committee was held at my home in the 1900 block of 'S' Street, Northwest, Sunday November, 2nd. The second meeting was held the next Tuesday at Morse's rooming place in the 1900 block of 3rd Street, Northwest."[4] A few days later, on November 13, the three soon-to-be founders of Phi Beta Sigma met and held further discussions with nine undergraduate colleagues from Howard University: S. P. Massie, J. A. Franklin, J. E. Jones, B. A. Matthews, W. F. Vincent, T. L. Alston, W. E. Tibbs, J. H. Howard, and I. L. Scruggs.[5] Taylor continued: "During the remainder of November and December, meetings were held on the 'Hill' (Howard University) during which time nine students were accepted for membership and plans for the fraternity were discussed and developed."[6]

On Friday evening, January 9, 1914, the three founders and nine initial members met in the Bowen Room of the YMCA's Twelfth Street Branch and officially organized the fraternity around the three principles of brotherhood, scholarship, and service. Taylor recounted the events of that meeting: "As chairman of the organizing committee, I reported how I had conceived the idea of the founding of the Fraternity and the three years of unrelenting toil I had given to the development of the plans. I closed the report by recommending that we form a permanent organization to be known as Phi Beta Sigma Fraternity. Upon a motion made by Charles I. Brown, seconded by William F. Vincent, the recommendation was accepted and Phi Beta Sigma became a national fraternity in fact as well as in our dreams."[7] The Board of Deans at Howard University recognized the new fraternity on April 15, 1914, and the *Howard University Journal* (the university's student publication) stated in its April 24 issue: "The Fraternity is the result of the efforts of Messrs. A. L. Taylor, L. F. Morse and C. I. Brown; and promises to be a vital force in the moral, social and intellectual life of the University."[8]

Just weeks later, on May 4, 1914, fourteen more members were added, and together, the twenty-six members of Phi Beta Sigma organized the fraternity's Alpha Chapter. During the summer of 1914, Scruggs procured a furnished, three-story brick house for the fraternity, located at 1907 Third Street, NW. The campus community was amazed by the rapidity of this acquisition, as well as by its size: it was the largest house among all the existing fraternal organizations at Howard at the time.[9]

Sigma was soon expanding its reach across campus. A. M. Walker, the first initiate of the fourteen-person pledge class, was elected associate editor of the

Howard University Journal, and Taylor was made its circulation editor. Other brothers soon held notable positions: Vincent was president of the debating society, W. H. Foster was president of the college YMCA, J. Berry was president of the Political Science Club, J. Camper became captain of the Howard football team, and E. Lawson was president of the Athletic Association. The presence of such noted undergraduate members was one factor that facilitated the fraternity's approval by the Howard Board of Deans, even though both Alpha Phi Alpha Fraternity and Omega Psi Phi Fraternity already existed on the Howard campus.[10] Seeking to further the fraternity's intellectual pool, several affluent African American scholars were inducted as honorary members: Dr. Edward Porter Davis, former dean of liberal Arts at Howard University; Thomas M. Gregory, noted orator, playwright, and theater director; Dr. Alain Leroy Locke, the first black Rhodes scholar; and Dr. Thomas W. Turner, nationally known botanist. These four men were the first graduate members of Phi Beta Sigma.[11]

The fraternity also aimed its expansion toward the racially divided South. On March 5, 1915, Professor Herbert L. Stevens, on the faculty at Wiley College in Marshall, Texas, was admitted as a graduate member by a special decree of the fraternity's general board. Later that year, on November 13, Stevens helped found the Beta Chapter at Wiley College.[12]

It was at this time that the fraternity had another unique opportunity to expand. In a letter dated December 11, 1915, Kappa Alpha Psi Fraternity founder and Grand Polemarch Elder W. Diggs offered to merge Kappa Alpha Psi with Phi Beta Sigma. At the time, Kappa was establishing itself in the Midwest, while Sigma was expanding in the East and South. The fraternity's general board considered the proposal, but in a reply dated December 18, 1915, Taylor turned down the offer.[13]

The fraternity kept progressing. One year later, Sigma held its first conclave (national convention) in Washington, D.C., on December 27–30, 1916. However, by 1917, the fraternity's chapters were beginning to be depleted due to the U.S. government's "call to arms" to serve in World War I. Only the Alpha Chapter still showed signs of activity, and "only one new chapter had been added. . . . That same year, 1917, was sadly memorable for the death of one of the most ardent and useful of the original twelve chartermen—W. F. Vincent. Brother A. Langston Taylor recalled the last words he heard from Brother Vincent . . . : 'Taylor, carry on for Sigma, until we meet again.'"[14] Taylor called on the national board to fill the vacancies created by members' military service.

By June 1919, the general board had reorganized itself, the Washington fraternity house had moved to a new location at 325 T Street, NW, and all but one of its chapters had been reactivated. It was largely through the efforts of Taylor and a few others that the fraternity continued to operate while numerous Sigma men served on the European battlefront.[15] Also due to their efforts, the fraternity was incorporated in Washington, D.C., on April 29, 1920, and the first issue of the *Phi Beta Sigma Journal* was printed in November 1921.[16] The next conclave was held in Atlanta, on December 27–31, 1921, at Morris Brown College, home of the Zeta Chapter of the fraternity. This meeting was also the first-ever interfraternity conclave (with Omega Psi Phi). As a result, an interfraternity conference was planned, and it took place on April 24–26, 1922, in Washington, D.C.[17]

Such momentous "firsts" characterized the fraternity's early years. Due to the continued support of the founders, Phi Beta Sigma was able to create a distinct fraternal praxis that would set the tone for the organization for many years to come. Today, Phi Beta Sigma has blossomed into an international organization and has established the Phi Beta Sigma Educational Foundation, the Phi Beta Sigma Housing Foundation, the Phi Beta Sigma Federal Credit Union, and the Phi Beta Sigma Charitable Outreach Foundation.[18]

The Founders of Phi Beta Sigma

Phi Beta Sigma viewed itself as "a part of" the general community rather than "apart from" society. In this sense, the fraternity was formed to exist as part of a greater brotherhood that would be devoted to the "inclusive we" rather than the "exclusive we." The founders believed that each potential member should be judged by his own merits rather than his family background or affluence and without regard to race, nationality, socioeconomic background, skin tone, or hair texture. In *Our Cause Speeds On,* Savage and Reddick recount the uncharacteristic intraracial diversity of the early members of Sigma:

> I. L. Scruggs. Short and dumpy with an enthusiasm that burned so brightly that today . . . he is still unsurpassed in ardor and zeal. W. E. Tibbs . . . Brown skin, slight of build . . . he talked fast, moved fast and thought with lightning speed. . . . Jacob E. Jones can best be described as a handsome black boy. Six feet tall, well-proportioned, "Jake" Jones was a tailor's model. . . . J. R. Howard. A smooth, round-faced boy, he always appeared for classes trim and neat as a pin. . . . S. P. Massie . . . the tallest of all the charter members. He was dark-skinned with large

feet. He spoke in a soft, quiet tone and always wore an infectious smile.
. . . [W. F.] Vincent was unassuming yet brilliant . . . tall, fair-skinned
with bushy, straight brown hair. . . . T. L. Alston was light brown and
a little freckled with reddish hair.[19]

Founder Morse summed up the entire group: "Each one was different in temperament, in ability, in appearance; but that was why they were chosen by the three Founders. We felt that a fraternity composed of men who were all alike in habits, interests and abilities would be a pretty dull organization."[20]

From its inception, the founders also conceived Sigma as a vehicle to deliver services to the general community rather than as a mechanism for nepotism or self-congratulatory betterment. In this sense, the founders were attempting to build a radically democratic organization predicated on respect for individual rights and privileging a noncoercive, consensus-building discourse in which participants could overcome egotistical or class-based agendas in favor of spiritually and rationally evenhanded agreement. For the founders, a significant tenet for African American self-determinism and autonomy was the implementation of critical self-reflection and discourse that would facilitate emancipation from myopic dogma and blind tradition.

Therefore, instead of following in the steps of what was becoming a "talented tenth"[21] cadre of separatist elites among many black organizations at the time, the founders believed that both the fraternity and society would best be served by pursuing more democratically inclusive methods of association. Rather than using the fraternity as a vehicle for the attainment of knowledge and skills to be utilized exclusively for themselves, the founders held a deep conviction that they should return their knowledge and ideas to the communities from which they came. Such an attitude was also tempered by the founders' idea that communities considered "at risk" or "impoverished" had valuable worldviews and understandings that had not been validated and thus were unjustly stigmatized. By taking a more inclusive approach to community uplift, the founders not only taught but also remained open to being taught by those communities. Hence, the founders shunned a paternalistic relationship with the "underclass" and recognized that many different values, norms, and logics composed various cultural standpoints and could be employed in various ways for the betterment of all people of African descent. This conviction was reflected in the fraternity's motto: "Culture for Service and Service for Humanity."

Although Phi Beta Sigma is emblematic for service today, the founders did not want the iconography of Greek letters to supersede the actions of the members who wear those letters. Further, the principles of brotherhood, scholarship, and service laid down by the founders were meant to be at the forefront of all fraternal activities. Accordingly, the philosophy of the fraternity is crystallized in the following:

> Service, service not only for the Fraternity, but for the general welfare of the society in which we live. Sigma believes further that symbols have no real meaning or function until they are put into everyday practice according to the meanings assigned them by the Fraternity. Symbols do not make the man, but are meaningful only when the interpretation of these become dynamic factors in determining everyday behavior. There is much that can be written and said about the philosophy of Phi Beta Sigma Fraternity, but nothing said or done will be of any real meaning or consequence unless the practice of that philosophy can be seen in terms of Brotherhood, Service and Scholarship in the daily living of its members.[22]

Yet none of this would have been possible if not for the foresight and commitment of the three founders of Phi Beta Sigma Fraternity Inc.

ABRAM LANGSTON TAYLOR

Abram Langston Taylor (1890–1953) was born in Summerville, Tennessee. As he reached adolescence, he was known for his height and lanky composure. "His eyes were set deep in a brown skin face that showed a square chin and prominent ears."[23] He was mentally keen and emotionally balanced, and his most distinguished characteristic was his slow and methodical style of speech and movement.[24] "He walked slowly, talked slowly, in a low monotone. But underneath his deliberate speech, thought and movement was an inner urge that drove him on to the completion of any task to which he once set his mind."[25] Taylor was rumored to be undefeatable in debate and argumentation, and as a consequence, he commanded the respect of his peers. They likewise admired his unwavering loyalty and devotion to his moral principles and his careful nurturing of friendships.[26] The fall 1964 issue of the *Crescent* (the fraternity organ) states of Taylor: "Although he joked and could trade punches in fun with the rest of us, there was a sense of seriousness and sincerity about him which was captivating."[27]

In 1909 Taylor graduated from the Howe Institute (now LeMoyne-Owen

College) in Memphis, Tennessee. It was in Memphis during the summer of 1910 that Taylor met a young alumnus of Howard University who recounted his appraisal of Greek-letter fraternities on campus. At that time, Taylor had already been accepted as a student at Howard and was scheduled to matriculate in the fall of 1910.[28] Taylor's talk with the young man germinated the idea for Phi Beta Sigma Fraternity. He wrote:

> If we are to be precise about it, the idea of the Fraternity had its origin not at Howard University, as might be expected, but in my hometown of Memphis, Tennessee. . . . One dull summer day in 1910, I was on my way home from downtown and paused for a while at Bumper Beale Street Grocery Store to pick up the latest news from the Squash Center, which usually held afternoon sessions there. I engaged in a conversation with a young man recently graduated from Howard University, and since I had decided to go to Howard, I was very much interested in what he had to say about the University. He dwelt at length on the activities of Greek Letter fraternities. His talk gave me an idea, and from that day on, Phi Beta Sigma was in the making.[29]

Taylor entered Howard University on November 23, 1910, and almost immediately began to lay the plans for a new fraternity.

As a member of the fraternity, Taylor gave twelve consecutive years of service as the first national president, national secretary-treasurer, and eighth member of the Distinguished Service Chapter (and later its president). Revered as a tireless worker, he constantly labored to ensure the retention of Sigma's early history by serving on the fraternity's history committee. In that capacity, he provided numerous notes, minutes, and oral histories. Most auspiciously, Taylor coined the fraternity motto: "Culture for Service, Service for Humanity."[30] For most of his adult life, Taylor lived at 1517 Vermont Avenue, NW, in Washington, D.C., and held many fraternity meetings there. Because of his studious ways and literary penchant, members of the Alpha Chapter habitually called Taylor "Prof." He carried reading material with him wherever he went, and in his free time he was constantly reading and writing.[31]

After graduation from Howard, Taylor took classes at Frelinghuysen University in Washington and chose real estate and insurance as his career. From 1917 to 1926, Taylor worked in those fields. He created the Allied Loan Association in 1920 and the Federal Life Insurance Company in 1922, directing the latter for three years. For six years he was secretary-treasurer of the Potomac

Investment Company. He also served for four years as president of the Taylor Tobacco Company. In 1922 he was instrumental in bringing together the Howard University BGLOs to discuss the possibility of forming a Pan-Hellenic Council. Although that meeting failed to yield an actual council, Taylor provided much of the ideological foundation for such an organization. This was characteristic of Taylor, for as Sigma brother Scruggs wrote of him: "When Taylor left the center of the stage, the main theme of the plot had been introduced. It would, of course, be developed, embellished, and varied in the years to come."[32] Six years later, another meeting took place at Howard at which various BGLOs decided to move forward with the idea of a council. The National Pan-Hellenic Council was founded on May 10, 1930, and still exists today.[33]

From 1928 to 1943, Taylor created many philanthropic, social, and service organizations, including the Derby Club (1928); the Banneker Research Society (1931), named in honor of Benjamin Banneker, a free African American mathematician, astronomer, clockmaker, and publisher; the Worthwhile Club (1933); Epsilon Phi Sigma Fraternity (1939); and the African Aid Society (1943). He was also a member of the Sharecroppers' Aid Committee, the Washington Labor Committee, the Inter-professional Association, the Federation of Civic Associations, and the American Industrial League. In 1945 Taylor began to expand his philanthropic interests to include aesthetic and artistic endeavors. He created the Taylor Art Museum in 1945 and the Guild of Associated Artists in 1949. In 1950 he founded the Progressive Therapy Association and the following year formed the Greek Letter Council. He also held offices in the Washington Art Society, Mu-So-Lit Club, Rhomboid Club, and Tennessee State Club of the District of Columbia.[34]

Taylor was involved in various other fraternal organizations. He was a member of the Independent Benevolent Protective Order of Elks of the World and a thirty-third-degree Mason. Taylor authored *The History of Negro Education in the State of Tennessee* and at one time was the Washington correspondent for the *Chicago Defender* (an African American–oriented newspaper). Later in life, Taylor worked as a federal employee with the Smithsonian Institution, from which he retired. Hailed as "the greatest name in Sigma," Taylor passed away on August 8, 1953. He is buried at Lincoln Memorial Cemetery in Suitland, Maryland.[35]

LEONARD FRANCIS MORSE

Leonard Francis Morse (1891–1961) was born in New Bedford, Massachusetts, to Mr. and Mrs. Frederick Morse, a distinguished New England family.

Morse is said to have been "handsome, shy, thin and dark."[36] He was valedictorian of his high school and later entered Howard University, where he shared a room with Taylor. Morse was later married and had five children, two of whom became brothers of the fraternity. Most recently, one of his grandchildren also joined the fraternity.

The longest surviving founder, Morse wrote the fraternity's first constitution and was its first national secretary, the sixteenth member of the Distinguished Service Chapter, the first president of Alpha Chapter, and a recipient of the rare Distinguished Service Key. Morse was also a well-versed student of the Greek language and assigned the fraternity its Greek letters. He worked as the fraternity's state director for Florida and personally organized nine chapters in that state.[37]

Morse was the first person to graduate from Howard in three years with both bachelor of arts and bachelor of education degrees.[38] While a student, he was the YMCA's director of social service from 1913 to 1914, president of the Young Men's Progressive Club from 1914 to 1915, and tutor of languages and history.[39] Extremely well educated, Morse went on to obtain bachelor of divinity degrees from both Wilberforce University and the Payne School of Divinity, a master's degree from Northwestern, and doctorates in philosophy and psychology from the College of Metaphysics in Indianapolis, Indiana. He received an honorary doctor of divinity degree from Allen University in Columbia, South Carolina, and an honorary doctor of laws degree from Edward Waters College in Jacksonville, Florida.[40]

Morse led a busy life, serving in many educational and religious institutions. He was principal of the Mobile County Training School and Emerson Institute, both in Alabama; principal of the Fesseden Academy in western Florida; and dean of theology at Edward Waters College in Jacksonville, where he later became president (1933–1934) and used personal funds to save the school from the hardships of the Depression. Morse also served as pastor of many metropolitan churches, including African Methodist Episcopal (AME) churches in Mobile, Jacksonville, Clearwater, St. Petersburg, St. Augustine, and Tampa. He also served as presiding elder of both the Madison and Lake City, Florida, districts of the AME Church.[41] At the time of his death on May 22, 1961, Morse was head of the Department of Religious Education and Humanities at Edward Waters College.[42]

CHARLES IGNATIUS BROWN

Charles Ignatius Brown is the most enigmatic of the three founders. He was born in Topeka, Kansas, in 1890 to the Reverend John M. Brown and Maggie

M. Brown. However, university records from 1910 show that Brown lived at 1813 Titan Street in Philadelphia, Pennsylvania, for quite some time before his enrollment at Howard. Brown was "of average size, [with] brown skin and princely in his manners. In dress, in movement, in speech Brother Brown was the 'perfect gentleman.'"[43] According to another source, "he had that gracious courtesy that is commonly associated with the Eighteenth Century ideal type; never hurried, never flustered, reticent and affable."[44] Brown graduated from Howard Academy in 1910; was class chaplain in 1913; was a member and president of the Chaplain Classical Club in 1912 and 1913, respectively; was president of the Classical Club in 1914; and wished to pursue postgraduate work in Latin. In addition, he was selected "The Most to Be Admired" for the class of 1914.[45] Accordingly, Brown was very popular with both the student body and the university administration. In the "Personals and Applied Quotations" section of the 1914 Howard University yearbook, Brown is quoted: "No legacy is so rich as honesty."[46]

Just seven weeks after Phi Beta Sigma was recognized by the university's Board of Deans, Brown graduated on June 3, 1914. He was the first national vice president and later became a member of the Distinguished Service Chapter. He is also credited with choosing the first nine members of the fraternity and writing its first rituals. Brown personally founded the Delta Chapter of Phi Beta Sigma at Kansas State University in Manhattan, Kansas, on April 9, 1917, shortly after moving there to work as an educator.[47] Delta Chapter ceased activity in the 1930s, after the Great Depression forced many members out of school (it was later reactivated). It was the first chapter of an African American fraternity at a mixed-race university west of the Mississippi River.

After the end of enslavement in the United States, Kansas State dedicated itself to the education of newly freed African Americans. Brown added to this commitment when he chartered Delta Chapter, whose presence on campus made Kansas State a welcoming place for many black men. The fraternity house (still standing at 1020 Colorado Street in Manhattan) became the primary residence for most of the black men who attended the university, and many of them became Sigma brothers.

Because of the strong relationship between the president of Kansas State and Sigma brother Dr. George Washington Carver, many of the Delta Chapter brothers majored in veterinary science and went on to establish the world-famous veterinary science program at Tuskegee University. For instance, Sigma brothers Dr. Thomas G. Perry headed the Department of Small Animal Medicine and Surgery, and Dr. George Thomas Bronson served as his assistant. These men and many others came to Tuskegee from Kansas State, and all of them, whether Sigmas or not, were influenced by the chapter created by Brown.

Sadly, the last correspondence received from Brown was a letter to Taylor in 1921 in which he indicated that he was enjoying his career as an educator in Kansas. It was discovered that Brown was working at the Kansas Industrial and Educational Institute, which was later renamed the Topeka Industrial and Educational Institute and finally the Kansas Vocational School.[48] Shortly afterward, Brown mysteriously disappeared from both the fraternity and his family, although census records and oral interviews show that he was alive in the Topeka area until 1931.[49] Many theories and myths surrounded his disappearance, including the conjecture that he had either moved overseas or become a victim of the reemerging violence of the Ku Klux Klan, which had a stronghold in Kansas in the 1920s and 1930s. Some oral histories reported that Brown had been murdered, although such claims were never validated. Accordingly, the fraternity was left with the words of Morse, who wrote in the spring of 1949, "We live in daily hope that we shall one day learn the fate of our beloved Brother and Founder."[50] An August 2006 "pilgrimage" by members of the fraternity to Kansas State resulted in the recovery of some information about Brown and the establishment of Delta Chapter, but it did not unearth the reason for his disappearance. However, groundbreaking discoveries in the summer of 2007 by Phi Beta Sigma historians included Brown's application for Social Security benefits, signed and dated by Brown on November 30, 1938. At the time, he was living in Pittsburgh, Pennsylvania. This research also unearthed a death certificate indicating that Brown passed away on December 21, 1981, of congestive heart failure at Thomas Jefferson Hospital in Philadelphia.[51] Future scholarship promises to elucidate, even more clearly, the last years of Brown's life.

Following World War I, the fraternity grew significantly and implemented its first official national program: Bigger and Better Business. Scruggs wrote:

> Philadelphia, 1924, Phi Beta Sigma Fraternity "arrived." We had a mob of people at this Conclave. There were representatives from twenty-eight chapters and all the trimmings. The introduction of the Bigger and Better Negro Business idea was made by way of an exhibit devoted to this topic. The Bigger and Better Negro Business idea was first tested in 1924 with an imposing exhibition in Philadelphia. This was held in connection with the Conclave. Twenty-five leading Negro Businesses sent statements and over fifty sent exhibits. . . . The response was so

great that the 1925 Conclave in Richmond, Virginia voted unanimously to make Bigger and Better Negro Business the public program of the Fraternity, and it has been so ever since. Phi Beta Sigma believes that the improvement and economic conditions of minorities is a major factor in the improvement of the general welfare of society.[52]

Through these programs and other facets of the fraternity structure, the founders' agenda and ideology spread to other influential members. Notable Sigma brothers James Weldon Johnson wrote "The Negro National Anthem," known as "Lift Ev'ry Voice and Sing"; A. Philip Randolph organized the Brotherhood of Sleeping Car Porters; and Howard University philosophy professor Alain Leroy Locke wrote "The New Negro," in which he described the emergence of a new zeitgeist in the 1920s—an innovative spirit that did not rely on older models but, rather, embraced a "new psychology" and "new spirit" toward social transformation. Johnson, Randolph, and Locke were also key thinkers in the Harlem Renaissance movement.

At the same time, other dramatic social changes were taking place. There was a rebirth of white nationalism that led to the passage of stringent anti-immigration laws, especially the Immigration Act of 1924. In 1920 the Volstead Act became effective, heralding the start of Prohibition, and on August 18 of that year, Tennessee became the crucial thirty-sixth state to ratify the Nineteenth Amendment, finally giving women the right to vote. With such changes taking place in society, many felt that it was an appropriate time to expand the options for black sororities. At the 1919 conclave, the brotherhood appointed founder A. L. Taylor and a new brother, Charles Robert Samuel Taylor, to search for a worthy sister organization. The memoirs of Charles Taylor provide a glimpse into what was to become Zeta Phi Beta Sorority:

As though moved by some pulling power, I recall how I thought of a sincere and enthusiastic young woman, who for me was the embodiment of our brotherhood in the sisterhood of which I dreamed. She had character and gifts. She had a beautiful spirit and intellectual effectiveness. She had appeal in her personality and in her words. I knew that if I won her, she would not give up until she had perfected a nucleus of a sisterhood for Phi Beta Sigma. Arizona Leedonia Cleaver was the chief builder and she asked fourteen others to join her. I shall never forget the first meetings held in the dormitory rooms of Miner Hall.[53]

Thus, in 1920, Phi Beta Sigma helped establish its sister sorority, Zeta Phi Beta Sorority Inc.

Zeta Phi Beta Sorority Inc.

Despite some advances, the Roaring Twenties were characterized by an entrenched system of de jure and de facto sexism and racism. Fifteen young women heeded the call for a new sorority to aid in African American women's social transformation. From the very beginning, these women tried to set a new course and set a higher standard. Unfortunately, the campus community was not very kind to these idealistic young women, and some branded them the "praying band" because of their religious character.[54] One by one, the group of fifteen dwindled until only five women remained to become the "Pearls" of Zeta Phi Beta: Arizona Cleaver, Myrtle and Viola Tyler, Fannie Pettie, and Pearl Neal. With the help of Phi Beta Sigma founder Abram L. Taylor (and the assistance of Sigma brother Charles Taylor), Zeta Phi Beta Sorority Inc. was established on January 16, 1920, at Howard University. Zeta Phi Beta's first formal introduction to the Washington, D.C., community was held at the Whitelaw Hotel, followed by a formal welcome to the campus by the sisters of the Alpha Chapter of Alpha Kappa Alpha and the Alpha Chapter of Delta Sigma Theta on the Howard campus.[55]

After gaining permission from the Howard University administration, the five founders of Zeta Phi Beta held their first boulé (convention) with their Sigma brothers in 1920 (an event repeated in 1936, 1957, and 1991) and immediately began to establish chapters all over the United States. In those early years of the sorority's existence, members understood the necessity of ensuring its permanence. Accordingly, Myrtle Tyler (Faithful) and four other Zeta sisters—Gladys Warrington, Joanna Houston, Josephine Johnson, and O. Goldia Smith—incorporated the sorority on March 30, 1923, in Washington, D.C. The sorority was also incorporated in the state of Illinois in 1939.[56] Based on the simple belief that sorority elitism and socializing should not overshadow the real mission of progressive organizations—to address societal ills, prejudices, poverty, and health concerns—the founders departed from the predominant models for elite black female coalitions and sought to establish a new organization predicated on scholarship, service, sisterly love, and finer womanhood.

Shortly after Zeta Phi Beta's inception, the founders established the *Archon* as the sorority magazine and began outreach programs with the NAACP and the

National Negro Congress. As noted earlier, Zeta Phi Beta Sorority Inc. and Phi Beta Sigma Fraternity Inc. share a unique bond among Greek organizations—a constitutionally bound relationship with each other. Both organizations' founding was based, in part, on the belief that the true mission of BGLOs is to address and correct the problems of society, particularly in the African American community. Years later, both Sigma and Zeta work together toward this goal of social justice and are highly visible in both their community outreach programs and their support of each other.

Today, Zeta continues its legacy of service to various communities. Since 1971, Zeta has partnered with the March of Dimes in an effort to encourage women to seek prenatal care in the first trimester of pregnancy, thereby increasing the prevention of birth defects and reducing infant mortality. Since the 1990s, the Z-HOPE (Zetas Helping Other People Excel) Program and the Zeta Organizational Leadership Program have assisted thousands of young women. Additionally, the Zeta National Educational Foundation operates exclusively for charitable and educational purposes and promotes activities that encourage the pursuit of higher education.

The Founders of Zeta Phi Beta

With the rampant changes in society and the challenges to traditional racial and gender roles that defined the beginning of the 1920s, many women initially expressed an interest in becoming members of Zeta Phi Beta. However, owing to the high academic standards, the inability to afford initiation fees (nominal, by today's standards), concern over a white or male backlash to black female empowerment, and uncertainty about a sorority that seemingly eschewed elitism and separatism, only a few followed through on their intentions to join. Of the twenty-five women who were eager to join the Zeta movement, only four aspirants—Gladys Warrington, Harriet Dorsey, Pauline Philips, and Nellie Singfield—obtained membership. This small cadre, influenced by the distinctive ideology of the sorority, labored to accelerate Zeta's growth. Whereas other organizations focused on establishing chapters at predominantly white educational institutions, Zeta (like Sigma) directed its attention to historically black colleges and universities, hoping to make inroads into the communities that would most benefit from their services. Therefore, instead of establishing chapters in the urban areas of Chicago, New York, and Detroit, they focused on racially divided cities in the South, including those in Alabama, Missouri, and North Carolina.

Zeta's first two chapters, after the one at Howard, were established at historically black universities (Morris Brown College and Morgan State College), followed by a citywide chapter in San Antonio, Texas. In 1923 (just three years after Zeta's founding), its Theta Chapter was established in Marshall, Texas, at Wiley College (the location of Phi Beta Sigma's Beta Chapter), making it the first black sorority to organize a collegiate chapter in Texas. Even after chartering chapters in more racially integrated cities, Zeta continued to make a concerted effort to develop chapters at the nation's historically black colleges and universities and in other areas of the South.[57] Because of the vision and continued work of the founders of Zeta Phi Beta Sorority Inc., such grand endeavors reached fruition.

ARIZONA LEEDONIA CLEAVER STEMONS

Arizona Leedonia Cleaver (1898–1980) was born in Pike County, Missouri. She was educated in the public schools of Hannibal, Missouri, and conducted her graduate and postgraduate work at Howard University and the Pennsylvania School of Social Work. She then taught in the Hannibal high school from which she had graduated. On June 1, 1928, Cleaver married James S. Stemons, an activist, author, and son of former slaves. In 1930 she was in charge of a Sunday school teachers' training class at St. Simon the Cyrenian Church in Philadelphia. In 1933 she accepted a position with the Philadelphia Department of Public Assistance. Stemons's other professional positions included director of a residence hall at Morgan State College in Baltimore, caseworker for the Philadelphia Society for the Prevention of Cruelty to Children, and juvenile court probation officer in Philadelphia. In 1935 Stemons entered the field of social work, serving in the Department of Public Assistance of Philadelphia as an investigator, a "message adjustor," and an interviewer.

Stemons was the first Basileus of the Alpha Chapter and the first Grand Basileus of Zeta Phi Beta Sorority Inc. She was a life member and affiliated with Beta Delta Zeta Chapter in Philadelphia. Stemons was responsible for chartering numerous undergraduate and graduate chapters throughout the United States. She passed away in March 1980 and was buried at Eden Cemetery in Philadelphia.[58]

PEARL ANNA NEAL

Pearl Anna Neal (?–1978) was born in Charlotte, North Carolina. Early on, she exhibited excellence in music and attended the Lincoln Academy in Kings

Mountain, North Carolina. Upon completion of her studies there, she entered Howard University and later graduated from its Conservatory of Music. She continued her graduate studies at the Julliard School of Music and the Chicago Music Institute and became the first black woman in New York to earn a master's degree in music from Columbia University.[59] Neal began her career in the field of education in Americus, Georgia, and then taught briefly in Crockett, Texas. An accomplished musician, Neal taught music in the North Carolina public schools and served as the director of seniors majoring in music at Teachers College in Winston-Salem, North Carolina. She ended her career in the Winston-Salem schools in 1966. She was extremely active in church and community activities and was awarded a life membership at the 1945 boulé for her founding role in Zeta Phi Beta Sorority Inc. She died on January 31, 1978, and was buried at York Memorial Cemetery in Charlotte, North Carolina.[60]

VIOLA TYLER GOINGS

Viola Tyler (1899–1983) was born on her family's farm near Flushing, Ohio. Her father was born a slave but, through extraordinary circumstances, was able to purchase the farm where he, his wife, and their nine children lived. Tyler was educated in the Ohio public schools and graduated from Howard University with a major in mathematics. After graduation, she taught in Smithville, North Carolina, and later accepted the position of assistant principal at Cambridge High School in Cambridge, Maryland. She married Fred Goings and had two sons and two daughters. She later moved with her family to Springfield, Ohio, and pursued her career as a teacher. She passed away in March 1983 in Springfield.[61]

MYRTLE TYLER FAITHFUL

Myrtle Tyler (1901–1994) was the younger sister of Viola Tyler and, like her sister, was born on the family farm near Flushing, Ohio. She was educated in the Ohio public schools, after which she matriculated at Howard University. At Howard, she was the secretary of her class, vice president of the Western Reserve Club, and assistant editor of the yearbook. After graduation, she taught high school mathematics in Annapolis, Maryland, for five years. She then moved to Springfield, Ohio, to take care of her parents. While in Ohio, Tyler taught mathematics and English and took an active interest in community affairs. She gave up teaching when she married Ross Faithful and raised two daughters, both of whom became members of Zeta Phi Beta.[62] Faithful was the second Grand Basileus of Zeta Phi Beta and became a life member in 1945. She later moved to Towson, Maryland, and passed away in April 1994. She was buried in Baltimore, Maryland.

FANNIE PETTIE WATTS

Fannie Pettie (?–1995) was born in Perry, Georgia, to attorney Foster B. Pettie and Fannie Rollins Pettie. She was educated in the public schools of Savannah, Georgia, and attended Georgia State College. Later she graduated from Howard University with a bachelor's degree in education. She pursued postgraduate studies in social work and in housing at New York University. She taught junior and senior high school in Savannah and also worked as a social worker in Brooklyn, New York. She was a life member and is credited with organizing the Delta Alpha Zeta and Omicron Beta Chapters in Brooklyn. She passed away on August 22, 1995, and was buried in Brooklyn.[63]

Given the rampant economic neoliberalism ushered in by the dismantling of the Keynesian welfare state; the rise of patriotism that obfuscates xenophobic, white supremacist discourses; the increased attention and loyalty paid to narratives that support black and brown "pathologies" as rationales for growing social inequalities; an anti-immigration discourse aggravated by white nationalism; and mounting hostility to the feminist and womanist movements and their subsequent victories, the need for BGLOs that will challenge such paradigms and propose and institute solutions is readily apparent. Taking into account that U.S. campuses are often "culture war" battlegrounds over race-, gender-, and class-related topics such as testing gaps, affirmative action, and even neo-minstrel "blackface" incidents, it is incumbent on organizations such as Phi Beta Sigma Fraternity Inc. and Zeta Phi Beta Sorority Inc. to remember their distinctive roots of opposing not just racial oppression but also class elitism, patriarchy, and various forms of xenophobia.

Notes

Gratitude for research assistance is extended to Donald Jemison, international executive director of Phi Beta Sigma Fraternity Inc.; Gerald D. Smith, executive director of Phi Beta Sigma Fraternity Inc. (1978–1990); the staff of the national headquarters of

Phi Beta Sigma Fraternity Inc.; and the staff of the Moorland-Spingarn Research Center at Howard University. I would be remiss if I did not acknowledge the rather unbalanced treatment of the two organizations in this chapter. Several attempts were made to obtain additional information from the national headquarters of Zeta Phi Beta in 2006–2007; however, none of these requests for information was acknowledged.

Epigraph from Abdu'l-Bahá. *Bahá'í World Faith* (1956; reprint, Wilmette, Ill.: Bahá'í Publishing Trust, 1976), 288.

1. The members of the NPHC (also known as the "Divine Nine") are Alpha Phi Alpha Fraternity (1906), Alpha Kappa Alpha Sorority (1908), Kappa Alpha Psi Fraternity (1911), Omega Psi Phi Fraternity (1911), Delta Sigma Theta Sorority (1913), Phi Beta Sigma Fraternity (1914), Zeta Phi Beta Sorority (1920), Sigma Gamma Rho Sorority (1922), and Iota Phi Theta Fraternity (1963).

2. Phi Beta Sigma Fraternity Inc., *The Sigma Light,* 4th ed. (1981), 17–18.

3. This date is incorrectly listed as October 8, 1913, in *Sigma Light,* 25. The actual date is October 18, 1913, as evidenced by A. L. Taylor's words: "It was in the afternoon of the next to the last Saturday of October 1913 . . . Saturday, October 18, 1913, therefore, is important in that at this time the idea of the new fraternity was proposed and agreed to by two persons." Quoted in Sherman W. Savage and L. D. Reddick, eds., *Our Cause Speeds On* (Atlanta: Fuller Press, 1957), 14.

4. Savage and Reddick, *Our Cause Speeds On,* 14.

5. Brother T. L. Alston's name is sometimes misspelled as "Austin." For instance, in *Sigma Light,* 10, his name is spelled "Austin," but in the *Crescent* 33, no. 1 (special ed., spring 1949): 9–10, his name is spelled "Alston" by both founders Taylor and Morse.

6. Savage and Reddick, *Our Cause Speeds On,* 14.

7. Ibid., 15.

8. Ibid.; Lawrence C. Ross Jr., *The Divine Nine: The History of African American Fraternities and Sororities* (New York: Dafina Books, 2000), 103.

9. Savage and Reddick, *Our Cause Speeds On,* 19. It is interesting to note that when I. L. Scruggs graduated from medical school in 1919, he married Ruth Trappe, a member of the Alpha Chapter of Zeta Phi Beta Sorority. Seven years later, in 1926, Ruth Trappe Scruggs was elected Grande Basileus of Zeta Phi Beta Sorority and served with distinction until 1930.

10. Ibid., 19, 21.

11. Ibid., 21.

12. Ibid., 7–8.

13. Ibid., 21.

14. Ibid., 32.

15. *Sigma Light,* 8.

16. Ibid., 13.

17. Ibid., 9.

18. Phi Beta Sigma Fraternity Inc. official Web site, "Who We Are," http://www.pbs1914.0rg/history/overview.asp (accessed May 6, 2007).

19. Savage and Reddick, *Our Cause Speeds On,* 15–16.

20. Ibid., 18.

21. The phrase "talented tenth" was written by W. E. B. DuBois in September 1903 and published in *The Negro Problem* (New York: James Pott and Company, 1903). DuBois argued that social change could be accomplished by developing the small group of college-educated, elite blacks he called the "talented tenth." He wrote: "three tasks lay before me; first to show from the past that the Talented Tenth as they have risen among American Negroes have been worthy of leadership; secondly to show how these men may be educated and developed; and thirdly to show their relation to the Negro problem." DuBois later recanted his words and advocated against the elitism of his prior argument.

22. Phi Beta Sigma Fraternity Inc., "The Philosophy of Phi Beta Sigma," in *Sigma Light,*17.

23. Savage and Reddick, *Our Cause Speeds On,* 13.

24. I. L. Scruggs, "I Knew A. Langston Taylor in His Early Years," *Crescent* 38, no. 1 (spring 1954): 15.

25. L. F. Morse, "As I Remember Them," *Crescent* 33, no. 1 (special ed., spring 1949): 8.

26. *Mirror,* Howard University Yearbook (1915).

27. I. L. Scruggs, "Our Founding Fathers," *Crescent,* 50th anniversary ed. (fall 1964): 4.

28. A. L. Taylor, "The First Four Years," *Crescent* 33, no. 1 (special ed., spring 1949): 10.

29. Savage and Reddick, *Our Cause Speeds On,* 14; Taylor, "The First Four Years."

30. "Taylor, A. Langston," *Crescent* 33, no. 1 (special ed., spring 1949): 92.

31. Phi Beta Sigma Web site, "Who We Are."

32. Scruggs, "Our Founding Fathers," 5.

33. Walter Kimbrough, *Black Greek 101: The Culture, Customs, and Challenges of Black Fraternities and Sororities* (Madison, N.J.: Fairleigh Dickinson University Press, 2003), 35.

34. Phi Beta Sigma Web site, "Who We Are"; *Sigma Light,* 12.

35. *Crescent* 37, no. 1 (spring 1953); *Crescent* 37, no. 2 (fall 1953); Phi Beta Sigma Web site, "Our Founders," http://www.pbs1914.0rg/history/founders.asp (accessed October 19, 2005).

36. Savage and Reddick, *Our Cause Speeds On,* 14.

37. Ibid., 236.

38. Ibid.

39. *Mirror,* Howard University Yearbook (1915).

40. *Crescent* 37, no. 1 (spring 1953): 7.

41. "Founder Morse Is Dead," *Crescent* 47, no. 2 (fall 1961): 4; Savage and Reddick, *Our Cause Speeds On,* 236.

42. *Crescent* 37, no. 1 (spring 1953): 7.

43. Ibid.

44. Savage and Reddick, *Our Cause Speeds On,* 14.

45. Morse, "As I Remember Them," 8.

46. Phi Beta Sigma Web site, "Who We Are."

47. Morse, "As I Remember Them," 8.

48. "Legend of Our Legacy: Reclaiming the Lost History of Sigma's Final Founder" (presented at the 2007 Phi Beta Sigma International Conclave, Charlotte, N.C.). The scholarship in this presentation was compiled by Phi Beta Sigma members Todd LeBon, Kevin Christian, Linden Houston, and Mark Pacich, in conjunction with the Phi Beta Sigma Historical Society

49. Phi Beta Sigma Web site, "Our Founders."

50. Morse, "As I Remember Them," 8.

51. "Legend of Our Legacy."

52. Savage and Reddick, *Our Cause Speeds On.* It is important to note that "Education" and "Social Action" were adopted as the additional two national programs in 1934 and 1945, respectively.

53. Taylor memoirs cited by Donald J. Jemison, international executive director, Phi Beta Sigma Fraternity Inc., "Founders' Day Speech," delivered at Tuskegee Institute, Tuskegee, Ala., 2006, originally written by Gerald D. Smith, executive director (1978–1990), Phi Beta Sigma Fraternity Inc.

54. Ibid.

55. Ibid.

56. Zeta Phi Beta Sorority Inc. official Web site, "Incorporators," http://www .zphib1920.0rg/heritage/incorporators.html (accessed May 10, 2007).

57. Zeta Phi Beta Web site, "Heritage," http://www.zphib1920.0rg/heritage/founders .html (accessed May 6, 2007).

58. Zeta Phi Beta Sorority Inc., *Torchbearers of a Legacy: A History of Zeta Phi Beta Sorority, Inc., 1920–1997* (Washington, D.C., 1998), 7–8.

59. Ibid., 8–9.

60. Zeta Phi Beta Web site, "Heritage."

61. Zeta Phi Beta, *Torchbearers,* 9.

62. Ibid., 10.

63. Ibid., 10–11.

6

The Pride of All Our Hearts
The Founders of Kappa Alpha Psi Fraternity

Michael E. Jennings

Kappa Alpha Psi Fraternity Inc. was founded on the campus of Indiana University on January 5, 1911. In describing the early years of the fraternity, its official history book asserts, "*The Story of Kappa Alpha Psi* is to a large extent the story of black students everywhere, whether organized or not, who attended predominantly white colleges or universities in America prior to World War II."[1] With this in mind, the history of Kappa Alpha Psi Fraternity Inc. can best be understood if examined within the sociohistorical context of the time and place of the fraternity's inception.

African Americans in Indiana: Life in the Heartland

From its recognition as a state in the early nineteenth century through the early years of the twentieth century, the state of Indiana fostered an atmosphere of hostility and violence toward its African American citizenry.[2] In his 1978 book about the history of Indiana, Howard H. Peckham (a noted historian of colonial and revolutionary America) observes that "Hoosiers were not racially tolerant: they didn't like Indians and they didn't like Negroes. They had largely ousted Indians from the area, and had, by stipulations in the new constitution, forbidden Negroes to enter the state."[3] Journalist John Bartlow Martin wrote of the "old tradition of intolerance" that existed in Indiana prior to Word War I and how it was exemplified by roadside signs that read: "Nigger, Don't Let the Sun Set on You Here."[4]

Further evidence of the specific hostility directed against African Americans can be found in the disturbing history of lynching in Indiana. Statistics show that at least twenty African Americans were lynched in that state between 1865 and 1903.[5] Even at a time when lynching was considered a southern phenomenon, Indiana stood out as a locale where violence against African Americans was pervasive.[6] In fact, Indiana's reputation for lynching was so well established during this time that the governor of Georgia used the record in Indiana to justify lynching in his own state.[7]

African American Students at Indiana University: The Early Years

It is within this context of racial intolerance and discrimination that a handful of African American students matriculated at Indiana University early in the twentieth century. The discrimination, alienation, and frequent indignities faced by these students provided the impetus for the organization of an African American fraternity on campus.

The first African American–sponsored Greek-letter organization at Indiana University was the Alpha Kappa Nu Greek society, created in 1903. Little is known about this organization, but it has been speculated that there were too few black students at Indiana University during this time to ensure the continuance of the organization. This speculation was fueled by the realization that the small number of African American students who attended Indiana University did so for only a short period before they withdrew to secure employment.[8] In subsequent years, however, a critical mass of African American male students at Indiana University sought to come together under the banner of fraternalism.

Howard University and the Creation of Kappa Alpha Nu

Seven years after the creation and dissolution of Alpha Kappa Nu, forces were set in motion that would lead to the creation of another African American fraternity on the campus of Indiana University. During the 1909–1910 school year, a young African American student at Indiana University named Irven Armstrong was visited by his cousin Byron Kenneth Armstrong, a student at Howard University in Washington, D.C. Byron Armstrong was so impressed with the Indiana University campus that he decided to transfer there in the fall of 1910. Byron persuaded close friend and fellow Howard University student Elder Watson Diggs to join him at Indiana University that same semester.[9]

Diggs's and Armstrong's experiences with Greek-letter organizations at Howard University have been the subject of some dispute in discussions of the early history of those organizations.[10] According to Crump, both Diggs and Armstrong "were approached by a fraternity, and both had declined pledgeship because they disapproved the attitudes and actions of certain members."[11] However, a somewhat different version of this story is related in an earlier publication of the fraternity. *The Hand Book of Kappa Alpha Psi Fraternity* states, "Elder W. Diggs and Byron K. Armstrong, had previously attended Howard University, and had come into contact with men belonging to the only national Greek-letter fraternity in existence among Negroes. Their experiences at Howard caused them to be the chief motivating spirits in the sowing of the seed for a fraternity at Indiana University and crystallizing the idea of establishing an independent Greek-letter organization."[12]

This earlier writing lacks the specificity of Crump's account and does not assert that Diggs and Armstrong were approached by any other fraternity on the Howard University campus for membership. Instead, it merely states that Diggs and Armstrong were aware of the existence of another historically black Greek-letter organization (Alpha Phi Alpha) and that their contact with this organization motivated them to pursue the idea of a fraternity at Indiana University. Although this distinction may be subtle, it provides interesting material to further the discussion about the relationship between two founders of Kappa Alpha Psi and the early members of the Beta Chapter of Alpha Phi Alpha.

By the fall of 1910, both Armstrong and Diggs were attending Indiana University. Crump contextualizes the life of these men and the other African Americans at Indiana University through his discussion of the isolation and racial indignities they endured on campus. He notes that African American students were routinely denied the use of entertainment and recreational facilities and that their sparse numbers led to a depressing isolation.[13]

In an effort to alleviate this condition, nine African American male students at Indiana University met to form a fraternal organization. The organization initially took the name Alpha Omega, until the necessary details of structuring a Greek-letter fraternity could be attended to. It is not known on what date Alpha Omega was founded or how much time elapsed before its members met again to solidify and permanently name their newly founded organization. However, Crump records that the members of Alpha Omega frequently spent time together and that "the depressing isolation earlier experienced was relieved as friendships solidified" among members.[14]

The Founders of Kappa Alpha Nu

Based on these positive experiences, the members of Alpha Omega met again on January 5, 1911, to solidify its existence as a permanent organization. At this meeting, three officers were chosen: Elder Watson Diggs was designated the permanent chairman, John Milton Lee was named secretary, and Byron Kenneth Armstrong was named sergeant at arms. One additional student, George W. Edmonds, was present at this meeting, bringing the total number to ten.[15]

From the outset, the members of the new fraternity were adamant about distinguishing Kappa Alpha Nu from other fraternities. They sought principles and practices that reflected Christian ideals and a purpose of achievement. Another important issue for the new fraternity was a desire to distinguish itself from other fraternities by not seeking members based on wealth or social position. Diggs took responsibility for creating the ritual and ceremonial forms for the fraternity, while Armstrong focused on developing the insignia and emblems. They both took their tasks seriously and pursued classes in Greek heraldry and Greek mythology to ensure that they collected enough information to "embody the major considerations." The name chosen for the new fraternity was Kappa Alpha Nu. There is no record of why this name was chosen, but it has been speculated that it was a tribute to the African American students who had organized Alpha Kappa Nu in 1903.[16]

The following biographical information for each of the founding members is based on Crump's book, unless otherwise cited.

ELDER WATSON DIGGS

Elder Watson Diggs (1890–1947) was a primary organizer and the first polemarch (president) of Kappa Alpha Nu. He was born in Madisonville, Kentucky, and graduated from Indiana State Normal School (currently Indiana State University) in the spring of 1908. Diggs entered Howard University in 1909 but left to attend Indiana University during the fall of 1910. While at Indiana University, Diggs oversaw the growth and expansion of the fraternity to several campuses throughout the Midwest. He earned his degree in 1916. During World War I, Diggs resigned his position as a high school principal in Indianapolis and served overseas with the 368th Infantry (U.S. Army) as a commissioned officer. After the war, Diggs returned to Indiana, where he worked as a public school administrator until his death in 1947. Because of his role in organizing the fraternity and his dedication to its ideals, Diggs was the first to receive the fraternity's highest award, the Laurel Wreath, in 1924.

BYRON KENNETH ARMSTRONG

Byron Kenneth Armstrong (1890–1980) was born in Westfield, Indiana, and enrolled at Howard University in 1909. He left Howard in 1910 to attend Indiana

University, where he studied philosophy, mathematics, and sociology. After finishing at Indiana, Armstrong attended Columbia University and received a master's degree in 1914. He worked in a variety of capacities throughout the United States and eventually earned his PhD from the University of Michigan in 1940. Because of his early and continued contributions to the fraternity, he received the fraternity's Laurel Wreath award in 1935.

GUY LEVIS GRANT

Guy Levis Grant (1891–1973) was born in New Albany, Indiana. He graduated from Indiana University in 1915 and later attended dental school there, receiving his DDS in 1920. In addition to his role in founding the fraternity, Grant served as its grand historian from 1951 until 1967. In 1967 the fraternity bestowed on Grant the title grand historian emeritus.

EZRA D. ALEXANDER

Ezra D. Alexander (1892–1971) was born and raised in Bloomington, Indiana. He received his bachelor's degree from Indiana University in 1917 and his MD in 1919. He practiced medicine for more than fifty years and served as a nonvoting member of the fraternity's Grand Board of Directors until his death in 1971.

EDWARD G. IRVIN

Edward G. Irvin (1893–1982) was born in Spencer, Indiana. He attended Indiana University but left to help support his family. Irvin eventually served in World War I as a combat medic, and he was cited for bravery in the performance of his duties. Later, Irvin pursued a career in journalism and worked for the *Gary Sun*, the *Indianapolis Freeman*, and the *Chicago Daily Bulletin*. Irvin also founded a weekly newspaper in Anderson, Indiana, called the *Shining Star*. Irvin served on the Selective Service Board during World War II and the Korean War. Among the awards and decorations he received were two Distinguished Service Awards (one from President Harry Truman and another from President Dwight D. Eisenhower) and the fraternity's Laurel Wreath.

PAUL W. CAINE

Paul W. Caine (1891–1922) was born in Greencastle, Indiana. He entered Indiana University in 1909, where he worked in several fraternity houses as a cook or housekeeper. The friendships he made through his work in these fraternity houses allowed him to gain information that contributed to the organization of Kappa Alpha Nu. However, Caine was forced to leave Indiana before finishing his sophomore year because of a fire in the fraternity house where he was employed. Caine later attended Columbia University and owned several catering businesses. He died suddenly in an explosion of gaseous materials at his business.[17]

MARCUS P. BLAKEMORE

Marcus P. Blakemore (1889–1959) was born in Franklin, Indiana, and attended public school in Anderson, Indiana. He entered Indiana University in the fall of 1910 but left in 1911. Blakemore organized and operated the Electric Engineering Company until his enlistment in World War I. Later, he attended the University of Pittsburgh and received his DDS in 1923. Blakemore practiced dentistry in Pittsburgh until his death in 1959.

HENRY T. ASHER

There is some dispute as to where and when Henry T. Asher (1890?–1963) was born. Crump asserts that Asher was born in Woodburn, Kentucky, in 1890, but *The Hand Book of Kappa Alpha Psi* states that he was born in Newbury, Indiana, in 1892.[18] Beyond this point of contention, the two sources are in agreement. Asher eventually moved to Bloomington, Indiana, where he attended high school and pursued higher education at Indiana University. He received his bachelor's degree in 1914 and a master's degree in 1917 from the University of Minnesota. In 1928 Asher received an LLB degree from the Detroit College of Law. He died in 1963 in Detroit, Michigan, where he had resided and taught in the public schools for several years.

JOHN MILTON LEE

John Milton Lee (1890–1958) was born in Danville, Indiana. He entered Indiana University in 1910 and completed three years of premedical study. Lee later attended Temple University but left because of deaths in his family. During World War I, he enlisted in the 349th Field Artillery and served overseas as a sergeant first class and gunner. Lee's unit was the first all-black battery to open fire on the enemy, and Lee had the distinction of firing the first shot. In later years, Lee lived in Philadelphia, where he helped organize the Fairview Golf Club (the city's first black golf club) and engaged in several vocational enterprises.[19]

GEORGE W. EDMONDS

The life of George W. Edmonds (1890–1962) was largely a mystery until 1978, when fraternity officials were finally able to piece together some scant information. Before that time, it was known that he was born in Vanderburgh County near Evansville, Indiana, and matriculated at Indiana University in the fall of 1910. However, once he left the university in the summer of 1911, he was not heard from again. Despite the best efforts of the fraternity's founders and other fraternity officials, no one was able to locate this "missing" founder. There were several reasons for their lack of success. First, Edmonds's last name was spelled incorrectly (i.e., "Edmunds") in fraternity records, making it difficult to locate the right man. Second, Edmonds never returned to Indiana because he was forced to support his family when his father died suddenly of pneumonia during the summer of 1911. Third, due to the circumstances of his life, Edmonds was prevented from moving in circles of higher education and was likely unaware that the fraternity had changed its name from Kappa Alpha Nu to Kappa Alpha Psi. Edmonds spent most of his life working in coal mines and for the railroad before dying of pneumonia in 1962.

From Kappa Alpha Nu to Kappa Alpha Psi

By the fall of 1914, Kappa Alpha Nu had established three new chapters on college campuses in the Midwest. Membership was increasing at a steady rate, and the first fraternity house was purchased in Bloomington, Indiana. Still, the members of Kappa Alpha Nu faced virulent racism at Indiana University and in the town of Bloomington.[20] During the fall semester of 1914, two members of the fraternity overheard a white student on campus refer to the fraternity as "Kappa Alpha Nig." It was obvious at that point that the name of the fraternity had become an important issue. Several months later, the fraternity took steps to change the name to Kappa Alpha Psi, ostensibly for the purpose of having a recognizably Greek character (versus the English-looking *N*, for Nu) in the fraternity's alphabetical designation. However, Crump records that fraternity members who were aware of the racial slur considered the adoption of a Greek character "a secondary consideration."[21] Thus, the name of the fraternity officially became Kappa Alpha Psi on April 15, 1915. With this new name, an important historical journey had come to an end. In just a few short years, what had started as a small group of African American students striving for dignity and respect amid racial hostility had grown and spread across the midwestern United States.[22]

Today, Kappa Alpha Psi is an international organization with more than 338 undergraduate and 337 graduate chapters in the United States, the Bahamas, Germany, England, Japan, Bermuda, the Virgin Islands, Korea, and South Africa.[23] The dream of ten young men on the campus of Indiana University, conceived nearly a century ago amidst racism and intolerance, has emerged as an international force emphasizing leadership development and achievement among African American men worldwide.

Notes

1. William L. Crump, *The Story of Kappa Alpha Psi: A History of the Beginning and Development of a College Greek Letter Organization, 1911–1991,* 4th ed. (Philadelphia: Grand Chapter of Kappa Alpha Psi, 1991), 1.

2. Ross F. Lockridge, *The Story of Indiana* (Oklahoma City: Harlow Publishing, 1957).

3. Howard H. Peckham, *Indiana: A Bicentennial History* (New York: W. W. Norton, 1978), 68.

4. John Bartlow Martin, *Indiana: An Interpretation* (Freeport, N.Y.: Books for Libraries Press, 1972).

5. William M. Lutholtz, *Grand Dragon: D. C. Stephenson and the Ku Klux Klan in Indiana* (Lafayette, Ind.: Purdue University Press, 1991).

6. James H. Madison, *A Lynching in the Heartland: Race and Memory in America* (New York: Palgrave, 2003).

7. Waldo E. Martin Jr. and Patricia Sullivan, eds., *Civil Rights in the United States* (New York: Macmillan Reference USA, 2001).

8. Crump, *The Story of Kappa Alpha Psi.*

9. Ibid.

10. Skip Mason, "Revisionist Fraternities: The Kappa, Omega, Sigma Conspiracy. Why Have You Omitted Alpha Phi Alpha Fraternity from Its Rightful Place in Your History Book?" Skip's Historical Moments #8, vol. 1, no. 8., http://www.skipmason.com/hm/hm08.htm (accessed October 15, 2006).

11. Crump, *The Story of Kappa Alpha Psi*, xxi.

12. Kappa Alpha Psi Fraternity Inc., *The Hand Book of Kappa Alpha Psi Fraternity*, rev. ed., vol. 2 (n.p.: Grand Chapter of Kappa Alpha Psi, 1936), 11.

13. Crump, *The Story of Kappa Alpha Psi*.

14. Ibid., 3.

15. Ibid.

16. Ibid., 3, 4.

17. Kappa Alpha Psi Fraternity Inc., "Our Founders," http://www.kappaalphapsi1911 .com (accessed October 1, 2006).

18. Crump, *The Story of Kappa Alpha Psi*; Kappa Alpha Psi, *The Hand Book*.

19. Kappa Alpha Psi, "Our Founders."

20. André McKenzie, "In the Beginning: The Early History of the Divine Nine," in *African American Fraternities and Sororities: The Legacy and the Vision*, ed. Tamara L. Brown, Gregory S. Parks, and Clarenda M. Phillips, 181–210 (Lexington: University Press of Kentucky, 2005).

21. Crump, *The Story of Kappa Alpha Psi*, 27.

22. McKenzie, "In the Beginning."

23. Crump, *The Story of Kappa Alpha Psi*.

7

Seven Schoolteachers Challenge the Klan
The Founders of Sigma Gamma Rho Sorority
Bernadette Pruitt, Caryn E. Neumann, and Katrina Hamilton

In the 1920s, African Americans found themselves the targets of widespread racial bigotry. Only a few years earlier, in 1918, scholar-activist W. E. B. DuBois, editor of the NAACP's *Crisis* magazine, had urged blacks to "close ranks" and, at least for the time being, support the Allied forces in their effort to defeat the Central Powers of Europe.[1] Blacks did just that: 400,000 of them in uniform, almost 1 million as wartime factory personnel, and many more as loyal supporters of the war effort. Regrettably, African American patriotism did little to damper racial hatred. Faced with random acts of violence, antiblack labor union strife, unemployment and underemployment, housing discrimination, poor city services, educational inequities, scientific racism, and condescending employers, African Americans turned inward and relied on the principle of self-help to secure autonomy, hope, and constructive resistance.[2]

In the city of Indianapolis, seven African American educators masked their anxieties, put aside their individual needs, and formed a self-help organization that sought to promote intellectual distinction among female schoolteachers and education majors. Either midwestern natives or southern migrants, these women, all from working-class backgrounds, recognized the power of agency for people of color. The teachers founded Sigma Gamma Rho Sorority in 1922 on the campus of Butler College (renamed Butler University in 1923). Community builders and idealists at heart, the educators refined their goals over the next few years. By 1925, they expanded their membership to include African American women outside the realm of education. In an effort to strengthen their collegiate programs and commitment to community agency and racial autonomy, the sorority in 1929 formed alumnae chapters and established scholarships for undergraduate members. A decade later, the organization comprised sixteen undergraduate chapters and four alumnae chapters in thirteen states.[3]

Interestingly, in the background of the sorority's genesis stood the very powerful and dangerous Ku Klux Klan (KKK), which had experienced a rebirth in 1915 in Stone Mountain, Georgia. Unlike the original KKK of the Recon-struction era, the second Klan targeted a variety of groups, including Jewish Americans, Catholics, recent European ethnic immigrants, Latinos, East Asians, and feminists. The new KKK of the twentieth century evolved from two national events in 1915: the anti-Semitic lynching of engineer Leo Frank in Atlanta, and the release of D. W. Griffith's film masterpiece *The Birth of a Nation.* The secret society grew to record proportions in the 1920s, especially in the Midwest, and Indiana stood out as a major center of Klan activity. With 300,000 members in the early 1920s, the Indiana Klan comprised one-third of the native-born white male population in the state. D. C. Stephenson, the Grand Dragon of the Indiana KKK since 1924, resided at 5432 University in Irvington, literally right next door to Butler University. Madge Oberholtzer, the educator that Stephenson raped and kidnapped in 1926, also lived in Irvington.[4]

The founders of Sigma Gamma Rho Sorority faced many aspects of racism on the campus of Butler College. Since its founding in 1855, Butler had been open to African American applicants. However, at least one Board of Regents member supported the KKK. The school itself practiced de facto segregation in numerous ways. The university adopted a quota system in 1927 that admitted only ten African American students annually. As a result, the university's African American enrollment declined from seventy-four in the 1926–1927 academic year to fifty-eight, including nine entering freshmen. The 1925 edition of the university yearbook, the *Drift,* placed photos of African American graduating seniors in the back of the book, separate from the alphabetical listing and pic-tures highlighting other seniors. These realities suggest that African Americans on campus encountered some degree of racial hostility.[5]

Nevertheless, the sorority's founders pressed on. Sigma Gamma Rho Soror-ity Inc. founders Mary Lou Allison, Nannie Mae Gahn, Vivian White, Bessie Downey, Cubena McClure, Dorothy Hanley, and Hattie Mae Dulin quietly began their society for teachers and sought to make a difference. In doing so, they indirectly challenged perceived early-twentieth-century notions about race and gender. They subtly defied the local KKK when they established their society for college-educated African American women. Ignoring the commonly held view that African American women were intellectually, culturally, and sexually inferior, the seven founders relied on racial autonomy, community building, and constructive activism in an effort to topple racism, poverty, and hopelessness.[6]

Mary Lou Allison Gardner Little

Mary Lou Allison (1896–1992) began life in Kentucky, but her family soon relocated to Indianapolis, Indiana, as part of the Great Migration of African Americans. Tragedy struck in late 1899 or 1900 when Allison's parents died suddenly, permanently altering the lives of the Allison children. Mary and her brother were separated and raised in different households; she remained in Indianapolis with family friend Katie Johnson.[7]

A precocious youngster, Allison had a passion for learning. She graduated from Clemmon Vonnegut School No. 9 in 1911. The aspiring artist then attended the Abram C. Shortridge High School and the John Herron Art Institute (on a scholarship). After graduating from high school in 1915, she entered the Indianapolis Normal School, earning her teacher's certificate in 1918. Allison began taking classes at Butler College in 1919.[8]

On November 12, 1922, the determined Allison, along with six of her classmates, colleagues, and dear friends, formed Sigma Gamma Rho Sorority, a professional society for African American female educators. Soon after the sorority's founding, Allison realized the urgency to develop an organization that appealed to a larger body of educated black women; she also stressed the importance of teachers continuing their education in an effort to obtain their four-year degrees. Equally important, Allison realized the value of establishing a group that promoted self-help activism, service, and racial autonomy in the larger African American community. Allison, the sorority's first Grand Basileus (national president) from 1925 to 1926, helped the organization evolve into a national community-service sorority in the mid-1920s. In 1929, members incorporated the club into a national collegiate sorority, establishing the Alpha Chapter on the Butler campus, and created the first of numerous community-service projects, the Sigma Gamma Rho National Education Fund. Sigma Gamma Rho's slogan, "Greater Service, Greater Progress," highlighted the founders' legacy of community building, charity, faith, and patience in the wake of extreme prejudice, turmoil, and poverty.[9]

Allison, who authored the sorority pledge, moved to Los Angeles with her husband, Wilford Gardner, in 1928 and eventually earned a bachelor's degree from the University of California at Los Angeles. After her husband's death in 1949, she married Roy Little. She taught in the Los Angeles school system for thirty-five years, retiring in 1967. Mary Lou Allison Gardner Little died in 1992 at age ninety-five. At each boulé (international biennial meeting), Sigma Gamma Rho Sorority Inc. awards the Mary Lou Allison Little Loving Cup Award to the most exceptional chapter of the biennium.[10]

Nannie Mae Gahn Johnson

A native of Indianapolis, Nannie Mae Gahn (?–1986) graduated from Abram C. Shortridge High School and the Indianapolis Normal School. She later received both bachelor's and master's degrees from Butler. While a student at Butler, she married and took the surname Foster. After divorcing her first husband, she remarried, taking the name Johnson. She began her successful teaching career in 1923, one year after Sigma Gamma Rho's founding. Following a career that spanned four decades, Johnson retired from the Indianapolis public schools in the mid-1960s as an elementary school principal.[11]

An active member of Allen Chapel African Methodist Episcopal Church in Indianapolis, Johnson dedicated her life to African American spirituality, intellectual development, and community service. This is especially evident in her volunteer work with Flanner House, a social service center that began serving Indianapolis's African American community in 1903. Flanner House, like similar institutions across the country, promoted nutrition, preventive medicine, job training, child care, senior citizen programs, social services, and cultural awareness. A member of the Flanner House Board of Directors after World War II, Johnson enthusiastically reached out to members of the African American working class in an effort to promote self-help, aesthetic awareness, socioeconomic autonomy, and racial responsibility in the African American community.[12]

Johnson remained a tireless organizer in Sigma Gamma Rho as well. She helped design the sorority's official pin—consisting of an open book with a torch as its foundation, ten pearls mounted on the edges, and two rubies at the base—which continues to be an integral part of the sorority's history and mission. After her retirement, Johnson remained active in the sorority and local community-building efforts. She had no children. Johnson died in 1986.[13]

Vivian Irene White Marbury

When the last surviving founder of Sigma Gamma Rho Sorority Inc., educator Vivian Marbury (1900–2000), died at age one hundred, she left a lasting legacy not only in her community-service organization but also in the field of education. Vivian Irene White was born in Oxford, Ohio, and, like her sorority cofounders, treasured knowledge. She graduated from Abram C. Shortridge High School and the Indianapolis Normal School.[14]

White and the other sorority founders viewed education as the most important instrument of racial autonomy, social justice, economic opportunity, and upward mobility. White married in 1929 and subsequently gave birth to two children. She eventually obtained a bachelor's degree in education from Butler in 1931. She received the Gregg Scholarship (named for benefactor and pioneer educator Thomas Gregg), a prestigious award given by the Indianapolis Board of School Commissioners to fund the intellectual endeavors of outstanding Indianapolis schoolteachers. The award was particularly gratifying for the young woman of color, since Indiana was a hotbed of KKK activity at the time.[15] Marbury earned her master's degree in education from Columbia University's Teachers College in New York City, but even after graduate school, she continued taking classes and expressed an interest in scholarly research. During her summer breaks, Marbury enrolled in continuing education courses at the University of Chicago and Cleveland's Western Reserve University (now Case Western Reserve University).[16]

Marbury compiled an impressive résumé as an educator. She taught at a number of institutions, including Morehouse College in Atlanta, Georgia. She also served as director of practice training for Butler University, the University of Indianapolis, and Indianapolis State University in Terre Haute. Mostly, the educator served Indianapolis schoolchildren. Marbury taught in the increasingly segregated Indianapolis school system for almost a decade before organizing Public School No. 87 in the 1920s. That institution grew from a four-room portable schoolhouse to an attractive eighteen-classroom building, and in 1928, Marbury was appointed its principal. She held that post for thirty-nine years, until her retirement in 1967.[17]

People revered the successful Marbury, and her sorority treasured her. Sorority sister Marbury outlived all her beloved friends, colleagues, and cofounders, and numerous chapters depended on her oral history accounts, astonishing memory, and intellectual integrity. On March 11, 2000, Marbury celebrated her 100th birthday. Sigma Gamma Rho Sorority Inc. commemorated the milestone with a proclamation; the grateful organization also dedicated its official magazine, the *Aurora,* to its illustrious surviving founder. Marbury died four months later in July 2000.[18]

Bessie May Downey Rhoades Martin

Like many women, educator and Sigma Gamma Rho founder Bessie Rhoades Martin (1900–1946?) spent numerous years caring for others, particularly her family. Bessie May Downey was born in Indianapolis, the youngest of six children. She exhibited a keen intellect at an early age, and her parents were especially astounded by their daughter's leadership skills. Young Downey joined the First Baptist Church of Indianapolis and became an active member. Her parents worked hard to nurture her natural gifts. After completing grade school in Indianapolis, the teen entered Emmerich Manual Training High School. Like many of her peers in Sigma Gamma Rho, she went on to the Indianapolis Normal School, graduating sometime in the 1920s. She later entered Butler University and eventually received a bachelor's degree in education in 1943.[19]

Downey faced a number of formidable trials as she worked to complete her college education. As she approached graduation, Downey's mother took ill. Torn between her love of learning and her dear mother, who had worked a number of jobs to pay for her daughter's schooling, Bessie made a difficult choice and cared for her ailing parent. She did, however, graduate from the teachers college. Regrettably, her mother died right after a jubilant Bessie secured her first teaching job at Indianapolis School No. 4, a position she kept for twenty-five years.[20]

The aspiring young woman eventually married twice but never had children. Nevertheless, she remained a fervent supporter of the family unit, as well as a devoted educator, wife, daughter, and community builder; she always put others first. Bessie Rhoades Martin joined Omega Rho, the sorority's chapter for deceased sisters, in late 1946 or 1947.[21]

Cubena McClure

Little is known about Sigma Gamma Rho founder Cubena McClure (1899?–1924), a talented educator who died of pneumonia only two years after the organization's founding. Born in Indianapolis in 1899 or 1900, McClure excelled academically. She graduated from Abram C. Shortridge High School during World War I and later the Indiana Normal School. In 1923 she began course work in education at Butler University. During the summer months, she attended Western Reserve University (now Case Western Reserve University) in Cleveland, Ohio. Undoubtedly, the beautiful young woman loved learning and community agency. McClure remained a constant presence in sorority affairs, and the organization's first initiation took place at her home. McClure also helped design Sigma Gamma Rho's pin, which reflected her artistic flair.[22]

McClure loved teaching as well. She taught at Indianapolis School Nos.

24 and 26 for three years. She was one of five instructors selected for a special supervisory project at School No. 24 in the early 1920s. McClure shined in the classroom, and her dedication to her craft paid off. Like fellow sorority sister Marbury, McClure was awarded the prestigious Gregg Scholarship by the Indianapolis Board of School Commissioners. Unfortunately, a debilitating illness prevented her from accepting the award.[23] McClure died on August 24, 1924.[24]

Dorothy Hanley Whiteside

Dorothy Hanley (1905–1985) entered the world in Paris, Tennessee, in Henry County. Young Dorothy moved to Indianapolis with her family in 1914. Like most of her sorority cofounders, Hanley graduated from Abram C. Shortridge High School in 1922 and then entered the Teachers College of Indianapolis (now Butler University College of Education), eventually obtaining her teaching certificate. She obtained a bachelor's degree in education from Butler University in 1942. While a first-year student at the Teachers College, Hanley met the other founders of Sigma Gamma Rho, who instantly became her closest friends.[25]

Hanley's enthusiasm for community building was reflected in her many decades of dedicated service to her students, sorority, city, and family. As an educator, she taught students in nearby North Vernon, Indiana, as well as in Indianapolis. Interestingly, although she loved teaching, she retired from the Indianapolis public schools in 1951, after twenty-five years of service. Her husband, an aspiring businessman, formed the Beard Delivery Service in the early 1950s, seeking greater opportunities for himself and his family, and in fact, his business prospered. Motivated by her husband's good fortune, Whiteside established a millinery shop in the 1950s. "Hats by Dorothy" thrived as sorority sisters, educators, church members, and others patronized her business. Of course, Whiteside remained a loyal supporter of Sigma Gamma Rho, donating some of her profits to the sorority's many charitable programs that benefited education, civil rights, the poor, and public health.[26]

Whiteside also devoted herself to the care of her family. Her father's health began to fail following a terrible accident. Her in-laws also needed Whiteside's assistance and support, especially as they got older. Then, Whiteside's loving husband of many years died in 1955. Devastated but not destroyed, Whiteside continued to operate both businesses through 1959. At that time, the rising cost of living and her growing financial obligations prompted the Sigma Gamma

Rho founder to return to the classroom. She continued to teach in Indianapolis until retiring in 1970.[27]

The multitalented Whiteside consistently put others first. Indeed, she eagerly served her community until her health failed in the 1980s. Originally a member of the African Methodist Episcopal Church, Whiteside later served on the vestry of St. Philip's Episcopal Church, on the Flanner House Board of Directors, and as Flanner House Guild president. The talented Whiteside also served her congregations as an organist and Sunday school teacher. In later years, she joined the Unity Trinity Center. She also served the community as a Moral Rearmament team member and garden club president. Whiteside continued to give to her sorority as well. Younger sorority sisters especially appreciated her thoughtfulness and generosity. Only her declining health slowed her community activities. She entered the Omega Rho Chapter on June 18, 1985, at the age of eighty.[28]

Hattie Mae Annette Dulin Redford

Hattie Mae Annette Dulin (1896–1990) was born in Greenville, Kentucky, to James and Mary Elizabeth Dulin. Her family, like a growing number of African Americans in the early twentieth century, left the South for the North. They moved to Indiana in 1898, first to Marion and later to South Bend. James and Mary Dulin were certain that the Midwest would offer their daughter a quality education. The ambitious Dulins also started a small hotel and restaurant in South Bend. Their independent daughter joined the Second Baptist Church, and she excelled in school. Hattie Mae graduated cum laude from South Bend Central High School during World War I. Eager to continue her education, she enrolled at Indiana State Teachers College (now Indiana State University). After graduating, the confident young woman immediately entered Butler College in the early 1920s. Redford eventually earned her master's degree in education in 1939. She titled her master's thesis "Student Government in the Elementary Schools of Indianapolis." Redford continued to enroll in continuing education courses at Western Reserve University in Cleveland, Ohio, and the Indiana University extension campus in Indianapolis.[29]

Redford taught in Indiana and served students for nearly forty years. First she taught in Terre Haute, the home of her alma mater, Indiana State Teachers College. Then she relocated to Indianapolis, where she did her graduate work and taught in the public school system. Like her sorority sisters, Redford loved education. She taught school for thirty-seven years in Indianapolis before retiring in the late 1960s. For most of her career, Redford taught at the Hazel Hart Hendricks School, Indianapolis Public School No. 37. Near the end of her teaching career, Redford proudly served under the leadership of principal and fellow Sigma Gamma Rho cofounder Nannie Mae Gahn Johnson.[30]

Redford served the community through her volunteer efforts in the sorority and at church. A member of Second Baptist Church, she worked as a dedicated clerk for many decades. Her work in the sorority was impressive as well. After founding the sorority in 1922, Redford took on numerous positions. As the sorority grew into a national organization of tens of thousands, Redford emerged as a central behind-the-scenes figure and source of strength. As Grand Epistoleus (sorority historian), Grand Tamiouchos (treasurer), and financial consultant, Redford actively sought new members; organized important documents and papers, especially financial receipts; and encouraged the sorority to commit itself to the new challenges facing African Americans in the latter twentieth century.[31]

Her uncompromising dedication earned her numerous awards over the years. The Blanche Edwards Award was presented to Hattie Mae Dulin Redford at the sorority's Silver Boulé in St. Louis, Missouri, in 1947 for her generosity and giving spirit. As one of the most beloved sisters in the organization in the 1940s, Redford was named Grand Boules. Other awards and honors included an exemption from the national head tax in 1959, an Alpha Lambda Sigma Achievement Trophy in Cleveland in 1961, and a silver bowl in recognition of her outstanding service as the national sorority's Grand Tamiouchos in 1969. Her generosity also reached outside the sorority. She earned a certificate of achievement from the Chicago Joint Council in 1964 and the Citizen Forum of Indianapolis's Certificate of Recognition in 1965.[32]

Redford, a dedicated and loving sorority sister, church member, and wife, remained active in volunteer work after her retirement. She inspired a new generation of sorors, reminding them of the importance of cooperation and community building. Redford continued to serve the sorority as financial consultant until her passing on July 9, 1990. Today, Sigma Gamma Rho Sorority Inc. awards several plaques in her honor at each boulé for exceptional exhibits highlighting chapter achievements.[33]

Amid the tumultuous racial climate of the 1920s, in a state well known for its Ku Klux Klan activities, seven young women formed a new self-help organization. The founders of Sigma Gamma Rho believed that their sorority could make a real difference in the African American community. The members saw mentoring, networking, and consoling as priorities, first among female educators of color, and second among female college students of African descent. This was especially necessary at a largely white university, where guidance for African Americans was largely absent. Targeting many groups by the mid-1920s, including female educators, college-educated women of color, eager schoolchildren interested in attending college, churchgoers, laborers, the poor, victims of racially motivated crimes, and civil rights groups, the women used their organization as a vehicle of constructive activism.[34]

Indeed, the programs, charities, projects, and causes supported by the sorority confirm this observation. Avid supporters of the NAACP, Sigma Gamma Rho and other members of the National Pan-Hellenic Council helped push for passage of the Costigan-Wagner Anti-Lynching Bill of 1935. Although unsuccessful, the women remained determined to work alongside other groups and the NAACP in formulating a mass movement to fight racial discrimination, especially de jure segregation in the South. The women who made up the undergraduate and alumnae chapters across the country also established employment bureaus for out-of-work sorority sisters in the 1930s, local literacy classes, and health programs. During World War II, the organization was a huge supporter of the Fair Employment Practices Committee. Though conservative to moderate in its sociopolitical tone, the organization's strong commitment to alleviating poverty, disease, and discrimination—at home and abroad—resonated loudly with campus groups, activists, middle-class reformers, integrationists, and civil rights advocates in the 1950s and 1960s.

As the organization approaches its ninetieth birthday, Sigma Gamma Rho Sorority members remain passionate about undergraduate scholastic excellence, human rights, racial equality, health care, and poverty. Still, like its peer organizations, Sigma Gamma Rho faces formidable challenges in the twenty-first century. The national body continues to address instances of illegal hazing practices, misconduct, and academic mediocrity in the undergraduate chapters. Furthermore, Sigma Gamma Rho, the youngest African American Greek-letter fraternal society and the smallest African American sorority in existence today, struggles to attract long-standing, financially active members in the alumnae chapters. Today, the organization claims five hundred chapters and ninety thousand active and inactive members around the world.[35]

Notes

The authors are grateful to the following individuals: Gwenette Parker, international Grand Epistoleus (historian), Sigma Gamma Rho Sorority Inc.; Jennifer Jones, executive director, Sigma Gamma Rho Sorority Inc.; Department of Education specialist and Sigma Gamma Rho member Deborah Walsh; Sally Childs-Helton, PhD, Special Collections, Rare Books, and University Archives librarian, Irvin Library, Butler University; Tom Krasean, Indiana Historical Society; Paul Diebold, former Irvington Historical Society board member and volunteer; Kim L. Hooper, assistant director of school and community relations, Indianapolis public schools; and Sondrea Ozolins, university registrar with the Office of Records and Registration, Butler University.

1. Mark Ellis, "'Closing Ranks' and 'Seeking Honors': W. E. B. Du Bois in World War I," *Journal of American History* 79 (January 1992): 76–124. Historian W. D. Wright, in *Black History and Black Identity: A Call for a New Historiography* (Westport, Conn.: Praeger, 2002), 1–21, makes a compelling case for the use of *Black* instead of *black* when defining people of African descent in the United States. According to Wright, middle-class and professional African Americans have, in recent years, urged society to capitalize the first letter of the word when describing African Americans of the United States. They argue that *Black* designates ethnicity, while *black* defines race and color. Wright believes that this designation must and should be determined by African Americans, and not by others. This use of *Black* over *black* challenges standard sentiment and standard dictionaries, which define the word as a color or a racial category. In Western culture, however, the term is largely associated with negativity. We have therefore decided to use, in most instances, *African American* in place of *black* (lowercase being the publisher's preferred style). See also John McWhorter, "Why I'm Black, not African-American," *Detroit News*, September 30, 2004.

2. Darlene Clark Hine, William C. Hine, and Stanley Harrold, *The African-American Odyssey,* 3rd ed. (Upper Saddle River, N.J: Pearson Prentice Hall, 2006), 354–56, 419–25, 432–35; Jacqueline Jones, Peter H. Wood, Thomas Borstelmann, Elaine Tyler May, and Vicki Ruiz, *Created Equal: A Social and Political History of the United States,* 2nd ed. (New York: Pearson-Longman, 2006), 702–3, 713–15, 724–25; Lawrence C. Ross Jr., *The Divine Nine: The History of African American Fraternities and Sororities* (New York: Dafina Books, 2000), 276. Increasingly, scholars are reevaluating the "accommodationist" label of Booker T. Washington and his supporters. Maceo Dailey, for example, defines Washington's political stance as one of "constructionalism," not accommodation. See Maceo Crenshaw Dailey Jr., "Neither 'Uncle Tom' nor 'Accommodationist,' Booker T. Washington, Emmett Jay Scott, and Constructionalism," *Atlanta History* 38, no. 4 (1995): 20–33.

3. Pearl Schwartz White, *Behind These Doors—A Legacy: The History of Sigma Gamma Rho Sorority* (Chicago: Sigma Gamma Rho Sorority Inc., 1974), 1–156; Katie Kinnard White, "Sigma Gamma Rho Sorority," in *Black Women in America: Historical Encyclopedia,* ed. Darlene Clark Hine, Elsa Barkley Brown, and Rosalyn Terbourg-Penn (Bloomington: Indiana University Press, 1994), 1030–32; John F. Kondelik, "Butler University and the Dream of Distinction" (PhD diss., University of Michigan, 1993), 45–103; Ralph D. Gray, *Indiana University–Purdue University of Indianapolis: The Making of an Urban University* (Bloomington: Indiana University Press, 2003), 21–22.

4. M. William Lutholtz, *Grand Dragon: D. C. Stephenson and the Ku Klux Klan*

in Indiana (West Lafayette, Ind.: Purdue University Press, 1993), 39–64; Paul Diebold, *Greater Irvington: Architecture, Places, and People on the Indianapolis Eastside* (Indianapolis: Irvington Historical Society, 1997), 117–20, 142; Hine et al., *African-American Odyssey*, 419–25; Jones et al., *Created Equal*, 713–15.

5. George M. Waller, *Butler University: A Sesquicentennial History* (Bloomington: Indiana University Press, 2006), 289–94; Butler University, "Butler University Sesquicentennial Timeline, 1855–2005," http://www.butler.edu/150/timeline_1.asp (accessed February 19, 2007). Butler University opened in 1855 as North Western Christian University; it was renamed Butler University in 1877. In 1896, the institution merged with the University of Indianapolis (no relation to the current University of Indianapolis) and became the latter's liberal arts or undergraduate college; that merger ended in 1906. In 1930 Butler acquired the Teachers College of Indianapolis and formed its College of Education. Even though the school was called "Butler University" in the nineteenth century, it existed as a single liberal arts school until vigorous fund-raising campaigns during World War I, the 1920s, and the 1930s spurred the institution's emergence as an elite midwestern university. See Kondelik, "Butler University and the Dream of Distinction," 45–103; "Butler University," in *The Encyclopedia of Indianapolis*, ed. David J. Bodchhamer and Robert G. Barrows (Bloomington: Indiana University Press, 1994), 372–74; Gray, *Indiana University–Purdue University of Indianapolis*, 21–22.

6. Hine et al., *African-American Odyssey*, 419–25; Jones et al., *Created Equal*, 713–15; Ross, *The Divine Nine*, 276; Emma Lou Thornborough, *Indiana Blacks in the Twentieth Century*, ed. Lana Ruegamer (Bloomington: Indiana University Press, 2000), 48–52; Richard B. Pierce, *Polite Protest: The Political Economy of Race in Indianapolis, 1920–1970* (Bloomington: Indiana University Press, 2005), 30–31. For other examples of community agency among professional African American women, see Jacqueline Ann Rouse, "Out of the Shadow of Tuskegee: Margaret Murray Washington, Social Activism, and Race Vindication," *Journal of Negro History* 81 (1996): 31–46; Glenda Elizabeth Gilmore, *Women and the Politics of White Supremacy in North Carolina, 1896–1920* (Chapel Hill: University of North Carolina Press, 1996); Jacqueline Jones, *Labor of Love, Labor of Sorrow: Black Women, Work, and the Family from Slavery to the Present* (New York: Basic Books, 1986); Paula Giddings, *When and Where I Enter: The Impact of Black Women on Race and Sex in America* (New York: Perennial, 1984); Stephanie J. Shaw, "Black Club Women and the Creation of the National Association of Colored Women," in *"We Specialize in the Wholly Impossible": A Reader in Black Women's History*, ed. Darlene Clark Hine, Wilma King, and Linda Reed (New York: Carlson Publishing, 1995), 433–42; Paula Giddings, *In Search of Sisterhood: Delta Sigma Theta and the Challenge of the Black Sorority Movement* (New York: Quill, 1988); Stephanie J. Shaw, *What a Woman Ought to Be and to Do: Black Professional Women Workers during the Jim Crow Era* (Chicago: University of Chicago Press, 1996),167; Naomi W. Ledé, *Precious Memories of a Black Socialite* (Houston: D. Armstrong, 1991); Audrey Y. Crawford, "'To Protect, to Feed, and to Give Momentum to Every Effort':

African American Clubwomen in Houston, 1880–1910," *Houston Review of History and Culture* 1 (fall 2003): 15–23.

7. Gwenette Parker, Grand Epistoleus, Sigma Gamma Rho Sorority Inc., tape-recorded interview by Katrina Hasan Hamilton, Los Angeles, Calif., July 15, 2006, in the author's possession; White, *Behind These Doors*, 1–26; Annie Lea Lawrence-Brown, Evelyn Hawkins Hood, Katie Kinnard White, and Lillie Wilkes, *The Legacy Continues . . . The History of Sigma Gamma Rho Sorority, 1974–1994* (Chicago: Sigma Gamma Rho Sorority Inc., 1994), 26, 229–30; André McKenzie, "In the Beginning: The Early History of the Divine Nine," in *African American Fraternities and Sororities: The Legacy and the Vision*, ed. Tamara L. Brown, Gregory S. Parks, and Clarenda M. Phillips (Lexington: University Press of Kentucky, 2005), 190–200; Ross, *The Divine Nine*, 286; Hine et al., *African-American Odyssey*, 354–56, 419–25; Jack S. Blocker Jr., "Midwestern States, Black Migration To," in *Encyclopedia of the Great Black Migration*, vol. 2 (Westport, Conn.: Greenwood Press, 2006), 528–32; Jason Carl Digman, "Black Migration before World War I, Patterns of," in ibid., 102–4; J. Trent Alexander, "Indianapolis, Indiana," in ibid., 425–27.

8. Parker interview; White, *Behind These Doors*, 1–55; Lawrence-Brown et al., *The Legacy Continues*, 26, 229–30; McKenzie, "In the Beginning," 190–200; Ross, *The Divine Nine*, 286; Mary Lou Allison's student transcripts and academic records, 1919–1924, Office of the Registrar, Butler University, Indianapolis, Ind.

9. Parker interview; White, *Behind These Doors*, 1–206; Lawrence-Brown et al., *The Legacy Continues*, 26, 229–30; White, "Sigma Gamma Rho," 1030–32; McKenzie, "In the Beginning," 198–210; Ross, *The Divine Nine*, 276–86; Sigma Gamma Rho Sorority Inc., "Illustrious Founders," *Sigma Gamma Rho, Greater Service, Greater Progress,* http://www.sgrh01922.0rg/founders.html (accessed May 29, 2006); Hine et al., *African-American Odyssey*, 433–35; Thornborough, *Indiana Blacks in the Twentieth Century*, 12.

10. Sigma Gamma Rho Sorority Inc., *Constitution By Laws Standard Operating Procedures Supplemental Information* (Chicago: Sigma Gamma Rho Sorority Inc., 1993), 8–7, 8–8; Lawrence-Brown et al., *The Legacy Continues*, 229–30; Ross, *The Divine Nine*, 286. For the obituary of Mary Lou Gardner Little, see *Aurora* 61 (spring 1992).

11. Parker interview; White, *Behind These Doors*, 1–206; Lawrence-Brown et al., *The Legacy Continues*, 26, 38, 56, 80, 149, 162; White, "Sigma Gamma Rho," 1030–32; McKenzie, "In the Beginning," 198–210; Ross, *The Divine Nine*, 276, 286–87; Sigma Gamma Rho, "Illustrious Founders." Although one source indicates that Nannie Mae Gahn Johnson graduated from Shortridge and Indianapolis Normal School, most others do not make this claim. Nannie Mae Foster's student transcripts and academic records—BS, 1932, MS, 1941, Office of the Registrar, Butler University.

12. Sigma Gamma Rho, "Illustrious Founders"; Ross, *The Divine Nine*, 286–87; Lawrence-Brown et al., *The Legacy Continues*, 26, 38, 56, 80, 149, 162; White, *Behind These Doors*, 1–55; "History," Flanner House Collection, 004, Philanthropy Manuscript Collections, Ruth Lilly Special Collections and Archives, Indiana University–Purdue

University at Indianapolis University Library, Indianapolis, Ind., www.ulib.iupui.edu/ Special/philcoll/coll/mss004.html (accessed December 28, 2006); Flanner House, "History of Flanner House as Written before 1946," Flanner House of Indianapolis, www .flannerhouse.com/1946.html (accessed December 28, 2006); Richard B. Pierce, *Polite Protest: The Political Economy of Race in Indianapolis, 1920–1970* (Bloomington: Indiana University Press, 2005), 15, 53, 62–64, 67–71, 140; Thornborough, *Indiana Blacks in the Twentieth Century,* 24–25, 36, 37–38, 95.

13. Sigma Gamma Rho, "Illustrious Founders"; Ross, *The Divine Nine,* 286–87; Lawrence-Brown et al., *The Legacy Continues,* 26, 38, 56, 80, 149, 162; White, *Behind These Doors,* 1–55; "History," Flanner House Collection; "History of Flanner House as Written before 1946."

14. Parker interview; Sigma Gamma Rho, "Illustrious Founders"; Ross, *The Divine Nine,* 286–87; Lawrence-Brown et al., *The Legacy Continues,* 26, 38, 49, 57, 59, 80, 89, 108–9, 119, 149, 162, 216, 259, 295; White, *Behind These Doors,* 1–55.

15. Parker interview; White, *Behind These Doors,* 1–65; Lawrence-Brown et al., *The Legacy Continues,* 216; Lydia R. Blaich, "The Gregg Scholarship of the Indianapolis Public Schools," *Elementary School Teacher* 12 (June 1912): 460–62; Ross, *The Divine Nine,* 276, 287; White, "Sigma Gamma Rho," 1030–32; Hine et al., *African-American Odyssey,* 433–35; Vivian White's student transcripts and academic records—BS, 1931, Office of the Registrar, Butler University; Pierce, *Polite Protest,* 26–55; Thornborough, *Indiana Blacks in the Twentieth Century,* 33–70.

16. Ross, *The Divine Nine,* 287; Sigma Gamma Rho, "Illustrious Founders"; Lawrence-Brown et al., *The Legacy Continues,* 216.

17. Ibid.

18. Parker interview; Ross, *The Divine Nine,* 287; Lawrence-Brown et al., *The Legacy Continues,* 26, 38, 49, 57, 59, 80, 89, 108–9, 119, 162, 216, 259, 295. For more on Sigma Gamma Rho's celebration of Vivian Marbury, see "Soror Vivian Irene White Marbury," *Aurora* 69, nos. 5 and 6 (winter–spring 2000).

19. Parker interview; White, *Behind These Doors,* 1–65; Ross, *The Divine Nine,* 287–88; Sigma Gamma Rho, "Illustrious Founders"; Bessie Martin's student transcripts and academic records—BS, 1943, Office of the Registrar, Butler University. Although sorority sources list City Teachers Normal as the teaching school attended by Bessie May Downey Rhoades Martin, this might be incorrect. Sources highlighting Sigma Gamma Rho's founders list several different normal schools that operated in the Indianapolis area in the early twentieth century. However, according to Indianapolis public schools community-relations personnel, the school was actually the Indianapolis Normal School. Some of the names given in source materials are as follows: City Normal School of Indianapolis, Indianapolis Normal School, City Teachers Normal, City Normal and Training School of Indianapolis, Indianapolis Normal and Training School, and Teachers College of Indianapolis. In 1930 Butler University acquired the bankrupted Teachers College of Indianapolis. The merger created the College of

Education on the Butler campus. Prior to this merger, Teachers College, which was the training center for primary school teachers, maintained an affiliation with Butler's program that trained high school instructors. Because all the founders were affiliated with Butler University in some way, either as undergraduate students or as normal school students at an institution connected with Butler, it is reasonable to suggest that those who attended normal schools independent of Butler University did their course work at a program similar to that of Teachers College of Indianapolis, which was in fact closely related to Butler. It is unclear whether these institutions existed separately, whether they evolved from one another, or whether people used different names to refer to a single institution. Most of the founders of Sigma Gamma Rho attended the Indianapolis Normal School. See *Encyclopedia of Indianapolis;* Sally Harvey-Kelvin, "Blaker, Eliza Ann," in *Learning to Give: An Action of the Heart, a Project of the Mind* (Center for Philanthropy, Indiana University), http://www.learningtogive.org/papers/index .asp?bpid=78 (accessed December 28, 2006); Ray E. Boomhower, "'The Thing Is Right!' Eliza Blaker and the Free Kindergarten Movement," *Traces of Indiana and Midwestern History* 16, no. 1 (2004): 28–37.

20. Parker interview; White, *Behind These Doors,* 1–65; Ross, *The Divine Nine,* 287–88; Sigma Gamma Rho, "Illustrious Founders."

21. Ibid.

22. Parker interview; White, *Behind These Doors,* 1–50; Ross, *The Divine Nine,* 88; Sigma Gamma Rho, "Illustrious Founders"; Cubena McClure's student transcripts and academic records, 1923, Office of the Registrar, Butler University.

23. Parker interview; White, *Behind These Doors,* 1–50; Ross, *The Divine Nine,* 88; Sigma Gamma Rho, "Illustrious Founders"; Blaich, "Gregg Scholarship," 460–62.

24. Sigma Gamma Rho, "Illustrious Founders"; Ross, *The Divine Nine,* 88; Lawrence-Brown et al., *The Legacy Continues,* 26, 38, 56, 80, 149, 162; White, *Behind These Doors,* 1–55; McKenzie, "In the Beginning," 198–99.

25. Parker interview; White, *Behind These Doors,* 1–65; Lawrence-Brown et al., *The Legacy Continues,* 26, 37, 38, 39, 80, 89, 108–9, 149, 162; McKenzie, "In the Beginning," 198–200; Ross, *The Divine Nine,* 289–90; Vivian Hanley's student transcripts and academic records—BS, 1942, Office of the Registrar, Butler University.

26. Parker interview; White, *Behind These Doors,* 1–65; Lawrence-Brown et al., *The Legacy Continues,* 26, 37, 38, 39, 80, 89, 108–9, 149, 162; McKenzie, "In the Beginning," 198–200; Ross, *The Divine Nine,* 289–90.

27. Ibid.

28. Flanner House of Indianapolis, www.flannerhouse.com/1946.html (accessed December 28, 2006); Lawrence-Brown, *The Legacy Continues,* 149; Ross, *The Divine Nine,* 88–89; "History," Flanner House Collection.

29. Parker interview; White, *Behind These Doors,* 1–65; Lawrence-Brown et al., *The Legacy Continues,* 26, 37, 38, 39, 80, 89, 108–9, 149, 162; Ross, *The Divine Nine,* 289–90; McKenzie, "In the Beginning," 199–200; Hine et al., *African-American Odyssey,*

354–56, 419–25; Blocker, "Midwestern States, Black Migration To," 528–32; Digman, "Black Migration before World War I, Patterns of," 102–4; Alexander, "Indianapolis, Indiana," 425–27.

30. White, *Behind These Doors*, 1–65; Lawrence-Brown et al., *The Legacy Continues,* 26, 33, 37, 38, 39, 49, 70, 80, 89, 108–9, 162, 204–7; Ross, *The Divine Nine*, 289–90; McKenzie, "In the Beginning," 199–200.

31. Sigma Gamma Rho, *Constitution By Laws,* 8–8; Lawrence-Brown et al., *The Legacy Continues,* 26, 33, 37, 38, 39, 49, 70, 80, 89, 108–9, 162, 204–7; Sigma Gamma Rho, "Illustrious Founders."

32. Lawrence-Brown et al., *The Legacy Continues,* 26, 33, 37, 38, 39, 49, 70, 80, 89, 108–9, 162, 204–7; Sigma Gamma Rho, "Illustrious Founders."

33. Ibid.

34. Sigma Gamma Rho, *Constitution By Laws,* 8–7, 8–8; Lawrence-Brown et al., *The Legacy Continues,* 229–30; Ross, *The Divine Nine*, 286; White, *Behind These Doors*, 2–42; Sigma Gamma Rho Sorority Inc., "National History," *Sigma Gamma Rho, Greater Service, Greater Progress,* http://www.sgrh01922.0rg/founders.html (accessed May 29, 2006).

35. Sigma Gamma Rho, *Constitution By Laws,* 8–7, 8–8; Lawrence-Brown et al., *The Legacy Continues,* 229–30; Ross, *The Divine Nine*, 286; White, *Behind These Doors,* 1–145; Sigma Gamma Rho, "National History"; Ricky L. Jones, *Black Haze: Violence, Sacrifice, and Manhood in Black Greek-Letter Fraternities* (Stony Brook: State University of New York Press, 2004); Elizabeth C. Fine, *Soulstepping: African American Step Shows* (Urbana: University of Illinois Press, 2003); Dorie Williams-Wheeler, *Be My Sorority Sister—Under Pressure* (Chicago: Sparkledoll Productions, 2003); Giddings, *In Search of Sisterhood.*

Part II

Social Activism

8

A Narrative Critique of Black Greek-Letter Organizations and Social Action

Jessica Harris and Vernon C. Mitchell Jr.

> Not the heights to which we have gone, but the depths from which we have come.
>
> —Alpha Phi Alpha slogan

Despite the varying colors, hailing calls, founding dates, and names, many things link black Greek-letter organizations (BGLOs). Beyond the aesthetic or descriptive elements on which their petty rivalries are based, there is a prevailing commitment to racial uplift embodied through social action. The nine intercollegiate BGLOs—Alpha Phi Alpha, Alpha Kappa Alpha, Kappa Alpha Psi, Omega Psi Phi, Delta Sigma Theta, Phi Beta Sigma, Zeta Phi Beta, Sigma Gamma Rho, and Iota Phi Theta—have worked extensively to improve the quality of life for African Americans. Through a social activist agenda, each organization has endeavored ardently to adhere to the ideals and vision set forth by their respective founders.

As we look back and take note of the success of BGLOs, there is much to be commended. However, despite the vastness and scope of what these organizations have achieved, there is still much left to be done. The purpose of this chapter is to examine the historical context behind the actions and programs of BGLOs and thus provide some meaningful insight into the early purposes of these organizations with regard to social action. The ultimate goal of this chapter is to discuss the most integral aspects of the social action programs of all nine BGLOs that constitute the National Pan-Hellenic Council (NPHC). Although not every aspect of every program can be mentioned, this by no means detracts from the influence of BGLOs not only on African American society and culture but also on the face of America as we know it. Those programs and members highlighted only help to place social action within the historical and organizational context of the BGLO movement. Social action programming by

BGLOs led the way to even larger programs and in some instances influenced the very fiber of the black freedom movement.

In addressing the subject of BGLOs and social action, we provide a narrative critique that not merely points the proverbial finger but allows for a more inclusive discourse to address the continued existence of BGLOs in the twenty-first century, going beyond the strictly descriptive, meaningless, self-exhaustion of members and their roles in the struggle. Our conclusion speaks to a question posed by Martin Luther King Jr.'s text, *Where Do We Go from Here? Chaos or Community.*[1] It is within this framework that we hope to provide ways to ensure that BGLOs continue to live up to the lofty ideals on which they were founded.

Famed historian Rayford Logan labeled the end of the nineteenth century the nadir of African American history.[2] Social Darwinist dogma was wedded to white superiority, as thoughts of African American inferiority dominated the racialized cultural and intellectual landscape of America.[3] Although faced with racial antagonism at every turn, African Americans, not shackled or stifled by these unwarranted circumstances, continuously fought back, forging notions of power and community. This was all in an effort to define and lay claim to their rightful place as citizens of this country. It is out of this heritage of resistance and perseverance that we find the formation of many civic and benevolent societies dedicated to racial uplift and, in the same spirit, the formation of BGLOs. The evolution of BGLOs throughout the decades has been emblematic of the changes occurring in the public sphere. From the articulation of the demands made by the Niagara movement in 1905 to the second March on Washington in 1963, BGLOs have been vessels for uplift through social action programs and initiatives.[4]

At the turn of the twentieth century, the notion of "uplift" was a hotly contested concept. According to historian Kevin Gaines, "for many black cultural elites, uplift described an ideology of self-help articulated mainly in racial and middle-class specific, rather than in broader, egalitarian social terms."[5] He posits that the black elite saw themselves as being chosen to usher the black masses—through the promotion of self-help and service—to respectability, thereby "uplifting the race." This idea of racial uplift by an exceptional few is aligned with the thoughts of W. E. B. DuBois, as set out in his 1903 essay "The Talented Tenth." There, DuBois suggested that "the negro race, like all races, is going to be saved by its exceptional men."[6] He conjectured that among the African American populace, a singular group of well-educated men and women would set the agenda for the progress of the entire race. Although DuBois would later revise his position on elite leadership, his view was at the center of the prevailing discourse at the turn of the century.[7]

The concept of racial uplift was a vital part of the formation of the eight oldest BGLOs. Access to higher education and entrance into the professional world placed the founders of these organizations among the elite of the race. Although afforded the opportunity to experience the full breadth of a college education, the very nature of their positioning in that exclusive sphere often meant that they were separated from the majority of their African American brothers and sisters. As such, reconciling their elite status with their desire to maintain a connection to the underprivileged masses would remain contested terrain. BGLOs often struggled to find balance between their interpretations of uplifting the race and creating social space for themselves. For BGLOs, the goal was not to champion normative structures of respectability but to create and define their own paradigms of success, fraternity, and sisterhood—paradigms built on the rock of a resilient cultural heritage. It was on this foundation that the service, philanthropic, and social action agendas of the organizations emerged.

Social action as a construction and a concept was more than just a novel idea for the so-called Divine Nine organizations. Much like the organizations themselves, the idea of social action was cultivated and underwent constant evolution. BGLOs blended, in the most Hegelian sense, the opposites of Booker T. Washington's pragmatic stance toward racial uplift and DuBois's idealism of equal opportunity. By adhering to philosophies of social action, BGLOs created a mechanism to lessen the schism between themselves and those who were not part of their elite caste.

Alpha Phi Alpha

Alpha Phi Alpha Fraternity was founded on the campus of Cornell University on December 4, 1906. Inspired by the organizational spirit of the 1905 Niagara movement, Alpha Phi Alpha fought against the societal structures that prevented African Americans from enjoying the promises of democracy. Fraternity historian and fourteenth general president Charles Harris Wesley chronicled that the "pressures of segregation, discrimination, mistreatment, prejudice, caste and neglect of consideration were being exerted on the black people in many places, as they were endeavoring to advance and improve their status."[8] At Cornell University, the seven founders of Alpha Phi Alpha created more than just an experiment in brotherhood; there was a constrained longing to "write our ideas in a movement for future benefit of Negro students everywhere," recalled founder George Biddle Kelley.[9] Another founder, Henry Arthur Callis, asserted, "Society offered us narrowly circumscribed opportunity and no security. Out of our need, our fraternity brought social purpose and social action."[10]

Alpha Phi Alpha, like the other four fraternities that emerged in subsequent years, labored to keep agendas that did not relegate their goals for social action and activism to mere flowery rhetoric. As the fraternities developed and the membership grew to encompass chapters throughout the East, Midwest, and South, fraternity initiatives grew in scope and reach. Most of the programming saw the light of day only after periods of consolidation as well as the formation of functional organizational structures.

Regardless, this did not prevent discussion and disagreement about the focus and aims of BGLOs. Alpha Phi Alpha was no exception. The fraternity faced internal criticism from the members, and even among the leadership there were factions opposed to the idea of civic or social action by an intercollegiate brotherhood. During the Thirty-first General Convention in Chicago, the twelfth general president, Raymond W. Cannon, extolled, "Let us leave to the NAACP the work that belongs to it, and the works of the Urban League to it. In other words let us stay within our boundaries and not encroach upon other organizations. . . . Greek letter College Fraternities should confine themselves primarily to scholastic endeavors."[11]

This narrowly defined scope was not a view shared by all; it must be remembered that these organizations are not monolithic. For that matter, neither are African Americans. Alpha Phi Alpha, as it grew and matured as an organization, dealt with changing currents and interpretations of how the fraternal body should be involved with the black community. Some had very narrowly circumscribed views, while others saw the fraternity as a catalyst for change. Roscoe C. Giles, the second general president, believed the latter. In 1915 Giles wrote an appeal to the brotherhood that emphasized how the fraternity could help in the effort to combat racial prejudice. Giles believed that the fraternity was not merely a social club or outlet. Rather, it could do much for black men in college as well as help further the cause of justice for the race. Giles wrote:

> Today the peace of certain sections of our country is disturbed by the clash of arms in an attempt to enforce so called white supremacy by the rule of the Iron Hand. . . . In the spot where Lincoln, Douglass, Sumner, Stevens and a host of other honest, unbiased men stood and fell in the defense of a then defenseless people, there stand Tillman,

Vardaman, and Wilson, seeking to undo all that has been done. We must not do as has been said of more than one organization, meet, eat, sleep, resolve and adjourn. No more representative, no more intelligent, no more worthy men exist in fraternal bond in the world today than we boast of within our ranks. . . . We must arouse the slumbering giant, Ethiopia.[12]

Giles's impassioned plea led to future endeavors. The question of where the fraternity should focus its efforts created an environment of self-examination.

Under the leadership of Rayford W. Logan, a tone was set in the organization that put the concepts of enlightenment and racial progress into action. Logan, an activist intellectual in his own right, used the fraternity as a "vehicle for militancy."[13] In December 1933, Logan was elected education director, a position that gave him the means to reshape the social activist agenda of the fraternity. Indeed, "a new chapter in the fraternity's history was in the process of development."[14] The continued de facto disenfranchisement of African Americans was of central interest to Logan, and he created a program of citizenship schools to be replicated throughout the nation. So successful was this campaign that the NAACP borrowed the idea.[15] As the director of education for the fraternity, his goal was to reshape and retool the way the fraternity functioned with regard to social action. The "Education for Citizenship" campaign was created to extend the fraternity's reach beyond the "more privileged sections of the African American community."[16] Logan was very much aware of the intrarace antagonisms based on class. His goal was to develop a program that blurred the lines between working class and black elite: "Such a program has to appeal not only to college men and women, but also to all other classes of our population. It is flexible enough to meet the needs of every community. In the South we would tackle squarely the problem of the Democratic white primary and the Lily White Republican caucus. In the North we would emphasize taking advantage of the opportunities for voting and strive to form the nucleus of an intelligent electorate."[17]

The campaign was later called "A Voteless People Is a Hopeless People" and became part of Alpha Phi Alpha's national program in 1936. The fraternity remained active with the black freedom movement throughout the first half of the century and into the second half as well. Of note is the fraternity's growing interest in civil rights litigation. Initial responses can be traced to financial support for the defense of the Scottsboro case in 1933.[18] Moreover, Alpha Phi Alpha was heavily involved in the drive to deal a deathblow to Jim Crow practices in public education. The fraternity saw the issue of education as of paramount interest, second only to suffrage, and a plan was initiated in 1934 during a session of a special convention. Alpha Phi Alpha believed that it should take the lead in this fight and dedicated its efforts toward this aim.[19] Fraternity members Charles Hamilton Houston (dean of Howard Law School), Thurgood Marshall (first African American Supreme Court justice), and Belford V. Lawson Jr. (assistant counsel to the fraternity and later elected sixteenth general president) led the charge to dismantle segregation through litigation.

This pre-*Brown* group of lawyers ushered in later civil rights gains. Alpha Phi Alpha realized that it would take some coalition building to accomplish the arduous task of integration, especially through the courts. Thus, working with the Washington chapter of the NAACP and the New Negro Alliance, a three-pronged attack was put in place to eradicate segregation. Houston was eventually called to New York and worked exclusively with the NAACP, while Alpha Phi Alpha took a less prominent role. The fraternity, however, was still very much involved with these matters.[20]

As president of the fraternity, Lawson continued its civil rights militancy. Challenging the organization in 1946, Lawson implored, "The great decision of this generation of Alpha men is whether we shall, with every ounce of energy, with every dollar in our treasury, with every fiber in our mind and soul, deny the gigantic conspiracy to preserve our segregated *status quo*, and destroy the mighty, monstrous mockery of human decency and dignity, the yoke of Jim Crow which hangs around our necks. To compromise is to evade the crucial issue. I call to action! Let us speak for the dawn."[21] This new "spirit of liberalism" was infectious and spread throughout the rest of the fraternal body, leading to increased involvement in securing rights for African Americans. The fraternity adopted a theme, "Desegregation the Mode—Total Integration the Goal," under the leadership of eighteenth general president Frank L. Stanley.[22] The road to equality was filled with toils and snares, both within the fraternity and outside as well. As the black freedom movement developed, culminating with the March on Washington in 1963, Alpha Phi Alpha played an important role in the litigation of liberation.

Alpha Kappa Alpha

Alpha Kappa Alpha Sorority (AKA), the oldest BGLO formed by and for African American women, was founded on the campus of Howard University on January 15, 1908. Using the words of their constitution as their guide, for nearly a century, Alpha Kappa Alpha has striven to "cultivate and encourage high scholastic and ethical standards, improve living conditions among African American people, and promote unity and friendship among college women."[23] Prior to its expansion into a national organization, the sorority's earliest programs were instituted primarily on the Howard campus.[24] However, with its incorporation on January 29, 1913, the sorority expanded its outlook and objectives beyond the walls of the academy.[25]

Throughout the 1920s and 1930s, the sorority developed programs of service and public betterment. For example, during the 1920s, the sorority's Vocational Guidance Program helped students qualify for entrance into the job market.[26] During the 1930s, the sorority introduced the Mississippi Health Project as a national initiative. The goal of this project was to improve conditions at the Saint's Industrial School in the town of Lexington, Mississippi, and to provide general health care for the residents of the community. Although such projects—those that "strengthened the bonds of friendships and promoted individual self-improvement"—remained very much a part of the sorority's national agenda, the 1930s would see AKA move in the direction of becoming more socially active.[27]

In evaluating and critiquing the components of its programs, the sorority began to question the effectiveness of these service projects, which treated only the symptoms of racism and discrimination rather than the disease itself.[28] Feeling the need to participate in activities directly related to the shaping of policy, the sorority accepted an invitation to become a member of the Joint Committee for National Recovery (JCNR).[29] An outgrowth of President Roosevelt's New Deal initiatives, the JCNR was a coalition of professional associations and national organizations committed to ensuring that African Americans had fair access to newly created government jobs.

In keeping with its push to become more socially active, in 1938 the sorority established the Non-Partisan Council on Public Affairs. Under the direction of Alpha Kappa Alpha founder and incorporator Norma Boyd, the sorority established a plan for a full-time lobby. Among the goals of the lobby were voter registration, the elimination of police brutality in the District of Columbia, the setting of a minimum wage for women in the laundry industry, and passage of antidiscrimination legislation in Congress. In addition to efforts to secure favorable legislation of national importance, the council attempted to collaborate with organizations with similar goals, such as the NAACP and the National Urban League. Although the National Non-Partisan Council was in operation for only ten years, it provided the underpinning for the sorority's continued involvement in the realm of social action.[30] In the summer of 1946, just two years before the final report of the Non-Partisan Council, the retiring Supreme Basileus Beulah Whitby invited the other BGLOs to participate in the Non-Partisan Lobby Program. As a result, seven of the eight BGLOs would organize to create the American Council on Human Rights (ACHR).[31] With Alpha Kappa Alpha sorority at the helm, this coalition of BGLOs was a moving force in the struggle for human rights and equality in this country.

Kappa Alpha Psi

At Indiana University, the founders of Kappa Alpha Psi (created on January 5, 1911) were committed to raising "the sights of black youths and stimulate them to accomplishments higher than otherwise might be realized or even imagined."[32] Community service was an integral part of the uplift component for Kappa Alpha Psi as well as the other organizations. Subjected to the same type of racial isolation that the founders of Alpha Phi Alpha endured at Cornell, the founders of Kappa Alpha Psi were as committed to the formation of a fraternity as they were to the larger issues related to furthering the race.

The Guide Right Movement of Kappa Alpha Psi was the culmination of the vision of the founders, who were seeking social action outside the fraternity. The program was created in 1925 as a "systematic endeavor to guide the youth of the race into successful careers of achievement."[33] Referred to as the "father" of the movement, Leon W. Steward coauthored the program with J. Jerome Peters.[34] The Guide Right Movement planned to accomplish its goals by "character, vocational, and educational guidance."[35] The program comprised a six-step process that would secure implementation by local chapters and the communities they served. Kappa Alpha Psi believed that "educational guidance will enable us to lay down the course of instruction and aid youth in making such decisions as choice of studies, choice of curriculums and the choice of schools necessary to be successful in any field which the youth may enter."[36] Although this was one of the organization's first programs, it was not its last. It is mentioned because of the scope with which the fraternity attempted to reach those African Americans cut off from educational opportunities.

Onetime Dillard University dean and later president of Lincoln University (Pennsylvania) Dr. Horace Mann Bond proclaimed, "the Fraternity must serve the Negro masses, not with burnt offerings nor with rare and precious incense, but with earnest and conscientious effort in their behalf." He continued, "We must make our education and our Fraternity the gateway to a new conciliation with the other half, rather than a barrier from it."[37] The comments made by Bond spoke directly to the significance of education for African Americans and provided insight into and validation for the very existence of Kappa Alpha Psi. Bond's remarks were among several profound statements of continued purpose that were uttered during the 1935 Grand Chapter in St. Louis, Missouri. Although the fraternity was marking twenty-four years of existence, the spirit of celebration would not overwhelm the continuing plight of African Americans.

BGLOs during the 1920s and 1930s pushed for innovative ways to combat racial inequality. For instance, in 1937 Lionel F. Artis, the editor in chief of the *Kappa Alpha Psi Journal,* implored his fraternity brothers to take seriously the antilynching legislation known as the Gavagan Bill. To show its support, Kappa Alpha Psi printed the bill in its entirety in the fraternity magazine in an effort to educate members about its specifics. In a heartfelt plea, Artis encouraged members to mobilize and contact their respective senators and stressed the importance of solidarity among African Americans on this issue. Artis informed the readership, "Legislation pending in the Senate must have the firm support of Negroes themselves if it is to pass."[38] Drawing on a sense of disillusionment, Artis pointed out the hypocrisy of African Americans' willingness to fight for the honor of the United States yet being denied the same freedoms that, as U.S. troops, they were seeking to secure for foreign nations. Thus, the organ of the fraternity was a tool of social action for the membership as well as those outside the ranks of Kappa Alpha Psi.

In keeping with the spirit of social action, the members of Kappa Alpha Psi moved to show that they "were not just a bunch of men miseducated and only interested in 'wine, women, and song'"—that they were active in such civic organizations as the NAACP.[39] Additionally, members of Kappa Alpha Psi openly supported the Congress of Industrial Organizations because of its stand against limiting membership in labor unions along racial and ethnic lines.

Conventions such as the Thirty-sixth Grand Chapter (1946) became forums for dialogue and resolutions to take social action against racially discriminatory practices such as restrictive covenants, to support the nondiscrimination policies of state agencies of the U.S. Employment Service, or to back the passage of legislation for the creation of a permanent Fair Employment Commission. The men of Kappa Alpha Psi used their Grand Chapters for more than just pomp and circumstance. They addressed fraternal as well and societal concerns, especially those that furthered the cause of African Americans and solidified the place of fraternities with the evolving civil rights movement.

Tom Bradley, former mayor of Los Angeles and Grand Polemarch, was dedicated to and embraced a more involved role for the fraternity in the civil rights arena. Speaking to the need for change in the 1960s, he implored his fraternity brothers: "The fraternity system can no longer function as the social outlet on a small tributary of the main stream of society. In the midst of scientific, technological, and social revolutions there is an urgent need for the fraternities to rethink their role in order that they be relevant to the times. We must look inward to identify our new responsibilities in view of our natural responsibility to mold leadership."[40]

Bradley further admonished his brethren to rethink the purpose of their brotherhood in terms of an abiding commitment to every aspect of society, from foreign policy to the economic disparities of the ghettos of America.[41] Tragically, the Watts riots occurred in August 1965 while Bradley was mayor, and the fraternity proudly recognized his leadership during that crisis, not only for the city but also for the black community in particular. With the ongoing changes that were occurring in American society due to the demands of the black freedom movement, as well as various challenges to public policy culminating with protests over the Vietnam conflict, Kappa Alpha Psi created a social action program. Led by Elmer Henderson, a committee was assembled to determine how the fraternity could best address the issues that pertained to its members and to the African American community.[42]

Omega Psi Phi

Omega Psi Phi, founded at Howard University on November 17, 1911, was the first fraternity established at a historically black college. The founders' inability to climb socially (they were "teachers, lawyers, physicians and clergymen") was linked to "barriers of race prejudice."[43] Committed to the four cardinal principles of "Scholarship, Manhood, Perseverance, and Uplift," the founders and members of Omega Psi Phi dedicated themselves to being more than mere scholars and expressed a sincere commitment to "lift up their down trodden brothers and sisters."[44]

The influence of BGLOs could not have come at a better time. In 1915, one of the most racist pieces of propaganda ever created was being hailed as a brilliant cinematic masterpiece.[45] D. W. Griffith's film *The Birth of a Nation* harmed the perception of African Americans and created a resurgence in the Ku Klux Klan that civic and fraternal organizations would have to speak out against. President Woodrow Wilson claimed that the damning film of the Civil War Lost Cause was like "writing history with lightning."[46] Thus the racial climate was quite antagonistic. The founders of Omega Psi Phi saw the need to address issues pertaining to people of color and worked to assist in the progress of their fellow Americans of African descent.[47]

Evidence of Omega's understanding of the importance of social action and support for racial progress is seen by the fraternity's life membership (purchased in 1926) in the Association for the Study of Negro Life and History, created by fraternity member and noted historian Carter G. Woodson. Omega Psi Phi also purchased a life membership with the NAACP and regularly contributed to the National Urban League.[48] The fraternity's involvement in these organizations was intended not only to support them but also "to help inspire in the Negro pride and to move him to creative action."[49]

An understanding of the need for self-knowledge highlighted the importance of African American history. Again, the words and urgings of Woodson made a profound impact on the fraternity. At the Ninth Annual Conclave, Woodson spoke about the need to address the ignorance of the masses of African Americans with regard to their own history. In his estimation, addressing this need would generate even more leadership among the masses. Simply put, knowledge of self would lead to self-determination, and the "Negro History Literature Achievement Week" project of Omega Psi Phi was born.[50]

Under the leadership of Linwood G. Koger, this new project began an intensive campaign both among fraternity members and among the African American masses. During the Ninth Annual Conclave, Koger claimed that Omega Psi Phi decided to "throw the strength of the entire organization behind an effort to inform the Negro of his past, to inspire race pride and thus stimulate noble race achievement."[51] To salute Woodson, Omega Psi Phi assisted in the development of future leaders and racial pride by engaging in a program of exposing African Americans to their own history. The fraternity recorded numerous successes with the program. "A great interest has been shown by the public," reported E. W. Green in 1921.[52] This program was run by the fraternity from 1921 until 1924, when Woodson took over its implementation. He changed the name to "Negro History Week" and moved the celebration from April to February (it eventually evolved into today's Black History Month). The fraternity, however, reinstated a similar program called "Negro Achievement Week," with a focus on contemporary accomplishments rather than past achievements. One important aspect of the new program was the identification of its target audience. Whereas the initial program had been geared toward undergraduates, the new one was constructed not "for the wise and the sophisticated, but for the boys and girls, young men and women, and the untutored, in order that they might be inspired to noble achievement through the example of their forefathers and the achievement of contemporaneous Negroes."[53]

The program was so successful, in fact, that it was made a formal program on November 10, 1935, sponsored by the Alpha Chapter at Howard University. Part of the program consisted of a radio broadcast, and of note is an address given by Dr. William J. Thompkins entitled "The Rise of Negro Business."[54] A discussion of business and African Americans' place within it was of paramount interest to the men of Omega. The fraternity believed that African Americans would fully rise and move forward as a people once their economic condition was lifted. Every African American institution from the church to politics was, in the fraternity's view, in a dilapidated state because African Americans were poor.[55] The fraternity thus began to circulate pamphlets not just on African American history but also on ways to secure economic independence for descendants of transplanted Africans. In their attempt to inspire racial pride, Omega Psi Phi diligently worked to show "the manhood of the race in the aspirations of the Negro generally."[56]

Delta Sigma Theta

From its founding on January 13, 1913, on the campus of Howard University, the twenty-two founders of Delta Sigma Theta Sorority envisioned an organization that would advance the scope and span of sorority life. The founders believed that "the times demanded of women everywhere evidence of their emancipated thinking and acting."[57] Seeing themselves as women destined to make lasting contributions to the struggle for racial and gender equality, Delta's founders knew that it was imperative to "set for themselves new goals which would lift the sorority to higher and wider levels of endeavor than mere fraternal comradeship."[58] Toward that end, in March 1913, just two months after its founding, the sorority participated in a march for women's suffrage in Washington, D.C. That public act, aside from making visible the racial and gender consciousness of the founders, also placed the sorority among the vanguard in social activism at the turn of the twentieth century and beyond.

As a new sorority looking to fortify itself, the first decade of Delta's existence focused on nationalization and programmatic structure. In 1913, the charter of the sorority stipulated that the "particular purpose and object of [Delta Sigma Theta] shall be to establish and maintain high standards of morality and scholarship among women generally."[59] As such, the sorority's earliest programs emphasized education. In addition to instituting numerous scholarship funds for members and nonmembers, under the leadership of first national president Sadie T. M. Alexander, the sorority implemented "May Week," the objective of which was to stress the importance of higher education for young women. First observed in 1921, May Week remains an integral part of Delta's tradition.[60]

Aside from its emphasis on service and philanthropy, the sorority held fast to its social activist roots. Throughout the national conventions held during the 1920s, the women of Delta Sigma Theta resolved to take critical stands on issues of racial concern. Under the direction of third president Ethel LaMay Calimese, the sorority introduced its National Vigilance Committee. The goals of the committee were to address political issues relevant to African Americans, endorse the appointment of African Americans to policy-making positions, and lobby the federal government on a number of issues of international and domestic concern.[61] Among the issues addressed by the committee were antilynching legislation, anti–poll tax bills, and foreign policy—specifically, the U.S. government's role in the affairs of Haiti.[62] In addition to the activities of the National Vigilance Committee, Delta continued its support of other groups that were committed to fighting inequality, such as the NAACP, the National Council of Negro Women, and the National Urban League.

With the attack on Pearl Harbor in 1941 and impending U.S. entry into World War II, the sorority turned its attention to the war effort. For Delta, as for many other civil and human rights organizations of the era, World War II was another opportunity to bring the nation's attention to racial inequality in the states. On the heels of A. Philip Randolph's proposed March on Washington in 1941 and President Roosevelt's executive order to end discrimination in defense industry employment practices, Delta saw an opportunity for even more expansion. During the war, Delta created its Job Analysis and Opportunities Project. This project not only brought attention to the racially charged climate of government and private industry but also emphasized "equitable exposure of Negro women to job opportunities."[63] The project sought to "utilize the wealth of leadership in Delta Sigma Theta in order to give direction, aid and advice in the economic problems of Negro women."[64]

As society moved into the period that many historians term the "modern civil rights movement," the sorority began to evaluate the effectiveness of its national programs. Aside from its active membership in the American

Council on Human Rights, the sorority, under the leadership of tenth national president Dorothy I. Height, implemented a five-point program. One of those points—political awareness and involvement—remains at the heart of Delta's social activist agenda today.

As the civil rights movement evolved, Delta would have to forge a response to calls for racial equality heard throughout the South and the rest of the nation. During the presidencies of Dorothy Penman Harrison, Jeanne Noble, and Geraldine Pittman Woods, the sorority indeed set a pattern for its involvement in the ongoing struggle for black freedom.[65] During the terms of these three Delta presidents, the sorority funneled financial resources to aid the Little Rock Nine in their efforts to desegregate Central High School, raised money to pay fines and bonds for those freedom fighters arrested during sit-ins and other demonstrations, and established its Social Action Commission—the current aegis of Delta's political awareness and involvement thrust. The Social Action Commission was, in many ways, the descendant of the National Vigilance Committee. Its primary mission was to lobby for civil rights legislation and provide information to sorority members and localities about issues of concern to the black community.[66]

As the movement progressed, the sorority continued to reassess its role. In 1963, the year of the sorority's golden anniversary, the sorority gathered in New York City for its Twenty-seventh National Convention. The theme of the convention—"The Past Is Prologue"— was quite appropriate.[67] In her presidential address, Jeanne Noble reminded her sorors, "We may have come to greet each other, to transact Delta business, but lest we forget the subordinate goals of our existence as an organization, we do well to remember that the single most pressing issue of 1963, as it was in 1913 and 100 years ago, is the need to expand the drive for freedom!"[68] With those words in mind, members of Delta Sigma Theta pledged their commitment to the August 28, 1963, March on Washington for jobs and freedom and proclaimed their support for impending civil rights legislation. During the 1963 march, the women of Delta Sigma Theta walked under the banner of Delta, as their founders had done in 1913 to obtain voting rights for women.

Phi Beta Sigma

Also at Howard University, Phi Beta Sigma Fraternity was founded on January 9, 1914. Cognizant of the racially charged and antagonistic flare of American society, A. Langston Taylor claimed that he had come to Howard in 1910 with the idea of creating a brotherhood. Driven by that urge, it was not long before Phi Beta Sigma was realized by Taylor, along with Charles I. Brown and Leonard F. Morse. Motivated by the motto "Culture for Service, Service for Humanity," the founders of Phi Beta Sigma set out to create a brotherhood that would uphold those high ideals. For the organization, that motto was "an idealistic phrase that is broad and suggestive enough to embrace middle class, liberal and revolutionary traditions."[69]

The first testing ground for "revolutionary traditions" was the drive to create camps for the training of African American officers in the military. The start of World War I ushered in a new phase in American history. Largely thought of as the epitome of isolationism, the United States thrust itself into the international stage and made the world safe for the ideals of democracy, or so the rhetoric went. African Americans saw this as another opportunity to show that they were truly American citizens and pledged themselves to assist in the war effort overseas. But as African Americans joined the armed forces, they found that Jim Crow rules of segregation prevented them from being integrated into the developing war machine.

Ultimately, to fight against their exclusion, African Americans created an organization to petition the federal government and military officials for black officers to lead black troops. If they could not be integrated, then surely they could lead each other. The group was known as the Central Committee of Negro College Men. Phi Beta Sigma viewed this social battle as the beginning of a movement against segregation and poured its energies into the initiative. This achievement was an interfraternal one, with all four existing black fraternities cooperating.

Created at Howard University on Tuesday, May 1, 1917, the committee was chaired by T. Montgomery Gregory, a member of Phi Beta Sigma, and consisted of influential members of two other BGLOs. Frank Coleman, one of the founders of Omega Psi Phi, and Charles Hamilton Houston, the great legal strategist and prominent member of Alpha Phi Alpha, were also part of the initial movement to create officer camps for African American men.[70] In an effort to keep up the spirits of those who did enlist, the Central Committee issued a statement of support whereby the cause for social action was infused with the call to arms: "The Government has challenged the Negro race to prove its worth, particularly the worth of its educated leaders. . . . We must succeed and pour into the camp in overwhelming numbers. Let no man slack."[71] Likewise, Phi Beta Sigma would not slack in its involvement with social action.

After the war's end, African Americans did not see any real lessening of their second-class status within the American democracy. Social equality seemed more of a disillusioning dream than ever before, since many African American soldiers had been treated as equals by foreign allies. Phi Beta Sigma approached the situation with concern and found ways to mobilize its members for what lay ahead. The war taught them and other African Americans that, "elsewhere, what started out to be a great crusade had changed into something very different indeed."[72]

Zeta Phi Beta

On January 16, 1920, Zeta Phi Beta Sorority was founded on the campus of Howard University. The founders' ideals, coupled with the ambitions of two members of Phi Beta Sigma Fraternity Inc.—Charles Robert Samuel Taylor and A. Langston Taylor—led to Zeta's founding as the fraternity's sister organization,[73] a relationship made official in their respective constitutions. The women of Zeta Phi Beta, bound together with the men of Phi Beta Sigma, pledged themselves to "furthering the cause of education by encouraging the highest standards of scholarship among college women; uplifting worthwhile projects on college campuses and within communities in which we may be located; furthering the spirit of sisterly love and promoting the ideals of finer womanhood."[74]

Throughout the 1920s and 1930s, much of the sorority's attention was focused on acclimating itself to the new world of black Greekdom.[75] Nonetheless, during its early years, Zeta Phi Beta created programs to serve the community. During its 1935 boulé, the sorority inaugurated its National Recreation Project, aimed at creating meaningful and wholesome leisure activities for children.[76]

Taking cues from social trends and events, Zeta Phi Beta also assembled strategies and developed programs to address the community's social, economic, and political problems. Zeta's first major venture into the arena of social action came during World War II, when the sorority developed its National Housing Project. With this project, the sorority was directly involved with the U.S. government and its efforts to find housing for employees in the defense industry. According to Zeta historian and twelfth International Grand Basileus Lullelia Harrison: "The sorors contacted homes where there were vacant rooms, homes from which men had gone into service, homes in which the housekeeper lived alone, and homes in which rooms were vacant because of death. The housekeepers of these homes were persuaded to open their doors to many war workers seeking shelter. The response was excellent."[77] Such a project directly addressed the issues of poverty, substandard housing, or the lack of housing for wartime workers. Moreover, in 1947, the sorority joined the ACHR and introduced another hallmark program, its National Juvenile Delinquency Project. Tackling the issue of juvenile delinquency, which was quite prevalent during the latter part of the 1940s, the sorority once again pressed forward to become more socially involved.[78]

As the civil rights movement evolved during the 1950s and 1960s, Zeta once again turned its attention to the issue of housing. This time, however, the sorority focused on the desegregation of public housing. Aside from working with legislators in an effort to pass laws favoring low-income persons, the sorority interviewed many of the underprivileged to hear their concerns and drafted resolutions based on those concerns—thereby calling for adequate housing on their behalf.[79]

Sigma Gamma Rho

The youngest sorority of the Divine Nine, Sigma Gamma Rho was founded on November 12, 1922, on the campus of Butler University in Indianapolis, Indiana. Originally founded as a professional sorority for teachers, Sigma Gamma Rho's initial purposes were, first, "to inculcate principles of high ideals and proficiency among teachers; second, to stimulate a feeling of sociability and to preserve in after years the friendship of college days; and third, to provide a common meeting ground where a selected group might meet to advance Negro citizenship, not as reformers but as educated women devoted to the preservation of American ideals."[80] Seeing a need to connect with persons outside of the teaching profession, the sorority would soon expand its ranks to include women from a variety of fields and occupations. With the founding of Sigma Gamma Rho, we see the black sorority movement in full operation—and with it, the formation of programs aimed at changing the very nature of society.

Nationalization and service played a major part in the early development of Sigma Gamma Rho. Members of the young sorority realized early on their responsibility as black women in the push for racial equality. Ethel Smith, past Grand Basileus of the sorority, urged her sorors to "make our future plan a contribution of our time to educational uplift of the masses."[81] And it was with such foresight that the women of Sigma Gamma Rho set forth to structure their national programs.

During the 1930s, the sorority implemented its National Vocational Guidance Program, through which members provided counseling services to skilled and semiskilled workers in myriad fields. During this same period, to support the efforts by other organizations to ensure a better quality of life for African Americans, the sorority pledged full cooperation with and affiliation to the NAACP and obtained a life membership in the Association for the Study of Negro Life and History.[82]

Like the Zetas during the 1940s, Sigma Gamma Rho also established a program aimed at curbing the rise in juvenile delinquency. That program, entitled "Sigma Teen Town," led to the opening of youth centers that offered young people alternative and productive activities.[83] Moreover, the sorority's Literary Contest Committee made juvenile delinquency the theme of its 1945 contest, with the following specific topics: "Delinquency, Its Treatment and Prevention," "Delinquency Threatens Victory," "Here's How Youth Can Curb Delinquency," "When the Night Has Passed, Then What?" and "Relationship of Delinquency to Early Marriage."[84] The overwhelming response from youth throughout the country proved that the sorority's efforts had been worthwhile.

During the 1950s and the 1960s, Sigma Gamma Rho expanded its scope to become actively involved in the civil rights movement. Besides becoming an active member of the ACHR—joining six other BGLOs—the sorority continued its avid financial support of the NAACP's legal defense and educational funds. The sorority also implemented national antipoverty programs and vocally supported President Lyndon Johnson's antipoverty campaign.[85]

Iota Phi Theta

The last of the Divine Nine BGLOs to be incorporated has an interesting and powerful story, not only because of the date of its founding but also because of its relevance to the ideal of social action. It could be argued that the founding of Iota Phi Theta Fraternity on September 19, 1963, at Morgan State University was itself an instance of social activism. That year was an important one for the black freedom movement in many ways. It signaled a new era in the movement and the push for civil rights. On the same day as the March on Washington, the charismatic intellectual W. E. B. DuBois, known for his many essays and countless speeches and books, passed away while in Ghana, estranged from the land of his birth. This is significant because, ostensibly, the proverbial torch was passed to the next generation of activists and intellectuals. As the culminating event of the civil rights movement in terms of protest, the March on Washington also ushered in a new era in the BGLO movement. The eight other existing organizations had been born during the turbulent turn of the century. Not too far past the midcentury point, the need to organize fraternally arose again.

The founders of Iota Phi Theta were determined to create an organization and structure it in a way that was emblematic of the egalitarian promise of America. Thus, the excitement generated by the March on Washington opened up new possibilities for social action. Iota Phi Theta focused its efforts not on African Americans but on Americans in general. However, it can still claim strong support for the NAACP, United Negro College Fund, Southern Christian Leadership Conference (SCLC), and National Sickle Cell Foundation, just to name a few. Considering themselves militant when it was unpopular to do so, the members of Iota Phi Theta were indeed committed to social action and have maintained an active role in the continuing struggle for equality for African Americans.

The Cause Continues

These glimpses of the social action programs and initiatives of the BGLOs from their inception through the latter part of the civil rights movement illustrate the importance of social action to each organization and its history. The formation of BGLOs, aside from creating a social space for many African Americans, has even more to do with their members' embodiment of racialized progress. At many points throughout the black freedom movement, BGLOs were instruments of social change. Moving past these brief examples allows for discussion about the continuing struggle of these organizations to remain dedicated to the causes of social uplift and racial progress, not simply as displays put on for potential new members but as integral parts of their identity. Moreover, it is not enough to glorify past achievements and movements or to revel and romanticize those members who have shone as luminaries of activism. For BGLOs to remain viable in these changing times, each organization must measure how far it is extending its effectiveness to meet the needs and obligations of the present day.

As Stephanie Y. Evans stated so eloquently in an article on BGLOs and civic responsibility, "The founders of BGLOs have laid down a challenge for contemporary members of their organizations. Meeting this challenge will further the legacy of BGLOs; however, failing to do so means squandering our potential political power and succumbing to the critique of organizational irrelevance at a time when political activism is most needed."[86]

According to statistics compiled by the Bureau of Labor, as of December 2005, the African American unemployment rate was 9.3 percent—far above the national average of 4.6 percent. In 2004, one in four—or 9 million—African Americans lived in poverty, the majority of whom were children.[87] According to a report from the Centers for Disease Control, in 2004, although African Americans accounted for less than a quarter of the U.S. population, they accounted for about half the people infected with HIV and AIDS. And according to information from thirty-three states, between the years 2001 and 2004, among women, more than half (68 percent) of the new cases of HIV/AIDS were among African Americans.[88] The issues of poverty, unemployment, and the AIDS epidemic are just a few that continue to plague our domestic and global communities.

As the Divine Nine continue to move forward—setting their agendas for the twenty-first century—the question remains: Where do we go from here? In his last presidential address to the SCLC, Dr. Martin Luther King Jr. asked this very question. He told his audience that in order to know where to go, "we must first honestly recognize where we are now."[89] The statistics he cited in 1968 to explain where African Americans were then were just as sobering as the ones mentioned here. Similar to King's beseeching of the SCLC to appraise its plans for the future is the call for BGLOs to evaluate where they are at this moment in history and where they see themselves going. As we approach the celebration of a century of intercollegiate fraternal and sororal involvement, a true assessment must ensue so that BGLOs can move beyond the rhetoric.

In 2004, *Black Issues in Higher Education* addressed the historic nature of the beginning of a new century for BGLOs and contextualized the moment by interviewing prominent members of several such organizations. One of these was Dr. Ricky Jones, author of *Black Haze: Violence, Sacrifice, and Manhood in Black Greek Letter Fraternities* and a member of Kappa Alpha Psi. Jones argued that "Black Greeks will be meaningless to Black Life overall until the BGLOs collectively work to establish a progressive, social, political and economic agenda."[90] Jones continued his critical assessment by positing a rhetorical query: Could anyone think of an issue on any level of politics where BGLOs had taken a strong stance?

Offering a rebuttal was Darryl Matthews Sr., executive director of the National Association of Black Accountants Inc. and the current general president of Alpha Phi Alpha Fraternity Inc. He mentioned how complex and difficult it is for

BGLOs to make political statements in a partisan way, owing to the complicated status of the membership. However, although in his current position he cannot be partisan, that does not keep him from being political. Speaking specifically to his own organization, he emphatically declared, "Our agenda transcends partisan politics."[91] All agendas of BGLOs should transcend partisanship based on their mottos, mission statements, and aims.

Carter G. Woodson noted, "One of the most striking evidences of the failure of higher education among Negroes is their estrangement from the masses, the very people upon whom they must eventually count for carrying out a program of progress."[92] This statement is very much aligned with the perspective of those who have criticized BGLOs over the years. According to Paula Giddings, "As one of the very few closed-membership organizations in the black community, and the only ones that required a college education, [African American fraternities and] sororities were particularly vulnerable to the stereotypes of a less than serious bourgeoisie class that was insensitive to the needs of the less fortunate."[93] Unfortunately, even today, these sentiments still ring true. Despite everything the organizations of the Divine Nine have done through the years in terms of service and activism, many nonmembers still perceive BGLOs as elitist and members as only superficially committed to social activism.

This perception exists partly because the projects and programs of BGLOs, though well orchestrated, are out of sight, whereas our soirées and other social events are quite visible. As BGLOs continue to evaluate their relevancy, they must work even harder to make known their foundational commitment to social action. BGLOs, in their position as long-standing social institutions of the black community, will undoubtedly continue to struggle to overcome the pitfalls of elitism. In making more of an effort to tailor their image and more efficiently address the issues currently facing African Americans, BGLOs must make strides to ally themselves with other bedrock institutions in our communities, such as the black church. Heeding the words of Dr. Martin Luther King Jr. when he affirmed, "we have been oppressed as a group and we must overcome that oppression as a group," BGLOs must not confine their efforts to mere organizational triumph but make the cause of social change a communal goal.[94]

BGLOs have gone through cycles in which their social activist foundations have been revisited and reevaluated. In an address by E. Franklin Frazier at Delta's Twenty-fourth National Convention, he stated the following: "Self-analysis and self-criticism are signs of maturity on the part of people, because they are an indication of a developed self-consciousness and the intellectual freedom which is a part of self-consciousness."[95] In 1938, writing for the *Oracle,* the national organ of Omega Psi Phi, John Aubrey Davis scolded BGLOs when he stated, "the Negro fraternity has become almost a meaningless hulk without vitality and even inadequately expressing the ideals and aims of the staggering Negro petty bourgeois." In his view, BGLOs were devolving into mere social clubs that spoke highly of past achievements but failed to press forward and live up to what they claimed to be through their mission statements, mottos, and aims. Addressing how they could gain back their "vigor," Davis implored his fraternal brethren and all BGLO members to ally themselves with "the most vital of the present social movements."[96] It is amazing that words spoken almost seventy years ago reverberate with even more clarity today.

While awaiting the pomp and circumstance of various centennial celebrations and dealing with continued threats to their existence due to litigation involving hazing, BGLOs should be focused on rededicating themselves to their original aims and plans and packaging themselves for relevancy in today's society. If steps are not taken to honestly evaluate where it is and where it needs to go, each BGLO runs the risk of becoming an organization "for the amusement of the undergraduate, a pawn for politicians seeking national recognition, a bourgeois club in an essentially working class race, and an anathema to its elder fathers."[97]

Notes

The epigraph was the slogan for the "Go to High School, Go to College" Program of Alpha Phi Alpha Fraternity in 1924.

1. Martin Luther King Jr., *Where Do We Go from Here? Chaos or Community* (New York: Beacon Press, 1968).

2. Rayford Logan, *The Betrayal of the Negro: From Rutherford B. Hayes to Woodrow Wilson* (New York: Da Capo Press, 1997), 52.

3. See the discussion of eugenicists Lothrop Stoddard and Madison Grant in Matthew Guterl's *The Color of Race in America, 1900–1940* (Cambridge, Mass.: Harvard University Press, 2001).

4. In January 1941, A. Phillip Randolph, president of the Brotherhood of Sleeping Car Porters, pushed for African Americans to march on Washington to demand employment of blacks in wartime industries. The march, scheduled to take place on July 1, 1941, alarmed many governmental officials, particularly President Franklin Roosevelt. After several meetings between the two men, Roosevelt assured Randolph that if he called off the march, Roosevelt would issue an order to address inequity in the defense industry. With that, the march was called off, and on June 25, 1941, Roosevelt issued Executive

Order 8802, which stated the following: "there shall be no discrimination in the employment of workers in defense industries or Government because of race, creed, color, or national origin." The executive order included a clause prohibiting discrimination in all defense contracts, and it created a Fair Employment Practices Committee to receive and investigate complaints of discrimination in violation of the order. See the discussion in John Hope Franklin's *From Slavery to Freedom: A History of African Americans* (New York: McGraw-Hill), 1994, 436–37.

5. Kevin K. Gaines, *Uplifting the Race: Black Leadership, Politics, and Culture in the Twentieth Century* (Chapel Hill: University of North Carolina Press, 1996), 20.

6. W. E. B. DuBois, "The Talented Tenth," in *The Negro Problem: A Series of Articles by Representative Negroes of To-day* (New York: James Pott and Company, 1903).

7. Joy James, *Transcending the Talented Tenth: Black Leaders and American Intellectuals* (New York: Routledge, 1997), 15–33.

8. Charles Harris Wesley, *The History of Alpha Phi Alpha: A Development in College Life*, 16th printing (Baltimore: Foundation Publishers, 1996), xiii.

9. Herman Mason Jr., *Talented Tenth: The Founders and Presidents of Alpha*, 2nd ed. (Winter Park, Fla.: Four-G Publishers, 1999), 390.

10. Ibid.

11. Ibid., 265.

12. Wesley, *History of Alpha Phi Alpha*, 100.

13. Kenneth R. Janken, *Rayford W. Logan and the Dilemma of the African American Intellectual* (Amherst: University of Massachusetts Press, 1993), 99.

14. Wesley, *History of Alpha Phi Alpha*, 210.

15. Ibid., 101–7.

16. Ibid., 204–5. See also the discussion in Janken, *Rayford W. Logan*, 103.

17. Janken, *Rayford W. Logan*, 103.

18. Wesley, *History of Alpha Phi Alpha*, 202. Worthy of mention is that some years later, twenty-ninth general president Milton C. Davis, as assistant attorney general for the state of Alabama, was a driving force for the pardon of the last of the Scottsboro Boys, Clarence Norris, in 1976.

19. Wesley, *History of Alpha Phi Alpha*, 217.

20. Ibid., 216–19.

21. Ibid., 280.

22. Ibid., 354.

23. Marjorie H. Parker, *The Past Is Prologue: The History of Alpha Kappa Alpha, 1908–1999* (Washington, D.C.: Author, 1999), 181.

24. Ibid., 184, 185.

25. Marjorie H. Parker, *Alpha Kappa Alpha: In the Eye of the Beholder* (Washington, D.C.: Alpha Kappa Alpha Sorority, 1979), 30.

26. Parker, *Past Is Prologue*, 187.

27. Ibid., 194.

28. Ibid.

29. Delta Sigma Theta Sorority Inc. was also a member.

30. Parker, *Past Is Prologue,* 195–96.

31. For more details, see Robert L. Harris Jr., "Lobbying for Civil Rights: The American Council on Human Rights, 1948–1963," in *African American Fraternities and Sororities: The Legacy and the Vision,* ed. Tamara L. Brown, Gregory S. Parks, and Clarenda M. Phillips (Lexington: University Press of Kentucky, 2005).

32. William L. Crump, *The Story of Kappa Alpha Psi: A History of the Beginnings and Development of a College Greek Letter Organization, 1911–1991,* 4th ed. (Philadelphia: Kappa Alpha Psi Fraternity International Headquarters, 1991), 5.

33. "The Guide Right Movement of Kappa Alpha Psi," *Kappa Alpha Psi Journal,* April 19, 1925, 11.

34. Crump, *Story of Kappa Alpha Psi,* 135.

35. "Guide Right Movement of Kappa Alpha Psi."

36. Ibid.

37. Crump, *Story of Kappa Alpha Psi,* 134.

38. "Anti-Lynch Legislation," *Kappa Alpha Psi Journal* 23, no. 6 (April 1937): 153.

39. "Kappa Alpha Psi Aids N.A.A.C.P. Cause," *Kappa Alpha Psi Journal* 23, no. 6 (April 1937): 155.

40. Crump, *Story of Kappa Alpha Psi,* 293.

41. See "State of the Fraternity Message for Fifty-third Grand Chapter," in ibid., 361, 362.

42. Ibid., 362–63.

43. Herman Dreer, *The History of Omega Psi Phi Fraternity, Inc.* (Washington, D.C.: Omega Psi Phi, 1940).

44. "Supplement to History of the Omega Psi Phi Fraternity," in ibid., 25.

45. The film, based primarily on the novel *The Klansman* by Thomas Dixon, became a rallying cry for the second resurgence of the Ku Klux Klan. The influx in membership ushered in a new era of racial hatred and violence toward African Americans. Griffith's motion picture labeled black men as rapists, criminals, and subhuman creatures bent on all manner of debased activity and the defilement of white women. For a more involved discussion, see Glenda Gilmore, *Gender and Jim Crow* (Chapel Hill: University of North Carolina Press, 1996).

46. Lewis Jacobs, *The Rise of the American Film* (New York: Harcourt, Brace, 1939), 175.

47. Dreer, *History of Omega Psi Phi,* 13.

48. Ibid., 143–45.

49. "Supplement to History of Omega Psi Phi," 25.

50. Dreer, *History of Omega Psi Phi,* 153.

51. Ibid.

52. Ibid., 155.

53. Ibid., 160.

54. Ibid., 168–69.

55. Ibid., 175–76.

56. Ibid., 179.

57. Mary Elizabeth Vroman, *Shaped to Its Purpose: Delta Sigma Theta: The First Fifty Years* (Random House: New York, 1965), 12.

58. Ibid.

59. Paula Giddings, *In Search of Sisterhood: Delta Sigma Theta and the Challenges of the Black Sorority Movement* (New York: William Morrow, 1988), 125.

60. Vroman, *Shaped to Its Purpose*, 25–26.

61. Ibid., 40.

62. Giddings, *In Search of Sisterhood*, 129–30.

63. Ibid., 195.

64. Ibid.

65. Ibid., 241.

66. Ibid., 262.

67. Ibid., 261.

68. Ibid.

69. W. Sherman Savage and L. D. Reddick, *Our Cause Speeds On—An Informal History of the Phi Beta Sigma Fraternity* (Atlanta: Fuller Press, 1957), 23.

70. Emmett J. Scott, *The American Negro in the World War* (New York: Arno Press, 1969), 84.

71. Ibid., 88–89.

72. Savage and Reddick, *Our Cause Speeds On*, 31.

73. Lullelia W. Harrison, *Torchbearers of a Legacy: A History of Zeta Phi Beta Sorority, Inc., 1920–1997* (Washington, D.C.: Zeta Phi Beta Sorority Inc., 1998), 1.

74. Ibid., 5.

75. Ibid., 29.

76. Ibid., 160.

77. Ibid.

78. Ibid., 161.

79. Ibid., 165.

80. Pearl Schwartz White, *Behind These Doors—A Legacy: The History of Sigma Gamma Rho Sorority, Inc.* (Chicago: Sigma Gamma Rho Sorority, 1974), 190.

81. Ibid., 14.

82. Ibid., 18.

83. Ibid., 40.

84. Ibid., 42.

85. Ibid., 101.

86. Stephanie Y. Evans, "Black Greek-Lettered Organizations and Civic Responsibility," *Black Issues in Higher Education*, October 7, 2004.

87. U.S. Census Bureau Web site, www.census.gov.

88. Centers for Disease Control Web site, www.cdc.gov.

89. James M. Washington, ed., *A Testament of Hope: The Essential Writings and Speeches of Martin Luther King, Jr.* (San Francisco: HarperSanFrancisco, 1991), 245.

90. Paul Ruffins, "Looking toward the Future: New Research Helps Black Sororities and Fraternities Consider New Governing Structures for the Next 100 Years," *Black Issues in Higher Education,* June 17, 2004.

91. Telephone interview with Darryl Matthews, July 2, 2006.

92. Carter G. Woodson, *The Mis-Education of the Negro* (Washington, D.C.: AMS Press, 1933), 52.

93. Giddings, *In Search of Sisterhood,* 144.

94. King, *Where Do We Go from Here?* 125.

95. Vroman, *Shaped to Its Purpose,* 153.

96. John A. Davis, "The Social Function of the Negro Fraternity," *Oracle,* March 1938, 23.

97. Ibid.

9

Black Feminist Thought in Black Sororities
Caryn E. Neumann

To many people, the idea of an essay on black feminist thought in black sororities is problematic. Sororities have a reputation—not entirely deserved—for being conservative organizations that engage chiefly in social activities. Many African American women, many of whom belong or belonged to historically black sororities, refuse to identify as feminists because they define feminism as a white women's movement that often excludes women of color. They also note that feminism seems to be anti-male, and as black women, they have more in common with black men than white women. However, feminist thought is evident in the histories of Alpha Kappa Alpha (AKA), Delta Sigma Theta, Sigma Gamma Rho, and Zeta Phi Beta.

Feminism is the idea that the structure and institutions of society need to be modified to enable women to achieve equality with men. The implication behind this belief is that men and women have equal abilities. Black feminism is different from white feminism, in that it emphasizes the freedom of people of color. This blend of black nationalist thought with feminism has been called "womanism" by Alice Walker and others. In her 1983 book *In Search of Our Mother's Gardens,* Walker coined the term from the folk expression, "You are acting womanish." It applies to women who behave in a bold, courageous, responsible way as agents of social change for the wholeness and liberation of black people and the rest of humanity. As self-described womanist Geneva Smitherman has noted, a womanist is rooted in the black community and is committed to the development of herself and the entire community.[1] These women are thus linked to earlier generations of "race women" who worked on behalf of black civil society. They celebrate the culture and beauty of black women.

The term *womanist* is a more comfortable fit for black women who do not identify as feminist but who support gender equity. It reflects the complexity of how black feminist practice actually operates. It suits such sorority members as Vanzetta Penn Durant of Sigma Gamma Rho, who emphatically declared in

1981 that she was not a feminist. Durant, an attorney, supported greater opportunities for women and believed that sex discrimination needed to be outlawed. However, she did not see herself as a feminist because she worked mostly with black males. She stated, "History has not been kind to them. To engage in further barrage would be unkind."[2] Womanism is a less radical political concept than feminism in the eyes of many African American women.

To recognize the unique dimensions of black feminist thought, I use the term *womanist* to describe the activities of the members of historically black sororities. Other scholars have noted that women affiliated with organizations that empower black women are more racially astute and display less conservative attitudes about gender roles.[3] However, the specific womanist histories of the sororities have not been examined. After sketching the histories of the four black sororities, I describe how their activities on behalf of the black community involved elevating the status of black women.

Sorority Beginnings

All the black sororities were founded in the age of Jim Crow in the first decades of the twentieth century. They came about because, in a society based on the dominance of the white race, black women struggled to carve out a place for themselves. Even well-educated and professional African American women were not wholeheartedly welcomed into liberal women's organizations. The many sorority members who also belonged to the American Association for University Women, the American Nurses Association, or similar groups were often members at large because few local chapters would accept blacks.[4] Sororities offered social opportunities, and most women joined for these reasons. However, black sororities also offered sisterhood, strategies for surviving in a racist world, and the opportunity to promote social justice.[5]

Begun in 1908 at historically black Howard University, AKA was the first sorority for African Americans and has enjoyed a long history of activism. The sorority quickly expanded to mixed-race campuses, part of a widespread effort by African American Greek organizations to foster community, self-respect, and a cohesive culture for black students who were greatly outnumbered on campus by their white peers.[6] Much more than a club for the African American elite, AKA promoted social and political service as part of its mission.[7] It marched for women's suffrage and provided critical financial support to the NAACP. The stated purpose of the sorority involved cultivating high ethical and scholastic standards, alleviating problems concerning women, and being of service to all people.[8] This goal did not change over time.

Delta Sigma Theta also began at Howard University. Formed on January 13, 1913, the sorority was created by disgruntled members of AKA who wanted a more politically active organization. Later that year, the Deltas became the first black sorority members to march for women's suffrage. In 1915, the Delta oath called for sorority members to pledge to never belittle the race and to "protest against the double standard of morals."[9] Interestingly, the oath was penned by Mary Church Terrell, an honorary Delta who had helped found the National Association of Colored Women in 1896. One of the best-known black leaders in the world, Terrell felt strongly that she had a duty to work for the benefit of the black race, including black women. She believed that social problems would be ameliorated with the advancement of women.[10] Befitting an organization that would honor Terrell, Delta has long had the reputation of being the most political of all the sororities. In the 1970s, it became explicitly a social service organization instead of a social organization. Historically, it has the largest membership of the four sororities.

The women of Zeta Phi Beta also accepted responsibility for uplifting the black race. This sorority began at Howard University on January 16, 1920, as the sister organization to Phi Beta Sigma Fraternity. It subscribed to some of the same tenets as AKA and Delta but based its constitution on that of the Sigmas. The Zetas aimed to develop the ideals of service, educational and scholastic achievement, civic and cultural involvement, sisterhood, and finer womanhood. From the start, Zeta has sought to remove blocks intended to retard the growth and progress of black women. With its credo of "Enhance, Accomplish, Serve," the sorority members have recognized their obligations as educated black women. To promote community uplift, Zeta has addressed the topics of unwed mothers, juvenile delinquency, and indigent families. The sorority has emphasized racial pride and was the first sorority to establish international chapters in West Africa.[11] It is the smallest of the sororities.

Sigma Gamma Rho, the youngest of the sororities, was organized on November 12, 1922, on the campus of Butler University in Indianapolis, Indiana. Unlike the other sororities, Sigma was founded at a predominantly white institution. It also began in a state that, in the 1920s, was the center of Ku Klux Klan activity. African American students were not permitted to join the all-white Greek sororities at Butler, and considering the climate of the era, it would have been unwise to press the matter. The seven founders of Sigma were all teachers who wanted to promote sisterhood among black women. They envisioned a sorority composed entirely of teachers that would offer support as well as professional de-

172 Caryn E. Neumann

velopment. However, they soon realized that teaching went far beyond the walls of the classroom and that community service was essential to educating black children. Sigma would become the sorority most concerned with education. It began the Sigma Gamma Rho National Education Fund to give scholarships to students and has long supported the United Negro College Fund.[12]

What a Woman Should Be and Do

While men in the twentieth century focused on public protests and a legalistic strategy, women's organizations often took a different approach to the betterment of the black race. Less involved with formal politics, black women devoted the majority of their attention to promoting change within the black community. The family roles of women made them responsible for helping the family adapt to a hostile environment. This emphasis on community work shaped much of sorority activism throughout the twentieth century.

All the sororities sought to promote "finer womanhood." But what should a fine woman be and do? Such a woman earned a college degree and used it to better the lives of others. Decade after decade, sorority leaders declared that the educational achievements of sorority members obliged them to participate in community affairs.[13] In 1949, AKA Supreme Basileus Edna Over Gray congratulated new graduates by telling them that they had a great responsibility to use their training to attack prejudice and develop better human relations. Twenty-one years later, Barbara Davis, editor of AKA's *Ivy Leaf,* echoed Gray's call: "Few would deny the general belief that we as black women of high moral, scholastic, and ethical standards are accountable, liable, and responsible to our fellow blacks, our youth, our conscience and our sorority in terms of how well we have examined the issues, defined the tasks, organized the strategies, and implemented the action for . . . greater service to mankind." In 1955, the Deltas established leadership institutes to train sorority members in the various components of leadership.[14] As the educated elite within the black community, the sorority women bore the responsibility for betterment of the race.

Uplifting the Race

Boosting the quality of African American home life and educating the mothers of the race were goals traditionally held by the black women's movement. Social justice involved racial uplift. A popular self-help ideology that emerged in the years after Reconstruction and remained strong into the twentieth century, racial uplift offered an opportunity to prove that blacks deserved to take a respected position within American society.[15] For women in particular, this ideology meant much more than political and economic opportunities.

Racial uplift had its basis in a theory that whites judged blacks according to the lowest elements of the race. Therefore, for blacks to be able to acquire rights, the standard of living of the working class had to be raised. Since women bore primary responsibility for maintenance of the home and care of the children, the fate of all African Americans depended on the ability of the distaff side to perfectly perform the domestic arts. Therefore, working-class blacks received cooking, cleaning, and personal care lessons from their betters. As both Floris Barnett Cash and Deborah Gray White have argued, to many black women activists, the local focus on uplift activities seemed to be an inadequate response to the disastrous position of African American families during the Great Depression and a tepid response to the inadequate help provided to blacks by the New Deal.[16]

Pressures to abandon racial uplift in the face of Depression fears and New Deal inadequacies did not banish this objective from the minds of black sorority activists, but the criticisms may have prompted a shift to less patronizing activities. To African American elites, including the sorority women, racial uplift continued to mean an emphasis on self-help, racial solidarity, temperance, thrift, chastity, social purity, and the accumulation of wealth. It also commonly involved an emphasis on patriarchal authority, but the history of sororities shows that some women refuted this aspect of the ideology.

Black Women's Movement

By the 1930s, the sororities wanted to do more than just address specific issues as they arose. They wanted to build a movement of African American women to open all sorts of doors. The massive and conservative National Association of Colored Women (NACW) promoted racial uplift, primarily through good works at the local level. It did not prepare a comprehensive attack on the institutional and political structures that permitted racism. In 1935, the sororities joined with ten other women's organizations to establish a new group, the National Council of Negro Women (NCNW), to promote black women's concerns at the national level.

The NCNW aimed to eliminate segregation and discrimination, especially as they affected black women. Specifically, the council's founders thought that constant publicity and lobbying would make it impossible for businesses and government to ignore black women and, as a result, leadership positions would become available for these women to fill.[17] AKA backed the NCNW in the belief that the council would "give our Negro women a status." Just before making the first parliamentary motion to establish the new organization, AKA Addie Hunton bluntly stated her reasons for doing so: "There is not a great group behind our women to push them."[18] The NACW had become too deeply involved in local matters and too oriented toward self-help for it to serve as an authoritative national voice, in the opinion of sorority leaders.

The sororities never offered much more than ritual cooperation to the NCNW. However, Dorothy Height, longtime head of the Deltas, became the fourth president of the NCNW in 1957 and continued in that office for decades. Womanist leaders of the NCNW, including Height, used the large organizational membership to give them leverage in dealing with others. Black women, handicapped especially by income, gender, and race, had not traditionally exercised such leverage.[19] As sorority support of the NCNW indicates, sorority members believed that enhanced status for black women brought them the benefit of a substantial role on the national stage.

Despite the shared emphasis on a greater role for women, the black women's movement differed qualitatively from the movement led by white women. Whereas white men had obvious advantages over white women, African American men were not significantly better off than the women of the race. The belief that racial issues were more urgent than gender issues influenced the activities of African American women, including the members of the four black sororities.

Civil Rights Organizing

The success of the NCNW prompted AKA to consider forming other umbrella organizations. Like the other sororities, it often worked through coalitions of organizations with similar goals. The push for civil rights that came out of World War II prompted the development of a new organization—the American Council on Human Rights (ACHR)—which was begun in 1948 by AKA to unite the Greek organizations in a nonpartisan civil rights lobbying effort and help blacks fight for democracy at home. It had its origins in AKA's National Non-Partisan Council on Public Affairs, which had been created in 1936 to lobby Congress for civil rights. The ACHR developed in the wake of President Harry S. Truman's 1948 request that Congress enact a civil rights program and the national Democratic Party's endorsement of such a program. The four sororities joined together with Kappa Alpha Psi and Alpha Phi Alpha to create the ACHR.[20]

The ACHR, with AKA Edna Over Gray as its head and Elmer Henderson as director of staff, represented a membership of more than 70,000 people.[21] ACHR objectives matched some of Truman's goals, including passage of the Fair Employment Act; abolition of segregation and the assurance of equality of training and opportunity in the various armed services; desegregation of the armed forces, public transportation, and public accommodations; passage of antilynching, anti–poll tax, and voting rights bills; federal aid to education, with protections against discrimination; revision of the cloture rule to eliminate the filibuster in the U.S. Senate; abolition of racial discrimination in immigration and naturalization; and federal appointments of African Americans.[22]

Sorority leaders urged the membership to support the ACHR by forming local councils on human rights, lobbying congressional representatives and senators, and making every sorority woman and fraternity brother a registered voter.[23] The ACHR took credit for a number of achievements, including passage of a 1954 expansion of the Social Security Act to cover domestic workers, many of whom were African American women.

The sororities also offered crucial financial support to the NAACP, helping to keep that organization alive to pursue legal remedies for racial discrimination. The NAACP could not have fought so fiercely without the backing of women's groups. As other scholars have noted, the organizational base provided by black women helped the NAACP survive the onslaught of racial terror and red-baiting that followed the civil rights victories of the early 1950s, which had dramatically reduced the organization's membership rolls.[24] Many of the founding members of sororities had worked for the NAACP, and as time passed, the membership continued its legacy of support for this civil rights group.[25] Vashti Turley Murphy, one of the founders of Delta, argued in 1956 that the sorority should require its members to hold NAACP membership cards as well, to remain in good standing. One of AKA's fund-raising drives for the NAACP in the early 1960s collected $440,000, a substantial amount at the time.[26]

Sorority members supported the NAACP because, as educated women, they believed that they had a special responsibility to lead. As Murphy wrote, "What a tragedy it would be . . . if the best educated women in the United States, the flower of American womanhood, stood in a struggling, hesitant mass, undecided, unwilling to take the first step."[27] To make the structures and institutions of American life more equitable to women and to blacks, African American women needed to step up and take charge.

The sororities, to varying degrees, also independently offered support to the civil rights movement. The Deltas responded to the dismantling of the ACHR in 1963 by creating a Student Emergency Fund. Money raised by more than a thousand Delta chapters across the nation paid the fines and bonds of those arrested during sit-ins and other civil rights demonstrations. The fund also paid tuition for students who promoted integration.[28]

Unlike the leaders of predominantly white women's organizations, black sorority officials did not believe that membership in male-dominated organizations weakened the clout of women. They never hesitated to work with the NAACP or with the fraternities that also joined the ACHR. Unlike white feminists, sorority members did not see the interests of black men as being essentially different from the issues of black women. All African Americans wanted to advance the race.

Promoting Education

Advancement is dependent on education. Scholar Patricia Hill Collins has argued that emancipation, liberation, or empowerment for black women as a collective rests on the ability of black women to self-define or name their own reality and the ability to self-determine or decide their own destiny.[29] As AKA Alison Harris Alexander declared in 1995, "There are many means by which a people may be enslaved. The easiest way to gain control over other individuals is to keep them uneducated."[30] Accordingly, Sigma Gamma Rho joined the Assault on Illiteracy Program in 1992; its goal was to enable adults who had been failed by the educational system to read at a fourth-grade level, at least. The sorority's chapters worked through Sunday schools to promote the program.[31]

Knowledge produced by and for African American women is critical for empowerment, as the leaders of sororities fully realized. The Delta Education and Research Foundation, created in 1967, provides funds to support the research and educational projects of African American women scholars. The National Education Foundation, a Zeta project that began in 1975, encourages scholarship, educational research, and community education programs. In 1995, AKA developed the Partnership in Mathematics and Science to educate young people from toddlers on up.[32]

Just as educated women were necessary for the black community to thrive, the education of young people was critical as well. The Delta Academy was created out of an urgent sense that bold action was needed to save girls aged eleven to fourteen from the perils of academic failure, low self-esteem, and crippled futures. The program provides an opportunity for local Delta chapters to enrich and enhance the education that girls receive in public schools across the nation. Specifically, it augments their scholarship in math, science, and technology and their opportunities to provide service in the form of leadership through service learning. Typical of a sorority program, the Delta Academy promotes sisterhood among the girls and tries to prepare them to be future leaders.[33]

Mentoring is part of the process of educating young African American women so that they can make a contribution to the community. The sororities have engaged in various mentoring projects over the years. In the early 1960s, the Deltas established Teen Lift to provide guidance to teenage girls. AKA took a more innovative approach when it joined President Lyndon B. Johnson's War on Poverty.

AKA has a long-standing belief in ameliorating the effects of poverty through employment opportunities. As one of its first efforts, AKA launched a Vocational Guidance Program in 1923 to prepare young people who were not on a college track for new and varied avenues of employment. AKA was not the only historically black sorority to become involved with vocational education. Sigma Gamma Rho began its Vocational Guidance and Workshop Center in 1950 to aid minority youth.[34]

White America may have ignored the poor, as social critic Michael Harrington persuasively argued in his 1962 book *The Other America*, but black America could not forget the less fortunate, because so many of them were part of the African American community. Harrington claimed that while most Americans enjoyed rising affluence, more than 40 million people had surrendered all hope of bettering their lives in the knowledge that they had no realistic chance to enter the ranks of the middle class. Economic concerns ranked just below racial problems as the main topic of conversation among African Americans in the 1960s.[35] In this decade, poverty also began to attract considerable attention from the federal government, which would lead AKA into the antipoverty Job Corps.

The Job Corps, part of the War on Poverty, provided young men and women with the skills necessary to succeed in the workplace. In its peak year of 1967, the Job Corps had 42,000 enrollees. Most of these enrollees were male, and a substantial proportion were African American. Women were underrepresented, at less than 25 percent of participants. Job Corps planners had focused on male unemployment, based on the assumption that women's workforce participation would be interrupted by marriage and pregnancy. U.S. Representative Edith Green, a longtime women's advocate, pushed the planners to consider the prospects of young women destined to become heads of households. The Job Corps would provide basic education and work experience to advance youths as far as they could go in six months' to a year's time.[36] In 1966, there were 6 large (1,000 to 3,000 enrollees) men's centers, more than 80 smaller (100 to 250 enrollees) conservation centers that were exclusively for men, and 17 women's centers of medium size (300 to 1,000 enrollees). All these centers provided residential facilities, health care, and counseling, in addition to their educational and vocational programs. Participants received monthly living allowances.[37]

In the 1960s, AKA leaders decided that the organization should again embark on some type of antipoverty program. Domestic service and farmwork, the traditional occupations of the black poor, paid poorly and offered no hope of advancement. Additionally, and just as importantly to AKA, such workers generally lacked the educational skills that would enable them to work for the advancement of the race.[38] In 1965, the sorority joined President Johnson's plan for a Great Society, leaping at this chance to pull women into better economic circumstances. Supreme Basileus Julia Purnell obtained a contract to operate a Job Corps center that would serve 325 women annually; they would be housed in the University House, a six-story residence hall located near University Circle on the east side of Cleveland, Ohio.[39] Purnell announced AKA's sponsorship of the Job Corps to members by declaring that women had a special responsibility to mold the future so that the next generation would not "fritter away the values we cherish so much."[40] Purnell's successor as Supreme Basileus, Larzette G. Hale, voiced her support for the Job Corps by arguing that AKA must promote equality in all areas of life by helping women and girls become "more economically productive and socially useful" citizens of the United States.[41]

The War on Poverty gave AKA an opportunity to directly and significantly change the fate of generations of Americans, at little comparative risk. The government, not the sorority, financed the Job Corps center on a cost-plus basis. This program was expected to open new opportunities for young men and women, aged sixteen to twenty-one, who lacked the basic education and work skills to find permanent employment. To become eligible for the Job Corps, a young woman had to be both out of school and unable to find work.[42] In short, AKA members attempted to better the lives of a challenging population.[43] AKA officials did not choose the women who enrolled in its Jobs Corps. A private organization, Women in Community Service (WICS), recruited and screened applicants. WICS included representatives from Church Women United, a nationwide ecumenical and interracial association, and the NCNW. Both organizations counted AKA members among their ranks, so the sorority had an indirect say in Job Corps recruitment.[44]

AKA members remained dedicated to the Jobs Corps for thirty years, despite cutbacks in the program. In 1995, the sorority ended its involvement.[45] The Job Corps showed the sorority's commitment to educational achievement, particularly in the minority community. The program was a means of giving young black men and women the freedom to make choices to obtain better futures.

Helping the Black Child

Sorority members, all college-educated women aspiring to put their degrees to good use by serving as community leaders, clearly understood that the demands of child care would reduce a woman's ability to engage in activities outside the home. In Oklahoma in 1966, the Wewoka Alumnae Chapter of Delta opened a day-care center for mothers. In Baltimore that same year, Deltas began counseling unwed mothers, before the issue of single mothers captured national attention.[46] In 1981, Delta brought various black women's groups together to address poverty among black single mothers and their children. More than many political leaders, black women understood that poverty and single motherhood had many dimensions. The Deltas believed that black women were being blamed for forces beyond their control. After a second Black Women's Political Forum in 1987, which was attended by all four sororities, Delta chapters linked single mothers to appropriate agencies and services while continuing to challenge the societal stigma of unwed motherhood. Zeta chapters focused on political change. Chapters sponsored political awareness programs on upcoming legislative issues such as education, child care, public health, and social services. Zeta members developed and offered workshops to the black community on lobbying and campaigning for issues affecting black families, especially single mothers.[47]

Zeta Phi Beta and Sigma Gamma Rho did not neglect social service concerns. One of Zeta's major programs has long been the Stork's Nest, a prenatal program run in cooperation with the March of Dimes. Stork's Nests are nonprofit education and distribution centers for expectant mothers who are referred by cooperating agencies and clinics. Maternity clothes, layettes, and infant furniture are available at minimal or no cost. The centers promote early and continuing prenatal care as means of helping the black community. Since the first center opened in Atlanta in 1972, more than 300 centers have opened around the United States.

Sigma Gamma Rho has run Project Reassurance since the 1970s, when the program was pioneered by two St. Louis, Missouri, chapters. It came about because statistics on adolescent pregnancy alarmed the sorority members. When teenagers have babies, the consequences are experienced throughout society. Children born to teenage parents are more likely to be of low birth weight and to suffer from inadequate health care, more likely to leave high school without graduating, and more likely to be poor. As the sorority stated, such offspring perpetuate "a cycle of unrealized potential." Project Reassurance sought to de-accelerate the feminization of poverty through the provision of prenatal care, the promotion of effective parenting skills, and improvements in the collection of child-support payments.[48]

Black History Models

Giving role models to young black women was another method of helping the black community. Such women could demonstrate to girls that they too possess limitless potential. It was yet another example of womanist activism. In the 1960s and 1970s, all the sororities touted the accomplishments of black women to inspire girls and young adults. The books and pamphlets produced by the sororities were different from most of the women's history books of the era, which were written by whites and profiled only famous women, such as suffragist Susan B. Anthony.

These black women's works of history had a womanist goal. They told black undergraduates and high school students to rise above the racial and gender limitations imposed on them, while emphasizing that even ordinary women could make a significant impact on a community. The Zeta publication, *Biographical Directory of Zeta Women,* included only women who had worked to better the community through involvement with professional associations or charitable groups such as Big Sisters or the Girl Scouts. A Delta publication by its St. Louis chapter highlighted Missouri-born stars such as singer Josephine Baker and opera star Grace Bumbry alongside mortician Nettie Cunningham and social worker Vallateen Dudley Abbington. The AKA heritage series, which included *Women in Dentistry* as well as *Negro Women in the Judiciary,* also emphasized that young women had new opportunities outside the home to make an impact on African American life.[49]

Womanist Debutantes

Although womanism and feminism always had critical differences, these differences were becoming more apparent as the women's rights movement of the 1960s began to flower. One of the most striking differences between womanists and feminists has to do with beauty contests. The 1968 protest of the Miss America contest at Atlantic City, New Jersey, was one of the defining moments of the women's liberation movement. Yet at the same time, several blocks away, black women were holding the first Miss Black America contest. African Americans had historically been excluded from beauty pageants, and the black pageant was an attempt to redress this wrong.[50] The black sororities have also celebrated the beauty of black women as a way of showing racial pride. For much of their history, they have sponsored debutante cotillions.

Accomplishments take a backseat to beauty and pageantry on the day of the debutante ball, but strong community involvement is a requirement for becoming a debutante. AKA chapters, like the branches of other sororities, require prospective debutantes to state their volunteer activities, honors and awards, and other recognitions.[51] In this respect, the requirements mirror those for becoming sorority members.

The cotillions differ from beauty contests, in that the debutantes, who are high school students, typically complete several months of bonding, etiquette training, and college preparation. Training in public speaking is also offered. On the day of the ball, the sorority chapters bring together dignitaries and other notable black community members to welcome debutantes to society. The balls are among the highlights of the sorority's year. Sigma Gamma Rho regularly features Miss Rhomania balls in the pages of its journal and occasionally uses the debutantes as cover girls. One of its chapters, Eta Sigma of Greater Atlanta, has sponsored debutante balls since 1950, and accounts of these events note that the young women long remember their introduction to adult society while dressed in highly fashionable gowns. The Omicron Gamma Zeta Chapter of Zeta Phi Beta so values its Buds of Royalty Revue that it sought and received a proclamation from the state of Texas for holding the ball.[52]

The debutante balls held by the sororities evidence pride in the accomplishments and potential of young black women. The sororities use the balls as a way of advancing black women by training them in the skills they will need to develop both themselves and the African American community. Although the focus on appearance would shock feminists, these balls are an integral part of a womanist community.

Organized black women never focused solely on the problems of women but instead addressed concerns related to being black in America. The four historically black sororities promoted the education of black women so that such women could uplift the race. The organizations supported vocational education, mentoring programs, and prenatal education to give women and mothers a chance to lift black families out of poverty. They devised community solutions to community problems of poverty and hopelessness.

Although the sororities engaged in activities that could be described as feminist, its members shied away from that label. They helped create a climate in the black community in which womanism could flourish. The activities of the sororities certainly constituted a direct challenge to barriers to women's participation in the world beyond the family and household. They kept a focus on developing successful young African American women to uplift the community. Women historically served as the backbone of the family, and an improvement in the status of women would also improve the status of the race. The uplift of African Americans began with black women.

Notes

1. Geneva Smitherman, "A Womanist Looks at the Million Man March," in *Million Man March/Day of Absence,* ed. Haki R. Madhubuti and Maulana Karenga (Chicago: Third World Press), 104.

2. Susan Sandord, "Darling, You're Just Like Me," *Aurora* 51, no. 2 (winter 1981): 101.

3. Katrice A. Albert, "Why Is She so Womanish? The Relationship between Racial Identity Attitudes and Womanist Identity Attitudes in African American College Women" (PhD diss., Auburn University, 2002).

4. See Caryn E. Neumann, "Status Seekers: Long-Established Women's Organizations and the Women's Movement in the United States" (PhD diss., Ohio State University, 2006).

5. In 1998, Kylynnedra Wilcots compiled data on the reasons why people join sororities: affiliation, status, and social activities. Black sorority women were more interested than white ones in issues of social justice. Clarenda M. Phillips reached the same conclusions about black sororities in earlier decades and noted that many women joined to advance racial uplift. See Wilcots, "The Relationship between Level of Afri-

can-American Acculturation and Affiliation with Fraternities and Sororities" (master's thesis, University of North Texas, 1998), and Phillips, "Sisterly Bonds: African American Sororities Rising to Overcome Obstacles," in *African American Fraternities and Sororities: The Legacy and the Vision,* ed. Tamara L. Brown, Gregory S. Parks, and Clarenda M. Phillips (Lexington: University Press of Kentucky, 2005).

6. Anthony W. James, "The College Social Fraternity Antidiscrimination Debate, 1945–1949," *Historian* 62, no. 2 (winter 2000): 304.

7. The national organization sometimes moved ahead of the membership, some of whom would have apparently preferred to be just a social club. Civil rights pioneer Septima Clark complained in 1980 that "quite a number of my sorority members are still afraid of me and still worry about the articles that come out in the paper saying I helped to get black teachers in Charleston or I helped to get equalization of salaries for black teachers." See Cynthia Stokes Brown, ed., *Ready from Within: Septima Clark and the Civil Rights Movement* (Navarro, Calif.: Wild Trees Press, 1986), 121.

8. The sorority repeatedly uses the word *mankind.* I have chosen to modernize the terminology except when quoting directly. Walter Anderson, *Ivy: An Unauthorized History of Alpha Kappa Alpha* (Arlington, Tex.: Milk and Honey, [2002]).

9. Robert Ewell Greene, *Delta Memories: A Historical Summary* (Washington, D.C.: Robert Ewell Greene, 1981), 5.

10. See Mary Church Terrell, *A Colored Woman in a White World* (London: Prentice Hall International, 1940).

11. Xi Zeta Chapter of Zeta Phi Beta, *Biographical Directory of Zeta Women,* (n.p.: Zeta Phi Beta Sorority, 1976), xi; Zeta Phi Beta Sorority, *Zeta Phi Beta Sorority, Inc.: An Organization for the Twenty-first Century* (Washington, D.C.: Zeta Phi Beta, [1997]).

12. Pearl Schwartz White, *Behind These Doors: A Legacy, the History of Sigma Gamma Rho Sorority* (Chicago: Sigma Gamma Rho Sorority, 1974).

13. Nan E. McGehee, "A Report on the Convention Exhibitor Information Survey," *Ivy Leaf* (March 1964): 5. Note that the volume numbering of the AKA journal was not consistent over time, thereby making it difficult to find a particular article by volume. For this reason, I am omitting volume numbers.

14. Edna Over Gray, "Soror Gray's Challenge to the 49ers," *Ivy Leaf* (June 1949): 5; Barbara Davis, "Across the Editors Desk," *Ivy Leaf* (March 1971): 3; Paula Giddings, *In Search of Sisterhood: Delta Sigma Theta and the Challenge of the Black Sorority Movement* (New York: Quill William Morrow, 1988), 236.

15. Kevin K. Gaines argues that racial uplift ideology cannot be regarded as an independent black perspective because elite blacks sought the support of white political and business elites. However, he fails to consider the members of historically black sororities, who had a tradition of independence and who were not always beholden to white opinion. See Gaines, *Uplifting the Race: Black Leadership, Politics, and Culture in the Twentieth Century* (Chapel Hill: University of North Carolina Press, 1996).

16. Floris Barnett Cash, *African American Women and Social Action: The Club-*

women and Volunteerism from Jim Crow to the New Deal, 1896–1936 (Westport, Conn.: Greenwood Press, 2001); Deborah Gray White, *Too Heavy a Load: Black Women in Defense of Themselves, 1894–1994* (New York: Norton, 1999).

17. White, *Too Heavy a Load,* 149, 151.

18. Addie W. Hunton spoke for AKA at the founding meeting of the NCNW. See Audrey Thomas McCluskey and Elaine M. Smith, *Mary McLeod Bethune: Building a Better World* (Bloomington: Indiana University Press, 1999), 169, 172.

19. Giddings, *In Search of Sisterhood,* 238; McCluskey and Smith, *Mary McLeod Bethune,* 138.

20. Howard H. Long, *The American Council on Human Relations: An Evaluation* (n.p.: American Council on Human Relations, 1953); Robert L. Harris Jr., "Lobbying Congress for Civil Rights: The American Council on Human Rights, 1948–1963," in *African American Fraternities and Sororities.*

21. "Your ACHR News—Statement of Elmer W. Henderson," *Ivy Leaf* (December 1952): 6.

22. "Your ACHR News," *Ivy Leaf* (March 1951): 8; Giddings, *In Search of Sisterhood,* 222.

23. "How to Support Your American Council on Human Rights," *Ivy Leaf* (June 1949): 3; "Your ACHR News," *Ivy Leaf* (December 1951): 5–6.

24. Greene, *Delta Memories,* 35.

25. Lawrence C. Ross Jr., *The Divine Nine: The History of African American Fraternities and Sororities* (New York: Kensington, 2000), 167; Warren D. St. James, *NAACP: Triumphs of a Pressure Group, 1909–1980* (Smithtown, N.Y.: 1980), 144.

26. Marjorie W. Turner, "Lottie Pearl Mitchell," *Crisis* 81 (December 1974): 351; Elizabeth Murphy Moss, *Be Strong! The Life of Vashti Turley Murphy* (Baltimore: Elizabeth Murphy Moss and A. Paul Moss, 1980), 9.

27. Moss, *Be Strong,* 9.

28. Giddings, *In Search of Sisterhood,* 241–42.

29. Patricia Hill Collins, *Fighting Words: Black Women and the Search for Justice* (Minneapolis: University of Minnesota Press, 1998), 45.

30. Alison Harris Alexander, "Reach for Education and a Brighter Future," *Ivy Leaf* (winter 1995): 2.

31. Catherine D. Thomas, "Our Role in the Continued Development of Assault on Illiteracy Program (AOIP) Divisions and Units," *Aurora* 55, no. 1 (fall 1984): 51.

32. "Partnership in Mathematics and Science," *Ivy Leaf* (winter 1995): 10.

33. Omicron Rho Chapter of Delta Sigma Theta, "Five Point Thrust and National Involvement," http://www.gmu.edu/org/delta/fivept.html (accessed August 9, 2006).

34. Kate Hicks, "Vocational Guidance and Workshop Center," *Aurora* 55, no. 1 (fall 1984): 7.

35. Donald R. Mathews and James W. Prothro examined the public problems talked about by black and white southerners. In order, whites focused on community

(22 percent), economic (17 percent), political and governmental (16 percent), racial (15 percent), international (15 percent), and vague, generalized problems (7 percent). Blacks were concerned with racial (26 percent), economic (23 percent), community (20 percent), and political and governmental problems (9 percent). Community concerns included such matters as roads. See Mathews and Prothro, *Negroes and the New Southern Politics* (New York: Harcourt, Brace, 1966), 42–43.

36. U.S. Congress, Senate Committee on Labor and Public Welfare, *Hearings on the Economic Opportunity Act of 1964,* 88th Cong., 2nd sess. (Washington, D.C.: Government Printing Office, 1964), pt.. 1, 147–48.

37. Sar A. Levitan and Benjamin H. Johnston, *The Job Corps: A Social Experiment that Works* (Baltimore: Johns Hopkins University Press, 1975), 4, 16.

38. Nan E. McGehee, "A Report on the Convention Exhibitor Information Survey," *Ivy Leaf* (March 1964): 5.

39. Marjorie H. Parker, *Past Is Prologue: The History of Alpha Kappa Alpha, 1908–1999* (Washington, D.C.: Alpha Kappa Alpha, 1999), 183.

40. Julia Purnell, "Supreme Basileus Speaks," *Ivy Leaf* (June 1965): 2.

41. Parker, *Past Is Prologue,* 184.

42. U.S. Government, *Every Girl Needs a Chance to Become Somebody* (Washington, D.C.: Government Printing Office, 1966).

43. Levitan and Johnston, *Job Corps,* 187–88.

44. WICS consisted of women from the National Council of Catholic Women, the National Council of Jewish Women, the National Council of Negro Women, and United Church Women. "Alpha Kappa Alpha Embraces the Challenges of the Sixties: Residential Training Center for Women a Reality," *Ivy Leaf* (February–March 1965): 9.

45. "Alpha Kappa Alpha Says Goodbye to the Cleveland Job Corps Center," *Ivy Leaf* (winter 1995): 17.

46. Giddings, *In Search of Sisterhood,* 271.

47. Ibid., 271, 300–301; Zeta Phi Beta, *Zeta Phi Beta Sorority,* 9.

48. Karla D. Smith, "Project Reassurance," *Aurora* 55, no. 2 (winter 1984): 7–8.

49. Xi Zeta Chapter, *Biographical Directory of Zeta Women;* St. Louis Alumnae Chapter of Delta Sigma Theta Inc., *Profiles in Silhouette: The Contributions of Black Women of Missouri* (St. Louis: St. Louis Alumnae Chapter of Delta Sigma Theta Inc., 1980); Alpha Kappa Alpha Sorority, *Women in Dentistry* (Chicago: Alpha Kappa Alpha, 1972); Alpha Kappa Alpha Sorority, *Negro Women in the Judiciary* (Chicago: Alpha Kappa Alpha Sorority, 1968); Alpha Kappa Alpha Sorority, *Women in Business* (Chicago: Alpha Kappa Alpha Sorority, 1970); Alpha Kappa Alpha Sorority, *Women in Medicine* (Chicago: Alpha Kappa Alpha Sorority, 1971); Alpha Kappa Alpha Sorority, *Women in Politics* (Chicago: Alpha Kappa Alpha Sorority, 1969).

50. Maxine Leeds Craig, *Ain't I a Beauty Queen: Black Women, Beauty, and the Politics of Race* (New York: Oxford University Press, 2002).

51. Alpha Kappa Alpha Sorority Inc., Rho Psi Chapter, Charlotte, N.C., "Debutante

Greetings," March 23, 2006, http://www.rhopsiomega.org/debutantegreetings.htm (accessed August 8, 2006).

52. Stone Mountain-Lithonia Alumnae Chapter of Delta Sigma Theta, "Upcoming Events," http://www.smlacdst.org/events.htm (accessed August 8, 2006); "Phi Sigma's Debutantes, Washington, D.C.," *Aurora* 55, no. 2 (winter 1984): cover; Gertrude Hobby, "Western Region: Epsilon Pi Sigma Chapter's Rhomania," ibid., 45; "Beauty, Pageantry, and Choreography Portrayed in the 34th Annual Debutante Ball," ibid., 51; Mae Wesley, "Sigma Gamma Rho Sorority, Inc. Eta Sigma Chapter Presents 54th Debutante Ball," *Atlanta Inquirer,* December 11, 2004; Texas State Legislature, Senate Resolution No. 608, April 13, 2005, http://www.capitol.state.tx.us/tlo/79R/billtext/SR00608F.htm (accessed August 8, 2006).

Alpha Phi Alpha Fraternity members at Howard University, 1966. Courtesy of Howard University Archives, Moorland-Spingarn Center.

W. E. B. DuBois (center, in light suit) and other Alpha Phi Alpha members at Howard University, 1932. Behind him is Alpha Phi Alpha's sixteenth general president, civil rights attorney Bedford V. Lawson Jr.

Andrew Zawacki, white member of Alpha Phi Alpha Fraternity, Rhodes scholar, Fulbright fellow, PhD student in social thought at the University of Chicago, assistant professor of English at the University of Georgia. Courtesy of Andrew Zawacki.

Kappa Alpha Psi Fraternity Scrollers at the University of Maryland–Eastern Shore, 1976. Courtesy of University of Maryland–Eastern Shore Archives.

Kappa Alpha Psi Fraternity Scrollers at Howard University, 1986. Courtesy of Howard University Archives, Moorland-Spingarn Center.

Kappa Alpha Psi Fraternity members at the University of Iowa, 1921. Courtesy of University of Iowa Archives.

(Above) Omega Psi Phi members at Hampton University, 1975. Courtesy of Hampton University Archives. *(Below)* Omega Psi Phi Fraternity members at Virginia Union University, 1942. Courtesy of Virginia Union University Archives.

(Above) Phi Beta Sigma Fraternity Crescents at Howard University, 1986.
Courtesy of Howard University Archives, Moorland-Spingarn Center.
(Below) Phi Beta Sigma Fraternity members at the University of North Carolina
at Greensboro, 2006. Courtesy of Geoffrey Miller and the Rho Beta Chapter of
Phi Beta Sigma Fraternity Inc.

(*Above*) Iota Phi Theta Fraternity members at Hampton University, 1970. Courtesy of Hampton University Archives. (*Below*) Alpha Kappa Alpha Sorority members at the University of Kansas, 1930. Courtesy of Spencer Research Library, Kansas Collection, University of Kansas.

(Above) Alpha Kappa Alpha Sorority members at West Virginia State College, date unknown. Courtesy of West Virginia State University Archives.
(Below) Alpha Kappa Alpha Sorority "plugs" at Howard University, 1958. Courtesy of Howard University Archives, Moorland-Spingarn Center

(Above) Delta Sigma Theta Sorority "probates" at the University of Maryland–Eastern Shore, 1975. Courtesy of University of Maryland–Eastern Shore Archives. (Below) Delta Sigma Theta Sorority members at Hampton University, 1972. Courtesy of Hampton University Archives.

(Above) Delta Sigma Theta Sorority members at Howard University, 1996.
Courtesy of Howard University Archives, Moorland-Spingarn Center.
(Below) Zeta Phi Beta Sorority members in Nashville at the Tenth Boulé, 1929.
Courtesy of Zeta Phi Beta Sorority Inc.

(Above) Zeta Phi Beta members in Brooklyn, 1950. Courtesy of Zeta Phi Beta Sorority Inc. *(Below)* Sigma Gamma Rho Sorority members, Howard University Founders' Day, 1945. Courtesy of Sigma Gamma Rho Sorority Inc.

Sigma Gamma Rho Sorority members at the First Boulé, 1925. Courtesy of Sigma Gamma Rho Sorority Inc.

Sigma Pi Phi Fraternity members, 1921. Courtesy of Denver Public Library.

10

Giving and Getting
Philanthropic Activity among
Black Greek-Letter Organizations

Marybeth Gasman, Patricia Louison, and Mark Barnes

African American giving is rooted in efforts to overcome oppression. The history of black philanthropy shows that those who gave did so to help others in the community. In response to pleas by influential community members, African Americans gave to causes that made a difference in their immediate environments. Black philanthropy has been a response to discrimination—in the past, due to slavery and segregation, and today, due to educational and workplace inequality. Among the most prominent philanthropic organizations for African Americans are sororities and fraternities—organizations that have, since their establishment, been dedicated to philanthropic service, specifically self-help and educational advancement.

This chapter illustrates the philanthropic efforts of black Greek-letter organizations (BGLOs) to support and further the lives of African Americans. These organizations, in formal and informal ways, have worked to serve and shape their community. By studying them, we can learn much about civic leadership and contributions to public life among African Americans. Too often, the work of these historical organizations is overlooked by scholars. Even though their insular nature is often cited as an explanation, they may have been passed over because they are viewed as social, not philanthropic, organizations. This chapter examines the service orientation woven deeply into the fabric of BGLOs. First, we provide an overview of African American giving. Then we explore the philanthropic actions taking place within black sororities and fraternities.[1]

History and Background of African American Giving

The tradition of giving "tithes and offerings" began as early as the colonial period, when free blacks in the North established black churches to aid needy

African Americans. According to C. Eric Lincoln and Lawrence H. Mamiya, "The tradition of mutual aid lay deep in the African heritage, which stressed a greater communalism and social solidarity than either European or American customs allowed. These incipient traditions of mutual aid and self-help in the slave quarters were formalized and legitimated with the Christianizing of the slaves in the eighteenth and nineteenth centuries."[2] The growth of separate black churches gave African Americans the opportunity to establish the "first black-owned and operated institutions."[3] Since its inception, the black church has been the single most important institution involved in black philanthropy.[4] It has also been the chief beneficiary of the black community's giving efforts. According to Ann Abbe, "Clergy are often the most influential members of their communities, and church members are expected to support the church with frequent and/or large gifts."[5]

The majority of African Americans are taught from a young age that they have an obligation to give to the church. Through personal engagement and the establishment of a trusting bond, black preachers convey the needs of the church and consistently encourage their parishioners to support the work of the church—the will of God.[6] This obligation to give has provided the backbone for many black social movements in the United States, including the civil rights movement.[7] Black ministers were cognizant of the effect of racism on economic mobility in the United States and sought to create a sound financial base from which political and social change could take place.[8] Since their beginnings, black churches have acted as collection points for money, services, and goods that are pooled and redistributed.[9] According to Bradford Smith and colleagues, "the creation and evolution of the black church has been the most significant factor in the political, social, cultural, spiritual, educational and philanthropic development of African Americans in this country."[10] Thus, the black church is a key example of African American agency. Although forced on blacks by white slave owners, in the hands of black leaders, Christianity became an instrument for black emancipation.[11]

Often started as an arm of the church, mutual aid societies were also among the earliest organizations created by African Americans.[12] These societies began in the North and were typically founded by freedmen. In addition to meeting the spiritual needs of blacks, they addressed their physical and social needs.[13] The first recorded mutual aid society was the Free African Society, which was established in 1787 in Philadelphia by the African Methodist Episcopal and African Protestant Episcopal churches. Other organizations included the New York Society, the Union Society of Brooklyn, the African Union Society, the Wilberforce Benevolent Society, the Woolman Society, and the Clarkson Society.[14] Eventually, the mutual aid societies developed into cultural, economic, and political forces that helped advance blacks. Under the aegis of these organizations, African Americans joined together—trusting and relying on one another in dire circumstances. According to Lincoln and Mamiya, these loosely organized societies were the forerunners of national organizations such as the Urban League and the NAACP.[15] Further, Smith and colleagues note that influential black businesses such as the "National Benefit Life Insurance and the Central Life Insurance companies also owe their origins to mutual aid organizations."[16]

Beginning in 1775 with the establishment of the Prince Hall Masons, fraternal organizations began to work closely with the black church. These organizations were, first and foremost, communal and social, but they were also committed to healing social ills and contributing to the community. They often secured funds and gifts in kind from their members for poor and indigent women and children. Black fraternal organizations consisted of two types: those that were black chapters of already existing white organizations, and those that were established specifically for African Americans. Blacks created their own versions of the Masons (as mentioned), Odd Fellows, Knights of Pythias, Eastern Star, Household of Ruth, Foresters, Shriners, and Elks. Those organizations created by blacks for blacks included the Grand United Order of Galilean Fisherman, Colored Brotherhood and Sisterhood of Honor, Friends of Negro Freedom, International Order of Twelve, African Blood Brotherhood, Colored Consolidated Brotherhood, African Legion, and Knights of the Invisible Colored Kingdom. Many of the fraternal organizations established an auxiliary group of women, such as the Daughters of the Eastern Star for Masons.[17] Fraternal organizations were most prevalent in northeastern cities, including Boston, Philadelphia, and New York. These organizations contributed to a culture of "giving back" and "uplifting the race."

During the antebellum period, black women devised a variety of means of supporting causes that were important to the community. For example, they participated in "fairs" with white abolitionist women to support antislavery legislation. These black women also sponsored their own fairs to support the African Methodist Episcopal Church, abolitionist Frederick Douglass, and the Union Anti-Slavery Society. Other African American women's organizations held fairs to support the black press or orphaned black children.[18] These efforts by black women are yet another example of the importance of uplifting the race as a motivation for giving.

African American elites (those in business and professional circles) have also created many social and service organizations for themselves. Because of the insular nature of these organizations and the fact that their membership is exclusively black, their philanthropic efforts go unnoticed by nonblacks and are often overlooked in discussions of African American philanthropy. Among the women's groups in this category are the Links, Girl Friends, National Smart Set, Drifters, and Northeasterners. For men, the organizations include the Boulé (Sigma Pi Phi), Comus Club, Reveille Club, Ramblers, Bachelor-Benedicts, and Guardsmen. African American children also belong to elite organizations—the most prominent being Jack and Jill.

According to a member of the Links, "Once you are a part of one of these groups, you end up knowing many more people in all the other groups too."[19] Because most of the elite organizations were founded on the premise of volunteerism and charitable giving, the potential for black philanthropy in these groups is obvious. For example, the Links proudly claim, "[Our] tradition is based on volunteerism. For over fifty years, the organization has gathered momentum, continuously redefined its purposes, sharpened its focus, and expanded its program dimensions in order to make the name 'Links' synonymous with not only a chain of friendship, but also a chain of purposeful service."[20] Within these elite organizations, giving is an expectation—a requirement, in fact, of membership. The success of these black elite organizations in supporting a wide variety of philanthropic endeavors is made possible by the strong bonds of trust within the organization.[21] The historical origins of African American giving have shaped the current practices of the BGLOs.

Philanthropy among African American Sororities

Like other Greek-letter organizations, African American sororities are often considered elitist by outsiders.[22] Membership is perceived not only as shrouded in secrecy but also as exclusive, owing to the financial commitment involved.[23] What is missing from critical assessments of black sororities is a discussion of the members' philanthropic activities. Members of the four black sororities are trained to help whenever they can, and this principle extends to the organizations' membership and beyond. Each of the sororities has mechanisms—both formal and informal—that serve the individual needs of members in crisis. When a sorority member is unemployed, homeless due to fire or other calamity, or in need of financial assistance for herself or her family, she can rest assured that her sorority will help her. When tested, the bonds of sisterhood produce the same generosity to those on the inside as they do to those on the outside.[24]

In this section, we focus on what it means to care about a community so much that women are willing to pour their hearts and souls into an organization that expects nothing less than their full economic, physical, and spiritual support in return. Although philanthropy is typically seen as a way of giving financially to those in need, the philanthropic efforts of America's black sororities go beyond this definition. What does it mean to voluntarily give for the benefit of human welfare? The members of African American sororities can easily answer this question. It is why they joined their organizations and why they remain active over their lifetimes.

A LIFETIME COMMITMENT

When members of the four black sororities pledge to serve and affiliate for a lifetime, it is no small undertaking. Before joining their respective sororities, the women we interviewed for this essay made a conscious effort to observe the members of their chosen organizations, noting the bonds of sisterhood and the dedication to service. This was their chief reason for affiliating. And they remain active because their sororities own real estate in their lives and hearts.[25]

To understand the power of affiliation, one must consider the founding principles of each organization. Alpha Kappa Alpha Sorority Inc. endeavors to be "supreme in service to all mankind."[26] Delta Sigma Theta Sorority Inc.'s hallmark is to "use their collective strength to promote academic excellence and to provide assistance to persons in need."[27] Zeta Phi Beta Sorority Inc. promotes "scholarship, service, sisterly love and finer womanhood" above all else.[28] And, Sigma Gamma Rho Sorority Inc. "aims to enhance the quality of life within the community" while providing "greater service, greater progress."[29] In short, each sorority has pledged to build and leave behind a legacy of social responsibility through action, as well as to give to and foster community.[30]

Collectively, these organizations boast a membership of more than 600,000 women devoted to shaping their communities locally, nationally, and internationally. Twenty-five percent of their membership is active at any given time. The largest share of members is employed in the field of education, followed by law, business, medicine, and social service professions. Even though each sorority was established at the collegiate level, estimates place graduate-level membership at more than 70 percent of the total.

REMAINING ACTIVE

In many cases, the decisions that sorority members must make differ from those made by fraternity members, owing to traditional gender roles in the African American family. For instance, women in sororities often consider the impact of their involvement on their spouses (regardless of whether they are fraternity members) and children. Some choose to suspend their membership until their children are older and home life is more stable.[31] Financial stability is also a factor for newly graduated sorority members. For some, the requisite financial commitment (annual dues, fund-raisers, tickets to events, and other assessments) is too high, and these members decide to take a hiatus from service. Consider the following observation shared by an Alpha Kappa Alpha (AKA) member: "Each member is compelled to maintain a constant balance between fun, funds, family and friends when making membership and activity decisions. Sorority members often are required to have a line item in their personal budget, get the family sign-off on sorority expenditures, create a separate budget altogether to handle sorority duties, and juggle their personal resource expenditures (e.g., time, talent, etc.)."[32] Retaining members thus becomes an important issue for the viability and sustainability of sororities beyond college.[33] Because they seek a lifetime commitment, such attrition is of great concern to black sororities. It leads not only to a loss of valuable talent but also to a loss of institutional memory—a critical commodity in all organizations.

PERSONAL AND GROUP DEVOTION

An examination of individual effort yields a rich picture of devotion to service and community through the giving of time, energy, and financial resources. For example, Mahlene Duckett Lee, president of Rho Theta Omega Chapter of Alpha Kappa Alpha in Philadelphia, spends more than thirty hours a week in service activities, planning meetings, and administering the business of the chapter. In addition to operating a business and other professional obligations, Lee has to juggle the requirements of her family, church, and other civic responsibilities. In her words, "AKA is 24 hours a day," and the gift of service never stops.[34] This commitment is magnified among those who provide regional, national, or international leadership. To serve their sorority, many women add the equivalent of a full-time job to their already busy professional lives. Additionally, this volunteer role calls for regular travel for board meetings with the president and other members of the governing body. Those with the most flexible schedules are the presidents of the organizations, who typically do not have outside jobs due to the hefty time commitment. Alpha Kappa Alpha estimates that members collectively donated more than 1 million hours of their time during the period July 2002 to July 2004.[35]

All the sororities can boast of their influence on the philanthropic efforts of the communities around them. Sigma Gamma Rho has institutionalized its impact in this area by allowing auxiliary groups, called Philos (meaning friends), to form and operate in support of their mission. Members of a Philo club operate in service to the goals and ideals of Sigma Gamma Rho, but they are not members of the sorority. Since being officially recognized in 1954, these groups have given countless hours and thousands of dollars to the betterment of others through their affiliation with local chapters of Sigma Gamma Rho.[36]

Although undergraduate members lack financial resources, they are just as committed as their alumna counterparts. They also give of their time, energy, talents, and financial wherewithal. Fund-raising drives, programming, and service activities, both on and off campus, characterize the collegiate sorority experience. These young women traditionally support the NAACP and the United Negro College Fund and serve as campus leaders through student government, inter-Greek councils, and other student groups.[37] Among the undergraduates' recent service accomplishments are a worldwide clothing donation effort (1999–2000) in which AKA members distributed 37,000 coats to the homeless.[38]

Within the undergraduate ranks, leadership development is paramount. Sororities treat the undergraduate years as a training ground for civic and graduate-level sorority leadership. Graduate chapters organize mentoring programs, sisterly gatherings, and day-to-day service efforts for undergraduates.[39] An example is Alpha Kappa Alpha's Leadership Seminar and Fellows Program, which seeks to cultivate future leaders among young women by inviting undergraduates to participate in an annual conference focused on leadership, political action, and economic development.[40] Likewise, Zeta Phi Beta sponsors the Zeta Organizational Leadership Program, which trains and certifies its undergraduate as well as graduate members for current and future leadership roles within the sorority.[41]

Without this mission-driven service through individual and group devotion, black sororities would not be able to sustain themselves. To become a more formidable force in service, leadership, and philanthropy, the nine BGLOs (four sororities and five fraternities) came under the umbrella of the National Pan-Hellenic Council (NPHC).[42] Together, they tackle issues of mutual import and strategize about how to increase social, economic, political, and educational capital for the communities they serve. Separately, the sororities concentrate on three central community concerns: education, health, and civil rights.

EDUCATIONAL ENDEAVORS

Since their founding, black sororities have focused on education as a gateway to economic and community advancement.[43] They have formalized this effort by creating foundations that offer grants, scholarships, and fellowships. Since their establishment, these organizations have raised millions of dollars in scholarships for African Americans as well as other students of color. Organizations such as the United Negro College Fund have benefited greatly from the philanthropic contributions of black sororities. In addition to the headquarters-based foundations, legions of chapters within each sorority operate charitable arms that give to educational causes and individuals. Sigma Gamma Rho pioneered chapter-based scholarships shortly before the Great Depression.[44] Below, we outline the significant individual and organizational impact of black sororities with respect to educational empowerment.

During their 1937 national convention, the sisters of Delta Sigma Theta launched a nationwide library project. Their efforts addressed an urgent need in the black community—especially in rural areas—for reading education. Of the 9 million African Americans living in the South, two-thirds were without public library services and thus had little or no exposure to books.[45] The national chapter of Delta Sigma Theta asked all its chapters to donate a minimum of ten books, worth approximately $2.50 each. Each local chapter was equipped with a "book basket with a lock and key to facilitate the transportation of the books."[46]

The project was aided by the contributions of Delta member Mollie Lee, who held teaching positions at Atlanta University and North Carolina College. Lee advised the library project and asked local teachers and principals to support it by assisting with the distribution of books. Perhaps one of the most innovative aspects of the program was the emphasis on providing books about black history and black achievement to people in rural communities, a strategy that gave African American children a glimpse of the past and of the possibilities that lay ahead. After the first year of the program, many teachers and parents wrote to the Deltas to express their appreciation for the library project. Even more significant, several of the rural towns continued the sorority's efforts by creating permanent libraries.[47] In areas that could not support the infrastructure of a library, the Deltas offered help—sometimes providing furniture, film projectors, and trained personnel. The Deltas were also instrumental in lobbying state legislatures in Georgia, North Carolina, and Alabama for library funds, and when none were allotted, they provided bookmobiles with librarians.[48]

In the 1940s, the Grand Basileus of Zeta Phi Beta, Lullelia Harrison, initiated the Prevention and Control of Juvenile Delinquency Project. The Zeta sisters were cognizant of increasing problems with juvenile delinquency and wanted to launch a national effort to provide young people with an alternative to crime. In conjunction with U.S. Attorney General Tom Clark, the Zetas designed neighborhood-specific programs to aid youth.[49] Involvement with children, especially young girls, has been a cornerstone of Zeta activities. For example, the Manhattan alumnae chapter in New York City, chartered in 1950, formed a cohesive partnership with Gompers High School in the Bronx. In cooperation with the school's administration, the Zeta volunteers taught reading, math, and science to African American and Hispanic girls in after-school programs. Over time, the sorority's volunteer efforts expanded to include an emphasis on writing, which culminated in scholarship competitions. From the outset of their scholarship program, the Zetas tracked the recipients, following their careers after college and often bringing them into the sorority as undergraduate or graduate members.[50] By stressing academics, the Zetas encouraged women to strive for greater achievement in education, especially in nontraditional areas.

Between 1964 and 1989, Alpha Kappa Alpha joined the war on poverty through its management of the Cleveland Job Corps, a residential education and vocational training agency for young people aged sixteen to twenty-four.[51] Today, one of the sorority's signature education programs is the Ivy Reading AKAdemy, which supports the literacy needs and development of students in kindergarten through grade three. This is made possible by a $1.5 million grant from the U.S. Department of Education and through the support of local chapters.[52] In partnership with the National Science Foundation, Delta Sigma Theta provides learning enrichment in science and math for parents and caregivers of students in kindergarten through grade eight. Sigma Gamma Rho's programming centers on children and families, placing an emphasis on education, teen pregnancy, and economic development. Among the Sigma Gamma Rho programs are Operation Big Book Bag, which provides tutoring, mentoring, school supplies, computers, and other resource materials to homeless children and young adults living in homeless shelters across the nation.[53]

HEALTH MATTERS

In addition to education, health is a major component of each sorority's national program. For example, as one of its five program targets, Alpha Kappa Alpha tackles health issues in the black community at large through education and broad advocacy strategies. Its major national initiatives deal with diabetes, sickle cell anemia, HIV/AIDS education and awareness, the collection of family history to prevent and treat cancer, and senior health and safety related to housing.[54] Delta Sigma Theta, through its Health Task Force, encourages its members and women in the black community to live mentally, physically, and spiritually fit lives. As part of its Lifestyle Change Initiative, Delta Sigma Theta targets obesity and heart disease.[55] Since 1972, Zeta Phi Beta has, in conjunction with the March of Dimes, sponsored its Stork's Nest program, which educates and serves thousands of pregnant women.[56] In this way, sorority members have stepped up to fill a need in the black community for earlier and more consistent prenatal care, as well as education about self-care during pregnancy, childbirth, and the postpartum period.[57] Sigma Gamma Rho operates a similar program called Project Reassurance aimed at educating teens through workshops and other activities about pre- and postnatal care, infant care, and child development.[58] In addition to this effort, Sigma Gamma Rho works hard to support education, research, and activism through its Cancer Awareness and National Bone Marrow Donor programs.[59]

CIVIL AND HUMAN RIGHTS

From their inception, African American sororities have played a critical role in advancing the cause of civil rights and social justice.[60] From their participation in the 1913 women's suffrage march to the enduring fight for equal voting rights, their involvement in this area has been constant.[61] On March 3, 1913, Delta Sigma Theta members joined a national march on Washington on behalf of women's suffrage. The sorority members marched with women of all backgrounds and ethnicities and endured taunts and insults by an angry crowd. According to the *Baltimore Afro-American,* "The women, trudging stoutly along under great difficulties, were able to complete their march only when troops of cavalry from Fort Myers were rushed into Washington to take charge of Pennsylvania Avenue."[62] By participating in the march, the Deltas were acting in defiance of the Howard University administration and, in many cases, against the wishes of their parents.[63]

At the request of Norma Boyd, a founder of Alpha Kappa Alpha, the Non-

Partisan Lobby for Economic and Democratic Rights was established in 1938 to make our "power felt in the halls and on the floors of Congress."[64] Some of the lobby's activities centered on eradicating police brutality, discrimination in public life, lynching, and inequities in federal housing and hospitalization programs. Today, similar civic and lobbying activities fall under the Alpha Kappa Alpha Connection committees that exist in each chapter to eliminate injustice and protect civil liberties. Similarly, Delta Sigma Theta holds "Delta Days" in the nation's capital, an annual legislative conference to increase member participation in the public policy-making process.[65] Making national headlines, Delta Sigma Theta pledged a major gift to the Legal Defense Fund of the NAACP to support voting rights programs, commemorating the fortieth anniversary of the 1965 Voting Rights Act.[66]

As a conglomerate, the nine NPHC organizations joined forces with the National Coalition on Black Civic Participation for the "Unity 04 Empowerment Campaign" to increase the number of registered voters nationwide and then mobilize voter turnout on election day 2004.[67] Importantly, all BGLOs seek to be seen and heard through statewide days at their respective state capitals and other public policy forums. For instance, on April 19, 2006, during Red & White Day at the capitol in Baton Rouge, Louisiana, Dr. Louise White, Delta Sigma Theta's national president, announced a $1 million pledge to aid historically black colleges and universities affected by Hurricane Katrina.[68]

Through their service in education, social justice, and economic empowerment, black sororities have established a foundation of high-impact and multilevel philanthropic service.[69] The enthusiasm and allegiance of their undergraduate and graduate members have helped these organizations grow and prove themselves to be powerful forces for social change, educational advancement, and community outreach. The wisdom of their founders and presiding officers at all organizational levels, along with the dedication of their members, has propelled each organization to achieve greater successes than anyone could have imagined at the outset. They remain vital to the next phase of the fight for equality, civil liberties, and rights. The women who have answered the call remain steadfast in their pledge to serve and give their all.

Philanthropy among African American Fraternities

The story of African American fraternities began in 1905 in Ithaca, New York, on Cornell's bitterly cold and racially intolerant campus. Pressured to "ascend" the "proscriptions of color common to American institutions of this era, and hampered by limited means of the average 'poor' student," the founders of the nation's oldest intercollegiate black fraternity (Alpha Phi Alpha) "faced the future and boldly endeavored to find a way out of their difficulties, scarcely realizing, however, the import of their action on subsequent generations"[70] Whether they found themselves stranded on historically white college campuses in New York, Indiana, or Ohio or among their own people in Washington, D.C., or Baltimore, the founders of each fraternity set out to establish a mission and adhered to the basic principles of education, political involvement, and economic empowerment to advance the race.

Initiates of Alpha Phi Alpha, Kappa Alpha Psi, Omega Psi Phi, Phi Beta Sigma, and Iota Phi Theta have, from their organizations' inception, taken solemn oaths to serve one another and humankind.[71] The modus operandi of each fraternity is expressed clearly in its motto. Thus, the Kappa's aim is to produce "achievement in every field of human endeavor." The Omega knows that "friendship is essential to the soul" and uses it to serve others. Establishing a "culture for service and service for humanity" is the Sigma's creed. The Iota believes in "building a tradition, not resting one" as he works to advance social change. Being "servants to all" is what Alphas strive to do.[72]

This review of philanthropy in black fraternities highlights the historical models that the five organizations have used to increase blacks' participation in education, engage them in political processes, stimulate their entrepreneurial ambitions, and establish a tradition of giving through fraternity-based foundations. We point to the driving influences behind their philanthropy, noting why and how black fraternities have given support to the greater good.

MODELS OF PHILANTHROPY

In fraternity histories, the formation of "movements," or what would later be called "national programs," was often a response to the crisis of the day or the vision fraternity men had for future generations.[73] It is important to remember that during the earliest years of black fraternities, between 1906 and 1914, black men and women had limited access to higher education. Few African Americans were aware of the benefits of higher education, and discrimination was widespread.[74]

The black fraternities' methods for solving what many referred to as the "Negro problem" focused on balancing inequities in public and private education, creating businesses, participating in political processes, establishing foundations, and building strategic alliances. Early debates routinely questioned the efficacy and sustainability of responding to fraternal and community calls for action. These debates, however, helped lay permanent foundations on which future generations of fraternity men could stand and thus advance themselves, their families, their communities, and their fraternities.[75]

Within black fraternities, philanthropic endeavors typically began at the local level and spread throughout each organization with the aid of national conclaves and conferences. Iota Phi Theta places this fact in the proper perspective on its national Web site: "In the initial stages of the Fraternity's existence, the Fraternity's service initiatives were local in nature as reflected by the size of the Fraternity and the scope of its resources. As the Fraternity began to take on a National dimension, it became evident that its programmatic thrust would have to be adjusted accordingly. This adjustment was complicated however, by the fact that many chapters have had historical ties to service organizations and causes in their local areas."[76] Tremendous overlap in philanthropic focus exists across each fraternity. Also, it is important to note that each organization awards scholarships to members and nonmembers at the chapter, district or state, and national levels, amounting to millions of dollars spent on African American education. No one fraternity concentrates on only one national initiative, and efforts often overlap within chapters.

EDUCATIONAL ENDEAVORS

The brothers of Alpha Phi Alpha agree that a college education is the "single best predictor of future economic success."[77] As such, they developed the national Go-to-High School, Go-to-College campaign in 1920, which used speakers, pamphlets, and personal letters to advertise the benefits of a college education.[78] Today, Alphas deliver their message year-round through a curriculum that concentrates on time management, study skills, goal setting, violence and conflict prevention, building self-esteem, historical perspectives of African and African American peoples, gender in society, and current events.[79]

Omega Psi Phi's national talent search awards scholarships to young people each year. The search began in the fraternity's Sixth District, which covers North and South Carolina. Since 1953, Omegas have organized talent contests in local communities and at their national conclaves.[80] Likewise, Phi Beta Sigma "focuses on programming and services to graduates and undergraduates in the fraternity" through its National Education Program.[81] Tutoring, scholarship awards, and lectures are its core objectives.[82]

SOCIAL ENTREPRENEURSHIP

Before the Great Depression, and before the discovery of "black capitalism" and the federal Office of Minority Business Enterprise in the late 1960s, the fraternity men of Sigma introduced the "Bigger and Better Negro Business" exhibition in 1924 to showcase to members and the public the achievements of the race. At the first convention in Philadelphia, more than twenty-five leading black businesses entered more than fifty exhibits. The response from local visitors was supportive, and as a result, the fraternity voted unanimously in 1925 to make "Bigger and Better Negro Business" a regular program. This program is consistent with Phi Beta Sigma's commitment to improving the economic conditions of minorities and the welfare of society at large.[83] Today, the program's mission includes "the promotion and fostering of ideas for the effective organization, improvement and expansion of business and the dissemination and propagation of information for the advancement of sound business principles and practices."[84] Partnering with organizations such as the NAACP and the National Urban League, Sigma offers financial and home ownership information to its members and their families through its Project SEED (Sigma Economic Empowerment Development). It also runs "an all-volunteer board, manager and staff" credit union for "the blue and white family" of Sigmas and the women of Zeta Phi Beta.[85] Deposits in the credit union are insured up to $100,000, and it provides low-cost mortgages for fraternity and sorority members, as well as loans for home improvement, education, and weddings.

COMBATING IGNORANCE AND INDIFFERENCE

An old joke asks: "What's the difference between ignorance and indifference?" The answer: "I don't know and I don't care." Each fraternal organization has endeavored to inform communities about pressing social issues that must be addressed through political and legislative processes, including getting people out to vote in local, state, and national elections.

Social action is the term most of the fraternities use to describe activities aimed at registering voters and increasing their knowledge of political issues.[86] Alpha Phi Alpha professes that "A Voteless People Is a Hopeless People." Its campaign began in the 1930s and was led by chapters across the country. Over the years, the Alphas have maintained and strengthened their belief in the power of voting.[87] In fact, in 2005 they began an effort to raise awareness of the expiration of the Voting Rights Act. Members of the organization testified before Congress and worked in local communities to educate African Americans about the importance of the act's reauthorization.[88] Likewise, the brothers of Omega Psi Phi are dedicated to a national platform aimed at increasing political involvement and voting. According to the national office, "all levels of the fraternity are expected to facilitate, participate and/or coordinate activities that will uplift their communities through the power of the vote."[89]

HEALTH MATTERS

Another way the fraternities work to combat ignorance and educate the African American community is through their health-related initiatives. For example, Omega Psi Phi chapters aim to uplift their local communities through the promotion of good health practices. Specifically, the chapters participate in the Charles Drew Blood Drive each June, the American Diabetes Association, and several HIV/AIDS awareness initiatives.[90] This last effort is particularly important because African Americans represent 50 percent of all new AIDS cases in the United States.[91] Phi Beta Sigma chapters, like the Omegas, spend considerable time raising money and educating their local communities on issues that are detrimental to the health of African Americans, such as diabetes.[92]

Eliminating health disparities in the black community has been a major thrust for fraternal organizations. In 2002, Iota Phi Theta launched a national Sickle Cell Anemia Awareness Campaign with St. Jude Children's Research Hospital in Memphis, Tennessee. According to Scott Seward, Iota Phi Theta's Pennsylvania state director, "Children are a significant reason for me to do community service. My chapter has donated several thousand dollars to the St. Jude's Cancer Foundation for Children."[93]

Alpha Phi Alpha forms a national partnership with the March of Dimes each year. Both organizations work cooperatively to educate teenagers about sexual health and responsibility. Males and, in some cases, females between the ages of twelve and fifteen participate in workshops designed to let them explore their attitudes about their sexuality, increase their awareness of sexually transmitted diseases, and improve their self-esteem. Also, both organizations raise funds for research on birth defects and educational programs through Walk America. "Every day 1 in 8 babies born in the U.S. arrives too soon," reports the March of Dimes.[94] Alpha brothers team up and engage in fraternal competitions to determine which chapter can raise the most funds and get the most members to participate in the walk.

JOINT EFFORTS

Over the years, fraternities have partnered with national nonprofit organizations and well-known for-profit corporations to advance their fraternal missions.
In some cases, the fraternities were invited to participate in the development of
nationwide programs and strategies to deliver educational curricula and resources
aimed at reducing the plight of low- to moderate-income communities.

Iota men help communities "succeed in a digital age" through a joint effort
with Africana.com and Microsoft Corporation to bridge the digital divide. The
digital divide has been described as a social, racial, class, and even political
problem in society that further separates the haves from the have-nots with
regard to technology and information access. In 2001, Iota men set out to deliver
black culture and history to schools through Henry Louis Gates Jr. and Kwame
Anthony Appiah's *Africana Encyclopedia* and Microsoft's *Encarta Africana*, the
CD-ROM version.[95]

The preponderance of single-parent households is a critical issue in urban
and rural communities. National organizations such as the Big Brothers/Big
Sisters of America have sought to ease the stress in these homes by providing children with "Bigs" to serve as mentors, counselors, and guides. In 1990,
Alpha Phi Alpha signed an agreement with Big Brothers/Big Sisters to assist in
its efforts to create environments where single parents and their children can
increase their growth options and opportunities.[96] The fraternity also partnered
with the Boy Scouts of America to create additional opportunities for boys to
receive career guidance from accomplished black males.

Fraternities have partnered with or donated to the causes of such organizations as the NAACP, National Urban League, and United Negro College
Fund. Omega Psi Phi has an extensive history of giving to these organizations.
At Omega Psi Phi's Los Angeles Grand Conclave in 1955, it was decided that
"each graduate chapter would purchase a Life Membership from the NAACP,"
and "between 1955 and 1959, chapters contributed nearly $40,000" to the
organization.[97] In the 1980s, the fraternity contributed $250,000 to the United
Negro College Fund and authorized an "annual gift of 50,000 dollars to that
organization in perpetuity."[98]

PERSONAL AND GROUP DEVOTION

Determining what drives people to give of their time, talents, and treasures
to help others is no easy task. Although there are many reasons why a person

might express a philanthropic spirit, it is clear that purpose is what drives black fraternity men. They connect on a number of levels with the missions of their organizations. Isaac Fraisier, an Omega Psi Phi brother for fifty-plus years, says his fraternity encourages him to "produce a better society where there are more and better young people being prepared to become leaders. It's an inward feeling that I get when I'm helping Omega to be the best. You are a servant of the community."[99] Fraisier has been a dues-paying member since he was initiated in 1949 on the campus of Claflin College. Born in 1925, he is currently a very active member of Nu Alpha Graduate Chapter in Charleston, South Carolina.

Iota Phi Theta member Scott Seward remarks, "My inspiration to serve comes from the knowledge that somebody will be better educated or better prepared in life because of my efforts and the efforts of my brothers. There is no other reason why I do this than the promotion and positive movement of the black race."[100] Seward was initiated at West Chester University in Pennsylvania in 2001 and is thirty years old. He is a member of the Chi Omega Chapter in Philadelphia.

Although the black church has often been cited as a reason for participating in philanthropic activities, some members do not understand this notion. According to Seward, "I am a Christian. I don't believe there is a spiritual influence in this work. Some of the [philosophies] connect with my fraternity's ideals, but I don't confuse them. We have partnered with churches and faith-based organizations on several occasions. It helps promote our brothers' work to people we wouldn't connect with through our other events and community service efforts." On the campuses of black colleges and universities, religion was a strong influence in the development of a service orientation. According to Fraisier, "Claflin was supported by the Methodist Church. The president demanded that everyone put on clean shirts and pants, and line up to go to church every Sunday. We marched with the Deltas to the church. Service wasn't a hard thing for me to do because of my background. It was a demanding sort of thing at Claflin."[101]

Since pledging was officially abolished in 1990, the fraternities have put service at the core of their process to initiate new members.[102] In all cases, "aspirants" are required to design and implement a community service project or program during the orientation period. Some believe that membership intake does not instill philanthropic values, but others disagree. "After some members pay for membership and use up their advanced payment, they don't come around anymore, and are not to be counted on to give time and money," said Fraisier. He continued, "It depends on brothers that sponsor new members to help them embrace that promotion [philanthropy]." Seward has a different point of view: "When service projects are properly implemented, intakes get to see that philanthropy is second nature for a brother. When they're done improperly, it has a negative effect and intakes see service as a chore. I believe engaging intakes in the service project or fund-raising development process helps him to better understand that this is our fraternity's primary purpose, and it's what's most important to the brotherhood." According to Seward, "Tradition goes hand in hand with philanthropy."[103] Each fraternity prides itself on what it has done to serve others. Service is their raison d'être. Each of their creation stories points to a void that was present in their communities and the steps they took to improve themselves and society. Tradition is a powerful influence in the black fraternity, especially among the more senior members.

In addition to the imperatives to give, there are certainly factors that have a negative impact on giving. Membership fees and dues at the chapter and national levels have the potential to dampen the philanthropic spirit. "Even though it's sad to say, membership fees, local and national dues, and convention costs have a negative effect on the willingness and ability of a member to donate money to scholarship causes," Seward observed. Established members are more likely to make direct donations to scholarship funds. These members are typically alumni who have achieved a modicum of success in their careers. Fraisier points to economic reality when he says: "Young people in the fraternity are still in debt after graduating from college. They have small children, mortgages, etc. That situation has a negative effect on their ability to give time and money, but sometimes they manage to do it. More established alumni brothers are different altogether."[104] Socioeconomic background, lifestyle, living arrangements, and even hobbies are all factors in a fraternity member's ability and willingness to participate in his organization. There are many more reasons that push and pull these men to give up the things that matter to them to help others.

It is evident that BGLOs play an intensely significant role in American philanthropy, specifically in the lives of African Americans. As demonstrated, in formal and informal ways, black sororities and fraternities have worked to serve and shape their local, regional, and national communities. Too often, the work of these organizations has been overlooked by historians and scholars with little access to organizational papers and key stakeholders. As noted, this is often due to the secretive nature of these organizations. However, through the scholarship of insiders and those who are willing to invest the time, a rich, wonderful story of love of humankind can be told. Telling this story is essential to establishing the relevance of BGLOs, especially in light of recent criticism surrounding hazing issues. The African American community and the general public need to be made aware of the multilayered, complex history and operation of BGLOs in order to have a more informed understanding of their contributions to society.

Notes

1. To more fully understand the actions of these organizations, we drew on their published histories and secondary sources. To augment this knowledge, we conducted interviews with members of BGLOs—capturing the voices of those closest to the philanthropic action.

2. C. Eric Lincoln and Lawrence H. Mamiya, *The Black Church in the African American Experience* (Durham, N.C.: Duke University Press, 1990), 242. This idea is reiterated in James A. Joseph, *Remaking America: How the Benevolent Traditions of Many Cultures Are Transforming Our National Life* (San Francisco: Jossey-Bass, 1995).

3. Bradford Smith, Sylvia Shue, Jennifer Lisa Vest, and Joseph Villarreal, *Philanthropy in Communities of Color* (Bloomington: Indiana University Press, 1999), 10.

4. Ibid.; Alicia Byrd, ed., *Philanthropy and the Black Church* (Washington, D.C.: Council on Foundations, 1990); E. Franklin Frazier, *The Negro Church in America* (New York: Schocken Books, 1963); C. Eric Lincoln, *The Black Church since Frazier* (New York: Schocken Books, 1974); E. Franklin Frazier, *Black Bourgeoisie* (New York: Free Press Paperbacks, 1997).

5. M. Ann Abbe, "The Roots of Minority Giving: Understand the Philanthropic Traditions of Different Cultures to Solicit Them More Effectively," *Case Currents* (July 2002): 4.

6. Lincoln and Mamiya, *The Black Church.*

7. David Garrow, *Philanthropy and the Civil Rights Movement* (New York: Center for the Study of Philanthropy, 1987).

8. Eric Anderson and Alfred A. Moss Jr., *Dangerous Donations: Northern Philanthropy and Southern Black Education, 1902–1930* (Columbia: University of Missouri Press, 1999).

9. Lincoln and Mamiya, *The Black Church;* Evelyn Brooks Higginbotham, *Righteous Discontent: The Women's Movement in the Black Baptist Church, 1880–1920* (Cambridge, Mass.: Harvard University Press, 1993).

10. Smith et al., *Philanthropy in Communities of Color*, 9.

11. Anderson and Moss, *Dangerous Donations.*

12. Lincoln and Mamiya, *The Black Church.*

13. For more information, see Emmett D. Carson, *A Charitable Appeals Fact Book: How Black and White Americans Respond to Different Types of Fund-Raising Efforts*

(Washington, D.C.: Joint Center for Political Studies, 1989); Emmett D. Carson, *A Hand Up: Black Philanthropy and Self-Help in America* (Washington, D.C.: Joint Center for Political and Economic Studies Press, 1993); Emmett D. Carson, "Black Philanthropy: Shaping Tomorrow's Nonprofit Sector," *NSFRE Journal* (summer 1989): 23–31; Emmett D. Carson, "Despite Long History, Black Philanthropy Gets Little Credit as 'Self-Help' Tool," *Focus* 15, no. 6 (June 1987): 3, 4, 76.

14. Smith et al., *Philanthropy in Communities of Color.*

15. Lincoln and Mamiya, *The Black Church.* More information on mutual aid societies can be found in V. P. Franklin, *Black Self-Determination: A History of African American Resistance* (New York: Lawrence Hill Books, 1992).

16. Smith et al., *Philanthropy in Communities of Color,* 11.

17. Lawrence Otis Graham, *Our Kind of People: Inside America's Black Upper Class* (New York: HarperPerennial, 2000).

18. Beverly Gordon, *Bazaars and Fair Ladies: The History of the American Fundraising Fair* (Knoxville: University of Tennessee Press, 1998).

19. Graham, *Our Kind of People,* 113.

20. Links Inc. publicity materials, 2001.

21. Graham, *Our Kind of People.*

22. E. Franklin Frazier, *The Black Bourgeois* (New York: Free Press, 1957).

23. Tamara L. Brown, Gregory S. Parks, and Clarenda M. Phillips, eds., *African American Fraternities and Sororities: The Legacy and the Vision* (Lexington: University Press of Kentucky, 2005).

24. Ibid. See also Annie Lawrence-Brown and Pearl S. White, *The Legacy Continues: The History of Sigma Gamma Rho Sorority, 1974–1994,* vol. 2 (Chicago: Sigma Gamma Rho Sorority, 1994); Marjorie Parker, *Alpha Kappa Alpha: In the Eye of the Beholder* (Washington, D.C.: Alpha Kappa Alpha Sorority, 1978); Lullelia Wittarrison, *Torchbearers of a Legacy: A History of Zeta Phi Beta Sorority, Inc., 1920–1997* (Washington, D.C.: Zeta Phi Beta Sorority, 1998); Paula Giddings, *In Search of Sisterhood: Delta Sigma Theta and the Challenge of the Black Sorority Movement* (New York: William Morrow, 1988).

25. Lawrence-Brown and White, *The Legacy Continues;* Parker, *Alpha Kappa Alpha;* Wittarrison, *Torchbearers of a Legacy;* Giddings, *In Search of Sisterhood.*

26. Parker, *Alpha Kappa Alpha;* Marjorie Parker, *Past Is Prologue: The History of Alpha Kappa Alpha, 1908–1999* (Washington, D.C.: Author, 1999).

27. Giddings, *In Search of Sisterhood.*

28. Wittarrison, *Torchbearers of a Legacy.*

29. Lawrence-Brown and White, *The Legacy Continues.*

30. Ibid.; Parker, *Alpha Kappa Alpha;* Wittarrison, *Torchbearers of a Legacy;* Giddings, *In Search of Sisterhood.*

31. Giddings, *In Search of Sisterhood.*

32. Mahlene Duckett Lee, interview with Patricia Louison, March 7, 2006.

33. Brown et al., *African American Fraternities and Sororities.* See also Lawrence-

Brown and White, *The Legacy Continues;* Parker, *Alpha Kappa Alpha;* Wittarrison, *Torchbearers of a Legacy;* Giddings, *In Search of Sisterhood.*

34. Lee interview.

35. Alpha Kappa Alpha Web site, www.aka1908.com (accessed March 16, 2006).

36. Sigma Gamma Rho Web site, www.sgrh01922.org (accessed March 17, 2006); Pearl S. White, *Behind These Doors: A Legacy. The History of Sigma Gamma Rho Sorority* (Cary, N.C.: Sigma Gamma Rho Sorority, 1974).

37. Giddings, *In Search of Sisterhood;* Parker, *Alpha Kappa Alpha.*

38. AKA Web site, www.aka1908.com.

39. Cynthia Shelton, "We Are What We Do: The National Program of Alpha Kappa Alpha Sorority, Incorporated. A Post-modern Corporatist Interpretation of African American Women's Philanthropy" (doctoral diss., University of Kentucky, 2003); Brown et al., *African American Fraternities and Sororities.*

40. Parker, *Alpha Kappa Alpha;* Shelton, "We Are What We Do."

41. Wittarrison, *Torchbearers of a Legacy;* Zeta Phi Beta Web site, www.zphib1920 .org (accessed March 29, 2006).

42. Brown et al., *African American Fraternities and Sororities.*

43. Marybeth Gasman, "Sisters in Service: A History of Black Sororities and Education," in *Women, Philanthropy, and Education,* ed. Andrea Walton (Bloomington: Indiana University Press, 2004); Giddings, *In Search of Sisterhood;* Parker, *Alpha Kappa Alpha.*

44. Lawrence C. Ross Jr., *The Divine Nine: The History of African American Fraternities and Sororities in America* (New York: Kensington, 2001).

45. Giddings, *In Search of Sisterhood;* Charles S. Johnson, *Patterns of Negro Segregation* (New York: Cronwell, 1943).

46. Giddings, *In Search of Sisterhood,* 183.

47. Ibid.

48. M. E. Vroman, *Shaped to Its Purpose: Delta Sigma Theta—The First Fifty Years* (New York: Random House, 1964).

49. Tom C. Clark Papers, organizations material 1945–1977, series IV, Tarlton Law Library, Jamail Center for Legal Research, University of Texas School of Law, Austin.

50. Ross, *The Divine Nine.*

51. Parker, *Alpha Kappa Alpha;* White, *Behind These Doors.*

52. AKA Web site, www.aka1908.com.

53. Sigma Gamma Rho Web site, www.sgrh01922.org.

54. AKA Web site, www.aka1908.com; Ross, *The Divine Nine;* Parker, *Past Is Prologue.*

55. Delta Sigma Theta Web site, www.deltasigmatheta.org (accessed April 1, 2006); Ross, *The Divine Nine;* Giddings, *In Search of Sisterhood.*

56. March of Dimes Web site, http://marchofdimes.com (accessed March 23, 2006).

57. L. Sylver, interview with Patricia Louison, March 10, 2006.

58. Sigma Gamma Rho Web site, www.sgrh01922.org.

59. Lawrence-Brown and White, *The Legacy Continues.*

60. André McKenzie, "Community Service and Social Action: Using the Past to Guide the Future of Black Greek-Letter Fraternities," *NASPA Journal* 28, no. 1 (1990): 30–36.

61. Giddings, *In Search of Sisterhood;* Johnson, *Patterns of Negro Segregation.*

62. *Baltimore Afro-American* quoted in Giddings, *In Search of Sisterhood,* 58.

63. Ross, *The Divine Nine.*

64. White, *Behind These Doors;* Parker, *Alpha Kappa Alpha,* 235.

65. Delta Sigma Theta Web site, www.deltasigmatheta.org.

66. Black Enterprise Web site, www.blackenterprise.com (accessed March 22, 2006).

67. NPHC Web site, www.nphchq.org (accessed March 22, 2006).

68. Delta Sigma Theta Web site, www.deltasigmatheta.org.

69. Gasman, "Sisters in Service"; Giddings, *In Search of Sisterhood;* Parker, *Alpha Kappa Alpha.*

70. Charles H. Wesley, *The History of Alpha Phi Alpha: A Development in College Life* (Baltimore: Foundation Publishers, 1996), 15.

71. Brown et al., *African American Fraternities and Sororities.*

72. Ibid.; Herman Dreer, *The History of Omega Psi Phi Fraternity: A Brotherhood of Negro College Men, 1911–1939* (Washington, D.C.: Omega Psi Phi Fraternity, 1940); W. S. Savage and L. D. Reddick, *Our Cause Speeds On: An Informal History of the Phi Beta Sigma Fraternity* (Atlanta: Fuller Press, 1957); John Slade, *The Centaur Rising: Iota Phi Theta Fraternity, Inc.: Ascending to the Next Millennium* (Washington, D.C.: Nations Capital Publishers, 1999).

73. McKenzie, "Community Service and Social Action."

74. John Hope Franklin and Alfred Moss, *From Slavery to Freedom: A History of African Americans* (New York: McGraw-Hill, 1994).

75. Brown et al., *African American Fraternities and Sororities;* Walter Kimbrough, *Black Greek 101: The Culture, Customs, and Challenges of Black Fraternities and Sororities* (Teaneck, N.J.: Fairleigh Dickinson University Press, 2003).

76. Iota Phi Theta Web site, www.iotaphitheta.org (accessed April 9, 2006).

77. Go-to-High-School, Go-to-College curriculum guide, www.alphaphialpha.net (accessed April 8, 2006).

78. Wesley, *History of Alpha Phi Alpha.*

79. Ross, *The Divine Nine.*

80. Dreer, *History of Omega Psi Phi.*

81. Phi Beta Sigma national Web site, www.pbs1914.org (accessed April 27, 2006).

82. Welton Scott, *History of Phi Beta Sigma Fraternity* (Savannah, Ga.: Savannah State College, 1970).

83. Ibid.; Phi Beta Sigma Web site, www.pbs1914.org.

84. Phi Beta Sigma Web site, www.pbs1914.org.

85. Ibid.

86. McKenzie, "Community Service and Social Action."

87. Wesley, *History of Alpha Phi Alpha.*

88. Alpha Phi Alpha Web site, www.alphphialpha.net (accessed April 30, 2006).

89. Omega Psi Phi Web site, www.oppf.org (accessed April 30, 2006).

90. Ibid.; Dreer, *History of Omega Psi Phi;* Robert Gill, *The Omega Psi Phi Fraternity and the Men Who Make Its History* (Washington, D.C.: Omega Psi Phi Fraternity, 1940).

91. Centers for Disease Control, www.cdc.gov (accessed April 30, 2006).

92. Savage and Reddick, *Our Cause Speeds On.*

93. Scott Seward, written response to survey questions.

94. March of Dimes corporate Web site, www.marchofdimes.com (accessed April 29, 2006).

95. Iota Phi Theta Web site, www.iotaphitheta.org.

96. Alpha Phi Alpha Web site, www.alphaphialpha.net.

97. Gill, *Omega Psi Phi Fraternity;* Omega Psi Phi Web site, www.oppf.org.

98. Omega Psi Phi Web site, www.oppf.org.

99. Isaac Fraisier, telephone interview with Mark Barnes, March 9, 2006.

100. Seward, written response to survey questions.

101. Ibid.; Fraisier interview.

102. Brown et al., *African American Fraternities and Sororities.*

103. Fraisier interview; Scott Seward, interview with Mark Barnes, March 9, 2006.

104. Seward interview; Fraisier interview.

Part III

**Groups outside the National
Pan-Hellenic Council**

11

Strategic Essentialism and Black Greek Identity in the Postmodern Era

Cynthia Lynne Shelton

> In a world which daily becomes more complex and confusing, where materialism, automation, population concentration and competition are increasing the spiritual isolation which is so destructive to human personality, there is a need for organizations which cut across racial, national, physical and social barriers to help individuals develop constructive relationships with others.
>
> —Marjorie H. Parker

An organization is essentially a reflection of its members' needs at a specific historical moment. Human needs in both the modern and postmodern eras have included a sense of belonging, self-validation, and space for self-actualization. Organizational membership facilitates the fulfillment of these needs and, in so doing, constructs identity. Historically, the black Greek-letter organization (BGLO) is a tool to achieve personal goals and professional acumen. BGLOs are also vehicles for the construction of self.

This chapter explores black Greek identity in the postmodern era as it relates to nonmembers of the National Pan-Hellenic Council (NPHC). The groups referenced in this research are social service organizations that use Greek nomenclature and are dedicated to fellowship, sisterhood, or brotherhood. This analysis is structured according to historical consequence, using theoretical frameworks that attempt to explain the postmodern experience.

Essentialism

Twentieth-century BGLOs created and maintained elaborate rituals and activities to inculcate members with a prescribed identity. They used modernist strategies to combat the negative representations placed on people of African descent. During the first half of the twentieth century, for members of BGLOs, group identity became synonymous with the repression of individual identity. The creation of a collective or "sameness" became a primary objective to achieve the association's larger goal.

The essential (albeit often unconscious) goal of BGLOs was to contest the negative representation of African American people. The goal was to facilitate, validate, and construct a positive image of blackness. Thus, BGLOs employed essentialism for strategic purposes. The goal has not changed in the current postmodern era.

Essentialism is the belief that humans have fixed and innate attributes. Essentialism posits that the attributes of group members are the same. Diana Fuss in *Essentially Speaking* asserts that essentialism is "a belief in the real, true essence, fixed properties that define the whatness of a given entity."[1] Most often, *essentialism* is used in a negative sense. It is often reductionist and exclusionary and can be dangerous. Essentialist thought has been used to justify political projects ranging from benign neglect to tyranny, from oppression to annihilation.

Essentialism was particularly useful in the modern era (1400–1945). This epoch was characterized by value-laden dualisms that attempted to produce order and maintain control. Conventional modernist discourse employed dichotomy as a means of understanding. There was no inconsistency between opinion and truth. Untruths, evil, and immorality inhabited the opposite side of the dichotomy.

The centrality of race in modernist projects is important to the analysis of essentialism. Blackness was always on the contrary side of the dichotomy. Dichotomous divisions and cohesions were (and still are) sustained by the dialectic or intellectual exchange between race and representation.[2] For example, slavery and legalized segregation in the United States were justified by essentialist notions of human superiority and inferiority. Counterfeit representations of blackness such as minstrelsy were employed to reinforce essentialist notions.

African Americans formed associations in order to negotiate hegemonic forces of essentialist thought. In the process of organizing, group identity was formed. Racial solidarity or its perception was a critical organizing strategy. Thus, BGLOs employed essentialism strategically.

Strategic essentialism differs from essentialism, in that the marginalized group imposes "essential attributes" on itself and acknowledges that these essential attributes are constructs.[3] Gaytari Spivak defines strategic essentialism as "a sort of temporary solidarity for the purpose of social action."[4] BGLOs produced an identity that was subversive to negative representations of blackness.

Identity Politics

Black people's organizations consciously invoked and reified constructs of erudition and refinement. They used societal etiquette derived from post-Reconstruction middle-class African American families to institute a utilitarian ideology that included social reform, community activism, and institution building.

Within this mantle of racial uplift, appropriate behavior, dress, occupation, and demeanor were attempts to ward off negative stereotypes. The "politics of respectability" was a modernist response to racism and sexism. It has been duly noted that the centrality and "overdeterminacy" of race subsume all other constructions. To counter this particular manifestation of essentialism, class distinctions among African Americans were perceived as strategically important.[5] Identity politics of the time necessitated that organizing occur along class lines.

However, class stratification created a "false universalism." Kevin Gaines argues that it produced a "bourgeois conception of the qualifications of rights and citizenship." Universalism led to specific qualifications for membership in certain organizations.[6] Black women's clubs, Sigma Pi Phi (the Boulé), and the "Elite 8" fraternities and sororities are products of this response. Members of these groups used modernist strategies such as "lifting as we climb" to counter negative representations of blackness.[7] The historical exclusivity and selectivity of these organizations stem from this type of modernist identity construction.

BGLOs founded in the first half of the twentieth century reinforced late-Victorian-era values that were crucial to attaining professional status. For many college-educated African Americans, these values included the performance of unpaid public work.[8] Community service became the distinguishing feature of African American collegiate organizations. Simultaneously, these organizations functioned to increase the status, income, and leadership skills of its members. They also served to contest policies and practices designed to limit the opportunities of all black people.

The performance of "race work" enabled African American professionals to refute their proscribed role and image in American society. Indeed, Darlene Clark Hine asserts, "a distinct feature of United States black culture is a moral ethic of race service as critical to a fully evolved consciousness."[9] Affiliation with an organization of like persons helped mitigate the effects of "living behind the veil."

For many members, belonging to a BGLO helped sustain the fiction that respect was being conferred by dominant society. Membership distinguished them as positive representatives of the race. Consequently, many of the inducted perceived themselves as arbiters of an authentic black identity. Middle-class economic status, education, and professional occupation became necessary credentials to assert authentication.[10]

African Americans who matured in the Progressive Era witnessed the expansion and maturation of the professional association. This post-emancipation generation of African Americans inextricably linked identity with occupation.[11] Ostracized from most professional associations, African Americans employed strategic essentialism and formed their own organizations. For example, African American attorneys were actively engaged in "race work" during the first decades of the twentieth century. Black attorneys were excluded from the American Bar Association (ABA), and in 1912, the ABA passed a resolution that "members of the colored race" were not to be admitted. The resolution stemmed from the discovery that three black attorneys were members of the ABA and were allowed to remain so by order of the U.S. attorney general. No new black members were admitted for more than thirty years.[12] Two years after the ABA resolution, twelve law students at Howard University formed Tau Delta Sigma; by 1925, this BGLO had become the National Bar Association. The National Bar Association, like its complement the National Medical Association, was not just a social organization but a critical entity created to advance the profession and legitimize credentials.[13]

Chi Delta Mu Fraternity (1913) is another example of a collegiate organization created to strengthen a profession. Founded on Howard's campus, the fraternity consisted of students matriculating in the allied health professions. The fraternity justified its existence and diverse membership as follows: "in response to this age of specialization, the Chi Delta Mu Fraternity enjoys the unique distinction of being the only Negro fraternity of its kind in the world that accepts for membership only those men who are active in the pursuit of Medicine, Dentistry, Pharmacy or Doctors who have been graduated in these professions."[14] By 1923, the fraternity boasted twelve chapters. Similarly, Tau Delta Sigma had two chapters: Beta in Detroit, and Gamma in Chicago.

Craig Torbenson identifies the 1920s as "a decade of growth and expansion unequaled in the annals of fraternity history."[15] As evidenced by Chi Delta Mu and Tau Delta Sigma, BGLOs established during this second wave of fraternal organizing reflected Progressive Era association building. They also served to expand professional space for African Americans.

Isomorphism

The process known as normative isomorphism is one in which members of a profession receive similar training and thus share a similar worldview.[16] BGLOs of the Progressive Era were heavily invested in this process. Collegiate organizations thus prepared their members for professional work and enhanced their professional lives.

Isomorphism also helped sororities strengthen professional space for women. In the 1920s, female students at Howard founded BGLOs dedicated to the medical and legal professions. Rho Psi Phi Sorority was established in 1922 for female medical students. Within the year, the Beta Chapter was chartered at the University of California, and the Gamma Chapter was organized in New York City. Howard's women law students established Epsilon Sigma Iota Sorority in 1920. The sorority's original mission—"to encourage women of color to pursue the study of law with the focus of advancing women in the law profession"—still resonates. Epsilon Sigma Iota has a prestigious history of collective and individual accomplishments.[17] Ekwutozia Nwabuzor described Epsilon Sigma Iota as "women-centered and dedicated to helping women excel, especially in the legal profession." Nwabuzor described herself as the "anti-sorority girl" and chose not to join a sorority as an undergraduate. However, upon her arrival at Howard, the women of Epsilon Sigma Iota welcomed her and helped her acclimate to campus life. After observing the organization's outreach activities, service projects, and campus activism, Nwabuzor reconsidered sorority affiliation and became convinced that membership in the organization would enhance her professional capacity.[18]

This decision-making process to pursue membership is not uncommon. Many college students engage in mimetic isomorphism to make the decision. Uncertain about college life or professional choice, some opt to mimic a successful peer. Observing individuals one admires helps negotiate the construction of self. BGLOs support this process.

By the mid-twentieth century, societal isomorphism became a valid option for some African Americans. The Supreme Court, the agency and activism of black people, and the egalitarian rhetoric of the postwar consensus mitigated the virulent racism of the earlier decades of the century. This confluence of factors began to dismantle the American system of racial oppression. Consequently, some African Americans supported integration as a viable means to achieve equality.

Adherence to integration ideology convinced many African Americans that their interspersion into dominant society would create widespread oppor-tunities for social mobility. This condition would lead to a process of thought transmutation in which racial taxonomic theories would wane. While this process is taking place, social conflict dissipates. Integration ideology dictates the removal of impediments to integration, which will spur progress in human security. Eventually, society recognizes human commonality.

The establishment of Phi Beta Kappa chapters at Howard and Fisk universi-ties in 1953, and the *Brown v. Board of Education* decision in 1954, convinced African American integrationists that law and mainstream society were com-plicit in expanding the "vital center."[19] In the immediate postwar era, many Americans became obsessed with conformity and the concept of isomorphism.[20] African American college students considered themselves part of the vital center as well. Their acts of civil disobedience, designed to confront societal structures and transform behavior, were also efforts to validate their worthi-ness of inclusion into mainstream society. With the investment in integration ideology, African American membership in traditionally white fraternities and sororities increased.[21]

Gamma Sigma Sigma National Service Sorority (1952) attracted a signifi-cant number of African American women during the mid-twentieth century. Chapters were established at many historically black colleges and universities (HBCUs). Gamma Sigma Sigma's official history indicates that Alpha Xi (1965) at Morgan State was the first chapter at an HBCU.[22] Former Gamma Sigma Sigma members Courtney Carter and Maxine Hardin, now members of Al-pha Kappa Alpha Sorority and Delta Sigma Theta Sorority, respectively, were initiated into the sorority in the early 1970s at an HBCU. They cite multiple reasons for joining. They wanted to be Greek and emulate their friends, and since Gamma Sigma Sigma had an open membership policy, they could join as freshmen. This classic example of mimetic isomorphism, coupled with the sorority's emphasis on service, made it an attractive option for many African American women.[23]

Other organizations that attracted African American members on HBCU campuses during the mid-twentieth century are Kappa Kappa Psi (KKΨ) and Tau Beta Sigma, the National Honorary Band Fraternity and Sorority, respec-tively. KKΨ was established during the Jazz Age (1919) "to serve the college or university band programs through service projects, fundraisers, social events and other projects." The first KKΨ chapters were established on historically black campuses in 1957 at Langston University (Delta Alpha) and Texas Southern University (Gamma Omega). Chapters at other HBCUs include Delta Iota at

Florida A&M University (1969), Zeta Eta at South Carolina State (1971), and Iota Mu at Kentucky State University (1990 or 1999).[24]

Brandon Green, president of Iota Mu Chapter, stated that his high school band director, a KKΨ member, introduced him to the fraternity. Green's decision to join is further evidence of mimetic isomorphism. As a college freshman, he observed that the KKΨ members in the Kentucky State University marching band were the "best and most disciplined musicians."[25]

Given the predominance and importance of marching bands at HBCUs, band fraternities and sororities were perhaps inevitable. Roosevelt Shelton's theory of "testification" explicates the emotive influence of participatory performance. He posits, "The perfection of the ritualistic expression, i.e., the music, the dance, etc. requires an inordinate amount of preparation. Much of this preparation is group or member generated, that is, the ideas of expression arise from the group. Thus, group membership is self-selective and meta-critical. Engagement in such preparation results in organizational bonding and melding." Shelton argues that the band associations represent a by-product of this experience and remain peripheral to the overall marching band experience. "The fraternity and sorority are reflective of the experience but they are not the experience."[26] This analysis is consistent with mimetic experiences and the operation of strategic essentialism employed by black organizations. The organization functions to aid, support, and perpetuate the values of the larger unit.

KKΨ and Tau Beta Sigma (TBΣ) chapters are coed, owing to Title IX and their own nondiscrimination policies. However, on most HBCU campuses, the confusion of "male sisters" and "female brothers" is avoided. Like traditional BGLOs, black chapters of KKΨ and TBΣ remain gender specific. Understanding this preference proved to be an issue for KKΨ's Southeast District governor, Chris Haughee. In 2003, Haughee asserted that if KKΨ president Melanie Muldrows (an African American woman) had matriculated at an HBCU, "she would have never been elected." He stated, "I . . . understand and appreciate that many (most, really) black men and women attending HBCUs prefer to join gender-based chapters, even if that does not reflect the membership of the national organization. It is difficult for me to accept that no black bandswoman at any HBCU would choose to seek membership in Kappa Kappa Psi over the 25-year history of our non-discriminatory membership policy."[27]

By choosing to defy the national norm and remain gender specific, African American chapters of KKΨ and TBΣ have employed essentialism for strategic purposes. These chapters have decided that it is important to maintain consistency with traditional BGLOs.

Postmodern Blackness

The successful incorporation of African Americans into traditionally white sororities and fraternities demonstrates the virtue of integration ideology. Social mobility was a possibility for some, and for these individuals, integration mitigated some of the effects of racism. Cultural critic bell hooks asserts that in the postmodern era, class mobility "altered the collective black experience so that racism does not necessarily have the same impact."[28] Consequently, uniting black people via a shared struggle against social ostracism, political disenfranchisement, and economic degradation was no longer sufficient.

By the mid-1960s, the attention of many turned to urban and economic issues as class stratification widened and became more salient within the African American community. Black intellectuals espoused the rhetoric of identity politics and advocated a "triple front." The social dynamic of the black arts movement, the defiant public political posture of the Black Panther Party, and economic literacy and community development were the operatives of the revolution. The penultimate goal of black and cultural nationalists was to "unite the black community on the basis of common descent."[29]

Intellectuals began to deconstruct the notion of fixed essences and underlying laws as industrialized societies entered the postmodern era. This new era, characterized by the compression of time and space and the cold war, resulted in major and unprecedented social and cultural formation. In the United States, the passive resistance of the civil rights movement, which was the foundation of integration ideology, transformed into social unrest and militant action.

Asserts hooks, "Part of our struggle for radical black subjectivity is the quest to find ways to construct self and identity that are oppositional and liberatory."[30] Other critical theorists note that once members of an oppressed or marginalized group receive recognition from the dominant society, they are denounced by their group members as unrepresentative.[31] During the mid-twentieth century, the authenticity and (some would argue) the hubris of the first wave of BGLOs were challenged. New groups challenged those that chose integration and the existing power relations within BGLOs by creating their own organizations and deconstructing extant knowledge and discourse. Some groups identified themselves as more authentically representative of the African American experience. Many of these groups chose to identify themselves as Greek-letter organizations and questioned the validity of traditional BGLOs as "speaking for the subaltern."[32]

Motivated by the activism and rhetoric of El-Hajj Malik El-Shabazz (Malcolm X) and Kwame Turé (Stokley Carmichael), Groove Phi Groove Fellowship Inc. and its sister organization, Swing Phi Swing, brought cultural nationalism to the college campus.[33] Groove Phi Groove, founded at Morgan State College in 1962, offered a postmodern critique. Part of the group's articulated purpose is "to study and help alleviate social and economic problems concerning society in order to improve the status of mankind."[34] Groove Phi Groove attempted to decenter the self from Western ideology by its embrace of Afrocentricity. Lee D. Baker asserts that Afrocentricity must be understood "as an empowering counter-hegemonic philosophy, which questions epistemological considerations which are based in European cultural realities."[35] Groove Phi Groove exemplifies this definition. For example, the fellowship asserts that *Phi* is not Greek but Egyptian. It is a symbol of the Khemit people and represents "reproduction in endless series."[36]

The *Phi* in Swing Phi Swing is not Greek either. *Phi* is an acronym for "promoting higher intelligence." According to Cheryl Konegay, current chairwoman of Swing Phi Swing Social Fellowship, the group's founders "dared to be different." They were invested in Afrocentricity and Black Power and were "unafraid of doing dirty work," engaging in "hands-on community projects." Kornegay stated that she "rejected the pearls and white gloves," broke the family tradition of pledging Delta Sigma Theta, and joined Swing Phi Swing in 1971 at Bennett College. She started a new family tradition, as her sister was initiated at Shaw College in 1976, and her daughter joined the fellowship in 2005.[37]

Despite its declarations of solidarity, the fellowship has had issues. Kornegay recalled that in the mid to late 1980s, all initiation was stopped. The membership believed that new members were too close in age to the founders and thus did not show deference to their elders. Resiliently, the fellowship reactivated in the 1990s and has functioned much better as the membership has matured. Konegay admitted that the image of the fellowship was tarnished and that reactivation has been an "uphill battle that has been overcome."[38]

The fellowship's commitment to public service work has never been questioned. Members boast an extensive record of community work. Still unafraid to "get their hands dirty," Konegay's chapter in Raleigh, North Carolina, volunteers at the local women's center, where they "feed and pray with the women, and then clean the kitchen."[39]

Swing Phi Swing members do not have to be college educated. However, undergraduate prospects must be in college, and self-actualization is strongly encouraged. Konegay asserted that candidates for fellowship must be recommended by a current member and should possess "dignity, pride, be articulate or have such potential." She stated that although her organization is not a sorority, it is "open and willing to work with all organizations [BGLOs] in common goal." However, she and her colleagues often feel "held back" because they are not affiliated with the NPHC and "do not get national attention and recognition."[40]

Currently, Swing Phi Swing boasts 50 chapters with 20,000 members. Groove Phi Groove has 30,000 members in 150 undergraduate, graduate, and affiliate chapters.[41] The continuation of Groove Phi Groove and Swing Phi Swing demonstrates the often-cited notion that cultural nationalism was the major legacy of the twentieth-century civil rights movement.

Multiculturalism

BGLOs founded in the postmodern era did not present a monolithic oppositional project. By the end of the twentieth century, collegiate groups had transformed isomorphism and integration ideology into multiculturalism. These groups rejected the homogeneity of conventional fraternities and sororities and employed strategic essentialism to differentiate themselves. In theory and practice, many have reified the construct of multiculturalism by blending the conventional demarcations between particularistic and mosaic multiculturalism.[42]

Multicultural sororities and fraternities purport to have multiethnic memberships; however, most groups are predominantly African American or Latino, with a few Asian members. There are even fewer white members in these groups. Conversely, many of these groups are predominantly white, with a few nonwhite members.[43] This is evidence that many multicultural Greek associations have adopted a particularistic perspective of multiculturalism, in which distinctions between groups are preserved, even though pluralism is espoused.

Overwhelmingly, Greek organizations prefer self-segregation. One study revealed that "62% of non-Greeks disagreed with segregated housing, while only 37% of Greeks disagreed." Sixty percent of Greeks and a significantly higher percentage of non-Greeks (87 percent) "liked hanging out with other races and cultures."[44]

The case of Melody Twilley, an African American who twice "rushed" the all-white sororities at the University of Alabama (UA) and was rejected, illustrates the Greek preference for segregation. UA has long been the site of racial unrest. Examples include the dismissal of Autherine Lucy Foster in 1953 for her "own safety" and the 1986 cross-burning incident when Alpha Kappa Alpha moved to all-white Sorority Row. Most African American students at UA supported

Twilley's cause. Yet many demonstrated the penchant for isomorphism when they queried, "Why would anyone want to do that?" Despite pressure from the UA administration and alumni on its "Greek Machine" to integrate, Twilley was not accepted.[45] Various proposals to force integration were rejected and opposed by members of both black and white collegiate organizations. The solution was to create a new multicultural sorority on campus, Alpha Delta Sigma Sorority Inc. (2002), of which Twilley was a founding member.[46]

Christina Houston surreptitiously integrated UA's Sorority Row by joining Gamma Phi Beta the year prior to Twilley's attempts. Houston's mother is white and her father is black, facts she did not divulge during the rush process. One can speculate that Houston's revelation was used by UA to temper the furor surrounding its segregation issues.

In 2005, UA boasted several multicultural collegiate organizations. In addition to Alpha Delta Sigma, the Kappa Chapter of Delta Xi Phi (1994) had eight members, two of whom were identified as black. Delta Xi Phi is a member of the National Multicultural Greek Council and was established at the University of Illinois–Urbana-Champaign. According to UA's campus history, after the Twilley incident, Dean of Students Tom Strong was interested in establishing a multicultural sorority, and Delta Xi Phi was invited to the campus. When the interest group split, both Alpha Delta Sigma and Delta Xi Phi were created.

UA has also expressed interest in establishing the first chapter of Sigma Lambda Beta (1986) in the state. Sigma Lambda Beta was founded at the University of Iowa with an emphasis on Latino culture. The "Purple Nation" now claims to have between 500 and 1,200 members in forty-three chapters and twenty colonies. UA students found the group attractive because "of its success nationally and because it was not exclusively Latino."[47]

In the postmodern era, the seemingly dichotomous concepts of the mosaic and the melting pot have converged, but issues of race remain central. Multicultural collegiate organizations are reflective of the multiple ethnic identities of black people in the United States. Many members embrace multiple heritages and choose not to live with a hyphenated identity. Michael Omi asserts that white Americans exercise the ethnic option, picking and choosing what suits them in a given time and space.[48] As Christina Houston at UA demonstrates, this is also true of many black or multiracial people in the twenty-first century.

Many students in multicultural organizations are first-generation American or first-generation college educated, reflecting the increase in minority student enrollment in colleges and universities. It is difficult to determine whether these groups are engaged in identity politics or whether they are developing a political framework based on identity. Twilley maintains that she did not have a political agenda and was unaware that no black women were admitted to UA's Sorority Row.[49]

The motto of Mu Sigma Upsilon Sorority (1981), founded at Rutgers University, articulates the complexity of postmodern identity. Its goal is to "recognize that culture is not just about country borders; culture is about language, symbols, technology, institutions and beliefs." In conjunction with eleven other predominantly East Coast groups, Mu Sigma Upsilon Sorority formed the Multicultural Greek Council in 1988. Council member Gamma Omega Delta Fraternity extends W. E. B. DuBois's twentieth-century proclamation and asserts that the "problem of the color line" is still apparent. This group has merged pluralistic multiculturalism with the preservation of particularistic attributes, as its stated purpose is to acknowledge "the barrier of race" and insist that "diversity is not the exception, it is the rule."[50]

The modernist issue of race and the strategy to emphasize community service continue into the postmodern era. Collegiate groups exhibit other continuities between the modern and postmodern eras. Most multicultural organizations are similar to conventional collegiate organizations, in that most have adopted the jargon, public calls, stepping, hand signs, and handshakes of African American fraternities and sororities.

Cultural Relativism

As Western industrialized society became more affluent with the embrace of advanced capitalism, the choice between "bread and butter" issues became less dominant in the discourse. With the "end of history," the belief that liberal democracy will forever reign encouraged the ascendancy of cultural issues in Western society.[51] Issues such as the control of reproductive capacity, marriage rights, and privacy rights became fodder in the culture wars and began to inform identity in the twenty-first century.[52]

By the end of the twentieth century, the postmodern challenge to modernity was fulfilled as the principle that beliefs, activities, and behaviors are axiomatic became a heuristic tool. The concept of relativism—the notion that beliefs, activities, and behaviors have no absolute reference and must be assessed only in terms of their historical or cultural context—became the prevailing academic epistemology. Cultural relativism, designed for the comparative assessment of cultures, was routinely employed to ward against cultural bias or ethnocentrism. Unfortunately, moral relativism—which asserts that there are no absolute morals and standards by which to assess an ethical proposition—has converged with cultural relativism. The concept of cultural relativism has been transformed into an ideology with its own discourse that asserts, "Everything is relative," which is negatively transformed to mean "anything goes." This rhetoric dominates the ideologically driven culture wars of the post–cold war era. Within its proper context, cultural relativism is an appropriate tool to assess the postmodern phenomenon of religious and sex-specific Greek-letter organizations.[53]

CONSTRUCTS OF SEXUALITY

The tenets of postmodernity, which assert the validity of multiple truths and all perspectives, empower individuals whose lifestyle and sexuality differ from perceived societal norms. Again, collegiate organizations use strategic essentialism as a means of maintaining and creating identity, and as a vehicle to create and legitimize political and institutional space. King-To Yeung asserts that homosexual men and women have challenged the "heterosexual model of fraternities while preserving key elements of the tradition." Yeung's research reveals that homosexual fraternities provide comfortable space "that encourage[s] brotherly, non-erotic relations lacking in the mainstream gay culture."[54]

Two significant sex-specific collegiate organizations were established in Tallahassee, Florida: Delta Phi Upsilon (1985) and Beta Phi Omega (2000). Despite its relatively recent establishment, Beta Phi Omega, also known as the National Feminine Minority Lesbian Sorority, has eight chapters. Its service projects focus primarily on health and health education while promoting lesbian pride and identity. According to its Web site, Delta Phi Upsilon was the first Greek-letter fraternity established for "Gay Men of Color." The Delts claim more than 300 initiated members in community-based chapters in Florida and Georgia. Delta Phi Upsilon is committed to correcting the disconnect between civil and human rights, and a main criterion of membership eligibility is being a registered voter. Its Project WATCHCARE supports "the legalization of same-sex marriage and the elimination of discriminatory policies in employment and life."[55]

These fraternal and sororal associations are actively engaged in identity politics to refute the absolutism of the modern era. Their political engagement distinguishes cultural and moral relativity as it asserts the postmodern adage that "politics is personal" and the ethical position that civil rights are human rights.

CONSTRUCTS OF RELIGION

In his post–cold war treatise *Clash of Civilizations and the Remaking of World Order,* Samuel Huntington argues that culture and religion will dominate geopolitics.[56] Despite his many critics and the obvious flaws in the thesis, religion has become an organizing principle of postmodern society. Christian principles have always been a fundamental part of most BGLOs. Reverence and obedience to God serve as guiding principles. Prayers are a ritualistic component of most ceremonies. By the late twentieth century, as in society, religion had become the focus of many collegiate organizations.

According to its Web site, the purpose of Alpha Nu Omega Inc. (1988) is "to present a Christian alternative to the students and/or faculty on college/university campuses, to minister to the needs of the whole person (spirit, soul, and body), and to promote an attitude of academic excellence among its members." As an "alternative" organization, Alpha Nu Omega demonstrates isomorphism by rejecting the secular worldview that characterizes most Greek-letter organizations. Founded at Morgan State by Shirley K. Russell, the organization fulfills postmodern objectives of helping to "make sense" of contemporary black experience, in that the organization embraces professionalism and is uniquely cogendered. President Curtis M. Brown asserts that Alpha Nu Omega is "one organization with a single constitution with fraternity and sorority components."[57] It has rejected the modernist construction of traditional African American religious groups in which men dominate and women serve as an auxiliary. This model appears to have appeal, as the organization currently has chapters in several states.

Christian-centric organizations are an attempt to address the spiritual isolation that Marjorie Parker refers to in the epigraph of this chapter. The reascendancy of religious fundamentalism is a global phenomenon, perhaps in reaction to increased capitalism. In any case, the passionate desire to insert religiosity into everyday life, inclusive of dress, speech, discourse, and politics, often results in intolerance.

Intolerance, in part, led Althia F. Collins to create a sorority that would respect and support her faith. According to Collins, she was "forced to leave a job she enjoyed" because coworkers would not accept her difference. Concerned that other professional women (especially young women) would encounter similar circumstances, she and her daughter, Imani Abdul-Haqq, formed Gamma Gamma Chi Sorority in Greensboro, North Carolina, in 2005. Collins, who serves as the organization's president and executive director, contends that

Gamma Gamma Chi is the first Islamic-based sorority. Its goal is to "improve the image of Muslim women and Islam in general" and to "unify collegiate and professional Muslim women." Consistent with BGLOs of the first half of the twentieth century, this is an example of associative organizing in an attempt to counter negative representation of this group. Yet, consistent with the postmodern construct of strategic essentialism, religious identity is the means. The sorority's motto—"Striving for the pleasure of Allah through sisterhood, scholarship, leadership and community service"—is also consistent with Sharia (Islamic law). The sorority is actively engaged in expansion and aims to have a chapter in every region of the United States by 2015.

Students at the University of Kentucky purportedly contacted Collins and expressed interest in forming a chapter on campus, generating considerable media buzz. Although the university's Office of Student Affairs confirmed the students' interest and indicated that the university was willing to give any support necessary, no application has been made.[58] The sorority is making progress toward its goal, however. Exactly one year after its founding, the sorority established its second chapter in Atlanta, Georgia, and six women from various Georgia colleges were inducted on April 23, 2006. Given the increasing number of Muslims in the United States, Gamma Gamma Chi has a good chance of reaching its goal.[59]

In the postmodern world, the constructs of religion and sexuality function to facilitate organizing and associative activity. These constructs are also used as an isomorphic tool to facilitate group identity for college students. The production of this collective identity helps individuals negotiate personal and professional space.

Essentialist conceptualizations of race have been constant, regardless of the historical moment. Thus, the use of strategic essentialism has been critical to the development of positive human relationships with others and with self. Marjorie Parker's words, written during the middle of the twentieth century, delineate the continual need for humans to form associations. Associative activity facilitates the understanding of reality. The varied and multivalent manifestations of BGLOs broaden conceptualizations of African American identity. By creating group identity, the BGLO has assisted individuals in negotiating the complexities of their lives, from emancipation to contested citizenship to full participation in a global society. By maintaining relevant strategies and adopting new ones, BGLOs make sense of the African American experience.

Notes

Epigraph from Marjorie H. Parker, *Alpha Kappa Alpha: Sixty Years of Service* (Washington, D.C.: Alpha Kappa Alpha Inc., 1966), 51. Parker's statement also addresses the concerns of postmodern critics who assert that the moment has resulted in fragmented, schizophrenic personalities.

1. Diana Fuss, *Essentially Speaking: Feminism, Nature and Difference* (Oxford: Routledge, 1990).

2. Extrapolating from the work of poststructuralists, Jacques Derrida and Jacques Lacan critique the Western preoccupation with finding the truth. Lacan decenters the self by deconstructing Descartes' concept of self, asserting that the self is constructed in language. See Ellie Ragland-Sullivan and Mark Braeher, *Lacan and the Subject of Language* (New York: Routledge, 1991). See also Jacque Derrida, *Of Grammatology*, ed. Gaytari Chakrovorty Spivak (Baltimore: John Hopkins University Press, 1984).

3. http://academic.reed.edu/english/Courses/English558/Week2.html.

4. Gaytari Chakrovorty Spivak, *The Post-Colonial Reader*, ed. Bill Ashcroft (Oxford: Routledge, 1995).

5. See James Grossman, *Chicago, Land of Hope, Black Southerners, and the Great Migration* (Chicago: University of Chicago Press, 1991). See also William H. Harris, "The Grand Boulé at the Dawn of a New Century: Sigma Pi Phi Fraternity," in *African American Fraternities and Sororities: The Legacy and the Vision*, ed. Tamara L. Brown, Gregory S. Parks, and Clarenda M. Phillips (Lexington: University Press of Kentucky, 2005), 105–6.

6. Kevin Gaines, *"Uplifting the Race: Black Leadership, Politics, and Culture in the Twentieth Century* (Chapel Hill: University of North Carolina Press, 1996), 5.

7. Although often criticized for its lack of social activism, the Boulé instituted a Committee on Public Welfare in 1915 and reaffirmed it in 1919. See Harris, "The Grand Boulé," 105–6.

8. See Stephanie Shaw, *What a Woman Ought to Be and to Do: Black Professional Women Workers during the Jim Crow Era* (Chicago: University of Chicago Press, 1996), 170.

9. Darlene Clark Hine, *Speak Truth to Power: Black Professional Class in United States History* (New York: Carlson Publishing, 1996), xxvii.

10. Cornel West asserts that these responses were advanced by "anxiety-ridden, middle-class black intellectuals (predominantly male and heterosexual) grappling with their sense of double-consciousness—namely their own crisis." Cornel West, "Race and Modernity," in *The Cornel West Reader* (New York: Basic Civitas Books, 1999), 56. This emerging and increasing black middle class differed from the "aristocrats of color," for whom complexion, religiosity, and often antebellum ancestry were criteria for inclusion. Many of the founders of the Elite 8 were one generation removed from slavery.

See Willard Gatewood, *Aristocrats of Color: The Black Elite* (Bloomington: Indiana University Press, 1990), 57.

11. Cynthia Lynne Shelton, "We Are What We Do: The National Program of Alpha Kappa Alpha Sorority, Inc." (PhD diss., University of Kentucky, 2003).

12. There has been some contention about the specific date when black attorneys were officially admitted into the ABA. See Tony Mauroamerican, "ABA Poised to Take Long Overdue Step," *Texas Lawyer,* February 2, 2002.

13. Credentials (or the lack thereof) were often used to prohibit black people from full participation in their chosen professions. See Shelton, "We Are What We Do."

14. Howard University *Bison,* 1922.

15. Craig L. Torbenson, "The Origin and Evolution of College Fraternities and Sororities," in Brown et al., *African American Fraternities and Sororities,* 56.

16. Mark Mizruchi and Lisa Fein, "The Social Construction of Organizational Knowledge: A Study of the Uses of Coercive, Mimetic, and Normative Isomorphism," *Administrative Science Quarterly* (December 1999).

17. In 2006, the sorority earned Howard University's "Organization of the Year" award. The twenty-six members of Epsilon Sigma Iota are highly visible on Howard's campus. Currently, the editor in chief of the *Howard Law Review,* four board members of the law journal, the vice president of the Black Students Law Association, and the president of the Howard Public Interest Society are members of ESI.

18. Ekwutozia Nwabuzor, interview by author, June 1, 2006.

19. The "vital center" terminology is used by consensus historians of the mid-twentieth century in an attempt to de-emphasize societal conflict and highlight what they purport to be the nation's "long tradition of shared ideas, principles and values." See Arthur Schlesinger, *The Vital Center: The Politics of Freedom* (Edison, N.J.: Transaction Press, 1997).

20. Mizruchi and Fein, "Social Construction of Organizational Knowledge."

21. There have always been black people in white fraternities and sororities; of particular note is Phi Beta Kappa.

22. Charlotte Chipper Debuskey, *Gamma Sigma Sigma Pledge Handbook,* 1972–1973 ed.

23. Courtney Carter and Maxine Hardin, interview by author, June 15, 2006. Open membership meant that there was no class year or grade point requirement.

24. KKY Web site, www.kkytbs.org/. KKY boasts Count Basie, Neil Armstrong, Ray Charles, Wynton Marsalis, and Bill Clinton as members. There is contention over the founding date for the Iota Mu Chapter.

25. Brandon Green, interview by author, Kentucky State University, Frankfort, June 12, 2006.

26. Roosevelt Shelton, interview by author, July 29, 2006.

27. Chris Haughee, "Women in Kappa Kappa Psi—My Evolving Perspective," http://harmony.gatech.edu/iota/eighthnote/printer.php?year=2003&semester=fall.

28. bell hooks, "Postmodern Blackness," *Postmodern Culture* 1, no. 1 (1990): 6.

29. Ibid.

30. hooks asserts that radical postmodernism calls attention to sensibilities, which are shared across boundaries of class, gender, and race. It calls for a construction of empathy to promote common commitments that can serve as a new strategy of resistance. See ibid., 1.

31. Spivak, *The Post-Colonial Reader.*

32. Ibid.

33. See Harold Cruse, *The Crisis of the Black Intellectual: A Historical Analysis of the Failure of Black Leadership* (New York: New York Review of Books, 2005), and Scot Brown, *Fighting for the US: Maulana Karenga, the US Organization and Black Cultural Nationalism* (New York: New York University Press, 2005). Cultural nationalism is the conceptual or aesthetic return to Africa in an effort to reclaim a heritage that has been distorted, omitted, and otherwise maligned and marginalized.

34. Groove Phi Groove Web site, www.groovephigroove.org.

35. Lee D. Baker, Department of Anthropology, Temple University, http://www.africa.upenn.edu/K-12/Afrocentric_Racism_16168.html.

36. Ibid.

37. Cheryl Konegay, interview by author, May 15, 2006.

38. Ibid.

39. Ibid.

40. Ibid.

41. Groove Phi Groove Web site, www.groovephigroove.org.

42. For definitions of multiculturalism, see Diane Ravitch, *The Language Police: How Pressure Groups Restrict What Students Learn* (New York: Vintage, 2004).

43. Most of these organizations do not keep official records regarding racial and ethnic data. Categorization would defeat the purpose of such groups.

44. "Members of Greek Groups Unlikely to Seek Diversity," *Women in Higher Education* 12, no. 11 (November 2003): 38.

45. Eric Hoover, "New Scrutiny for Powerful Greek Systems," *Chronicle*, June 8, 2001.

46. The members opted for the description of diversity instead of multiculturalism, which, they argue, "encompasses so many more things, such as socio-economic background and sexual orientation, as well as just race and religion." See the Alpha Delta Sigma Web site, www.alphadeltaasigma.org.

47. "Hispanic, Diversity-Based Greek Organizations Raising Cultural Awareness on Campus," *Diverse Issues in Higher Education* 22, no. 22 (December 15, 2005): 12.

48. Michael Omi and Howard Winant, *Racial Formation in the United States: From the 1960s to the 1990s* (Oxford: Routledge, 1994).

49. Jason Zengerle, "The New Schoolhouse Door: Sorority Row," *New Republic*, February 3, 2002.

50. See Gamma Omega Delta Web site, www.gammaomegadelta.org.

51. See Francis Fukuyama, *The End of History and the Last Man* (New York: Free Press, 2006).

52. Legal positivism maintains that there are no rights other than those granted by the state.

53. Anthropologist Franz Boas and his protégés, especially Margaret Mead, are credited with the initial identification and implementation of cultural relativism. They used it as a methodology to make sense of their research and, specifically, to guard against ethnocentrism.

54. King-To Yeung, "Challenging the Heterosexual Model of Brotherhood: The Gay Fraternity's Dilemma" (unpublished manuscript, n.d.).

55. Delta Phi Upsilon Web site, www.dphiu.org/the-fraternity.html.

56. Samuel P. Huntington, "The Clash of Civilizations?" *Foreign Affairs* 72, no. 3 (1993).

57. Alpha Nu Omega Web site, www.alphanuomega.org.

58. Sean Rose, "Greek Letters, Islamic Principles, UK Students Aim to Found First Chapter," *Kentucky Kernel,* November 29, 2005.

59. The U.S. Census does not record religious affiliation. Based on independent studies, the number of Muslims in the United States is estimated at between 1 million and 3 million, or 0.4 to 0.09 percent of the population. The count of African American Muslims is even less accurate but is estimated at 100,000 to 2 million. See National Opinion Research Center, www.experts.com.

12

"I've Got All My Sisters with Me"
Black Women's Organizations in the Twenty-first Century

Shirley A. Jackson

This chapter explores the history and themes of black women's organizations, in particular, social and civic organizations. Historically, the ability of black women to engage in social and civic activism has been hampered by their exclusion from those organizations founded or dominated by their white counterparts.[1] In response, black women developed their own clubs, and these groups are the basis on which many black women still organize today. Black women patterned their organizations after and were inspired by those of white women. However, there were some important differences, in that black women knew the necessity of finding the type of work "that will be original, peculiarly suitable to our peculiar needs and that will distinguish our work from white women's clubs."[2]

Historical Overview

The coming together of black women to pursue a common interest or goal is not new. Women's collectives are evident throughout the African diasporas and have historically been visible when and where women have worked together to take care of their families, household tasks, and those chores that led them both to the market and into the fields. These activities in both the "public sphere" and the private or "domestic sphere" were often accomplished with the help and guidance of other women.[3] African women's lives were intertwined but not necessarily segmented; rather they encompassed a *worldview* of women's roles that included both private and public spheres.[4] This approach to organizing among women is still common today.

The degree to which black women work together to solve problems, whether personal, familial, political, economic, or social, is indicative of the many ways women are involved in the *process* of organizing and the activism that ensues. The organizing and activism of women demand a present-day consideration. Much of the study of black women's activism is, unfortunately, limited to the antislavery activism of black and white women abolitionists,[5] to the club movement of the 1890s to 1920s,[6] to their roles in the church,[7] or to their roles during the civil rights movement of the 1950s and 1960s.[8] These limited temporal snapshots discount the integral role that activism plays in the lives of black women today. In a reworking of the motto of the National Association of Colored Women's Clubs Inc., black women are still attempting to "lift as they climb," and much of this work is done under the auspices of social and civic sororities.

Black women's organizations often find their roots in informal gatherings. Some groups may then opt for a formal structure by establishing bylaws, appointing or electing an executive board, and developing a mission statement. The creation of formal organizations has the dual purpose of clarifying organizational missions and goals and bringing a degree of formal recognition to the women involved and by society at large. The latter is important because it often includes submitting requests for funding and other types of support from outside agencies. Organizations may find that they are unable to locate sources of funding, thus limiting their ability to establish or maintain the group. I address here the histories and missions of several black women's organizations and their current plans of action. I also discuss some of the problems faced by organizations in terms of membership and the perceived need for the continuing existence of black women's social organizations.

Politicizing Women's Civic Engagement

Club development for black women has been personal, public, and political. These three factors combine to help African American women's organizations address myriad political and social issues that affect them, their families, and their communities. In fact, historically, these organizations have been rooted in the very real need to aid black women and the black community at large, often during periods defined by hostile social, economic, and political climates.[9]

NATIONAL ASSOCIATION OF COLORED WOMEN'S CLUBS

Two separate organizations, the National Federation of Afro-American Women and the National League of Colored Women, joined forces in 1896 to become the National Association of Colored Women's Clubs Inc. (NACWC). The National Federation of Afro-American Women was founded in Boston in

1895, with Margaret Murray Washington as its first president. Similarly, also in 1895, "female members of Washington's black elite under the leadership of Mary Church Terrell—educator, lecturer, and politician—and the educator Anna Julia Cooper" organized the National League of Colored Women.[10]

Thus, a mere three decades after the end of slavery, one of the earliest black women's organizations still in existence today, the NACWC, was founded. The organization was established by Mary Church Terrell and other black women in response to a letter disparaging black womanhood.[11] Conspicuously, this was the same year that the U.S. Supreme Court handed down its landmark decision in *Plessy v. Ferguson,* determining that "separate but equal" facilities for whites and blacks was the law of the land. The new organization's primary function was to address the problem of the color line, which inhibited the members' ability to work directly with their white female counterparts due to segregated organizations. The NACWC worked to promote positive images and public perceptions of black women, utilizing a cadre of women committed to "the Republican motherhood, insisting that the future of the race was moored to African American mothers' moral guardianship."[12] Its motto, "Lifting as We Climb," attests to its mission of fostering support among black women and promoting the moral and racial uplift of their sisters. The NACWC also exemplifies W. E. B. DuBois's notion of a "Talented Tenth," those blacks who have the unique responsibility of engaging in the racial and moral uplift of the rest of the black population.[13] The organization's members continue to be obligated to do so through its mission of "respectability, that is, a standard of behavior expected of all blacks, especially of the women."[14] The NACWC has been at the forefront of bringing attention to the concerns of African American women through its platform. The following objectives are listed on its Web site:

- To work for the economic, moral, religious, and social welfare of women and youth.
- To protect the rights of women and youth.
- To raise the standard and quality of life in home and family.
- To secure and use our influence for the enforcement of civil and political rights for African Americans and all citizens.
- To promote the education of women and youth through the work of the departments.
- To obtain for African American women the opportunity of reaching the highest levels in all fields of human endeavor.
- To promote effective interaction with the male auxiliary.

- To promote interracial understanding so that justice and goodwill may prevail among all people.
- To hold educational workshops biennially at the convention.[15]

Although many of the women involved in the organization today may be reluctant to identify themselves and their activities as *feminist,*[16] the NACWC platform suggests otherwise. A look at the organization's current goals, as listed in its plan of action on its Web site, provides a glimpse of the contemporary issues affecting the organization:

- Increase membership—target young adults
- To initiate an AIDS Awareness Program
- Network with organizations
- Completion of Renaissance Project—1601 R Street
- Increase club involvement in fifty states
- Implement programs to strengthen the Black Family
- Increase scholarships and programs for our youth
- To initiate organ donor and blood donation program[17]

Of interest is the organization's aim to increase its membership, with a specific focus on young adults. For those African American women's organizations that require some type of annual dues or fee, however, membership may be out of reach for some young people. But organizations that find themselves with an increasingly aging membership and leadership realize the importance of replenishing their ranks with new, younger members, who also bring new ideas about activities, programs, and organizational direction.

The concerted effort to attract young members is directly linked to the NACWC's Youth Clubs. These clubs were designed for young women and young men in 1930 and 1984, respectively. Thus, whereas the connection to young women has been deeply entrenched within the organization's philosophy for many years, its inclusion of young men is a relatively recent development. Formerly titled the National Association of Girls Clubs and the National Association of Boys Clubs, both now make up the National Association of Youth Clubs.[18] Their joint inclusion in the organization's membership may have the unintended impact of addressing high membership costs, which might have discouraged young people's involvement. Additionally, as younger women are incorporated into the activism of "mother organizations," they, like their foremothers, are likely to maintain a history of sustained activism within such organizations.

Furthermore, with a current membership of 45,000 in thirty-eight states,[19] increasing club involvement nationally is a goal that can be linked to increased membership. More important, though, it speaks to the organization's attempts to fulfill many past goals and to develop new clubs to achieve the organization's new goals. The benefit is apparent for both the women who become involved and for the organization. Each needs the other to fulfill their objectives of supporting a history of activism and finding solutions to problems.

NATIONAL COUNCIL OF NEGRO WOMEN

Founded in 1935 by Mary McLeod Bethune, the National Council of Negro Women (NCNW) is what Audrey Thomas McCluskey describes as "the largest nonsorority black women's organization in America."[20] The organization's initial focus was on maximizing the "political and economic clout of black women."[21] More specifically, the organization states that its mission is "to lead, develop, and advocate for women of African descent as they support their families and communities."[22]

As the largest organization of black women, with almost 4 million members and a budget of more than $1.5 million,[23] the NCNW has a strong membership base, which increases its ability to provide a wide array of community programs. The emphasis on community includes what Cheryl Townsend Gilkes refers to as "community work" and includes "all tasks contained in strategies to combat racial oppression and to strengthen African American social, economic, and political institutions in order to foster group survival, growth, and advancement. . . . Community work also focuses on changing ideas, stereotypes, and images that keep a group perpetually stigmatized."[24]

The NCNW is committed to national and international projects that benefit women and children. Since its inception, it has been involved in providing a variety of services in the United States and in several African countries. Specifically, the NCNW provides "critical services to women, children and families designed to improve the quality of life in all communities. Currently, through domestic and international programs, NCNW is operating in urban and rural cities in the United States and in Eritrea, Benin, Kenya, and South Africa."[25]

Sisterhood and Service

There are numerous examples of African American women's organizations that function as social groups. Cases in point include the Links (which also considers itself a political organization), SISTUHS Inc., the Girl Friends, the Chums, and the Smart Set. These are national organizations with local chapters. What sets these organizations apart from others is that they limit memberships to small numbers of women, often by invitation only. They have been sharply criticized for their historical and, some would argue, current reliance on skin color and social class to weed out individuals who do not pass the "brown bag" test, which excludes blacks with skin darker than a brown paper bag. Diana Kendall notes the special place of such groups during the club era, writing that "black social clubs, fraternal organizations, and churches became the center of black social life, and it is in social organizations such as Jack and Jill of America, The Links, The Girl Friends, and the Boulé, which were organized to focus on tradition and pride in family background and accomplishment, that we find the roots for the black debutant presentation."[26] They provide an intimate network of women who pursue like interests but also serve as exclusive centers for black women's networking.

THE GIRL FRIENDS

The Girl Friends Inc. was founded in 1927 and is an organization of 1,300 women, with membership limited to a select few. The group began in New York City as "a club of young women with similar backgrounds and interests who could meet occasionally for social or intellectual purposes." The organization has forty chapters and focuses on "philanthropic, social, and cultural activities, raising money for local and national charities as well as sponsoring programs for its own members." These women, from some of the "oldest and best-respected families" in their communities, have followed the paths of their parents through their hypergamous marriage patterns, marrying well-educated, prominent, professional men with enviable occupations such as lawyers, doctors, and politicians. However, the Girl Friends themselves possess strong track records as "educators, attorneys, physicians, professors, high-profile fund-raisers, and government officials."[27]

The group has had its detractors. Historically, it has practiced both colorism and classism, limiting membership to those considered the black elite. Selective organizations such as the Girl Friends that engage in segregation based on class and skin color may actually limit the number of women participating in other prominent elite organizations, such as the Smart Set or the Links, due to their tendency to exclude women who do not meet membership requirements related to class and skin color. Lawrence Otis Graham quotes a Chicago Girl Friend member: "We're a lot smaller than the Links because we're a lot more selective than they are." The woman goes on to say, "They are all about money, power, and ambition these days. . . . The Girl Friends aren't into that kind of power."[28] Yet the Girl Friends continues to engage in social elitism; this is evident in the organization's membership directory, which includes photographs, occupations of members and their spouses, members' children's names, and whether their daughters are also members. The last is an example of nepotism and may provide insight into the number of women who generate members from within their own families. Because their mothers are already the "right kind of people," the daughters would likely be so as well. Graham notes:

> Unless you are the daughter of a member, getting into the Girl Friends is even more difficult than getting into the Links. Since the chapters are generally smaller (usually twenty to thirty members) than Links Chapters, and since no city has no more than one chapter, it really does require a wave of resignations or deaths before a woman's chances for acceptance improve. There is no membership office to call. You have to be sponsored by at least two members who know you well, and at least two-thirds of the members must vote for your admission. If a woman is turned down, she can never be proposed by that chapter again.[29]

Unlike some of its counterparts that have Web sites to provide members and, perhaps most importantly, *potential* members with information on the group's activities, none exists for the Girl Friends. This is due in large part to the selective membership process. In essence, they do not need to advertise their activities or their members, given the closed nature of the group. At work here is also the fact that local chapters have their own networking channels. Additionally, the national office publishes a journal, the *Chatterbox,* for its members. Although all this seemingly makes the Internet unnecessary, it only adds to the organization's secrecy, especially with regard to member selection. This close-knit organization of women in cities around the country is sometimes considered too close. As one detractor states, "Those Girl Friends are almost *too* intimate."[30] The implication here is that the close networks of women involved in the organization know too much about the personal lives of others involved. This also adds to the difficulty of outsiders gaining entrance into the organization. Thus, the organization appears to espouse a type of exclusivity whereby women who are not already involved in the network find it difficult to gain access. It is exactly this type of characterization that may work against the group's continued existence and influence. One wonders whether the group will be able to continue to draw in the kinds of people it wants to attract.

THE CHUMS INC.

The Chums Inc. is also considered a socially elite group. Few primary sources discuss the foundation of the organization or its membership, mission, and current activities. Nonetheless, its secrecy, like that of the Smart Set and others, provides an example of the surreptitious elite black organizations that still survive today.

According to Gloria Toxey Jones of the Philadelphia Chums,[31] the organization has thirty-eight chapters, each of which is responsible for implementing projects that revolve around children. These projects may include adopting schools, tutoring, and taking students on field trips. In this capacity, the group's members serve as mentors for young people. Toxey Jones notes that although the Chums (and specifically her chapter) has no particular problem either attaining or maintaining its mission, the group is always looking to increase its membership. Following the trend of organizations such as the National Council of Negro Women, the Chums is engaged in outreach to young people. This suggests the importance of reaching youth as well as the adults who interact with youth on a regular basis (parents, teachers, school administrators). I contend that various methods of outreach may be instrumental in convincing adults to join or support an organization's mission, activities, and goals.

THE LINKS INC.

The Links Inc. was founded in 1946 in Philadelphia by Margaret Hawkins and Sarah Scott. It boasts 10,000 members in 274 chapters in 42 states and has an annual budget of more than $500,000. According to the organization's Web site, the goal of this organization in the 1940s was to build "an organization that would respond to the needs and aspirations of Black women in ways that existing clubs did not. It was their intent the club would have a threefold aim—civic, educational, and cultural. Based on these aims, the club would implement programs which its founders hoped would foster cultural appreciation through the arts; develop richer inter-group relations; and help women who participated to understand and accept their social and civic responsibilities."[32]

The group is considered both social and political, as evidenced by its activities in local chapters and nationally.[33]

Graham notes, "Although not as old as other elite black women's groups like the Girl Friends or the National Smart Set, the Links is by far the largest and the most influential."[34] Nonetheless, like its counterparts, the Links works with and for youth, in addition to addressing national and international concerns and supporting the arts. Youth services focus on seven social problems: "teenage pregnancy, juvenile crime and delinquency, alcohol and substance abuse, mental and emotional illnesses/disorders, breakdown of the family, unemployment, and education. Because the target areas are so intertwined, prevention/intervention efforts in any of the seven areas would generalize to have generic preventative effect. Drug and alcohol abuse appears to permeate each area, regardless of cause or effect relationship. Therefore, drug and alcohol abuse prevention has been our primary focus since the 1982–84 biennium."[35] Also worthy of mention are the organization's current national concerns: organ and bone marrow donations and providing much-needed support to storm-ravaged areas in the aftermath of Hurricanes Katrina and Rita in 2005.

The women of the Links provide uplift to their local communities, as well as extending their philanthropic efforts to women outside the United States by funding projects in South Africa, Germany, and the Bahamas.[36] Nonetheless, there appears to be some inconsistency among regions of the United States with regard to the group's visibility and activism. For example, based on the organization's regional calendars and other information available on its Web sites, the Eastern Region is notably less active, while the Western Region seems to be the most active. The exclusivity of the organization may hinder weaker chapters from garnering support from existing members and inhibit the introduction of new members, thus negatively impacting the ability to engage in and support regional activities as a whole.

SISTUHS INC.

SISTUHS Inc., founded on the campus of Florida State University in 1992, is the newest of the organizations described here. Collegiate and professional chapters have been formed on various campuses in Florida since the organization's inception. The most recent chapter, a professional one, was chartered in 2003. According to its Web site, SISTUHS (an acronym derived from the following traits: strength, initiative, spirituality, tenacity, unity, health, and substance) strives to do the following:

- Promote spiritual growth.
- Promote personal growth and develop knowledge of thyself.
- Promote a positive image of African-American women and anything that positively enhances the survival and well being of African-American women.
- Seek guidance from Elder African-American women.
- Foster an environment amongst ourselves that is conducive to learning about the history and the role African-American women have played and continue to play in developing this and other nations.
- Develop local leadership to respond to the community's needs, particularly those of African-American women.
- Provide moral and educational guidance to other young African-American women in the community.
- Provide unity among People of Color.
- Provide opportunities to educate ourselves as well as the community on political issues that affect the well being of African-American women.
- Provide encouragement and support to African-American men.[37]

What sets SISTUHS Inc. apart from some of the other organizations discussed thus far is that it has a membership application, and its membership dues and fees are relatively reasonable for college or university women interested in joining. The organization provides answers to frequently asked questions on its Web site that clarify the membership process, noting, "A Prospective Member must be of good moral character, attend an accredited college or university or be 21 years of age or a graduate of an accredited college or university. A Prospective Member must also be willing to participate in the Rites of Passage program and Induction Ceremony." The fees are also explained by the organization: "The Application Processing fees total a range from $35–$60 depending on the Chapter. The Chapter dues range from $20 per year to $150 per year depending on the Chapter. Each Chapter levys [*sic*] its own dues, fines, and assessments in its local by-laws; however the National Headquarters assesses all other fines for Annual Returns and New Membership."[38]

Because many universities are beginning to implement a service learning component as a requirement, SISTUHS stands out in this regard. In response to a question about how the organization differs from others, it notes, "Each of us is required to give back to our community, through our time, talent, or monetary effort. SISTUHS, Inc. is an organization that gives members an opportunity to join in a collaborative effort to support our communities."[39] The organization conducted a brief survey asking members why they joined. For many college-aged women, the choice to become a member of SISTUHS was based largely on the ability to maintain their individual identities. For example, one woman wrote, "I chose to become a member of SISTUHS, Incorporated because I liked what the organization stands for. I wanted to join an organization that I could create its history rather than have the history of the organization overburden my personal identity." Another woman remarked in a similar fashion, "I decided to become a member of SISTUHS, Inc. because I was interested in joining an organization on campus that was not Greek-affiliated and was involved on the campus as well as in the community." Notably, this young woman mentioned the tendency to become overwhelmed by a Greek affiliation, which can be strong, especially on black college campuses. She also noted the importance of being involved in the community as well as on campus. She is not alone in this regard. Another student stated, "I was impressed that there was an organization besides a sorority that stressed community service and education as well as SISTERHOOD." Other young women expressed a desire to be affiliated with an organization that promoted a connectedness with other black women, black pride, uplift of black women, and spirituality. Finally, one young woman summed up her decision by stating, "I wanted to be a part of something that [was] special."[40]

The women of SISTUHS Inc. tend to be much fewer in number compared with their counterparts in other organizations on college campuses, particularly black Greek organizations. The traditional black Greek sorority system has a long and protracted history of separatism based on race and class.[41] Whether this separatism is as strong today as it was in the past, the women of SISTUHS Inc. have overcome the peer pressure to pledge a sorority. It is obvious through their comments that they perceive SISTUHS Inc. as offering its members something unique.

Children as the Center of Organizing Activities

The central focus on children and mothers is best epitomized by Jack and Jill of America and Mocha Moms. These two organizations support those who nurture and care for children. The two organizations are quite different, in that Jack and Jill of America was founded some sixty years prior to Mocha Moms and is considered a staple among middle-class black parents. Jack and Jill is also financially out of reach for many black women and their children. Mocha Moms, in contrast, is only a little more than a decade old and, because of its Internet accessibility and financial practicability, may be more accessible to women of various social classes, occupations, and ethnicities and in regions of the country where few blacks reside.

JACK AND JILL OF AMERICA

Jack and Jill of America, "a membership-by-invitation-only social group, was founded in 1938," according to Kendall. It has 220 chapters and serves as a "national network for black children and their families, providing them with opportunities for social service, education, and other projects."[42] With an annual budget of $400,000 and more than 30,000 parents and children involved in the organization in its various chapters in the United States and Germany, the organization has maintained an impressive presence over the years.[43] Kendall notes, "Although it is the mothers who are invited to membership, this organization primarily benefits middle- and upper-class African American children."[44] Graham characterizes the organization as "a non-profit service organization [that] . . . focuses on bringing together children aged two to nineteen and introducing them to various education, social, and cultural experiences. In addition to sponsoring public service projects in their communities, the various Jack and Jill chapters raise money for local nursing homes, shelters, hospitals and educational institutions."[45]

As an elite social group, Jack and Jill has also been criticized for its classist and colorist membership pattern. According to Graham:

> [The organization] attracted a negative reaction from many blacks who lacked the resources, the pedigree, or the physical appearance to be considered for membership. History shows that some chapters, particularly the ones in the larger southern cities, were clearly guilty of placing a great emphasis on these characteristics, but others were unfairly attacked for doing the same thing when what really was happening was that they were just nominating people who were in their social circle, their church, their bridge club. And not surprisingly, these darker, less-pedigreed people had long before been shut out of those institutions.[46]

Graham points to the clear relationship between skin color and class that existed during the early years of the organization. These same factors may still play a role today in determining who receives entrée and who does not, although once again, the degree to which this occurs varies regionally and may not be as widespread as it once was. Graham observes, "I would imagine that most former members would agree that the Jack and Jill of today is less status-conscious and less color-obsessed than the Jack and Jill of my childhood."[47]

The elitist attitudes of some of the organization's members are apparent in the types of activities sponsored and the focus on academic and social achievements. Based on his childhood experiences, Graham asserts that the focus is not on sports or dance as a way to achieve success; rather, it is on academic ability and the avoidance of mediocrity.[48] Jack and Jill's critics assert that the organization's founders, leadership, and membership are "light-skinned professional blacks with money." Others rebut this assertion, pointing out the more diverse composition of the organization today and the decline in traditions that were instrumental in separating the black elite from their not so successful counterparts.[49]

MOCHA MOMS INC.

Mocha Moms Inc. is one of the newest black women's organizations, having been established in 1997. Although it does not formally claim to be an organization specifically for black women, its name implies that it is by and for women of color, which includes black women and Latinas. The organization started with a newsletter published by two women, Jolene Ivey and Karla Chutz. They were subsequently joined by a third and a fourth, Cheli English-Figaro and Joby Dupree, with all contributing in some way to the founding of Mocha Moms. One of the interesting characteristics of Mocha Moms Inc. is its use of the Internet to reach mothers. The dissemination of a wide range of materials and the low cost of membership ($40 per year) make the organization accessible to many women. Also, because there is no requirement to belong to a local chapter, mothers can find support through "virtual" relationships with other mothers.[50]

Mocha Moms Inc.'s platform consists of seven pillars. The first is based on nonexclusivity, and all who support the organization's mission are accepted, regardless of race or ethnicity, religion, social class, employment status, or even gender—fathers are welcomed as well. The second pillar is civic engagement, which includes involvement in community activism and volunteerism; a "giving back" to the community in which one lives is central. The third pillar, support for work-at-home mothers, recognizes that stay-at-home moms need as much support as their counterparts who work outside the home. Acknowledging that work-at-home mothers require their own form of networking, the organization provides a database with information on home businesses. Fourth is nonpartisanship, which affirms the nonpolitical nature of the organization. This pillar is also linked to the organization's acceptance of all, regardless of religious beliefs. The fifth pillar is the commitment to marriage and the support of spouses, and the sixth pillar recognizes women's need to take care of themselves. The last pillar involves the education of their children.[51]

Mocha Moms Inc. is helping to educate women. Its members serve as mentors to other stay-at-home mothers. In a society where women who opt to stay at home to raise their children are often perceived as unemployable, lazy, overly traditional, and submissive to their husbands, Mocha Moms provides them with the support they need to counter such negative perceptions. The organization's activities and newsletter are instrumental in providing members with information and advice on parenting and how to be effective wives and partners. Members also learn the importance of taking time for themselves; each chapter holds a monthly mothers-only event, where the women get to enjoy the company of other mothers without their children.[52] These meetings afford stay-at-home mothers the opportunity to get out and meet and befriend others like themselves.

Issues for the Future

Although no particular organization seems to have pressing financial difficulties that threaten to limit its future existence or its ability to carry out projects, other concerns have been alluded to throughout. One problem is the exclusive nature of some social groups. This, along with their lack of visibility, may prevent them from finding "suitable" new members when they need to replenish their declining and aging membership base.

A second issue is that several groups are perceived to be holdovers of the old "color-struck" aristocracy. Women who are "high" not only in class but also in color are perceived as more worthy of membership; others are denied entrée into the inner circle. Although some of the elite black women's groups of the past still exist, they may find that, as time goes on, there is no real social benefit to the pattern of exclusivity that characterizes their organizations. A move toward inclusiveness may be desired by women who are interested in camaraderie and community service but no longer support the skin color and class hierarchies that still exist in some black women's organizations. The increasing numbers of black women who attend black and predominantly white colleges and universities in the post–civil rights era and who have varying skin colors and hair textures and styles may have something to do with the changing face of *who* belongs to *what* organization.

Third, although some individuals advocate the use of the Internet in promoting knowledge about an organization, there are limitations. For example, when seeking information on the Girl Friends, I was shocked to find a pornographic Web site on my first try. Like the Smart Set (not discussed here because of my inability to locate recent information on the group), the Girl Friends' aging membership and lack of knowledge about the Internet and Web site development may limit its ability to inform potential members of its existence. But as stated earlier, perhaps this is intentional.

Black women's civic and volunteer activity continues today. This is evidenced through a wide array of organizations with myriad mission statements and goals. Their variety may constitute a crucial factor in bringing together like-minded women. Women who choose not to participate in community service via organizations may be more comfortable in organizations that focus on social activities. Women who are childless may be interested in organizational activities that differ from those whose primary focus is their roles as mothers, and so on.

Finally, some colleges and universities have implemented service learning requirements to help students develop and foster a sense of community responsibility. This aspect of social engagement at the college level encourages students' involvement in community organizations during their academic careers, and some, it is hoped, will continue their involvement long after graduation.

Although some organizations continue to promote racial uplift as part of the "Talented Tenth" concept[53] through church groups, school mentoring programs for young girls that affirm the politics of respectability,[54] sororities, social clubs, and civic involvement, black women are steadfast in their participation in a wide variety of organizations that reflect their myriad interests and address the specific problems plaguing their communities. Regardless of the method of involvement, it is clear that social sororities remain an important and integral part of the lives of women. However, it must be noted that class and other barriers may prevent some women from benefiting from these organizations. Thus, black women's organizations may mean little or nothing to these women. This is especially so for those women who lack the funds to join, lack the networks to be invited to participate, or are unaware of the existence of local and national black women's organizations. This is in sharp contrast to those women who are able to afford the benefits of organizational involvement. These black women build and maintain strong bonds of sisterhood with their peers in organizations that they find meaningful. Historically relevant in the nineteenth century, black women's social sororities remain a significant part of many women's lives in the twenty-first century.

Notes

1. Paula Giddings, *When and Where I Enter: The Impact of Black Women on Race and Sex in America* (New York: Bantam, 1984); Glenda Gilmore, *Gender and Jim Crow: Women and the Politics of White Supremacy in North Carolina, 1896–1920* (Chapel Hill: University of North Carolina Press, 1996); Rosalyn Terborg-Penn, "Discrimination against Afro-American Women in the Women's Movement, 1830–1920," in *The Black Woman Cross Culturally*, ed. Filomina Chioma Steady (Cambridge: Schenkman, 1981), 301–16.

2. Giddings, *When and Where I Enter*, 97.

3. Michelle Zimbalist Rosaldo and Louise Lamphere, *Women, Culture, and Society* (Stanford, Calif.: Stanford University Press, 1974).

4. Darlene Clark Hine, *Hine Sight: Black Women and the Re-Construction of American History* (Bloomington: Indiana University Press, 1994), 51.

5. Anne Boylan, *The Origins of Women's Activism: New York and Boston, 1797–1840* (Chapel Hill: University of North Carolina Press, 2002).

6. Giddings, *When and Where I Enter*; Anne Meis Knupfer, *Toward a Tenderer Humanity and a Nobler Womanhood: African American Women's Clubs in Turn-of-the-Century Chicago* (New York: New York University Press, 1996).

7. Marla F Frederick, *Between Sundays: Black Women and Everyday Struggles of Faith* (Berkeley: University of California Press, 2003); Evelyn Brooks Higginbotham, *Righteous Discontent: The Women's Movement in the Black Baptist Church, 1880–1920* (Cambridge, Mass.: Harvard University Press, 1993).

8. Aldon Morris, *The Origins of the Civil Rights Movement* (New York: Free Press, 1984).

9. Floris Barnett Cash, *African American Women and Social Action: The Clubwomen and Volunteerism from Jim Crow to the New Deal, 1896–1936* (Westport, Conn.: Greenwood Press, 2001).

10. Nina Mjagki, ed., *Organizing Black America: An Encyclopedia of African American Associations* (New York: Garland, 2001), 392.

11. Diana Kendall, *The Power of Good Deeds: Privileged Women and the Social Reproduction of the Upper Class* (Lanham, Md.: Rowman and Littlefield, 2002); Knupfer, *Toward a Tenderer Humanity*, 12.

12. Knupfer, *Toward a Tenderer Humanity,* 12.

13. W. E. B. DuBois, "The Talented Tenth," in *The Negro Problem A Series of Articles by Representative American Negroes of Today,* ed. U. Lee (New York: J. Pott, 1903), 33–75.

14. Ibid.

15. National Association of Colored Women and Girls Clubs Inc., "Objectives," www.nacwc.org/about/objectives.php (accessed March 15, 2006).

16. Shirley A. Jackson, "'There's Something about the Word': Feminism and African American Women," in *Radical Women,* ed. Kathy Blee (New York: New York University Press, 1997), 38–45.

17. National Association of Colored Women and Girls Clubs Inc., "Plan of Action," www.nacwc.org/about/objectives.php (accessed March 15, 2006).

18. National Association of Colored Women and Girls Clubs Inc., "The National Association of Youth Clubs," www.nacwc.org/programs/youth.php (accessed March 15, 2006). One source notes that the ninth president of the NACWC, Rosa L. Gragg, changed the name in 1962 to avoid a direct reference to race. This is interesting, given that the club was founded with the specific intent to counter negative images of black girls by promoting "the moral, mental, and material development of black girls" and teaching "black girls how to lead moral lives and make their homes a bulwark in the defense of black womanhood." Mjagki, *Organizing Black America,* 388.

19. "National Association of Colored Women's Clubs (NACWC)," in *Encyclopedia of Associations,* 45th ed. (Detroit: Thomson Gale, 2008), vol. 1, pt. 2, 1564.

20. Audrey Thomas McCluskey, "Multiple Consciousness in the Leadership of Mary McLeod Bethune," *National Women's Studies Association Journal* 6, no. 1 (1994): 69–81.

21. Ibid., 75.

22. National Council of Negro Women, "Our Mission," www.ncnw.org/aboutncnw .htm (accessed June 9, 2006).

23. Ibid. (Other sources list the organization's members at 40,000.)

24. Cheryl Townsend Gilkes, "'If It Wasn't for the Women . . .': African American Women, Community Work, and Social Change," in *Women and the Politics of Empowerment,* ed. Anne Bookman and Sandra Morgen (Philadelphia: Temple University, 1994), 229–46.

25. National Council of Negro Women, "Our Programs," www.ncnw.org/NCNW-Programs.htm (accessed June 9, 2006).

26. Kendall, *The Power of Good Deeds,* 128. The Boulé is another name for Sigma Pi Phi Fraternity.

27. Lawrence Otis Graham, *Our Kind of People: Inside America's Black Upper Class* (New York: HarperPerennial, 2000), 116, 117, 119.

28. Ibid., 114.

29. Ibid., 120.

30. Ibid., 120, 115.

31. Gloria Toxey Jones, survey response to author, February 28, 2006.

32. The Links, "About the Links, Incorporated," www.linksinc.org/about/about.html (accessed March 5, 2006).

33. Marjorie H. Parker, *The History of the Links, Incorporated* (Washington, D.C.: National Headquarters of the Links, 1981).

34. Graham, *Our Kind of People*, 102.

35. The Links, "Services to Youth," www.linksinc.org/community/youth/youth2.html (accessed March 5, 2006).

36. The Links, "About the Links Foundation, Incorporated," www.linksinc.org/foundation/foundation (accessed March 5, 2006).

37. SISTUHS Inc., "About Us," www.sistuhs.org/about_us.html (accessed April 25, 2006).

38. SISTUHS Inc., "FAQS," www.sistuhs.org/faqs.html (accessed April 25, 2006).

39. Ibid.

40. SISTUHS Inc., "Member Feedback," www.sistuhs.org/m-_feedback.html (accessed April 25, 2006).

41. Lullelia W. Harrison, *Torchbearers of a Legacy: A History of Zeta Phi Beta Sorority, Inc., 1920–1997* (Washington, D.C.: Zeta Phi Beta Sorority, 1998), 12.

42. Kendall, *The Power of Good Deeds*, 148.

43. "Jack and Jill (JJA)," in *Encyclopedia of Associations,* vol. 1, pt. 2, 11449; Graham, *Our Kind of People*, 22.

44. Kendall, *The Power of Good Deeds*, 148.

45. Graham, *Our Kind of People*, 22.

46. Ibid., 39.

47. Ibid., 42. Jack and Jill is one of many organizations described at length in Graham's book, which is one of the most instructive works on the African American upper class. Graham discusses his own involvement in Jack and Jill as a child and interviews others who were involved as children.

48. Ibid., 39.

49. Ibid., 43.

50. Mocha Moms Inc., "Our History," www.mochamoms.org/about.html (accessed May 1, 2006).

51. Mocha Moms Inc., "Platform," www.mochammoms.org/about.html (accessed May 1, 2006).

52. Ibid.

53. DuBois, "The Talented Tenth."

54. Higginbotham, *Righteous Discontent.*

Part IV

Organizational Functioning

13

Sisterhood beyond the Ivory Tower
An Exploration of Black Sorority Alumnae Membership

Marcia D. Hernandez

Black sorority members share an understanding that membership is something one grows in to, not out of. Most of the active members of black sororities are in graduate chapters, not undergraduate ones.[1] In his study of the black elite, Lawrence Graham notes that members of black Greek organizations use their affiliations as social and professional networks and as an avenue for philanthropic efforts. He writes, "Black fraternities and sororities play a much more important role later in life and serve as a vehicle for black alumni to contribute money and time to civic projects, scholarships, and other programs to aid disadvantaged blacks in the United States and abroad."[2] Alumnae membership in black sororities has consistently grown, unlike undergraduate membership, which has fluctuated over time.[3] Today, many major metropolitan areas in the United States, as well as large international cities, have alumnae chapters of black sororities.[4] To gain a sense of how important alumnae membership is for sororities, 76 percent of Delta Sigma Theta's membership is alumnae, as is 72 percent of Alpha Kappa Alpha's.[5]

Research on black Greek life is in its infancy; there are few published works that offer holistic discussions of the black sororities.[6] Although women are active in black sororities after college, scholarship on Greek life portrays sorority membership almost as an exclusively undergraduate phenomenon. Within this literature there is a tendency for researchers to compare predominantly black and white organizations, which limits the scope of investigation because membership in predominantly white sororities consists mostly of undergraduates.[7] Scholars often use the same research questions to study both black and white groups, resulting in an emphasis on the potentially destructive aspects of membership, such as hazing and substance abuse, at the expense of the positive elements of Greek life, such as camaraderie and community service.[8] Studying alumnae membership provides an opportunity to investigate aspects of Greek life that have not been adequately addressed by scholars. For example, researchers tend to neglect the intricate dynamics of alumni membership, particularly the challenges and rewards of building relationships among sorority sisters once a shared campus environment is no longer part of daily life.

This chapter presents an analysis of women's experiences as alumnae members of black sororities. This is exploratory research that focuses primarily on three different yet related stages of sorority membership. My discussion begins with women's motivation to join an organization, which in turn influences the second stage, when membership is actually sought. The final stage includes acceptance as a member and the careful, deliberate strategizing to balance the expectations of being a good sister with other responsibilities.

Black Sororities as a Social Movement

Once they graduate from college and begin their professional careers and start their own families, many black sorority members seek to continue the camaraderie, community activism, and networks provided by their sororities.[9] Paula Giddings argues that the development of alumnae chapters signified the maturity of the black sorority movement, as members realized the good they could do in their communities as part of a sisterhood that continued after college.[10] Alumnae chapters form whenever there are enough interested individuals to seek a charter from national headquarters. Black sororities chartered graduate chapters as early as the 1920s.[11]

Once a woman joins a black sorority, she is always a member, at least in spirit. Alumnae membership is not required, and a woman can choose not to join a chapter after graduation. However, she has the privilege of continuing to self-identify as a member of the sorority, and others may refer to her as a "sister" even if she has little or no official contact with a graduate chapter. To enjoy full benefits, such as the ability to vote and hold office, a woman must pay dues and attend various functions on a continual basis.

Women are allowed to seek membership in a black sorority at any point in their lives if they have a college degree; in fact, some women wait to seek membership until after graduation.[12] Alumnae membership allows women to continue fostering the relationships created with their sisters as undergraduates, and it provides social support and resources for new members who join an established sisterhood.

Black sorority alumnae chapters function similarly to professional organizations and benevolent societies. Collectively, the groups contribute innumerable hours of community service. Their work follows in the spirit of the black women's club movement from the early 1900s, after which the sororities were originally modeled.[13] Two key elements from the women's club movement—individual empowerment and the uplifting of black communities—were adopted as the foundation for sorority activities. Giddings writes that the black sorority was intended as "a sisterhood, and an enabler that helps individuals to grow through cooperation, leadership development, 'culture' and exposure to the leading figures and issues of the times."[14] Because sororities focus on transforming individuals, not social institutions or society as whole, the membership has enjoyed a fairly consistent organizational structure that few other black social and political organizations enjoy. The individualistic focus is a benefit for the organizations as well, since the groups have not had to change their goals or model of leadership after de jure segregation ended. Giddings notes that this is part of the reason why black sororities have thrived while other organizations have not.[15]

Giddings was one of the first researchers to propose that black sororities be understood as part of a social movement, not simply as social organizations that occasionally perform good deeds. Placing black sororities within a social movement framework highlights community service as the organizations' prominent activity. This is a constructive move to understand the practical appeal of membership for women who believe that community service should be part of their lives after college, when additional responsibilities may lead them away from such work. The more skills and expertise a woman has, the more resources she can share with her sisters to do the work of the alumnae chapter, including volunteering, fund-raising, and creating educational programming.

Unfortunately, social movement research has not adequately addressed the role that sororities play in black communities.[16] Social scientists engaged in serious research have either ignored or deemed insignificant organizations associated with or supported by African Americans.[17] Black women's work is rarely considered a viable research topic, even though, as Bernice McNair Barnett notes, "'feminist' organizational patterns [were a distinguishing part of] Black women's roles as 'organizers' in the churches, in work- and school-based organizations, in sororities such as Delta Sigma Theta and Alpha Kappa Alpha."[18] Social movement research fails to capture many other important aspects of membership for individuals as well as the structural organization of black sororities. For example, the process by which members negotiate their responsibility to do "good deeds" without neglecting their commitments in other areas of their lives is an issue I explore later in this chapter.

Data and Method

The research presented in this chapter is based on fifteen interviews conducted between 2003 and 2005. Ten of my respondents joined a sorority as undergraduates and entered an alumnae chapter, and five women joined after college. I used snowball sampling to acquire participants for the study. Snowball sampling allowed the respondent pool to be one of convenience—a distinct advantage, because the earliest interviews occurred in a northeastern city with a relatively small African American population. The initial sample was drawn from my former students and professional acquaintances, who were then asked to refer other women to participate in the project. This sampling technique eventually allowed me to recruit sorority members from the southern, midwestern, and western regions of the United States for interviews. Members from three of the four national black sororities are represented in this study: Alpha Kappa Alpha, Delta Sigma Theta, and Sigma Gamma Rho. To respect the anonymity of my respondents, I use pseudonyms when directly citing a sorority member in this chapter.[19]

During the interviews, women used two terms interchangeably—*graduate* and *alumnae*—to refer to membership in postcollege sorority chapters. For clarification, I make a distinction between women who pledged as undergraduates and joined alumnae chapters after graduation, and those who first joined a sorority as alumnae members (those who "go grad"). I refer to women who have both undergraduate and graduate experience as *continuous members* and women who first joined an alumnae chapter as *graduate only members*. Although the sample size is modest, and I cannot provide generalizable results about alumnae membership, this exploratory research illuminates the experiences of women seeking to enter, and striving to maintain, a sisterhood in black sorority alumnae chapters.

Motivations for Joining: Seeking Sisterhood and Doing Good Deeds

For alumnae members, sororities offer a unique experience to blend community activism and leadership skills, expand their networks, and socialize with other like-minded individuals. Respondents cited a desire to give back to their communities and to connect with other professional, college-educated women as reasons for joining an alumnae chapter. For example, Crystal, a continuous member for approximately fifty years, viewed alumnae membership as not a "necessity to satisfy [my] life, but it provides aspects of life that I enjoy which are community activism and socialization and culture. It provides these three things that the other groups that I belong to don't."[20]

A couple of respondents were initially drawn to alumnae chapters primarily as a means of improving their social networks. Alana claimed that membership fulfills multiple purposes in her life; in particular, it provides a network to help her achieve personal and professional goals: "I can say with Alpha Kappa Alpha, wherever you are, whatever your career, you can always strive higher to achieve . . . you have so many sisters around you who will aid you, advise you, and will help you when you're down."[21] Brittany, a graduate-only member, echoed Alana's sentiments and explained, "I'm an only child, so I was hoping to get involved in a lot of friendships, it was a more like sisterly kind of thing . . . and networking [to improve] my social life."[22] Although Brittany's primary motivation was to enter an established social network, she also did a lot of work for her chapter.

Respondents who chose to go grad understood that obtaining alumnae membership meant that they were there "to do business." Imani explained the difference between women who join the graduate chapter and those who joined as undergraduates:

> I think there is a big difference in what people are hoping to get out of it. Are you joining more for social purposes and status? Which at the college level, it's awesome you get in as part of a group, you have people to talk to, you always have something to do, and you're never alone by yourself, there's kind of this group mentality. . . . You know it's like a status thing. But once you enter into a graduate level that status is gone because you are not in an enclosed area like a college campus, you're not wearing your stuff on your sleeve and people do not see you as a member of a Greek organization first. And even if they do know you are a member of a Greek organization that does not necessarily mean anything, so it's really about the community service, about the real work, the hard part.[23]

Cherise, a continuous member, explained that because joining as an alumna requires such a great commitment to community service, the intake process at that level should "be very long, at least a year . . . so that they understand what they are getting into. And I think, informally people should volunteer to work with us on anything that we are doing." She believes that women interested in joining the group need "to get to know us or get to know more about the organization . . . they can work on any project . . . to get an idea of what we are about." Cherise said that there are some women who have done this for a year or two and are still involved with the group. "They know it's a lifetime commitment, they know it's constant, you don't ever get a break. And so they can accept those things before they apply and are given membership."[24]

Deciding When to Join: Continuous Membership versus Going Grad

When they decided to seek membership had a qualitative impact on the sorority experiences of my respondents. Becoming a member during college is the only choice that makes sense for some women, and it was the most popular choice among my respondents. For others, waiting to join an alumnae chapter was the best course of action and the only way to join the sorority of their choice. The option of inducting women directly into an alumnae chapter helps maintain the vitality of black sororities, but it is also a source of tension between continuous members and graduate-only members. The opportunity to join an alumnae chapter without first being an undergraduate member was criticized by some of the respondents as an "easy way" to become a sister.[25] Yet there are many reasons why a woman might wait to join a sorority's alumnae chapter rather than an undergraduate one.

The three most common explanations cited by respondents for waiting to "go grad" were institutional ones over which the women had no control: no chapter of the sorority of choice on campus, suspension of the chapter, or prohibition of social Greek organizations on campus. Continuous members were less critical of their graduate-only peers if any of these reasons prevented them from joining during college. Other reasons cited for going grad had to do with the behavior of the sorority members at their colleges. Because one has to be invited to join a sorority, respondents were mindful of how well they "fit" with a particular group of women. If the undergraduate members appeared to be unwelcoming, respondents were often deterred from seeking sorority membership. In addition, apprehension about pledging motivated some women to bypass undergraduate membership, even if the sorority members seemed to complement their own interests and personalities. Continuing a family legacy also played a role in when membership was sought.

INCOMPATIBILITY

Incompatibility with members in the undergraduate chapter on campus was a common explanation for waiting to go grad. Imani, a graduate-only member, described the undergraduate women in the sorority of her choice as "cold." Her first encounter with sorority members occurred during Welcome Week in her freshman year. Imani stated, "I was very hopeful, and I approached the table of the organization that my mother belonged to because I figured if I were going to join anything it would be the one my mother belonged to. However, my initial experience is that they were cold, not necessarily very friendly . . . which was unfortunate, because the other organization that my mother was not a part of seemed very warm and friendly." Imani's impression of the women did not improve over time. She said, "it was a combination of, you know, whether or not I believed I could interact with that particular group of individuals in a comfortable setting while at the same time working through school, and I made a decision at that time that it was not the best decision for me to pursue."[26]

For Imani, joining the sorority *of her choice* with members that she could envision calling sisters overrode any other consideration. She chose not to join the other black sorority on campus, even though its members were friendlier and more approachable. When Imani did seek membership, it was to the same alumnae chapter in which her mother was active. She explained that joining her mother's chapter strengthened their relationship, which made sorority membership all the more meaningful.

FAMILY PRESSURES

Like Imani, other women felt a desire to join a sorority if their mothers or grandmothers were members, to maintain the family's legacy within a group. Pressure from family to seek membership in a specific organization played a part in Linda's decision. Linda's family strongly encouraged her to seek membership in Alpha Kappa Alpha (AKA); however, her sorority of choice was Delta Sigma Theta (DST). She stated, "I thought of joining [DST] but my mother said 'NO WAY' would we . . . change from the family. So I went with the AKAs because that's what my sister had already pledged." Linda began the intake process but dropped out because she found the sisters' treatment of the pledges "a bit ridiculous." She said, "the things they did to them, I knew I wasn't going to allow that. And rather than pledge and not get in at all, I dropped out. I just didn't bother with it one way or the other. I found out you can pledge as a grad and I decided to pledge in the grad chapter."[27]

PLEDGING AND HAZING

Knowledge that they might have to endure a difficult (and often unregu-lated) intake process deterred some of the women who were interested in becom-ing members during college and were qualified to do so.[28] Whether a woman's fear of hazing and pledging rituals was real or imagined, this aspect of Greek life played a significant role in my respondents' experiences.

Jill, who joined as an undergraduate in the early 1990s, explained, "People who pledge a grad chapter are a lot more concerned about the hazing process than the people I know who pledged undergrad." For her, women who chose to go grad took the easier path to membership because they were "fearful or anxious about what it [the undergraduate intake process] might have been like." As a comparison, she noted that she and the women she joined with understood that "there was some possibility of it [being hazed], but we weren't turned off at all about it." Jill summed up her feelings as follows: "I think those who go grad are afraid. They're afraid of being demeaned, or someone acting condescending toward them."[29]

Although Jill's beliefs were not universally shared, there was a consensus that women who go grad have a different, less meaningful intake experience than those who pledge as undergraduates. Gregory Parks and Tamara Brown write that pledging "provides a source of institutional continuity."[30] Several of my respondents echoed those sentiments, declaring that there is a lack of connection between women in their chapters who pledged and those who did not. Continuous members informed me that graduate-only members missed out on the bonding experience, but just as important, they did not have access to the important knowledge about their respective organizations that is dis-seminated during pledging. Furthermore, continuous members often believed that their graduate-only peers were less prepared to be full members or not entitled to enjoy all the perquisites of membership because they did not earn their letters through pledging. Both continuous and graduate-only members recognized that this divide can exist not only in social situations but also when doing chapter work.

Kim, a continuous member, acknowledged that pledging is not always safe but defended the process as necessary because it provides women with the opportunity to learn about their sisters and their organizations. She stated,

"Some people go to extremes, which is pledging gone wrong. . . . It's never to hit or to hurt anybody, it's there to teach, and there are some things that you cannot learn unless you pledge. There are things that if you're not somebody who pledged AKA you wouldn't know even if you are a card-carrying member."[31] Parks and Brown write that, for pledged members, there is supposed to be an "almost instantaneous connection because of the shared pledged experience . . . [due to] their common knowledge of organizational secrets." However, the authors question whether pledging truly achieves the goal of common knowledge, because "there is no guarantee that all the members have been taught the same information."[32]

Additionally, Kim explained that in terms of social events, there is "a big difference between those who were pledged members and those who were not. The write-ins [people who did not pledge] tend not to come to social stuff, and there are like these social rules, norms or whatever within the organization concerning people who pledge and people who wrote in. So then there are some things that if you were a write-in you can't participate, on a social level I mean. On a chapter level, hey you have another set of hands that can come and do the work, so that's fine."[33] As Kim's statement illustrates, continuous members may have conflicting views of their graduate-only sisters. Throughout the interviews, continuous members reiterated their sorority's motto of sisterhood, doing community service, and being a role model for others (particularly younger women) as the ultimate signs of being a good sister. Yet clearly, the respondents did not rate all members of their alumnae chapters as equal. This delicate issue affecting the relationships among members was not lost on the women who decided to go grad.

STATUS AND COMMITMENT

Continuous members were vocal regarding the importance of having uninterrupted membership, and they recognized a clear distinction between joining an undergraduate versus a graduate chapter. Perhaps because their personal identities have been tied to their sororities longer, continuous members had stronger feelings than graduate-only members about the differences in the quality and depth of relationships between the two groups.[34] Here, I explore respondents' views on the challenges of building sisterhood in alumnae chapters.

Respondents explained that, to a certain degree, the hierarchy within an alumnae chapter is based on who has earned the most respect from her peers, which is used as social capital among the sisters. Those with the most social capital in a group may informally dictate the social relationships within a chapter. According to these women, in the Greek world, few other experiences or achievements bring more acclaim than successfully completing an extended pledge process.[35] To an outsider, the distinction between joining as an under-graduate and joining as an alumna may seem minute if the expressed purpose is to do community service and enter a sisterhood. However, women who first join as alumnae might be judged as less sincere in their commitment because they did not earn their membership by pledging. For those, like Linda, who find pledging "ridiculous," they can avoid that experience by going grad. Hence, some graduate-only members made a calculated decision to avoid what continuous members see as a more difficult yet rewarding path to sisterhood.

The five graduate-only members in my study claimed that the work they did in their respective alumnae chapters rivaled the contributions of their continuous peers. And as Kim stated, graduate-only members offered "another set of hands," so their work ethic was difficult for continuous members to chal-lenge. Yet women who chose to go grad were often at a disadvantage owing to the widely held belief that they were less sincere in their commitment to the sorority and should not be treated as equal to members who had pledged. This was a frustrating perception that the graduate-only members had to deal with on a regular basis.

One way that graduate-only members tried to negotiate their new status as sorority sisters was to show a lot of respect to longtime members and to be humble. Jessica, a graduate-only member, said, "When I came in, I felt ashamed. And I think me going in feeling ashamed made me more humble. So I didn't necessarily run into any tension because they saw I was committed."[36] Although humility was a key component to being a good sister, particularly for younger, less experienced women, not all the graduate-only members believed that it was the best route to take. Some of them believed that respect should be a given based on one's contributions to the sorority. Imani's encounter with an inactive member of her sorority illustrates this point.

Imani recounted a conversation she had had with an inactive sorority member who chastised her for going grad. The woman believed that to be a real member of the group, one had to be pledged. Imani disagreed, arguing that a better judge of commitment and loyalty to a sorority was a member's contributions to her chapter. Although the woman questioning Imani's status was no longer involved with the sorority and viewed herself as "too old for that foolishness," that did not stop her from criticizing Imani's choice. Imani exclaimed, "Some people just believe it's better to be inactive and come through as an undergraduate than it is to be active as a grad even though one of you is still working with the organization and one of you is not."[37] This was obviously a frustrating experience for Imani, who felt that her contributions to the chapter made her worthy of respect; yet the woman's reaction had been based solely on how and when Imani had joined. Clearly, a pledged member does not have to remain active in a sorority to pass judgment on women who go grad.

Continuous members believed that they were inherently more knowledgeable about their sororities and therefore better and more "real" sisters compared with their graduate-only peers. Yet it is telling that the continuous members did not offer to enlighten their less informed sisters about some of the protocols they might have missed by not pledging. No continuous member said that this inequity in knowledge among members was something that the organizations should address as a high priority either within chapters or at the national level. Only one continuous member believed that the sorority should take full responsibility for enforcing safe, harmless activities to encourage community building among pledges during the membership intake process, but she was not sure how to do this and had not raised the issue with her peers. Continuous members may be suspicious of graduate-only members' ability to be equal sisters, but their failure to challenge the sorority leadership to make structural changes allows the division between them to remain.

Yet, sisterhood even among the continuous members is not guaranteed; rather, it is a constant negotiation and balancing act for members. How respondents attempt to meet the requirements of membership in sororities is explored next.

Balancing Competing Demands

Alumnae chapters enjoy the benefits of having new members as well as a continuous membership pool that spans multiple generations. Yet sororities can be greedy institutions, and the demands they make on their members are not always easy to meet. This is particularly so for alumnae members, who must balance the competing needs of family, work, and often school, in addition to their sororities.

The work ethic of alumnae members is laudable, but the amount of work it takes to be considered a good sister can be overwhelming, and this work is not always evenly distributed in a chapter. Some of the respondents are members of large chapters, where the work can easily be shared; others are involved in much smaller chapters, where it is difficult to achieve a balance between one's interests and strengths and the sorority's workload.

Alana, a graduate-only member, said, "Sometimes it feels like it's another full-time job . . . of course, it depends on the committees you are in. I would say in a month, [I spend] about twenty hours" doing sorority activities.[38] For the women in my study, it was not unusual to hear that they served on more than one committee at a time, which meant that they were paying dues to an organization for the privilege of giving up their free time.

Besides time, being a good sister demands energy and other resources, often at the expense of the women's individual personalities and personal lives. Brittany proclaimed that although women are chosen for their unique personalities and achievements, the dynamics of sisterhood dictate engaging in a group mentality. She stated, "It's a paradox of Alpha Kappa Alpha, each person, I think they forget that everyone has their own lives, is an individual. I think people forget that. I think we're so caught up in AKA, or in other groups that sometimes we're not able to do everything when we think we should be."[39] Demanding the sacrifice of members' personal resources and individuality is a common trait of a greedy institution.

Sororities as greedy institutions came up many times in the interviews. Lewis Coser defines greedy institutions as groups that "make total claims on their members . . . they seek exclusive and undivided loyalty." They are characterized by voluntary involvement, and they encourage loyalty and commitment by offering members a desirable social identity and status.[40] Scholars have most recently used this concept in discussing women's experiences trying to meet the demands of both academic careers and domestic responsibilities. Patricia Gouthro and Andrew Grace explore how women may feel trapped between two (or more) institutions that conflict with each other, where the work in one place is not valued in the other. As a result, "many women must not only work exceptionally hard to prove that they are meeting the demands of each institution, but they must also do it in a way that this work is invisible, so as not to draw attention to the time and energy expended upon it."[41] This concept aptly describes women's experiences in alumnae chapters. Respondents described the difficulties of balancing the demands of friends, family, work, and school (if students) while remaining active in their sorority. In discussing how respondents negotiate the demands of sisterhood and other responsibilities, two themes emerged: generational differences in meeting the expectations of sisterhood, and opting out if the demands of membership become too much.

GENERATIONAL DIFFERENCES

The community service work at the graduate level requires more commit-ment and planning than that expected in undergraduate chapters. For example, Cherise noted that as an undergraduate member, "you are looking more to please your peers. . . . Helping is on another level, like, giving food away in soup kitchens. And then at the graduate level it develops into a much more sophisticated, and more involved process. It's more than a one-day effort. Like, we've had our youth group for about fifteen years."[42]

Continuous members insisted that membership at the graduate level is more demanding of one's time and that the newest members are expected to do everything and to do it well. However, as members of a greedy institution, alumnae cannot complain to the older sisters in the group if the workload is too much. Learning to balance respect for the older women while contributing to the chapter on one's own terms is a delicate process, and Jessica's experience provides an example of this balancing act:

> They were here before me. And, they made their changes; they ruffled some of their older sorors when they came about too. As long as there is a fine line between being respectful and trying to get some new ideas across to older members. . . . And sometimes we do get ahead of our-selves. You know, the younger crowd wants older members to sit back and let us handle it, but that's not going to be the case. There's always got to be a compromise. And sometimes they're not as appreciative of our efforts. And vice versa, sometimes we are not as appreciative of theirs. . . . They try to tell us, "Slow down, wait!" And we say, "Oh we got this," [but then find] . . . we didn't follow protocol. It was the thing they pointed out. It was like, "See, I told you."[43]

Although showing respect to older members was a primary concern of the respondents, some also explained that women remained active out of obliga-tion and loyalty to real or fictive kin relationships. Such was the case for one of Linda's friends, a younger woman and a relatively new continuous member of an alumnae chapter. She joined the same alumnae chapter as her mother and grandmother, making her part of a legacy in the sorority. According to Linda, her friend puts in "110 percent and it is not enough. . . . Some of the older members . . . never offered help, never offered guidance, [but say to the younger members] 'This work needs to get done.'" Even after Linda's friend married and had a child, her time commitment to the sorority remained high. She felt as if she had to do the work because of her family's legacy in the chapter. Linda said that her friend's mother "sits back and glows [because her daughter is] doing all of the work."[44]

Graduate-only members admitted to knowing that membership would entail a lot of work, but they were unprepared for the unfair division of committee work and responsibilities. The graduate-only respondents understood, however, that it was acceptable to say "no" to their sorority. For example, Linda explained, "When I came here [the members] opened up to me, but they also thought that I was gonna do ALL of those things [e.g., committee work]. I did more than I needed to do really as it was. But if I had done all they wanted me to do, there's no time for you to have a life."[45]

As stated earlier, the graduate-only respondents were just as active in their chapters as the continuous members, but their attitude and approach to work were different. Perhaps because these respondents entered the sorority later in their lives, their contributions seemed more strategic than that of the continuous members. The graduate-only members were more likely to shy away from acting as a "Jill of all trades," attempting to do a little bit of everything for their sorority; instead, they tended to focus on doing work at which they had some expertise. For example, one member with an MBA served on a committee dealing with the appropriation of chapter funds and participated in the creation of an educational program to teach children to be financially responsible, because these tasks allowed her to showcase her skills.

Respondents also said that the cost of alumnae membership was just as burdensome as the amount of work required. The membership dues are higher and the events are more costly than the undergraduate members were accustomed to. Many of the younger alumnae found this monetary requirement cumbersome, while their older, professionally established sisters were able to fulfill their financial responsibilities with relative ease. Serena, a continuous member, stated, "A lot of older women they just throw out money. They have husbands. They've been teachers and doctors and attorneys for thirty years, so it's not an issue. But for some of the younger members who are still establishing themselves, when they are asked to pay dues it's like, 'Whoa, okay, let me work on it. I want to eat Friday.'"[46] The expense of joining an alumnae chapter kept some women from paying dues and officially joining for many years, even though they maintained relationships with their sisters. Financial concerns are one of many reasons listed by women for opting out.

OPTING OUT

A positive structural feature of black sororities is that inactive sisters are welcomed back into the fold whenever they are ready to be official (i.e., dues-paying) members again. This feature of alumnae chapters allows them to grow and remain vibrant by maintaining a steady flow of women who are willing to work. If a woman's lifestyle or economic situation does not allow her to participate in the way she wants, she can negotiate her relationship with the sorority. Women can continue their membership and do less work for the chapter, or they can opt out of the sorority.

Many women opt out of membership to pursue other interests or to meet the demands of other greedy institutions, such as family or work. They return to the sorority later when there is more time to devote to the group. Charlene's situation illustrates this phenomenon. She joined Alpha Kappa Alpha in the 1960s and remained active for some time after graduating from college, but she opted out after getting married and having children. She found that holding a full-time job and being a wife and mother were too time-consuming to allow her to be an active alumnae member. Yet Charlene renewed her alumnae membership five years ago when she started to plan for retirement, wanting "something to do, to be with friends and keep active."[47] Leaving the paid labor force meant that Charlene would lose contact with many of her friends, and the sorority provided an ideal environment where she could be part of a new supportive social network and spend time volunteering.

Some members choose to opt out if they were never very well integrated into the sorority in the first place. Brittany's experience provides an example. She said, "I thought that I'd have a closer bond with my sorors than I do. I really don't feel that. I even left the chapter for a year. I was kind of tired of all their attitudes . . . and just a few years ago my dad died, and I was really hurt by the lack of support I got from my sorors. Some people didn't call or anything. That really hurt me. I think that kind of added to my bitterness." Despite being disappointed that membership failed to meet her expectations, Brittany mentioned the possibility of rejoining the sorority. She explained, "I hope after I relax for a while, and I come back, it will be more positive. I hope we continue to do more. I think we're doing really well with the community service. I really like what we're doing and I hope we continue on that road."[48] Brittany's language reveals that she continues to identify as a member of the group, even though she has opted out. Perhaps more poignantly, Brittany, whose primary motivation for joining was to have a larger social network and camaraderie, discovered that it is the social activism she admires most. Her attitude exemplifies why women continue to join alumnae chapters despite the difficulties of bonding with and earning the respect of other members, and why they are willing to share their resources with groups that act as greedy institutions. If being part of a sisterhood ultimately improves the lives of others, alumnae membership will continue to be a popular choice for women who believe that this work just "needs to get done."

Conclusion

Alumnae members are the backbone of black sororities. The sheer number of alumnae members and their collective resources make these women a significant force for change in their communities. This research demonstrates that community service, philanthropy, sisterhood, and professional development are motivating factors for women to maintain an active status in their college organizations or to join sororities after graduation. Given the wide variety of philanthropic, professional, and social organizations that black women can join today, the fact that alumnae membership continues to grow highlights the importance of these groups in contemporary society. Moreover, the disproportionately high percentage of graduate members in black sororities speaks to members' individual commitment to maintain the vitality of the groups through different stages of their lives and across generations. However, research on Greek organizations continues to neglect the relevance of these organizations for members after college, while social movement literature ignores the complexity and multipurpose goals of sororities.

My research indicates that membership in alumnae chapters involves a variety of negotiations, including when to seek membership, the nature of relationships with peers, and decisions to opt out. Most of my respondents believe that the opportunity to join later in life or to rejoin a sorority is beneficial for themselves as well as for the organizations. Membership in an alumnae chapter can be a complicated process to navigate, however. Continuous members hold complex and often contradictory views of their graduate-only peers. There was almost uniform agreement among the continuous members that pledging not only makes them better informed but also facilitates the creation of bonds among women. My findings indicate that graduate-only members may experience a social disadvantage due to their more limited membership intake process.

All alumnae members have to negotiate how much of their personal resources they are willing to share with a sorority. Generosity with one's time, expertise, energy, and money is a sign of one's devotion to the group and is part of being a good sister. However, if the expectations of sisterhood are unrealistic or become too much, women may elect to opt out, at least for a limited time.

My research indicates that further investigation is essential to better understand the dynamics of alumnae membership in black sororities. Research into intragroup class-based inequalities would provide more information on the diversity of membership as well as motivations for joining a sorority.[49] Each sorority has nationally mandated community service goals, but each chapter can perform these goals according to the needs of the local community. Understanding the decision-making process alumnae members go through in terms of acting on these goals might uncover structural changes that could alleviate the pressure of sororities acting as greedy institutions. Also, longitudinal research on opting out and reentry would be useful in understanding at what point in life women are most likely to do either. Scholars studying community service, social movements, and Greek-letter organizations should explore these issues to expand the understanding of membership in black sorority alumnae chapters and their continued relevance in contemporary society.

Notes

1. Paula Giddings, *In Search of Sisterhood: Delta Sigma Theta and the Challenge of the Black Sorority Movement* (New York: William Morrow, 1988); Lawrence Otis Graham, *Our Kind of People: Inside America's Black Upper Class* (New York: Harper-Collins, 2000).

2. Graham, *Our Kind of People*, 70.

3. Rhoda Pickett, "Blacks Find Bonds, Networks in Post-Graduate Sororities and Fraternities," in Newhouse News Service, *The Race and Ethnicity Beat*, 2000, http://www.newhouse.com/archive/story1b051500.html (accessed March 6, 2005).

4. Lawrence C. Ross Jr., *The Divine Nine: The History of African American Fraternities and Sororities* (New York: Kensington, 2000).

5. Delta Sigma Theta Inc. national Web site, "Membership Demographics," www.deltasigmatheta.org (accessed April 25, 2006); Alpha Kappa Alpha Inc. national Web site, "Membership Demographics," www.aka1908.com21 (accessed April 25, 2006).

6. For example, see Walter M. Kimbrough, *Black Greek 101: The Culture, Customs, and Challenges of Black Fraternities and Sororities* (Cranbury, N.J.: Rosemont, 2003); Tamara L. Brown, Gregory S. Parks, and Clarenda M. Phillips, eds., *African American Fraternities and Sororities: The Legacy and the Vision* (Lexington: University Press of

Kentucky, 2005). The underdeveloped scholarship on black Greek life also applies to fraternities. The aforementioned works offer the most extensive research on black fraternities as well as sororities.

7. Alexandra Berkowitz and Irene Padavic, "Getting a Man or Getting Ahead: A Comparison of White and Black Sororities," *Journal of Contemporary Ethnograph* 27, no. 4 (1999): 530–57; Mindy Stombler and Irene Padavic, "Sister Acts: Resisting Men's Domination in Black and White Fraternity Little Sister Programs," *Social Problems* 44, no. 2 (1997): 256–75.

8. For example, see Ricky L. Jones, *Black Haze: Violence, Sacrifice, and Manhood in Black Greek-Letter Fraternities* (Albany: State University of New York Press, 2004); Hank Nuwer, "Violence in Historically African American Greek Groups," in *Wrongs of Passage: Fraternities, Sororities, Hazing and Binge Drinking,* by Hank Nuwer (Bloomington: Indiana University Press, 1999).

9. Giddings, *In Search of Sisterhood;* Graham, *Our Kind of People;* Kimbrough, *Black Greek 101.*

10. Giddings, *In Search of Sisterhood.*

11. André McKenzie, "In the Beginning: The Early History of the Divine Nine," in Brown et al., *African American Fraternities and Sororities,* 181–210; Giddings, *In Search of Sisterhood.*

12. Stombler and Padavic, "Sister Acts."

13. Michael H. Washington and Cheryl L. Nunez, "Education, Racial Uplift, and the Rise of the Greek-Letter Tradition: The African American Quest for Status in the Early Twentieth Century," in Brown et al., *African American Fraternities and Sororities,* 137–80; Clarenda M. Phillips, "Sisterly Bonds: African American Sororities Rising to Overcome Obstacles," in ibid., 341–59.

14. Giddings, *In Search of Sisterhood,* 21.

15. Ibid.

16. Rachel Einwohner, Jocelyn Hollander, and Toska Olson, "Engendering Social Movements: Cultural Images and Movement Dynamics," *Gender and Society* 14, no. 5 (2000): 679–99.

17. Myra Marx Ferree and Silke Roth, "Gender, Class and the Interaction between Social Movements: A Strike of West Berlin Day Care Workers," *Gender and Society* 12, no. 6 (1998): 626–48.

18. Bernice McNair Barnett, "Black Women's Collectivist Movement Organizations: Their Struggles during the 'Doldrums,'" in *Feminist Organizations: Harvest of the New Women's Movement,* ed. Myra Marx Ferree and Patricia Yancey Martin (Philadelphia: Temple University Press, 1995), 203–4; Patricia Hill Collins, *Black Feminist Thought: Knowledge, Consciousness, and the Politics of Empowerment* (New York: Routledge, 1991); Shirley Jackson, "'Something about the Word': African American Women and Feminism," in *No Middle Ground: Women and Radical Protest,* ed. Kathleen M. Blee (New York: New York University Press, 1998).

19. To protect the anonymity of my respondents, the Institutional Review Board at the University of Albany, SUNY, required the use of pseudonyms for my dissertation research. Therefore, the citations for the interviews contain minimal information.

20. Interview with Crystal, June 20, 2003.

21. Interview with Alana, April 18, 2005.

22. Interview with Brittany, May 2, 2005.

23. Interview with Imani, August 20, 2003.

24. Interview with Cherise, December 12, 2003.

25. For a detailed discussion of pledging, see Hank Nuwer, *The Hazing Reader* (Bloomington: Indiana University Press, 2004); Nuwer, *Wrongs of Passage*; Gregory S. Parks and Tamara L. Brown, "'In the Fell Clutch of Circumstance': Pledging and the Black Greek Experience," in Brown et al., *African American Fraternities and Sororities*, 437–64.

26. Interview with Imani.

27. Interview with Linda, June 17, 2003.

28. See Parks and Brown, "In the Fell Clutch of Circumstance"; Kimbrough, *Black Greek 101*; Nuwer, *Wrongs of Passage*; Nuwer, *The Hazing Reader*.

29. Interview with Jill, April 15, 2005.

30. Parks and Brown, "In the Fell Clutch of Circumstance," 451.

31. Interview with Kim, October 24, 2003.

32. Parks and Brown, "In the Fell Clutch of Circumstance," 451.

33. Interview with Kim.

34. See Parks and Brown, "In the Fell Clutch of Circumstance"; Kimbrough, *Black Greek 101*; Nuwer, *Wrongs of Passage*; Nuwer, *The Hazing Reader.*

35. See Parks and Brown, "In the Fell Clutch of Circumstance"; Nuwer, *Wrongs of Passage.*

36. Interview with Jessica, May 7, 2005.

37. Interview with Imani.

38. Interview with Alana.

39. Interview with Brittany.

40. Lewis Coser, *Greedy Institutions* (New York: Free Press, 1974), 4, 6, 7.

41. Patricia Gouthro and Andrew Grace, "Feminist Pedagogies and Graduate Adult and Higher Education for Women Students: Matters of Connection and Possibility," http://www.edst.educ.ubc.ca/aerc/2000/gouthrop&grace1-final.PDF (accessed March 3, 2005).

42. Interview with Cherise.

43. Interview with Jessica.

44. Interview with Linda.

45. Ibid.

46. Interview with Serena, June 16, 2003.

47. Interview with Charlene, June 15, 2003.

48. Interview with Brittany.

49. For information on sororities and elitism, see Diana Kendal, *The Power of Good Deeds: Privileged Women and the Social Reproduction of the Upper Class* (Lanham, Md.: Rowman and Littlefield, 2002).

14

Exploring Black Greek-Letter Organizations through a Positive Organizing Lens

Laura Morgan Roberts and Lynn Perry Wooten

From their inception, black Greek-letter organizations (BGLOs) have provided a forum for African Americans to fulfill their personal need for affiliation and belongingness, to develop leadership abilities, and to collectively engage in social action for the betterment of the black community. This chapter draws on theory from positive organizational scholarship to analyze the enabling properties of BGLOs throughout their history. Through this lens, we view BGLOs as social movement organizations and explore how they are organized to achieve their goals. By taking this approach, we seek to understand how these organizations enable human excellence and mobilize the collective action of extraordinary individuals for the purposes of social support, scholarship, political activism, economic development, and community service—organizational aspects of BGLOs that are often overlooked.

Positive Organizational Scholarship

Positive organizational scholarship (POS) is an umbrella term that provides a frame for current and future research on positive states, outcomes, and generative mechanisms in individuals, dyads, groups, organizations, and societies.[1] POS is an alternative lens that places positive dynamics at the center of organizational research, in contrast to the dominant approach toward understanding and improving organizational behavior. The traditional concept of enhancing the quality of organizational life focuses on identifying what is not working in organizations and assessing the relative impact of such problems on individual and organizational outcomes. This deficit-based approach is oriented toward identifying the mechanisms that prevent organizations from reaching optimal functioning, rather than highlighting those that push beyond such barriers. Positive organizational scholars contend that the deficit orientation falls short of generating the entire range of solutions to enable flourishing.[2] The POS lens prompts researchers to expand the focus; rather than asking only what is wrong in organizations, positive scholars pose the complementary question: what is right in organizations, and what can we learn from these positive examples?

It is essential to incorporate POS principles into the interpretation of BGLO history. The POS lens informs our understanding of how collective action can enable flourishing in a variety of work and community service contexts. The vast majority of research on diversity, and on race in particular, in organizational studies has emphasized the problems that emerge when people of different cultural backgrounds attempt to form working relationships with one another and advance in their careers.[3] This body of work on racial conflict and inequity in organizations overshadows the discussion of individual and collective strengths that people of color bring to organizations as a function of their sociocultural experiences. A recent report by the Center for Work-Life Policy suggests that employers underutilize the organizing and leadership skills that people of color develop through their civic, community, and religious involvement.[4]

This chapter's POS analysis illustrates how African Americans' strengths have been put to use in BGLOs to provide social support, foster education and leadership development, and initiate social change. We employ a traditional organizational life-cycle model to capture the positive organizing routines that shaped the evolution of BGLOs. We then explore the future of BGLOs and discuss how these organizations might maintain relevance for members and society at large.

Organizational Life Cycles

The organizational life-cycle model provides an excellent framework to examine the positive organizing routines of BGLOs. This model proposes that, over time, organizations move through a series of developmental stages. It is based on a biological metaphor—that organizations mimic living organisms by demonstrating cyclical patterns of development. The model's stages are sequential and occur as a hierarchical progression.[5] Each stage involves leadership committing to a range of activities and structures designed to help the organization accomplish its goals. Furthermore, at each stage of an organization's life cycle, its behavior is a response to opportunities and threats, both internal and external. This is reflected in the cognitive orientation of the organization's members, the organization's structure, and the organization's relations with external stakeholders.

Organizational theorists propose three major developmental phases associated with the life cycle of an organization. The birth phase encompasses the founding years of an organization and is characterized by organizing members, marshaling resources, attaining goals, and forming an ideology.[6] Also, during the founding years, the organization works innovatively to establish a niche among its peer group and adapt to its external environment.[7] During the second phase of the organizational life cycle, known as the growth years, organizations concentrate on expansion, efficiency, and goal attainment. This emphasis on expansion demands that the organization formalize its structure and governing rules. Formalization occurs through control and coordination mechanisms that regulate organizational activities. In the third phase of the life cycle, the organization matures and directs its attention to maintaining the status quo and institutionalizing governance structures. In this mature stage, the organization becomes more conservative and predictable in its responses to external environmental pressures. In the next sections, we link the organizational life-cycle model to the positive organizing routines of BGLOs.

In the Beginning: The Visionary Years

The beginning of the twentieth century created a favorable climate for the founding of BGLOs. By that time, the founders of BGLOs were one generation removed from slavery and had begun to pursue college education. The African Americans attending predominantly white institutions viewed fraternities and sororities as social support vehicles on their college campuses. Through their observations of white fraternities and sororities, they recognized the privileges associated with memberships, such as housing, study groups, and social networks. In addition, the founders of BGLOs were influenced by the organizational mission and ritualistic practices of black fraternal and benevolent societies that emphasized social change, assistance with living needs, and spiritual guidance.[8] Thus, the formation of BGLOs is an example of mimetic isomorphism, which is an organizing strategy based on the adoption of established systems and processes. By adopting the best practices of existing organizations, BGLOs brought legitimacy to their emerging organizational form and validated their practices.

In creating the initial vision for BGLOs, however, founders sought something more meaningful than their predecessors' organizations. This desire was manifested in the founders' passionate drive to create collegiate organizations based on an ideology of improving the African American race through scholarship, community service, and kinship networks. Because of their dedication to this ideology, the founders were intrinsically motivated to take action, even when confronted with risk and the knowledge that they were deviating from the expected behavior of African American college students. Furthermore, the ideology provided the founders with a means to differentiate their organizations from white fraternities and sororities. In other words, their organizing behavior was an example of positive deviance—intentional behavior that departs from the norm in an honorable way.[9]

For instance, because of the importance of education as a means of social and economic mobility for African Americans, BGLOs required members to have college credits and strong grade point averages. This positive deviance was evident in their commitment to community service as well. Thus, the founders of BGLOs were individuals who envisioned their organizations to be positively deviant not only internally, by way of admission standards and the socialization of members, but also externally, by the goal of being "other focused" through servant leadership. Servant leadership focuses on others first by encouraging collaboration, trust, and empowerment.[10]

In the case of BGLOs, this servant leadership was manifested in the motto "Lift as We Climb." This motto encouraged African American intellectual elites to use their education and talents to help improve the quality of life for other African Americans. This was especially important, because the societal context of the early 1900s was characterized by segregation, poverty, and women's rights issues. Because of these factors, in the founding years, members of BGLOs were indoctrinated with the importance of community service and social action. For example, early on, the fraternity Kappa Alpha Psi inaugurated the Guide Right national service project, whose purpose was to mentor high school students.[11] Local chapters of the fraternity implemented the Guide Right program by sponsoring chapel services, tutoring sessions, and lectures for high school students. In addition to chapter-led service projects, the founding ideology of BGLOs supported service leadership through partnerships with other organizations engaged in community service, such as the NAACP, YWCA, and Colored Merchant Associations.[12] Interestingly, a by-product of the servant leadership behavior in the early years of BGLOs provided members with a leadership legacy that future generations would strive to imitate. Moreover, leadership experience gained through BGLO participation has served as an informal training academy for career preparation and aided in the development of social capital for its members.[13]

BGLOs' strong emphasis on brotherhood and sisterhood also exemplified their positive deviant behavior. From the beginning, founders created organizing routines that reinforced the kinship networks of the black community.[14] Historically, kinship networks—webs of immediate and extended family, friends, neighbors, and church members—have been used by African Americans for the exchange of support, goods, services, and knowledge. BGLOs' membership intake processes (formerly known as pledging) and organizational structures were designed to imitate an extended family. Unlike white fraternities and sororities, an explicit assumption of the BGLOs' founders was that the kinship networks formed during college would provide the foundation for lifelong relationships and would strengthen the bond of brotherhood or sisterhood. Furthermore, these kinship networks helped BGLO members cope with racism and provided another safe haven to celebrate black traditions.

Consistent with the organizational life-cycle model, the beginning years laid the groundwork for creating the organizational identity of BGLOs. It was inspired by visionary leadership. This identity served as the basis for the future organizational behavior of BGLOs. It defined the mission of BGLOs, membership requirements, and important stakeholders. However, an organizational vision is useless without an infrastructure; to achieve organizational goals, the infrastructure and vision should be aligned.[15] Organizational infrastructure encompasses both formal and informal aspects. The formal organizational arrangements include the explicit processes, structures, systems, and procedures developed to organize the work and activities of individual members so that they are consistent with the vision. Coexisting with the formal organization, the informal infrastructure, often known as the organizational culture, consists of unwritten guidelines that influence the behavior of groups or individuals. It is reflected in practices and relationships that reinforce acceptable behavioral norms and the shared values of members. The informal organization is the glue that holds members together.

During the first two decades of BGLOs' existence, many actions were taken by the leadership that provided vehicles to achieve organizational goals and aligned the structure and culture with the vision of the founders. Incorporation was one of the first formal organizing actions taken by BGLOs. Incorporation legalized these organizations as separate financial entities and ensured their continuation beyond the lives of the founders. In addition, legal incorporation gave BGLOs the power to institute subordinate chapters. Beyond legal incorporation, much of the focus was on creating organizational culture through symbols and the socialization of new members.

For BGLOs, symbols are a major aspect of their organizational culture, and in many instances, they reinforced the vision of their founders. The majority of the constructs associated with organizational culture are invisible practices of its shared ideology. However, symbols bring an organization's ideology to life by providing a concrete representation for members to associate with what the organization values.[16] People learn through association, so organizational symbols act as cues to guide behavior.[17] Moreover, organizational symbols provide outsiders with an internal view of the organization by publicly acknowledging its principles and its differentiating characteristics.

In other words, the organizational symbols of BGLOs were crafted as "triggers" to represent the inspired values and norms of the founders. For the fraternity Omega Psi Phi, the selection of certain Greek letters highlighted the importance of symbols representing the visions of its founders. The name Omega Psi Phi was derived from the Greek initials for "Friendship is essential to the soul." Similarly, the initials of Alpha Kappa Alpha Sorority represent the first letters of the Greek words that formed the sorority's motto, "By culture and by merit." In addition to Greek letters, BGLO mottos were often created as written organizational symbols to reinforce values, such as the public motto "Intelligence is the torch of wisdom" for the sorority Delta Sigma Theta.

However, the organizational symbols created over the years to communicate the vision of the founders are more than the Greek letters and the mottos associated with each BGLO. They include colors, mascots, songs, and coats of arms. For example, Sigma Gamma Rho's badge symbolizes the sorority's principles and pays homage to the sorority's founders. The open book on the sorority's badge represents knowledge. The ten pearls symbolize the seven founders and the three virtues of faith, hope, and love. Also, illustrated on Sigma Gamma Rho's badge are two rubies representing light and achievement.[18]

The socialization of new members is another organizational mechanism that was adopted early in the life cycle of BGLOs for the purposes of aligning members' behavior with the vision of each fraternity or sorority. In organizations, the socialization of new members entails a process for transmitting expectations associated with their roles and is designed to eliminate uncertainty and ambiguity.[19] Thus, it is a system for internalizing expectations so that members voluntarily and willingly contribute to an organization's goals. The socialization of new members facilitates assimilation into the organization. This results in an efficient process of integrating new members into the organization, and they learn rapidly which behaviors the organization rewards.

The pledge process became the dominant model for socializing new members and the defining characteristic of the black Greek experience.[20] Over time, the pledge process evolved into a period during which prospective BGLO members could bond with one another and learn about the fraternity's or sorority's history.[21] To establish bonding and the formation of the kinship networks, prospective members attended chapel as a group, ate meals together, and dressed alike. Furthermore, prospective members were educated on topics such as parliamentary procedure or organizational governance, and they were usually encouraged to participate in chapter service projects and fund-raising activities. Hence, from a POS perspective, the pledge process created fertile ground to sow seeds in prospective members, with the potential for these seeds to bloom into a lifetime psychological contract of commitment to the organization's vision.

Growing the Organization: Expansion and Viability

In the growth years of the organizational life-cycle model, BGLOs directed their energies toward expansion and capacity building. Each BGLO sought to charter collegiate chapters and graduate chapters throughout the United States. Eventually, chapters outside the United States were established as current members moved to new countries and members desired to bring BGLOs to Africa and the Caribbean. The growth of BGLOs had an evangelical spirit, because members believed that the extensive presence of chapters not only extended the chain of brotherhood or sisterhood but also sparked grassroots efforts for local community service programs. Moreover, the expansive growth validated the existence of these organizations and further ensured their survival. This growth was also generative, since it enabled each BGLO to reach a size that allowed it to achieve economies of scale and scope. Economies of scale resulted in more cost-efficient processes as these organizations grew, and economies of scope permitted the pooling of resources and sharing of knowledge.

With growth came the need for leadership to work toward capacity building. Capacity building involves the activities that enhance or improve a nonprofit organization's ability to achieve its mission.[22] It encompasses a systematic approach to fusing the organization's strengths and co-constructing the architectural design for its future. The capacity-building activities of the BGLOs were purposeful, involved reflective planning, and were action oriented. To manage these capacity-building activities, BGLOs invested in national offices and professional staffs who were responsible for financial management, membership records, training programs, convention planning, and the documentation of rituals and protocols. With the investment in national headquarters, BGLOs were able to transform the tacit knowledge that defined their operating procedures into explicit systems. This expedited organizational learning and further supported the efficient establishment of new chapters. In addition to an administrative national headquarters, a large proportion of capacity-building work during this phase of the organizational life cycle entailed acquiring the funds needed for survival. Hence, for the BGLOs, this challenged them to create innovative means of generating financial resources beyond membership dues. Many local chapters began "signature" fund-raising programs, such as fashion shows, step shows, debutante balls, and formal parties.

Another aspect of capacity building was the formation of the National Pan-Hellenic Council as an umbrella organization for BGLOs. This council, composed of the nine BGLOs, evolved for the purposes of expressing unanimity of thought and action and to provide a collective platform to address problems of mutual interest to its member organizations.[23] Through governance by representative leadership, the National Pan-Hellenic Council promotes forums and meetings where information is exchanged. Additionally, the organizations in the council work together on activities that support cooperative programming and initiatives. As the BGLOs grew, the council gave them a unified voice that reinforced their historical purpose and black roots. This strengthened the chain of community service and the web of social networks. Furthermore, on college campuses and communities where BGLO chapters are small in number, the National Pan-Hellenic Council empowers them with a presence and a critical mass to make a difference.

In summary, from a POS perspective, the growth phase of BGLOs not only involved the initiation of new chapters but also fostered growth in the organizational thought process. This thought process brought a deeper meaning by empowering connections through expansion. These empowering connections were reinforced with the National Pan-Hellenic Council, which became the overarching community of practice for BGLOs, and the common interests of member organizations promoted social learning.

The Mature Years: Producing and Sustaining

Organizational behavior in the mature years of the BGLOs focused on strengthening the community service ethos and their identity. As BGLOs adopted formalized approaches for community service, programming became the heart and soul of their organizing strategy. It became necessary to think strategically when implementing service projects. This strategic thought process was built on the work accomplished in the other phases of the organizational life cycle by activating energy toward community service.[24] In contrast to most organizations that rest on their laurels, the BGLOs used their experiences to push forward their community service initiatives. In addition, partnerships were created with other nonprofit organizations, such as the March of Dimes, Habitat for Humanity, the United Nations, and the United Negro College Fund, to help BGLOs advance their community service goals. These partnerships are another example of BGLOs' ability to create high-quality relationships that are outside of their organizational boundaries. Also, members of BGLOs in high-power positions, such as Dr. Martin Luther King and Mary Church Terrell, were used to validate the significance of their community service projects and as icons when seeking support from the broader community.

Consistent throughout the history of BGLOs, community service projects focused on education and empowering the black community.[25] However, the actual projects adapted over time to address political issues, the economic environment, and sociocultural trends.[26] For example, in the 1950s, Alpha Kappa Alpha Sorority partnered with the Job Corps to provide young African Americans with vocations, for the purpose of attacking poverty. During the same era, Delta Sigma Theta Sorority and Zeta Phi Beta Sorority were on the front lines of the civil rights movement, participating in protests and helping to pay the expenses of students arrested at nonviolent demonstrations.

After the passage of the Civil Rights Acts, BGLOs continued their community service efforts, with a special focus on youth. Youth became an important aspect of community service projects because they represent the future, and African Americans believe that "it takes a village to raise a child." All of the "Divine Nine" BGLOs have some type of community service project targeted toward youth. For instance, to address the crisis of African American adolescents dropping out of school, Iota Phi Theta developed a mentoring program for boys between the ages of eight and thirteen. Delta Sigma Theta Sorority designed an academy for girls aged eleven to fourteen to promote the principles of sisterhood, learning, and service. Other BGLOs focused on health issues; Sigma Gamma Rho assisted the March of Dimes with a Healthy Start program for African American children, and Phi Beta Sigma waged a campaign to reduce the incidence of teenage pregnancy.

Similar to the expansion of chapters, community service did not stop in the United States. The BGLOs viewed Africa and the Caribbean countries as an important part of their heritage and became concerned about the challenges facing other African descendants. International endeavors of BGLOs included the World Policy Council of Alpha Phi Alpha and Sigma Gamma Rho's Program for Africa, which finances grain grinders for female African farmers.

The Future: Organizational Resilience and Renewal

The preceding organizational life-cycle analysis illustrates the positive organizing routines that set BGLOs apart and made them models of servant leadership and collective action. The development and growth of BGLOs were fueled by the energizing common vision and the networks of social relationships within and among organizations. The vision and networks inspired members to contribute and anchored each local and campus chapter to a long-standing history of strength and wisdom among people of African descent. The establishment of well-aligned structures, systems, and norms sustained the BGLOs as they maintained prominence during the Jim Crow, civil rights, postsegregation, and globalization eras of American history. Symbols and values remained relatively unchanged, but leadership structures and programming expanded to include thousands of new members and serve black communities around the globe.

As we look into the future, we question whether the positive routines established and implemented in the past century of BGLOs are sufficient to withstand the contextual changes these organizations must address. The basic principles on which BGLOs were founded may be timeless. Yet the collective sense of urgency to address racial inequities and attain social justice through education and service is far less palpable today than it was fifty years ago, when African Americans prepared for and carried forth the civil rights movement. The questionable existence and necessity of a collective "black" identity permeate scholarship and public discourse.[27] Meanwhile, the experiences of African Americans have become increasingly diverse and stratified; as many black professionals move into suburban areas to take advantage of higher-quality school systems and profitable housing markets, an urban, largely black underclass has emerged in the inner cities and rural areas.[28] Such socioeconomic and geographic dispersion makes service partnerships among African Americans more difficult to execute, since they are based less on personal connections with those in need of academic and financial assistance and more on benevolent social agendas that must compete with other extracurricular and professional development activities.

We propose that BGLOs must continue to be resilient in order to maintain relevance for members and society at large. Organizational resilience is the process of responding to changes in both the internal and external environments so that the organization can thrive.[29] Thus, we challenge BGLOs to develop an infrastructure that supports reconstruction and renewal of organizational values, processes, and behaviors. This demands tackling difficult issues and cultivating membership engagement.

BGLOs are designed to meet members' personal needs for affiliation and belongingness, to develop leadership abilities, and to collectively engage in social action for the betterment of the black community. Despite the thousands of remarkable men and women who have been initiated into BGLOs, the percentage of active, financially supportive members is shockingly low. The infrastructure of BGLOs was established such that the national leadership hierarchy would be mirrored within local chapters. Local chapters submit several extensive reports to their regional directors and national headquarters, so that the national organization is aware of all activities that occur on the regional and local levels. National officers are challenged by the overwhelming amount of information they attempt to process; only recently have they begun to collect forms and maintain membership records using sophisticated technology. Manual processing has led to long delays in registration, initiation, and reporting about organizational activities.

The primary mechanism for working collectively across chapters is through regional and national conferences. The reality is that people tend to cluster with those they know and with whom they have things in common,[30] which poses a challenge for creating cross-chapter and cross-generational bonds, even within the same sorority or fraternity. Due to our rapidly changing economy, college graduates can expect to change jobs at least five times during their careers, and it is quite likely that these job changes will require members of BGLOs to relocate at least once during their working lives. BGLOs must establish positive organizing routines for managing the transitions between undergraduate and alumni chapters and from one alumni chapter to another. For example, the current protocol is for members to find a local chapter in their new location and introduce themselves. It would be more efficient for the national headquarters to establish a relocation database so that local chapters could reach out and assist sorority sisters or fraternity brothers who are new to the area.

Since the founding of the BGLOs, black college graduates have created or joined a variety of professional and service organizations. To sustain relevance and cultivate member engagement, BGLOs must gain clarity about how to positively differentiate themselves from other black organizations such as the National Society for Black Engineers, National Association of Black Accountants, National Black MBA Association, and National Medical Association, as well as historically white organizations that now welcome African American professionals into their membership. BGLOs were traditionally differentiated from other organizations through their mission and strong socialization practices that were intended to create a sense of sisterhood and brotherhood. Tragedies involving injury, harm, and loss of life, as well as lawsuits, have called many of these initiation practices into question, resulting in permanent expulsion for members found guilty of hazing and suspension of chapters in which such activities occur. Several organizational and social psychological studies reinforce the critical roles of formal and informal socialization in creating role clarity and organizational commitment.[31] A POS perspective calls for humanizing the initiation and orientation of new members in ways that build confidence, commitment, and teamwork without demeaning newcomers. How can BGLOs pass on the rich tradition of sisterhood and brotherhood to one another without alienating or harming current and future members?

In addition to establishing practices that effectively socialize members, BGLOs may need to revisit their missions to ensure that they still embody the positive deviance that has energized member engagement and activity. Founded shortly after the *Plessy v. Ferguson* ruling of "separate but equal" in 1896, BGLOs maximized the benefits of unification to oppose racial inequality and social disadvantage.[32] One century later, Jim Crow laws are no longer in effect, and racial discrimination has been deemed illegal in higher education admissions and workforce hiring. The dramatic increase in black enrollment in higher education, particularly in predominantly white institutions, has led to an increased level of participation in and leadership of integrated professional and civic organizations. What will continue to differentiate BGLOs from other organizations and compel younger African Americans, who have experienced the civil rights movement only via film, to sustain these organizations?

According to social psychological and organizational behavior research, people remain psychologically engaged and active members of organizations because of the sustainable resources they provide. Historically, BGLOs have fulfilled African American college students' and alumni's need for a sense of belonging and high-quality relationships, which often generate emotional, physiological, and financial benefits.[33] People choose to form new groups or join existing groups so that they can achieve a sense of collective identity while also maintaining an optimal level of distinctiveness from other people.[34] Optimal distinctiveness is an important mechanism that BGLOs have utilized; the Divine Nine have effectively connected members to common principles and practices, but the colors, symbols, mottos, and Greek letters have enabled them to differentiate themselves from members of other organizations. Myths and stereotypes have emerged about personality differences between the members of certain BGLOs, and these have been used by members to describe the positive distinctiveness of their own organizations, with indirect negative implications about other organizations. For example, oft-cited stereotypes distinguish the women of Alpha Kappa Alpha from the women of Delta Sigma Theta, despite the fact that structural and sociocultural experiences are more similar than different for members of each organization, and strong friendship and family ties have always existed across organizations. Honorary memberships for trailblazers in entertainment, politics, health, and education have also been used as a means of elevating the status of BGLOs and providing mechanisms for members to personally identify with the achievements of prominent black leaders (as well as a select few of other ethnic backgrounds).

The critical question we pose is: How can BGLOs leverage the unique strengths that have been developed out of the black experience in the nineteenth, twentieth, and twenty-first centuries? We suggest that BGLOs must adopt positive organizing routines to ensure their relevance and viability in the twenty-first century. Positive organizing refers to "a process consisting of a set of generative dynamics at the collective level that can enable organizational resourcefulness and can lead to positive states or outcomes such as enhanced strengths and capabilities, expanded organizational action repertoires, optimal functioning, flourishing or simply organizational excellence."[35] Positive organizing routines are required to renew BGLOs' visions so that they are relevant to twenty-first century challenges and opportunities. Despite previous successes, it may be time for a new organizational form to emerge that will align BGLOs' individual and collective missions with the current context that people of African descent experience in the United States and abroad, where segregation no longer exists, but stratification is ever present. BGLOs must be ambidextrous; that is, on the one hand, they must leverage the efficiency they have established in their rich and proud histories, and on the other hand, they must chart a new course that addresses new issues that will emerge in the future.[36]

Positive organizing routines are also needed to reinforce members' identification and engagement with BGLOs. Given the increasing social and geographic mobility of African American college graduates, the transformation of initiation and socialization practices, and the expanded range of professional and civic organizations to which African Americans belong, it is critical for BGLOs to provide a compelling experience of optimal distinctiveness through symbols, local friendships, and high-profile members. In addition, positive organizing routines are needed to inspire and equip people of African descent to exemplify the leadership principles that transformed American and world history in the twentieth century. In the past twenty years, BGLOs have established different forums for leadership development, particularly for sisters and brothers who belong to such organizations. To remain relevant and vital, BGLOs must engage in strategic succession planning, with the deliberate intent of passing the mantle of leadership from senior elders to more junior torchbearers. This will require intergenerational collaboration—a deep appreciation for the positive organizing routines of the past, and an openness to new leadership models that envisions what younger members of BGLOs can bring to the future. As organizational scholars, we eagerly await the next stage in the life cycle of BGLOs and the positive organizing routines that will emerge.

Notes

1. Laura Morgan Roberts, "Shifting the Lens on Organizational Life: The Added Value of Positive Scholarship," *Academy of Management Review* 31 (2006): 241–60.

2. S. Bernstein, "Positive Organizational Scholarship: Meet the Movement: An Interview with Kim Cameron, Jane Dutton, and Robert Quinn," *Journal of Management Inquiry* 12 (2003): 266–71; K. Cameron and A. Caza, "Contributions to the Discipline of Positive Organizational Scholarship," *American Behavioral Scientist* 47 (2004): 731–39; K. S. Cameron, J. E. Dutton, R. E. Quinn, and A. E. Wrzesniewski, "Developing a Discipline of Positive Organizational Scholarship," in *Positive Organizational Scholarship: Foundations of a New Discipline,* ed. K. S. Cameron, J. E. Dutton, and R. E. Quinn, 361–70 (San Francisco: Berrett-Koehler, 2003).

3. K. Jehn, G. Northcraft, and M. Neale, "Why Differences Make a Difference: A Field Study of Diversity, Conflict and Performance in Workgroups," *Administrative Science Quarterly* 44 (1999): 741–63; S. Jeanquart-Barone, "Implications of Racial Diversity in the Supervisor-Subordinate Relationship," *Journal of Applied Social Psychology* 26, no. 11 (1996): 935–44; A. Mehra, M. Kilduff, and D. Brass, "At the Margins: A Distinctiveness Approach to the Social Identity and Social Networks of Underrepresented Groups: Race and Sex Differences in Social Identity, Friendship and Network Position," *Academy of Management Journal* 41, no. 4 (1998): 441–52; A. S. Tsui, T. D. Egan, and C. O'Reilly,

"Being Different: Relational Demography and Organizational Attachment," *Administrative Science Quarterly* 37, no. 4 (1992): 549–79.

4. Sylvia Ann Hewlett, Carolyn Buck Luce, Cornel West, Helen Chernikoff, Danielle Samalin, and Peggy Shiller, "Invisible Lives: Celebrating and Leveraging Diversity in the Executive Suite" (Center for Work-Life Policy, 2005).

5. R. Quinn and K. Cameron, "Organizational Life Cycles and Shifting Criteria of Effectiveness: Some Preliminary Evidence," *Management Science* 29 (1983): 33–51.

6. J. R. Kimberly, "Issues in the Creation of Organization: Initiation, Innovation and Institutionalization," *Academy of Management Journal* 22 (1979): 437–57.

7. F. Lyden, "Using Parsons' Functional Analysis in the Study of Public Organizations," *Administrative Science Quarterly* 20 (1975): 59–70.

8. A. Butler, "Black Fraternal and Benevolent Societies in Nineteenth-Century America," in *African American Fraternities and Sororities: The Legacy and the Vision,* ed. Tamara L. Brown, Gregory S. Parks, and Clarenda M. Phillips (Lexington: University Press of Kentucky, 2005).

9. G. M. Spreitzer and S. Sonenshein, "Positive Deviance and Extraordinary Organizing," in Cameron et al., *Positive Organizational Scholarship.*

10. R. K. Greenleaf and L. Spears, *Servant Leadership: A Journey into the Nature of Legitimate Power and Greatness* (Mahwah, N.J.: Paulist Press, 2002).

11. Lawrence C. Ross, *The Divine Nine: The History of African-American Fraternities and Sororities* (New York: Kensington, 2000).

12. Ibid.

13. S. A. Hewllet, C. B. Luce, and C. West, "Leadership in Your Midst: Tapping the Hidden Strength of Minority Executives," *Harvard Business Review* 83 (2005): 74–81.

14. C. M. Phillips, "Sisterly Bonds: African American Sororities Rising to Overcome Obstacles," in Brown et al., *African American Fraternities and Sororities,* 341–59.

15. D. A. Nadler and M. L. Tushman, *Competing by Design: The Power of Organizational Architecture* (New York: Oxford University Press, 1997).

16. H. M. Trice and J. M. Beyer, *The Culture of Work Organizations* (Englewood Cliffs, N.J.: Prentice Hall, 1993).

17. A. Rafaeli and M. Worline, "Symbols in Organizational Culture," in *Handbook of Organizational Culture and Climate* (Thousand Oaks, Calif.: Sage, 1999).

18. A. McKenzie, "In the Beginning: The Early History of the Divine Nine," in Brown et al., *African American Fraternities and Sororities,* 181–210.

19. Trice and Beyer, *The Culture of Work Organizations.*

20. W. Kimbrough, *Black Greek 101* (Cranbury, N.J.: Associated University Press, 2003).

21. G. S. Parks and T. L. Brown, "'In the Fell Clutch of Circumstance': Pledging and the Black Greek Experience," in Brown et al., *African American Fraternities and Sororities,* 437–64.

22. Daniel Rickett, "Capacity Building. Global Mapping International," http://www.gmi.org/research/capbuild.htm (2000).

23. National Pan-Hellenic Council Web site, http://www.nphchq.org/about.htm.

24. D. Cooperrider and L. Sekerka, "Toward a Theory of Positive Organizational Change," in Cameron et al., *Positive Organizational Scholarship*.

25. National Pan-Hellenic Council Web site, http://www.nphchq.org/about.htm.

26. Ross, *The Divine Nine*.

27. Kwame Anthony Appiah, *The Ethics of Identity* (Princeton, N.J.: Princeton University Press, 2005); Tommie Shelby, *We Who Are Dark: The Philosophical Foundations of Black Solidarity* (Cambridge, Mass.: Belknap Press, 2005).

28. William J. Wilson, *When Work Disappears: The World of the New Urban Poor* (New York: Alfred A. Knopf, 1997).

29. K. Sutcliffe and T. Vogus, "Organizing for Resilience," in Cameron et al., *Positive Organizational Scholarship*.

30. P. Byrne, "The Ubiquitous Relationship: Attitude Similarity and Attraction: A Cross-Cultural Study," *Human Relations* 24 (1971): 201–7.

31. G. R. Jones, "Socialization Tactics, Self-Efficacy, and Newcomers' Adjustments to Organizations," *Academy of Management Journal* 29, no. 2 (1986): 262–79; R. L. Moreland and J. M. Levine, "Newcomers and Oldtimers in Small Groups," in *Psychology of Group Influence*, 2nd ed. (Hillsdale, N.J.: Lawrence Erlbaum Associates, 1989); J. Van Maanen and E. Schein, "Toward a Theory of Organizational Socialization," in *Research in Organizational Behavior*, ed. B. M. Staw and L. L. Cummings (Greenwich, Conn.: JAI Press, 1979).

32. Ross, *The Divine Nine*.

33. R. F. Baumeister and M. Leary, "The Need to Belong: Desire for Interpersonal Attachments as a Fundamental Human Motivation," *Psychological Bulletin* 117, no. 3 (1995): 497–529; J. Dutton and E. Heaphy, "Coming to Life: The Power of High-Quality Connections at Work," in Cameron et al., *Positive Organizational Scholarship*.

34. M. B. Brewer, "The Social Self: On Being the Same and Different at the Same Time," *Personality and Social Psychology Bulletin* 17, no. 5 (1991): 475–82.

35. K. Cameron, "Organizational Virtuousness and Performance," in Cameron et al., *Positive Organizational Scholarship*, 48–65; L. M. Roberts, "Shifting the Lens on Organizational Life: The Added Value of Positive Scholarship [response to Fineman, 2006]," *Academy of Management Review* 31 (2006): 292–305; M. A. Glynn and J. E. Dutton, "The Generative Dynamics of Positive Organizing," working paper prepared as an invited article for *Organization Science* (2007).

36. Cristina Gibson and Julian Birkinshaw, "The Antecedents, Consequences and Mediating Role of Organizational Ambidexterity," *Academy of Management Journal* 47, no. 2 (2004): 209–26.

Part V

Diversity

15

Not on My Line
Attitudes about Homosexuality in Black Fraternities

Alan D. DeSantis and Marcus Coleman

No issue is more controversial or taboo in black fraternities than male homo-sexuality. As John, a third-year brother and business major, remarked, "That shit is just wrong, you know. You can't bring that shit anywhere near us. No, no, no, no." For John and the other brothers we interviewed, homosexuality in their fraternal ranks challenges their fundamental ideas about brotherhood, loyalty, trustworthiness, and, most importantly, masculinity.

Although there has been no published research on the attitudes of black fraternity members toward homosexuality, there is compelling evidence that the black community is more homophobic than its white counterpart.[1] A number of scholars have found that blacks are more likely than whites to view homosexual relations as wrong and immoral. Similarly, Lisa Schulte found that blacks were more willing than whites to express negativity toward gays and lesbians.[2]

These differences can best be accounted for by white-black religious and educational differences. Beliefs about homosexuality and support for gay rights vary substantially by religion and by the intensity of religious feeling. Disapproval is highest among those who attend religious services frequently, who pray often, and who view religion as important in their lives.[3] Blacks are substantially more religious and are more likely to adopt a fundamental interpretation of the Bible than whites are.[4] Education also seems to have a significant impact on white-black attitudinal differences about homosexuality. Higher educational levels have been shown to result in greater acceptance of differences, a more liberal sexual attitude, more contact with gays and lesbians, and a heightened sense of democratic values and civil liberties.[5] Blacks are only two-thirds as likely as whites to be college gradu-ates.[6] The available research, however, tells us only in broad demographic strokes how the general black population feels about homosexuality. What we do not know is how certain segments of the black community conceive of homosexuality and whether their attitudes result in discriminatory practices.

Our specific concern here is how homosexuality is viewed by black fraternity members and whether these attitudes result in the exclusion of potential members. The importance of understanding the attitudes and actions of this specific subsegment of black culture is underscored when one considers the disproportionate economic and political power wielded by the members of these organizations. Their beliefs and judgments have ramifications that permeate far beyond the fraternity and into the seats of cultural and social decision making.[7]

We used two methods of gathering data. First, we conducted eighteen face-to-face, audiotaped interviews with thirteen student and five alumni members of the four oldest black fraternities—Alpha Phi Alpha, Kappa Alpha Psi, Omega Psi Phi, and Phi Beta Sigma.[8] All members were active brothers affiliated with one of three educational institutions in the South: a primarily white state university, a primarily black state university, and a historically black state university.

Since this topic is fraught with legal and confidentiality concerns, the authors and the interviewees agreed to a series of guidelines designed to protect the latter's anonymity. Consequently, the interviewees in this study were assigned pseudonyms; their organizations, when the nature of the interviews allowed, were referred to by arbitrary, noncorresponding Greek letters (Beta, Gamma, Eta, and Theta)[9]; and their affiliated universities were ascribed arbitrary, non-corresponding roman numerals (University I, II, and III). Additionally, any third-party names or identifying events that might jeopardize the anonymity of our subjects were changed or removed. Finally, to facilitate the readability of this chapter and to avoid needless repetition within the text, only the subjects' pseudonyms are referenced. See table 15.1 for each interviewee's pseudonym and fraternity and university affiliation.

We also gathered data through an online questionnaire soliciting the opinions of black fraternity brothers from around the nation.[10] An invitation to the Listserv was sent to the National Pan-Hellenic Council (NPHC) national Listserv, where members were encouraged to share the invitation with other NPHC members. Respondents to this questionnaire had the choice of either sending their answers to a groupwide Listserv, which was maintained and monitored by us, or e-mailing their responses directly to us.

We received sixteen completed, thoughtful, and highly credible questionnaires from members of black Greek-letter organizations (BGLOs).[11] Although subjects were not asked to disclose any personal or demographic information, four of the sixteen respondents voluntarily told us that they were homosexual; two are openly gay; two are covertly gay. All four admitted, however, to "passing" as heterosexual men while pledging.

Although the online questionnaire format inhibited our ability to engage in

Table 15.1. Interviewees' Pseudonyms and Fraternity and University Affiliations

Name	Organization	University	Status
John	Beta	I	Student
Michael	Beta	I	Alumnus
Raymond	Beta	II	Student
Greg	Beta	I	Student
Mark	Beta	II	Student
Ron	Beta	III	Alumnus
Alex	Gamma	II	Alumnus
Robert	Gamma	II	Student
Muhammad	Gamma	III	Student
Benjamin	Eta	I	Student
Leroy	Eta	I	Student
Wallace	Eta	II	Student
Martin	Eta	III	Alumnus
Fred	Eta	III	Student
William	Theta	I	Student
James	Theta	II	Alumnus
Jefferson	Theta	II	Student
Brian	Theta	III	Student

extended conversational exchanges with our subjects, it afforded certain other advantages. First, since no names or demographic information (e.g., fraternity or university affiliation, regional location, age) was supplied by the respondents, anonymity was guaranteed. Second, these questionnaires allowed us to gather more data, widen the scope of our investigation, and expand the geographic range of the study. Given the nature of the Internet, our survey was available to anyone with access to the World Wide Web, regardless of location.

In what follows, we detail how these thirty-four men conceive of black masculinity in relationship to sexual orientation, view homosexual integration in their organizations, and justify their homophobia and exclusion of black gay men from their fraternities.

Defining Masculinity

To understand how these men view *homosexuality*, it is first necessary to understand how they conceive of *masculinity*. As Julia Woods asserts, these two ideas have created a symbiotic relationship in contemporary America.[12] Masculinity is conceptualized, first and foremost, in binary relationship to homosexuality: to be "manly" is to be virile, attracted to women, and hyper-heterosexual. As other authors have warned, however, we must be careful about presuming a universal notion of black manhood.[13] Wizdom Powell Hammond and Jacqueline S. Mattis, in fact, uncovered fifteen masculine attributes detailed by a diverse group of African American men living in five metropolitan areas in the United States.[14]

Given the insular nature of Greek life and the highly discerning process of selecting new members, however, we should not be surprised that many of the same motifs of masculinity were shared by these fraternal brothers. Many of our subjects agreed, for example, that "real men" provide for their families, protect the people they care about, and remain active in their communities. These attributions were especially important to the older alumni brothers in our study. As James, a fifty-five-year old alumni member, claimed, "A man takes care of business, home and away. You have to have character and love for your race."

For the college brothers, however, such familial and societal concerns were far less important. Instead, many celebrated a hip-hop–inspired hypermasculinity that privileged the individual over the collective. "We don't want to be Dr. Kings or Stokley Carmichaels," asserted Raymond. "We, they [correcting himself], my brothers want to be Jay Z or Snoop or, God help us, Fifty Cent." Michael agreed that hip-hop "has an impact on every element of black culture, including college life and our organizations. Our men want to be thugs, not doctors."

Though Michael may have exaggerated the point, it is true that most of the undergraduates we interviewed conceived of ideal black masculinity as physical, sexual, hard, and street or urban smart. Most disturbingly, their ideas of manhood stood in binary opposition to anything chaste, sensitive, studious, and refined. These attributes were viewed as not only feminine characteristics but also white and gay traits. Specifically, their conceptions of masculinity may best be understood in three maxims.

MAXIM ONE: BE PHYSICALLY STRONG AND DOMINATING

All our undergraduates agreed that an important part of ideal black masculinity is manifested in the body. "Our bodies have always been important; it is the only thing that they [white society] can't take," asserted Martin. "It is why the black male is a symbol of strength, physical strength." Jefferson, a junior communications major, concurred and claimed, "For the black male persona it is all about the body . . . what you have, what you own, what you look like, the type of image you project." Muhammad believes that this trait is the primary allure of Omega men. "I mean, let's be real, the Omegas is just that. We all know it, and I am not even a Q. They are the jocks, the athletes. They have that side covered, for real. We all respect that."

For these men, however, it is not just the body in isolation. The physicality and contact of the male body with other male bodies is equally important. It is tied into community and identity building. As one of us (Marcus Coleman) has often claimed, "If we don't touch you, we don't love you." This aphorism is especially true during "underground pledging," where physical contact is central to many of the hazing rituals.[15] "Going through it, hard, is what makes us men. If you don't get the shit beat out of you, you ain't one of us," argued Robert. "The physical part is what tests you, tests to see if you're a man, your manhood." William, being more explicit in his description of the role of physical contact, sees violence as a natural, if not necessary, extension of this first maxim. "Male against male violence is seen as being extremely masculine. Quite often there is a lot of stuff that goes on in our underground pledge processes. You know, paddling is very traditional for us. Our line got it, woooo. I have met brothers who have been hit a hundred times in one night. . . . It separates the boys from the men." It is not simply paddling that ties these men together, however. William indicated that "other things happen too. People get punched, slapped. Usually it is not in the face, but in the chest and the back and they end up with extremely bruised chests and back or arms."[16]

Because of this intimate physical relationship formed on the pledge line, gay or effeminate men are anathema. "It's just fact," Ron, remarked. "We are close, physically. I can't go into everything, you know, but believe me, you can't have a homo [he laughs], a homosexual [he corrects himself] on line. We close, face-to-face. You can't have it, believe me." Similarly, Alex worried that the dynamics of brotherhood would change with gay pledges: "I'm concerned. We bring young men together in close proximity experiencing things where they might be nude, they might be half-exposed, they are closely lined up, sometimes pressed chest to back. It is highly intolerable that someone be homosexual within that mix."

For these men, therefore, ideal masculinity is not simply about the muscular black male body as a symbol of strength and virility; it is also about physical and, at times, violent contact with one another. This male-on-male connection serves both to bind brothers together and to demonstrate a hypermasculine endurance in the face of pain. These outcomes, however, are believed to be jeopardized by the presence of gay brothers. As John wondered, "Is that gay dude looking at me, checking me out? Is he rubbing on me in line? Is he, you know, liking it?" The body, therefore, ceases to be an extension of masculinity and becomes a possible object of unwanted desire. As John speculated, "Everything would change."

MAXIM TWO: BE HYPERSEXUAL AND PROMISCUOUS

Each of the men we interviewed also saw a man's worth marked by his ability to "handle the ladies" (Wallace). When we asked Alex what type of man he wanted in his fraternity, he responded by saying that he "looks for guys who will have a good rapport with the women. Not too pushy, but you know, they have to be able to charm, to handle himself around the ladies." In posing the same question to Fred, we received an almost identical answer: We "want guys who get the girls and things of that nature. He should be smooth with the women." Brian also wants "bros who can bring in the ladies. You got to have it. You don't want bookish guys, you want the men who can get the party started, get them to show up, you know, and keep 'em happy [laughs]."

This attribute is likely to pay dividends outside the social context. Alex told us, "The guys who are good with women have the right persona. They are more likely to get in where they want, wherever. They get placed in positions of leadership because of that 'ladies' man' kind of persona that they present." "Sure it is prized," affirmed Jefferson, "everyone wants to be able to do that . . . it is just a must with us. It is all part of having a total package, and yah, you need it to be a leader, to be respected, I guess I should say."

Just as maxim one (be strong and physical) was seen as being closely associated with the public persona of the Omegas, maxim two was perceived to be most closely aligned with the Kappa image. "Kappas are seen as the pretty boys, smooth, ladies' men," claimed Michael. "They are the playboys. That's them. Now, that don't mean we don't get the women too, right, but that's them." John, Greg, Alex, and James also agreed with this association. Brian even went so far as to say, "If you want to get the ladies, if that is your thing, then you go Kappa. They may not be the best in sports or grades, but, you know, the girls."

For the undergraduates in this study, therefore, being successful with women is as important as being strong and physical. In many ways, in fact, maintaining the body is a means to successful sexual ends. Wallace, a brother who has spent considerable time in the gym, confessed that he does "it all for the women. They love this [pointing to his chest]. They always rubbin' on me [laughs]. I'm the man!"

This primary criterion of judging masculinity, however, would be challenged by homosexual integration into black fraternities. First and foremost, it would mean that these men would have to reconsider their traditional ideas of masculinity and brotherhood. Simply put, can a man date another man and still be masculine? Can heterosexual and homosexual men create an authentic bond of brotherhood? It would also mean that these brothers, whose activities with one another revolve around heterosexual interactions with women (e.g., flirting, dating, partying), would have to alter their social lives to accommodate homosexual lifestyles. More questions arise: Could gay and straight social agendas coexist? Would straight women be willing to attend a mixed heterosexual-homosexual function? Would gay men be willing to attend a mixed function? It is little wonder that integration is such a hot-button topic for these men. As Martin, a thirty-seven-year-old alumnus wondered, "Are we ready for this yet?"

MAXIM THREE: NEVER BE OVERLY REFINED OR ACADEMIC

For these men, masculinity involves more than what a man looks like and how promiscuous he is; it is also how a man carries himself, how he maintains an image, and how "real" he keeps it. Part of keeping it real is being hard, emotionally controlled, and "cool."[17] Most disturbingly, it also means the avoidance of being overly refined and academic—traits that these men see not only as "selling out" (i.e., not keeping it real) but also as feminine, white, and gay.

Robert, a second-year graduate student, for example, conceives of this (soft) white versus (hard) black dichotomy as a mind versus body proposition: "Intellect for white males as opposed to physical attributes for black males. For the black male persona is all about the body . . . the type of image you project. For white males, it's not as manly, it is about what you know, how well reasoned your decisions are, how economic or how efficient you are. And that shows through in financial considerations, even in academia. It shows through in writing in academia who can be the efficient and say this the most pedantic way. For us, it is about the self, the physical self as opposed to the intellectual self."

But there is more to this conception of masculinity than just the punctuation of the body over the mind. There is also what John McWhorter has called anti-intellectualism running through black male consciousness.[18] Too many of our respondents associated being academic—or what Greg called "bookish" and John called "nerdy"—with being both white and gay.

This dangerous bifurcation is also seen in the career choices brothers make once they leave campus. "Being street," according to Leroy, "means that you have not forgotten, that you know, you know? You don't want to be like the 'business type.' They are the sellouts. It is also, like I said before, a gay image." A thoughtful Alex agreed with this perception in the black community but posited an explanation grounded in historical forces. "You see, white men have been able to define their manhood by their career, but in many instances, we were limited, or thought we were limited." He asserted that because of this lack of opportunity, "black men turned to something they can control (e.g., their image, their body, their attitude). They became hypermasculine. If you are not that way, though, you are viewed as feminine. A soft brother."

As many of these men claimed, however, it is not just the positive aspects of masculinity that must be accentuated; there are certain feminine qualities that must be eschewed. One cannot be too "refined," "immaculate," or "well dressed." Benjamin, for example, sees men who are "well dressed and well versed as being suspect. You know, there is a chance he is homosexual." Raymond voiced the same suspicions: "It is almost, for a man to be refined, well dressed, . . . speaking white, unless he is over the age of forty, . . . a given he is gay or just a complete geek."

Speaking directly to this concern, James, a refined, well-dressed alumnus, related his personal experience of not fitting into this limited mold of masculinity: "There is one time when I was pledging and a big brother came in and asked me if I had 'sugar in my tank.' I said, 'Excuse us big brother, what do you mean?' 'I mean are you gay?' But this happens. . . . Just recently again, I was talking to one of my brothers and he said he thought I was gay when we first met because I was too polished and I spoke the queen's English and I am fairly reserved."

Just as with the first two maxims, this third law of masculinity was also associated with a particular fraternity. "The Alphas," Jefferson claimed, "they are the smart ones, the immaculate ones. They are very precise, and of course, there is the stereotype that they are the gay ones." Robert sees the Alphas as "bookish, straight. I think that's why people think they are more nonmasculine, feminine right. Not that it is bad, you know. It is just different."

Even the Alphas we spoke with were aware of their reputation. Some argued that this perception is new. "We are more traditional. We are Dr. King and Thurgood Marshall. The younger brothers don't know their history so that's not cool to them." Others Alpha brothers think it stems from the culture that is strategically cultivated by the organization: "We work on our image as gentlemen.

So I think a different type of brother comes to us. We are also not interested in gang bangers. So it goes both ways. We look and they look for us."

Not all Alphas, however, are proud of their contemporary public perception. "I try to flip the script," explained one younger Alpha. "People meet us [his chapter] and they think geeks or nerds. After they meet us, they say, 'I thought Alphas was like this, now I changed my mind.' So I try to work on that. I don't glorify the stereotype."

This anti-intellectual spirit, however, did not go unchallenged. In fact, an uneasy dialectical tension marked most of our discussions about academic achievement and masculinity. On the one hand, these men viewed manhood as being antithetical to a life of the mind. Being too intellectual, refined, or well-spoken cast doubt on both their commitment to the race (i.e., they were perceived as selling out to the white culture) and their heterosexual status. On the other hand, these men were proud to be at college and competitive about their grades. This sense of pride was especially pronounced among brothers who had overcome myriad social and personal obstacles to gain admission to their universities. This dialectical push and pull compelled many of these men, therefore, to walk the thin line between being too refined and too street. Chuck D, from Public Enemy fame, aptly termed this paradoxical clash of identities as life of the "college thug." We have been assured by many of the older alumni in this study, however, that "these young brothers will outgrow this stage" of life (Ron).

The Decision-Making Process

Given this tripartite, and often homophobic, conception of masculinity, we wondered whether homosexual integration in BGLOs is possible. As we suspected, an openly gay student stands almost no chance of gaining admission into a college chapter. In unequivocal terms, most brothers echoed Benjamin's sentiments: "A guy who is gay is not getting in my frat." "There is an unwritten rule," explained Alex, "that homosexuals are forbidden to be in the fraternity. It is not part of the official laws, but a part of the principles." "In the eighteen years that I have been a brother," Raymond confessed, "no openly gay brother affirming that before joining has ever joined. I am not sure if it will ever happen to tell you the truth."

Even given exceptional circumstances, like the one recently faced by Wallace and his brothers, gay men are persona non grata: "There was this great guy on campus who [was] openly gay and he wanted to be part of a black fraternity, mine in particular. He is the most polished guy on campus. President of student government, can you believe it? He was not welcome. He knew it. We never saw him again." We heard a similar story of rejection from a former student who contacted us online. "I am openly gay," he wrote, but he thought that pledging a fraternity would be a "good thing socially." So "I submitted to the Thetas, after having done everything and beyond what they asked and expected of any other . . . I had a 4.0, was president of several campus organizations." Yet he was rejected, presumably "for being gay. They never said it, but they could not even give me a legitimate reason for the denial, especially when compared to the boys they did choose."

There was one undergraduate, however, who crafted a scenario—improbable and humorous as it may be—in which a homosexual would probably be welcome. "Let's say Tiger Woods put an application into X fraternity. . . . We can say the same thing about Michael Jordan," explained Brian. "Because of his notoriety, because of his popularity, what he can do for the brothers, you find out that he is a *little* gay . . . he would probably get in."

But what if an aspirant does not openly admit to being gay? Would brothers be any more tolerant of a prospect who remained "in the closet"? Surprisingly, a few of our subjects were "cool with it," as William put it. Some even viewed fraternity life like the military. "Don't ask, don't tell, is my motto," said Fred. "What you do away from me and behind your own locked door is your business."

For Lewis, one of our online respondents, it was about more than just remaining quiet; it was also about public image. "If he is flamboyant and feminine, then absolutely not. We have enough pressure and issues to deal with being black men in a fraternity. If he is discreet, then I don't see a problem. It's all about discretion. But I am probably out there alone on this one." Jamal, another online respondent, saw the issue of remaining in the closet differently, calling it a matter of honesty. "I would rather have an openly gay fraternity brother than a closet bisexual brother [referring to down-low brothers]. Then the relationship with the fraternity is based on deception." For Jamal, truth is more important in the equation of brotherhood than sexual preference.

Most men in this study, however, did not want a homosexual brother in their ranks, whether openly or clandestinely gay. This position, of course, raises a whole new set of problems for black fraternities. The most obvious, of course, is how to determine whether a prospect is gay. As the previous section highlighted, some search for physical characteristics, personality traits, and habits. "You can tell most of the time," said Martin. "You know the stereotypes, the way they walk and talk. Guys who are feminine." "Generally," theorized William, "if they are too studious, clean, you know, well dressed . . . if you don't see them with women . . . that is always a pretty good sign too."

Many of the men we interviewed, however, were not as confident as they once were about their ability to identify homosexuals. "The 'down-low' thing keeps you guessing," remarked Raymond. "Down low" is often used to describe black men who have sex with other men as well as women but do not identify themselves as gay or bisexual. This is also referred to as being "on the down low," "on the DL," or "on the low low."[19] As Ray put it, "It has changed everything. You don't know anymore about anyone."

For some of the brothers, the DL has made traditional means of identification obsolete. "I kind of just gave up," claimed William. "You never know. They might be very masculine, but they might just be like that. They might go out and play a pick-up game of basketball and dunk on you and talk smack on the court, and ask you to go to bed afterwards. There is just no way to tell anymore." For Muhammad, the phenomenon has also made it a "futile effort for a guy to be hypermasculine and use that as a justification for why people shouldn't see him as homosexual. You know, 'the guy can't be gay, he has women and plays ball.' Damn, that don't mean nothing. I just give up [laughs]."

For other brothers, the DL has heightened their homophobic suspicions. Jefferson now thinks that "everyone is a possible 'fag.' The down low puts a question mark on everyone. Nobody escapes the question mark these days. I'll be honest, right, I look at everyone a little different, you know." Similarly, Fred admitted, "This whole thing has made everyone paranoid. Even if you don't want to be having it in the back of your mind they can sort of just shove it there. . . . Everything is suspect."

So where does this leave these fraternities? Since they can never be sure about the sexual orientation of an initiate, have they given up their scrutinizing search for "real men"? The answer from most was a resounding no. Most claimed, in fact, to be more diligent in their interrogation and investigation of prospects. Some have chosen a more honest and forthright approach. Michael said that when he is in doubt, he "will just ask. Not to say it is the right way to do things, but I will just bring it up." He is well aware, however, that the prospect will "probably . . . deny it regardless. But at least I asked. The rest is on him, you know." Adopting a similar strategy, Benjamin also asks, albeit in a more intimidating context. "There is always an underground interview and most of the time there is always a direct question about sexual orientation. I will just come out and ask. It's hard to lie in situations like that . . . brother yelling at your face."

Many of the brothers we talked with, however, opted for a less direct and personal approach to information gathering. One of the more common sources of background information is letters of recommendation. Leroy sees these endorsements as crucial in weeding out unwanted elements. "We know, if you can't get a good letter from brothers, something is wrong. And brothers won't write one if they know something's wrong [referring to being gay]. So it is not necessarily a direct method of trying to intimidate them not to be in, you see. [Etas] just look out for each other and the fraternity. They won't write one for a gay homosexual."

Some, like Brian, also "monitor" the actions of their prospective brothers. "Just watch and listen, you can tell. Keep your eyes and ears open. It's a vibe, a certain vibe I catch." Or they might actually question students on campus. "I ask people," said Brian. "Women know what's what, so if you ask women about him and they say he is straight, he's straight. If they have a question mark, then uh oh, it's trouble." Similarly, Robert's and Alex's chapters "do background investigations." "Yea, we investigate. We dig to make sure we are getting a Beta man. A Beta man has to be a certain type. And yea, part of what we looking for is whether they right [heterosexual]."

Making it successfully through the cross-examinations, obtaining the right letters of recommendation, and having a clean investigation are not always enough, however. If there are still suspicions, regardless of a lack of actual proof, a prospect might not get in. Ron told of one case in which conjecture and gossip were enough for exclusion: "Like I said, this one guy that we thought, but we had no proof. We investigated it to see whether or not we could prove he was a homosexual and we couldn't, but we voted him down. More than one guy too, that we knew were homosexuals, that tried to join the frat."

What often happens, however, is that a questionable prospect makes it through the first aboveground stage of acceptance—letter, grade point average, dues—only to receive greater scrutiny during the later underground pledge process. "I've seen it a few times," stated Robert. "I didn't like it, but what was I gonna do? The brothers just beat these guys down until they quit. If they want you to quit, you will. They all did. Gone." Benjamin recalled when they "beat down" one of his own line brothers. "It was bad, every day, at him and at him, bam, bam, bam." After a few weeks of this abuse, Ben came to the aid of his brother. "Wow. I just tried to say he was cool. And they were like, 'You his bitch?' And all of a sudden I was like [long pause] whatever." By the end of the process, "The kid dropped, just left. I don't blame him though. He got it hard."

On rare occasions, some make it through the abuse. Mark still carries emotional scars from the hazing he received for being too feminine. When Mark first arrived on campus, it was his "dream to be a brother." Despite being gay, he wanted to experience the authentic college life, especially being a member of a fraternity. The way he saw it, "it shouldn't have mattered" that he was gay. "I kept my business, my business." In an effort to be more welcomed, in fact, he "even tried to keep a female always about—just to keep some visibility. You know, do something that they can see . . . to keep them off my back." It quickly became evident to Mark, however, that he was not overtly masculine enough for his older brothers. He began to be subjected to increasing verbal and physical abuse on his line. He recalled: "I got badgered on a daily basis. It came to my face every day. I didn't let them see my anger and my frustration. When I got back to my apartment and it was just me, you know, that's when I let my emotions kind of get the best of me and I am kind of ashamed to say that I let them get to me like that. When you are badgered and it is brought to you on a daily basis, you know, it got to get to you. But I never let them see that. I never let them see my hurt." Mark finally made it through and became a brother, but he is still bitter about how he was treated. At the end of the interview, we asked him whether it was worth it. "No," he responded without hesitation. "I feel ashamed that I stooped to their level, just to keep them off my back. No, I don't feel it was worth it. It made me [long pause] feel even worse about myself."

The preceding cases focus primarily on the actions and thoughts of undergraduate chapters. Would alumni and graduate chapters be less homophobic and more accepting? Most in our study agreed that they would be. James, for example, believes that a gay man has a "fifty-fifty" chance, "as opposed to twenty year ago, [when] it would have been ten-ninety." "Because of time," he continued, "because of the society that we live in, the playing field is almost level as far as accepting gay people into [alumni] sororities and fraternities."

For Michael, this greater acceptance is due to the maturity of its members. "Many of the men in our alumni realms," he claimed, "are older, more professional. We get older and we mellow. We have families, jobs. That stuff [homosexuality] is less important." In a similar vein, Martin attributed greater acceptance to the different criteria used. "Alumni chapters generally have different standards for picking members. Sexual orientation is not one of the more important criteria. It's about being productive. Our alumni chapters are looking for a bro who is willing to work, who is willing to be financial, who is willing to be responsible to the black community."

Not all the subjects in our study, however, agreed that alumni or graduate chapters would *necessarily* be more tolerant of homosexuals. "I think it really is about where the location is," asserted Muhammad. If we lived in "a more liberal area such as Florida or New York or Chicago, in a big metropolitan city, we'd see more of it and it is acceptable because it is out there." Others speculated that the degree of acceptance would also be correlated with the ages of the alumni members. "There are some chapters out there," claimed Leroy, "that have a bunch of old, old men, old farmer types. They are from a different era . . . homosexuality is taboo." Young professional men are "more liberal minded when it comes to sexual orientation."[20]

This greater tolerance in alumni or graduate chapters, however, was not always seen as a positive social advancement. Some brothers disapproved of the lowering of fraternal standards. Stephen, an online respondent from the Washington, D.C., area, detailed the "declining" state of his chapter: "Yes, I shun them, try to stay away from them and limit my contact with them. Most of the other brothers are also gay (or closeted, or sympathizers), so they all treat each other like the little gay dudes that they are. The straight brothers have stopped being active because of all the gay dudes. We've all basically left our local chapters and are inactive because we're sick of all the gay dudes."

Based on the information we collected, it is clear that homosexual students at the undergraduate level are systematically excluded from the black fraternal experience. It is less clear, however, to what degree and under which situations gay alumni or graduate members are discriminated against. In the final section, we investigate how the exclusion of gay prospects is justified and why so many brothers view homosexuality as anathema to the mission and vision of BGLOs.

Justification for Homophobia

One of our goals in undertaking this project was to understand how fraternity brothers view homosexuality and how that perspective is informed by their ideas of masculinity. For the men involved in this study, however, no source was more important in informing their opinions about homosexuality than the Bible. "A *real* man," asserted Mark, "is a God-fearing and Bible-believing Christian." In fact, all twenty-eight (of thirty-four) brothers in this study who believe that homosexuality is "wrong" used religion to justify their belief.

"God makes it clear," Robert elaborated, "the Bible is clear-cut. Clear-cut as stealing and as murder. . . . It is wrong and it's not supposed to take place." "Yes, I think it is wrong," James asserted. "I do not think it is what God intended for men. I think it is sinful." For Jacob, one of our online respondents, the sin is not simply being gay—an affliction he believes a person is "born" with or has forced on him by "molestation"—but "acting" on those impulses. "These guys have the choice of *living* the gay lifestyle, and that's where I have a problem. I hate to see men carrying on like women or with a bunch of feminine characteristics—*especially* if they are sporting my fraternity letters. . . . I do not think it is what God intended for men."

The historical Christian foundation of BGLOs is often used as a salient rationale for the exclusion of gay members. A Sigma brother defined this interconnected relationship: "Most fraternal African-American organizations have a Christian value. . . . Their members at some point or another affirm that these are Christian organizations. Their rituals have Christian rituals embedded in them. So we're talking now about a Christian value system . . . that members were attracted to."

Speaking to his specific organization's historical roots, an Omega brother attributes his chapter's stance on gay men to "one of the four founders, . . . who was a bishop and so the Bible like intermingles in everything that we do and what we think." Similarly, a Kappa brother told us, "The Bible is used as our key, from the beginning. It [homosexuality] is against the Bible, a sin. So we trust that as brothers."

Many that we spoke with, however, did not view "sin" in such monolithic terms. For Raymond, there is a difference between long-term and short-term sin. "Short-term sins," he detailed, "are the sins that will pass over such as lying, cheating . . . things that can be easily taken care of." Long-terms sins, like homosexuality, "affect people for a long time, and people will never forget about that." Others relied on a ranking system to give order to their moral code. For Wallace, homosexuality is "one of the top ones [he pauses to think]. It is bad to say that. 'Murder' is the top one, but then 'homosexuality' is probably right underneath that." Similarly, Jefferson uses a "hierarchy of sin" based on the Bible to determine the degrees of immorality. "Homosexuality," he told us, "is pretty high" on the list. "A lot of other sins are not as bad, like you won't go to hell for drinking."

Not all the brothers we interviewed, however, were comfortable using the Bible to prioritize sin or justify exclusion. In one of the more thoughtful responses, Benjamin explained, "Slave owners justified slavery by citing biblical scripture—does that make it right? During the Jim Crow era, whites used the Bible to keep black and white people separate. So when people say they know what God wants, watch out [laughing]." Others were skeptical of using literal interpretations of the Word because of human politics and intervention. "King James omitted a couple of books of the Bible," Michael wrote. "I think we put too much trust in a document that has been written/translated by man." Using a similar line of reasoning, Joshua detailed the historical politics that fuels his misgivings about literalism: "Remember that the Bible conveniently leaves out Gospels that the Church deemed inconsistent with the tenets it wished to enforce. Thus, the Gospel of Mary that gives women greater prominence is not there, nor is the Gospel of Thomas by Didymos Judas Thomas with other recorded sayings from Jesus."

But religion was not the only source used by these brothers to justify their homophobia. The "laws of nature" also informed their attitudes about sexual orientation. "You are a man," explained Mark, "you are to reproduce with a woman. . . . My defining argument [against homosexuality] is production and the conduct of it. You know, we need to produce other human beings. It is pure and simple; it goes against the laws of nature." John concurred, noting, "It is a natural thing. If everybody was gay the world would end because we couldn't create, you know, so it is a natural order of life that I see." "Look at all animals," asserted Mark, "you don't see gay animals because it is unnatural. It is like poison in human society—something from outside of the normal."

Brothers also relied on social norms and cultural codes of acceptable behavior to inform their belief system. Regardless of what our pretty new "Will and Grace society" tells us, explained Wallace, "our social norms still tell us that it is wrong. We, especially black people, think it is wrong. Look around you. People are against it. That should be enough." For Greg, obeying social rules is part of being a good fraternity brother. "Our objective is to gain the public interest and to do things in the public interest, so if we are doing things like homosexuality that are against the social norms then we are a contradiction. Think about it, right? If we are good citizens, then we can't be gay." Similarly, Mark said, "The social norms is a man and a woman being together. . . . The majority of people, the way the world is, the way that society says, is homosexuality is wrong."

Not all the justifications raised by these men dealt with the abstract world of religion, nature, and social norms. Many of their concerns focused on the day-to-day pragmatics of homosexual integration. As previously discussed, for example, brothers expressed concern over the effect gay men would have on underground pledging. "We pretty close on line," explained Leroy. "We spend a lot of time with our shirts off, pretty close to each other. Paddling. It would just be weird to have a gay dude there. I would feel weird."

This physical intimacy could also engender unwanted sexual advances—

"being hit on." Explained Wallace, "I don't want a gay dude trying to holler at me. I'm not interested in that, that's being disrespectful." According to Robert, "There would always be a small amount of doubt put in your mind by this person." He would always be wondering, "Is this person close to me because we are pledging together or does he want to be close to me intimately? That small amount of doubt could cause a problem, a larger problem." "You always have that fear and kind of question," concluded Fred. "Is he trying to hit on me? . . . What are his true intentions? [Does he have] some other ulterior motive?"

Brothers were also concerned about the impact gay men would have on the organizational climate and culture of their fraternities. An online respondent viewed integration as being most "dangerous because they would cause division and destabilize the very unity of the organization." Michael feared that a gay presence could create "division within the fraternity" and "alienate" members, facilitating a "negative environment."

The threat to fraternal bonding and friendships was also raised. "As a group of guys," explained Mark, "we are all men of like-minded interests, because it gets down to interests. We like similar things, like we like to drink, we are going to like sports, we're going to like women." What, he wondered, would unite straight and gay brothers? This dissimilarity, from Martin's perspective, also threatens the brothers' ability to bond. "It's a different culture, so when you have different beliefs and different cultures you don't have a bond." And from the perspective of the brothers in this study, "it is all about the bond of brotherhood."

Finally, many in our study feared that public ridicule and ostracism would accompany homosexual integration. For some of our respondents, the concern was how they as individuals would be perceived. "I don't want people to think I am gay," worried Greg, to think that "because I have a homosexual guy in my chapter or multiple homosexual men, . . . I might be gay too." William was also anxious about his reputation. "I would be like, 'Hey, meet my frat brothers,' and he is openly gay, and, at least in theory, we would have this strong relational tie with each other. People would begin to think that I'm gay . . . I can't go for that, now."

Brothers were equally concerned about what a gay presence would do to their organization's public image. "You don't want to be known as the gay chapter on campus," warned Greg. "There is one kind of [fraternity] like that here [his university] and it's bad. They are a joke." Some, like John and Raymond, feared that the chapter would be seen as "weak" by the other fraternities, citing this as "a major fear that drives . . . discrimination." Explained Muhammad, "If you take one in, will everyone think everybody's gay too? You know, like why did they take that guy anyway?" An online respondent similarly worried about such misconceptions. "Fraternities gather men who share common interests; if you get one or two gay guys, people will assume that [the] whole fraternity is gay."

It was not just "perception," in and of itself, that concerned these men, however. How you are seen is "tied in with everything. It is your life blood." Admitting homosexuals "would have serious consequences for how we operate on our campus," said Alex. "We will be scrutinized," expanded Ben. "Folks will not come to our functions, our parties, community service projects." "We will be the laughingstocks of the campus with this gay dude in our chapter," claimed Leroy, and "our numbers would decline . . . we would probably be seen as the *wack* fraternity. . . . Other people won't join." For Robert, "the process goes like this, now listen: So you take one gay guy, right? And next, less guys on campus want to join. Now, with fewer brothers, you have less money, less talk about you, less and smaller parties and so forth. The women stop coming by. When that happens, less guys want to join, cause it's about the women."

Conclusion

For the men in this study, homophobia is not an unexamined attitude, nor is it simple blind obedience to tradition. Their belief system about homosexuality has been discussed, debated, and refined. They have acquired support and evidence, albeit some a bit suspect, from pop culture, their parents, ministers, classes (e.g., social norms, natural order), and one another. What is most interesting is how similar the statements, metaphors, examples, and justifications are. Many of these men, in fact, used identical phrases and expressions when detailing their attitudes and beliefs about homosexuality. It is obvious that these rationales for homophobia are collectively shared and crafted within these very isolated and insulated fraternal groups.

It is also apparent that the organizations represented in this study have constructed a set of normative rules and procedures that are informally taught to new initiates and collectively embraced by existing members. These lessons not only supply most brothers with a rationale for their homophobia; they also create expectations for proper masculine behavior and strategies for homosexual exclusion (e.g., investigation, interrogation, intimidation on line). It is not an overstatement, therefore, to conclude that (1) antihomosexual bias is deeply ingrained in the rules, laws, and collective psyche of these organizations and that (2) true integration, at least in the foreseeable future, is extremely unlikely without some ideological augmentations to fundamental Christianity and structural changes to contemporary (hip-hop inspired) notions of masculinity in the black culture.

Although this study examined the homophobic attitudes of fraternity brothers, we would be remiss not to address the concerns of the rejected and discriminated against homosexuals from these organizations. To begin with, the intense degree of homophobia exhibited in fraternal organizations could result in higher degrees of "stigmatization," which in turn "causes more 'closeted' behaviors" and stress for these gay men.[21] This stigmatization, according to Horace Griffin, "also creates an inescapable feeling of unworthiness and low self-esteem" that, if not monitored, could create a climate of "denial that can develop into rage and hostility by those who experience psychic pain."[22] Finally, "Understanding with the intent of abolishing homophobia is not only a psychological issue but arguably, a public health one as well. With the increasing prevalence and incidence of HIV/AIDS in African-American communities," this stigmatization, and the closeted behavior that accompanies it, creates a climate of silence and ignorance that "prevents the control of HIV/AIDS."[23]

When word got out that this volume would include a chapter dealing with black fraternities and homosexuality, more than one source took umbrage. This book's editor received requests to exclude this chapter, and we were strongly encouraged to discontinue the project and questioned as to its purpose and value. Alex, one of our online respondents, sent us this message: "What is the purpose of dredging up this topic? As homophobic as Greeks are, don't you foresee a backlash from them. . . . Greeks know how they feel and live with it quite well. There is a deeply religious and conservative air ever present in black life in general and Greek life in particular. I cannot conceive of a change in attitude amongst us. However, right now, we don't 'Witch Hunt' and I think most of us would rather keep it that way."

As academicians and fraternity brothers, our goal is not to "witch hunt" or to create a "backlash" in BGLOs but to cast an analytical lens on a culturally taboo issue. We should be worried not about the light that thoughtful discussion engenders but about the intellectual darkness that accompanies silence and censorship. It is our hope, therefore, that this work will generate conversations within the black Greek community about contemporary notions of masculinity; the intellectual, social, financial, and spiritual costs of excluding homosexuals; and issues of justice and discrimination. As Griffin reminds us, "African American gays, like their heterosexual counterparts, simply seek the freedom to establish and maintain . . . relationships, without the burden of heterosexual harassment, ridicule, and restrictions."[24]

Notes

1. For purposes of this study, we use the word *homophobia* to mean an "irrational fear of, aversion to, or discrimination against homosexuality or homosexuals." It can also mean "hatred of and disparagement of homosexual people, their lifestyle, their sexual behavior, or culture." *Merriam-Webster's Dictionary* (2006).

2. Walter W. Hudson and Wendell A. Ricketts, "A Strategy for the Measurement of Homophobia," *Journal of Homosexuality* 5, no. 4 (1980): 357–73; William Schneider and I. A. Lewis, "The Straight Story on Homosexuality and Gay Rights," *Public Opinion* 7 (February–March 1984): 16–20; Gregory B. Lewis, "Black-White Differences in Attitudes towards Homosexuality and Gay Rights," *Public Opinion Quarterly* 67 (2003): 59–78; Lisa J. Schulte, "Similarities and Differences in Homophobia among African Americans versus Caucasians," *Race, Gender, and Class* 9, no. 4 (2002): 71–93.

3. Lewis, "Black-White Differences in Attitudes," 59–78; Christopher G. Ellison and March A. Musick, "Southern Intolerance: A Fundamentalist Effect?" *Social Forces* 72 (1993): 379–98; Gregory M. Herek, "Heterosexuals' Attitudes towards Lesbians and Gay Men: Correlates and Gender Differences," *Journal of Sex Research* 25, no. 4 (1988): 457–77; Richard Seltzer, "AIDS, Homosexuality, Public Opinion, and Changing Correlates over Time," *Journal of Homosexuality* 26, no. 1 (1993): 85–97.

4. Robert Joseph Taylor, "Structural Determinants of Religious Participation among Black Americans," *Review of Religious Research* 30, no. 2 (1988): 114–25; Robert Joseph Taylor and Linda M. Chatters, "Black and White Differences in Religious Participation: A Multisample Comparison," *Journal of the Scientific Study of Religion* 3, no. 4 (1996): 403–10.

5. Ellison and Musick, "Southern Intolerance," 379–98; James L. Gibson and Kent L. Tedin, "The Etiology of Intolerance of Homosexual Politics," *Social Science Quarterly* 69, no. 3 (1988): 587–604; G. M. Herek and J. P. Capitanio, "Black Heterosexuals' Attitudes towards Lesbian and Gay Men in the United States," *Journal of Sex Research* 32 (1995): 95–105.

6. Lewis, "Black-White Differences in Attitudes," 59–78; U.S. Bureau of the Census, *Statistical Abstract of the United States 2001,* http://www.census.gov/compendia/statab/.

7. Some of the more high-profile members include the following: Dennis Archer, former mayor of Detroit (Alpha); Barry E. Beckham, founder, Beckham House Publishers (Sigma); Guion Bluford, first black astronaut in space (Omega); George Washington Carver, world-famous scientist (Sigma); Johnnie L Cochran, attorney (Kappa); William H. Cosby, comedian, actor, educator, philanthropist (Omega); Charles Drew, doctor

(Omega); W. E. B. DuBois, author, historian, civil rights activist (Alpha); Dr. Bernard Harris, astronaut, first black to walk in space (Kappa); Robert Johnson, founder and CEO, Black Entertainment Network (Kappa); Michael Jordan, former Chicago Bulls basketball player (Omega); Kwame Kilpatrick, mayor of Detroit (Alpha); Dr. Martin Luther King Jr., civil rights activist (Alpha); Thurgood Marshall, civil rights activist, Supreme Court justice (Alpha); Adam Clayton Powell Jr., civil rights activist (Alpha); Andrew Young, former mayor of Atlanta, former U.S. ambassador to the United Nations (Alpha). This list was obtained from http://www.learningtogive.org/papers/index.asp?bpid=171.

8. Iota Phi Theta Fraternity was not included in this study because it did not have chapters at all the universities under investigation.

9. In several places in this chapter, organizational pseudonyms were *not* used, so as to protect the coding system. In these cases, well-known organizational stereotypes were being discussed that would be easily recognizable to any informed member of a BGLO and could be used to decipher the codes.

10. The questionnaire was posted from August 2005 through March 2006 on Yahoo .com as a user group entitled "Homosexuals in Black Fraternities." The questionnaire consisted of six questions dealing with homosexuality in black fraternities: (1) Do you think openly gay men should be allowed to join your fraternity? Why or why not? (2) Do you think down-low (closet bisexual) men should be allowed to join your fraternity? Why or why not? (3) Do you think covertly gay (closet homosexual) men should be allowed to join your fraternity? Why or why not? (4) Do you think being gay is wrong (morally, socially, ethically, religiously)? Please elaborate. (5) What are the national stereotypes of each NPHC fraternity? Do these notions influence membership? (6) Do you know of any openly gay members? How are they treated by other brothers?

11. The group received 166 responses. Many of these, however, came in the form of short replies, spam mail, and erroneous messages.

12. Julia T. Woods, *Gendered Lives: Communication, Gender, and Culture*, 3rd ed. (Belmont, Calif.: Wadsworth, 1999).

13. Maxine Baca-Zinn, "Chicago Men and Masculinity," *Journal of Ethnic Studies* 10 (1984): 29–44; Clyde W. Franklin, *Men and Society* (Chicago: Nelson-Hall, 1988); David D. Gilmore, *Manhood in the Making: Cultural Concepts of Masculinity* (New Haven, Conn.: Yale University Press, 1990).

14. Wizdom Powell Hammond and Jacqueline S. Mattis, "Being a Man about It: Manhood Meaning among African American Men," *Psychology of Men and Masculinity* 6, no. 2 (2005): 114–26.

15. Any form of hazing is officially prohibited by all nationally recognized black fraternities, including the four that we investigated. Many local chapters, however, still pledge "underground." For more information, see Ricky Jones, *Black Haze: Violence and Manhood in Black Greek-Letter Fraternities* (Albany: State University of New York Press, 2004).

16. Many brothers have divided themselves into two groups: "Paper" brothers

are men who received their letters of recommendation, maintained their grade point averages, paid their dues, and completed their community service but were not illegally pledged or hazed underground. "Real" brothers are the men who went "on line" with their pledge brothers and completed the underground hazing segment of initiation. In the eyes of most real brothers, paper brothers lack legitimacy.

17. Richard Majors and Janet Mancini Billson, *Cool Pose: The Dilemmas of Black Manhood in America* (New York: Simon and Schuster, 1992); bell hooks, *We Real Cool: Black Men and Masculinity* (New York: Routledge Press, 2003).

18. John H. McWhorter, *Losing the Race: Self-Sabotage in Black America* (New York: Free Press, 2000).

19. Keith Boykin, *Beyond the Down Low: Sex, Lies, and Denial in Black America* (New York: Carroll and Graf, 2005); J. L. King and Karen Hunter, *On the Down Low* (New York: Harlem Books, 2005); Centers for Disease Control, *HIV/AIDS Surveillance Report, 2004,* vol. 16 (Atlanta: U.S. Department of Health and Human Services, CDC, 2005), 1–46.

20. Lewis concurs, arguing that "older African Americans tend to be less politically and socially tolerant than younger Americans, probably due more to the eras in which they were socialized than to the aging process." Lewis, "Black-White Differences in Attitudes," 66.

21. Anthony J. Lemelle and Juan Battle, "Black Masculinity Matters in Attitudes toward Gay Males," *Journal of Homosexuality* 47, no. 1 (2004): 40.

22. Horace Griffin, "Their Own Received Them Not: African American Lesbians and Gays in Black Churches," in *The Greatest Taboo: Homosexuality in Black Communities,* ed. D. Constantine-Simms (Los Angeles: Alyson Books, 2001), 120.

23. Lemelle and Battle, "Black Masculinity Matters," 41.

24. Griffin, "Their Own Received Them Not," 120.

16

"I Did It for the Brotherhood"

Nonblack Members in Black Greek-Letter Organizations

Matthew W. Hughey

In May 1904, Philadelphia bore witness to the birth of Sigma Pi Phi Fraternity, the first black Greek-letter organization (BGLO). Since their genesis a century ago, BGLOs have based their ideals on a synthesis of different organizational models and traditions. BGLOs incorporate African customs, principles, and social models of exclusive membership, along with attributes that mirror white-dominated fraternities and sororities.[1] This synthesis has led to BGLOs' iconic stature within the black community, marking themselves as institutions integral to W. E. B. DuBois's infamous "Talented Tenth"—a moniker for the cadre of elite, upper-class, college-educated African Americans.

In today's era of educational reform, just past the half-century mark of *Brown v. Board of Education* (1954), scholars, practitioners, and students have begun to question a U.S. system of higher education that is still largely segregated by race, despite federal efforts to promote desegregation. BGLOs are increasingly being sought out not only by members of a diverse and heterogeneous black population but also by people across the color line, with many whites, Latinos, and Asians seeking membership as well. Although the law prohibits de jure membership exclusion based on race in U.S. college fraternities and sororities, racial separation prevails de facto through custom, tradition, and preference in a Greek system comprising racially homogeneous groups. Analysis of the phenomenon of nonblack BGLO members has significant import and points toward a necessary examination of the role Greek organizations play in the foundation, development, and deployment of campus racial politics.

Why does nonblack BGLO membership matter? Why is this topic worthy of scholarly consideration? To answer these questions, we must first consider the significance of nonblack membership as contextualized by the increasing, and now institutionalized, rhetoric of multiculturalism in contemporary society. In a post–civil rights era in which many proclaim that racism has "ended," that the significance of race is "declining," and that whites are now subject to

313

victimization by "reverse racism," this study both adds to and contests these racialized assessments.

Although naming, locating, and dissecting "race" in the critical tradition has achieved a powerful purchase on the significance of power, culture, and representations, I aim to extend this perspective into the "local" uses of nonblack racial identities to make sense of conflict, power, desire, and racial anxiety in the culturally distinct spaces of BGLOs. Rather than revealing a set of common core dynamics that define why and when nonblacks join BGLOs, I sketch the local uses to which many members put differing rationales, ideologies, and discursive frames and how these same components reflexively constrain and enable their role as nonblack BGLO members.

Differences between Black and White Greek Organizations

Many scholars identify substantial differences in terms of value orientations, postcollege commitment, academic importance, and membership intake proce- dures between the BGLOs under the National Pan-Hellenic Council (NPHC)[2] and the predominantly white Greek organizations under the National Inter- fraternity Conference (NIC) and the National Panhellenic Conference (NPC).[3] First, Whipple, Baier, and Grady's study of more than 620 fraternity and sorority members found that "Black Greeks generally come from a lower socioeconomic background, are more academically motivated, more liberal, more socially con- scious, and more peer independent than White Greeks."[4] They conclude that there are fundamentally different value orientations, family backgrounds, and educational objectives between the two Greek systems. Berkowitz and Padavic, by means of twenty-six in-depth, open-ended interviews, investigated white and black women's reasons (in terms of academic, social, and career plans) for join- ing sororities. They found that white sorority members seemed more focused on using the Greek structure to "get a man," whereas black sorority members were more focused on community service and career advancement.[5]

Second, Berkowitz and Padavic found that black sorority members con- sidered membership to be a lifelong commitment, as opposed to most white sorority members, who regarded it as a college activity. Consequently, BGLOs have a much larger percentage of alumni who remain active in alumni chapters and act as formal and informal advisers to undergraduate chapters.[6]

Third, white Greeks place less value on academic achievement than do their nonwhite Greek counterparts.[7] Further, BGLOs provide much of the major social structure for the black community on campus, while their white Greek counterparts generally do not extend their programs or activities beyond the Greek social network.[8] BGLOs also appear to be more service oriented than white Greeks, and some estimates claim that BGLOs devote five times as many hours to community service compared with white Greeks.[9]

Fourth, and most notably, both the traditional and post-1990 membership intake processes of white and black systems are very different. Walter Kimbrough writes that pledging "could be defined as a cultural appendage that has taken on a life of its own. It has evolved over time into a complex culture that has birthed numerous customs and traditions associated with Black Greek life. . . . It is an integral part of the Black fraternal experience."[10]

These differences in the black and white systems of Greek life add to a complexity that both enables and constrains or, as Giddens states, "structurates" the initial appeal, recruitment, and retention of nonblacks who cross the color line into BGLOs.[11] Kimbrough writes, when "Whites . . . go against the grain of societal norms and seek membership in groups founded to serve the Black community . . . this is definitely a controversial subject."[12] This is so contentious because, as E. Franklin Frazier points out, BGLOs were founded in direct response to white Greek organizations' refusal to allow blacks to join.[13] However, unlike their white counterparts, fraternities established for particular minority groups began to accept members who were not people of color only three or four decades after their founding. Despite the introduction of nonblack members, BGLOs still understood their mission as a black-centered endeavor that was a reaction to white racism. When questioned about the need for minority student fraternities in 1949, Alpha Phi Alpha president Wilbert Whitsett responded, "If we are not permitted to join other fraternities, we must form a fraternity of our own. We have no other choice."[14]

The History of Nonblacks in BGLOs

Probably the first induction of a nonblack member in a BGLO occurred on June 21, 1946, when Alpha Phi Alpha pledged senior Bernard Levin at the University of Illinois College of Dentistry. A 1946 article in *Ebony* magazine states: "Pledging a white student, the opposition maintained, would violate an ancient Alpha tradition of seeking recruits from the cream of college-bred Negroes. Supporters of the admission of Bernard Levin attacked these arguments as smug bigotry. To oppose creation of an interracial fraternity amounted to justifying Jim Crow, they said. After hours of heated wrangling, the interracialists finally triumphed and Levin was pledged."[15]

The trend of nonblack members slowly continued. In 1949, Mrs. Marjorie T. Ware and Miss Olive Young became the first two white women initiated into Alpha Kappa Alpha Sorority. Both members attributed their choice of membership in the black sorority to their belief in human rights and racial integration. In 1953, at the University of Kansas, a white man named Roger L. Youmans pledged Alpha Phi Alpha and moved into the fraternity house during the next fall semester. After Youmans gained media attention for his move, a cross was burned on the front lawn of the fraternity house.[16] In an interview about his decision to join Alpha rather than a white fraternity, Youmans stated, "White fraternities were more arrogant. [Alpha Phi Alpha] was far more interested in providing community service."[17]

Chi Delta Mu (one of the first BGLOs, but no longer in existence) and Omega Psi Phi Fraternity at Howard University admitted white members in 1949.[18] A decade later at the Omega Psi Phi conference, Herbert E. Tucker, the assistant attorney general of Massachusetts, urged all BGLOs to encourage interracial membership. He stated, "Negro fraternities had only token white membership . . . [and] should all do whatever they can to attract whites, who now represent less than 5 per cent of the membership."[19] These patterns of sporadic nonblack membership continued in more recent years. In 1986, a white student made headlines when she joined the University of Alabama (UA) chapter of Zeta Phi Beta Sorority. In 1987, Mark Brafford became a white member of Zeta Phi Beta's brother organization—Phi Beta Sigma Fraternity. Jeff Choron became a white member of Phi Beta Sigma at UA in 1990 because he felt "they are more tolerant, because differences are to be expected." The next semester, Everett Whiteside, another white student, also became a member of Phi Beta Sigma at UA. Whiteside stated, "Being part of a trend never crossed my mind. . . . Make your own reasons why I joined."[20]

The December 2000 issue of *Ebony* included the article "Whites in Black Sororities and Fraternities," which examined both white and black members' perceptions of cross-racial membership in BGLOs and made special note of white heterogeneity. "White members fit no easy stereotypes. Instead, they come from all backgrounds. . . . Some grew up surrounded by Blacks, while others had little contact with African Americans before college."[21] Brodey Milburn, a white student who pledged Kappa Alpha Psi Fraternity at Indiana University, stated, "There are black people who don't appreciate my presence in a black fraternity, just as there are white people who can't understand why I did it in the first place." Accordingly, L. R. Stains wrote, "It's rarely the black fraternity members who resent whites; it's the bystanders who are bothered."[22] Researchers report that much of the harshest criticism of nonblacks who join BGLOs comes not from blacks but from individuals within the racial group of the nonblack member.[23] Some white members receive challenging looks from other whites and become involved in verbal confrontations. This is not the only area where race-related anxiety exists, however; there is often a notable tension between black and nonblack BGLO members. Lisa Terrell, who became a white member of Alpha Kappa Alpha Sorority at Texas Tech University, stated, "Most people didn't want me to be a part of the chapter. They didn't want to be known as the ones who allowed a White soror to slip in."[24] Davina Brown, a black member of Zeta Phi Beta Sorority, remarked, "We service the special needs of our Black communities—it just makes me feel uncomfortable in knowing that, here again, is a tradition that is slowly being taken away from us."[25] Yet Lawrence Ross, author of *The Divine Nine*, argues that the fear of whites taking over BGLOs is unfounded and virtually impossible; even though white membership in BGLOs has grown, it is far from a "white stampede."[26]

Whites who join BGLOs are not the only nonblack members. Some Hispanic and Asian students seek membership across the color line and present their own distinct challenges to the issues of integration, acceptance, and identity. In the mid-1990s at the University of Florida, Rhonda Chung-DeCambre was invited to an academic forum by Sigma Gamma Rho Sorority. She knew that she wanted to be involved in the Greek system, but she was not interested in the traditional white groups. She later became a member of Sigma Gamma Rho, joining two Hispanic women who were also members of the traditionally black sorority.[27]

As Elizabeth Chen writes of her study at a large Pacific Coast university (dubbed "PCU"): "At least ten Asian American women participated in African American sororities at some point between 1992 and 1997 at PCU. Their participation illustrates another form of incorporation that departs from the classical model of assimilation. The participation of Asian American women . . . reveals social processes that underly [sic] one form of incorporation, in which minority members become integrated into another minority community that is not socially defined as their own."[28] Chen goes on to identify the process of Asian American women joining BGLOs as a strategy to both further develop their identities as women of color and directly challenge racial hierarchies in which Asianness is juxtaposed against blackness and whiteness. Specifically, the subjects of her study used their membership in a BGLO to construct a nonwhite identity, identify with other racial minorities, and articulate an Asian American identity. These all work together to foster oppositional racial identities. Accordingly, critical race theorist Mari Matsuda writes: "If white, as it has been historically, is the top of the racial hierarchy in America, and black, historically, is the bottom, will yellow assume the place of the racial middle? . . . [What] if it refuses to be the middle, if it refuses to buy into racial hierarchy, and if it refuses to abandon communities of black and brown people, choosing instead to forge alliance with them[?]"[29] Perhaps Asian Americans who join BGLOs are expressing a form of subtle resistance to racial categories. After all, the women in Chen's study had already developed a sense of racial consciousness prior to joining and did not view black and Asian struggles as completely separate.

Regardless of the kind of nonblack membership, the context and cultural processes of these racial boundary transgressions must be studied for their import in relation to racial identity, racism, and the political economies of both multiculturalism and racial homogeneity. With the decline of formal segregation, the proliferation of the "new racism" is a more mystified, but no less oppressive, social and cultural phenomenon. Are BGLOs reproducing racism against whites, or is their attempt to remain culturally and ontologically black centered as an imperative against racism now being criminalized as racist itself? Are whites, who are generally more privileged than others in society, feeling a loss of power that engenders an attitude that they, not people of color, are the predominant victims of racism? As our mainstream discourse becomes more centered on "color blindness" as the predominant logic, what role does cross-racial membership play in masking or illuminating racial agendas? This chapter addresses these questions and adds nuance to the predominant account of diversity within U.S. college fraternities and sororities by identifying, describing, and constructing a picture of nonblack BGLO membership.

The Cultural Contradictions of Nonblack Members

In analyzing the culture of nonblack BGLO members, I employed a qualitative analysis operationalized through interviews with thirty nonblack BGLO members.[30] From these interviews I constructed a typology of four different kinds of nonblack BGLO members. In almost every interview I conducted, nonblack members described the desire for a brotherhood that extended past their racial, national, or religious identities and social circles. They stated that prior to pledging, they had perceived BGLOs as possessing an authentic connectivity for which they yearned. In fact, many of them "did it for the brotherhood" and claimed that their BGLO membership is something they treasure and would never take for granted. However, when I asked the respondents whether they thought of their identity as primarily (1) their racial or ethnic group, (2) their nationality, (3) their religion, or (4) their BGLO, most respondents did not identify their BGLO membership as the primary aspect of their identity. In fact, it was the least popular choice. Only two respondents (7 percent) identified their BGLO membership as their primary identity. Fourteen respondents (47 percent) identified their race as primary, nine respondents (30 percent) said nationality, and five (17 percent) said religion.

These results seem confounding and inconsistent. Yet the world of nonblack BGLO members is a world of cultural contradictions: a desire to serve the black community but with a quest for leadership positions, a commitment to multiculturalism with a simultaneous desire for black homogeneity, a view of race as a relative social construction while approaching blackness as an essentialized, "authentic" racial identity, or a desire to achieve a "post-race" political utopia while immersed in an inherently racialized organization. As a nonblack member of a BGLO for more than ten years, I have watched myself and others struggle to navigate these social tensions.

Therefore, there is no one culture of nonblack BGLO members. Rather, there are many cultures. The question is, how many different ideologies, rationales, repertories, and epistemic frames do we find, what forms do they take, and in what ways are they formed? To say that all nonblack BGLO members are actively and consciously aware of their decision to join a BGLO as a political, antisegregationist move is reductive. So it is also incorrect to label all nonblack members as racially unconscious, status-seeking hyperindividualists. Yet, the idea that both attitudes exist is both correct and significant.

Accordingly, I describe four kinds of nonblack BGLO members who illustrate the most prominent (and often overlapping) patterns I observed.[31] This typology is not meant to be exhaustive. I certainly recognize the reductive potential and how such diminution could be dangerous if interpreted in the wrong way. The BGLO community is already stigmatized by incredibly violent stereotypes, and I do not wish to add to this. I emphasize the social structure of race and racism as shaping the meanings nonblack members ascribe to their organizations and themselves. Unlike many scholars, however, I do not consider the member-organization relationship a functional one—that is, that nonblacks choose certain ideologies for defensive or "rational" purposes. Rather, I theorize that processes that both complicate and constitute the paths taken

mediate the relationships of nonblack members and their organizations. I urge
the reader to understand that nonblack BGLO members' engagement in their
specific subculture involves—as with any cultural dynamic—interpretive labor.
I move from the assumption that these interpretive processes are embedded in
ruling discourses of racial inequality that were the raison d'être for the creation
of BGLOs and that now structure, but without guarantees, the thoughts and
actions of members.

These nonblack BGLO members have particularly interesting stories to
tell—precisely because they represent striking forms of cultural reactions to
massive changes in racial boundaries over the past five decades. For shorthand
purposes, I describe the four types of nonblack members as follows: (1) the
"John Browns," who want to serve the black community and radically improve
race relations but who also usurp leadership positions, indicative of neoliberal
paternalism; (2) the "color-blind collaborators," who desire a post-race political
utopia but are immersed in inherently racialized organizations; (3) the "cultural
capitalists," who view race as a relative social construction while approaching
blackness as an essentialized, "authentic" racial identity; and (4) the "multicultural nationalists," who navigate a desire for racial diversity with a simultaneous
defense of BGLOs as black-controlled and -dominated. Although these labels
are surely reductive, they capture a certain version of the realities that have led
these members and others like them to develop culturally specific strategies
for rationalizing, and even coping with, the decision to cross the racial line in
such dramatic fashion.

John Browns

John Brown, the white abolitionist who led twenty-one men on a raid of a federal
arsenal at Harpers Ferry in 1859, has become a symbol for radical white commitment to improved race relations and equal rights. In this vein, many white
BGLO members have deep-seated commitments to African American social advancement. Many respondents reported race-conscious ideologies and professed
extreme opposition to the racist practices of either individuals or institutions.
Several respondents recounted emotionally laden stories about wanting to help
black organizations achieve their goals. Many are cognizant of the rampant racial
inequalities that exist and wish to use BGLOs as a vehicle toward their resolution.
John Browns feel an incredible "calling" in their membership. They simply must
work for racial justice because, to them, there is little alternative.

However, these John Browns are caught in a distinct tension: they wish to serve the black community and labor to eradicate racism, but they also feel a sense of entitlement to leadership positions. Said a thirty-two-year-old white member of Kappa Alpha Psi, "I love Kappa. I would do anything for it . . . and I often do. I'm glad I'm a member because I get to influence a lot of procedures. I mean I try to lead on every committee and position I can get because, well . . . Kappa, like all of us, makes a lot of mistakes and I like to think that I can set some things straight."[32] In all but three interviews with the twenty-one white respondents, they either directly mentioned or alluded to a feeling of resentment that they would never be president of the BGLO because of their color. "Brian," a thirty-seven-year-old white member of Phi Beta Sigma (ΦΒΣ), stated:

> I think my race hurt me. . . . My aspiration was to be the president of the chapter but my race placed a glass ceiling on me. VP [vice president] was as good as I was ever going to be. I remember that I was told . . . that we could not have a nonblack representing ΦΒΣ (e.g., in the NPHC meetings and on campus). Although I will never feel the full brunt of being black in America, I do not believe that many whites can say that they have had a personal experience with . . . how discrimination feels . . . [yet] I was also voted to a position on the regional board. . . . Some brothers refused to even give me the grip and . . . there was always that glass ceiling there. No matter what I did I knew that I could never be the national president of ΦΒΣ.[33]

Brian's disappointment that he will never be the chapter or national president and his perception that his race placed a "glass ceiling" on his social mobility are very telling. He expressed a desire to lead and to give as much guidance as he could to the organization. Stories like Brian's were common.

A white woman I call "Grace," who is a twenty-five-year-old member of Delta Sigma Theta, stated, "I joined Delta because of the phenomenal work they do and I wanted to contribute toward that tradition, but as a white woman I have a different perspective on race and come from a different culture than most of my sorors. It's hard to get them to follow what I suggest."[34] Grace feels a particular tension between admiration for her sisters and her sorority's tradition of service and her frustration at being unable to convince her sorority sisters to follow her advice—advice that she believes is meritorious because she is "different." Such a statement indicates a sense of white entitlement.

Recently, scholarly discourse has exploded with studies of "whiteness" and white privilege. Since the advent of the modern civil rights movement, people of color have usually been responsible for leading the debate and discussion about race and racism. In contrast, forced to evaluate the status of their race in relation to the prejudice they experience, most white people, even the most liberal, are oblivious to the sociological and political weight of their own color. Whiteness is invested with a great deal of political, social, economic, and cultural entitlement and privilege. Writes Ronald Hall: "Succinctly put, by virtue of power enabled by significant and tenacious historical events, White[s] experience entitlement fantasies. . . . Entitlement fantasies can have a major effect on all human interaction. Hence, males of European descent—and to some extent females—developed a universal sense of ownership and superiority that has imposed on their human interaction for subsequent centuries. Yet, having the ability to dominate without any formidable balance in power may encourage White American males to a universal sense of entitlement ultimately pathological and self-destructive to all."[35]

White entitlement does not have to be conscious and is most often enacted with the best of intentions. Melanie Bush's work *Breaking the Code of Good Intentions* explores the mechanisms that reinforce white adherence to dominant narratives and the reproduction of racialized structures of inequality.[36] Akin to Bush's study, I found that many race-conscious whites saw their role as one that involved leadership and being responsible for their black brothers and sisters. For example, "Carter," a thirty-four-year-old white member of Omega Psi Phi, stated, "I feel it is my duty to lead. I was allowed the privilege of Omega and I owe something back." Carter's logic is admirable and well placed amidst a rationalization of service and responsibility. However, many members were incredibly lacking in introspection. Many felt that their presence in BGLOs did not usurp the position of or take leadership opportunities away from deserving black members. Carter continued, "I have always looked up to Omega men, but I also see where we can do better and need to adjust our mission."[37]

Along these lines, twenty-eight nonblack BGLO members (93 percent) responded that they have felt admiration for black BGLO members, and nineteen (63 percent) stated that they have felt sympathy toward black BGLO members. Among these nineteen respondents, fifteen (79 percent) expressed that they often felt like they "knew better" than their black fellow members in relation to the BGLO's course of action. When the responses from the twenty-one white BGLO participants were correlated with the desire for change in BGLOs, it revealed potential tensions between white and black members. To clarify these issues, I present a simplified scheme in table 16.1, showing how white members' desire

Table 16.1. Intersection between White BGLO Members' Goals and Their Feelings toward Black Members

White Members' Goals	White Members' Feelings toward Black Members	
	Admiration	Sympathy
Maintain status quo in BGLO	(1) Adherent	(2) Reconcilist
Make changes in BGLO	(3) Conflictual	(4) Paternalist

for change in the actions or ideology of their BGLOs can intersect with feelings of admiration or sympathy toward black BGLO members.

In the first intersection ("adherent") a functional relationship exists when white members are in accord with the black-determined goals of the organization and they express admiration for black members. This kind of relationship is nonconflictual. The second intersection between desiring stasis and feeling sympathy for black members is called "reconcilist." That is, white members do not wish to change anything about the goals or makeup of the BGLO, but they feel pity, regret, or sympathy for wrong turns or misdoings by black fellow members. Therefore, they constantly have to reconcile these feelings of pity with their willingness to maintain the status quo. The third intersection ("conflictual")—the compounding of desire for change and admiration for black members—leads to dissonance, whereby white members face internal conflicts between their admiration for those who set the organizational agenda and their desire to change that agenda. In this case, white members often desire change in the organization but are met with resistance from the black majority. Last, the white desire for change is combined with sympathy for black fellow members, which often results in a "paternalistic" attitude toward black members and the BGLO chapter. This kind of "benevolent paternalism" is exhibited by white BGLO members who want to make the black community "better." They have many ideas and are often excited about sharing and implementing them.

There have been many studies on paternalism applied to many settings,[38] but VanDeVeer rules out callousness or maliciousness as a motive for paternalistic actions.[39] Specifically, Jackman in *The Velvet Glove* maintains, "The presumption of moral superiority over a group with whom one has an expropriative relationship is thus flatly incompatible with the spirit of altruistic benevolence, no matter how much affection and breast-beating accompanies it. . . . Their unequal relationship is swathed in a morality that identifies subordinates' worth and value within the terms of that relationship."[40] It is this form of moral superiority that John Browns often enact, but it is rationalized by a belief that they are leading the organization and the black community at large in a positive direction. Although the ideology of paternalism is geared toward eliciting deference from subordinates—warm feelings of close brotherhood coupled with an agenda to maintain or usurp directional control of an organization—I am not convinced that these subjects consciously engage in such a plot.

Rather, the John Brown syndrome is indicative of a desire for positive goals and control. It is precisely this marriage that engenders ambiguity and subtle forms of deception in power relations, making this kind of paternalism an insidious form of social control. It effectively allows white members to enjoy expropriation while feeling that they are taking nothing away from black self-determination. Far from causing dissonance, John Browns express affection and sympathy. In the end, John Browns are able to trade a distinctly valuable commodity for compliance to their agenda—brotherhood. If the social order of the BGLO chapter becomes predicated on such an underpinning, black members become subordinate to the fulfillment of this emotional need for brotherhood. In this context, brotherhood becomes an extremely potent weapon with which to extract compliance.

Color-blind Collaborators

Color-blind collaborators labor to have a world, or at least a BGLO, in which race is a nonissue. Said one thirty-year-old Latina member of Alpha Kappa Alpha, "I joined AKA to make a difference. To be a part of a tradition of greatness, and that is what we do. . . . It's not right that some members of black Greek organizations are judged by their color. This is something to move past to get beyond . . . not just racism, but race."[41] This member wishes for a post-race political utopia. However, she is also immersed in the inherently hyperracialized culture that is black Greekdom. Color-blind collaborators often said that they do not "see race." They often took issue with my questions about race and their own race-consciousness and made it clear that their membership in a black organization is not an issue with anyone except for, as one respondent put it, "people making too big of a deal about it." Some nonblack members even stated that questions about race had no bearing on them! Fifty-seven percent said that their BGLOs are not perceived in a different or negative light because of their membership. They stated that they were not attracted to their organizations because of any race-related factor but rather because of the high principles of the organization. Color-blind collaborators were more often female and included many Asian and Latino members.

I found that the color-blind collaborator often depoliticized and dehistoricized their membership. They spoke of BGLOs in such a way as to minimize any connection to issues of race; hence, their membership represented nothing racial or different—only "normal." And "normal" to them signifies some state of being in which race is somehow absent. Thirty-three percent said that their race played no role while pledging, and 20 percent said their race had no effect on them as nonblack BGLO members.

Many color-blind collaborators approach their BGLO membership as an incredible chance to network. Their membership is framed as a catalyst for social mobility. Much like the John Browns, the color-blind collaborators seek success and leadership positions in their BGLOs. However, in contrast to the John Browns, they do not see their color as a barrier to advancement; rather, they believe that it plays no role at all. One Indian American woman named "Nina," a twenty-seven-year-old member of Alpha Kappa Alpha, stated, "I have been asked to speak at various national programs. I was selected as Miss AKA for the North Atlantic Region, I was selected as a leadership fellow. I was selected based on my credentials and love for the sorority, not my ethnic background."[42] She continued in a follow-up telephone conversation: "My race has no effect on my membership. Color has no bearing on my success in the organization. . . . I was chosen because I embodied the qualities of my sorority. It was a part of me before I joined."[43] "Carla," a white, twenty-three-year-old member of Sigma Gamma Rho Sorority, stated:

> There are no differences [between races] really, I mean, obviously there is a difference, but I believe that people are products of their environment and that they are who they are because of what happened in their lives. So it's hard to say, because each individual is different, maybe that's naive to say but I like to believe that. . . . But I do think that nonblack NPHC members do have, in a certain way, a different viewpoint in the organization. Being a white member, I guess I get to feel what it is like to be a minority so that is a difference. I don't think there is a role that white members play that is different.[44]

When "James," a twenty-nine-year-old white member of Omega Psi Phi, was asked about the differences between black and nonblack members, he responded:

"I don't know, not a lot of differences I don't think. Maybe black members act differently out of a black power thing or as a sign that they are really 'down,' but I'm not sure what whites do. Maybe we want to be accepted in something that feels really real? I'm not sure."[45] What is striking about James's response is that he placed the "burden" of difference on black members. His belief that black members act differently from whites, and his uncertainty about what whites do to be different, labors to normalize whiteness, even though whites are the racial group that is "out of place."

This normalization of whiteness, Asianness, and Latinness in distinction to blackness was a common theme among the color-blind collaborators. Members also responded that racial differences are only skin deep; what really makes one different, they said, is personality traits. When asked, "What do you feel are the main differences between black and nonblack BGLO members?" a white, twenty-eight-year-old member of Alpha Phi Alpha named "Lucas" stated: "Only skin color, if the two individuals are in the organization for the 'right' reasons. I see myself, fraternally and personally, working for the same goals as my brothers. If you aren't in it for the right reasons, the differences could be vast. Ultimately, on average, skin color, where you are from, and goals in life are what really make you different."[46]

The inability of many color-blind collaborators to recognize how their nonblack subjectivity plays out in the day-to-day realities of life as a BGLO member is counterbalanced by their hyperattention to "moving past" race. Many members offered harsh and vehement appraisals of how their race was made an issue while pledging. Their analysis of racial politics during the pledge process was focused on hypocrisy and power differentials. That is, as nonwhite members with diminished power, they often saw how intake processes worked to their detriment. This type of focus on their personal afflictions with regard to racial politics is what motivates the color-blind collaborators to argue for a post-race society. One twenty-six-year-old Latina member of Zeta Phi Beta Sorority that I call "Gloria" stated, "It would be so much easier if we could simply get past 'race.' I mean, putting people in categories is something I never liked. I try to step outside of boxes. We shouldn't talk about race, we should be human."[47] Appeals to "get past" or "forget" race, or even to associate race-consciousness with racism itself, were all rationales used by color-blind collaborators to take focus away from their difference. As "Mark," a white twenty-two-year-old member of Kappa Alpha Psi, stated, "To make a big deal of race is to engage in racism itself. It has no place in today's society. Its presence only divides us."[48]

Such rationales and strategies commonly serve to naturalize what Eduardo Bonilla-Silva has called "color-blind racism." Color-blind racism is often thought of as "unintentional racism." In this setting, it is exactly these members' distaste for racism that leads them into a social reproduction of racist ideologies. When a color-blind approach is adopted, white people tend to dominate because the experiences are defined in terms to which white people can more easily relate and that reflect and support many white interests. These common worldviews tend to bolster the white self-image and increase, not decrease, racial inequality. As Bonilla-Silva writes: "In contrast with Jim Crow, color blind racism's major themes are (1) the extension of the principles of liberalism to racial matters in an abstract manner, (2) cultural rather than biological explanation of minorities' inferior standing and performance in labor and educational markets, (3) naturalization of racial phenomena such as residential and school segregation, and (4) the claim that discrimination has all but disappeared."[49] Bonilla-Silva contends that many whites utilize these frames both independently and collectively to argue against measures that talk about race. As the preceding analysis demonstrated, many nonblack BGLO members use these frames to speak of racism when they are victims of it, and to foreclose the possibility of its discussion when they might not benefit. Ironically, these actions were most often motivated by an abstract liberal desire to "end racism."

Cultural Capitalists

Cultural capitalists are nonblack BGLO members who view their own race as a relative, fabricated, and political identity—a "social construction"[50]—while viewing blackness as an essentialized, "authentic" racial identity. In so doing, many cultural capitalists are in search of authenticity; they view their white, Asian, or Latin racial identity as something lacking or as partially out of touch. They often explain that they were attracted to BGLOs because of how "real" those black organizations are. One twenty-five-year-old white member of Zeta Phi Beta said, "In being a part of Zeta I feel alive. I feel like I have changed myself from something fake into something real."[51]

Many cultural capitalists are attempting to identify and support a social and political marginality that they associate with black organizational forms. As a consequence of this intent, many attempt to rebuild their racial identity through close contact with black fellow members and the BGLO. A twenty-six-year-old Latino member of Alpha Phi Alpha that I call "Calvin" stated:

It's hard being an Alpha and I get a lot of strange looks and some brothers are less than accepting, but that is okay, that is to be expected. The
thing that actually doesn't really bother me is how some Latinos think
I have "sold out" by joining Alpha. But that is the catch, right there!
So many people in the Latino community are becoming conservative,
trying to assimilate, it's not real, and I think it's hurting the community.
So, I mean, I think, by joining Alpha I'm trying to fight that trend, you
know? I took sociology classes, I get that race is socially constructed or
whatever, but my decision to join Alpha was political, but it's personal.
. . . I guess it's both . . . I just know it's real.[52]

Calvin's comment establishes a connection between his view of race as a social
construction and the authenticity of black "others." I questioned how he could
identify this difference, and he responded: "It's like that weird feeling you get
when people buy into the artificiality character of the mainstream; I can't stand
it. A lot of people talk about race and about being political, but it's just talk. So
many aspects of nonblack cultures, whether it's white or Indian, or Hispanic
. . . whatever, it's not challenging the status quo. It's that it's somehow fake; I
know you get what I'm saying."[53] Again, Calvin emphasizes that many aspects
of nonblackness are on a par with a lack of authenticity. Additionally, by being
an Alpha, he stops talking about race in politically correct terms and begins
living a life where he is "challenging the status quo."

"Chris," a thirty-seven-year-old member of Phi Beta Sigma, stated:

I think that I grew up like most typical white kids. The difference started
when I was in high school. That was when I began to gravitate toward the
African American race. I played basketball on the JV team and began to
hang out with the "brothers" on the team. That is when I began to make
the transformation from your typical white kid. I began to embrace the
African American culture/way of life. In terms of music, women, food
. . . clothes, hairstyle. . . . During high school it was more of the social
aspects. It wasn't until I went to college that I began to understand that
African American culture was more than just these things.[54]

Cultural capitalists profess to reject what they believe is their own racial
inauthenticity through their contact with the political and aesthetic valuation
of BGLO culture. Chris's description of his life undergoing a "transformation"
is telling. To cultural capitalists, this border-crossing is like an act of racial de-

territorialization. Many envision themselves as nouveau desegregationists of unauthenticated racial lifestyles. Many members try to gain access to "authenticity" by relating to the "cultural capital" of blackness.[55] Jennifer, a thirty-year-old white member of Alpha Kappa Alpha, stated:

> When I first came to college I didn't have a lot of friends. Most of my friends I made growing up were friends I had through sports or the church. So, when I got to college I started going to [Catholic] Mass, but something was missing . . . it felt like people there were not very kind or real. I felt repelled by it all. Then I went to this movie night that AKA was putting on, and I met the nicest women there. Years later, here I am, and I am still the chapter historian. I feel great about researching and knowing everything about the sorority and its role in civil rights—important things. . . . It gives me that feeling I had when I was growing up, I feel connected to something real and I feel like I am resisting something bad as well.[56]

Mary Waters's landmark work *Ethnic Options* demonstrates the changing nature of ethnic whiteness in the United States among a sample of suburban Roman Catholics.[57] Her research validates Herbert Gans's suggestion that "symbolic identification" with racial and ethnic identity is akin to a leisure-time activity for many whites.[58] Finding that ethnic homogeneity varies directly with age, Waters's work disputed prevalent sociological theory that saw ethnicity as fluid but as not changing within the lives of particular individuals. But whereas Waters's population believed in the biological fixity of race, many of these nonblack BGLO members believe in the social construction of race and actively seek to re-create their racial identities through contact with black cultural capital. They want their ideology to constitute their identity.

"Michael," a thirty-four-year-old white member of Alpha Phi Alpha, stated, "If people simply tried to get themselves outside of their comfort zones . . . if they tried to re-create their whiteness, then they could make a lot of change and do a lot of good." I asked Michael to clarify what "re-create their whiteness" meant and he replied, "I'm not entirely sure, I don't know if it's an event or a process, but by joining a BGLO, you get in touch with many black things, and you should learn from them . . . capitalize on it!"[59]

While the cultural capitalists are attempting to fight what they believe is a conservative, racist, inauthentic racial status quo among nonblacks, they are unintentionally essentializing blackness as a very narrowly conceived form of racial identity. Additionally, if blackness becomes a coveted gateway for resistance that credentials nonblack members with status, then access to that identity must be restricted if it is to retain value. The work of both Parkin and Collins analyzed the processes of monopolizing or usurping resources within and across group boundaries, with an emphasis on "credentialism."[60] The logic of the cultural capitalists links this form of resistive, pro-black credentialism to BGLO racial boundaries. Thus, embracing inclusivity becomes something that must be exclusively guarded. Ironically, among the eighteen respondents who expressed a cultural capitalist ideology, sixteen (89 percent) expressed a strong view that BGLOs should remain almost all black. How can nonblack members argue that their organizations should remain almost all black? They see themselves as exceptions. And this restrictive membership works to make cultural breadth a highly valued resource.

Scholars such as Bryson, Lamont, and Peterson and Kern found that attitudes of inclusivity do not abolish restrictive borders but simply realign them.[61] Specifically, I point to Bryson's work on "multicultural capital," which illuminates how displaying familial attitudes of racial tolerance and openness is a form of status credential.[62] Along these lines, if nonblack BGLO members claim familiarity with black Greek cultural styles as a gateway to the end of racism, then access to that familiarity must be restricted if their status is to retain value. This multicultural capital serves as the basis for social exclusion by mystifying cultural contradictions and reifying racially exclusive boundaries based on attitudes of inclusion.

This multicultural capital then serves as the basis for a symbolic boundary of social exclusion. By displaying certain "cultivated dispositions"[63] (in this case, a distaste for the "inauthentic mainstream"), symbolic boundaries of morality are (re)drawn to credential the nonblack BGLO member with racial authority. These processes of capital exchange and transformation illuminate that nonblack BGLO members' actions are, at first glance, transgressive, progressive, and antiracist. However, they do not destroy racial boundaries; they merely transform and reestablish them. Bryson writes, "Cultural tolerance should not be conceptualized as an indiscriminate tendency to be non-exclusive, but as a reordering of group boundaries."[64] Power and boundaries are never separate; they constitute each other.

Multicultural Nationalists

Multicultural nationalists may provide a glimpse into one of the most striking cultural contradictions of nonwhite BGLO subcultures. Multicultural nationalists express a committed support to making organizations, institutions, or any setting that possesses a coherent social order as racially diverse as possible. This feeling is not atypical; rather, it is indicative of one of the pillars of our cultural logic in the neoliberal West: diversity is good. Yet, among the multicultural nationalists, this principle is wedded to a commensurate support of black-dominated and -centered organizations. For example, a twenty-four-year-old Latino member of Alpha Phi Alpha said, "I think that black Greek organizations should be black, but not exclusively . . . they shouldn't be dominated by nonblacks however. . . . Diversity makes organizations stronger, but too much makes it weaker. I think there is a balance."[65] Many multicultural nationalists outwardly express a Black Nationalist–like ideology that BGLOs should be dedicated to keeping their populations majority black and black led.[66] They express the fear that if BGLOs became less black, their focus and goals would change, possibly to the detriment of the black community.

When asked whether BGLOs should worry about remaining majority black, many nonblack members expressed a fear of blacks becoming a minority in their own organizations. "David," a thirty-year-old white member of Phi Beta Sigma, stated, "It would concern me if a chapter were to become a black minority due to losing . . . its purpose and ideals, [but] this is probably a silly fear to have."[67] Still others are ambivalent about the issue. Thirty-year-old "Gwinn," a white member of Alpha Kappa Alpha, stated, "I think the chapter should do whatever is best, I don't know."[68] Many others are adamant about the issue and see it as a matter of discrimination. A white, twenty-six-year-old member of Alpha Phi Alpha named "Marcus" stated, "This is a middle ground question. It is like saying, should you be excluded from this organization on the basis of your race, and I say resoundingly, 'NO!'"[69]

These nonblack members are trying to synthesize the tension of an anti-discrimination logic, a multicultural yearning for diversity, and a simultaneous defense of BGLOs' core "blackness." How do the multicultural nationalists navigate this tricky terrain? They hyperregulate other nonblack aspirants' access to their BGLOs. "Jonathan," a thirty-two-year-old white member of Kappa Alpha Psi, stated, "I know what a lot of other white people think and how they view black Americans. I think they would want to pledge for the wrong reasons . . . it's part of my responsibility as a white person to be harder on those possible pledges. I wouldn't say that I stop them from pledging, but I make sure that they prove themselves and demonstrate their merit."[70]

"Katherine," a thirty-four-year-old white member of Delta Sigma Theta, stated, "If you are going to be white and pledge Delta, you had better know your stuff and be ready to be challenged. I feel like that is part of my responsibility, but I feel like I need to test those potential members. I guess I am protective of the sorority."[71] Is this simply a case of nonblack members having their cake and eating it too? Where should the line be drawn? When asked how many nonblack members would be too many in a chapter, thirty-five-year-old "Carl," a white member of Phi Beta Sigma, said, "I don't know, that's not something you can put a number on. I might say more than half, but I'm not sure, I don't think that is possible to answer."[72] A Latino member of Alpha Phi Alpha, twenty-four-year-old "Juan," stated, "I don't agree with it being all black membership, but I don't think they should have all nonblack membership either, because then those members may not have . . . a responsibility to the black community. . . . I also feel that black members can relate better if they have more connections to the community."[73] Multicultural nationalists have a difficult time rationalizing their views. They often simply give up and admit that they do not know how this should be reconciled. What they do know is that neither extreme—either all black or less than majority black—is acceptable.

Among the quantitative data, one of the relationships between variables had a strong correlation. The most striking relationship was between the desired level of black membership and political activism (table 16.2). First, when respondents were asked to rate the importance of BGLOs remaining majority black (on a scale from 1 to 7, with 1 meaning they should not worry about maintaining a black majority and 7 meaning that BGLOs should stay as black as possible), the average of the responses was 4.66, indicating that the average nonblack BGLO member would most likely express moderate support for BGLOs remaining majority black. Second, when respondents were asked whether their particular BGLO chapters were more or less politically active (on a scale from 1 to 7, with 1 meaning less active and 7 meaning more active), the average was 4.3, demonstrating that most nonblack BGLO members see their organizations as moderately political.

Alone, these two responses meant very little. However, when these two individual responses were correlated, they were directly related. That is, non-black members who responded that BGLOs should remain majority black also responded that their chapters were more politically active. In other words, respondents who thought the organizations should be black also thought of their organizations as political vehicles. Conversely, one could say that possessing a multicultural BGLO ideology delimits the chapter's potential to be politically active.[74] As figure 16.1 demonstrates, there is a clear linear relationship (moving from the bottom left to the upper right) between the desire for majority black BGLOs and the identification of BGLOs as political vehicles.

Table 16.2. Relationship between Desired Level of Black BGLO Membership and Political Activism

Black Majority Membership	No.	Percentage	Political Activism	No.	Percentage
1 (not a worry)	5	16.7	1 (less active)	4	13.3
2	3	10.0	2	6	20.0
3	3	10.0	3	1	3.3
4 (neutral)	0	0.0	4 (active)	4	13.3
5	4	13.3	5	4	13.3
6	8	26.7	6	7	23.3
7 (keep as black as possible)	7	23.3	7 (most active)	4	13.3

Figure 16.1. BGLO Blackness Related to Political Activism*

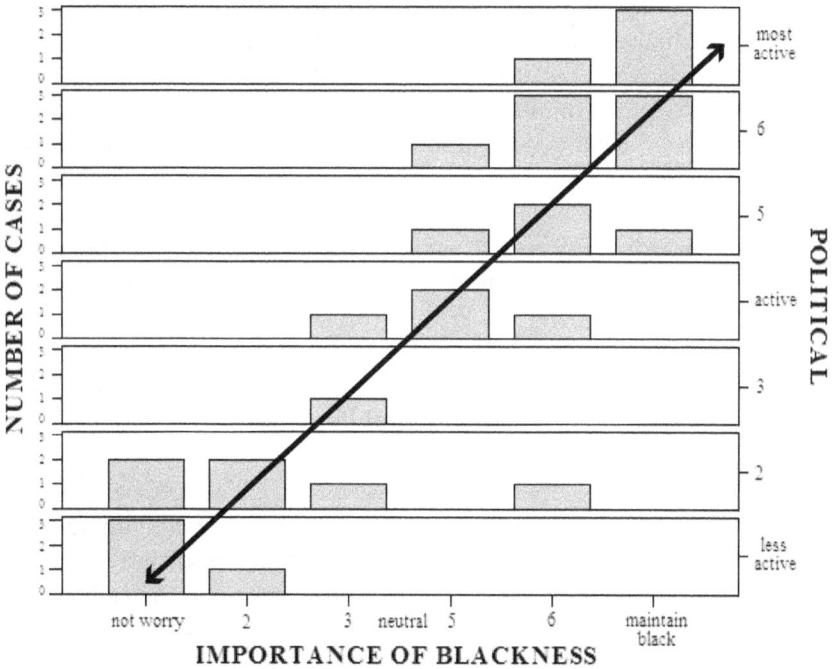

*The X axis does not include an increment of 4, because there were no observed data for that value. For further clarification, see table 16.2.

As "Sean," a twenty-nine-year-old, white member of Phi Beta Sigma Fraternity, stated:

> We were founded under the auspices of a political cause . . . African Americans were simply not allowed to join white Greek organizations. Look at Huey Newton, Alain Leroy Locke, James Weldon Johnson . . . all Sigmas, all black, all political. If we should lose any one of these facets of our organization, then I am afraid that we may warp or twist this organization into something it was not meant to be. . . . we may have already done that. I hope we have not . . . I pray we have not. In the meantime, brothers like me have to be very careful, whether or not we should have pledged or not is now irrelevant, not that it should not be thought about and analyzed like you are doing, but we are here now, so the question remains: what is to be done?[75]

Sean's response emphasizes that present nonblack BGLO members have a responsibility to shape the future significance of their membership. Multicultural nationalists espouse differing views—from a liberal support of racial diversity to a more Black Nationalist stance. They are trying to reconcile divergent and often antithetical ideologies. This should not be regarded as atypical "incoherence" but rather as indicative of this specialized subculture. These members are navigating loaded cultural politics and are often demonized or deified by both blacks and whites for their decision to cross the color line in such dramatic fashion. This type of multiple-subject positioning is indicative of the racial politics of the present—a decidedly unstable time caught between the transition from the modern to the postmodern.

Integrated Spectacles and Bicultural Performance

In constructing the narratives about these nonblack BGLO members, I hoped to make clear that these types are not exclusive; they can overlap. Although the thirty individuals are at times embodiments of the four types I have delineated, these types are also reflections of the social and cultural ideologies that labor to make sense of this specific racial-political formation. The typology should be understood as personified ideologies—ideologies with faces created to facilitate an understanding of these different approaches to BGLO membership. We must be vigilant not to transform these stories into essentialized commodities devoid of the politics of racial boundary transgressions. Rather, we must work to shift both the criteria and the perspectives of canonization itself to speak of the cultures of nonblack BGLO members without rehearsing the naturalization of a particular form of nonblack BGLO culture. Otherwise, the search and expansion of work on this topic will result only in the stylization of history though a recycling of tokenism and narrow nostalgia. A way out of this paradox is to search for the conditions and mechanisms of epistemic logics that produce these very claims to nonblack BGLO membership authenticity, representation, and performativity.

I have been a white member of Phi Beta Sigma Fraternity Inc. since 1996. In looking back, I see that I have moved through all four types and have tried to advance an antiracist agenda, although I have also unintentionally reproduced that very racism. In this vein, I have approached this topic with both a deep emotional connection and the rigor of a cultural sociologist. I have attempted to be both critical toward, and sympathetic to, others and myself. Accordingly, my own story, and the thirty stories assembled here, should raise questions of appropriation, authenticity, and authority from the critical reader. As Alcoff points out, "Persons from dominant groups who speak for others are often treated as authenticating presences that confer legitimacy and credibility on the demand of subjugated speakers; such speaking for others does nothing to disrupt the discursive hierarchies that operate in public spaces."[76] From this, one might conclude that it is better not to speak for others at all. Such representative recoil is intellectually detrimental. As Henry Louis Gates Jr. stated, "Like it or not, all writers are 'cultural impersonators.'"[77]

Within the social sciences, it has become difficult to speak of such subjectivity in scholarly fashion, because life stories are currently unfashionable.[78] Yet there are glimpses of a renewed interest in personal narratives, life histories, and autobiographies due to the changing nature of methodological fieldwork and the types of questions posed owing to the influence of the "cultural turn."[79] As Reed-Danahay writes: "One of the main characteristics of an autoethnographic perspective is that the autoethnographer is a boundary-crosser, and the role can be characterized as that of a dual identity. . . . It is associated with the late nineteenth-century ideas of 'double consciousness.' . . . The notion of autoethnography foregrounds the multiple nature of selfhood and opens up new ways of writing about social life."[80]

Although I do not engage in a full exposition into, or interrogation of, my own "double consciousness" as a nonblack member of a BGLO, I take this opportunity to assert, "To write of individual experience is to write of social experience."[81] Applied to BGLO membership, my own experience, and that of the thirty others described here, resists reductive, dualistic views of "self" and "other" distinctions. Our experiences are not accumulated in a social vacuum, nor do they escape the operations of social hierarchies and power differentials.

The main question raised is what nonblack membership foreshadows for the future of BGLOs, black intelligentsia, and black leadership. Is diversity within BGLOs a further indication of our attainment of a postmodern, postracial state characterized by the "death of the subject" and the demise of identity politics? Or is it an aberration of late-capitalist development, in which liberal multicultural-ism is an ideology that masks the "continued significance of race"? Nonblack BGLO members show socially conflicting instances of multiracial contact at the level of an intimate brotherhood. The difficulty of interpreting these cases is aggravated by the complexity in interpreting their context. These organiza-tions are both utopias and dystopias; nonblack BGLO members are what I call "integrated spectacles." This represents one of the main paradoxes within our multiracial, postmodern moment: an attempt to function in the presence of mainstream social production based on racial cooperation and diversity, while disguising a continued racial conflict of hegemonic proportions. Does nonblack BGLO membership create a stronger and more diverse cadre of young thinkers and unified persons, or does it weaken and commodify the tradition of BGLOs as creators of black intelligentsia, leadership, and social service endeavors?

In a society in which racism is profoundly rooted in our cultural logic, it would be disingenuous and politically myopic to propose a utopia of racial harmony or a society without racial frameworks. Simply engaging in color-blind politics labors to justify the continued second-class status of minorities as the product of market dynamics, naturally occurring phenomena, and "cultural deficiencies." Alternatives to this utopian leap can be understood as a practical politics constituted by "soft borders"—not a harsh and unyielding segrega-tion, but the maintenance of public black spheres that contest institutional manifestations of racism, while also defending autonomous, alternative, and heterogeneous black communities. Such a space would be constructed on the basis of an economy of authentic cooperation in social production—on socially, culturally, and politically conscious brotherhood. This proposal, without the exacerbation of social antagonisms, aims to recognize the material conditions of racism in order to begin a process of putting the marginalized in control of their own destiny. We cannot simply say that the phenomenon of nonblacks joining BGLOs is either wholly progressive or oppressive. It is essential to deconstruct and rearticulate the tension between committed nonblack antiracist support and the unintentional reproduction of racial paternalism, co-optation, and fetishism that could have a significant impact on BGLOs, especially if we are concerned with BGLOs' future role in realizing black autonomy and equality.

We must turn more attention to considerations of power. How does power operate in the intersections of traditionally marginalized peoples who create their own organizations and then allow the former (or current) oppressor membership? We cannot simply say that this is a case of good or bad, moral or immoral, utopian or dystopian racial contact. Research on these "integrated spectacles" is a fruitful field that is just beginning to be opened up to critical theory. As research continues, we must resist the specific canonization of narrow versions of this form of border crossing. We must rethink the historical and contemporary dimensions of the regime of dominant knowledge on BGLOs through a plurality of geopolitical registers of reasoning, particularly those that acknowledge and defend humans residing on the margins.

Notes

Portions of this chapter were first published as "Crossing the Sands, Crossing the Color-Line: Non-Black Members of Historically Black Greek Organizations," *Journal of African American Studies* 11 (2007). I offer thanks to Neela Pall for editing assistance; to Tristan S. Bridges, who aided me in the coding and correlation stages of this research; and to Marian Callaham, who served as my research assistant. For access to data, I extend special gratitude to Phi Beta Sigma Fraternity Inc. international executive director Donald J. Jemison; Kappa Alpha Psi Fraternity Inc. executive director Richard L. Snow; Kappa Alpha Psi Fraternity Inc. director of undergraduate and university affairs Andre G. Early; Alpha Phi Alpha Fraternity Inc. general president Darryl R. Matthews; Alpha Phi Alpha Fraternity Inc. executive director Willard C. Hall Jr.; and the editor of this volume, Gregory S. Parks.

1. Examples include the all-male secret societies composed of Cuban-African slaves and laborers (Abakuás and cabildos de nación, respectively) and white fraternal secret societies (Masons, Knights Templar, Eastern Stars).

2. The members of the NPHC (also known as the Divine Nine) and their founding dates are Alpha Phi Alpha Faternity (1906), Alpha Kappa Alpha Sorority (1908), Kappa Alpha Psi Fraternity (1911), Omega Psi Phi Fraternity (1911), Delta Sigma Theta Sorority (1913), Phi Beta Sigma Fraternity (1914), Zeta Phi Beta Sorority (1920), Sigma Gamma Rho Sorority (1922), and Iota Phi Theta Fraternity (1963).

3. The National Interfraternity Conference (NIC) and the National Panhellenic Conference (NPC) are the governing bodies for traditionally white fraternities and sororities, respectively.

4. E. G. Whipple, J. L. Baier, and D. Grady, "A Comparison of Black and White Greeks at a Predominately White University," *NASPA Journal* 28, no. 2 (1991): 146.

5. A. Berkowitz and I. Padavic, "Getting a Man or Getting Ahead: A Comparison of White and Black Sororities," *Journal of Contemporary Ethnography* 27, no. 4 (1999): 530–57.

6. Ibid.

7. See R. Binder, M. B. Schaub, W. Seiler, and T. Lake, "Greek Academic Achievement Update: Gamma Sigma Alpha and Bowling Green State University Partnership" (paper presented at the annual meeting of the Association of Fraternity Advisors, Columbus, Ohio, December 2002), and J. Kunjufu, *Black College Student Survival Guide* (Chicago: African American Images, 1997).

8. C. W. McKee, "Understanding the Diversity of the Greek World," in *Fraternities and Sororities on the Contemporary College Campus*, ed. R. B. Winston Jr., W. B. Nettles III, and J. H. Opper Jr. (San Francisco: Jossey-Bass, 1987), 21–35.

9. L. R. Stains, "Black Like Me," *Rolling Stone*, March 24, 1994, 69–72.

10. Walter Kimbrough, *Black Greek 101: The Culture, Customs, and Challenges of Black Fraternities and Sororities* (Madison, N.J.: Fairleigh Dickinson University Press, 2003), 38, 41–43.

11. Sociologist Anthony Giddens's "structuration theory" is one of his best-known ideas. At its center is a cyclical relationship between social structure and human action. For more, see A. Giddens, *The Constitution of Society* (Berkeley: University of California Press, 1984).

12. Kimbrough, *Black Greek 101,* 41.

13. E. Franklin Frazier, *Black Bourgeoisie* (New York: Simon and Schuster, 1957).

14. R. Plotkin, "A Brief History of Racial and Ethnic Discrimination in Greek-Letter Organizations," *Alternative Orange* 2, no. 6 (April 1993): 12.

15. "Negro Frat Admits 'White Brother,'" *Ebony,* October 1946, 24, 26.

16. "White Student Belongs to Negro Frat at K.U.," *Lawrence Daily Journal-World,* October 24, 1953, 2.

17. Interview via post-mail, March 24, 2006.

18. "Negro Joins Fraternity," *New York Times,* March 25, 1949; "Admits White Student," *New York Times,* April 12, 1949.

19. "Negro Clubs Told to Enroll Whites," *New York Times,* December 28, 1959.

20. Stains, "Black Like Me," 70–71.

21. "Whites in Black Sororities and Fraternities," *Ebony,* December 2000, 173.

22. Stains, "Black Like Me," 72.

23. As a white member of the BGLO Phi Beta Sigma Fraternity Inc., my experiences support most of the research on this topic. For the ten years I have been a member, the harshest challenges have come from other whites. Whether this means that whites possess more negative attitudes about my racial boundary crossing or whether they simply feel more of a right to confront me about my BGLO membership calls for more qualitative inquiries on the subject.

24. "Whites in Black Sororities and Fraternities," 174.

25. Ibid.

26. Lawrence C. Ross Jr., *The Divine Nine: The History of African American Fraternities and Sororities* (New York: Dafina Books, 2002).

27. A. Burkdoll, "Greek Differences: Black, White," Alligator On-Line, University of Florida, October 7, 1996, http://www.alligator.org.

28. Elizabeth Wen-Chu Chen, "The Continuing Significance of Race: A Case Study of Asian American Women in White, Asian American, and African American Sororities" (doctoral diss., University of California–Los Angeles, 1998), 106.

29. Mari Matsuda, *Where Is Your Body? And Other Essays on Race, Gender and the Law* (Boston: Beacon Press, 1996), 150.

30. From January to April 2006, I conducted both telephone and e-mail interviews with thirty nonblack BGLO members. My population was obtained using a "snowball sampling" technique. These interviews uncovered how nonblack BGLO members make sense of their positioning, what rhetorical strategies they use to discuss or rationalize their actions, and how they reflexively view themselves and their organizations as social phenomena. As a result, I was able to draw many conclusions about the culture of nonblack BGLO membership. Although this small sample is not a cross section of nonblack BGLO members in the United States, it includes people of many different backgrounds. The sample has eleven women (37 percent) and nineteen men (63 percent). Sixteen respondents (53 percent) had graduate-level education (in the form of graduate school or law or medical degrees), and eleven respondents (37 percent) had bachelor's degrees. Three (10 percent) reported an annual income below $20,000 a year; twelve (40 percent) reported income of $21,000 to $40,000; six (20 percent) reported income of $41,000 to $80,000; and nine (30 percent) reported an income of more than $81,000. An overwhelming portion of the sample—twenty-five of thirty (83 percent)—reported themselves as Christian (with five identifying specifically as Methodist, five as Catholic, and three as Baptist); there were also two Baha'is, one Sikh, one "spiritual," and one "unaffiliated." Political views were dominated by Democrats (50 percent), followed by no political affiliation (40 percent), Independent (7 percent), and Republican (3 percent). Of the thirty respondents, twenty (67 percent) were or are married, and fifteen (50 percent) married people of a different race. The average age of the respondents when interviewed was thirty-three years (born in 1973), and the ages ranged from twenty-three to seventy-three. Twenty-one of the respondents (70 percent) were white or Caucasian, seven (23 percent) were Latino (one identifying as Puerto Rican, one as Cuban, and five as Hispanic), and two (7 percent) were Asian American. Eight of the nine NPHC organizations were represented in my sample: Delta Sigma Theta Sorority Inc. (two respondents), Kappa Alpha Psi Fraternity Inc. (two), Omega Psi Phi Fraternity Inc. (two), Sigma Gamma Rho Sorority Inc. (two), Zeta Phi Beta Sorority Inc. (three), Alpha Kappa Alpha Sorority Inc. (four), Phi Beta Sigma Fraternity Inc. (seven), and Alpha Phi Alpha Fraternity Inc. (eight). My account aims to be as accurate as possible. I did not alter

organizational affiliation or other demographic information; however, I use pseudonyms to refer to the respondents. I offer no blatant or hidden clues to the true identity of my subjects in order to protect them and the ethical soundness of this study.

31. I draw inspiration for this typological framework from Sharon Hays, *Flat Broke with Children: Women in the Age of Welfare Reform* (New York: Oxford University Press, 2003). Her chapter "Cultures of Poverty" is particularly insightful for a delineation of the types of women on welfare.

32. Interview via e-mail, April 18, 2006.

33. Interview via telephone, March 22, 2006.

34. Interview via e-mail, April 5, 2006.

35. Ronald Hall, "Entitlement Disorder: The Colonial Traditions of Power as White Male Resistance to Affirmative Action," *Journal of Black Studies* 34, no. 4 (March 2004): 571–72.

36. Melanie Bush, *Breaking the Code of Good Intentions: Everyday Forms of Whiteness* (New York: Rowman and Littlefield, 2004).

37. Interview via telephone, April 16, 2006.

38. The notion of "paternalism" has occupied a marginal role in the analysis of intergroup boundary transgression mainly because of an overriding concern with forms of direct conflict and hostility. However, Pierre Van den Berghe discusses the term in the context of preindustrial societies whereby a small minority dominates a large majority. See P. Van den Berghe, *Race and Racism: A Comparative Perspective* (New York: John Wiley and Sons, 1967). Gunnar Myrdal's classic study of black-white relations regards paternalism as (dys)functional for social cohesion. See G. Myrdal, *An American Dilemma: The Negro Problem and the Modern Democracy* (New York: Harper and Brothers, 1944). Genovese applied the concept to master-slave relationships in the antebellum South, and others have applied it to the assessment of industrial enterprise. Some authors see paternalism as a system fraught with contradictions. See E. D. Genovese, *Roll, Jordan, Roll: The World the Slaves Made* (New York: Random House, 1974); D. Lockwood, "Sources of Variation in Working Class Images of Society," *Sociological Review* 14 (November 1966): 249–67; H. Newby, "Paternalism and Capitalism," in *Industrial Society: Class, Cleavage, and Control,* ed. R. Scase (London: Allen and Unwin, 1977), 59–73; W. Staples and C. L. Staples, *Power, Profits and Patriarchy* (New York: Rowman and Littlefield, 2001).

39. D. VanDeVeer, *Paternalistic Intervention* (Princeton, N.J.: Princeton University Press, 1986).

40. M. R. Jackman, *The Velvet Glove: Paternalism and Conflict in Gender, Class, and Race Relations* (Berkeley: University of California Press, 1994), 14–15.

41. Interview via e-mail, January 19, 2006.

42. Interview via email, March 31, 2006.

43. Interview via telephone, April 6, 2006.

44. Interview via telephone, January 25, 2006.

45. Interview via telephone, February 9, 2006.

46. Interview via e-mail, March 4, 2006.

47. Interview via e-mail, January 8, 2006.

48. Interview via telephone, January 18, 2006.

49. Eduardo Bonilla-Silva, "The Linguistics of Color Blind Racism: How to Talk Nasty about Blacks without Sounding 'Racist,'" *Critical Sociology* 28, nos. 1–2 (2002): 42.

50. A "social construction" is a concept that denotes the process of "inventing" or "constructing" images, identities, ideologies, institutions, and so forth by participants in a particular culture or society. The term was first used by Peter L. Berger and Thomas Luckmann in their book *The Social Construction of Reality* (Garden City, N.Y.: Anchor Books, 1966). Social constructs include such things as language, money, class, race, and morality. Within sociology, it is a school of thought that attempts, to varying degrees, to analyze seemingly natural and given phenomena in terms of social constructs. However, social constructions are very real, as they are a central part of our lived reality.

51. Interview via telephone, January 22, 2006.

52. Interview via telephone, February 12, 2006.

53. Ibid.

54. Interview via e-mail, April 18, 2006.

55. Sociologist Pierre Bourdieu coined the term *cultural capital* in "Cultural Reproduction and Social Reproduction," in *Knowledge, Education and Social Change,* ed. Richard K. Brown (London: Tavistock, 1971). Cultural capital can be understood as forms of knowledge, skill, education, and any advantages a person has that convey a higher status in society, including high expectations.

56. Interview via telephone, March 21, 2006.

57. Mary Waters, *Ethnic Options: Choosing Identities in America* (Berkeley: University of California Press, 1990).

58. Herbert J. Gans, "Symbolic Ethnicity: The Future of Ethnic Groups and Cultures in America," in *Majority and Minority,* ed. N. Yetman (Boston: Allyn and Bacon, 1991), 416–29.

59. Interview via e-mail, January 25, 2006.

60. F. Parkin, "Strategies of Closure in Class Formation," in *The Social Analysis of Class Structure* (London: Tavistock, 1974), 1–18; R. Collins, *The Credential Society* (New York: Academic Press, 1976).

61. B. Bryson, *Making Multiculturalism* (Stanford, Calif.: Stanford University Press, 2005); B. Bryson, "'Anything but Heavy Metal': Symbolic Exclusion and Musical Dislikes," *American Sociological Review* 61 (1996): 884–99; M. Lamont, *Money, Morals, and Manners* (Chicago: University of Chicago Press, 1992); R. A. Peterson and R. Kern, "Changing Highbrow Taste: From Snob to Omnivore," *American Sociological Review* 61 (1996): 900–7.

62. Bryson, "Anything but Heavy Metal."

63. Lamont, *Money, Morals, and Manners.*

64. Bryson, "Anything but Heavy Metal," 895.

65. Interview via e-mail, March 21, 2006.

66. Black Nationalism is a political and social movement that arose in the 1960s and early 1970s mostly among African Americans in the United States. Black Nationalism is antiassimilationist and seeks to maintain and promote a separate identity among people of African ancestry. Overall, it is a complex set of beliefs emphasizing the need for the cultural, political, and economic independence and self-determination of African Americans.

67. Interview via e-mail, April 16, 2006.

68. Interview via e-mail, April 27, 2006.

69. Interview via telephone, March 2, 2006.

70. Interview via e-mail, March 21, 2006.

71. Interview via e-mail, March 23, 2006.

72. Interview via e-mail, April 8, 2006.

73. Interview via telephone, March 27, 2006.

74. My chi-square of 48.576 is significant to the .02 level (see table 16.3). Although this is not a standard accepted p-value, these results are reported because of the small number of cases ($n = 30$). However, this leads me to believe that there is in fact a relationship between self-reported level of political activity and self-reported desire for BGLOs to either remain black or become more racially diverse. The higher the self-reported level of political activity associated with the BGLO, the more its members wanted the organization to remain black. The lambda of .333 ($p < .05$) illustrates the strength of this relationship and the direction. This is a moderately strong relationship, especially considering the small sample size. A group t-test shows the results of the independent variable on the dependent as well (see table 16.4). This test was significant to the .001 level, indicating a very accurate correlation, and as one reads from the chi-square test, the relationship is also of moderate strength.

Table 16.3. Chi-Square Results

Chi-Square	48.576*
Lambda	.333***
No.	30

*** $p < .05$; ** $p < .01$; * $p < .02$

Table 16.4. T-Test Results

Blackness t-value	11.524***
Political t-value	10.856***
No.	30

*** $p < .001$; ** $p < .01$; * $p < .05$

75. Interview via e-mail, April 9, 2006.

76. L. M. Alcoff, "The Problem of Speaking for Others," in *Who Can Speak? Authority and Critical Identity,* ed. J. Roof and R. Weigman (Urbana: University of Illinois Press, 1995), 99.

77. D. Callaghan, "The Vicar and Virago: Feminism and the Problem of Identity," in Roof and Weigman, *Who Can Speak?* 196.

78. D. Bertaux and M. Kohli, "The Life Story Approach: A Continental View," *Annual Review of Sociology* 10 (1984): 231.

79. The "cultural turn" describes developments in cultural studies and the sociology of culture. It refers to a shift in emphasis toward meaning. This shift occurred over a prolonged period, but particularly since the 1960s. Due mainly to the introduction of "social constructionism," the shift toward meaning now wields a great deal of descriptive, conceptual, and explanatory power for the analysis of cultural processes and practices.

80. D. E. Reed-Danahay, *Auto/Ethnography* (New York: Oxford, 1997), 3.

81. E. Mykhalovskiy, "Reconsidering Table Talk: Critical Thoughts on the Relationship between Sociology, Autobiography and Self-Indulgence," *Qualitative Sociology* 19, no. 1 (1996): 140.

Part VI

Contemporary Debates

17
Eating Disorders within African American Sororities

Tamika C. Zapolski and Gregory T. Smith

In mainstream American society, female beauty or attractiveness is typically defined by thinness.[1] For example, studies indicate that the body sizes of winners of the Miss America pageants and of *Playboy* centerfolds have been steadily decreasing over the years.[2] It is then no surprise that for many women in the United States, there is an intense perceived pressure to be thin and a strong belief that thinness is a necessary ingredient for beauty.[3] For some women, the preoccupation with and the desire for thinness can lead to the development of both clinical and subclinical eating disorders, such as anorexia nervosa and bulimia nervosa. The *Diagnostic and Statistical Manual of Mental Disorders* (*DSM-IV-TR*) defines *anorexia nervosa* as an eating disorder characterized by extreme restriction of caloric intake for the purpose of weight control and fat avoidance.[4] Restrictive behaviors may also be accompanied by purgative methods such as induced vomiting and laxative use, in an attempt to avoid weight gain after eating. *Bulimia nervosa* is defined as an eating disorder characterized by binge-eating episodes in which large amounts of food are consumed, followed by purgative or nonpurgative compensatory behaviors. Patients with anorexia nervosa fail to maintain a normal body weight, whereas those with bulimia nervosa are often a normal weight or overweight. There is also a third classification of disordered eating referred to as *binge-eating disorder*. Individuals with this disorder experience extreme, uncontrollable episodes of food consumption over short periods of time. However, they do not resort to inappropriate compensatory behaviors such as vomiting, and they are more likely to be overweight. Although binge eating is not an official diagnosis in the *DSM-IV-TR*, it is a fairly prevalent disorder; some researchers suggest that it may affect as many as 20 percent of men and women.[5]

Prevalence of and Risk Factors for Eating Disorders

The prevalence of anorexia nervosa and bulimia nervosa is much higher in women than in men, with approximately 90 percent of those affected being female.[6] However, even among women, fully diagnosable clinical disorders are rare. In the general female population, the lifetime prevalence of anorexia nervosa is estimated to be 0.5 percent, and that of bulimia nervosa ranges from 1 percent to 3 percent.[7] Among college women, however, the rates may be as high as 5 percent.[8] In most cases, these prevalence rates are applicable only to Caucasian women, because historically, most research on eating disorders was conducted with Caucasian women. It was assumed that eating disorders took the same form and had the same prevalence rates in women of other ethnicities, but most studies comparing Caucasian and African American women have found differences between the two groups.[9] Striegel-Moore and colleagues report that the odds of detecting bulimia nervosa are six times greater for Caucasian women than African American women.[10] Consistent with that finding, a focus on specific symptoms demonstrates that African American women typically report fewer instances of restrictive dieting and self-induced vomiting than Caucasian women do.[11] Conversely, African American women have an equivalent or slightly higher likelihood of reporting binge eating in comparison to Caucasian women.[12]

Despite these differences, there is evidence that certain risk factors are common among the two groups. In particular, body dissatisfaction and concerns about body image are strong predictors of eating disorders.[13] Although body image is a complex phenomenon, researchers have found that it can be divided into two distinct and independent components: attitudinal and perceptual.[14] Attitudinal body image involves the degree of satisfaction with one's body and its parts. Perceptual body image refers to the self-perception of one's body size and parts, which may be either accurate or distorted. It is significant that African American women consistently exhibit lower rates of dissatisfaction for each type of body image. For example, pertaining to attitudinal body image, Caucasian women report more negative attitudes about their weight and overall appearance than do African American women, even when their weight is within the normal range. Concerning perceptual body image, Caucasian women believe themselves to be heavier than their ideal weight and overestimate their weight more often than African American women do.[15] Since African American women appear to have healthier body images and less dissatisfaction with their bodies, they are apparently at less risk for the development of the two eating disorders that emphasize thinness and weight control—anorexia nervosa and bulimia nervosa.

These findings are consistent with the evidence that African American women are less likely to engage in restrictive dieting or purgative behaviors.

Eating Disorders and Sororities

In general, women in the Greek-letter community are perceived as being overly concerned with their appearance. As a result of their social environment and the perceived pressure from others, these women may be at risk for engaging in potentially dangerous weight-control behaviors. Furthermore, it has been found that social groups, such as sororities, play a strong role in telling us who we are, what we should think, and how we should behave. If thinness is deemed to be an important, valued quality among sorority members, extreme behaviors such as restricting food intake and purging may arise. Additionally, it may be the case that disordered eating has a tendency to spread socially. That is, women tend to become more like their friends over time. Thus, if one woman in a sorority exhibits disordered eating and dieting behaviors, it is likely that other women will adopt similar behaviors over time—especially if the disordered behaviors are exhibited by a particularly popular member.[16]

Studies have found several trends among Caucasian sorority members. First, women who are members of Greek sororities generally have more disturbed eating behaviors than women who are not members. Second, sorority members generally report a stronger desire for thinness and a greater fear of becoming fat, are more preoccupied with their weight, and are more concerned with dieting in comparison to nonmembers.[17] Third, one study found that living arrangements played an important role in how preoccupied sorority women were with their bodies.[18] Women who lived in sorority houses had a greater fear of becoming fat, greater body dissatisfaction and weight preoccupation, and stronger worries about dieting compared with those who did not.[19]

Comparison of Black and White Sororities

Given the apparently higher risk among Caucasian sorority members, investigators have considered whether African American sorority members are also at increased risk—even though African American women in general appear to have fewer eating disturbances than Caucasian women do. Some researchers have engaged in the following reasoning: to the degree that African American sorority members tend to be of higher socioeconomic status and thus have more pervasive, daily contact with mainstream middle-class culture, perhaps they experience more perceived pressure to be thin and hence engage in more restrictive eating or purging behaviors. As plausible as this hypothesis may be, studies have found that African American sorority members are at no greater risk than their nonsorority counterparts for developing eating disorders.[20] In fact, African American sorority members may be at reduced risk because of specific protective factors in African American sororities.

Because African American women appear to engage in less restrictive eating and purging behavior and tend to be more satisfied with their bodies, researchers have sought to understand the reasons for their healthier status in comparison to Caucasian women. Several differences between African American culture and Caucasian culture have been identified as potential protective factors against the development of anorexia nervosa and bulimia nervosa in African American women. These factors include more positive feedback from one's family, less pressure to be thin, a tendency not to compare oneself to mainstream standards, and a broader, more flexible definition of beauty. There is evidence supporting each of these possibilities.

First, African American women receive more positive feedback about their looks and style from family and friends in comparison to Caucasian women.[21] African American women are encouraged to embrace their current body shape and be proud of their looks, style, and appearance. This social support appears to be effective: one study found that African American women had less fear of weight gain and were less likely to believe that a gain of five pounds would make a significant difference in their attractiveness.[22] Similarly, in comparison to Caucasian women, African American women reported that their immediate families placed significantly less emphasis on food and weight control. It thus appears that African American women are encouraged to take a more positive view of their bodies and their appearance, and indeed, they tend to be more satisfied with their current body shape, size, and weight and less concerned with weight, dieting, or being thin.[23]

Second, African American women are less likely to engage in self-evaluation of their physical attractiveness by comparing themselves to mainstream standards of beauty.[24] In part, this lack of comparison could be due to the encouragement of the black community to embrace one's body shape, regardless of size. Another factor may be that African American women tend to view women portrayed through the media as not being relevant to them or as not offering a realistic basis of comparison. Of course, the typical women held up as ideals of beauty tend to be Caucasian. In addition, the mainstream Western media image of women is typically portrayed by models who represent unhealthy ideals for any woman to strive for.[25] These ideals may be particularly oppressive for African American women, whose body size, shape, and facial features differ significantly from mainstream ideals. Therefore, African American women are less likely to compare themselves to Caucasian models and compare themselves to African American models instead.[26]

It appears to be true, however, that those African American women portrayed through various media outlets tend to resemble their Caucasian counterparts: they tend to be lighter skinned with "Anglo" features. Thus, for many African American women, neither Caucasian nor African American images represent the body types common to black women, so they may not be viewed as realistic goals to aim for. Therefore, although African American women are aware of the pressure to emulate the aesthetic ideals of mainstream culture, these maladaptive ideals are viewed as unattainable and undermined by the healthy encouragement of the black community to embrace and have pride in one's body.[27]

Third, African American culture appears to give a more positive view to larger body sizes. Thus, thinness is simply not as important as it is among Caucasians. This difference likely reduces African American women's risk for anorexia nervosa and bulimia nervosa. This apparent protective factor has been supported through research, which has found that even though African American women are larger on average than their Caucasian counterparts, they are more satisfied with their bodies, consider their figures to be attractive, and experience less discrepancy between their actual and ideal body sizes.[28] Additionally, one study found that African American women were less fat phobic; they had less strict criteria for perceptions of fatness and were less eager to pursue extreme thinness than Caucasian women were.[29] Their greater acceptance of larger body sizes may also be related to the perception that African American men prefer bigger or curvier women and find these body types more attractive. It has been shown that these perceptions appear to be correct. In a comparison of African American and Caucasian men, thinness in the women they dated was more important to Caucasian men. Further, African American men expressed more willingness to date larger-than-ideal women and expected less ridicule for doing so than did Caucasian men.[30]

Fourth, African American culture defines beauty as a more flexible, fluid, and multifaceted concept that is not based primarily on body size, shape, or weight.[31] Qualitative studies examining how African American women define beauty found that beauty encompasses more than just physical characteristics such as weight; it is also defined by nonphysical attributes such as personal style, self-confidence, spirituality, self-care, and personality traits. In this way, beauty is defined more by body ethics, such as values and beliefs regarding care and presentation of the body, rather than body ideals.[32] Central to the concept of attractiveness or beauty for African American women is the idea of "looking good." Thus, a large woman can still be viewed as attractive if she is able to look "put together"—that is, wear clothes that fit her shape and exude confidence in the presence of others. Studies have found similar definitions of beauty among African American female adolescents, with beauty being dependent on projecting a certain self-image or personal style, rather than body size.[33] All these findings support the belief that the more fluid, less weight-restrained image of beauty promoted by the African American community has helped guard African American women from the development of anorexia nervosa and bulimia nervosa.

Fifth, a stronger womanist or feminist identity among African American women may also be a protective factor. African American women are taught from a young age to be strong, independent, and self-reliant, in contrast to the traditional Caucasian feminine gender role, which tends to value passive, dependent, and deferential behavior.[34] Furthermore, African American women's gender identities are more androgynous than those of Caucasian women, which may allow them to develop greater senses of strength, self-efficacy, and agency, providing protection against poor body image.[35] Therefore, for African American sorority members, the presence of other strong, independent African American women may act as a positive socializing force and hence as another protective factor against the pressure to be thin in mainstream society. Members of sororities are constantly surrounded by other women who share similar ideals and beliefs, and as stated earlier, such social groups are important in determining attitudes and identity. Not surprisingly, whereas Caucasian sorority women may view their membership as a way to get a man, this is not the case for African American sorority women. African American sorority members see their sisterhood as a way to support their communities, network, and "get ahead."[36] Therefore, the strong womanist and cultural ideals embodied within the African American Greek community may help guard against eating disorders.

Comparison of Black Sorority and Nonsorority Women

In addition to distinctions between African American and Caucasian sorority women, there may be distinctions between African American sorority and nonsorority women. Factors that may distinguish the two groups with regard to eating disorders are racial and womanist identity development.[37] Racial identity is an important factor in the overall development of ethnic minority individuals. One challenge that they face is to establish a coherent sense of identity while also contending with and responding to the social and environmental pressures of minority status vis-à-vis a dominant culture.[38] Many models have been developed to explain the process of racial identity. The most widely studied models are Cross's four-stage model, which was expanded by Helms.[39] Both models illustrate the development of black racial identity as a movement from the mainstream white frame of reference to a positive black frame of reference through four stages: preencounter, encounter, immersion-emersion, and internalization.

The preencounter stage is identified as the precultural awakening or conformity stage. Individuals at this stage are thought to identify primarily with a Eurocentric frame of reference and devalue their own ethnoculture.[40] An African American woman in this stage may be more likely to embrace the mainstream ideal of thinness. The second stage, encounter, is characterized by an individual's awareness of the emotional conflict between self-depreciation and self-appreciation. At this stage, an individual's old Eurocentric frame of reference is challenged, though there is still a struggle to remove the old frame of reference and replace it with a new frame of reference based on one's own culture. Pertaining to body image, an African American woman at this stage would begin grappling with the understanding that there are differences between mainstream ideals and the black community's ideals of beauty.

The third stage of identity development, immersion-emersion, is characterized by self-appreciation through a complete immersion into the culture of origin. African American women in this stage typically devote themselves to black culture and reject mainstream culture. They embrace black standards of beauty and disparage the Caucasian cultural emphasis on thinness. The final stage of identity development, internalization, is marked by the integration of a healthy ethnocultural identity and positive attitudes about self and culture. Pertaining to body image, African American women at this stage accept the black culture's concept of beauty and are inclined to value themselves and to perceive themselves as beautiful. At the same time, they can acknowledge and appreciate that attractiveness is defined differently across cultures.[41]

Some studies have found that for African American women, the preencounter stage of identity development is positively related to symptoms of eating disorders, whereas the other three stages are not.[42] Studies examining black self-consciousness, which is similar to ethnic identity, found that women with lower self-consciousness have higher rates of body image dissatisfaction.[43] Of particular importance for understanding the role of African American sororities in this process is the possibility that involvement in black Greek life enables women to move from the preencounter stage to the immersion stage more quickly. Sorority members are able to develop stronger racial identities through their interactions with various African American women and their involvement with the black community. As a result, involvement in black Greek life may in fact reduce the risk for eating disorders, in sharp contrast to the finding that Caucasian Greek life may increase the risk.

A second factor that has received less attention is the relationship between having a strong womanist identity and eating disorders. Womanist identity development, a concept developed by Helms, has been defined as the movement from an externally based to an internally based definition of oneself as a woman.[44] Through this model, emphasis is placed on how a woman comes to value herself as a woman, regardless of how society defines femininity. This model emphasizes the individual's internal definition of her nature as a woman. In relation to sorority membership, it has been shown that women who are affiliated with organizations that empower black women have less conservative attitudes about gender roles than their nonaffiliated counterparts.[45] Thus, it has been theorized that the promotion of female empowerment within African American sororities may lead these women to develop stronger womanist views and racial identities and thus reduce the risk that they will internalize mainstream standards of beauty and develop eating disorders.

Potential Risk Factors for African American Sorority Women

Just as it was a mistake to assume that African American women's risk for eating disorders was the same as Caucasian women's risk, researchers have begun to emphasize that it may also be naïve and harmful not to consider how and why African American women may be at risk for some eating disorders. There are four different types of potential risk processes that researchers are now considering. First, some have suggested that African American women's risk for anorexia nervosa and bulimia nervosa is increasing as they assimilate into mainstream society, climb the corporate ladder, and become more strongly affiliated with individuals and institutions that embrace the typical emphasis on thinness.[46] Second, other appearance-related factors, such as dissatisfaction with skin tone and low self-consciousness, may operate in conjunction with more mainstream risk factors, such as body dissatisfaction and low self-esteem, to increase the risk for African American women.[47] Third, ongoing exposure to racism, classism, and sexism may influence African American women's eating and dieting behavior.[48] Fourth, although black culture appears to be a strong protective factor against anorexia nervosa and bulimia nervosa, the African American acceptance of larger body shapes may place African American women at higher risk for other eating disorders, such as binge eating and obesity.[49]

With greater economic and social opportunities, some African American women may become more vulnerable to the development of eating disorders. For these women, pressure to conform to the mainstream's standards may become increasingly potent as they become more upwardly mobile and increase their social status. This may occur in two ways. First, in Caucasian culture, there is evidence that women who are viewed as more attractive tend to be given more opportunities.[50] African American women who are seeking to succeed in largely Caucasian contexts may, perhaps accurately, perceive an advantage to conforming to Caucasian standards of beauty. Second, as African American women become more immersed in traditionally Caucasian cultural contexts, a higher percentage of their contacts, acquaintances, and perhaps friends are likely to model Caucasian beauty-based behaviors, such as eating low-calorie foods, joining exercise gyms, and the like. This modeling may influence the perceptions and behaviors of African American women.

Of course, conformity can involve multiple behaviors or perspectives. It may include internalizing mainstream beauty ideals, exhibiting more European characteristics such as straight hair, talking with a more "proper" dialect, and relinquishing some traits of one's Afrocentric heritage while at the workplace.[51] Some researchers have also found that social mobility and family concerns about ethnic and class assimilation are linked with concerns about dieting and thinness.[52] These findings and theoretical perspectives support the belief that for African American women, low self-consciousness or loss of ethnic identity caused by a disconnection with African roots can place them at higher risk for the development of symptoms of restrictive and purging eating disorders.

As stated earlier, body dissatisfaction is a strong predictor for eating-disordered behavior. For Caucasian women, body dissatisfaction is associated primarily with body size, shape, or weight. However, for African American women, body dissatisfaction may extend to their general appearance and encompass characteristics such as skin tone, facial features, and hair. Skin tone has long been an issue affecting the perception of attractiveness among African

American women.[53] Researchers have shown that skin tone is still an important factor in African American women's self-evaluation, with lighter skin tones being idealized.[54] Furthermore, studies have shown that greater skin color satisfaction is related to higher overall appearance satisfaction and lower internalization of mainstream views of attractiveness for African American college students.[55]

Researchers have also hypothesized that African American women are at increased risk for eating disorders if they become disconnected from their cultural roots.[56] Disconnection could be the result of several factors, including a lack of racial identity development and increased upward mobility. As stated earlier, African American women who are in the preencounter stage of racial identity are at a higher risk of developing eating disorders.

A third set of risk factors that are likely to contribute to the development of eating disorders in African American women is a trio of stressors in their daily lives: racism, classism, and sexism. Due to the constant stress of being a black woman in a racist, classist, and sexist society, maladaptive behaviors such as abstaining from food, binge eating, or purging might be used as a coping mechanism. In one qualitative study, researchers found that many African American women were struggling with sexual abuse, poverty, and gender and racial discrimination and that these traumatic experiences and the struggle to survive played a greater role in the development of eating disorders than did aspirations toward thinness.[57] At this point, this is only a hypothesis that remains to be evaluated by empirical research. We know very little about how these three mechanisms influence African American women's lives and how they interact with other protective and risk factors. A great deal more work needs to be done.

A fourth type of risk factor may stem from the black culture's de-emphasis on weight and thinness. African American women are disproportionately identified as being obese in the United States,[58] and it is possible that a positive view of large body types removes the incentive to keep one's weight down. There is also emerging evidence that African American women are at equal or increased risk for binge-eating disorder compared with Caucasian women. There are, of course, many health risks associated with obesity and binge eating, including hypertension, cardiovascular disease, diabetes, stroke, some cancers, osteoarthritis, sleep apnea, and gallstones.[59] These negative consequences of binge eating and obesity should not be lost in the focus on anorexia nervosa and bulimia nervosa. Studies have shown that African American women are also less likely to practice health-promoting behaviors, such as frequent physical activity, and they are less likely to perceive themselves as overweight.[60] Some researchers suggest that although overweight African American women tend to be weight conscious, the absence of strong negative social pressure combined with a relatively positive body image may limit the extent to which weight-loss efforts are sustained.[61]

At present, we know very little about how these risk factors might interact in any individual. Do racially identified African American women whose profession leads them to be immersed in a predominantly Caucasian cultural context feel conflict about their own appearance-related goals? Is any such process present in upwardly mobile African American sorority members? If so, does that sense of conflict have any negative consequences for eating and dieting behaviors? These questions identify potentially fruitful avenues for further research.

Culture and Body Dissatisfaction

To help clarify the remaining issues in the African American risk literature, we return to the oft-mentioned risk factor of body dissatisfaction. Although body dissatisfaction has been identified as one of the strongest risk factors for eating disorders, it may be that body dissatisfaction should be defined differently for each group.[62] For Caucasian women, body dissatisfaction is strongly connected to the central issue of body size and weight dissatisfaction.[63] For African American women, body dissatisfaction is hypothesized to be associated either directly or indirectly with a *combination* of factors, including dissatisfaction with skin tone, higher or lower weight, low self-consciousness, and dissatisfaction with appearance.

At present, we do not know whether the combination of beauty-related concerns typical of African American culture operates purely as a protective factor against anorexia nervosa and bulimia nervosa or whether it increases the risk for either another type of eating disorder or some other form of disorder altogether. As described, there is evidence that it operates as a protective factor against restrictive eating and purging, because thinness receives so much less emphasis. But could it increase the risk for some other disorder? On the one hand, the flexibility and fluidity of the African American view of beauty likely mitigate against dysfunction: one can achieve an attractive style in many different ways, so there is less reason for distress. On the other hand, women who have difficulty developing a coherent sense of style that they can be proud of may be at risk for some form of dysfunction, perhaps having nothing to do with eating. These questions merit careful scrutiny by informed researchers.

Conclusion

Based on the literature we have reviewed here, we offer the following conclusions concerning African American women and their risk for eating disorders. Eating disorders have become increasingly more prevalent due in part to societal pressure on women to be thin in order to be viewed as attractive. However, African American women appear to experience some cultural protection against the pressure for thinness and hence against eating disorders that emphasize weight control (anorexia nervosa and bulimia nervosa). Within African American culture, one attains beauty through one's personal style, one's personality, and one's pride and self-confidence. Thinness thus plays a far less important role for African American women. Moreover, there is less pressure by the community to fit into a narrow definition of what others consider beautiful. The African American community embraces greater acceptance of the female body, no matter the size, with the result that African American women tend to view their own bodies with greater acceptance and satisfaction. Furthermore, for those women who become members of black Greek sororities, an additional layer of protection is provided. The Greek community encourages its members to develop strong ethnic identities, so members may be less influenced by the pressures of mainstream society. In addition, black Greek sororities encourage their members to be proud of being strong African American women. We believe that this sense of strength in one's identity as a woman reduces one's vulnerability to external definitions of what is ideal or what is attractive. In sum, based on the research on eating disorders within the black Greek community, it appears that this group advocates a healthier outlook toward weight and dieting and a positive outlook toward ethnic identity. Thus, membership in black sororities can only aid in the quest for positive examples of ethnicity, body size, and shape, in turn reducing the risk for eating disorders within the African American community. Black Greek-letter organizations appear to be quite relevant with respect to this important health issue, and one can only hope that they will remain a viable source of support for the next generation of African American college women.

Although many researchers have found that disordered eating is generally less prevalent among African American women, this should not be taken to mean that African American women are immune to eating disorders. African American women may be at increased risk for eating disorders that do not emphasize thinness, such as binge eating and obesity. It is an important service to African American women to emphasize these disorders and to point out the lower rates of health-promoting behaviors and exercise among them. At present, we know nothing about African American sororities' impact on the risk for these disorders. Finally, it is essential to recognize that there are some African American women with anorexia nervosa and bulimia nervosa. Studies have shown that such women are often misdiagnosed or diagnosed late because these disorders are less frequent in African American women. This could have a strong adverse effect on these women, because the longer treatment is delayed, the more severe the eating problem becomes due to the extended process of starvation.[64] Therefore, it is crucial to encourage African American women who are experiencing eating disorder symptoms to seek help and be treated.

Notes

1. Lawrence D. Cohen and Nancy E. Adler, "Women and Men Perception," *Psychology of Women Quarterly* 16 (1992): 69–79; Christian S. Crandall, "Social Contagion of Binge Eating," *Journal of Personality and Social Psychology* 55 (1988): 588–98; C. Sue Lamb, Lee A. Jackson, Patricia B. Cassiday, and Doris J. Priest, "Body Figure Preferences of Men and Women: A Comparison of Two Generations," *Sex Roles* 28 (1993): 345–58; Philip N. Myers and Frank A. Biocca, "The Elastic Body Image: The Effect of Television Advertising and Programming on Body Image Distortion in Young Women," *Journal of Communication* 42 (1992): 108–34.

2. David M. Garner, Paul E. Garfinkel, Donald Schwartz, and Michael Thompson, "Cultural Expectations of Thinness in Women," *Psychological Reports* 47 (1980): 483–91.

3. Meg Lovejoy, "Disturbances in the Social Body: Differences in Body Image and Eating Problems among African American and White Women," *Gender and Society* 15 (2001): 239–61.

4. Allen Frances, Harold A. Pincus, and Michael B. First, *Diagnostic and Statistical Manual Of Mental Disorders—Text Revision,* 4th ed. (Arlington, Va.: American Psychiatric Association, 2000), 583–95.

5. Diane J. Harris and Sue A. Kuba, "Ethnocultural Identity and Eating Disorders in Women of Color," *Professional Psychology Research and Practice* 28 (1997): 341–47.

6. Linda Smolack and Sarah K. Murnen, "Gender and Eating Problems," in *Eating Disorders: Innovative Directions in Research and Practice* (Washington, D.C.: American Psychological Association, 2001), 91.

7. Frances et al., *Diagnostic and Statistical Manual,* 587, 593.

8. Felice D. Kurtzman, Joel Yager, John Landswerk, Edward Wiesmeier, and Diane Bodurka, "Eating Disorders among Selected Female Student Populations at UCLA," *Journal of the American Dietetic Association* 89 (1989): 45–53; David E. Schotte and

Albert J. Stunkard, "Bulimia vs. Bulimic Behaviors on a College Campus," *Journal of the American Medical Association* 258 (1987): 1213–15.

   9. Jana G. Atlas, Gregory T. Smith, and Leigh A. Hohlstein, "Similarities and Differences in Caucasian and African-American Women's Eating Disorder Symptoms and Risk Processes," *International Journal of Eating Disorders* 32 (2002): 326–34.

   10. Ruth H. Striegel-Moore, Faith A. Dohm, Helena C. Kraemer, C. Barr Taylor, Stephen Daniels, Patricia B. Crawford, and George B. Schreiber, "Eating Disorders in White and Black Women," *American Journal of Psychiatry* 160 (2003): 1326–31.

   11. Ruth H. Striegel-Moore and Linda Smolack, "The Influence of Ethnicity on Eating Disorders in Women," in *Handbook of Gender, Culture, and Health* (Mahwah, N.J.: Lawrence Erlbaum, 2000), 227–54.

   12. Marjorie Crago, Catherine M. Shisslak, and Linda S. Estes, "Eating Disturbances among American Minority Groups: A Review," *International Journal of Eating Disorders* 19 (1996): 239–48; Shannon O'Neil, "African American Women and Eating Disturbances: A Meta-analysis," *Journal of Black Psychology* 29 (2003): 3–16; Amy R. Pemberton, Sally W. Vernon, and Eun Sui Lee, "Prevalence and Correlates of Bulimia Nervosa and Bulimic Behaviors in a Racially Diverse Sample of Undergraduate Students in Two Universities in Southeast Texas," *American Journal of Epidemiology* 144 (1996): 450–55.

   13. Eric Strice, "Risk Factors for Eating Pathology: Recent Advances and Future Directions," in *Eating Disorders: Innovative Directions in Research and Practice* (Washington, D.C.: American Psychological Association, 2001), 55; Laurie B. Mitz and Nancy E. Betz, "Prevalence and Correlates of Eating Disordered Behaviors among Undergraduate Women," *Journal of Counseling Psychology* 35 (1988): 463–71.

   14. Lovejoy, "Disturbances in the Social Body," 239–61.

   15. Sharon M. Desmond, "Black and White Adolescents' Perceptions of Their Weight," *Journal of School Health* 59 (1989): 353–58.

   16. Crandall, "Social Contagion of Binge Eating," 588–98.

   17. Ellen D. Schulken and Paul J. Pinciaro, "Sorority Women's Body Size Perceptions and Their Weight-Related Attitudes and Behaviors," *Journal of American College Health* 46 (1997): 69–74.

   18. Sharon L. Hoerr, Ronda Bokram, Brenda Lugo, Tanya Bivins, and Debra R. Keast, "Risk for Disordered Eating Relates to Both Gender and Ethnicity for College Students," *Journal of American College Nutrition* 21 (2002): 307–14.

   19. Schulken and Pinciaro, "Sorority Women's Body Size Perceptions," 69–74.

   20. Amy Mulholland and Laurie Mintz, "Prevalence of Eating Disorders among African American Women," *Journal of Counseling Psychology* 48 (2001): 111–16.

   21. Crago et al., "Eating Disturbances among American Minority Groups," 239–48; James J. Gray, Kathryn Ford, and Lily M. Kelly, "The Prevalence of Bulimia in a Black College Population," *International Journal of Eating Disorders* 6 (1987): 733–40; Andrea Powell and Arnold Kahn, "Racial Differences in Women's Desire to Be Thin," *International Journal of Eating Disorders* 17 (1995): 191–95.

22. Gray et al., "Prevalence of Bulimia," 733–40.

23. Kay Kosak Abrams, La Rue Allen, and James J. Gray, "Disordered Eating Attitudes and Behaviors, Psychology Adjustment, and Ethnic Identity: A Comparison of Black and White Female College Students," *International Journal of Eating Disorders* 14 (1993): 49–57; Crago et al., "Eating Disturbances among American Minority Groups," 239–48; Cynthia M. Frisby, "Does Race Matter? Effects of Idealized Images of African American Women's Perceptions of Body Esteem," *Journal of Black Studies* 34 (2004): 323–47; Clifford E. Rucker III and Thomas F. Cash, "Body Images, Body-Size Perceptions, and Eating Behaviors among African-American and White College Women," *International Journal of Eating Disorders* 12 (1992): 291–99.

24. Mary Louise Cashel, Dana Cunningham, Clarinda Landeros, Kevin O. Cokley, and Grace Muhammad, "Sociocultural Attitudes and Symptoms of Bulimia: Evaluating the SATAQ with Diverse College Groups," *Journal of Counseling Psychology* 50 (2003): 287–96; Peggy Evans and Allen McConnel, "Do Racial Minorities Respond in the Same Way to Mainstream Beauty Standards? Social Comparison Processes in Asian, Black, and White Women," *Self and Identity* 2 (2003): 153–67; Frisby, "Does Race Matter?" 323–47; Maya Poran, "Denying Diversity: Perceptions of Beauty and Social Comparison Processes among Latino, Black, and White Women," *Sex Roles* 47 (2002): 65–81.

25. Lisa R. Rubin, Mako L. Fittrs, and Anne E. Becker, "'Whatever Feels Good in My Soul': Body Ethics and Aesthetics among African American and Latina Women," *Culture, Medicine and Psychiatry* 27 (2003): 49–75.

26. Frisby, "Does Race Matter?" 323–47.

27. bell hooks, *Outlaw Culture: Resisting Representations* (New York: Routledge, 1994), 178–80; Rubin et al., "Whatever Feels Good," 49–75.

28. Michelle R. Hebl and Todd F. Heatherton, "The Stigma of Obesity in Women: The Difference Is Black and White," *Personality and Social Psychology Bulletin* 24 (1998): 417–26; Shiriki Kumanyika, Judy F. Wilson, and Marsha Guilford-Davenport, "Weight-Related Attitudes and Behaviors of Black Women," *Journal of the American Dietetic Association* 93 (1993): 416–22; Marisol Perez and Thomas E. Joiner Jr., "Body Image Dissatisfaction and Disordered Eating in Black and White Women," *International Journal of Eating Disorders* 33 (2003): 342–50; Powell and Kahn, "Racial Differences in Women's Desire to Be Thin," 191–95.

29. Rucker and Cash, "Body Images," 291–99.

30. Jack Demarest and Rita Allen, "Body Image: Gender, Ethnic, and Age Differences," *Journal of Social Psychology* 140 (2000): 465–72; Beth Molloy and Sharon Herzberger, "Body Image and Self-esteem: A Comparison of African-American and Caucasian Women," *Sex Roles* 38 (1998): 631–43; Powell and Kahn, "Racial Differences in Women's Desire to Be Thin," 191–95.

31. Evans and McConnel, "Do Racial Minorities Respond in the Same Way?" 153–67; Kumanyika et al., "Weight-Related Attitudes," 416–22; Lovejoy, "Disturbances in the Social Body," 239–61; Poran, "Denying Diversity," 65–81.

32. Crago et al., "Eating Disturbances among American Minority Groups," 239–48; Poran, "Denying Diversity," 65–81; Rubin et al., "Whatever Feels Good," 49–75.

33. Sheila A. Parker, Mimi Nichter, Mark Nichter, Nancy Vuckovic, Colette Sims, and Cheryl Ritenbaugh, "Body Image and Weight Concerns among African American and White Adolescent Females: Differences that Make a Difference," *Human Organization* 54 (1995): 103–14.

34. Beverly A. Greene, "What Has Gone Before: The Legacy of Racism and Sexism in the Lives of Black Mothers and Daughters," *Women and Therapy* 9 (1990): 207–30.

35. Lovejoy, "Disturbances in the Social Body," 239–61; Molloy and Herzberger, "Body Image and Self-esteem," 631–43.

36. Alexandra Berkowitz and Irene Padavic, "Getting a Man or Getting Ahead: A Comparison of White and Black Sororities," *Journal of Contemporary Ethnography* 27, no. 4 (1999): 50–57.

37. Alane R. O'Reilly, "The Impact of Membership in Black Greek Letter Organizations on the Identity Development of Black Students on Predominantly White Residential Campuses" (PhD diss., Ohio University, 1990); Katrice A. Albert, "Why Is She so Womanish? The Relationship between Racial Identity Attitudes and Womanist Identity Attitudes in African American College Women" (PhD diss., Auburn University, 2002).

38. Britta D. Dinsmore and Brent Mallinckrodt, "Emotional Self-awareness, Eating Disorders, and Racial Identity Attitudes in African American Women," *Journal of Multicultural Counseling and Development* 24 (1996): 267–77.

39. Janet E. Helms, "An Update of Helms's White and People of Color Racial Identity Models," in *Handbook of Multicultural Counseling* (Thousand Oaks, Calif.: Sage, 1995), 181–98.

40. William E. Cross Jr., "Negro-to-Black Conversion Experience: Toward a Psychology of Black Liberation," *Black World* 20 (1971): 13–27.

41. Diane J. Harris and Sue A. Kuba, "Ethnocultural Identity and Eating Disorders in Women of Color," *Professional Psychology Research and Practice* 28 (1997): 341–47.

42. Abrams et al., "Disordered Eating Attitudes and Behaviors," 49–57.

43. Jameca Falconer and Helen Neville, "African American College Women's Body Image: An Examination of Body Mass, African Self-consciousness, and Skin Color Satisfaction," *Psychology of Women Quarterly* 24 (2000): 236–43.

44. Bonnie Moradi, "Advancing Womanist Identity Development: Where We Are and Where We Need to Go," *Counseling Psychologist* 33 (2005): 225–53.

45. Albert, "Why Is She so Womanish?" 2126.

46. Rubin et al., "Whatever Feels Good," 49–75; Becky W. Thompson, "'A Way Outa No Way': Eating Problems among African-American, Latina, and White Women," *Gender and Society* 6 (1992): 546–61.

47. Falconer and Neville, "African American College Women's Body Image," 236–43.

48. Thompson, "A Way Outa No Way," 546–61.

49. Lovejoy, "Disturbances in the Social Body," 239–61.

50. Allan Feingold, "Good Looking People Are Not What We Think," *Psychological Bulletin* 111 (1992): 304–41.

51. Rubin et al., "Whatever Feels Good," 49–75.

52. Thompson, "A Way Outa No Way," 546–61.

53. Angela M. Neal and Midge L. Wilson, "The Role of Skin Color and Features in the Black Community: Implications for Black Women and Therapy," *Clinical Psychology Review* 9 (1989): 323–33.

54. Madeline Altabe, "Ethnicity and Body Image: Quantitative and Qualitative Analysis," *International Journal of Eating Disorders* 23 (1998): 153–59; Neal and Wilson, "Role of Skin Color," 323–33.

55. Falconer and Neville, "African American College Women's Body Image," 236–43.

56. Rubin et al., "Whatever Feels Good," 49–75.

57. Thompson, "A Way Outa No Way," 546–61.

58. Fannie July, Dorthy Hawthorne, Janice Elliot, and Wanda Robinson, "Weight Management Behaviors of African American Female College Students," *American Board of Nutrition and Fitness Journal* (May–June 2003): 71–72; Lovejoy, "Disturbances in the Social Body," 239–61.

59. O'Neil, "African American Women and Eating Disturbances," 3–16; Striegel-Moore and Smolack, "Influence of Ethnicity on Eating Disorders in Women," 239, 219.

60. July et al., "Weight Management Behaviors," 71–72.

61. Kumanyika et al., "Weight-Related Attitudes," 416–22.

62. Mitz and Betz, "Prevalence and Correlates of Eating Disordered Behaviors," 463–71; Strice, "Risk Factors for Eating Pathology," 55.

63. Cashel et al., "Sociocultural Attitudes and Symptoms of Bulimia," 287–96.

64. Thompson, "A Way Outa No Way," 546–61.

18

Modern Fraternities, Ancient Origins
Charles S. Finch III

> Modern man does not understand how much his "rationalism"
> (which has destroyed his capacity to respond to numinous symbols
> and ideas) has put him at the mercy of the psychic "underworld."
> He has freed himself from superstition (or so he believes) but in
> the process he has lost his spiritual values to a positively dangerous
> degree. His moral and spiritual tradition has disintegrated, and he is
> now paying the price for this break-up in world-wide disorientation
> and dissociation.
>
> —Carl Jung

Psychocultural Background

There has always been a certain tendency in modern Western culture to disparage and dismiss the values and customs of the past; to view with condescen-
sion and scorn the lifeways, practices, and cultural perspectives of ancient and
traditional peoples. This attitude of derision and contempt has fueled most of
the systematic and relentless destruction of traditional cultures in every part of
the globe. Although the conquest and mass destruction of indigenous peoples
have produced devastating consequences, there are even more subtle effects that
have exerted negative repercussions on the perpetrators of such conquest. Carl
Jung realized this truth early in the twentieth century, when his investigations
into the human psyche revealed the existence of a common archetypal bedrock
in the "collective unconscious" of humanity out of which symbols emerged
that drove not merely human behavior but also the process by which humans
struggled to become psychically whole.[1] Jung realized that these symbolic and
mythical psychic substrates exerted a far greater impact on the evolution of human consciousness and "self-sense" than all the carefully constructed rational
edifices of Western learning ever did.

In the end, Jung came to a startling and, to him, alarming conclusion: Western science and philosophy, at least since the time of Descartes (seventeenth century), if not earlier, had systematically devalued and disempowered the symbolic essence of human existence. Myth, instead of being a consciously created symbolic expression of an otherwise inexpressible reality, was relegated to the realm of the fairy tale and puerile storytelling, artificially denuded of any and all truth it ever contained.[2] Jung observed that myths were "depersonalized archetypes," and archetypes were "personalized myths"; clearly, myths and unconscious archetypes were two ends of an unbreakable continuum of human psychic life. They were coactualizers and coenablers of human mental evolution. Looked at this way, there is no real way to discard or destroy myths or the symbols that constitute them, just as it is impossible to discard the human psyche.

Western civilization, however, had embarked on a systematic campaign to exterminate myth and symbol; among scientists, scholars, and clergy, myth was deactivated and anathemized. In institutionalized Christianity, symbolism was pared down to a handful of canonical figures, signs, and icons, the cross being the most paramount. But Jung realized that this eradication campaign carried with it a terrible cost to the eradicators: the archetypes that represented interior symbols and myths no longer had any appropriate outlet or means of expression. Consequently, they did not disappear but merely remanifested in revised and aberrant forms. Jung expresses it as follows: "They [cultural symbols] are important constituents of our mental make-up and vital forces in the building up of human society; and they cannot be eradicated without serious loss. Where they are re-pressed or neglected, their specific energy disappears into the un-conscious with unaccountable consequences. The psychic energy that appears to have been lost in this way in fact serves to revive and intensify whatever is uppermost in the unconscious. . . . Even tendencies that might in some circumstances be able to exert a beneficial influence are transformed into demons when they are repressed."[3] The archetypes were as active as they had ever been, but now, they were exteriorizing themselves in the most insidiously destructive ways imaginable. For example, the reworking of the sacred swastika of antiquity, a deep structural symbol in myriad lands around the world, became the defining emblem of the Nazis and their genocidal Aryan ideology, launching a war that would claim more than 50 million lives.[4] The color red—ancient symbol of the blood of the mother presiding over the production and sustaining of new life—became the color of revolutionary Marxism, whose seminal idea of abolishing the state was soon awash in rivers of blood. Stalin killed 20 million of his countrymen, Mao 20 million, and Pol Pot 2 million (these numbers may be conservative).⁵ And despite anticlerical themes, each new modern ideology produced its "savior," sacred scripture, "religious" symbol, and vision of paradise. For the Nazis, it was Adolf Hitler, *Mein Kampf,* the swastika, and the "thousand-year reich." For the Communists, it was Karl Marx, *Das Kapital,* the hammer and sickle, and the "withering away of the state"— a nirvanic ideal if there ever was one. As Jung put it, "Not only has civilized Germany disgorged its terrible primitivity, but Russia is also ruled by it."⁶

What does any of this have to do with modern fraternities? They are the remnants of ancient and traditional institutions for initiation and rites of passage, archetypal portals erected by ancient cultures. The passwords, secret knowledge, symbols, peer group bonds, and lifelong relationships of mutual support all reflect sociocultural institutions whose origins are discernible in the dim mists of antiquity. Fraternities, moreover, are distantly related to Masonic organizations, which consciously stress their role as the inheritors and keepers of ancient and secret knowledge. The archetypal drives that Western society has so diligently endeavored to de-energize and delete from modern culture are as strong as ever and still impel men to find an outlet for them in venues of reenacted initiation, ritual, symbol, and myth. The persistence of organizations like fraternities responds to our deepest and most ineradicable imperatives.

The hazing that is so characteristic of modern fraternities—and so tenaciously persistent—is but a simulacrum of the manhood trials emblematic of the rites of passage among traditional peoples in Africa, America, Asia, and the South Pacific. The physical trials in these tribal manhood rites involved, among other things, ritualized pain, deprivation, and suffering, often severe enough to lead to death. These initiation rites were designed to test and train young males for the rigors and responsibilities of manhood; indeed, the initiate was, in effect, undergoing a metaphorical and mythical "death" of his old child-self so that, through these trials, he could be "reborn" as a true man. Modern hazing—whether in fraternities, the military, or sports teams—is impelled by the same deep-seated, if unacknowledged, motives.⁷ However, fraternity hazing lacks the serious purpose of tribal manhood initiation; the life and sustainability of the tribe depended on producing strong, capable, resourceful men ready to give their lives to the service of family, clan, and community. In the tribal setting, boys became men without passing through adolescence. Put another way, adolescence was compressed into the two- to three-month period of the rite of passage. The extended teenage angst so characteristic of modern society—with its often destructive self-indulgence and rebellion—simply did not exist. There was no place for it; ancient and traditional societies did not have the luxury or the inclination to support it.

It can therefore be said that the roots of the modern fraternity can be traced to two related processes: the initiation into special occult or spiritual knowledge, and the rite of passage of manhood training. In traditional society, one could not be a full and participating member without initiation. In effect, *everyone* was initiated at some basic level. One could hardly consider oneself a real person without knowing where one belonged and what one's place in life was. Perhaps that is the reason that even today, there is a mild, detectable, but usually unexpressed disdain among fraternity members for those not in fraternities or those not "properly" initiated. This chapter concentrates on the first-named process—initiation into occult knowledge or the "mysteries," whose origins predate the beginning of the dynastic period in the Nile Valley (4300 B.C.), some say as early as 10,500 B.C.[8]

Ancient Mysteries: The Case of Egypt

In that part of the Old World west of the Indus River, all sages, scientists, and philosophers deferred to Egypt—called *Kemit* ("the black land") or *Ta-Meri* ("the beloved land") by its own people—and to the Nile Valley civilization generally. The latter encompassed the combined geocultural complex of Kemit and Cush, later called Egypt and Ethiopia. It is beyond the scope of this essay to explore the comprehensive Nile Valley civilization, except to say that Egypt's roots are traceable southward, and it is entirely appropriate to echo what the Ethiopian priests told Diodorus in the first century B.C.— that Egypt was in fact a colony of Ethiopia.[9] Egypt's temple system is the focus of this discussion because the learning accumulated and preserved there for more than four millennia garnered the awe and admiration of all lands.

It is evident that Egyptian learning, like a seamless spiritual, scientific, and philosophic fabric, reaches back beyond the dawn of history. But soon after the beginning of its dynastic period (4300 B.C.), a stupendous edifice of knowledge and learning organized itself inside Egypt's temple system. Although this process began unfolding much earlier, it becomes documentable from about that time. However, the Egyptians' outlook on dispensing this ever-burgeoning knowledge was entirely different from ours, for there was no belief in or provision for mass education. Thus, when we look at this ancient Nile world, we are seeing a mentality and a psychological perspective very unlike our own.[10] The

Egyptians simply did not see things the way we do, and failure to recognize this essential truism has created impossible conundrums for modern scholars who—with notable exceptions—fail to comprehend this ancient civilization in all its immensity.

Ancient Egyptian society was a hierarchal one, with well-defined castes and social categories. Through the ups and downs of a 4,000-year history, this hierarchal system was never overthrown; there was not even a trace of what we would call a democratic revolution. The pharaoh and his family resided at the top of this pyramidal structure, which then flared downward through the nobility and the various occupational castes of priest-scribes, artisans, merchants, and farmers. A man followed the profession of his ancestors and expected his descendants to do the same. However, there was an important exception to this social calculus: a young person of outstanding ability or talent could rise beyond the otherwise rigorous boundaries of his social class. In fact, both the pharaoh and the priesthood were always on the lookout for such rare and unusual individuals. From the Old Kingdom on, the annals of Egypt are filled with stories of "new men," commoners who, through extraordinary talent, diligence, and fidelity to the pharaoh, rose to the highest reaches of service in the pharaonic hierarchy. Moreover, it was not unheard of for a peasant boy to be plucked from the mud of the Nile-soaked agricultural fields and recruited into the temple to be trained as a priest-scribe. Thus, the seemingly unvarying social hierarchy provided an outlet, an "escape clause," for the truly talented. In this way, Egypt differed dramatically from Hindu India, where caste status was not only inherited but also rigidly permanent. No low-caste person, no matter how brilliant, could ever hope to rise above his station, to break through the inflexible bonds of caste membership.

Particularly in the high epochs, the number of priests was vast, especially at the "Vatican" of ancient Kemit, Karnak Temple in Thebes (modern-day Luxor). Karnak Temple was the most immense temple complex in antiquity, where, on any given day, 80,000 persons lived and worked.[11] But, mirroring society itself, there was a priestly hierarchy. Although every priest was literate, those at the lowest level were little more than copyists and functionaries. From among these priestly hordes, only a precious few were deemed worthy candidates for higher initiation. Members of the royal family and nobility might encounter fewer access barriers to the higher echelons of the priesthood, but no one passed upward through the ranks without passing the tests and trials of initiation, including the pharaoh. Most pharaohs, though of royal birth, had to be successful temple initiates. There was no automatic succession from father to eldest son; there was always a pool of royal sons to choose from. The initiation process began in childhood, and eventually, the most suitable candidate for rulership revealed himself. The higher one advanced, the more stringent and demanding the tests. The most rarefied levels of the priesthood were occupied by a few extraordinary men full of fathomless knowledge, wisdom, sagacity, and impeccable character.

The temples were filled with Egyptian *and* Nubian priests. This point is important, because until the late period, Egyptians did not admit foreigners into the temples. Nubians were no more foreigners in Egypt than Scotsmen are foreigners in England. In fact, after the eighth century, the most important center of Amon worship was located in Napata in Cush, and at various times, Egyptian priests migrated there to serve in that temple rather than remain in Egypt. Greeks began to visit Egypt in the eighth century b.c.—the poet Homer and Solon the lawgiver being two famous examples. The first Greek to be accepted for entry-level initiation in Egypt was Thales in the late seventh century b.c. Thales may have been admitted because he was actually of Phoenician extraction, and Phoenicians had been closely associated with Egypt since 1200 b.c. Pythagoras was the first—and only—Greek to be allowed to ascend to the highest levels of temple initiation, having spent twenty-two years studying in the Egyptian temple system. But it is worth pointing out that Pythagoras was only half Greek; his father (some say his mother) was Phoenician.[12]

The Pythagorean Initiation

Pythagoras is an important historical figure from a number of standpoints, but he is especially relevant to this discussion because his late biographers, most notably Iamblichus (circa a.d. 300), provided descriptions of his initiation—the only extant records of higher initiation in the Egyptian priesthood. It is hard to gauge just how accurate these reports are; certainly, some parts of the descriptions must be taken with the proverbial grain of salt. Nevertheless, when corroborated from other material, it may be possible to arrive at some semblance of what initiation in the inner temple looked like. One thing is certain: foreigners attempting to win admittance to the temple had a harder time than natives. The priests went out of their way to discourage Greeks, whose impatient and skeptical mentality simply made them unfit for the deeper knowledge the temple had to impart. Greeks always wanted to ask questions, and there was little tolerance of such questioning attitudes in the temple. Pythagoras was given all manner of demeaning and meaningless tasks to do as a way of discouraging him. His persistence, patience, humility, and cheerful willingness to accept whatever trial was put before him eventually won the priests over, but then, Pythagoras was a most unusual man.

Born in 570 B.C. and raised on the isle of Samos, Pythagoras was the son of a wealthy merchant and a woman named Parthenis, which probably accounts for claims that his was a virgin birth (*parthenos* means "virgin"). He proved to be unusually gifted from childhood, and as he grew older, he traveled around the islands of the eastern Mediterranean to study with the most learned Greeks of the period. It was Thales, usually considered the first Greek philosopher, and himself a student in Egypt for seven years, who encouraged Pythagoras to travel to Egypt for further education. Since he came from a prominent family and, though but a youth of eighteen, possessed a brilliant reputation, Pythagoras had no trouble securing a letter of introduction and recommendation from Polycrates, the tyrant of Samos who, on account of a thriving mercantile relationship, was a personal friend of the pharaoh Amasis. Upon seeing the introductory letter from Polycrates, Amasis provided the young Pythagoras with a letter of his own, bidding the priests of Heliopolis to accept the young Samian postulant into the temple for instruction. Greeks had been trickling into Egypt for some time, seeking higher knowledge. Orpheus, the acknowledged, semilegendary originator of the Greek religious system, was said to have studied in Egypt. As noted earlier, Homer and Solon reportedly traveled to Egypt, but the priests of the temple were far from welcoming to the unlettered interlopers from the Grecian isles. In fact, they told Solon, "You Greeks are but children, there is no such thing as an old Greek."[13] Hoary tradition, in fact, forbade the initiation of foreigners in Egypt. But by 600 B.C., Egypt's political circumstances had drastically changed, and after his accession in 568 B.C., Amasis depended on Greek mercenaries to fill his military ranks and Greek seafaring cities for much-needed trade. Not wanting to offend Polycrates, he allowed Pythagoras to receive instruction at the temple.

The priests of Heliopolis could not reject the pharaonic command outright, but they hit upon the stratagem of passing the buck. Insisting that all their learning had been lost and that their temple instruction was at a very low ebb, they sent Pythagoras to the Temple of Ptah in Memphis. These priests were no more welcoming than their confederates in the Temple of Ra, and continuing the ruse, they too insisted that they no longer possessed any significant knowledge and sent Pythagoras south to the Temple of Amon at Karnak. The priests of Amon were no more eager than their brethren to take in this presumptuous foreigner, but they had nowhere else to send him. So they decided to simply discourage him. For a solid year, they gave him meaningless and demeaning tasks, such as digging holes and then filling them in again. They did everything possible to make life uncongenial and unfulfilling for Pythagoras. But Pythagoras did everything he was told, and he did so with an efficiency and cheerfulness that astounded the priests. He would not give up, desist, or be discouraged; he accepted every humiliation with a joyful spirit. Finally, the priests of Amon recognized his extraordinary personal qualities and admitted him to the temple for initiation.

Pythagoras spent twenty-two years studying in Egypt, traveling to all the major temples and learning from the most celebrated sages and priests in the land. No other Greek was ever allowed to study in Egypt for so long, and Pythagoras doubtless would have stayed and studied even longer if he had not been taken captive and sent to Chaldea when the Persians overran Egypt (525 B.C.). He would stay in Chaldea another seven years (some say twelve), where he continued to receive instruction under the Chaldean magi. Thus, as a man of knowledge, Pythagoras went higher and farther than any Greek before or after his time. He was the quintessential philosopher and in fact coined the term *philosopher* to describe himself as a "lover of wisdom." It can be said that all Greek philosophy descends from Pythagoras. Eventually, he would open a famous school in southern Italy at Croton, and his students seeded the entire Greek world with the Pythagorean system. However, in about his hundredth year, his school was attacked, sacked, and burned by a local mob led by a spurned applicant. Some sources say that Pythagoras died in the fire; others claim that he escaped only to allow himself to starve to death in Tarentum.[14]

Despite the space devoted to the life of Pythagoras, his main import for this essay is that the steps of his initiation came to light much later and were preserved by his biographers. Although there is no way to guarantee the accuracy of these reports, they give us a glimpse into the inner workings of temple initiation. Each temple was dedicated to a particular *neter*, be it Ra, Ptah, Amon, or Osiris, but sacred learning was always under the tutelage of Thoth (e.g., *Djehuti*), the Divine Master of all wisdom and knowledge. Thoth was the reputed author of forty-two sacred books and was always referred to as the "Thrice Greatest." The Greeks called him Hermes, and sacred knowledge in late antiquity—even up through the Renaissance in Europe—was always thought of as *hermetic* knowledge.

Regardless of which temple a novice was assigned to, if he was selected for the "higher mysteries," it was inside the Great Pyramid that he was first initiated. Initiation of this kind was granted to very few, even among Egyptians.

Only in the late period was the rare foreigner such as Pythagoras granted such a privilege. Nineteenth-century French author Paul Christian says: "Initiation, the crown of knowledge, was not granted to all, even among members of the Egyptian priestly class. In the sacred colleges there was a hierarchy of aptitudes and functions, a scale of scientific grades, each of which had a test that had to be passed. Each test gave the measure of the degree of intelligence and moral strength possessed by the aspiring initiate. He who failed in one of these tests was never allowed a second chance."[15]

Even after the priests had agreed to consider Pythagoras for initiation, he was interrogated minutely concerning his background. If that interrogation had brought to light any untoward information about the applicant, he would have been refused admission by secret ballot, which could not be gainsaid even by the pharaoh. The earliest tests were grueling, designed to cause applicants with insufficient fortitude to turn back. However, once a postulant survived this phase and the sacred and secret symbols had been explained to him, he could not turn back. A series of tests awaited him, and if he failed to pass any one of them on the first try, he would never again see the light of day. Some say that he would quietly be put to death; others say that he would be confined within the walls of the temple for life. The Egyptian priests were known far and wide for their obsessive, life-or-death vows of secrecy concerning their sacred knowledge. In assuring the preservation of that secrecy, they were implacable. Pythagoras took that lesson to heart; he too became famous for the absolute secrecy in which he conducted his instruction. Subsequently, most Greek philosophers adhered to the Pythagorean rule—really, the priestly rule of the Egyptian temple—and refused to speak of certain matters deemed sacred.

The Mysteries of Initiation

Iamblichus gives the fullest description of what actually happened during the initiation process.[16] Given the ancient law of secrecy, it is hard to know how much of what he relates can be trusted, but his account certainly influenced the later Masonic and Rosicrucian systems to which modern fraternities are related. Iamblichus says that the true entrance to the initiates' arena was actually between the paws of the Sphinx, the massive human-headed lion statue—possibly as old as 12,500 years—that sits just east of and below the pyramid complex on the plateau of Giza. The Sphinx was connected to the Great Pyramid by an underground system of corridors. These corridors constituted a skillfully contrived maze such that anyone who managed to enter them without a trained guide would inevitably find himself back at the place where he started. The initiates who led and guided the novice on the first night of his journey were called (in Greek) *Thesmothetes,* or "guardians of the rites." The novice, eyes blindfolded, was commanded to maintain complete silence at all times and not to ask questions, no matter what he was told to do. The bronze door cut into the body of the Sphinx was opened by a hidden mechanism; one of the Thesmothetes led the way with a lamp, and the other guided the novice by hand down a flight of twenty-two steps.[17] Through another door invisible to the naked eye, the trio entered a circular cavern.

In this room, the formal trials commenced. The Thesmothetes led the postulant to the edge of what he was made to believe was the precipice of a deep chasm. He was informed that the abyss on whose edge he was standing surrounded the temple and was designed to swallow up any profane or unworthy person who sought to penetrate the holy mysteries. He was instructed to stand silently, cross his hands over his chest, and remain blindfolded or suffer the pain of death. Absolute obedience was the only chance he had of getting through the ordeal alive. Already, the increasingly uncanny and eerie quality of the experiences and sensations tested the postulant's will, fortitude, and strength of character.

While he stood and waited, full of trepidation of the unknown, each of the two Thesmothetes dressed themselves in white linen robes, tied with a gold belt for one and a silver belt for the other, and put on, respectively, a lion's mask and a bull's mask. The gold belt is a solar symbol; the silver, a lunar one. The lion's head represents Atum, under whose zodiacal sign in June–July the solar zenith occurs, which marks the beginning of the Nile flood (an important event in Egypt). The bull is Apis, representative of the Nile god Hapi and a figuration of the Taurean zodiacal age (4436 to 2275 B.C.)—the era in which the pyramids were built. The Thesmothetes in their respective garbs represented *Pi-Rā,* the Sun, and *Pi-Yāh,* the Moon (literally, "ascending sun" and "ascending moon," respectively). These powers governed the "evolutions" of the sun and moon that, as Christian states, exerted "the most direct influence on the creation, the dissolution, and the renewal of earthly things." The idea of ascension, from the word *pi,* embodied the postulant's progress through the initiation ordeal.

Next, in Christian's description, the blindfold was snatched off the postulant while, simultaneously, a trapdoor opened with a deep roar out of which rose a mechanical specter brandishing a scythe, loudly intoning frightful threats against anyone so presumptuous as to disturb the peace of the dead. The novice thus abruptly came face-to-face with three terrible-looking figures—including the masked Thesmothetes—just as the scythe brushed his head seven times. If he did not faint, the mechanical figure retreated and the trapdoor closed. The Thesmothetes then took off their masks, congratulated him on having passed the first test of courage, and prepared him for the next stage in his journey.

The novice was then handed a lamp, and yet another hidden mechanism opened a portal to the passageway through which he would continue his travels. The corridor was so low and narrow, however, that the only way to get through it was to crawl with the lamp in hand. This passageway—dark, narrow, cramped, and forbidding—was called the "tomb," and it engendered feelings of almost unconquerable claustrophobia. If the candidate could not, after a few minutes, overcome his hesitation, he was neither berated nor judged but simply blind-folded and led away. However, there would be no second chance; one failure was sufficient to bar the neophyte's progress in the mysteries permanently. If the Thesmothetes judged that he had not received or seen any important secrets, he might be released and allowed to return to the world; otherwise, the ex-postulant would spend the rest of his life as a menial laborer in the temple, never to leave its confines. However, if the postulant could summon the courage to embark on the next forbidding phase of this life-or-death journey, he entered the tunnel, crawling like a worm, as the bronze door fell back into place behind him. Almost as soon as he began moving through the crawlspace, another doom-laden voice boomed around him, promising death to anyone fool enough to covet such sacred knowledge and the power that came with it. The voice repeated the threat seven times at precisely spaced intervals, and as he crawled through the tunnel with the voice echoing in his head, the candidate imagined himself being entombed alive. He began to feel his grip on sanity loosening, and the only way to hold on to its strands was to force himself forward, hoping that the lamp did not go out. If that happened, he was done.

Finally, after seemingly endless crawling, the postulant noticed that the tunnel widened and the roof rose as the ground sloped downward. At last, he arrived at the edge of a deep cavity—an inverted cone—that appeared bottomless. An iron ladder was attached to the side of this cavity leading downward and disappearing into the darkness. Again, the postulant had to make what seemed to be a life-or-death decision—go back or descend into the unknown. He eventually realized that, whatever might be waiting at the bottom of the ladder, there was no other way to proceed. After climbing down seventy-eight rungs, he reached the bottom only to find that a fresh shock awaited him; below the bottom rung, there was nothing but another yawning chasm, and by now, his lamp was beginning to flutter. The postulant was paralyzed with indecision. With his light about to go out, he did the only thing he could—slowly climbed back upward, looking for another means of escape. As he mounted the ladder, rung by rung, he caught sight of a crevice in the flutter of the lamp's flame; looking more closely, he found that there was an opening large enough for a man. Inside the opening, another series of steps presented themselves, and with a certain desperation, he climbed into the crevice and began to walk up the stairs. Christian describes what happened next: "After a few moments of calming reflection he rises and enters this crevice. The stairway turns in a spiral. At the twenty-second step is a bronze grating through which the postulant can see a long gallery lined each side by . . . sculpted sphinxes: there are twenty-four. Between them the wall is covered with frescoes representing mysterious personages and symbols. These twenty-two pairs of pictures face each other, lit by eleven bronze tripods in a line running down the middle of the gallery. Each tripod carries a crystal sphinx in which burns an amianthus wick in incense-laden oil."[18]

Having attained this arena, the postulant was greeted by a hierophant called *Pastophore* ("carrier of the shepherd's crook"), the guardian of the sacred symbols. The postulant, now called "Son of Earth," was congratulated on having passed a test that caused most to perish, by having discovered the "path of wisdom." He was now an "aspirant" and came under the guidance and protection of Isis, although his trials were by no means over. For the first time, certain sacred symbols were revealed and explained to him. The aspirant was fully committed; unless he mastered all tests in front of him, he would never be allowed to leave the temple alive. The twenty-two symbols that confronted him were the *arcana* ("initiated knowledge") that embodied the Science of the Will, informing all true wisdom and producing all real power. Though debased, modern tarot derives from these arcana. The etymology of the word *tarot* even gives a clue to their function: in Egyptian, *Ta* means "earth" or "world," and *rud* means "a flight of stairs." Thus, the tarot symbol keys, as *Ta-rud,* are the twenty-two steps rising from the world.

Here, for the first time, the aspirant was given, one by one, an identification and explanation of each arcanum and its associated number and letter. Taken together, all twenty-two constituted a complete wisdom and knowledge system, hidden from ordinary view. Each arcanum could be visually meditated upon or uttered as a mantra, gradually bringing into the student's purview the authentic, interlaced reality of the divine, mental, and physical worlds. Each arcanum personified a law in the spiritual, energetic, and material domains that interacted with the contemplator to change him in permanent ways. These phenomena are fundamental to life itself and govern its evolution in the universe.

It is beyond the scope of this chapter to discuss the arcana in detail, but they consist of the following:

Arcanum I—The Magus: Will: Number 1
Arcanum II—Opening of the Secret Sanctuary: Knowledge: Number 2
Arcanum III—Isis, Queen of Heaven: Action: Number 3
Arcanum IV—The Cubic Stone: Realization: Number 4
Arcanum V—The Master: Occult Inspiration: Number 5
Arcanum VI—The Two Paths: Ordeal: Number 6
Arcanum VII—The Chariot of Osiris: Victory: Number 7
Arcanum VIII—Ma'at: Balance: Number 8
Arcanum IX—The Veiled Lamp: Prudence: Number 9
Arcanum X—The Sphinx: Destiny: Number 10
Arcanum XI—The Tamed Lion: Power: Number 20
Arcanum XII—Sacrifice: Death by Hanging: Number 30
Arcanum XIII—The Scythe: Transformation: Number 40
Arcanum XIV—The Sun: Initiative: Number 50
Arcanum XV—Seth: Unavoidable Fate: Number 60
Arcanum XVI—Tower Struck by Lightning: Ruin: Number 70
Arcanum XVII—Star of the Magi: Hope: Number 80
Arcanum XVIII—Twilight: Deception: Number 90
Arcanum XIX—Flaming Light: Earthly Happiness: Number 100
Arcanum XX—Reviving the Dead: Renewal: Number 200
Arcanum 0—Ammit, the Crocodile: Expiation: Number 300
Arcanum XXI—The Crown of the Magi: The Reward: Number 400

After having each arcanum carefully and fully explained, the ordeal continued. This time, the Pastophore led the aspirant to a door that opened onto a hallway leading to a blazing furnace. The Son of Earth was directed to take his courage in hand and go forth into the burning mouth of what looked like certain incineration. However, as he walked through the passageway, it became apparent that the fiery blaze was an optical illusion. But no sooner was the aspirant relieved by this discovery than he found himself at the lip of a large, dark pool. Just then, a real wall of flame leaped up behind him, making it impossible to turn back. Slowly he entered the pool, whose surface rose higher on his body until all but his head was immersed in the water. Just then, the bottom began to rise, and as he continued to move forward, he found himself moving upward and out of the pool. He had passed the twin ordeals of fire and water, the two elements whose interaction had formed the universe and the world. What is more, the evolution of the universe continues to be driven by this interplay of fire and water.

Upon moving out of the pool, the aspirant saw before him another flight of steps leading to a platform overshadowed on three sides by a high arcade. At the end of the platform was a brass door in which a large metal ring—in the shape of a snake with its tail in its mouth—jutted out from sculpted lion's jaws. Symbolically, the lion is associated with both fire and water. (As noted earlier, it represents the heat of the summer sun, especially at the solstice, and when the sun rises in the constellation of Leo, the Nile begins to flood.) The serpent ring—the *uroboros*—is the symbol of eternity. By now, the furnace behind him no longer breathed fire, and an oppressive darkness settled over the aspirant. Another disembodied voice assured him that death awaited him if he turned back; only by going forward was there the possibility of salvation. Not knowing what else to do, the aspirant grasped the ring, only to have the floor give way beneath him, leaving him suspended in midair as he held frantically to the ring. The danger was more apparent than real—although the aspirant did not know it—because several heavy cloths were strung across the pit beneath him to serve as a safety net should he fall. However, if he managed to hold on, the trapdoor would close under him, allowing him to set his feet down. The moment he did so, the brass door opened before him. In front of him stood a dozen *Neocores* ("guardians of the sanctuary"), who rebandaged his eyes and led him by torchlight through the last passageway into the Great Pyramid. At strategic points, the procession had to pass through doorways guarded by protectors to whom passwords and special signs had to be given to be permitted to pass. The entrance through each door required a separate password and sign.

At last the procession of thirteen—twelve Neocores and one aspirant—arrived at the center of the pyramid. It is worth digressing a bit to note that if the terminus of the initiation so far described was located in the compartments of the pyramid that are now known, it would most likely have been in the so-called King's Chamber. Moreover, if there is any truth in the foregoing description, it would explain why there were granite plugs permanently blocking the entrance to the Ascending Passage—the only possible passageway from outside into the King's Chamber (and the Queen's Chamber below it). That is, the Great Pyramid was *never* intended to be entered except by the secret passageway from the Sphinx itself, resting one-quarter mile away. No such passageway between the Sphinx and the Great Pyramid has yet been discovered, but ultrasound studies have detected hidden chambers beneath the Sphinx. As reported by Graham Hancock and Robert Bauval, an underground chamber beneath the Sphinx was discovered in 1982.[19] However, no further work in this domain has been done, with one exception: "The single exception was Thomas Dobecki's seismic work in the early 1990s. . . . This resulted in the discovery of what appears to be a large, rectangular chamber beneath the forepaws of the Sphinx."[20] If there are hidden chambers beneath the Sphinx, it is reasonable to assume that they also exist beneath the bedrock of the Great Pyramid.

The Neocores and the aspirant were now in the Central Crypt of the Great Pyramid, and assembled before them were the chief priest, or hierophant, and the entire College of Initiates. The hierophant was clothed in a rich purple robe, and on his forehead he wore a circular gold diadem decorated with seven stars; he sat on a silver throne resting on an upraised platform. The initiates, all wearing long, white linen cloaks with plain, undecorated gold diadems circling their heads, stood in three semicircular ranks below the supreme prelate, facing outward toward the aspirant. Purple, known from remote antiquity as the "royal color," was ordinarily reserved for the pharaoh alone. That the prelate also wore purple indicated that in this occult lodge—this spiritual sanctuary—he ruled as king. In this setting, the pharaoh himself would bow to him, much like a Christian king would kiss the ring of the pope when visiting the Vatican. However, even above this spiritual king ruled one greater: Isis, Queen of Heaven. A magnificent statue of Isis rose up behind and above the throne. She wore a triangular silver crown adorned with a fan of twelve golden rays. On her breast rested a golden rose, symbolic of the universe, fixed at the center of a golden cross. Her arms were stretched forward with the hands turned down, each with five golden rays pointing toward the earth. The ten golden rays emanating from the hands plus the twelve projecting upward from the crown totaled twenty-two—the number of the arcana.

What is striking here is the paramount role of the goddess Isis in the initiation to the higher mysteries. The supreme stature of Isis stems from her position as mother of the sun (Horus); personification of the moon; queen of heaven, whose abode is the star Sirius; and, above all, sister-wife of Osiris, whom, through her power and knowledge, she resurrected when he was killed and dismembered by Set, the Adversary. All these Isisian themes adumbrated the initiatory path, culminating in the climactic ceremonies enacted in the Central Crypt of the Great Pyramid.

As yet the Son of Earth saw none of this spectacle. He was brought before the throne of the prelate still blindfolded and compelled to stand motionless.

Then the hierophant began to speak, mocking the aspirant's pretensions, dismissing his presumption, dismantling every vestige of self-regard he might have brought into the ordeal. Even yet, the aspirant might find himself thrown into a dark dungeon to live out his days in bitter remorse, subsisting on nothing but bread and water. The hierophant fell silent for a space, as if pondering his next action—whether to carry out this dire threat or allow the initiation to continue. For all the aspirant knew, the entire ordeal might have been for nothing, and feelings of despair, anguish, fear, and exhaustion pushed him to the edge of madness. The tension was unbearable, but even this was a test: could the aspirant summon the strength of will to hold himself together when his nerves had been strained past the breaking point? "At last the Hierophant calls him forward. What came next was the oath of oaths: . . . our clemency deigns to show itself greater than your insincerity; all it will ask of you, even if you wish to be restored to liberty, will be your solemn oath that you will never reveal to anyone the least detail of what you have seen [and] heard this night. Will you give this oath?"[21] When the aspirant responded "I will," the Neocores forced him to his knees, whereupon the hierophant made him repeat an oath of secrecy that was inflexible, immutable, and deadly serious, the violation of which meant that he would be hunted down and have his tongue and heart cut out without mercy. This oath of sacred secrecy was never violated, even in Greece, until later Christian times. Greek authors such as Herodotus, Diodorus, and Plutarch, among others, refused to divulge certain sacred information covered by this oath in any of their writings. Though Pythagoras never invoked the pain of death as punishment, he was as rigorous and absolute about the oath of secrecy during his lifetime as any Egyptian hierophant. It is why it is said that he never wrote anything down. The aspirant, upon completing the oath, was now considered an entry-level member of the College of Wisdom and called a *zealot* ("fervent student"). However, his oath-giving was not complete, for the hierophant compelled him to swear an equally binding oath of absolute, unquestioning obedience to the hierophant himself, as the highest representative, practitioner, and protector of the mysteries.

A new scenario unfolded. The sound of popping, roaring, deafening thunder was produced using naphtha, calculated to rattle already overtaxed nerves. At this exact juncture, the bandage around the aspirant's eyes was abruptly torn away, and the sight that greeted him was bound to make him quail: in the weird, flickering light of the crypt, every Neocore stood over him with a long, sharply pointed sword aimed directly at him, almost touching his body. Even a slight thrust from a single sword would prove fatal. The display was meant to indelibly impress upon the aspirant's psyche the inexorable play of justice should any of his oaths be forsaken. Then, as the swords were lowered, two goblets were brought to him, one containing a fatal poison and the other a harmless liquid. He was commanded to take without thinking or hesitation one of the two goblets; fate would decide whether he was truly meant for initiation. Should he hesitate for even a second, a funereal drum roll sounded, a black shroud was thrown over him, and he was taken from the crypt, destined never to go a single step further in the mysteries. He was incarcerated for seven months and given certain books to read, filled with moral instruction. He was then brought before the hierophant again and given the same choice. If he followed through this time, he was released from his dungeon but must serve in the temple for the rest of his life in the lowly capacity of zealot. As was true of all these tests, the prospect of death, though terrifyingly real to the aspirant, was an illusion. Each cup contained wine mixed with a little myrrh to give it a bitter taste but was otherwise harmless.

A final test remained—deceptively enticing, yet the only one with an actual prospect of death. The zealot was congratulated on his success and sent to a room where he was washed, given luxurious clothes to wear, provided with a sumptuous meal and fine wine, and serenaded with beautiful, sensuous music. Unknown to him, the wine was slightly drugged; perfume and incense filled the air. Then a group of alluring females—all daughters of the priests—came into the room to begin a round of dancing calculated to inflame the zealot's passions. Two of them danced around him, ensnaring him with a garland of flowers, each making every effort to entice him to embrace her. Should he succumb to this weakness, one of the Neocores who had slipped in behind him would strike him dead with a knife. Should he remain unmoving while this pantomime was played out, eventually the music would stop and the dancers would disappear; a parade of initiates would file in to congratulate the zealot on passing this final and most difficult of tests, the test of self-control.

From then on, the zealot was allowed to progress as far as his ability and character could take him. There were nine grades of mysteries, and few could ascend all nine levels to the summit, which might take as long as forty-four years. But it is pertinent to question again the accuracy of the foregoing description of the initiation process of the Egyptian temple. It is supposed to reflect what Pythagoras (twenty-two years) and Plato (thirteen years) actually underwent. However, given the rigid penchant for secrecy—binding the initiate with fearful, unbreakable oaths—such a peek into this world would not have been possible until the collapse of the civilization of antiquity with the advent of Christianity.

Certainly, there is a strong element of the fantastic in this description—repeatedly creating a mise-en-scène that would put Hollywood to shame. But none of it was beyond the powers of the Egyptian priesthood to arrange. Just as clearly, the picturesque *tableaux vivants* presented are highly colored by Greek sensibility: all of the titles and names, for example, are Greek rather than Egyptian. But what is indubitably clear is that Pythagoras, Plato, and other Greek sages who were permitted to enter the temple in Egypt were the purveyors and transmitters of Egyptian thought, knowledge, and wisdom to the modern world. That Greek-letter fraternities even exist is due to the temple initiations of Pythagoras, Plato, and other Greek philosophers in Egypt.

Conclusion

This essay has summarized the occult initiation into the mysteries that developed to the highest degree in ancient Egypt and spread to other lands. In Phoenicia, Assyria, Greece, and Rome, the temple rites all carried the impress of ancient Egyptian wisdom and methodology. Even after the fall of Rome and the rise of Christendom, the Arabic-Muslim world did much to carry the knowledge of the past forward; it was, in fact, that world that would reeducate Europe in the ancient knowledge lost in the Dark Ages. Hermetic and Masonic lore owed a great deal to Arab-Moorish occult learning, and Muslim symbols still abound among the Masons. The fraternities of today are offshoots of Masons who—legitimately or not—consider themselves to be the keepers of the legacy of ancient Egypt. Thus, the seeds of the contemporary Greek-letter fraternity system can be traced to the banks of the ancient Nile—in truth, all the way back to the very sources of the Nile itself.

In the modern world, tradition and a sense of history have diminished markedly in the affairs of the world. There is a prevailing sense that those things that are new and "in the moment" must claim priority. However, the excessive emphasis on individualism and the present in all domains of life has contributed to a profound contemporary malaise and alienation. The youth, especially (though not exclusively), seem rootless and uncommitted to anything beyond self-indulgence and sensual gratification. Thus, to counteract these social and psychic centrifugal forces, many human beings reach out almost desperately to collective entities in search of stable moorings and psychological security. They join churches, causes, gangs, and, yes, fraternities. Fraternities, by their very nature, represent links to the past, however tenuous they sometimes seem.

Moreover, they promote peer bonds that enable members, in many instances, to function as productive, contributing members of society. Fraternities usually have programs of charitable giving, support for education, and social outreach; these altruistic aspects of fraternities might even be called their raison d'être.

We have seen that among ancient and traditional peoples, rites of passage fulfilled a dual function: initiation into special occult or spiritual knowledge, and manhood training. Modern fraternities came into being in response to these same deeply felt imperatives, attenuated though they may have been in recent times. These imperatives are at the heart of what it means to be a man and a person, even in contemporary society. Rites of passage, at their most effective, develop both the inner and the outer man—man in his spirituality and in his materiality—seamlessly and consistently. The effective procedures for enabling this twofold, indispensable development were fully realized in ancient and traditional societies. Something was lost in the heedless, headlong drive to enshrine progress and modernity as the prime determinants of life; men have sought to compensate for that loss, and the fraternity system is one result. It has been said that the only thing new is that which has been forgotten. Through the fraternity system, modern men are vouchsafed the small possibility of glimpsing something of the oldest, deepest, and most ineluctable part of themselves. For many such men, it makes all the difference in the world.

Notes

Epigraph from Carl G. Jung, "Approaching the Unconscious," in *Man and His Symbols* (Garden City, N.Y.: Doubleday, 1964), 93.

1. Carl G. Jung, *The Archetypes and the Collective Unconscious*, trans. R. F. C. Hull (Princeton, N.J.: Princeton University Press, 1968), 3–53.

2. Ibid.

3. Carl G. Jung, "Approaching the Unconscious," in *Man and His Symbols* (Garden City, N.Y.: Doubleday, 1964), 93.

4. See Mathew White, *Source List and Detailed Death Tolls for the Twentieth Century Hemoclysm*, http://users.erols.com/mwhite28/warstats.htm. White's total for World War II is actually 55 million, 42 million attributed directly or indirectly to the Nazis.

5. It is impossible to get exact numbers for the "democides" committed by certain Communist regimes, but the number of deaths is staggering. Prior to World War II, there is a consensus that Stalin was responsible for the deaths of 20 million countrymen by famine or execution. Mao was responsible for between 20 million and 50 million Chinese deaths during the Great Leap Forward and the Cultural Revolution. Pol Pot,

by comparison, caused the deaths of a "mere" 2 million Cambodians. See White, *Source List.*

   6. Jung, "Approaching the Unconscious," 94.

   7. See Malidoma Patrice Somé, *Of Water and the Spirit* (New York: Penguin Books, 1994), 191–302, for a description of Dagara manhood rites, including a descent into the underworld.

   8. Graham Hancock and Robert Bauval, *The Message of the Sphinx* (New York: Crown, 1996).

   9. *Diodorus Siculus, Book II,* trans. C. H. Oldfather (Cambridge, Mass.: Harvard University Press, 1929), 93.

   10. R. A. Schwaller de Lubicz, *Sacred Science*, trans. André VandenBroeck and Goldian VandenBroeck (New York: Inner Traditions International, 1961), 14–16.

   11. Serge Sauneron, *The Priests of Ancient Egypt*, trans. Ann Morrissett (New York: Grove Press, 1969), 55.

   12. See Kenneth S. Guthrie, *The Pythagorean Sourcebook and Library* (Grand Rapids, Mich.: Phanes Press, 1987), for biographical material on Pythagoras.

   13. Plato, *Timaeus and Critias*, trans. Desmond Lee (New York: Penguin Books, 1979), 35.

   14. See Edouard Shuré, *The Great Initiates*, trans. Gloria Rasberry (Blauvelt, N.Y.: Rudolph Steiner Publications, 1960), 265–369, for an extended discussion of the life, times, and mission of Pythagoras and his school.

   15. Paul Christian, *The History and Practice of Magic*, trans. James Kirkup and Julian Shaw (New York: Citadel Press, 1969), 88.

   16. The account in this section is drawn mostly from Christian, *The History and Practice of Magic,* 81–126. (See also note 9 above.)

   17. The number twenty-two is significant; it is the number of arcana that will be encountered later.

   18. Christian, *The History and Practice of Magic,* 93–94.

   19. Hancock and Bauval, *The Message of the Sphinx,* 93.

   20. Ibid.

   21. Christian, *The History and Practice of Magic,* 117.

19

"'Cuz I'm Young and I'm Black and My Hat's Real Low?"

A Critique of Black Greeks as "Educated Gangs"

Matthew W. Hughey

On a spring day in 2006, I was walking across the campus of the University of Virginia on my way to a regular meeting with a friend of mine, a young African American professor. Our weekly conversations generally ran the gamut from critical theory to the iconography of Ernesto "Ché" Guevara, from Africana philosophy to campus racism, from our take on the local political economy to the culture of black Greek life. The last was a personal topic, because he is an Alpha and I am a Sigma. We took a seat on a bench outside the campus library and began our ruminations. After a few minutes, a couple of my fraternity brothers walked by, and I rose to greet them. They immediately informed me that they had been involved in an altercation with a few Alphas the previous evening. "A fight? . . . You mean you got in an argument?" I asked. "No bruh, a real fight," they said. After they recounted the ins and outs of what had happened, I offered to introduce them to my friend. "He's a professor here, . . . and also an Alpha," I mentioned. "I don't even want to talk to an Alpha," one of my fraternity brothers stated abruptly. With disgust, I retorted, "You've got to be joking. Perhaps you should respect him as a professor rather than see him only as an Alpha." "Sorry," they both replied in unison, "but I just can't do it." Highly embarrassed by this divide-and-conquer, Greek-induced myopia, I gave them the fraternal handshake and ended our conversation. I rejoined my friend on the bench and apologized for my fraternity brothers' behavior. He suddenly interrupted: "Don't even worry about it. . . ." Then his voice trailed off. With his gaze fixed on the ground in front of him, he took a deep breath and said, "It's just that sometimes we act like educated gangs."

The issue of black Greek-letter organizations (BGLOs) as "educated gangs" is a controversial one, to say the least. On the one hand, many believe that BGLOs are funnel organizations for the inculcation of the new black elite. On the other hand, some see BGLOs as paradigmatic reflections of the decline of Western civilization and morality. There are many arguments on both sides of whether BGLOs are gangs, and it is necessary to define each entity independently.[1]

Black Greek-Letter Organizations

BGLOs are predominantly college-based social service organizations with a combination of foci: the development of African American identity, community uplift, brother- or sisterhood, and social justice. BGLOs' genesis stretches back to Freemasonry (especially Prince Hall); Phi Beta Kappa, the first Greek-letter organization; various African traditions; and the nature of collegiate demographics and racist beliefs and attitudes at the turn of the twentieth century.[2] BGLOs generally consist of the nine members of the National Pan-Hellenic Council (NPHC), the umbrella organization for historically black, international Greek-letter fraternities and sororities.[3] Both individually and collectively, BGLOs sponsor programs on the national and local levels.

There are many differences between BGLOs and gangs. Sociologist Talcott Parsons defines an *organization* as a social system that focuses on the contributions toward, and the attainment of, specific goals within the scope of the larger social system.[4] Max Weber writes that "an organization is a system of continuous purposeful activity of a specified kind."[5] Peter Blau and W. Richard Scott argue that the organization is a social unit "established for the explicit purpose of achieving certain goals."[6] Organizational forms, such as BGLOs, are intentional and purposeful, and they are in some state of continuity. Furthermore, there is a collective orientation toward the active realization of goals that is absent or much less developed in gangs.

Gangs

Gangs are groups of individuals who share a common identity and, in common parlance, engage in illegal activities. Some anthropologists believe that the gang structure is one of the most ancient forms of human organizations. The word *gang* is generally pejorative. The origin of the word is unknown, and the term lacks a clear definition even in the law. "There is no consensus across the large number of gang-involved cities on types of gangs . . . [and] efforts to establish a uniform definition of a gang suffer from a major dilemma—lack of consensus."[7]

The nominal term *gang* eliminates many other forms of social organization, leaving the core definition as an essentially criminal enterprise. Relying so heavily on an axiological definition is problematic for several reasons. First, if laws change, do certain groups become, or stop being, gangs? The penchant for a value-defined definition can lead to a great deal of conceptual slippage owing to the changing nature of jurisprudence. Second, because of the immoral or unethical underpinnings of the word *gang*, many organizations that would technically be included under the definition would not commonly be thought of as gangs. Many would probably heartily disagree if the Southern Christian Leadership Conference and the illegal marches and sit-ins led by Dr. Martin Luther King Jr. (a member of Alpha Phi Alpha) were classified as a gang and gang-related behavior. Many might consider the Black Panther Party of Dr. Huey P. Newton (a member of Phi Beta Sigma) a gang because its members carried guns and recruited heavily from the underclass, yet they were extremely vigilant in not only respecting the law but also educating people about it and upholding it. Given the increasing "gang involvement in legitimate business enterprises . . . such as . . . laundering money and participating in financial crimes,"[8] were Kenneth Lay and the others involved in the 2004 Enron scandal a gang? Third, gang definitions are complicated by the tendency toward tautological explanations. "Using delinquent behavior as a criterion makes a possible outcome of gang activity one of the defining characteristics."[9] That is, if criminal activity is a distinctive feature in the ability to differentiate gangs from nongangs, the logic is circular. Fourth, although they often engage in violent and illegal behavior, gangs are often responses to some social-structural precondition such as poverty, racism, unemployment, or miseducation, and that response is not always negative. As writer and activist Jacob Riis writes, "The gang is a distemper of the slums; a friend come to tell us something is amiss in our social life."[10] Many gangs—the Blackstone Rangers, Latin Kings, and even Crips and Bloods—have engaged in community service endeavors. Controversy over the positive attributes of gang behavior was manifested in the debate over the December 2005 execution in California of Crips cofounder Stanley Tookie Williams, who was an antiviolence activist and a Nobel Peace Prize nominee.

The Debate

Given the preceding definitions, why are BGLOs even mentioned in the same breath as gangs? Most scholars agree that gangs do not meet the basic definitional criteria of organizations. Yet the charge has been made that BGLOs portray many of the same stereotypical characteristics as street gangs—from the cultural expression and treatment of gang colors, signs, and verbal calls to the material manifestations of violence, substance abuse, and culturally entrenched patterns of misogyny.

   As with many contentious debates, there is evidence on all sides. Accordingly, this chapter does not try to either dispel or validate the critique per se, although it touches on both the similarities and differences between BGLOs and gangs. Rather, this chapter emphasizes the discursive move to call BGLOs "educated gangs," what this naming accomplishes or negates, and what systems of meaning (from racism to beliefs in cultural deficiencies) already exist to legitimate such a demarcation. It is not hard to believe that those who call BGLOs educated gangs are intentionally seeking to link this form of organized blackness with deviance. As Tom Hayden writes in *Street Wars: Gangs and the Future of Violence,* "No one is more vilified today than a 'gang member,' with the exception of an 'international terrorist' or a 'narco-terrorist,' . . . these shadowy personas are increasingly morphed into a single archenemy of society. The mainstream perceptions of order and well-being depend on the projection of an opposite, the barbarian."[11] Using "educated gang" as a disparaging pseudonym for BGLOs enacts a distinct labor of representation whose impact is made real by those who uncritically accept the nominal term. However, the thesis cannot be cavalierly dismissed, because BGLOs have adopted some of the negative aspects of gangs through their violent hazing, intergroup violence, and betrayal of their founders' missions.

Analytic Framework

Recent years have witnessed a resurgence of research on identity, culture, and power amidst the ontological constructions of blackness.[12] Many BGLOs are laboring to construct their missions in such a way as to physically, emotionally, and symbolically (re)claim blackness.[13] Although this recuperation of blackness in the face of an omnipresent white racism can lead to, protect, and propagate many negative ganglike and antidemocratic forms within BGLO culture, to posit that BGLOs construct *only* such narrow ontological manifestations of blackness is flatly inaccurate. The process by which certain images and discursive frames of BGLOs come to the pages of the press, television screens, and Internet journals and blogs, as well as the manner in which their style, scope, and substance are treated, is always a negotiation between competing interests. In acknowledging this conflict, a critical postmodern lens is offered to evaluate this debate. Combining the work of scholars Michel Foucault, Stuart Hall, bell hooks, and Cornel West, I argue that the present educated gang thesis is arrested within an axiological binary that delimits both a contextual (or cultural) and a relational (or critical) understanding of BGLOs.

West's discussion illuminates how representations of blackness are cast into simplistic binary oppositions of positive-negative and good-bad that privilege dominant ideology vis-à-vis white aesthetics and normative discursive frameworks.[14] In grappling with this particular form of "double consciousness," BGLOs are experiencing a postmodern crisis of identity: they are caught between a quest for white approval and the push to move past internalized racism and feelings of inferiority.

This is nothing new. BGLOs' origins are a conflicted combination of antiracist and anticlassist missions that are simultaneously incorporated into a highly assimilative, early DuBoisian "talented tenth" agenda.[15] In a more hopeful and positive sense, critiquing this tension offers a glimpse of those aspects of human experience and identity that may be used as a moral foundation to counter the dominant ideology that names BGLOs gangs in the first place.

There are three predominant responses to the educated gang thesis. First, many simply agree that BGLOs have devolved into quasi-gangs. Second, critics state that BGLOs should not worry about how they are perceived, because all organizations commit both positive and negative actions. Third, other critics claim that BGLOs should work to portray only positive actions and avoid exposing any "dirty laundry," so that they can combat predominant agendas, as well as unintentional forms, of antiblack racism.

Although these three approaches are common, they are all normative and axiologically driven. Comparisons between good and bad representations of BGLOs, even when based on the best of intentions to redress imbalances in the field of racial representation, are inherently reductive because they fail to address questions of ambivalence or transgression. Drawing on the work of scholar Stuart Hall, who writes that "'Black' is essentially a politically and culturally *constructed* category,"[16] this chapter argues that we must investigate the educated gang paradigm with the knowledge that BGLOs were founded, and can still work in large part, to *reconstruct* blackness as a nonfixed, fluid subject that can transcend white judgments of whether black actions are positive or not. Scholar bell hooks argues: "Discussions of representation among African Americans usually occur within the context of emerging identity politics, again with the central focus on whether images are considered 'good' or 'bad'. The idea of a good image is often informed simply by whether or not it differs from a racist stereotype. . . . Issues of context, form, audience, experience (all of which inform the construction of images) are usually completely submerged when judgments are made solely on the basis of good or bad imagery."[17] Reducing studies of BGLOs to the conclusion that they are either like gangs or not labors to reinstall the status of BGLOs within the scope of a reactive and counterproductive politics. Such politics are purchased in the field of representation at the price of the repression of counterhegemonic or even directly resistive and self-determinative BGLO actions.

In this sense, the act of representing BGLOs as an educated gang is what sociological theorist Michel Foucault refers to as a "truth game." Foucault aims "to sketch a history of the different ways in our culture that humans develop knowledge about themselves . . . [and] to analyze these so-called sciences as very specific 'truth games' related to specific techniques that human beings use to understand themselves." Accordingly, a critical understanding of BGLOs can occur through examining the four registers of "truth claims" laid out by Foucault:

(1) Technologies of production, which permit us to produce, transform, or manipulate things; (2) technologies of sign systems, which permit us to use signs, meanings, symbols, or signification; (3) technologies of power, which determine the conduct of individuals and submit them to certain ends or domination, an objectivizing of the subject; (4) technologies of the self, which permit individuals to effect by their own means or with the help of others a certain number of operations on their own bodies and souls, thoughts, conduct and way of being, so as to transform themselves in order to attain a certain state of happiness, purity, wisdom, perfection, or immortality.[18]

The critical interrogation of BGLOs depends not on an agenda of collecting acquisitions or concealments of "truth." It depends on the history of "veridictions," understood as the forms by which discourses capable of being declared true or false are articulated concerning a certain domain of things.

We must ask the necessary, but by no means absolute, questions regarding the processes of subjectivization and objectivization that made it possible for the subject qua subject (BGLOs as educated gangs) to become a valid object of knowledge in the first place. Of course, this is not a matter of ascertaining how this "knowledge" of BGLOs as gangs was constituted—doing so would be little more than a hallowed hagiography of history—but a matter of discovering why and how such a claim is being made in the present moment. Such an undertaking gestures toward the enormity of the task when one is attempting to comprehend and recuperate a critical, cultural, and reflexive understanding of BGLOs.

Examining the Truth Claim: Black Greeks as Educated Gangs

Few studies compare Greek organizations to gangs. One of the first was William J. Chambliss's study, which found that despite their participation in strikingly similar delinquent activities, Greek and gang differences in education and in economic and social positioning led to the labeling of the gang as deviant but excused the Greek organization.[19] Both Marcos Martínez's and Carol J. Pinkerton's studies found that Greek organizations and gangs are similar in several ways, from abusive hazing rituals to recognizable markings and symbols.[20]

Although these studies used empirical and direct observations to make their claims, we must consider that neither gangs nor BGLOs are static, monolithic entities. There are variations in both, and their understanding is dependent on context. Frederick Thrasher's study of gangs in Chicago found five types of gangs: diffuse, solidified, conventional, criminal, and secret.[21] Other researchers have demonstrated that many community members do not consider gangs as deviant.[22] Irving Spergel observes that gangs exist in a "bewildering array, complexity, and variability of structures. Gangs may not be simply solitary, loosely knit, or bureaucratic so much as variable small networks ... more or less cohesive or clearly structured at various periods of their development."[23] BGLOs are also vastly heterogeneous. However, the amount of scholarly attention paid to BGLOs is minuscule in comparison to gang research, although there is some diffuse scholarship on BGLO subtopics.

It is important to empirically delineate the key aspects used to underpin the educated gang thesis before the ideological and discursive move to align the two is appropriately deconstructed. The following sections concentrate on the themes of competition and conflict, hazing, rape and substance abuse, social constructions of black masculinity and femininity, social structure, cultural aesthetics, philanthropy and civic action, and collegiate versus alumni members.

COMPETITION AND CONFLICT

Both established gangs and BGLOs have chapters scattered throughout a specific geographic space. BGLOs as well as larger gangs stretch from coast to coast, but both are sometimes more concentrated in specific regions. When either gangs or Greeks are in close proximity to others of like kind, there is a strong likelihood for conflict and competition. Since the founding of the first Greek organizations, they have competed through athletics, grades, and campus awards.[24] More specifically, within the BGLO tradition, they have competed in step shows, to attain social dominance on campus, and to work out personality or leadership animosities. Like Greeks, gangs also compete, but generally over control of an underground economy based on stolen goods or illicit drugs. Spergel writes that "the development of drug enterprises by gang cliques or personal animosities by leaders of 'renegade' groups or sections frequently may result in more violence . . . between gangs."[25]

Both gangs and BGLOs exercise salutations and defamations of one another in the public sphere. As Elizabeth C. Fine writes, "Like other Greek organizations, black fraternities and sororities are intensely competitive and this competitive spirit comes to the fore in the crack or cut. Many cracks are based in the very strong African-American tradition of verbal dueling, expressed in such well-known folklore genres as the dozens (or sounding), rapping, and signifying and marking."[26] The performance of these salutations and criticisms creates, according to Richard Bauman, a "differential identity,"[27] whereby the user's verbal assaults reflexively help to define the user as well as the recipient, while also entertaining onlookers. The social performance of both saluting and defaming rival groups operates within two poles that are integral to the black community. Fine writes, "The first pole is a tendency toward identification and unity . . . the second pole is a tendency toward competition and difference."[28] Unfortunately, like gangs, BGLOs are sometimes involved in violent acts. This violence often stems from unresolved issues such as instances of public disrespect gone too far, conflicts over significant others, or personal antagonisms that grow and embroil the brotherhood of both groups.

HAZING

From the stages of initiation to prophyte (new member) hazing, both Greeks and gangs have notorious reputations. As Martínez writes, "it would be difficult to compare one group's customs and traditions to another. There are certain rituals in various social groups that one cannot compare with explicit detail, due to the uniqueness of each group's rituals, but looking at the group to see if a certain ritual is practiced is quite possible."[29] Both gangs and BGLOs have initiation ceremonies. According to scholars, the process in both venues involves elements of physical strength and endurance. However, gang initiation tends to be much more physically violent—referred to by Robert Rhoads as "street baptism"—whereas BGLO initiation tends to be more extended, can be just as violent, but is generally centered on emotional and mental stress.[30] Other similarities include alcohol and drug abuse, physically taxing activities, and destruction of property. "There is always a price to pay for admittance into these groups, whether it is monetary, physical, or illegal."[31]

Selecting members for initiation is also a similar process among gangs and Greeks. Pinkerton writes:

> The selection process served to implement a criterion, set by the organization. . . . These meaning units seem to support the experiences of fraternity, sorority, and gang members as having gone through a selection process in order to join their perspective organizations. . . . Numerous meaning units (e.g., "being paddled" and "walking the line") that reflected a sense of abuse during initiation for fraternity, sorority, and gang members were observed during the research. This category seemed to reflect fraternity, sorority, and gang members' experiences as participants in initiation rituals that were abusive and varied in severity ("being shocked" vs. "being forced to eat dog biscuits").[32]

BGLO hazing came to the forefront of public attention due in part to Spike Lee's film School Daze. Since the film's release in 1988, many scholars have affirmed that hazing in Greek organizations is a vicious problem. The works of Hank Nuwer, Ester Wright, Walter Kimbrough, Ricky Jones, and Gregory S. Parks and Tamara L. Brown all give a thorough review of hazing in general, as well as the specifics of BGLO hazing.[33] R. A. Schroth found that thousands of criminal offenses in Greek culture "virtually disappear . . . thus reinforcing the illusion of being both separate and special that is at the heart of the Greek mystique."[34] M. Geraghty found that in contrast to the high levels of physical violence in most fraternities, sorority hazing is much more likely to involve emotional and psychological abuse, along with alcohol consumption; however, physical violence among sororities is increasing, approaching the level in fraternities.[35]

Despite any contextual differences, most scholars maintain that hazing is having a severe impact on Greek organizations, and they conclude that BGLO hazing practices are posing much more severe risks to members than those of their white counterparts. It is no exaggeration that BGLO hazing has led to serious injuries and deaths in recent years. Many point to this aspect of BGLO culture as a prime reason why the "educated gang" label sticks. Scholars point to many reasons why hazing in its numerous forms (e.g., violent beatings, procurement of rare items, alcohol and drug abuse) persists: the secrecy of the process, which helps solidify an in-group–out-group symbolic boundary; the fostering of a community that is perceived as both institutional and longitudinal; the creation of self-respect; the search for a collective sense of meaning and identity that is reified through an intense mental and physical process. However, there has also been resistance to hazing from within BGLOs. Many of the organizations have tried to quell the violence through a variety of measures, including an across-the-board ban on pledging from the NPHC that took effect in the early 1990s. "Despite the radical change in the BGLO pledge process, there has actually been an increase in hazing incidents and reports of hazing incidents since this historic decision."[36]

RAPE AND SUBSTANCE ABUSE

Among Greeks and gangs, underage alcohol consumption and illegal drug use have strong parallels. Although alcohol and drug abuse is widespread on college campuses, one study found that members of Greek organizations were much more likely to abuse alcohol than their non-Greek counterparts.[37] Kuh and Arnold write, "the greatest disappointment is that fraternities, and those who choose to support them, have not taken action to address the cultural context of these groups so that the behavior of fraternity members is closer to the goals espoused by the fraternity."[38] In a particularly negative take on Greek life, Baier and Whipple discovered that "one reason fraternities have come under so much negative scrutiny is that in addition to discipline problems, legal liabilities, injuries, and deaths caused by fraternity hazing, sexual assaults, racism . . . and alcohol substance abuse, educators have been unable to find any evidence that fraternities contribute to the positive moral, ethical, and intellectual development of their members."[39]

According to Martínez, "As studies have shown, gangs may be in the business of selling more drugs than fraternities, and fraternities may have a higher degree of alcohol consumption than gangs, but the commonality between the two is that both of the groups have a high participation in the areas of drugs and alcohol."[40] Other researchers found that alcohol use might be a predictor of fraternity membership itself.[41] Ester Wright in *Torn Togas* states, "many fraternities glorify drinking and may deliberately encourage women to overdrink. . . . Clearly a strong link exists between the use of alcohol and rape, which explains how sexual assault has become so prevalent at fraternities.[42]

Some studies have shown that a woman's chance of being sexually assaulted as a college student is as high as 20 to 25 percent,[43] and others report that key fraternity practices such as group loyalty, group secrecy, alcohol use, and emphasis on competition create an atmosphere conducive to rape.[44] Martínez writes, "One of the most common crimes committed between the two groups is sexual assault on females."[45] Other scholars have found that one of the main reasons for joining a gang or a fraternity is the increased access to females that such membership is rumored to bring.[46]

BGLOs often have a better reputation than their white Greek counterparts in terms of both substance abuse and sexual harassment or assault. Tyra Black, Joanne Belknap, and Jennifer Ginsburg found several differences between the white and black Greek systems. The most notable with regard to alcohol abuse and sexual assault is that white Greek parties often occur in private settings, while BGLO parties are generally in public settings that disallow many forms of sexual assault. They write, "During parties, white fraternities can consume alcohol and drugs, play loud music, have access to bedrooms, and behave in a sexually aggressive manner in the privacy of their own houses, whereas black fraternity parties are formally supervised, which makes each fraternity member more accountable for his own behavior and that of his brothers and others."[47]

Most research shows that BGLOs do not engage in the same high-risk activities that promote alcohol and drug abuse and sexual assault as white Greek organizations or common gangs do. However, this does not mean that such actions are absent within BGLO circles. As Nancy Boyd-Franklin and A. J. Franklin write in *Boys into Men*, "One of the 'codes of the brotherhood' hinges on bragging about sexual conquests, real and imagined. 'Getting some' and then bragging about it to other brothers is a merit badge of masculinity that permits entry into black 'manhood.'"[48] In a similar fashion, S. B. Boeringer states, "Due to hypermasculine environments in which fraternities . . . exist and the strong peer influence to 'be a brother' . . . this peer acceptance may be more reinforcing than in other settings."[49] Within both gangs and Greek organizations, rape, sexual assault, and a hypermasculine, misogynistic bravado underpin much of the subcultural logic and, as a consequence, are often normalized.

SOCIAL CONSTRUCTIONS OF BLACK MASCULINITY
AND FEMININITY

The fourth facet used to draw parallels between BGLOs and gangs is the similarity in specific constructions of black masculinity and femininity. In *Cool Pose: The Dilemmas of Black Manhood in America*, Richard Majors and Janet Billson explore the coping strategies used by young black men to deal with social pressures. They write, "Of all the strategies embraced by black males to cope with oppression and marginality, the creation of the cool pose is perhaps the most unique . . . tough talk and aggressive posturing that value ways of expressing coolness."[50] The "cool pose" is often attributed to both gangs and BGLOs. Greg Dimitriadis writes in *Friendship, Cliques, and Gangs*, "When we do see notions of community among black men, it is usually through the relatively large and methodologically diverse body of work on contemporary gangs."[51] Similar to BGLOs, members of gangs act as though they are "brothers." Majors and Billson write, "all the members of the gang [are] brothers . . . [and] if members could come to think of themselves as brothers, they would be likely to develop more respect for fellow members and ultimately more empathy for the gang as a whole."[52]

Almost all discussions of black gangs include what Dimitriadis calls "'the brotherhood ideology' . . . with the very common and reductive notion that one's gang is one's 'family.'"[53] Likewise, many scholars view Greek organizations as a kind of familial structure.[54] Martínez writes, "Both types of members within these groups are usually in a delicate stage of development (14–24 years old), and often times without the guidance of their nearby family."[55] Although some scholarship has tried to dispute the claim that black collectives (especially groups of black men) automatically engage in a close-knit family-like relationship that leads to illegal behavior—for example, Mitchell Dunier's *Slim's Table*, an ethnographic look at older black men in Chicago[56]—such work often reinforces dominant ideas about black masculinity centered on physical and verbal aggression, hypermasculinity, sexual exploits, and lack of an Anglo work ethic. Other texts argue that in order for black men to "make it," they must shun social collectivities with other black men. One example is the critically acclaimed *Hope in the Unseen*, which chronicles how young Cedric Jennings escapes the "hood" to matriculate at an Ivy League school.[57]

If such an analysis is accepted, then, "'success' often means isolating oneself from others, pulling away from the dangers of unpredictable and open pernicious social networks. . . . 'Failure,' in turn, often means falling prey to the lure of 'peer pressure,' the 'brotherhood ideology' that marks nearly all accounts of gang life."[58] This hyperindividualism is predicated on a Eurocentric dualist logic, as epitomized by René Descartes' famous phrase *cogito ergo sum* ("I think, therefore I am"). Many of our social and political paradigms stem from this dualism and enable individualism, capitalism, egoism, fragmentation, alienation, and isolation. This runs counter to the African philosophical tradition of *Ubuntu* ("I am because we are"). The primary theme of this philosophy, which is often encoded in BGLO principles concerning brotherhood, is the idea that individual identity is never separable from one's sociocultural environment. As Jonathan Lee and Fred Hord write in *I Am Because We Are,* the move to articulate the communal rather than the individual "self" can be applied to "evaluate and counter the dehumanization to which people and ideas of African descent have been subjected through the history of colonialism and of European racism . . . [while] at the same time philosophy also holds the promise of helping to counter . . . self-dehumanization, a dehumanization that is the product of that same history of racism and manifests itself in the false universalism of so much European thought."[59]

This is applicable not only to black masculinity but also to the collective black femininity of black sororities and female gangs. As Sudhir Alladi Venkatesh states, when women have been studied in this context, "researchers portrayed women as little more than auxiliaries to male social roles." Venkatesh's study of Black Sisters United, a Chicago federation of "girl gangs," found that female gangsters were involved in stereotypical masculine and feminine activities as well as negative and positive endeavors—from drug sales to "bake sales, fashion shows, and political demonstrations."[60] Anne Campbell argues in *The Girls in the Gang* that female gang activity has been a neglected area of study. Further, she remarks that when women are studied, the scholarly findings reflect sexist ideologies, because women are portrayed as important only when they affect male members.[61] The effect is nothing short of an outrageous combination of racism and sexism that excuses whiteness, criminalizes blackness, and invisibilizes femininity regardless of race. In either case, both gangs and BGLOs become key institutions for the formation of masculinity and femininity, especially when they act as a surrogate family structure.

SOCIAL STRUCTURE

Martínez writes, "With gangs and fraternities having similar activities, closeness in ages, and contemporary attitudes, it is hypothesized that gangs and fraternities have very similar structures."[62] Both groups generally have a hierarchical leadership, are often spread out in different chapters, and are highly organized. In terms of leadership, Martin S. Janjowski's study of various gang structures found that the "vertical/hierarchical" model is predominant in gangs.[63] Most BGLO leadership style is the same, with the same functioning positions as gangs. National diffusion of gang and BGLO membership is also a similarity. The establishment of new chapters is a point of pride among members and also brings more visibility, income, and growth to the group. The highly organized nature of both groups is also an attractive incentive for potential members. Boyd-Franklin and Franklin identified ten reasons why African American youth join gangs: "protection, self-esteem, status, racial or cultural identity, friendship, a sense of belonging, excitement, power, reputation, and in some cases, money."[64] Much of the research into why black college students join BGLOs mirrors these findings.[65] Black students' membership in BGLOs revolves around community involvement and a sense of belonging,[66] and Tresa M. Saxton argues that these aspects extend to proving one's manhood, building a more self-confident identity, social bonding, gaining respect, and following tradition.[67]

The desire for social structure, as opposed to chaos and freedom, is what attracts some members to both gangs and BGLOs. In *Deadly Consequences*, Deborah Prothrow-Stith and Michaele Weissman argue that gangs have a social structure of rules, colors, and informal guidelines that young people both need and desire.[68] Many might think that this does not affect the dominant middle-class sensibilities that compose the centers of higher learning in which BGLOs are embedded. But Joseph White and James Coñes III address the notion of a "spillover effect" of gang mentalities into middle-class neighborhoods in *Black Man Emerging*. They argue that the excitement, adventure, and macho image of gang life exude a seductive aura.[69] As BGLOs convey similar characteristics, the same "spillover effect" can apply.

CULTURAL AESTHETICS

Gangs often claim public areas such as sidewalks and parks as their "turf." Such cultural conquest can be either a well-known "fact" or something unbeknownst to the general public. Such space is used to conduct "business" and also serves as a social boundary to keep rival gangs out. Similarly, BGLOs have "plots" of land that are viewed as physical representations of the BGLO community on campus. On many historically black college and university campuses, plots of ground are designated for specific black fraternities and sororities. They may differ in size and design, but they are places where members go to socialize, meet new members, or hold events. Because most BGLO chapters are too small to afford fraternity houses, BGLOs often treat their plots with a reverence that rivals white Greeks' treatment of their houses. Just as with gang territory, it is considered highly disrespectful to step foot on a plot if one is not a member or not invited. Again, among both BGLOs and gangs, such disregard of these folkways and mores can lead to severe verbal chastisement or even physical confrontation.

In addition to the cultural context of the "land" on which gangs and BGLOs stand, there are similarities in individual members' appearances and behavior. As bell hooks writes in *Art on My Mind,* "To break with the ruling hegemony that has a hold on images of the black male body, a revolutionary visual aesthetic must emerge that reappropriates, revises, and reinvents, giving everyone something new to look at."[70] The wearing of specific colors, the display of ornate jackets, and the use of hand signs all mark membership to both subcultural insiders and outsiders. Martínez writes, "It is common knowledge that fraternities are based on a Greek system, with Greek letters representing their organization. To give the distinction of their fraternity to others, they also often have their own fraternity colors. In similar fashion, gangs have their own signs, symbols, and colors to distinguish themselves."[71] Boyd-Franklin and Franklin write:

African American men have always used handshakes, words, and signals to bond with and communicate with one another. The black power handshake of the 1960s and 1970s and the "giving skin" of high- and low-fives are examples of handshakes and hand signals used by black men to show solidarity and loyalty. Black fraternities have a long history of secret handshakes, special colors, and codes of honor. It is all part of identifying with the brotherhood of black men. The gang then is the ultimate "cool pose" and appeals to the black adolescent's need for the signs and symbols of belonging.[72]

Such a striking comparison between the cultural aesthetics of gangs and BGLOs is undoubtedly one of the key points used to ground the educated gang thesis. Dr. Jawanza Kunjufu, coordinator of the SIMBA training program for young black manhood, draws on the work of Nathan and Julia Hare's *Bringing the Black Boy to Manhood.*[73] He remarks that mentoring programs must "adapt the symbols of solidarity that gang membership accords young men—such as logos, T-shirts, jackets, caps, a chant, song, or step routine—to a positive end.

He reminds us of the success of fraternities in our communities and on black campuses."[74] In both gangs and BGLOs, hand signs are used to identify members and to antagonize members of other groups. There is a distinct similarity of form and function between gang hand signs and BGLO hand signs: the Primo gang hand sign is the same as the hand sign of Alpha Phi Alpha Fraternity, the Brims and Phi Beta Sigma Fraternity share the same hand sign, and the universal hand sign is used by both the Bloods and Kappa Alpha Psi Fraternity.[75]

Another similarity involves names or nicknames. BGLO members often use their "line names," and gang members use their "street names." As Boyd-Franklin and Franklin write, "Gang members often use symbols . . . to signify membership . . . nicknames—such as 'Monster' or 'Killer'—that complete the show of solidarity."[76]

The display of membership is further extended to bodily adornment or even body modification via tattoos and branding. As Sandra Mizumoto Posey writes, "to the outsiders, branding might be associated with hazing or with historical parallels such as branding of cattle or slaves as a marker of ownership. . . . This is far from the case. . . . From beauty to belonging, the motivations for altering one's body are as diverse as the people who choose to do it."[77] Elsewhere she writes, "Fraternity members informally negotiate with brothers who do not support branding, family members who struggle with what it means to their own group identity, and most importantly, popular culture, which holds negative associations. The men who undergo branding, however, invert the narratives that explain branding as a mark of ownership and slavery and insist on defining its meaning for themselves."[78]

Body modification is not an uncommon thing, from plastic surgery to piercing. Pinkerton writes, "Being permanently marked to identity their membership in an organization was common to fraternities, and both male and female gang members ('being tattooed'). Both men and women in fraternities and gangs experience being tattooed."[79] Gang and BGLO tattooing and branding remind members "and others of what has happened not just to them, but also because of them."[80] In a (post)modern world filled with uncertainty and fractured, alienated identities, the permanence of body markings holds a meaningful place in both cultures.

Such cultural aesthetics extend not only to the visual appearance of members but also to the social arenas of auditory performance. BGLOs use verbal calls to demarcate membership or to signal some action. Marcella L. McCoy writes, "Calls, along with organizational colors, commonly serve as introductory features to BGLOs. Calls are vocal utterances, either words or sounds, coined for use by the respective organizations. They can be loud, bizarre, distinctive, disturbing, and imposing. At the same time, they can be comforting, exciting, and prideful expressions of their performers' license, skill, and very presence."[81] In addition, some gangs have verbal calls that they use to denote their affiliation or to provoke members of other gangs. One example is "Suuu-wup," a call used by certain Los Angeles Blood gang members.

PHILANTHROPY AND CIVIC ACTION

BGLO members generally serve in leadership positions, participate in service programs, and try to maintain high academic standards. Giving back to the larger community is a key principle for all BGLOs, which sponsor a multitude of service events that either raise money for or otherwise assist agencies in need. The first public service initiative completed by the newly founded Delta Sigma Theta Sorority Inc. was the 1913 women's suffrage march in Washington, D.C. Members of Sigma Gamma Rho Sorority Inc. also showed an interest in women's rights during the early years of their organization's existence. Phi Beta Sigma Fraternity Inc., founded in 1914, focused on antilynching laws and international issues occurring in the Republic of Haiti. According to C. William McKee, "Martin Luther King, Jr. attracted many of the staff members for the Southern Christian Leadership Conference from the ranks of black Greeks . . . today social action and civil rights projects will receive as high a priority as social functions."[82] Such philanthropy and social action among BGLOs persists today. Surprisingly, many gangs also involve themselves in community service, such as one gang collective in Chicago that "purchased groceries, clothes, and other necessities for young mothers"[83] However, research shows that this is the exception rather than the norm. Thus, the facet of engaging in philanthropy and civic action is a stark division between BGLOs and gangs.

COLLEGIATE VERSUS ALUMNI MEMBERS

Today, many undergraduate members of BGLOs, especially fraternity members, conceive of ideal black masculinity as overly sexualized, anti-intellectual, and possessing street or urban sensibilities. Many report that this is widening the gulf between collegiate members who are embracing a hip-hop culture and alumni members who have a more traditional and mainstream view of how BGLO members should "properly" present themselves. Both BGLOs and gangs claim to possess a respect for elders that is manifested in a reverence for "OGs" (original gangsters, or members who have lived through violence and crime) and "Old School" (BGLO members who have been active for ten years or more). However, both groups have witnessed a rampant acceleration of the view that elders are unnecessary, burdensome, and behind the times.

According to sociologist Elijah Anderson, when a community changes too rapidly or when social cohesion starts to loosen, the "old heads" lose their power and authority over younger members. An "old head," writes Anderson, "was a man of stable means who believed in hard work, family life, and the church. He was an aggressive agent of the wider society whose acknowledged role was to teach, support, encourage, and in effect socialize young men to meet their responsibilities regarding work, family, the law, and common decency."[84] According to Anderson, such models are disappearing. However, Anderson has delineated a new form, a "code of the street," whereby members "code-switch" from a "street" persona to a more accepted "decent" attitude. Anderson writes, "The inner-city success story . . . requires the ability to code-switch, to play by the code of the street with the street element and the code of decency with others."[85] Perhaps the critique of BGLOs as educated gangs carries so much credence because critics have essentialized the social performance of "code" into a reductive ontological singularization. That is, when critics see both gangs and BGLOs as little more than their contextual social performance, that calls for, in effect, a disallowing of the complexity of role playing and attitudinal heterogeneity that is simply part of the human experience, especially when that experience has been socially and politically marginalized.

Are BGLO members, like gang members, "code-switching"? It seems apropos that BGLO members follow the predominant social folkways and mores of their generation in order to exchange cultural and social capital with their peers. Some point to the rising influence of hip-hop culture and aestheticism that glorifies gangs, violence, misogyny, and various other socially destructive characteristics on young black men and women. Others argue that collegiate members of BGLOs are no different from many other college students who have embraced hip-hop, like earlier generations did with rock and roll and jazz. Further, not all hip-hop culture is negative or self-destructive; some of it is highly positive, antiracist, community minded, and socially conscientious. Still, this scenario begs the question: if BGLO members are claiming to be servant-leaders and scholars, should they not work to transcend negative aspects of society and serve as examples of some higher or different social order? It is a paradox stated no better than when Rudyard Kipling wrote: "If you can walk with crowds and keep your virtue, Or walk with Kings—nor lose the common touch, If neither foes nor loving friends can hurt you, If all men count with you but none too much; If you can fill the unforgiving minute With sixty seconds' worth of distance run, Yours is the Earth and everything that is in it, And—which is more—you'll be a man my son."[86]

Critiquing the Educated Gang Thesis

What is the actual work of framing BGLOs as educated gangs? What structures does such phrasing employ in order to give it legitimate meaning? BGLOs as educated gangs are inserted in contested discourses about blackness, and such a discursive framing labors to constitute a very large part of that discourse. As George Lipsitz writes, "Cultural forms create conditions of possibility, they expand the present by informing it within memories of the past and hopes for the future; but they also engender accommodation with prevailing power realities, separating art from life, and internalizing the dominant culture's norms and values as necessary and inevitable."[87] Too much of either an uncritical celebration or a defamation of new forms of black representation misses the point explicated by Lipsitz. That is, proclaiming BGLOs as either deities or demons distracts from the context of why BGLOs are taking up such a contentious place in the debate over cultural values and racial identity.

In a time of crackdowns on educational affirmative action programs—from Proposition 209 in California[88] to the recent Supreme Court decisions on the University of Michigan's admissions policies[89]—some expect that rationales linking criminality with blackness will increase. Accordingly, despite evidence and counterevidence, there are three modalities by which the educated gang thesis appeals to its supporters: a nouveau criminalization argument of BGLO culture vis-à-vis Oscar Lewis's "culture of poverty" thesis, the modus operandi of social "othering" that sociologist Pierre Bourdieu calls "symbolic violence," and techniques of defaming blackness in relation to normalization and privileging of whiteness.

THE CULTURE OF POVERTY

In 1966 Oscar Lewis published *La Vida: A Puerto Rican Family in the Culture of Poverty—San Juan and New York*.[90] The text argues that the poor have bad values and bad habits, which suggests that they remain in poverty because of their adaptations to the burdens of poverty. This argument has been mapped onto contemporary discussions of race. Although most people today do not believe that people of color are *biologically* inferior, many are of the opinion that nonwhites, especially African Americans, are *culturally* inferior. The idea is that social forces, from racism to poverty, create a culture of misery and an inability to defer gratification, such that the culture itself takes on a life of its own and works as a cycle of dependency. Due to reports, publications, and an increasingly publicized conservative agenda that first ascended in the 1960s, a new ideology toward race developed. This ideology was first intimated in a 1965 report by Patrick Moynihan entitled "The Negro Family: The Case for National Action."[91] It was reproduced in black scholarship such as Kenneth Clarke's *Dark Ghetto* and persists today in Richard J. Herrnstein and Charles Murray's *The Bell Curve*, as well as in the vitriolics against affirmative action.[92] The new conservatism stresses that there is plenty of opportunity in the nation, but minorities simply fail to take advantage of it. This logic undergirds the educated gang thesis. Although it is true that BGLOs develop self-destructive habits, one cannot discount the social structures of capitalism and white supremacy that work to criminalize people of color despite any meritocracy sensibilities.[93] The tragedy is that both popular culture commentators and average white U.S. citizens have adopted this theory of poverty as mapped onto race. They have transformed it into a new excuse for racism by simply dropping or de-emphasizing the role of the social structure and white racism,[94] as well as ignoring the everyday experiences of prejudice and discrimination in the lives of people of color.[95]

SYMBOLIC VIOLENCE

Framing BGLOs as educated gangs commits a certain "symbolic violence" against not only the BGLO system but also blackness itself. Sociologist Pierre Bourdieu has analyzed the effect of this "naming" or sanctioning of events by a legitimated group on a supposedly "deviant" group. He writes: "all the symbolic strategies though which agents aim to impose their vision of the divisions of the social world and their position in that world . . . [compel] the *official naming,* a symbolic act of imposition which has on its side all the strength of the collective, of the consensus, of common sense, because it is performed by . . . the holder of the *monopoly of legitimate symbolic violence.*"[96] The naming or the qualification of specific actions committed by BGLOs becomes an act that is more durable than the intrinsic characteristics of BGLOs themselves. It is not the relative value of the BGLOs' action that determines the value of the naming. Instead, the institutionalized value of the event *once named* acts as an instrument to serve and defend the value of the *namer,* the holder of the legitimated knowledge—the white mainstream. Naming and (de)legitimating such events are acts of symbolic violence toward nonwhite agency. The struggle over the educated gang thesis's racial meaning and how BGLOs are thus named is not a struggle between mere subjectivism and objectivism. No matter how much evidence is weighed, there will be some on both sides. Rather, the view of BGLOs as educated gangs is actually mediated by the stake between social agents who are equipped to attain the social markers that legitimate claims to absolute and self-verifying knowledge and those who do not possess cultural capital of the dominant racial discourse.

WHITE NORMALIZATION

If we examine the context that surrounds the discourse of BGLOs as educated gangs, we open up new possibilities for viewing the striking hegemonic power of such a framing that is able to reinstall white normality and superiority. It is able to do so through three distinct valences. First, portraying black Greeks as a gang gives the collective memory of personal hatred and fear, as well as structural racism, an easy target. That is, if even the elite, college-attending black youth act like a gang, they can be used to make the case for extending black biological inferiority to black cultural deficiency. Second, the striking irony of framing BGLOs as educated gangs is that the black exceptionalism of these organizations becomes refigured as a deficient form of "otherness." Behavior that, under a white face, would be ignored, excused, or explained away by personal, rogue, or "bad apple" elucidations becomes a sociological accounting book for the "true nature" of BGLO ontology. Third, race operates relationally. That is, race holds both meaning and power not only by the category in which it is placed but also by how the boundary of difference is drawn between those types. By taking discussions of BGLOs outside the discussion of the political economy of identity and power, there is a singular, reductionist focus on BGLO shortcomings. Many of these shortcomings exist, and their deleterious effects both inside and outside the African American community should not be excused. However, such a myopic focus destabilizes one's ability to theorize how conditions got to be that way, how they are maintained, and, most important, how others get away with, or are praised for, similar actions.

The focus on BGLOs, rather than on the entire Greek system; the mysterious absence of discussions about how colleges and universities treat students of color as commodities for the credentialism of ivory tower demographics; and the entire delimiting of bad value choices and unethical behavior by mainstream whites—all these work together to establish blackness as a criminal enterprise and ontology, no matter what grand or ethical accomplishments BGLOs can claim. Do BGLOs engage in criminal, dangerous, and self-destructive behavior? Yes, as do many Greek organizations regardless of their racial makeup, as well as many other institutions, from day-care centers to the federal government.

Moral Panic and the Janus Face of Axiology

One of the main themes throughout the corpus of BGLO scholarship is the notion of a dual responsibility: BGLOs must both uplift the black community and engage in self-critique. Ironically, it is the notion of BGLO responsibility that helps drive the critique of BGLOs as educated gangs. This is nothing new. As William M. Banks writes in *Black Intellectuals,* "Black thinkers . . . noted the main failings of a people only recently freed from bondage and still oppressed everywhere, but they did not question the race's essential fitness. Their balanced critique made little difference to most white Americans. White racial attitudes blended with a huge popular myth—that the U.S. drive for empire was simply an unfolding of the natural order. Like people of color elsewhere in the world, African Americans were victimized by the myth—and the reality—of empire."[97]

This myth has been reified in the culture of poverty, symbolic violence, and the normalization of whiteness, and it is leading to a "moral panic." According to Stanley Cohen, a moral panic occurs when "a condition, episode, person or group of persons emerges to become defined as a threat to societal values and interests."[98] Such can be said of both BGLOs and gangs. Attention to gangs has increased due to concern over "innocent bystanders, the intimidation of potential witnesses to gang-related activities, reports of increasing gang violence in schools, gang graffiti, drug-related commitments to local facilities, and drug-related arrests."[99] Scholar Simon Cottle writes: "This 'moral panic' . . . [which] helped pave the (ideological) way for a new form of state 'authoritarian populism' (neoconservative politics) that itself was a response to processes of national economic representations of 'race' to wider state interests and processes of ideological reproduction[,] has proved seminal through its explanation of the exact mechanisms linking media institutions, professional practices and cultural representations to political forces of change."[100] The same "neoconservative politics" prompts the educated gang thesis. Although motivated by a genuine desire to protect the ivory tower, the labeling of BGLOs as gangs is done in a diminutive fashion and functions largely as an "ideological state apparatus."[101] The auxiliary effect of this label captures the social imagination of the public and distracts them from larger, more widespread issues such as rising unemployment, the skyrocketing prison rates and the privatization of those prisons, and the changing nature of racism. As Hall and colleagues argue, "The first phenomenal form which the experience of social crisis assumes in public consciousness, then, is the moral panic. . . . In this form, a society famous for its tenacious grasp on certain well-earned rights of personal liberty . . . screws itself up to the distasteful task of going through 'iron times.'"[102] The rising moral panic over BGLOs as educated gangs operates as an excuse for the future introduction of new policing policies that allow the state or other institutions to clamp down on black resistance, self-determinism, or leadership.

BGLOs have a tradition of supporting viable communities in which black institutions are stronger than the ideologies that denigrate them. To this end, the BGLO tradition is an attempt to enter the public sphere and participate in full. This tradition seems naturally opposed to and suspicious of the postmodern lens used to deconstruct the educated gang thesis. Due to postmodernism's perception as an elitist, abstracted, theory game, as well as its denial of the "reality" of racial constraints in the lives of many African Americans, postmodernists' call for the recognition of "multiple subjectivities" seems not to be taken seriously when African Americans are still largely defined by their singular position as an inferior "other," even when they are members of BGLOs. It is BGLOs' latent underpinning of black self-determinism and quasi-nationalism that works to resist oppressive paradigms and makes many suspicious of their ability to interact amicably with postmodern thought. Yet, as Regina Austin writes of nationalism's connection to postmodernity:

> There is a renewed interest in nationalism, but possibly as a reflection of the influence of postmodernism, it is not weighed down or conditioned with demands that everyone follow one overriding credo. Blacks do not seem to be searching for a single macro-ideology. The calls for community, commitment, and caring are fluid . . . greater influence is placed on creativity . . . there is lots of nostalgia . . . black nostalgia has a political purpose born of a material need. The resort to historical figures is a response to the dominant society's invocation of black exceptionalism. . . . We do not need any more bogus icons.[103]

Further, hooks writes, "Given a pervasive politic of white supremacy which seeks to prevent the formation of radical black subjectivity, we cannot cavalierly dismiss a concern with identity politics. Any critic exploring the radical potential of postmodernism as it relates to racial difference and racial domination would need to consider the implications of a critique of identity for oppressed groups."[104]

The antiracist mission of BGLOs also constitutes an opposition of the dominant moral and ideological framework that dictates what constitutes a Janus-faced "good-bad" white value judgment of blackness. As West states, "The moralistic and communal aspects of the initial black diasporan responses to social and psychic erasure were not simply cast into simplistic binary oppositions of positive-negative, good-bad images that privileged the first term in light of a white norm so that black efforts remained inscribed within the very logic that dehumanized them."[105]

When BGLOs submit to either assimilative or image-corrective agendas, they allow themselves to fall prey to the critique that they are educated gangs. Accordingly, Adolph L. Reed Jr. argues that self-determined black movements such as BGLOs have "construed racial politics within the ideological universe through which the containment of the black population was mediated. Acceptance of this model . . . prevented Black Power from transcending the social program of the indigenous administrative elite."[106] So long as the predominant BGLO strategy seeks not to transcend such prostitution of self-determination, representations of their blackness will continue to fit neatly into a framework that is indispensable for the justification of racial inequality.

Conclusion: Where to Now?

Given the tense history of race relations, it would be an egregious error to allow uncritical discourse that fosters the inference that no matter what the cultural condition—be it gangster or Greek—groups of African Americans are violent, aggressive, superpredators.[107] At the same time, we must address certain dynamics of BGLO culture if these organizations are to remain pertinent. To foster that relevance, I outline three major tribulations and suggest courses of action.

First, attention to hazing, abuse, and other forms of violence (which often take a skin-tone, classed, or gendered form) cannot be understated. In 1989, Joel Harris died while pledging Alpha Phi Alpha at Morehouse College. In response to his death, the NPHC voted to completely ban the traditional pledging process at its 1990 convention, and within a few years, all members of the NPHC had banned pledging in favor of a short (three-day to three-week) "member intake process." However, as anyone attuned to BGLO issues has witnessed, this has failed to stop hazing. In recent years, BGLOs have faced an avalanche of hazing-related incidents and lawsuits.[108] Thus, the problem is not that there is too much focus on violence; rather, there is not enough attention on postinitiation instruction that encourages member consolidation and political awareness. "Solutions" to these problems have thus far mirrored the dynamics of colonialism, whereby a foreign power (alumni chapter or executive office) issues authoritarian mandates to its subjects, only to be surprised when that repression breeds resistance. More attention must focus on developing interchapter partnerships and undergraduate-led solutions so that collegiate members are fully invested in and wholeheartedly committed to plans and goals.

Second, we must carefully and boldly examine how BGLO elitism (which may stem from a fetish of bourgeois proclivities) may produce a retroactive effect. That is, many younger undergraduate members perceive the alumni chapters, administrative affairs, and executive operations (and even occasional fiscal scandals) of their organizations as completely alienated from their everyday concerns of educational attainment, economic pressure, social justice, and identity formation. They thereby understand many aspects of their own organizations as "inauthentic" and hypocritical. As a consequence, many members are not simply engaging in wanton disregard or disrespectful behavior; they are trying to "keep it real" via overromanticized and imagined conceptions of what they believe to be truly authentic: the harshness of the impoverished lower classes, anti-intellectualism coupled with emotional detachment, hypermasculinity, and the aesthetics and practices glorified in many forms of hip-hop, including the objectification of women, promiscuity, and a craze for capitalist forms of "conspicuous consumption."[109] Simply put, many young BGLO members are compensating for their very real organizational marginalization by constructing their BGLO identities against a perceived inauthentic (br)other.

Third, a fundamental rethinking of the effectiveness of the NPHC must occur. As it stands now, the NPHC is the BGLO version of the United Nations, inclusive of its political flaccidity: it has the ability to issue edicts and official pronouncements, but it has no real power. Such a realization gestures toward a rethinking of interfraternity and -sorority cooperation. Perhaps because of the blinders of competition, BGLOs do not presently acknowledge that what negatively affects one will have the same effect on the others down the line. To begin the conversation concerning a new unified coalition, a starting point is to consider how BGLOs can act as political vehicles for the resistance of white supremacy, build economic self-determinism in impoverished locales, and serve as catalysts for the revival of the welfare state, which is being dismantled by neoliberal tactics that can only spell disaster for the "identity politics" foundation on which BGLOs stand.

BGLO members clearly have an incentive to address these issues to ensure their organizations' impact and perpetuity. However, their willingness to engage in critical self-reflection is the catch. After all, it is much easier to label a young black man a "gangster," attribute social problems to psychological pathologies, criminalize his actions, and wash one's hands of the entire matter. It is a tried-and-true game, but one that will hopefully reach its conclusion before it is too late.

Notes

The phrase in the chapter title is appropriated from the rap artist Jay-Z and his song "99 Problems," found on *The Black Album* (Def Jam, November 2003). Portions of this chapter were published as "Brotherhood or Brothers in the 'Hood? Debunking the 'Educated Gang' Thesis as Black Fraternity and Sorority Slander," *Race, Ethnicity, and Education* (2008).

1. It is important to mention that I concentrate mainly on black Greek fraternities, not sororities, because the critique of BGLOs as educated gangs is usually directed at male members. However, this does not discount or exclude female members. I recognize the gender dynamics that make the fraternity and sorority lived experiences very different from each other, although they are still lived within the overarching context of blackness. Still, one must acknowledge, "From the very beginning of the sociology of deviance, women had been neglected, treated as biological entities to whom sociology did not apply, reduced to appendages or confined to the home. Their absence from the field is nothing short of spectacular. It is a silence so stunning that it demands examination for what it reveals." Colin Sumner, *The Sociology of Deviance: An Obituary* (New York: Continuum, 1994), 94.

2. Walter Kimbrough, *Black Greek 101: The Culture, Customs, and Challenges of Black Fraternities and Sororities* (Cranbury, N.J.: Rosemont, 2003); Tamara L. Brown, Gregory S. Parks, and Clarenda M. Phillips, eds., *African American Fraternities and Sororities: The Legacy and the Vision* (Lexington: University Press of Kentucky, 2005).

3. The members of the NPHC (also known as the Divine Nine) and their dates of founding are as follows: Alpha Phi Alpha Fraternity (1906), Alpha Kappa Alpha Sorority (1908), Kappa Alpha Psi Fraternity (1911), Omega Psi Phi Fraternity (1911), Delta Sigma Theta Sorority (1913), Phi Beta Sigma Fraternity (1914), Zeta Phi Beta Sorority (1920), Sigma Gamma Rho Sorority (1922), and Iota Phi Theta Fraternity (1963).

4. Talcott Parsons, "Suggestions for a Sociological Approach to the Theory of Organizations," in *Classics of Organization Theory*, 2nd ed., ed. Jay M. Shafritz and J. Stephen Ott (Chicago: Dorsey Press, 1987).

5. Max Weber, *The Theory of Social and Economic Organization* (New York: Free Press, 1997), 151.

6. Peter M. Blau and W. Richard Scott, *Formal Organizations: A Comparative Approach* (Scranton, Pa.: Chandler, 1962), 1.

7. Deborah Lamm Weisel, *Contemporary Gangs: An Organizational Analysis* (New York: LFB Scholarly Publishing, 2002), 3, 34.

8. Ibid., 1.

9. Robert J. Bursik and Harold G. Grasmick, "The Use of Contextual Analysis in Models of Criminal Behavior," in *Delinquency and Crime: Current Theories,* ed. J. David Dawkins (New York: Cambridge University Press, 1996), 245.

10. Jacob Riis cited in Frederick Thrasher, *The Gang: A Study of 1,313 Gangs in Chicago* (1927; reprint, Chicago: University of Chicago Press, 1963), 342.

11. Tom Hayden, *Street Wars: Gangs and the Future of Violence* (New York: Free Press, 2004), 86.

12. Elijah Anderson, *Code of the Street* (New York: W. W. Norton, 1999); Michael Duneier, *Slim's Table: Race, Respectability and Masculinity* (Chicago: University of Chicago Press, 1992); Joe Feagin and D. Wilkinson, "Guns, Youth Violence, and Social Identity in Inner-Cities," *Crime and Justice* 24 (1998): 105–88; R. J. Sampson and W. J. Wilson, "Toward a Theory of Race, Crime and Urban Inequality," in *Crime and Inequality,* ed. J. Hagan and R. D. Peterson (Stanford, Calif.: Stanford University Press, 1995), 37–54; R. Staples, *Black Masculinity: The Black Male's Role in American Society* (San Francisco: Black Scholar Press, 1982); R. Staples and L. B. Johnson, *Black Families at the Crossroads: Challenges and Prospects* (San Francisco: Jossey-Bass, 1993).

13. S. S. Estes, *I Am a Man! Race, Manhood, and the Civil Rights Movement* (Chapel Hill: University of North Carolina Press, 2006).

14. Cornel West, "The New Cultural Politics of Difference," in *The Cornel West Reader* (New York: Basic Civitas Books, 1999), 119–48.

15. W. E. B. DuBois, "The Talented Tenth," in *The Negro Problem: A Series of Articles by Representative Negroes of Today,* ed. Booker T. Washington et al. (New York: J. Pott, 1903).

16. Stuart Hall quoted in Issac Julien and Kobena Mercer, "De Margin and De Centre," in *Stuart Hall: Critical Dialogues in Cultural Studies,* ed. David Morley and Kuan-Hsing Chen (London: Routledge, 1996), 443.

17. bell hooks, *Yearning: Race, Gender, and Cultural Politics* (Boston: South End Press, 1990), 72.

18. Michel Foucault, *Technologies of the Self: A Seminar with Michel Foucault,* ed. L. H. Martin, H. Gutman, and P. H. Hutton (Amherst: University of Massachusetts Press, 1998), 17, 18.

19. William J. Chambliss, "The Saints and the Roughnecks," *Society* 11, no. 1 (1973): 24–31.

20. Marcos Martínez, "Analyzing College Fraternities and Gangs to Investigate and

Compare" (master's thesis, University of Colorado, 2001); Carol J. Pinkerton, "Fraternities, Sororities, and Gangs: A Grounded Theory Comparison" (master's thesis, State University of West Georgia, 2000).

21. Thrasher, *The Gang.*

22. William F. Whyte, *Street Corner Society* (Chicago: University of Chicago Press, 1943); Gerald D. Suttles, *The Social Order of the Slum* (Chicago: University of Chicago Press, 1971); Joan Moore, *Homeboys* (Philadelphia: Temple University Press, 1978); James D. Virgil, *Barrio Gangs* (Austin, Tex.: University of Austin Press, 1988).

23. Irving Spergel, *Violent Gangs in Chicago: Segmentation and Integration* (Chicago: University of Chicago, 1983), 19.

24. Jane M. Goettsch and Michael A. Hayes, "Racism and Sexism in Greek Events: A Call for Sensitivity," *NASPA Journal* 28, no. 1 (fall 1990): 68.

25. Irving A. Spergel, *The Youth Gang Problem* (New York: Oxford University Press, 1995), 80.

26. Elizabeth C. Fine, "Stepping, Saluting, Cracking, and Freaking: The Cultural Politics of African-American Step Shows," *Drama Review* 35, no. 2 (summer 1991): 48.

27. Richard Bauman, "Differential Identity and the Social Base of Folklore," in *Toward New Perspectives in Folklore,* ed. Americo Paredes and Richard Bauman (Austin: University of Texas Press, 1972), 31–41.

28. Fine, "Stepping, Saluting, Cracking," 56.

29. Martínez, "Analyzing College Fraternities and Gangs," 8.

30. Robert A. Rhoads, "Whales Tales, Dog Piles, and Beer Goggles: An Ethnographic Case Study of Fraternity Life," *Anthropology and Education Quarterly* 26, no. 3 (1995): 306–23; James Diego Virgil, *Barrio Gangs* (Austin: University of Texas Press, 1988); James Diego Virgil, "Street Baptism: Chicano Gang Initiation," *Human Organization* 55, no. 2 (summer 1996): 149–53.

31. Martínez, "Analyzing College Fraternities and Gangs," 9.

32. Pinkerton, "Fraternities, Sororities, and Gangs," 46–50.

33. Hank Nuwer, *Broken Pledges: The Deadly Rite of Hazing* (Athens, Ga.: Longstreet Press, 1990); Hank Nuwer, *The Hazing Reader* (Bloomington: Indiana University Press, 2004); Hank Nuwer, *Wrongs of Passage* (Bloomington: Indiana University Press, 1999); Ester Wright, *Torn Togas: The Dark Side of Campus Greek Life* (Minneapolis: Fairview Press, 1996); Kimbrough, *Black Greek 101;* Ricky Jones, *Black Haze: Violence, Sacrifice and Manhood in Black Greek-Letter Fraternities* (Albany: State University of New York Press, 2004); Gregory S. Parks and Tamara L. Brown, "'In the Fell Clutch of Circumstance': Pledging and the Black Greek Experience," in Brown et al., *African American Fraternities and Sororities,* 437–64.

34. R. A. Schroth, "Brotherhood of Death," *America* 177 no. 11 (1997): 6.

35. M. Geraghty, "Hazing Incidents at Sororities Alarm Colleges," *Chronicle of Higher Education* 43, no. 41 (1997): 38.

36. Parks and Brown, "In the Fell Clutch of Circumstance," 444–45.

37. G. D. Kuh, E. T. Pascarella, and H. Wechsleer, "The Questionable Value of Fraternities," *Chronicle of Higher Education* 434, no. 4 (1996): A68.

38. G. D. Kuh and J. C. Arnold, *Brotherhood and the Bottle: A Cultural Analysis of the Role of Alcohol in Fraternities* (Bloomington: Center for the Study of the College Fraternity, Indiana University, 1992), 97.

39. J. L. Baier and E. G. Whipple, "Greek Values and Attitudes: A Comparison with Independents," *NASPA Journal* 28, no. 1 (1990): 53.

40. Martínez, "Analyzing College Fraternities and Gangs," 5.

41. R. M. O'Conner, S. E. Cooper, and W. S. Thiel, "Alcohol Use as a Predictor of Potential Fraternity Membership," *Journal of College Student Development* 37, no. 6 (1996): 669–76.

42. Wright, *Torn Togas,* 53.

43. Nicholas J. Hennessy and Lisa M. Huson, "Legal Issues and Greek Letter Organizations," in *New Challenges for Greek Letter Organizations: Transforming Fraternities and Sororities into Learning Communities,* ed. Edward G. Whipple (San Francisco: Jossey-Bass, 1998), 61–77.

44. S. Copenhaver and E. Grauerholz, "Sexual Victimization among Sorority Women: Exploring the Link between Sexual Violence and Institutional Practices," *Sex Roles* 24, no. 102 (1991): 31–41.

45. Martínez, "Analyzing College Fraternities and Gangs," 4.

46. Craig T. Palmer and Christopher F. Tilley, "Sexual Access to Females as Motivation for Joining Gangs: An Evolutionary Approach," *Journal of Sex Research* 32, no. 3 (1995): 213–17; Rhoads, "Whales Tales, Dog Piles, and Beer Goggles," 306–23.

47. Tyra Black, Joanne Belknap, and Jennifer Ginsburg, "Racism, Sexism, and Aggression: A Study of Black and White Fraternities," in Brown et al, *African American Fraternities and Sororities,* 386.

48. Nancy Boyd-Franklin and A. J. Franklin, *Boys into Men: Raising Our African American Teenage Sons* (New York: Dutton Books, 2000), 145.

49. S. B. Boeringer, "Associations of Rape-Supportive Attitudes with Fraternal and Athletic Participation," *Violence against Women* 5, no. 1 (1999): 85.

50. Richard Majors and Janet M. Billson, *Cool Pose: The Dilemmas of Black Manhood in America* (New York: Touchstone, 1992), 8, 29.

51. Greg Dimitriadis, *Friendship, Cliques, and Gangs: Young Black Men Coming of Age in Urban America* (New York: Teachers College Press, Columbia University, 2003), 18.

52. Majors and Billson, *Cool Pose,* 86.

53. Dimitriadis, *Friendship, Cliques, and Gangs,* 18.

54. Baier and Whipple, "Greek Values and Attitudes," 43–53; Ronald Huff, ed., *Gangs in America, III* (Thousand Oaks, Calif.: Sage Publications, 2002); Rhoads, "Whales Tales, Dog Piles, and Beer Goggles," 306–23; Jean-Marie Lyon, Scott Henggeler, and James A. Hall, "The Family Relations and Criminal Activities of Caucasian and Hispanic-American Gang Members," *Journal of Abnormal Child Psychology* 20, no. 5 (1992): 439–49.

55. Martínez, "Analyzing College Fraternities and Gangs," 10.

56. Mitchell Dunier, *Slim's Table: Race, Respectability, and Masculinity* (Chicago: University of Chicago Press, 1992).

57. Ron Suskind, *Hope in the Unseen: An American Odyssey from the Inner City to the Ivy League* (New York: Broadway Books, 1998).

58. Dimitriadis, *Friendship, Cliques, and Gangs*, 33.

59. Jonathan Scott Lee and Fred L. Hord, eds., *I Am Because We Are: Readings in Black Philosophy* (Amherst: University of Massachusetts Press, 1995), 5.

60. Sudhir Alladi Venkatesh, "Gender and Outlaw Capitalism: A Historical Account of the Black Sisters United 'Girl Gang,'" *Signs* 23, no. 3 (1998): 687, 705.

61. Anne Campbell, *The Girls in the Gang* (New York: Blackwell, 1984), 687.

62. Martínez, "Analyzing College Fraternities and Gangs," 6.

63. Martin S. Janjowski, *Islands in the Streets: Gangs and American Urban Society* (Berkeley: University of California Press, 1991).

64. Boyd-Franklin and Franklin, *Boys into Men*, 187.

65. W. E. Sedlecek and G. C. Brooks, *Racism in American Education: A Model for Change* (Chicago: Nelson-Hall, 1976); J. Burt and G. Halpin, "African American Identity Development: A Review of the Literature" (paper presented at the meeting of the Mid-South Educational Research Association, New Orleans, 1998).

66. Walter Kimbrough and P. Hutcheson, "The Impact of Membership in Black Greek-Letter Organizations on Black Students' Involvement in Collegiate Activities and Their Development of Leadership Skills," *Journal of Negro Education* 67, no. 2 (spring 1998): 96–105.

67. Tresa Mitchell Saxton, "The Hazing Practices of Black Fraternities Located on White Campuses: The Interplay of Racism, Masculinity, and Male Violence" (PhD diss., University of North Carolina at Greensboro, 2003).

68. Deborah Prothrow-Stith and Michaele Weissman, *Deadly Consequences: How Violence Is Destroying Our Teenage Population and a Plan to Begin Solving the Problem* (New York: HarperCollins, 1993).

69. Joseph White and James Coñes III, *Black Man Emerging: Facing the Past and Seizing the Future in America* (New York: Routledge, 1999).

70. bell hooks, *Art on my Mind* (New York: New Press, 1995), 211.

71. Martínez, "Analyzing College Fraternities and Gangs," 9.

72. Boyd-Franklin and Franklin, *Boys into Men*, 193.

73. Nathan Hare and Julia Hare, *Bringing the Black Boy to Manhood: The Passage* (San Francisco: Black Think Tank, 1985).

74. Jawanza Kunjufu, cited in Boyd-Franklin and Franklin, *Boys into Men*, 217.

75. Usually these signs are made by using the fingers on one or both hands to form some sort of symbol or letter. It can also relay more specific information, such as what set they represent within a larger gang or in which activities they are currently taking part. The hand sign of Primo and Alpha Phi Alpha is performed by extending the thumb

and pinky finger; this is also the American Sign Language symbol for the letter Y. The Phi Beta Sigma and Brims gang sign is performed by extending the index and pinky fingers, and the universal Blood and Kappa Alpha Psi sign is performed similarly to the "okay" symbol of touching the index finger to the thumb and holding the remaining three fingers upright.

76. Boyd-Franklin and Franklin, *Boys into Men*, 192.

77. Sandra Mizumoto Posey, "The Body Art of Brotherhood," in Brown et al., *African American Fraternities and Sororities*, 269–93.

78. Sandra Mizumoto Posey, "Burning Messages: Interpreting African American Fraternity Brands and Their Bearers," *Voices* 30, nos. 3–4 (fall–winter 2004): 1; also available at http://www.nyfolklore.org/pubs/voic30-3-4/burnmsgs.html.

79. Pinkerton, "Fraternities, Sororities, and Gangs," 58.

80. Posey, "The Body Art of Brotherhood," 289.

81. Marcella L. McCoy, "Calls: An Inquiry into Their Origin, Meaning, and Function," in Brown et al., *African American Fraternities and Sororities*, 295–313.

82. C. William McKee, "Understanding the Diversity of the Greek World," in *Fraternities and Sororities on the Contemporary College Campus*, ed. Roger B. Winston Jr., William R. Nettles III, and John H. Opper Jr. (San Francisco: Jossey-Bass, 1987), 27–28.

83. Venkatesh, "Gender and Outlaw Capitalism," 694.

84. Elijah Anderson, *Streetwise: Race, Class, and Change in an Urban Community* (Chicago: University of Chicago Press, 1990), 3.

85. Elijah Anderson, *Code of the Street: Decency, Violence, and the Moral Life of the Inner City* (Chicago: University of Chicago Press, 1999), 310.

86. Rudyard Kipling, "If—," in *Rewards and Fairies* (New York: Doubleday, Page, 1910).

87. George Lipsitz, *Time Passages: Collective Memory and American Popular Culture* (Minneapolis: University of Minnesota Press, 1990), 16.

88. Proposition 209 was a 1996 California ballot proposition that amended the state constitution to prohibit public institutions from discriminating on the basis of race, sex, or ethnicity. It was supported by the California Civil Rights Initiative Campaign, led by University of California regent Ward Connerly, and was opposed by pro–affirmative action advocacy groups. Proposition 209 was adopted on November 5, 1996, with 54 percent of the vote.

89. On June 23, 2003, in a six-to-three decision, the Supreme Court ruled that the University of Michigan's point system for its undergraduate affirmative action admissions policy was too mechanistic and therefore unconstitutional (*Gratz v. Bollinger*, 539 U.S. 244). However, that same day, the Supreme Court upheld the affirmative action admissions policy of the University of Michigan Law School, by a decision of five to four (*Grutter v. Bollinger*, 539 U.S. 306). Justice Sandra Day O'Connor wrote: "We expect that 25 years from now, the use of racial preferences will no longer be necessary."

90. Oscar Lewis, *La Vida: A Puerto Rican Family in the Culture of Poverty—San Juan and New York* (New York: Random House, 1966).

91. See Gordon MacInnes, *Wrong for All the Right Reasons: How White Liberals Have Been Undone by Race* (New York: New York University Press, 1996).

92. Kenneth B. Clarke, *Dark Ghetto: Dilemmas of Social Power* (New York: Harper and Row, 1965); Richard J. Herrnstein and Charles Murray, *The Bell Curve: Intelligence and Class Structure in American Life* (New York: Free Press, 1994).

93. For instance, Princeton sociologist Devah Pager's recent study sent evenly matched pairs of black and white job applicants to 350 interviews for entry-level positions. The only difference was that some applicants listed an eighteen-month prison sentence for cocaine possession on their résumés. For the black applicants, the callback rate was 5 percent for those with criminal records and 14 percent for those without. For the white applicants, it was 17 percent for those with criminal records and 34 percent for those without. Therefore, whites with felony records were more than three times as likely to be hired than blacks with felony records, and white applicants with clean records were more than twice as likely to be hired than black applicants with clean records. See Devah Pager, "Walking the Talk: What Employers Say versus What They Do," *American Sociological Review* 70, no. 3 (2005): 355–80; Devah Pager, "Double Jeopardy: Race, Crime, and Getting a Job," *Wisconsin Law Review* 2 (2005): 617–60; Devah Pager, "The Mark of a Criminal Record," *American Journal of Sociology* 108, no. 5 (2003): 937–75; Devah Pager, "Blacks and Ex-Cons Need Not Apply," *Contexts* 2, no. 4 (2003): 58–59. In another study by Marianne Bertrand and Sendhil Mullainathan, stereotypically white and black names were affixed to résumés and sent to employers. White names got about one callback per ten résumés; black names got one per fifteen. "Carries" and "Kristens" had callback rates of more than 13 percent, but the rates for "Aisha," "Keisha," and "Tamika" were 2.2 percent, 3.8 percent, and 5.4 percent, respectively. See Marianne Bertrand and Sendhil Mullainathan, "Are Emily and Brendan More Employable than Lakisha and Jamal? A Field Experiment on Labor Market Discrimination," NBER working paper series no. 9873 (Cambridge, Mass.: National Bureau of Economic Research, 2003).

94. For an excellent critique of the culture of poverty thesis, see Stephen Steinberg, *The Ethnic Myth: Race, Ethnicity, and Class in America* (Boston: Beacon Press, 1981).

95. Andrew Hacker, *Two Nations: Black and White, Separate, Hostile, and Unequal* (New York: Scribners, 1992).

96. Pierre Bourdieu, "Cultural Power," cited in Lyn Spillman, *Cultural Sociology* (Malden, Mass.: Blackwell, 2002), 72 (emphasis in original).

97. William M. Banks, *Black Intellectuals: Race and Responsibility in American Life* (New York: W. W. Norton, 1996), 66.

98. Stanley Cohen, *Folk Devils and Moral Panics* (London: Palladin, 1973), 9.

99. Pat Jackson and Cary Rudman, "Moral Panic and the Response to Gangs in California," in *Gangs: The Origins and Impact of Contemporary Youth Gangs in the United*

States, ed. Scott Cummings and Daniel J. Monti (Albany: State University of New York Press, 1993), 259.

100. Simon Cottle, *Ethnic Minorities and the Media* (Philadelphia: Open University Press, 2000), 11.

101. Richard C. McCorkle and Terance D. Miethe, *Panic: The Social Construction of the Street Gang Problem* (Upper Saddle River, N.J.: Prentice Hall, 2001). There are many different institutions in society that socialize us to accept dominant ideas and values. The Marxist scholar Louis Althusser refers to such institutions as ideological state apparatuses (ISAs), which operate alongside the material structures of courts, police, prisons, the military, and so forth. Althusser argues that ISAs function for the management and consent of society's members, trying to persuade us to accept as legitimate for the whole society that ideology which in fact best serves the interests of the dominant class. In this context, if BGLOs were to challenge dominant practices, the defamation of them as educated gangs would be an ISA. See Louis Althusser, *Lenin and Philosophy and Other Essays* (London: New Left Books, 1977).

102. Stuart Hall, Chas Critcher, Tony Jefferson, John Clark, and Bryan Roberts, *Policing the Crisis* (London: Macmillan, 1978), 323.

103. Regina Austin, "Left at the Post: One Take on Blacks and Postmodernism," *Law and Society* 26, no. 4 (1992): 752.

104. bell hooks, "Postmodern Blackness," in *Yearnings* (Boston: South End Press, 1990), 23–31.

105. West, "The New Cultural Politics of Difference," 129.

106. Adolph L. Reed Jr., "Black Particularity Reconsidered," in *Is It Nation Time? Contemporary Essays on Black Power and Black Nationalism,* ed. E. S. Glaude Jr. (Chicago: University of Chicago Press, 2002): 51.

107. Steven R. Cureton, "Introducing Hoover: 'I'll Ride for You, Gangsta,'" in Huff, *Gangs in America, III,* 100.

108. Paul Ruffins, "'Greek' Pride and Pain," *Black Issues in Higher Education* 16, no. 3 (August 1999): 103–4.

109. *Conspicuous consumption* is a term used to describe lavish spending on goods and services acquired mainly for the purpose of displaying income or wealth. In the mind of a conspicuous consumer, such displays are a means of attaining or maintaining social status. See Thorstein Veblen, *Theory of the Leisure Class: An Economic Study in the Evolution of Institutions* (New York: Macmillan, 1899).

Part VII

Advising Undergraduate Chapters

20

Black and White Greeks

A Call for Collaboration

Edward G. Whipple, Martin Crichlow, and Sally Click

Although the histories and traditions of black and white Greek-letter organizations are distinct, these organizations are also similar. Undergraduate Greek-letter groups, whether historically black or white, have enough in common that the suggestion that the two systems work together is not unrealistic. It is doubtful, however, that this convergence will come to pass on its own. To achieve a unified Greek system, it is likely that host institutions and alumni will need to commit time and resources toward this end.[1]

In considering the interaction between black and white Greek-letter organizations, a good starting point is their commonalities. Only when similarities are recognized is collaboration possible. Furthermore, when collaboration occurs, the environment for community building is enhanced. Strong, unified Greek systems promote the health and effectiveness of each group, provide rich experiences for individual members, and contribute to positive educational outcomes.[2] Energies dedicated to community building in this setting are not wasted. Academic institutions' missions speak to the role of higher education in preparing students for the challenges of responsible citizenship in both a local and a global perspective. Students working together in a defined community composed of what may seem at first to be diverse entities can lead to the discovery of similar conditions and interests. Greek membership provides a laboratory for citizen training. Seeing other points of view, developing empathy, mediating conflicts, coming to consensus, and persisting when challenged are critical skills and experiences that students need to successfully navigate an increasingly complex world.

We start this chapter with the premise that collaboration is the desired state of affairs. The philosophical perspective of structural functionalism embraces consensus and equilibrium, defining these societal characteristics as the ultimate symbols of human interaction and progress.[3] Structural functionalism represents a consensus view and suggests that groups naturally seek shared norms and values.[4] In this vein, building and preserving agreement are powerful forces that motivate individual and collective behavior. In essence, we assume that people want to work together and that the benefits of such an approach are clearly visible. Absent stability, control, and some predictability, it is difficult for institutions of higher education to advance their stated missions.

A consensus approach feels better to most student affairs administrators. Working collaboratively in all aspects of campus life helps establish and maintain an environment conducive to learning. With respect to Greek life, we know that a collaborative climate is likely to encourage prospective members to consider becoming involved and that involvement in campus life contributes to student success and persistence. Alexander Astin's research on student involvement generally notes that how students feel about their undergraduate experiences influences their success. He defines involvement as "the amount of physical and psychological energy that the student devotes to the academic experience."[5] Opportunities to become involved on campus increase the chance that students will persist and complete their degrees.[6]

Fraternities and sororities are examples of organizations that can influence students' personal and academic success. Astin also asserts that peer influence is one of the most important factors in student growth and development during the undergraduate experience.[7] The Greek experience, with its intense emphasis on personal relationships, can have a powerful impact on the quality of the students' experience. For black students, membership in black Greek-letter organizations (BGLOs) can be extremely important. At historically black institutions, the Greek experience provides greater social outlets and a more supportive environment. The membership experience contributes positively to social, cultural, and academic adjustment. This is especially true for black students attending predominantly white institutions. BGLOs provide a major support system, connections to other black students, and a main avenue for the delivery of social programming. Fraternity or sorority membership, depending on the institution, can also provide a safe haven from discrimination and isolation. Regardless of the campus type, the connection to BGLOs is a positive factor in retention and graduation.[8]

Historical Distinctions

The first Greek organization, Phi Beta Kappa, was founded in 1776 at the College of William and Mary. It was an all-white, all-male group. It "had all the characteristics of the present-day fraternity: the charm and mystery of secrecy, a ritual, oaths of fidelity, a grip, a motto, a badge for external display, a background of high idealism, a strong tie of friendship and comradeship, an urge for sharing its values through nation-wide expansion."[9] Phi Beta Kappa later expanded to Yale, Harvard, and Dartmouth and became the prototype of the early fraternity.

In the first quarter of the nineteenth century, literary societies developed with classical names such as Adelphian, Calliopean, Ciceronian, Erosophian, and Philolethean.[10] In 1825, a more socially oriented organization, Kappa Alpha Society, was founded at Union College. Characteristics such as secrecy, the wearing of badges, and the Greek-letter name emerged. Despite the opposition that Kappa Alpha Society encountered, two more Greek organizations were founded as a result of that campus tension. The expansion and growth of men's Greek-letter organizations slowed during the Civil War but escalated considerably after the war's end.[11]

By the latter part of the nineteenth century, college student demographics radically changed, with increasing numbers of female, black, and Jewish students seeking a place in campus life. Women's Greek organizations began in 1851 with the establishment of a secret society, Alpha Delta Pi.[12] Even though college women had engaged in their own battle of exclusion, they also maintained all-white membership. Women's groups were initially referred to as "fraternities," as no gender-specific term existed. The word *sorority* was coined by an adviser for Gamma Phi Beta in 1882, in deference to the Latin word *sorors,* meaning "sister."[13]

Intercollegiate BGLOs arose in response to black students' feelings of discrimination and isolation and the desire to uplift the race.[14] Generally, these feelings developed from societal racism in general and campus racism in particular. This was especially true at predominantly white institutions. Alpha Phi Alpha Fraternity was founded at Cornell University in 1906, followed by Kappa Alpha Psi Fraternity at Indiana University in 1911. Howard University was the founding site of several groups: Alpha Kappa Alpha Sorority, the first black Greek women's group, in 1908; Omega Psi Phi Fraternity in 1911; Delta Sigma Theta Sorority in 1913; Phi Beta Sigma Fraternity in 1914; and Zeta Phi Beta Sorority in 1920. Sigma Gamma Rho Sorority was established at Butler University in 1922.[15]

The early white and black Greek organizations shared commonalities with early Masonic organizations. The first African American Mason, Prince Hall, was initiated in 1775 by European Masons. These European Masons allowed African American members to establish separate lodges, but they shared their secrets and instructions for performing the various rituals. Black Masons who emanated from these early lodges would become pillars of African American society, aiding those distressed by America's oppressive economic and social systems.[16]

Cultural Distinctions

With the exception of the common practices of recruitment, pledging, and certain events such as dances, philanthropy programs, and alumni events, white fraternities and sororities have few traditions that are common to all groups. BGLOs also engage in many of the same activities, but they have established unique traditions such as branding, calls, hand signs, and stepping that are arguably based on African customs and culture.[17] BGLOs also recruit members differently, often requiring them to have some college credits and an established grade point average before joining. Additionally, one of the major differences between black and white groups is BGLOs' emphasis on service. In response to racial discrimination, BGLO undergraduates and alumni place a premium on community building and social justice: "From the beginning, the organizations' original purposes were to provide a harbor for . . . members from hatred and isolation, to pull together the best trained African-American minds, and to give leadership to the African-American community in its struggle for freedom and justice. . . . Today, scholarship, service, and political action to the community are likewise expected from this most educated, highly trained, influential, and politically connected sector of society."[18] BGLOs donate millions of dollars in educational scholarships each year, and they are involved in a broad spectrum of service programs, ranging from tutoring to career fairs to building houses for the poor.

Recent research on differences between black and white Greeks reminds us that the ownership of a chapter house can alter the internal dynamics of a group as well as influence its status on campus. White organizations, especially fraternities, are more likely to own houses and consequently operate with more privacy and seclusion.[19] Groups without houses or other privately owned space may be scrutinized to a higher degree because their activities are more public. Black groups tend to fall into this category.

Structural Distinctions

The national coordinating organizations for black and white Greek organizations emerged from differing needs. For historically white Greek groups, the North-

American Interfraternity Conference (NIC) for fraternities and the National Panhellenic Conference (NPC) for sororities were founded to discuss issues common to their constituent organizations. In the NPC's formative years, the women's groups focused on rush and pledging issues. The men's groups needed to sort out intense rivalries before they could settle into conversations about common interests.[20] For BGLOs, the National Pan-Hellenic Council (NPHC) reflects the unique history of black college students in the United States and the context of discrimination in which BGLOs exist.[21]

In 1902, seven women's Greek-letter organizations met to discuss issues of cooperation and mutual assistance. Out of that meeting the NPC was born. Presently, there are twenty-six NPC member groups bound by guidelines known as mutual agreements. Other than legislation for its own meetings, the NPC does not enact rules or policies. Its mission focuses on being an advocate and support organization for its members, member groups, and local college and alumnae councils and a proponent of women's sorority membership.[22]

The seeds of the NIC were planted in 1909 when twenty-six fraternities met to discuss pertinent issues. The next year, the Interfraternity Conference was formed; its name was changed in 1931 to the National Interfraternity Conference and in 1999 to its present name. Today there are sixty-four member chapters that have adopted nine basic expectations. The NIC's mission is "to advocate the needs of its member fraternities through enrichment of the fraternity experience; advancement and growth of the fraternity community; and enhancement of the educational mission of the host institutions."[23]

The NPHC is composed of nine international fraternities and sororities and exists to provide a strong, unified voice and representative body for its member groups. The council was founded at Howard University in 1930, with the purpose of promoting civic and service engagement by members and chapters. The NPHC mission differs somewhat from the missions of its white counterparts. It takes a stronger stand in articulating the values of service and a commitment to lifetime membership: "NPHC affiliates and their respective members have pledged to devote their resources to service in their respective communities, realizing that the membership experience of NPHC organizations goes beyond organizational membership during an individual's college career. A lifetime commitment to the goals and ideals of each respective organization is stressed." The NPHC does not advocate a separatist philosophy and does not advocate disassociation from the NIC, NPC, or National Association of Latino Fraternal Organizations (NALFO). Local NPHC councils maintain a distinct identity as service-based organizations, as opposed to those that may be strictly social in nature.[24]

Early Collaboration

Interaction and community building between black and white Greek organizations are relatively recent phenomena. Historically, white Greek groups excluded people of color. As BGLOs became established, the exclusionary practices of long-standing white Greek-letter organizations became more firmly entrenched. Craig Torbenson states, "Many of the older fraternities reacted by implementing exclusionary clauses, limiting membership to white, male, Protestant students to ensure a homogeneous group of individuals of like mind, religion, and race."[25] Brotherhood involved compatibility, and the differences of race and religion were perceived as obstacles to that end.

In response, people of color formed parallel organizations to foster the friendship and support they so desperately needed, especially those students living in overwhelmingly white environments. Once BGLOs began to form as separate entities, further barriers to full participation in campus life were imposed by administrators who refused to recognize these student groups. The founding of Kappa Alpha Psi at Indiana University in 1911 provides one example. Kappa Alpha Psi was initially denied a charter and university recognition and had difficulty securing a meeting place, even in members' rooming houses.[26] According to the NPHC, some colleges and universities required newly formed on-campus organizations to belong to a national organization, and that national organization had to belong to a national umbrella organization.[27] White Greek groups, which were well established by the early 1900s, were not affected by that requirement. This dualistic treatment is not surprising, given the social and political context. Around the same time, the Supreme Court sanctioned the "separate but equal" doctrine in *Plessy v. Ferguson*. Clearly, black and white Greek groups were viewed differently, and the early years of Greek-letter organizations did not produce the kind of climate needed for the groups to work together. It would be another sixty years before the nation would begin to wrestle with its racial inequities.

Until the civil rights movement of the mid-twentieth century caused discriminatory practices to be questioned, many white Greek organizations maintained their racially restrictive membership clauses. Most had statutes or bylaws prohibiting nonwhites and Jews from joining.[28] The Civil Rights Act of 1964 made it illegal for student organizations at institutions that received federal funds, such as financial aid, to prohibit membership based on race. With changing demographics, particularly in the latter part of the twentieth century, Greek-letter organizations had to rethink their once exclusionary membership policies if they wanted to survive. Although integration has occurred slowly, on campuses that host both white and black Greek organizations, segregation is still prevalent. The groups often have separate governance structures; they rarely collaborate or interact. Events such as recruitment and Greek Week seldom include both white and black Greeks. College administrators attribute this separation to many possible factors: the historical development of each system, alumni attitudes, fear of change, reluctance on the part of student members, and lack of skills and motivation on the part of college staff.

Research on current collaborative efforts between black and white Greeks is sparse. In one campus study, Erin King found that the black and white groups had different priorities that prevented them from working in partnership. BGLOs' tendency to be more service oriented did not mesh with the white organizations' social priorities. King also reported that black and white Greeks' failure to collaborate could be traced to a lack of understanding of each other's values and histories. Finally, even though students articulated the importance of collaboration, they did not want to accept responsibility for planning and implementing programs that promoted working together.[29]

Current Issues Facing Greek-Letter Organizations

Over the years, fraternities and sororities, whether historically white or black, have wrestled with many of the same issues. These include (but are not limited to) the role of Greek life on campus, the relationship of fraternities and sororities to the host institution, the misuse and abuse of alcohol and drugs, hazing, and retention of members. More than ever, Greeks must address issues of importance to their host institutions.[30] As external pressures mount for accountability by colleges and universities, Greeks must be identified as true partners in a learning community—demonstrating values and behaviors consistent with the institution's educational priorities.[31] Furthermore, as student populations become more racially and ethnically diverse, Greek groups will be challenged to embrace the concepts of openness and the appreciation of differences. The greatest threat to the persistence of all Greek groups, however, is the potential liability related to high-risk behaviors. Infrequent cases of hazing reported in the media remind us that these embedded practices of new member initiation survive despite bans by educational institutions and national organizations and state laws prohibiting them. Lawsuits brought by grieving families in response to students' injury or death from hazing or abusive drinking are a real threat to a chapter's financial solvency. Ricky Jones speaks to the prevalence of hazing in BGLOs and asserts that BGLO hazing is differentiated from that of other groups because of the intensity of the physical violence endured by initiates. These practices have roots in ancient rituals and are deeply ingrained in the psyche of black fraternities.[32] Attempts by the NPHC to prohibit such practices have not been successful. A concerted study of the origins and culture of black male organizations is needed to address this problem.

In a call to realign Greek-letter organizations so that they have respect for the values of the academic community and act accordingly, Robert Ackerman warns, "Greeks have long held a special place in campus life. But without a *concerted* renewal effort indicating that fraternities and sororities can adapt to the changing campus environment, that place may soon be forfeited."[33] Given the many issues facing both white and black Greeks on campuses, it is imperative for all these groups to work together. Cultural change will not be successful if only a few groups recognize the challenges and move toward reform.

Creating a Collaborative Climate

One perspective on facilitating interaction among groups, especially those of unequal status, provides a framework as we seek to establish a climate of collaboration between black and white Greeks. In early conversations about school desegregation in the late 1950s, Gordon Allport suggested that racial stereotypes would not end simply because black and white students were occupying the same schools. He asserted that educational institutions influence the social norms related to how people interact and that successful integration would occur when four conditions were met.[34] Since then, others have built on Allport's contact theory and reinforced these four conditions necessary for optimal intergroup contact: (1) equal group status within the situation, (2) common goals, (3) intergroup cooperation, and (4) the support of authorities, law, or custom.[35] When these conditions are violated, negative outcomes, such as increased prejudicial attitudes, can occur.[36]

Applying the contact theory framework to the Greek system, advisers and administrators should strive for the following: First, black and white organizations should expect, receive, and perceive equal status. All Greek groups should be entitled to the same resources, including support services, programming, advising, attention, and recognition. Outreach should be conducted with groups that do not readily seek support. Second, local Greek coordinating groups—the

Interfraternity Council (IFC), NPC, and NPHC—should articulate systemwide goals and then actively work together to realize them. Such goals need to be consistent with, and integrated into, institutional priorities so that Greek groups are helping the institution move forward with its agenda. In today's climate, that would entail the inclusion of goals related to the appreciation of diversity, service learning, and civic engagement. Third, the Greek environment needs to be generally noncompetitive. All Greek members should perceive a win-win climate. Positive accomplishments and progress toward stated goals should be recognized in a timely and appropriate fashion, especially those achievements that involve cooperation and collaboration. Finally, Greeks must hear, see, and sense the institution's desire for a collaborative Greek system. Due to the constant turnover of student leaders, administrators need to revisit the history of institutional support, recite language in relationship statements, demonstrate interest and availability, and envision with students a future that is collaborative in nature.

Institutions can be supportive by providing structures that facilitate Allport's four conditions. Helen L. Mamarchev, Julie A. Sina, and Debbie E. Heida have devised an oversight plan for improving Greek programs that can be adapted by campuses to help black and white groups increase their collaborative efforts.[37] An oversight plan defines the relationship between Greek groups and the institution and explicitly states how behavior will be evaluated. Key aspects of a collaboration plan include vision, resources, program variety, and evaluation.

With regard to vision, both black and white Greeks should have open and honest discussions concerning what it means to collaborate, what issues and barriers may hinder effective collaboration, and what an effective plan for collaboration entails. This is an appropriate topic to discuss during a retreat, taking advantage of the extended time available in that setting. A skilled facilitator can help guide the conversation toward tangible results. In addition, students and institutional representatives need to ask what kinds of resources are necessary for effective collaboration, particularly human resources. For example, what is the role of the alumni, the institution's administration, and undergraduate members? Collaboration can take many forms, and effective community building can be accomplished with programs that are well balanced and meet different needs. For example, relationship building is less threatening and can be most effective when centered around joint social events. Once students get to know others as individuals and form relationships, they can disregard the labels attached to particular groups. When this basis for communication is established, more sophisticated educational programming and initiatives can be tackled. Because both black and white Greeks have service and volunteerism embedded into their rituals and traditions, this area provides a natural collaborative bridge. Finally, to measure the effectiveness of students' efforts, specific programs and initiatives must be assessed. Additionally, there should be a mechanism to measure how students have grown and developed from the experience.

Greek-letter organizations extend their allegiances beyond campus borders, and we cannot omit important partners in this endeavor. All stakeholders need to participate in developing a plan for collaboration if the process is to yield lasting coalitions that are both meaningful and productive. In addition to the undergraduate chapters, the local Greek coordinating councils and representatives from the institution, local alumni, and national organizations must be participants in the process.

Best Practices

Successful programs at a number of colleges and universities are achieving significant results through plans that empower student leaders to collaborate on mutually beneficial activities. An examination of cases in which collaboration between black and white Greek organizations is a priority has revealed several "best practices." Areas most commonly addressed by collaborative programming include leadership development, community involvement and service, general program administration, and social events.

At the University of North Alabama, Greeks come together in three ways: participation in a two-day retreat, formation of an all-Greek council, and creation of a joint Greek information session for incoming students. During their retreat, participants focus on "their similarities, appreciating and understanding their differences, and making a plan to grow from there." One outcome of the retreat was the decision to implement an all-Greek council that would share information, openly discuss issues, and plan Greek-wide community programming. Student leaders agreed to keep the lines of communication open and assist each other in philanthropic events. During summer orientation for new students, black and white Greek organizations had previously presented their recruiting information at separate sessions. To ensure that the process is inclusive, all the Greek organizations have streamlined their information and now hold one combined session for potential members. At the University of North Alabama, Greeks clearly believe that it is more impressive, as well as more beneficial for growth, to demonstrate the existence of a unified Greek community at the institution.[38]

Bowling Green State University in Ohio addresses the issue of collaboration between black and white Greeks in two ways. First, there is a weekly IFC, NPC, and NPHC presidents' dinner meeting throughout the year. At the dinner, the council presidents share their monthly calendars as well as items of interest and mutual concern. These weekly dinners serve, in many respects, as a unified Greek council. Second, noncouncil chapter presidents meet for dinner and dialogue once a month. At these meetings, the chapter presidents get to know one another and use the time to discuss joint social or philanthropic activities. To assist in building a Greek community, the university provides campus housing to all Greek-letter organizations based on availability of space.[39]

One collaborative effort at the University of North Carolina at Wilmington is called You Got Served (named after a popular hip-hop dance film). This program is sponsored by NPC and NPHC groups and focuses on women's health issues. A second bridging approach between white and black groups involves acknowledging faith and religion as a common bond. Joint Bible studies serve as a springboard for the design and implementation of philanthropic projects. A third effort that seeks to empower participation in decision making was initiated by the Greek Affairs Office. A Greek Student Advisory Council comprising nonofficeholding members from Greek councils provides a forum for discussion and fosters their emerging leadership potential.[40]

At the University of South Florida, the Greek Life Office sponsors a community service project that requires 10 percent of each Greek organization's membership to participate. University administrators form community service project groups. At the conclusion of the work, Greek members debrief one another on their experiences and then consider ways to work together in the future. A second collaborative effort is the institution of monthly Greek enrichment meetings, at which members of black, white, and multicultural Greek-letter organizations discuss communication, identity development, cultural diversity, fraternal histories, leadership development skills, and the importance of academics. Each Greek-letter organization is required to send 10 percent of its chapter membership to these meetings. The Greek enrichment meetings are one way to bring together different groups to counter existing stereotypes. These informal gatherings teach respect for diversity while opening new channels of communication. Finally, the university's Greek Week committee includes members representing white, black, and multicultural organizations. In the past, this planning committee consisted primarily of NPC members, but since the composition of the committee has changed, more Greeks from all types of groups in the South Florida community have participated in Greek Week activities.[41]

At the University of Texas at San Antonio, the Greek Life Office hosts a sisterhood and brotherhood social event and an all-Greek community social event to allow members to get to know one another in a relaxed setting. The All-Greek Council is another avenue for students to communicate and collaborate within the Greek community. All three councils' executives meet every other week to program a calendar of upcoming events and to discuss mutual campus concerns.[42]

Southeastern Louisiana University's collaboration initiative was started by the black and white Greek-letter organizations themselves. Initially, BGLOs were paired with white organizations to teach the latter's members how to step—a rhythmic dance style that combines footsteps, claps, and chants and has long been a tradition in black fraternities and sororities. These white groups then had an opportunity to perform during the Greek Week Step Show. The success of this event paved the way for other joint Greek-related activities during the academic year.[43]

The Greek Affairs Office at Western Carolina University facilitates many opportunities for black and white Greeks to socialize, work together, and collaborate on projects and activities. They participate in the Greek Council, a body made up of representatives of all Greek organizations. This group meets to discuss issues of concern and to maintain an ongoing dialogue. During open IFC, NPC, and NPHC sessions, information is disseminated to the respective groups. Greek housing on the Western Carolina campus accommodates fraternities and sororities with smaller memberships. In addition, because all Greeks are housed in the same general location on campus, black and white members live in close proximity, helping to foster a sense of community.

Western Carolina University also addresses Greek leadership development each spring semester. Upper-level undergraduate members conduct a "Greek Advance," which is an opportunity for new members to be properly indoctrinated into the Western Carolina Greek community and receive information about Greek life on campus. These upper-division Greeks receive special training to facilitate their sessions with the new members. In addition, BGLOs offer Black Greek 101, an introductory course to create more awareness and understanding of the African American Greek community. This course also serves as an effective recruitment tool.[44]

Key Areas for Collaboration

We started with the assumption that agreement is preferable to conflict and that a consensus-seeking agenda benefits all parties that share an interest in Greek organizations on campus. While respecting the different histories and traditions of the various groups, collaboration can be fostered when we focus on group similarities and shared interests. Employing our knowledge of theories, group dynamics, and current practices, black and white Greek-letter organizations should be directed to the following key topics as they work toward building a strong and positive Greek system:

- Developing Greek community activities
- Developing campus and surrounding community activities
- Working together on common issues involving chapter operations (e.g., officer training, parents' programs, alumni events)
- Forming an all-Greek council to address issues of mutual concern within the Greek community
- Providing the opportunity for a universal ritual—for example, a Greek convocation held at the beginning of the academic year that emphasizes similarities, intergroup cooperation, and a commitment to the institution
- Developing a joint leadership program for students focused on collaboration, culminating with a joint community service project
- Realizing the opportunities for enhanced alumni collaboration

Administrators should encourage Greeks to engage in community building efforts. The process starts with the identification of common interests and goals, with an emphasis on those areas that mesh with the host institution's mission and imperatives. A culture of collaboration is likely to flourish in a supportive environment that ensures the equal status of all Greek-letter organizations and facilitates the development of common goals that all groups can actively pursue.

Notes

1. Ongoing concerns about alcohol abuse, hazing, and sexual misconduct; escalating accountability imposed by the courts; and heightened public interest have led institutions and alumni to actively engage with Greek-letter groups. The administrative approach of in loco parentis (in lieu of a parent) may have gone by the wayside, but concern for students' safety and their personal growth and development has not.

2. John Hayek, Robert Carini, Patrick O'Day, and George Kuh, "Triumph or Trag-

edy? Comparing Student Engagement Levels of Members of Greek-Letter Organizations and Other Students," *Journal of College Student Development* 43, no. 5 (2002): 643–63; Shaun R. Harper, Lauretta F. Byars, and Thomas B. Jelke, "How Black Greek-Letter Organization Membership Affects College Adjustment and Undergraduate Outcomes," in *African American Fraternities and Sororities: The Legacy and the Vision*, ed. Tamara L. Brown, Gregory S. Parks, and Clarenda M. Phillips (Lexington: University Press of Kentucky, 2005), 393–416.

3. An alternative view includes a Marxist perspective whereby conflict, not stability, is the impetus for community change. A world in which Greek advisers purposefully adopt a Marxist approach is nearly impossible to imagine; thus, we advocate the more optimistic route.

4. Patricia K. Kubow and Paul R. Fossum, *Comparative Education: Exploring Issues in International Context* (Upper Saddle River, N.J.: Merrill Prentice-Hall, 2003), 28–30.

5. Alexander W. Astin, *What Matters in College: Four Critical Years Revisited* (San Francisco: Jossey-Bass, 1993); Lee Upcraft and John Gardner, *The Freshman Year Experience: Helping Students Survive and Succeed in College* (San Francisco: Jossey-Bass, 1989).

6. Vincent Tinto, *Rethinking the Causes and Cures of Student Attrition*, 2nd ed. (Chicago: University of Chicago Press, 1993).

7. Astin, *What Matters in College*, 363.

8. Harper et al., "How Black Greek-Letter Organization Membership Affects College Adjustment."

9. William Baird, *Baird's Manual of American College Fraternities*, 20th ed., ed. Jack Anson and Robert Marchesani Jr. (Indianapolis: Baird's Manual Foundation, 1991).

10. Ibid., 1–10.

11. John S. Brubacher and Willis Rudy, *Higher Education in Transition: A History of American Colleges and Universities, 1636–1976*, 3rd ed. (New York: Harper and Row, 1976), 127.

12. Alpha Delta Phi founders page, www.alphadeltapi.org/contentmanager/page.asp?webpageid=197 (accessed May 31, 2006).

13. Gamma Phi Beta history page, www.gammaphibetaneworleans.com/History.html (accessed May 31, 2006).

14. Michael H. Washington and Cheryl L. Nunez, "Education, Racial Uplift, and the Rise of the Greek-Letter Tradition: The African American Quest for Status in the Early Twentieth Century," in Brown et al., *African American Fraternities and Sororities*, 137–79.

15. Walter M. Kimbrough, "Historically Black Fraternal Organizations," in *The Administration of Fraternal Organizations on North American Campuses: A Pattern for the New Millennium*, ed. Dennis E. Gregory et al. (Asheville, N.C.: College Administration Publications, 2003), 79–80.

16. Joanna Brooks, "Prince Hall, Freemasonry, and Genealogy," *African American Review* 34, no. 2 (2000): 197–216; Prince Hall et al., "Documents Relating to Negro Masonry in America," *Journal of Negro History* 21, no. 4 (1936): 411–32; Alvin J. Schmidt and Nicholas Babchuk, "The Unbrotherly Brotherhood: Discrimination in Fraternal Orders," *Phylon* 34, no. 3 (1973): 275–82.

17. Brown et al., *African American Fraternities and Sororities.*

18. D. Gadson, "Greek Power! African American Greek Letter Organizations Yield Massive Influence after School Days," *Black Collegian* 20, no. 1 (1989): 36.

19. Tyra Black, Joanne Belknap, and Jennifer Ginsburg, "Racism, Sexism, and Aggression: A Study of Black and White Fraternities," in Brown et al., *African American Fraternities and Sororities,* 385–86.

20. Washington and Nunez, "Education, Racial Uplift, and Rise of the Greek-Letter Tradition," 137–79; Peter Smithhisler, "The Role of the North-American Interfraternity Conference (NIC)," in Gregory et al., *Administration of Fraternal Organizations on North American Campuses,* 117–35.

21. National Pan-Hellenic Council, "About the NPHC," http://www.nphchq.org/about.htm (accessed May 24, 2006).

22. National Panhellenic Conference, "About NPC," http://www.npcwomen.org/about/an_mission.php (accessed May 24, 2006).

23. North-American Interfraternity Council, "Who We Are and What We Do," http://www.nicindy.org/index.html (accessed May 24, 2006).

24. National Pan-Hellenic Council, "About the NPHC."

25. Craig L. Torbenson, "The Origin and Evolution of College Fraternities and Sororities," in Brown et al., *African American Fraternities and Sororities,* 37–66.

26. André McKenzie, "In the Beginning: The Early History of the Divine Nine," in Brown et al., *African American Fraternities and Sororities,* 181–210.

27. National Pan-Hellenic Council, "About the NPHC."

28. Clyde Sanfred Johnson, *Fraternities in Our Colleges* (New York: National Interfraternity Foundation, 1972), 208; Ron Binder, "Historically White Men's Fraternal Organizations," in Gregory et al., *Administration of Fraternal Organizations on North American Campuses,* 35.

29. Erin T. King, "All Greek Together? An Examination of Sorority and Fraternity Members' Attitudes about Collaboration" (master's thesis, University of Toledo, 2004).

30. Edward G. Whipple and Eileen G. Sullivan, "Greeks as Communities of Learners," in *New Challenges for Greek Letter Organizations: Transforming Fraternities and Sororities into Learning Communities,* ed. Edward G. Whipple (San Francisco: Jossey-Bass, 1998), 87–94.

31. Jon C. Dalton and A. M. Petrie, "The Power of Peer Culture," *Educational Record* 78, nos. 3–4 (1997): 18–24.

32. Ricky L. Jones, *Black Haze: Violence, Sacrifice, and Manhood in Black Greek-Letter Fraternities* (Albany: State University of New York Press, 2004).

33. Robert Ackerman, "The Survival of Greek Life: Concerns and Solutions," *NASPA Journal* 28, no. 1 (1990): 81.

34. Gordon W. Allport, *The Nature of Prejudice* (Reading, Mass.: Addison-Wesley, 1954).

35. Tabbye M. Chavous, "An Intergroup Contact-Theory Framework for Evaluating Racial Climate on Predominantly White College Campuses," *American Journal of Community Psychology* 36, nos. 3–4 (2005): 239–57.

36. Thomas F. Pettigrew, "Intergroup Contact Theory," *Annual Review of Psychology* 49 (1998): 65–85.

37. Helen L. Mamarchev, Julie A. Sina, and Debbie E. Heida, "Creating and Maintaining a Campus Oversight Plan: Do They Work? What Are the Alternatives?" in Gregory et al., *Administration of Fraternal Organizations on North American Campuses*, 199–213.

38. Amy G. Ellis, University North Alabama, e-mail to researcher, March 27, 2006.

39. Ron Binder, Bowling Green State University, personal communication, February 2006.

40. Tracie M. Massey, University of North Carolina at Wilmington, e-mail to researcher, March 28, 2006.

41. Dyonne M. Butler, University of South Florida, e-mail to researcher, March 28, 2006.

42. Kristal C. Statler, University of Texas at San Antonio, e-mail to researcher, April 3, 2006.

43. Jim McHodgkins, Southeastern Louisiana University, e-mail to researcher, April 5, 2006.

44. Bart H. Andrus, Western Carolina University, e-mail to researcher, April 3, 2006.

21

Advising Black Greek-Letter Organizations
A Student Development Approach

Ralph Johnson, Darnell Bradley, LeKeisha Bryant,
Darren M. Morton, and Don C. Sawyer III

The saga of the American college fraternity and sorority is replete with triumph and tragedy. It is one that speaks of the exuberance of youth and their desire for meaningful relationships. Moreover, the saga speaks of the human need to care for others and the reciprocal need to feel cared about. This is expressed through the groups' emphasis on brotherhood and sisterhood. Since its inception in 1776, members of the American collegiate Greek system have sought to live out the ideals embodied in their creeds and credos and have fostered a sense of camaraderie and esprit de corps. Greek membership "expresses a bond founded on intense interpersonal, transpersonal and metaphysical affection."[1] This has been their strength and is the reason that Greek-letter organizations have survived for generations.

As American higher education changed and began to reflect the broader society, so did the Greek-letter organization movement. By the turn of the twentieth century, what had once been a relatively monolithic phenomenon evolved into a relatively diverse phenomenon when a college fraternity for men of African descent, Alpha Phi Alpha, was founded on December 4, 1906, at Cornell University in Ithaca, New York.[2] The men who enrolled at Cornell in 1906 were ardent scholars who were determined to succeed, both individually and collectively. To assist with that goal, they created a society for their mutual benefit and ushered in the black Greek-letter organization (BGLO) movement.[3]

Like their counterparts in 1776, the founders of Alpha Phi Alpha were attracted to the idea of a fraternity because of the special bond it would create. Through this bond, they could foster a spirit of cooperation, collaboration, and genuine caring for their fraternity brothers, all of whom faced the vicissitudes of being men of color at a practically all-white institution at the beginning of the twentieth century. The founders of the other BGLOs at predominantly white institutions (PWIs) were like-minded, having faced similar circumstances at Indiana and Butler universities. All these students, as well as those who introduced the BGLO concept to historically black colleges and universities (HBCUs), were trailblazers and made significant contributions to higher education and American society in general. Although they were among the elite, they maintained a strong desire to reach back and bring along others from their communities. Gloria Dickinson comments on this sentiment: "The founders of the first eight BGLOs were scholarly activists slightly more than one generation removed from slavery. . . . The earliest of them entered college during the decade following the historic *Plessy v. Ferguson* (1896) Supreme Court decision that affirmed both the doctrine of 'separate but equal' and the permanence of Jim Crow. So, like their elders, they became enmeshed in organizing 'for the race.'"[4]

By the 1960s, the BGLO had become a major fixture on American college and university campuses. And although the initial expansion of some of the groups occurred at PWIs, the explosive growth took place at the country's HBCUs. These two environments interfaced differently with the BGLOs, although in both cases, administrators wondered just how much institutional support, if any, the groups should be given. It is safe to say that both types of institutions have wrestled with the challenges and issues that come with hosting BGLOs, with the overarching question being how best to advise them.

In this chapter, we discuss the most effective ways to advise BGLOs. We outline the similarities and differences of the BGLO system in PWIs versus HBCUs. Moreover, we discuss what has been done to advise and support these groups and what needs to be done to assist their members in their overall growth and development. Student affairs practitioners, student development specialists, and other higher education professionals, as well as the national and international leadership of the constituent groups of the National Pan-Hellenic Council (NPHC), should find this information helpful. It is through the use of appropriate student development theory, coupled with the dedication and commitment of caring professionals, that the work of developing students who affiliate with BGLOs will be enhanced.

Who are the students who join BGLOs? What types of experiences have contributed to their desire or need to affiliate with these groups? What challenges or developmental issues do they face, and what contributions do they bring to this unique campus culture? Perhaps a cursory look at the burgeoning literature about students of color will shed some light on and give some context to the social phenomenon explored here.

Students of Color and College Participation

The literature on students of color, academic achievement, and college attendance rates is full of theories and articles with divergent views. It is difficult to paint one picture that incorporates all the issues these students face and illustrates how these issues affect their attainment of postsecondary education. To get an accurate picture of the reasons for high and low academic achievement in college and the lower rates of attendance by blacks, we must look at the living environments of minority and nonminority students and their levels of preparation for postsecondary education.

The family environment in which a child lives has an impact on many aspects of that child's life, including educational performance. The National Center for Education Statistics (NCES) reports that black children are more likely than white children to live in poverty, to live in single-parent households, and to live in urban areas. Family structure and poverty level are associated with an increased risk for dropping out of high school or not attending college after high school graduation. Children with a low socioeconomic status have lower than normal achievement rates and higher than average dropout rates. Recent research indicates that students who attend urban schools are more likely to encounter problems that hinder educational achievement than are those who attend schools in other areas. The majority of all blacks in grades one through twelve in the United States live in areas characterized as central cities. In contrast, the majority of white students live in the suburbs. The NCES's 1999 report shows that parents' level of educational achievement may be the reason for increased achievement levels among suburban children.[5]

Some of the current literature finds that the peer group is influential on the academic achievement of black students. Studies suggest that, in contrast to other minorities, blacks are less likely to receive support from other blacks for academic excellence. Jawanza Kunjufu found that, in an effort to cope with this lack of support, some high-achieving African Americans become class clowns to conceal their academic abilities.[6] M. L. Clark identified other students who live dual lives—adopting the norms and values of the majority culture to achieve success in school, while embracing black peer group cultural norms outside of school to be accepted socially.[7]

Even with all these obstacles in place, the number of students of color on campuses has increased in the United States. Students of color have also been graduating at higher rates, although the rate is still only 42 percent—20 percentage points below that of their white counterparts.[8] It is understood that, nationally, students of color do not make up the majority of college students in this country. All the issues related to students of color in higher education have a direct impact on BGLO membership, which consists primarily of students of color. There are a multitude of issues facing students of color on college campuses, but for purposes of this chapter, we concentrate on the issues facing students of color (mostly blacks) who are BGLO members.

One of the biggest factors facing BGLOs at PWIs is the number of students in the chapters on campuses. Some institutions have a variety of the nine NPHC organizations represented on campus, while others have few or none of these groups. On some campuses, there are often too many BGLO chapters to be supported by the limited number of students of color enrolled there. Walter Kimbrough reports an average of fifteen students in BGLO chapters at one of the PWIs where he conducted his research.[9] Having fifteen members in a chapter at a PWI (especially in the Northeast) would be considered a grand accomplishment by today's standards. But one has to ask why fifteen members in an undergraduate chapter is currently a stretch for some BGLOs at PWIs.

Kimbrough notes that students of color once viewed these organizations as a way to become part of the mainstream campus culture. They also viewed these groups as a support system to help them survive and thrive on predominantly white campuses across the nation. During this "golden age" of BGLO activity, there was no perceived need to "recruit" new members. Everybody wanted to be Greek—or so it was assumed.[10] However, this has changed. College students are still interested in becoming members of BGLOs, but there are now many more options from which to choose. With the explosion of Latino and Latina organizations and other multicultural organizations on college campuses, BGLOs are no longer viewed as the only outlet for black college students. With the presence of other non-Greek organizations, such as National Association of Negro Business and Professional Women's Club, National Society of Black Engineers, and other cultural, academic, and civic groups, BGLOs face considerable competition. The members of these non-Greek organizations seem to reap the benefits of being in a supportive affinity group without having to go through any type of sanctioned or underground new member initiation process.

The Institutional Context

Many PWIs struggle to find a balance between fully integrating BGLOs into the campus's fraternity and sorority community and maintaining the fundamental differences of the groups. There is often a surface-level understanding that the members of the National Interfraternity Conference (NIC), National Panhellenic Conference (NPC), and National Pan-Hellenic Council (NPHC) have both similarities and differences. This constant balancing act has a profound impact on the advisement that BGLOs receive on a given campus. Campuses have addressed this same issue differently across the country. There are PWIs where BGLOs have a local NPHC chapter, campuses where all organizations are housed in one council, and campuses where BGLOs are grouped with multicultural and Latino organizations in a multicultural Greek council. There are also campuses where BGLOs are not housed in the Greek Affairs Office but are located instead in the Multicultural Affairs Division.

The quest for culturally aware advisers at PWIs has led to a structure in which some NPHC organizations are advised out of a campus diversity unit (e.g., Multicultural Affairs, Black Cultural Center, Minority Affairs). In most cases, this move was initiated by students who felt that their advisers knew too little about their experiences. The assumption was that someone of color, even if not a member of a BGLO, could at least understand what it was like to be a student of color at a PWI.

White advisers at PWIs must be prepared to advise BGLOs, with the understanding that students of color experience greater feelings of alienation than do white students at PWIs.[11] Researchers have attributed such feelings of alienation to the perceived racial climate on campus, which includes factors such as racism and discrimination in the policies, attitudes, and procedures of the institution of higher education.[12] This research paints a picture that is both daunting and replete with opportunity. By having regular contact with chapter members and building relationships within the organizational structure (chapter presidents, alumni advisers, regional directors, state directors, and so forth), advisers can become allies to these students and their organizations. In the past, NPHC organizations did not receive the full benefits of having advisers and thus had to seek out their own advisers who were culturally sensitive to their needs.

To what extent this organizational arrangement affects the success and failure of these groups remains unclear. Anecdotal evidence is all we have, and it shows mixed results. Some NPHC organizations have flourished under the advisement of the campus diversity unit, while others have experienced success under the larger Greek umbrella. As campuses become more diverse, advisers and other administrators are becoming more culturally aware, and they are now doing a better job of advising students of color. However, this task is far from complete, and it still involves only a few individuals who have responsibility for advising BGLOs. With all these different council structures come different issues that members of BGLOs must face. Some may argue that one structure is better than another, but that is difficult to prove because of the various factors that must be considered both collectively and in isolation.

Because BGLO chapters do not have as many members as NIC and NPC chapters, their issues are often placed on the "back burner" of the campus administrators who are responsible for their advisement. The council structure issue gets more complicated when dealing with the notion of campus advising practices. Some institutions have a specific adviser for each council; at others, advisers are shared based on the historical focus of the fraternity or sorority councils. Attendance at a national fraternity- or sorority-related conference often reveals a great deal of misunderstanding about the advising of BGLOs at PWIs. New advisers often have no clue how to reach the students they have been charged with advising. This is not always the fault of the adviser, but in some cases, colleges and universities have not done a good job in terms of hiring people with expertise in the affairs of BGLOs. This is clearly demonstrated with a deeper look into the structure of fraternity and sorority communities.

As stated previously, BGLO issues are often misunderstood and swept under the carpet. However, institutions are not solely at fault. Students in BGLOs have done their part to remain out of sight and out of mind. Their small numbers have allowed some organizations to operate under the radar and carry out activities that would not be permitted if they were appropriately advised.[13] Many BGLO representatives collectively attempt to pull the wool over the eyes of campus advisers by operating under a false sense of cultural Greek secrecy. They say, "It's a black Greek thing, you wouldn't understand." For an inexperienced adviser, this is an easy trap to fall into. Since BGLOs generally do not have traveling consultants, and national officers rarely visit the campus, advisers are left to blindly navigate the road of proper BGLO advisement on their own. This can be disastrous for all involved. On campuses that have white advisers for BGLOs, this problem is usually more pronounced. It has been found that among white, African American, and Mexican American students, all groups disclosed more personal information to faculty members who shared the same ethnicity.[14] This was especially true among black students when the topic related to something of a racial, academic, or sensitive nature. This finding underscores the fact that white advisers have an additional hurdle to overcome when dealing with BGLOs. However, this hurdle should not be used as an excuse; it simply means that staff members have to be extremely diligent in gathering the appropriate information and best practices concerning the advisement of BGLOs.

Research indicates that for students of color, particularly blacks, positive interactions with university staff and faculty members can maximize their educational experience.[15] Alexander Astin supports this notion, observing that faculty and staff can help integrate students into the social and academic culture of the institution.[16] The quality of the college experience for blacks is strongly impacted by their interactions with agents of the institution; therefore, agents of the institution must be aware of how to serve these students.

Recent research in the area of BGLOs has focused on the membership intake process,[17] members' cognitive development,[18] and the social development of BGLO members at PWI and HBCU campuses.[19] But what are the implications of these studies on individuals who advise NPHC groups on campuses? Does this mean that advisers who serve chapters at HBCUs have an easier task than those serving at PWIs? Should advisers take a different approach based primarily on a single institutional descriptor?

The search for cultural sensitivity is seen as a less daunting task at HBCUs.[20] There, students have administrators and faculty who look like them, and they have a sense of a support network to help them adjust to college life. These elements of comfort also create an advantageous situation for the individuals advising these students. There are fewer cultural barriers to overcome; the students already feel a connectedness to the institution, and they are eager to participate.

For campus professionals at PWIs and HBCUs, as well as alumni, one of the most outstanding problems plaguing NPHC organizations is their academic performance. With the exception of Shaun Harper's study,[21] there has been little scholarly research on how this particular segment of the minority student population navigates the undergraduate academic experience. Students of color are encouraged to get involved and carve their own niche on campus; however, when members of BGLOs do so, they often experience a decline in academic performance. One potentially large contributor to this trend is the hazing culture prevalent in BGLOs. Since the 1990 NPHC ban on pledging, there have been numerous incidents of bodily harm as a result of illegal pledging and hazing on college campuses. Despite attempts by student affairs professionals to educate students on the negative aspects of hazing, the practice continues. The sleep deprivation, physical abuse, and mental pressure involved in hazing almost certainly have an impact on students' academics. Although the scientific evidence may be inconclusive, there is enough anecdotal evidence to safely argue the case.

Another argument specific to PWIs is overinvolvement in BGLOs, which creates time-management problems. In contrast to chapters at HBCUs (which have a larger pool of members to draw from), BGLO chapters at PWIs tend to have fewer members and, as a result, smaller chapters. This means that there are fewer people to perform all the tasks of organizing and running BGLO activities, along with juggling involvement in other student organizations and, of course, doing course work. Although previous research provides conclusive evidence that involvement in BGLOs by minority students is beneficial, it might be the case that overinvolvement can be detrimental.[22]

Perhaps the most striking difference between BGLOs at PWIs and those at HBCUs is the level of institutional control over the groups. BGLOs at PWIs are often considered a low priority or may be completely ignored. Even when advisers make a conscientious effort to provide effective oversight to BGLOs, the contact and institutional expectations are far less intense at PWIs compared with HBCUs. For example, at PWIs, membership recruitment rules for fraternities are more flexible and allow for variation in the schedules of pledge periods and initiations. Although women's recruitment tends to be more structured, that structure is governed more by NPC rules than by institutional mandate. At HBCUs however, the university typically determines the exact timing of recruitment and membership intake, even to the point of deciding when initiations must occur. This approach is rarely, if ever, used at PWIs. Moreover, HBCUs may impose academic requirements beyond the criteria set by BGLOs' national offices for participation in the membership intake process and subsequent initiation. This approach is reminiscent of the days when the philosophy of in loco parentis permeated American colleges and universities. Again, such practices beg the question of what are the most effective ways to advise student organizations and, more pointedly, BGLOs.

Advising Student Organizations

The job of advising students became a major focus after World War I, when university administrators wanted students to build a bridge between academics and the cocurricular aspects of student life. That led to the formal institutional recognition of student organizations. Faculty members played a vital role in establishing the advising role until the growth of graduate programs in the late 1960s and early 1970s that trained student personnel professionals.[23] During this period, students spent much out-of-class time focusing on leadership and volunteer activities that enhanced their classroom experience.

Higher education literature repeatedly states that involvement in cocurricular activities is vital to the improvement and expansion of the whole student. Astin defines involvement as the amount of energy a student puts into the academic enterprise, whether in the classroom or in cocurricular activities.[24] Edward Whipple states that student affairs staff "must be directed toward, and committed to, the growth and development of students. They must have the resources to assess and enhance programs, and staff must be well aware of the thin line between control and autonomy. Researchers have discovered many characteristics of good advisors. They are knowledgeable, enthusiastic, self-starters, available, energetic, emotionally supportive and directive."[25] These characteristics are consistent with many standards set by the institution to ensure that student organizations are complementing the academic mission.

Some individuals are unaware of the true benefits of being an adviser. These benefits include "a better understanding of students' lives, an opportunity to observe students' growth and development, and the goodwill that quality advising generates on campus."[26] Student affairs professionals believe that advising an organization is an expected part of working with students, but faculty and other staff who are asked to serve as advisers tend to be more reluctant due to the potential challenges they may face.[27] Norbert Dunkel and John Schuh list a number of challenges and rewards that advisers experience:

Challenges
- Time management and the tendency to over-commit.
- Minimal adviser training available.
- Clarification of their role in the organization.
- Potential to over-control in matters of the group.
- Keeping abreast of important actions and decisions taken by the organization.
- Exercising patience in the growth and developmental processes of students.

Rewards
- Being able to observe the development of students during college.
- Recognition by the institution, organization, and students for a job well done.
- Serving as a mentor for students.
- Ability to observe fads, cultures, and subtle changes that occur in student life.

- Opportunity to teach, lead, and coach students.
- Opportunity to form networks with colleagues involved as advisers of similar organizations.
- Opportunity to participate in an organization whose purpose you enjoy.[28]

The negative aspects of advising student organizations may overwhelm some individuals. These include evening and weekend hours, the high demands of many students, and the potential for conflict.

Since the late nineteenth century, advisers have been debating the connection between the Greek system and the institution. This debate centers on the founding history of the Greek-letter organizations and their influence on student life. The 1990 Greek system was seen as a "campus subculture for students to associate with others who are affluent, have relatively undefined academic and vocational goals, and place a higher priority on social life rather than intellectual pursuits."[29] This perception is still prevalent on campuses that have a dominant Greek system.[30] The roles that currently define the adviser include consultant, information source, clarifier, counselor, and facilitator.[31] The adviser must consult with the individual chapters in creating purposeful programs and increasing their presence for recruitment purposes. Advisers serve as information sources in helping students develop relationships with other departments for possible collaborative programming. Advisers become clarifiers when it comes to disseminating new policies and procedures and getting organizations to revisit their missions and constitutions annually. Advisers are often seen as counselors because of the advice they give pertaining to chapter development and programming; they serve as facilitators when dealing with inter- and intragroup misunderstandings. They must use an unbiased approach in helping students work through various issues and concerns. Student affairs administrators must understand the changing culture of fraternities and sororities, and their advisers must be knowledgeable about the current generation of students joining fraternities and sororities, including what that generational profile looks like. This knowledge will guide advisers in developing a plan to help fraternities and sororities understand their role in the institution and help them change the prevailing negative perception about Greeks.

Every Greek adviser must be knowledgeable of the history of the emergence of BGLOs on college campuses. By joining the Greek-letter movement, black students developed a sense of purpose that incorporated their racial identification, cultural heritage, and social uplift; they merely imitated the white fraternities and sororities in terms of organizational structure.[32] Once these organizations began to grow and develop chapters on other campuses, the NPHC, established in 1930, provided a governing council for the nine organizations still in existence today.

Advisers must understand the differences among the NPC, NIC, and NPHC, which include visible culture, organizational culture, socioeconomic status of members, time of initiation, and purpose.[33] The visible culture for the NPHC includes line jackets, audible calls, hand signs, probate shows, and step shows. The organizational culture includes the presence of alumni activity and the local, regional, and national presence of the NPHC. Socioeconomic status involves the percentage of students involved in NPHC groups that come from a lower socioeconomic status than students involved in predominantly white fraternities and sororities. The NPHC organization conducts more social events benefiting black students and the wider black community. Kimbrough and Hutcheson assert, "Scarcity of research on BGLOs handicaps administrators who are unfamiliar with the Greek system, but who contend with the serious problems by which these organizations are beset."[34] These problems include hazing, alcohol and drug abuse, and poor academic performance.

The challenges facing advisers also include the contribution and support black Greek organizations provide to the institution, which in turn determines how valuable they are to the institution. Michael Shonrock declares that campus administrators "must emphasize that it is a privilege, not a right, to be on a campus and if chapters do not contribute to the college or university's educational mission and the standards the institution espouses, these organizations will not be welcome."[35] On certain campuses, this notion leaves the NPHC at a crossroad: either shape up or be removed.

Student Development Theory and Advising BGLOs

Although specific faculty members were assigned the task of handling student issues outside the classroom early in American higher education, the concept of "student affairs" as we know it today was set forth pursuant to a meeting of student personnel workers in 1936–1937. The historic American Council on Education document that emerged from this meeting is known as the "1937 Student Personnel Point of View," and it encouraged colleges and universities to provide appropriate programs and services that would assist students with their total development and help them become positive citizens in the community. There are four basic assumptions of the "Student Personnel Point of View":

1. The individual student must be considered as a whole.
2. Each student is a unique person and must be treated as such.
3. The total environment of the student is educational and must be used to achieve his or her full development.
4. The major responsibility for a student's personal and social development rests with the student and his or her personal resources.[36]

Inherent in this philosophy is the premise that students have a right to succeed and that trained university staff should be employed to assist them in maximizing their success. It is also believed that students have a right to fail, as long as those failures are used as "teachable moments" to aid in students' overall growth and development. As such, student affairs practitioners prescribe to and utilize student development theories to impact student learning and to foster the holistic development of students through their cocurricular involvement.

Marylu McEwen writes: "Since the primary goals of student affairs practitioners are to serve students, to be student-centered, to understand and design academic environments, and to be experts about organizations and how they function, it is of utmost importance, both professionally and ethically, for them to know and understand the individuals, groups, and institutions they work in. One way to do this is through theory."[37] As a rule, theory helps predict the issues and challenges that students will experience and guides the practitioner in creating programs and offering services that will assist students as they confront these developmental tasks.

Theodore Miller and Judith Prince ask: "And what about *student development* itself, the heart of our enterprise? Obviously, at the most basic level, this term simply means the development of the whole college-going human being. But it is defined more specifically as *the application of human development concepts in postsecondary settings so that everyone involved can master increasingly complex developmental tasks, achieve self-direction, and become interdependent.* It is, then, both a philosophical goal and the means for achieving it."[38] Student affairs professionals use theory in their work because it helps make sense of a complex environment. McEwen states, "Every one of us has our own informal theories about people, environment, students, human development, and how to work with students, although these theories or perspectives may not always be a conscious or clear part of our awareness. Thus people turn to theory—both formal and informal—to make the many complex facets of experience manageable, understandable, meaningful, and consistent rather than random."[39]

The use of student development theory can assist advisers in providing a more purposeful direction for the BGLOs under their advisement. Student affairs professionals, whether at PWIs or HBCUs, must become familiar with these theories and employ them as a matter of course when developing plans for student leadership training and chapter consultation. Moreover, the national and international leadership of the nine BGLOs should employ these theories when working with their collegiate chapters. Although not everyone would agree, we believe that the applicability of theories is particularly relevant in terms of BGLOs' identity and moral development, inasmuch as BGLO collegians often struggle with these developmental tasks, as do students from all backgrounds. There is probably greater agreement, however, that Astin's theory of involvement, the theory of service learning, and the social change model are particularly salient for BGLOs.

Putting these theories into practice in BGLOs is not difficult. It is simply a matter of identifying alumni and alumnae members who are student affairs professionals, and thus have training and experience in using these theories, and engaging their services to infuse a student development philosophy into the administration of their collegiate chapters. This is already being done by one of the NPHC groups. In 1998, Alpha Phi Alpha Fraternity became the first Greek-letter organization of any kind to create and offer a collegiate leadership training opportunity that intentionally and deliberately uses student development theory as a framework. The Alpha College Chapter Leadership Academy was designed by an alumni member of the fraternity who is a seasoned student affairs professional. Additionally, several of the academy faculty who teach and facilitate the myriad workshops and sessions are student affairs professionals. Through this academy, Alpha Phi Alpha's collegiate members participate in a weeklong training experience and are exposed to student development theories while learning about principles of leadership, ethical decision making, moral development, social change, and the inner workings of the fraternity. The program is highly successful and has proved to be an effective way of training the organization's future leaders.

Education and Training for Effective Greek Advisers

The advisement of BGLOs on college campuses continues to be an issue of tremendous concern. The role of the adviser is essential to breaking down barriers and developing organizations that can be fully integrated into campus life. The adviser must have a clear understanding of the overall system—how it works, its historical context and organizational dynamics—along with a deliberate focus on student development practice.

In general, campus administrations have failed to provide adequate support and structure for BGLOs. As a result, these organizations have been underadvised and poorly assisted. Given the complexity of these organizations, the adviser must be a highly trained professional with experience in developing Greek-letter organizations. The professional preparation must transcend the basic requirements for becoming a general student organization adviser. Depending on the individual and the institution, the qualifications can be as varied as the number of Greek-letter organizations on a campus. With few exceptions, professionals appointed as advisers to BGLOs lack the proficiency to progressively transform the black Greek experience. The adviser has traditionally been categorized as an entry-level administrator, a recent graduate, or a semiexperienced administrator with an expressed interest in working with these organizations. In some situations, the adviser may be a graduate member of a BGLO who is working on campus.

The vast majority of these individuals have a peripheral acquaintance with BGLOs' history, culture, organizational norms, and nuances. Most advisers hold a bachelor's degree and have received no advanced education or training focused on advisement or the development of these organizations. In many instances, these advisers have even less experience in student development theory or fraternal organizations. About student advisement, Dunkel writes, "The advisers usually relied on the observable experience they had as an undergraduate student working with their organization's advisor as the sole basis for how they currently advise an organization."[40] The same is disproportionately true of BGLO advisers; they have received limited, if any, training to serve as effective advisers for these organizations. The result is a lack of understanding about how to shape a positive or transformative experience.

Until recently, a substantial number of institutions, both predominantly white and historically black, have hired entry-level professionals or assigned the advisement role to graduate students as part of their assistantships. At PWIs, these entry-level professionals may be emblematic student affairs or student activities generalists. They have a diverse portfolio of responsibility with no specialization in BGLO affairs, or they are administrators of color working in other areas within the institution, such as multicultural affairs, a cultural center, and the like. These administrators are, by and large, freelancing in this area and possess even less knowledge or training than the entry-level student affairs professional.

At many PWIs, there are varying models for advisement of Greek-letter organizations. In some cases, the NPHC organizations have a different adviser from the NIC and NPC organizations. Regardless of the advisement structure, BGLOs must be closely linked to the institutional Greek life system. Carlos Cortes points out, "Colleges and universities need to continue to seek innovative ways to promote positive cross-cultural and intergroup relations, particularly among students. These efforts should include at least two dimensions; the development of better understanding of difference; and the recognition, sometimes the discovery, of underlying commonalities."[41]

Since BGLOs have both a fraternal and a black cultural aspect, it is necessary for the adviser to have a comprehensive knowledge of the groups' cultural norms, including ethnic and fraternal customs. Advisers to BGLOs must have an aptitude for fostering the cultural and fraternal core values in a balanced manner. Otherwise, these organizations will self-identify with the ethnic affinity group. Cortes states, "Universities face the challenge of facilitating healthy, supportive and affirming group aggregation while simultaneously trying to inhibit calcification into self-segregation."[42] An advisement structure that separates NIC, NPC, and NPHC organizations only limits these organizations' ability to become mainstreamed into the overall Greek system and often restricts the growth and development of these organizations within the framework of a comprehensive Greek system. Only within the last decade or so have BGLOs begun to receive advisement from the same professionals who advise the NIC and NPC organizations; therefore, professional education and training must prepare these advisers for fraternal and cross-cultural challenges.

HBCU campuses face the same challenges, except they may have a more homogeneous Greek system. Nevertheless, the same entry-level professionals are typically advising fraternities and sororities. If there are fraternal organizations other than African American ones, they are most likely advised by the same professional. Frequently, the adviser is a student affairs generalist with limited training and is most likely a graduate member of an NPHC organization.

Professionals serving as advisers to BGLOs across institutional types generally have comparable qualifications. Notwithstanding the type of institution (PWI or HBCU), professional education and training of the adviser should not be substituted for membership in one of these organizations. Although experienced professionals may have a better understanding of the higher education field, all advisers should receive the proper training to effectively execute their responsibilities. Nothing can replace the perfect combination of formal education, training, and experience.

Today, advisers to these organizations must be carefully selected and hold the appropriate credentials. Kimbrough points out, "If Black Greek-letter organizations are to thrive on college campuses in the next century, a new paradigm must be employed with regard to advising."[43] The campus adviser must be part of this paradigm shift. Highly qualified professionals with adequate education, organizational and cultural knowledge, and practical skills who partner with the national organizations are necessary for an effective paradigm shift. For this reason, advisers must have the aptitude to master the organizational dynamics unique to these organizations.

Professionals working with BGLOs should have a master's degree or higher, preferably from a graduate program specializing in a student development or higher education administration field. Graduate school course work provides a foundation for effective advisement skills through cognitive and theoretical knowledge. Likewise, a combination of practicum, internship, assistantship, or full-time work experience in the field can develop the requisite practical skills. Dunkel notes, "The emphasis at many programs is to hold assistantships in supervisory positions all while attempting to advise a student orgnazation."[44] Graduates of these programs acquire expansive theoretical and practical knowledge specific to student affairs. Although assistantships are extremely beneficial in preparation for a career in student affairs, close supervision by an experienced professional in the area is crucial.

Typically, professionals with graduate school training are more proficient and have competencies in student development practice, cross-cultural paradigms (organizational and ethnic), various college and university dynamics, and techniques for developing institutional goals to benefit BGLOs' aggregation into campus life. Kimbrough observes, "A much more hands-on approach is needed in working with these students, and student affairs educators must begin to discuss how this can occur."[45] Only explicitly educated and sufficiently trained professionals with graduate school preparation can provide this type of principled approach to qualitative and quantitative assistance.

The ongoing acquisition of knowledge through participation in professional associations and development opportunities is just as critical. These experiences help revitalize the stale, regimented, ineffective advisement of these organizations. Effective advisers must have a current awareness and understanding of issues and trends facing all fraternities and sororities, including NIC and NPC organizations. A unified advisement structure in which the same professional advises NPHC, NIC, and NPC organizations is optimal, but the professional preparedness of the adviser is most important.

Professional associations such as the Association of Fraternity Advisors (AFA) are also tremendous resources for gaining a breadth of knowledge about the Greek system. A balanced professional development experience can expand the knowledge base and enable advisers to implement a holistic approach to advisement. Participation in the NPHC, NIC, NPC, and AFA can provide a 360-degree view of fraternity and sorority life on college campuses.

Advisers to BGLOs should involve themselves in a diverse portfolio of professional development experiences, including those provided by the National Association of Student Affairs Professionals, National Association of Student Personnel Administrators, American College Personnel Association, Fraternity Executives Association, and Leadershape Institute. Within the context of the collegiate fraternal experience, Fraternity and Sorority Affairs Knowledge Communities and professional development institutes (e.g., Interfraternity Institute, Greek Leadershape) offer invaluable resources for the development of a "best-in-class" advisement program for BGLOs. These professional associations provide opportunities for the advisers to network, exchange ideas, gain new perspectives, and participate in educational programs. Constant growth and development, both in the student affairs profession and in the changing culture of BGLOs, are the only way to effectively advise these organizations. The adviser must be knowledgeable about current issues regarding student development theory, membership, cross-cultural awareness, Greek organizational dynamics, programming, and risk management. Critical thinking can be acquired only through continual education and professional development.

Recommendations for Effective Advisement of BGLOs

In keeping with recent trends occurring at various campuses around the country, we recommend that NPHC chapters receive the full benefits of the campus Greek adviser. Although the diversity unit might be a suitable place for student development to occur, the administrators there are often not professional Greek advisers. The campus Greek adviser, in most cases, is a professional hired to ensure that fraternities and sororities on campus are fulfilling their respective purposes. This person should be trained in the rules, regulations, and norms of every council he or she serves on campus. This training should begin in graduate school and continue throughout the person's career in the form of professional development. As campuses commit resources to Greek life, the NPHC and other cultural organizations must be included.

There are two avenues for professionals and alumni alike to better serve NPHC groups. The first involves all stakeholders attaining a level of cultural competence. At many campuses, Greek life has a "culture," and within that larger picture, the NPHC has its own culture. Alumni advisers need to be cognizant of student development theory when dealing with undergraduate chapters. These individuals, who are often volunteers, do a great service for the organization, and this service would be greatly enhanced by a nominal amount of student development theory. Although advising is not an exact science, and much is gained through the process of learning from one's mistakes, having the ability to reference concepts such as moral development, women's ways of knowing, and racial identity development, among others, would enable alumni advisers to do their jobs in a much more informed manner.

To better serve students in BGLOs, institutions have to require every person working in the Greek Affairs Office to have a general knowledge of NPHC- and BGLO-related issues. It is not fair for an institution to expect an understanding of NIC and NPC chapters without expecting the same understanding for BGLOs. If BGLOs are valued on campus, considerable resources must be used to ensure that everyone has a basic understanding of the issues facing students in these organizations.

Greek Affairs Offices have to hold the national and international organizations accountable for assisting with their chapters on campus. And office staff at the national and international level must be responsive to these institutional calls for assistance. Why would an institution want to use valuable human resources to maintain chapters on its campus if high-level support is lacking? It is recommended that BGLOs' national and international offices seek and value the input of undergraduate members. Officers must be viewed as a source of support, not just a group of alumni or alumnae charged with handing out sanctions and collecting dues. This recommendation is also offered to the national office of the NPHC. Undergraduate members of BGLOs often struggle to understand the purpose of the NPHC governing body and the need to pay NPHC dues for services that are perceived as absent.

Greek Affairs Offices at PWIs must also hold BGLO members accountable for the size of their chapters. With so much competition from other organizations on campus, BGLOs have to realize that recruiting is not only acceptable but also essential to their longevity. Recruitment does not mean that BGLO members should walk around campus waving banners and asking people to join; however, they must become more active in seeking the most qualified students to be members of their respective organizations.

Conclusion

The BGLO movement has always been a dynamic phenomenon. Black students at the turn of the twentieth century had the vision and the fortitude to create organizations for their mutual support and for the uplift of a race of people. Those luminaries were simply collegians engaged in the academic enterprise, yet they constructed social organizations that have lasted for a century. As colleges and universities accepted them, these institutions had to struggle with how best to support these groups. As BGLOs evolved, it became evident that adequate institutional resources were needed so that the members could be supported and nurtured into outstanding alumnae and alumni. In fact, we argue that if BGLOs are to remain viable entities in the future, they must invest the necessary resources to train and develop their members and utilize university student affairs professionals in that enterprise.

BGLO alumnae and alumni, whether initiated at a PWI or an HBCU, dominate the list of who's who in black (indeed, American) history. From Thurgood Marshall of Alpha Phi Alpha to Dorothy Height of Delta Sigma Theta, countless individuals were affirmed by these organizations and emerged to become leaders and ardent scholars on the national and international scene.

It is hoped that we have made a compelling case for a student development approach to advising BGLOs. In conclusion, we offer this final point: Effective advisement of these groups will yield great benefits to the members and the institutions that host them. Moreover, effective advisement will help minimize the tragedies and multiply the triumphs of these groups and their members as they move resolutely into another century of service to all humankind.

Notes

1. William K. Amiott and E. Maurice Cottingham Jr., *Brotherhood: Myth or Mystique? Reflections on Two Hundred Years of Greek-Letter College Fraternities* (Sigma Nu Foundation, 1976), 17.

2. Charles H. Wesley, *The History of Alpha Phi Alpha Fraternity: A Development in College Life*, 17th ed. (Baltimore: Foundation Publishers, 2000), 27.

3. Ibid.; Walter M. Kimbrough, "The Membership Intake Movement of Historically Black Greek-Letter Organizations," *NASPA Journal* 34, no. 3 (spring 1997): 230; Clyde S. Johnson, *Fraternities in Our Colleges* (New York: George Banta, 1972), 41.

4. Gloria Harper Dickinson, "Pledged to Remember: Africa in the Life and Lore of Black Greek-Letter Organizations," in *African American Fraternities and Sororities: The Legacy and the Vision*, ed. Tamara L. Brown, Gregory S. Parks, and Clarenda M. Phillips (Lexington: University Press of Kentucky, 2005), 11–12.

5. National Center for Education Statistics, *Education Digest* (1999), http://nces .ed.gov/programs/digest.asp; National Center for Education Statistics, *Education Digest* (2001), http://nces.ed.gov/programs/digest/d01/dt207.asp.

6. Jawanza Kunjufu, *To Be Popular or Smart: The Black Peer Group* (Chicago: African American Images Press, 1988).

7. M. L. Clark, "Social Identity, Peer Relations, and Academic Competence of African American Adolescents," *Education and Urban Society* 24, no.1 (1991): 41–52.

8. "Black Student College Graduation Rates Remain Low, but Modest Progress Begins to Show," *Journal of Blacks in Higher Education* 50 (2005–2006): 88–96.

9. Walter M. Kimbrough, "Self-assessment, Participation, and Value of Leadership Skills, Activities, and Experiences for Black Students Relative to Their Membership in Historically Black Fraternities and Sororities," *Journal of Negro Education* 64 (1995): 63.

10. Walter M. Kimbrough, *Black Greek 101: The Culture, Customs, and Challenges of Black Fraternities and Sororities* (Madison, N.J.: Fairleigh Dickinson Press, 2003).

11. W. Allen, "The Color of Success: African-American College Student Outcomes at Predominantly White and Historically Black Public Colleges and Universities," *Harvard Educational Review* 62 (1992): 26–44; D. Allen, "Desire to Finish College: An Empirical Link between Motivation and Persistence," *Research in Higher Education* 40 (1999): 461–85; R. J. Steward, S. Germain, and J. D. Jackson, "Alienation and Interactional Style: A Study of Successful Anglo, Asian, and Hispanic University Students," *Journal of College Student Development* 33 (1992): 149–56.

12. A. F. Cabrera, A. Nora, P. T. Terenzini, E. T. Pascarella, and L. S. Hagedorn, "Campus Racial Climate and the Adjustment of Students to College: A Comparison between White Students and African-American Students," *Journal of Higher Education* 70, no. 2 (1999): 134–60.

13. Lori Patton and Fred Bonner, "Advising the Historically Black Greek Letter Organization (HBGLO): A Reason for Angst or Euphoria?" *NASAP Journal* 4, no. 1 (2001): 24.

14. R. C. Noel and S. S. Smith, "Self-Disclosure of College Students to Faculty: The Influence of Ethnicity," *Journal of College Student Development* 37 (1996): 88–94.

15. G. D. Kuh and S. Hu, "The Effects of Student-Faculty Interaction in the 1990s," *Review of Higher Education* 24 (2001): 309.

16. Alexander Astin, *What Matters in College: Four Critical Years Revisited* (San Francisco: Jossey-Bass, 1993).

17. Walter M. Kimbrough and E. M. Sutton, *The Persistent Pledging of Black Greeks: A Student Development Approach for Understanding and Challenging the Culture* (Washington, D.C.: National Association of Student Personnel Administrators, 1998); H. Nuwer, "Violence in Historically African American Groups," in *Wrongs of Passage: Fraternities, Sororities, Hazing, and Binge Drinking*, ed. H. Nuwer (Bloomington: Indiana University Press, 1999).

18. Shaun R. Harper and M. A. Wolley, "Becoming an 'Involving College' for African American Undergraduate Men: Strategies for Increasing African American Male Participation in Campus Activities," *Bulletin* 70 (2002): 16–24.

19. D. Jason DeSousa and George D. Kuh, "Does Institutional Racial Composition Make a Difference in What Black Students Gain from College?" *Journal of College Student Development* 37 (1996): 259–67; Walter M. Kimbrough and P. A. Hutcheson, "The Impact of Membership in Black Greek-Letter Organizations on Black Students' Involvement in Collegiate Activities and Their Development of Leadership Skills," *Journal of Negro Education* 67 (1998): 96–105; E. Michael Sutton and Walter M. Kimbrough, "Trends in Black Student Involvement," *NASPA Journal* 39 (2001): 30–40.

20. W. Allen, "The Color of Success: African-American College Student Outcomes at Predominantly White and Historically Black Public Colleges and Universities," *Harvard Educational Review* 62 (1992): 26–44.

21. Shaun R. Harper, "The Academic Standings Report: Helping NPHC Students Make the Grade," *Perspectives* (fall 2000): 14–17.

22. Kimbrough and Hutcheson, "Impact of Membership," 96–105.

23. Norbert W. Dunkel, "The Responsibilities of Advising a Student Organization," *NetResult* 6 (January 2004); Edward Whipple, *Student Activities* (Springfield, Ill.: Charles C. Thomas, 1996).

24. Alexander Astin, "Student Involvement: A Developmental Theory for Higher Education, *Journal of College Student Development* 40 (1999): 518.

25. Edward G. Whipple, "Student Activities," in *Student Affairs Practice in Higher Education,* ed. A. L. Rentz (Springfield, Ill.: Charles C. Thomas, 1996); Edward G. Whipple and Eileen Sullivan, "Greek Letter Organizations: Communities of Learners?" *New Directions for Student Services* 81 (1998): 7–17.

26. Norbert W. Dunkel and John Schuh, *Advising Student Groups and Organizations* (San Francisco: Jossey-Bass, 1998).

27. Carmen Neuberger and G. Hanson, "The Greek Life Self Study: A Powerful Process for Change on Campus," *NASPA Journal* 34, no. 2 (winter 1997): 91.

28. Dunkel and Schuh, *Advising Student Groups and Organizations,* 15.

29. Whipple, "Student Activities," 313.

30. Neuberger and Hanson, "The Greek Life Self Study," 91.

31. Association of Fraternity Advisors, *A How-to Guide for Advisor Training* (Carmel, Ind., n.d.).

32. André McKenzie, "In the Beginning: The Early History of the Divine Nine,"

in *African American Fraternities and Sororities: The Legacy and the Vision*, ed. Tamara L. Brown, Gregory S. Parks, and Clarenda M. Phillips (Lexington: University Press of Kentucky, 2005).

33. Anthony Crenshaw, "Undergraduate Members' Perceptions of the Current Membership Intake Process among Selected Black Greek-Lettered Organizations" (master's thesis, Virginia Polytechnic Institute and State University, 2004).

34. Kimbrough and Hutcheson, "Impact of Membership," 96–105.

35. Michael Shonrock, "Standards and Expectations for Greek Letter Organizations," *New Directions for Student Services* 81 (1998): 79–85.

36. Theodore K. Miller and Judith S. Prince, *The Future of Student Affairs* (San Francisco: Jossey-Bass, 1976), 4.

37. Marylu K. McEwen, "The Nature and Uses of Theory," in *Student Services: A Handbook for the Profession*, 3rd ed., ed. S. R. Komoves, D. B. Woodard Jr., et al. (San Francisco: Jossey-Bass, 1996), 148–49.

38. Miller and Prince, *The Future of Student Affairs*, 3.

39. McEwen, "Nature and Uses of Theory," 148.

40. Dunkel, "Responsibilities of Advising a Student Organization."

41. Carlos E. Cortes, "Building Community from Communities," *NetResults*, January 1, 1999, http://www.naspa.org/membership/mem/nr/article.cfm?id=341 (accessed June 17, 2006).

42. Ibid.

43. Kimbrough, *Black Greek 101*, 164.

44. Dunkel, "Responsibilities of Advising a Student Organization."

45. Walter Kimbrough, "Guess Who's Coming to Campus: The Growth of Black, Latin and Asian Fraternal Organizations," *NetResult,* January 22, 2002, http://www.naspa.org/membership/mem/nr/article.cfm?id=563 (accessed June 17, 2006).

Afterword

Marc H. Morial, National Urban League

The recent mobilization of thousands of African Americans to protest the unequal treatment of six black teens in Jena, Louisiana, illustrates the importance of black Greek-letter organizations in advancing equal rights and justice in the twenty-first century. This event helped transcend some of the current media stereotypes of black fraternities and sororities and raised awareness of their role in the black community as agents of social and political change. The Jena demonstration conjured up images of the great civil rights marches of the 1950s and 1960s rather than stepping and hazing—two practices associated with BGLOs in Hollywood movies and pop culture.

BGLOs helped provide the momentum behind the Jena Six movement and propel the issue to national prominence. Briefly, in a small town in Louisiana, six black teenagers were initially charged with attempted murder for attacking a white classmate. The incident was the culmination of months of escalating racial tensions touched off when three white students at Jena High School hung nooses from a tree on school grounds. The unfolding trial of Mychal Bell, who was originally convicted of aggravated battery, eluded the national radar for months until university students sounded the call for equal justice.

In doing so, they brought the mission of black fraternities and sororities back to its civil rights roots. In the years following Reconstruction at the end of the nineteenth century, African Americans, especially those in the South, watched the promise of equality and equal opportunity provided by ratification of the Fourteenth and Fifteenth Amendments to the U.S. Constitution, which gave them citizenship and the right to vote, disappear as southern states began to lay the foundation for Jim Crow laws. That gave rise to the Niagara movement led by black intelligentsia such as W. E. B. DuBois, who fought racism with their intellect, and the "uplift" movement championed by Booker T. Washington, which united the black middle class and elites in support of their less-affluent brethren.

Established in 1906 at Cornell University, the first black fraternity, Alpha Phi Alpha, grew out of both movements. It was created to help the few black students on campus combat the isolation, racism, and skepticism they faced and pursue a path of excellence in academics and service to the nation's downtrodden. It kicked off the establishment of eight additional black fraternities and sororities.

As African American fraternities and sororities pass the century mark, they have been forced to reflect on their role in black culture and decide where to go next. The Jena protest made them realize that the civil rights movement of their grandparents' generation has not disappeared but has merely evolved. And despite great progress in race relations in the United States, much still needs to be done to narrow the gaps between minorities and mainstream America, especially economically.

They have been forced to realize that the extent of their future influence on the African American community will hinge on their ability to leverage their power in the social, political, and cultural arenas to remain strong through the twenty-first century. Much like the civil rights movement, black Greek-letter organizations face a new stage in their evolution. They can either embrace it and persevere, or fade into the background.

Contributors

MARK BARNES   MA, Temple University. Adjunct professor in the Department of Geography and Planning, West Chester University. Alpha Phi Alpha Fraternity Inc.; Area II director and college adviser to the Pennsylvania Association of Alpha Chapters.

DARNELL BRADLEY   BA and MA, Eastern Illinois University; MA and EdD candidate, Northern Illinois University. Director of Diversity Student Services, Northern Michigan University. Phi Beta Sigma Fraternity Inc.

STEFAN BRADLEY   BA, Gonzaga University; MA, Washington State University; PhD, University of Missouri–Columbia. Assistant professor of history, Southern Illinois University, Edwardsville. Alpha Phi Alpha Fraternity Inc.

LEKEISHA BRYANT   BA and MEd, University of Oklahoma. Academic adviser, University of Central Oklahoma. Sigma Gamma Rho Sorority Inc.

SALLY CLICK   BA, University of Washington; MEd, Oregon State University; PhD student in higher education and student affairs, Bowling Green State University.

MARCUS COLEMAN   BA, University of Southern Mississippi–Hattiesburg; MA, University of Kentucky. Kappa Alpha Psi Fraternity Inc.

MARTIN CRICHLOW   BA, Oral Roberts University; MS, Colorado State University. Alpha Phi Alpha Fraternity Inc.

ALAN D. DESANTIS   BA, James Madison University; MA, University of Alabama; PhD, Indiana University. Associate professor of communications, University of Kentucky. *Inside Greek U: Fraternities, Sororities, and the Pursuit of Pleasure, Power, and Prestige.*

STEPHANIE Y. EVANS   BA, California State University–Long Beach; MA and PhD, University of Massachusetts–Amherst. Assistant professor of African American studies and women's studies, University of Florida. Alpha Kappa Alpha Sorority Inc. *Black Women in the Ivory Tower: 1850–1954;* "Black Greek-Lettered Organizations and Civic Responsibility," in *Black Issues in Higher Education.*

CHARLES S. FINCH III   BA, Yale University; MD, Jefferson Medical College.

Former director of international health, Morehouse School of Medicine. Alpha Phi Alpha Fraternity Inc.

MARYBETH GASMAN   BA, St. Norbert College; MS and PhD, Indiana University. Assistant professor of higher education, University of Pennsylvania. "Sisters in Service: African American Sororities and the Philanthropic Support of Education," in *Women, Philanthropy, and Education.*

KATRINA HAMILTON   BA, California State University, Dominguez Hills; MA, Pepperdine University. Educator and writer.

JESSICA HARRIS   BA, Dillard University; PhD candidate in history, Cornell University. Delta Sigma Theta Sorority Inc.

MARCIA D. HERNANDEZ   BA, University of California–Santa Barbara; PhD, State University of New York. Assistant professor, University of the Pacific.

MATTHEW W. HUGHEY   BA, University of North Carolina–Greensboro; MEd, Ohio University; PhD student in sociology, University of Virginia. Adjunct instructor in African American studies, media studies, and sociology, University of Virginia. Phi Beta Sigma Fraternity Inc. "Virtual (Br)other and (Re)sisters: Authentic Black Fraternity and Sorority Identity on the Internet," in *Journal of Contemporary Ethnography;* "Brotherhood or Brothers in the 'Hood? Debunking the 'Educated Gang' Thesis as Black Fraternity and Sorority Slander," in *Race, Ethnicity, and Education;* "Rushing the Wall, Crossing the Sands: Cross-Racial Membership in U.S. College Fraternities and Sororities," in *Diversity in American Greek Organization;* "Crossing the Color-Line: Non-Black Members of Historically Black Greek Organizations," in *Journal of African American Studies;* "Black, White, Greek . . . Like Who? Howard University Student Perceptions of a White Fraternity on Campus," in *Educational Foundations.*

SHIRLEY A. JACKSON   BA, Wayne State University; MA and PhD, University of California–Santa Barbara. Associate professor of sociology, Southern Connecticut State University.

JUDSON L. JEFFRIES   BA, Old Dominion University; MPP, State University of New York–Binghamton; PhD, University of Southern California. Professor of African American and African studies and director of the Community Extension Center, the Ohio State University. Omega Psi Phi Fraternity Inc.

MICHAEL E. JENNINGS   BA Hampton University; MA and PhD, University of

North Carolina–Chapel Hill. Associate professor of educational leadership and policy studies, University of Texas–San Antonio. Kappa Alpha Psi Fraternity Inc.

RALPH JOHNSON   BS, University of Alabama; MS, Florida State University; PhD, University of South Carolina. Associate dean of student life, Johns Hopkins University. Alpha Phi Alpha Fraternity Inc.; former interim national executive director, initiator, and director of the Alpha College Chapter Leadership Academy; chairman of the Alpha Phi Alpha Education Foundation.

PATRICIA LOUISON   AB, Cornell University; MSEd and EdD, University of Pennsylvania. Director of undergraduate studies, Temple University College of Education. Alpha Kappa Alpha Sorority Inc.

VERNON C. MITCHELL JR.   AB and MA, University of Missouri–Columbia; PhD student in history, Cornell University. Alpha Phi Alpha Fraternity Inc.

DARREN M. MORTON   BBA, Hofstra University; MS, St. John's University. Assistant vice president for student affairs, St. John's University. Former Eastern Region executive director and vice president, Alpha Phi Alpha Fraternity Inc.

CARYN E. NEUMANN   BA and MA, Florida Atlantic University; PhD, Ohio State University. Visiting assistant professor of history and special assistant to the associate dean for community relations, Miami University of Ohio at Middletown.

GREGORY S. PARKS   BA, Howard University; MS, City University of New York; MA and PhD, University of Kentucky; JD candidate, Cornell University. Alpha Phi Alpha Fraternity Inc. *African American Fraternities and Sororities: The Legacy and the Vision; Diversity within American College Fraternities and Sororities.*

BERNADETTE PRUITT   BA and MA, Texas Southern University; PhD, University of Houston. Assistant professor of history, Sam Houston State University. Sigma Gamma Rho Sorority Inc.

LAURA MORGAN ROBERTS   BA, University of Virginia; MA and PhD, University of Michigan. Assistant professor of organizational behavior, Harvard University Business School. Alpha Kappa Alpha Sorority Inc.

DON C. SAWYER III   BA, Hartwick College; MS, Syracuse University; PhD candidate in sociology, Syracuse University. Alpha Phi Alpha Fraternity Inc.

CYNTHIA LYNNE SHELTON   BA, Wayne State University; MPA, Kentucky State

University; MA and PhD, University of Kentucky. Assistant professor, Kentucky State University. Alpha Kappa Alpha Sorority Inc.; The Links Inc.

Gregory T. Smith   BA, Kalamazoo College; MA and PhD, Wayne State University. Professor of clinical psychology, University of Kentucky.

Edward G. Whipple   BA, Willamette University; MA, Northwestern University; PhD, Oregon State University. Adjunct associate professor of higher education and student affairs and vice president for student affairs, Bowling Green State University. Past president, Phi Delta Theta Fraternity; national president, Order of Omega; president, National Association of Student Personnel Administration Foundation.

Lynn Perry Wooten   BA, North Carolina A&T; MBA, Duke University; PhD, University of Michigan. Clinical assistant professor of strategy and management, University of Michigan Ross School of Business. Delta Sigma Theta Sorority Inc.; The Links Inc.; Jack and Jill of America.

Tamika C. Zapolski   BA, University of Missouri–Columbia; MA, University of Kentucky; PhD student in clinical psychology, University of Kentucky.

Index

Tuskegee Institute, 20
Tuskegee University, 104–5
Twilley, Melody, 222–23, 224
Tyler, Myrtle, 107, 110–11
Tyler, Viola, 107, 110

Ubuntu, 397
undergraduate BGLO members:
    versus alumni members, 401–3;
    commitment and service, 193
underground BGLO pledging, 295, 306
Underground Railroad, 25
unemployment, 162
"unintentional racism," 327
Union Anti-Slavery Society, 189
Union College, 423
United Negro College Fund: Omega
    Psi Phi and, 202; Sigma Gamma
    Rho and, 172; sorority support for,
    193, 194
U.S. Army: Frank Coleman in, 68–69;
    Edgar Love in, 73
U.S. postage stamps: Ernest Just and, 72
"Unity 04 Empowerment Campaign," 197
universalism, 215
University of Alabama, 222–23
University of Illinois Press, 11
University of Kentucky, 227
University of North Alabama, 430
University of North Carolina at
    Wilmington, 431
University of South Florida, 431
University of Texas at San Antonio, 432
University of Toronto, 25, 29, 34
university presses, 11–12
University Press of Kentucky, 11
unwed mothers, 179
Uplifting the Race (Gaines), 21
"uplift" movement: Alpha Phi Alpha
    and, 19–20, 21, 25; Booker T.
    Washington and, 19, 459. *See also*
    racial uplift
uroboros, 378

Valley of the Poor, The (Weaver), 89
Van den Berghe, Pierre, 340n38
Velvet Glove, The (Jackman), 323–24
Venkatesh, Sudhir Alladi, 397
verbal calls, 400–401
vertical/hierarchical leadership, 398
veterinary science, 104
Vincent, W. F., 96, 97, 99
violence: black masculinity and, 295
Virginia Union University, 29
vocational education programs, 149, 177
Vocational Guidance and Workshop
    Center (Sigma Gamma Rho), 177
Vocational Guidance Program (Alpha
    Kappa Alpha), 149, 177
Volstead Act, 106
Vosges Mountains, 73
"Voteless People Is a Hopeless People,
    A" (Alpha Phi Alpha), 25, 147, 200
voter registration programs, 25
Voting Rights Act, 200–201
Vroman, Mary, 89

Walk America, 201
Walker, A. M., 96–97
Walker, Alice, 169
Walker, C. J., 34–35
Ware, Grace White, 91
Ware, Marjorie T., 316
War on Poverty, 177–79
Warren, Francis E., 32
Warrington, Gladys, 107, 108
Washington, Booker T.:
    "accommodationist" label,
    135n2; National Negro Business
    League and, 34; notions of black
    advancement, 20–21; Vertner
    Tandy and, 33; "uplift" movement
    and, 19, 459
Washington, George, 57
Washington, Margaret Murray, 235
WATCHCARE project, 225
Waters, Mary, 329

www.ingramcontent.com/pod-product-compliance
Lightning Source LLC
Chambersburg PA
CBHW020447270326
41926CB00008B/518